THE OFFICIAL

Price Guide to

COLLECTING BOOKS

THE **OFFICIAL**

Price Guide to

COLLECTING BOOKS

FOURTH EDITION

MARIE TEDFORD AND PAT GOUDEY

HOUSE OF COLLECTIBLES
The Crown Publishing Group
New York

House of Collectibles is a registered trademark and the HC colophon is a trademark of Random House, Inc.

Published by: House of Collectibles
The Crown Publishing Group
New York, New York

Distributed by the Crown Publishing Group,
a division of Random House, Inc., New York,
and simultaneously in Canada by Random House of Canada Limited, Toronto.

www.randomhouse.com

Printed in the United States of America

ISBN: 0-609-80769-2

10 9 8 7 6 5 4 3 2 1

Fourth Edition: January 2002

ACKNOWLEDGMENTS

Our thanks to the many booksellers who responded to our request for information and to Swann Galleries, Pacific Book Auction Galleries, and Donna Howard of The Eloquent Page bookshop in Vermont, who provided information for the market review.

We thank the Vermont Antiquarian Booksellers who allowed us to use photographs from Pomfret Book Shows; to Gary Austin of the Vermont Antiquarian Bookseller's Association, who provided comments on the Internet; and thanks to photographer Ilan Fisher of Sharon, Massachusetts, for the continuing use of his pictures. Our gratitude goes, also, to Ken Andersen of Middlebury, Vermont, for his unfailing assistance; to Alan and Mary Culpin, booksellers from Austin, Texas, and Boulder, Colorado; Stephen Smith of Fair Haven, Vermont; Cattermole Books of Newberry, Ohio; Monroe Street Books of Middlebury, Vermont; Roger and Joan Bassett, Booksellers of Fullerton, Nebraska; Barry and Hillary Anthony of The Milford Book Cellar and Church Street Books in Milford, Pennsylvania; and Barbara Harris Books of Guilford, New Hampshire. Thanks to Richard and Jane Adelson of North Pomfret, Vermont. And thank you to Joe Spoor, publisher of *Bookseller Monthly* and *Bookseller Marketplace* and owner of the Internet book site www.bookgraveyard.com.

And once more, special thanks to Donna Howard at The Eloquent Page in St. Albans, Vermont, for her constant encouragement and for her information on children's books and on the Internet.

CONTENTS

INTRODUCTION TO THE FOURTH EDITION

Interest in antiquarian and collectible books continues to grow. The market has always been brisk and steady, but it was a somewhat esoteric interest—well known to those who participated, all but invisible to those who didn't. Not so now, as we move into the 21st century.

Newcomers to the field have swelled the ranks of collectors and dealers alike, many of them entering the industry lured by the Internet and the commerce site, eBay. The success of eBay as an outlet for auctioning—and now direct selling—anything from cars to bric-a-brac, has propelled many a dabbler into the used book business. Collectible books have been carried along on this wave.

The general public now is more aware of rare and collectible books as valuable items for trade and investment. This heightened interest is propelling ever greater numbers of dealers and collectors to search out those unique volumes to round out a collection, or to list on the Internet for sale.

This book is designed to help in that search. No one research volume can contain all the information an antiquarian book dealer or collector will need. The literature available, and the new cyberspace web sites, include a considerable body of reference material for publication and price data. Cross-checking information on a book will help to ensure you've got the best price and accurate statistics. And searching multiple references can net you valuable information on a book that's hard to find.

For this edition, we've combed our listings, updated prices, provided additional publication information, and added new volumes. We've written a new overview chapter on the workings of the collectible book business and one identifying popular collectible genres. We suggest you use the information we provide and consult many other sources. We've provided a list of resources at the back of the book.

We want this book to do more than tell you the going rate for a particular title. Books are much more than a commodity with a price tag. As always, our intention is to inform you, pique your interest, and even entertain you a bit. Because we still think the best reason for developing an interest in books is for the sheer fun of it.

MARKET REVIEW

W hen last we visited the markets, we saw a new world economy developing as countries negoatiated multinational trade agreements and the European governments aligned themselves into a single trading and financial entity. Add to these the global changes brought on by the meteoric rise of the Internet as a venue for buying and selling goods and services, and our emergence into the 21st century can be called truly revolutionary.

So, how does all this change affect the market for collectible books? We're happy to report that, as in the past, the market is strong and vibrant. Now as before, the business of antiquarian and collectible bookselling is brisk and profitable, though the lay of the land has changed considerably with an influx of new blood interested in trading on-line. Much of this new commerce focuses on used books and lower-end (less pricey) collectibles, but a presence on the web has become a necessity for the larger booksellers carrying the best in antiquarian and fine collectible books.

Sotheby's, Christies, Pacific Book Auctions, Zubal—all have prodigious listings on their own web sites on-line, maintaining catalogues for upcoming auctions as well as reporting past auctions and prices realized. Their in-person events remain popular, as do the larger book fairs around the country. Smaller bookfairs report a drop-off in clientele, however, with some visitors

At the Vermont Antiquarian Booksellers Fair in Pomfret, Vermont.

Photo by Ilan Fisher

browsing, taking notes, and then going home to buy on-line copies of the books they've seen at the show.

Many independent bookstores maintain individual web sites, while hundreds of smaller shops list books on collective sites like the Advanced Book Exchange's www.abebooks.com. Book listings and dealer sites can be found, too, through search services like the one maintained by 13th Generation Media at www.bookfinder.com. These services are well used by dealers and collectors of good collectible books, though they often provide information on used, out-of-print, and reading copies, as well. At all times when dealing with the Internet, a buyer is advised to inquire about the credentials of the seller and to confirm that the book in question is a quality purchase.

The web megasite, eBay, includes extensive book listings, though many of these consist of used and reading copies. Collectible titles are among the huge volume of books listed there, but again, it's buyer beware when purchasing since anyone can list items for sale on this highly popular site.

As for trends at the turn of the millennium, the trick remains to be aware of genres that are rising and those that are falling off. Children's books have been highly prized during the latter years of the 20th century and they remain strong, along with science fiction and mysteries.

Modern first editions are still a risky business when dealing with living authors. Among current books, a hot prospect this year could be next year's ho-hum title. When purchasing the newer authors, buying low and waiting out the verdict on how the prices hold over time is about the best strategy.

Booksellers Richard and Jane Adelson in North Pomfret, Vermont, tell us that books on travel and exploration continue to draw strong interest, especially Antarctic explorations. Ernest Shackleton material and Capt. James Cook's 2nd voyage have jumped in value in the past five years, they report. For collectors of women's books, they say Isabella Bird's travel accounts of Japan, Hawaii, and the Rocky Mountains are quick to move off the shelves.

Swann Galleries reported a strong response to their travel literature auction in November of 2000 featuring fine older books on world travel. A first edition copy of *Journey into Greece* by George Wheler (Lon., 1682) brought $3,910, while a first edition of Richard Pococke's *A Description of the East* (Lon., 1743-45) brought $3,680.

Also in November, 2000, Swann featured 20th century literature, including a copy of William Faulkner's first novel, *Soldier's Pay* (NY, 1926) which realized $32,200. A first edition, first binding copy of his *Sanctuary* (NY, 1931) sold for $6,900, and a first edition of *Light in August* (NY, 1932), with a bright dust jacket, went for $4,830. Other works sold at the same auction included a signed edition of Ernest Hemingway's *Green Hills of Africa* (NY, 1935) that went for $8,050, and a first edition of Robert Penn Warren's *All the King's Men* (NY, 1946), with first issue dust jacket, that brought $10,350.

Modern first edition authors such as these have survived the test of time and become highly collectible literary authors. Another who has moved into this genre is Jack Kerouac, whose most well-known title, *On the Road* (NY, 1950), in first edition, went for $7,475 at a Swann auction.

Pacific Book Auction Galleries realized $3,162.50 on an advance copy of Kerouac's *Dharma Bums* in September, 2000, under the modern litarature rubric. At the same auction, a first edition of John Steinbeck's *Grapes of Wrath* went for $2,300. At another Pacific Book Auction modern literature event in October of 2000, a first edition of William Faulkner's *The Hamlet* sold for $850.

Pacific reported successful on-line auctions run by their own Auction Galleries that are open to public bidding. They offer books priced from $10 and up, often including rare collectible titles. Recent on-line auction results include the sale of a first edition of Cormack McCarthy's *All the Pretty Horses* that sold for $253, while the Western Americana title *The Arrest and Killing of Sitting Bull* by John M. Carroll sold for $201. Pacific reports that on-line prices realized are often on a par with in-person auctions.

Swann Galleries offered art and architecture books in December of 2000, including a copy of Giuseppe Tucci's *Tibetan Painted Scrolls* (ltd 750, Rome, 1949), which sold for $3,680.

In February, 2001, Swann featured modern press and illustrated books, offering Robert Louis Stevenson's *The Black Arrow* (NY, 1920), illustrated and signed by N. C. Wyeth, that sold for $5,060.

Clearly, the world of collectible books is changing with a changing world, but the true bibliophile who remains diligent and observant will find the markets as exciting and rewarding as ever.

A CLOSER LOOK AT
THE BOOK TRADE

Books are the legacies that a great genius leaves to mankind,
which are delivered down from generation to generation,
as presents to the posterity of those who are yet unborn.
                                        —THE SPECTATOR, 1711

We have long suspected the world contains many would-be bookmen needing only a nudge to get them started. During the past five years, modern technology has given them that nudge. With the rise of the Internet, bookmen are on-line by the thousands. And with their arrival, the whole climate of the collectible book business has changed.

The Internet has had a greater effect on the book trade than any other factor in the latter half of the 20th century. Instant access to markets the world over has changed the way many dealers buy and advertise their stock and the way collectors search for their treasures. For instance, with instant Internet access to buyers all over the world, dealers can now easily market regional books direct to the customer, rather than to a dealer in a distant locale.

There was a time when, if you wanted a book on Flatbush, you would depend on a bookseller in New York to find it for you. He was there, on-site. He could search for books in his region, and people would come to him because he had developed channels for buying and selling regional books. Now you can put out your own search on the Internet and you'll find books listed all over the world on every subject you can imagine.

By the same token, you can market your regional and specialty books directly to collectors all over the world using the Net. However, by bypassing a bookseller who is a specialist in the field, you lose valuable counsel and you risk underpricing a book for sale or paying too much for a book you might not want in your collection simply because you did not have the opportunity to talk it over with an experienced professional. This can apply to any specialty.

With the proliferation of books on-line, many books once labeled rare, hard to find, or scarce have lost their status. These titles may once have been uncommon in Albuquerque, but technology has expanded the reach of a collector and he soon discovers that there are many more copies offered for sale than he once thought. This in turn affects price, for buyer and seller alike. When a previously rare title comes up in a search, you may find that the treasure you were looking for is common, and that fact may gain you the book at a lower price. On the other hand, if you are selling a so-called rare title, you may find the competition on the Internet a little discouraging. Buying and selling at the right price is important if you don't want to lose your shirt.

Remember the adage "You can't teach an old dog new tricks"? Well, as time goes on, the dogs young and old who manage to stay in business are the ones who learn new tricks.

Donna Howard of The Eloquent Page in St. Albans, Vermont, now lists her considerable stock of science fiction, fantasy, and horror—collectible books as well as many reading copies or paperbacks—on her Internet web site. She has always attracted a clientele of collectors and readers alike and she does a brisk business in these genres, even more so now that she's featured in cyberspace.

Marie's web site, too, has brought the world to her doorstep here in rural Vermont. In the past two years, she has made the acquaintance of many bibliophiles in the far corners of the globe, including a professor in Australia and a World War II enthusiast from the Netherlands, whose correspondence over the subject of sought after books often brightens her day in the bookshop.

WHEN IS AN OLD BOOK COLLECTIBLE?

A reasonable question. Instead of thinking in terms of "old," consider your books used, out-of-print, or rare. These descriptions apply to books of any age. Rather than age, think about content: what is the book about, or who wrote it?

If you must choose between two books, one printed in London in 1632 by an obscure British poet, and the other a 19th-century tome on the American Indian published in New York, choose the one on the American Indian. There's a lively market for Native Americana and the book will likely find a customer in the collectible book market. The poetry is merely fun to have on the shelf. It isn't automatically a collector's item.

We don't think anybody knows the cut-off date for "antiquarian" books. Is it the 19th century? Early 20th? Unless you are a rare-book dealer focusing on the earliest printed material—incunabula or the first printed books in the New World—put actual age out of your mind and learn which books are

The Land of Oz, *a sequel to* The Wizard of Oz, *was printed by Reilley & Lee, Chicago, no date given. The book is not a first edition, but its condition is good for a children's book. It is illustrated by J. R. Neill.*

Photo by Jonathan Draudt, Tamarac Arts

sought by dealers and other collectors. You'll discover a busy trade in books from past centuries and books from last year, indeed from yesterday, from antiquarian volumes to modern first editions.

WHERE WILL I FIND GOOD BOOKS?

The first source that comes to mind is the antiquarian and collectible book dealer. For many genres, used book stores will yield exactly what you're after, often at bargain prices. Throw in a little conversation with the bookseller, and you've learned something about your subject, too. A book bought from a reputable dealer has been pre-screened and you won't have to do further research to verify your find.

However, another source has been thrown into the mix, the Internet. The collector is on his own when he treads onto this new territory. He now must bone up on his subject before he starts his quest. He will have far more volumes at his fingertips. But absent is the bookseller's wealth of information gathered through years of experience. The collector must place his faith in information administered by someone he has never seen. Not to say that many, many reputable booksellers cannot be found on the Internet. But how to discern who knows his business and who is a novice? There's the rub.

WHERE CAN I FIND BOOKS ON THE INTERNET?

New web sites make it easy for the novice to find books by providing search services that scour the Net for authors, titles, and topics. Several large web sites have moved to the forefront of the industry, including Advanced Book Exchange at www.abebooks.com, Alibris at www.alibris.com, and BookFinder at www.bookfinder.com. Barnes and Noble includes antiquarian titles among its offerings at www.barnesandnoble.com, as does the Internet bookselling giant Amazon.com. Not to forget the general merchandise auction and retail megasite, eBay (www.ebay.com), where both beginner and experienced booksellers market titles ranging from new or used reading copies to pricey collectibles.

Independent booksellers can subscribe to one of several group sites, set up a web page and post their own books for sale, advertise wants and perform searches for clients, all for reasonable monthly fees usually based on the number of books posted or the amount of activity at the site. For newcomers to the Internet, technical support for managing the pages is usually available. Thousands of booksellers have availed themselves of these services or set up their own sites. They include experienced dealers, long established auction houses, and brand-new entrepreneurs.

A buyer can log on to these sites and search the dealer lists for specific books, or just browse among the many titles offered. As a buyer, know your books well and learn something about the dealer you're working with before committing your money to a sale. Check to see if the dealer has a return policy. For dealers, if you're new to the field, learn about the books, how to evaluate their rarity and condition, and how to properly describe them to a potential buyer before putting a price on them and posting them for sale to the world. We have included terms for describing books in the glossary in Appendix A at the back of this book.

If you are looking for a particular Hopalong Cassidy title, the number of items that may come up in a search will amaze you. A search may call up hundreds of volumes of a title being offered on the Internet, from books in pristine collectible condition to dog-eared reading copies. And the prices will range from "I can afford that" to "You've gotta be kidding!" At most search sites, you can refine your quest by limiting the search, asking to see only first editions, signed copies, or hardcover books with dust jackets.

Booksellers themselves have long considered other dealers a prime source of good stock bought directly through bookstores, dealer catalogues, advertisements, industry periodicals, and at book fairs. These practices haven't completely fallen out of favor, even though many also take advantage of the larger marketplace that the Internet affords them.

Catalogue advertising and dealer-to-dealer selling have evolved with this new technology, as has attendance at bookshows and fairs. Many dealers no longer spend considerable time and resources to create and mail comprehensive print catalogues when so many serious collectors have access to the Internet, though some have begun to return to catalogues to communicate their best titles to select customers.

Bookshows continue to draw dedicated bibliophiles who enjoy the opportunity to see and examine a multitude of books and who appreciate the opportunity to talk to knowledgeable dealers. Casual buyers and investment-oriented collectors, however, are increasingly attracted to the ease of cyber-commerce and dwindling attendance at some smaller regional shows reflects this.

The pros and cons of the Internet for booksellers can be legitimately argued. One of the advantages of the Net is the wealth of book titles available, including titles heretofore completely unseen in some regions and so thought to be scarce. Prices can also be an eye-opener. Competition, keen among dealers, seems to be guiding prices now, bringing them into a more competitive range. The consumer profits from this adjustment.

On the other hand, dealers are now able to reach a broader audience with information about their wares, increasing the pool of buyers for truly scarce books in excellent condition.

A note of caution: A new breed of buyer and seller has entered the market with the Internet. Many are speculators who have little expertise or interest in the books per se. With these newcomers, prices vary greatly as does their knowledge of the books they're trading in and the quality of their wares. Serious dealers and collectors should tread carefully when dealing with unknowns in cyberspace.

Will this trend continue? Differing opinions make the rounds of book-trade newsletters, e-mail, and in conversation whenever two booksellers or collectors get together. The only consensus is that the Internet has brought great changes to the collectible book world. Whether or not this cyberspace bookselling and collecting has a future, and what shape that future might take, remain anyone's guess.

Marie's experience and that of her colleagues in Vermont and elsewhere has been that buying and selling on the Internet is an increasingly important

Children's books on display at the Vermont Antiquarian Booksellers Fair in Pomfret, Vermont, in the booth of Royu and Jean Kulp of Hatfield, Pennsylvania.

Photo by Ilan Fisher

element of the book business. Some dealers resist the "on-line" mania, but the Internet has changed every facet of commerce on the planet and there's no turning back.

Nonetheless, the Internet is just one venue for buying and selling books. The true enthusiast can also attend regional fairs and shows, many of which remain popular around the country. They're an education unto themselves. Nothing is more satisfying than to hold a book in your hand and take the time to examine it for yourself. If you have a question, dealers can give you an answer right then and there.

Other excellent sources are flea markets, estate sales, auctions, the Salvation Army, antique stores, and garage sales. These are the places where professionals continue to find books.

But some of us are involved with collectible books for reasons other than merely earning a living. Traditional bibliophiles enjoy the hunt through the stacks, scouring the countryside for books long out of circulation, leafing through private collections to find the one or two treasures among them, holding history in their hands even if only for a moment. They enjoy the heft and feel of a book almost as much as the words and images on a page. They enjoy the people they meet and the opportunities for invigorating conversation on topics of shared interest. These are among the esoteric pleasures of antiquarian bookselling and collecting that the Internet cannot replace.

HOW GOOD ARE AUCTIONS FOR BUYING AND SELLING BOOKS?

Books at local auctions are still plentiful and a good source of collectibles, but you can't be sure of picking up a bargain any longer unless the crowd is dull about books. In too many cases, except perhaps at the larger, more exclusive rare book and collectible houses, the popularity of auctions has brought with it a kind of recreational bidder. In the heat of competition for an item, prices may be driven much higher than a careful buyer would be willing to pay in a bookstore or in a private transaction.

Great books can still be had for excellent prices if buyers exercise caution, know how much they are willing to pay ahead of time, and sit on their hands when the bidding gets rowdy.

If you're selling books, auctions and dealers are on a par, each having their strong and weak points. On a particular day, if an auction attracts a spirited audience, you could do well. On an off day, you risk your books selling for less than you hoped. Selling through dealers requires more of your time and effort, but dealers have pipelines to collectors who may be looking for just the book you're selling. In the final analysis, we can only tell you what is available. You must choose what's right for you.

WHAT BOOKS SHOULD I PICK UP?

There's no one answer to this question. Before you ask it, you have some decisions to make, and then the question will begin to answer itself. Are you buying books for investment or fun? Are you a collector? A dealer? Will you specialize or be a generalist?

Carefully bought collectible books hold their value well and grow in value at a steady rate of up to 10 per cent per year. They're a safe investment, but with rare exceptions, they're not speculative and won't make you a killing.

As an example of the quality of investment, consider the sale of the Raymond Epstein collection, placed on the block at Swann Auction Galleries in April, 1992. Mr. Epstein had carefully recorded the purchase prices of his books, which were maintained in excellent condition, providing a unusual opportunity to compare market price over an approximately thirty-year period. A copy of *Dracula* bought in 1965 for $46 was maintained in a specially made case costing $38. The book realized $11,000 at auction in 1992. A copy of *Ulysses* bought for $400 in 1965 and maintained in a $350 case sold for $19,800. Mr. Epstein acquired *Tom Sawyer* in 1966 for $1,250 and it sold for $9,350. An $885 *The Wizard of Oz* acquired in 1972 sold for $20,900.

This is clear evidence that careful collecting is a solid investment. Still, as often as not, even those who collect for investment wind up excited by the hunt and end up collecting for fun, too.

If you decide to specialize, whether bookseller or collector, learn all you can about your subject. Don't neglect allied subjects that broaden your knowledge. Visit bookstores, talk to dealers, read dealer catalogues to see what's being offered and what someone else wants. Visit libraries.

Michael Ginsberg, a bookseller from Massachusetts and past president of the Antiquarian Booksellers Association of America (ABAA) told us he likes to read the bibliographies in the back of books related to his specialty to discover other books to read and some he might want to collect or resell.

CATEGORIES, OR ANA

When you get more involved as a dealer or collector, you'll become familiar with references to the common genres and specialties, sometimes called "ana" (see Glossary). These will include topics like the settling of the Americas, native peoples, Black studies, maritime trades, foreign countries, children's books, medicine, science, sporting books, zoology, anthropology, magic, antiques, the military, cooking, poetry, railroads, billiards, the radical labor movement, and on and on. Add to that limited editions, fine presses, fine bindings, illustrated books; the list doesn't end. And each genre has sub-genres, ad infinitum.

These categories help dealers and collectors communicate. Dealers use them to describe their specialties and collectors use them to define their area of interest. But genres are not mutually exclusive; there's enormous overlapping, and they are just one tool for evaluating books. We go into greater detail in our chapter on Popular Genres.

We have also included a list of collectible titles and authors, by genre, at the end of this book.

AMERICANA VS. US-IANA

A very popular specialty is Americana, but what do bookmen mean by the term? Do they refer to books on the discovery, exploration, political and cultural development of the United States? Or do they adopt the broader and truer meaning of the term and include all the Americas from Canada to Argentina?

In modern vernacular, the meaning of Americana has narrowed to refer to the United States and its territories, though some dealers use it in the more inclusive form. To be technically correct when referring to the United States, the term US-iana was coined by bibliographer Wright Howes, author of *Howes USIANA* issued in 1954, but the term is less widely used.

WHAT ABOUT CONDITION?

This is probably the most important judgment you will make about a book you're buying or selling. Depending on its condition, a book can be a collector's item or just a nice book to read. We often see the same look of perplexity on the faces of people not in the trade when we reject the old book in their hand. "But it's old!"

No matter.

Unless the book is an Eliot Bible, or another great rarity, it must be in good condition—bindings attached, pages all there, illustrations accounted for, no underlining, no tears, and clean covers. If the book was issued with a dust jacket, the jacket must be present and in good condition, especially for modern first editions. The absence of the jacket radically reduces the value.

Sounds cranky, doesn't it? But we can't stress enough the importance of condition in collectible books. Still, don't throw away that intact book in less than good condition. Scholars, researchers, and recreational readers are another market for inexpensive reading copies.

HOW IMPORTANT ARE FIRST EDITIONS?

Rare book collectors want first editions because they reflect the first time these particular thoughts of an author appeared in print. They are percieved to be closest to the author's true intent. As further editions are issued, the supply of books is increased, thereby diminishing the value of succeeding editions. But relative scarcity of firsts remains constant.

As often as not, collectors don't read their first editions, but buy them to enjoy the possession of something rare and special, something others don't have. Scholars and readers will pay a price for later editions, but it will be a mere shadow of the price paid for a first edition.

Now, after having said that, let us confuse you further. Popular titles are often re-issued in limited editions. Printed on high quality papers, with fine bindings and slipcases, these commonly include illustrations by noted artists. Limited editions may command higher prices than first editions, since most are numbered and signed by the author, the artist, or both.

And then you have modern first editons, published in the past year or two and already commanding a collectible price, which nullifies the idea that age determines price. See more on this subject in our discussion on collecting popular genres.

HOW DO I PRICE A BOOK?

The plain truth is, there is no one right price for a used book. It's all subjective. The law of supply and demand is in play. During flush times, prices

Chapbooks were popular fare during the 19th century, often sold door-to-door by traveling salesmen commonly called chapmen. This collection is included in Special Collections at the Bailey-Howe Library at the University of Vermont. Shown are (top row) The Farm House, *Mhalon Day printer, early 1800s;* The Red Squirrel, *A. Phelps, Greenfield, 1846;* Cinderella of The Glass Slipper, *H & E Phinney, Cooperstown, 1834; (bottom row)* Stories for Children About Whales, *Rufus Merrill, Concord, NH, 1843;* Cock Robin's Courtship and Marriage, *Sidney's Press, New Haven, 1824;* The Young Sailer, or The Sea Life of Tom Bowline, *Kiggins & Kellogg, NY, 1840s.*

and sales soar, and in a lagging economy, they come back down. Market correction.

With a book in your hand, you'll do the research and then settle on a number. In the end, the value of a book is only what you or your customer are willing to pay. You will notice for some books we've listed, the price range is narrow. According to our sources, including dealers' pricing and auction records, folks agree on the current value of those books. For others, the range is hundreds or even thousands of dollars. These are actual prices people have asked for and paid. They reflect differing opinions from one dealer to another, or from one part of the country to another. Such disparities are common.

We've listed some titles more than once to show the difference in price between, for instance, trade and limited editions, the first edition and a later edition, a first edition with dust jacket and one without, or a signed copy and an unsigned one. We've assigned our prices assuming very good to fine condition, with the rare exceptions noted. Where you don't find the actual title you're after, but we list other titles by the same author, you've verified the author as important if not collectible. You have more research to do, however, before you can price the book in your hand. Some authors have many titles to their credit, not all prized. The whole subject is fraught with cautions.

Talk to people in the business, consult price guides and dealer catalogues, visit antiquarian bookstores. Learn as much as you can and then learn some more.

Pricing stock for a shop begins when you buy the books. Will your initial investment be tied up for months or a year, or do you have a ready customer for the book? Do you have a shop with overhead costs or do you mail order?

As dealers, when we know exactly what book we're looking for, the quickest way to find it is through other professionals. That means we dealers often buy from each other and the price goes up as a book passes from hand to hand before it ever reaches the public. How many times can that happen?

You must make these judgments based upon your growing knowledge of the business. In the end, you're bound to make some mistakes. It's that kind of business.

WHAT TO COLLECT IN POPULAR GENRES

All the world knows me in my book and my book in me.
                                    —MICHEL DE MONTAIGNE

The collector learns about collecting by collecting. So advises John Winterich in his entertaining book, *A Primer of Book Collecting*, published in 1926. We think his sage words ring as true today as they did in yesteryear. There is much to learn and it is best learned through hands-on experience.

"But what will I collect?" you may ask. That is an impossible question to answer in simple terms. You may be interested in books for your own collection or you may specialize in books for sale. You may look for titles based on your favorite authors, on fine bindings, or on topics of special interest to you. These are some of the ways we define the myriad genres among collectible books, genres like medicine, mysteries, science fiction, modern first editions, and the like. Many collectors limit their attention to a specific genre. In this chapter, we will provide an introduction to some of today's more popular genres.

In earlier books on collecting, the emphasis was on literature and specific writers along with books of incunabula, which is the term for books printed before the year 1501.

We don't want to go into a sociological analysis here, but suffice it to say that tastes have changed since writers like Henry James were in demand. Certainly there are still collectors of Mr. James, but today's collector is more apt to go for the late 20th century writers, Larry McMurtry, Joyce Carol

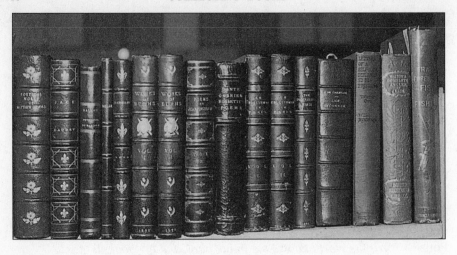

Fine bindings on display at the Antiquarian Booksellers Fair in Pomfret, Vermont.

Photo by Ilan Fisher

Oates, Henry Miller, Tobias Wolff and a host of other commendable writers. We do not want to leave the impression that many of the older writers are not collectible, but let's say the audience for them has slimmed down.

While some once popular authors have been abandoned by today's markets, still others continue to interest the collector down through the decades. The works of Hemingway, Faulkner, Fitzgerald, Steinbeck, Crane, and Harte are certainly models of collectible books. Along with these old venerables have been added the masters of mystery, science fiction, children's, science, exploration, and others which we will address in this chapter.

The number of titles and authors that cross over genres are legion. Arthur C. Clarke, August Derleth, Theodore Sturgeon, Jules Verne, Ray Bradbury— these are only a few of the top science fiction writers who also swell the list of collectible literary authors and modern first editions.

Clearly, the topic of collectible genres can fill a book of its own. In these pages, we provide an introduction to the subject and list some of the most collectible authors and titles, those the fledgling book enthusiast is likely to find. If collecting in specific genres is your primary interest, we urge further research and study.

MODERN FIRST EDITIONS

Today, one of the top genres for collecting is modern first editions. If any area of book collecting is in danger of falling victim to fads, this is it. Modern First Editions prove the fact that a book can be published in the past year or two and already have a collectible price affixed.

Sue Grafton's crime novels have been popular with collectors of modern first editions over the past decade. Her first book, *"A" is for Alibi*, published in 1982, is currently offered on the Internet for $600. But interest in her books waxes and wanes, especially those titles further down the alphabet. Writers like John Galsworthy, once a popularly collected author, now get scant attention from collectors. The prolific writer Stephen King's first novel, *Carrie,* in first edition with dust jacket, is offered for $600 to $1200 as universities begin to offer courses on his works.

Whether Grafton and other popular writers of today like King, Tom Clancy, John Grisham, Ann Tyler, and Ann Rice will have staying power as collectibles remains to be seen.

Those authors who move into the literature category have the best chance, said Paul Jung, auctioneer and cataloguer for Kane Antiquarian Auctions of Pottstown, Pennsylvania. Collectors buy literary modern firsts and put them aside, hoping the authors will be studied.

"The standbys are always there, Hemingway, Faulkner, Steinbeck," Jung said. "They're always collected."

And then there are cases like the first edition of Raymond Chandler's 1939 mystery, *The Big Sleep*, introducing the character of detective Philip Marlowe. In a near perfect dust jacket, the book sold for $7,150 in 1992, more than twice what experts had estimated it would bring. By 1996, experts were setting the price closer to $5,000. In the year 2001, the book with its dust jacket is offered for $8,000 to $15,000 on the Internet. The difference in price is due to the book's condition. Considered a classic in the genre for its era, *The Big Sleep* was dramatized in a movie starring Humphrey Bogart as detective Philip Marlowe. Was it exposure that brought the price up? What really sets the pace for what a book is worth? We suspect that whimsy has a lot to do with it. On the other hand, *The Big Sleep* is considered by many to be a literary classic, having crossed over from the mystery genre.

This is the way it is with modern first editions. Either the books become classics, part of the popular culture—most notably, through movies these days—or they are recognized as literature and are studied in the classroom, and their value remains high. Or they pass into oblivion and are relegated to the Penny Box.

Percy Muir had a wonderful discussion on the subject in his delightful commentary *Book Collecting As a Hobby*, published in 1945. He says when a contemporary author is "hot" the demand for first editions will drive up the price. When the demand is satisfied, prices decline. If the author's work has lasting substance, collectors will rediscover him and prices will rise again.

Muir cautions, "Never, never collect an author when he is in the height of fashion." He advises anticipating who will be the next to rise, if you can, or wait until authors have weathered the test of time. We believe this advice remains relevant today.

The bottom line is, take care in buying and pricing, especially with modern first editions. Watch trends, understand them, plan for them, but don't be swept up in them.

CHILDREN'S BOOKS

Collectible children's books range from the scarce and hard-to-obtain chap books to modern Golden Books and J. K. Rowling's *Harry Potter*.

In between, a collector's dream would include early pop-ups, books illustrated with chromolithographs and tipped-in plates by Edmund Dulac, N. C. Wyeth, Arthur Rackham, Kate Greenaway, Maurice Sendak, Jessie Wilcox Smith and many others.

Whatever the motivation for collecting, desirable classic authors—Carroll, Milne, Potter, Wiggin, Burgess and others too numerous to mention—take the lion's share of the market, but series books like the Hardy Boys, Nancy Drew, Dick & Jane, Dana Girls, The Campfire Girls, Mickey Mouse Club, Motor Cycle Boys and Boy Scouts are back in circulation and enjoying a renaissance.

And of course the Oz books, especially first editions with color plates, are perennial favorites that fetch high prices.

Unlike collectors who covet first editions, collectors of series books don't always consider it important, and, besides, determining a first edition series book isn't so easy. The copyright page tells you little about which edition you're holding. Nostalgia motivates many children's book collectors who search for titles from their childhood.

To the hard-core collector all the points are important; dust jacket, first edition, very good condition, rarity—and that applies to the series books, as well.

We consulted Donna Howard at The Eloquent Page in St. Albans, Vermont, for clarification. Children's series books can be known by their titles and by their number in the series. "In the children's series, often, though not always, the last number or the last few numbers are considerably more expensive than earlier numbers," Donna said.

This is because fewer books were published later in the series. As each new book in a series is produced, more copies of earlier titles are printed to meet a continued demand. The result, she says, is "the last numbers are usually issued only once as the series goes out of print, therefore fewer copies are available to collectors and dealers."

The higher-number rule doesn't apply to all the series books, however. Popular Hardy Boys and Nancy Drew books, most notably, have ongoing publication and follow the standard rule—the earlier the edition, the better.

Valuable and collectible children's books are out there if you know what to look for, and condition is most important. Some flaws are acceptable, such

A copy of Puck of Pook's Hill, *NY, Doubleday Page, 1906, illustrated by Rackham;* Live Boys, or Charlie and Nasho in Texas, *by Arthur Morecamp, Boston, Lee & Shepard, 1879, 1st ed. (Difficult to find, this book written by Thomas Pilgrim under a pseudonym, is one of the earliest to mention cowboys);* The Poor White or The Rebel Conscript, *Boston, Graves & Young, 1864, 1st ed., a Civil War novel.*

Photo by Jonathan Draudt, Tamarac Arts

as cover wear or an owner's signature on a flyleaf, even a dust jacket can be missing, but a collector draws the line on books that are falling apart or have torn and scribbled pages.

Don't spurn a reprint, especially one in good condition. Unlike modern first editions, juvenile reprints hold a higher percentage of their value. Clean, crisp books with clean dust jackets sell fast and best. And prices can be considerable. Beginners in the children's category are amazed how a dust jacket can add to the price of a book.

The mid-1930's through the 1950's were the true Golden Age of children's books in America. Among the ten most requested authors from the 1930's to the present are: Margaret Wise Brown, Lois Lenski, Roald Dahl, Jean DeBrunhoff, Marguerite De Angeli, Robert Lawson, William Steig.

The most-wanted series books are: The Bobbsey Twins, Nancy Drew, Hardy Boys, Tom Swift, Judy Bolton, Rick Brant, Black Stallion Series, Thornton Burgess, Dr. Dolittle, Landmark Books, and the Scribner's Illustrated Classics.

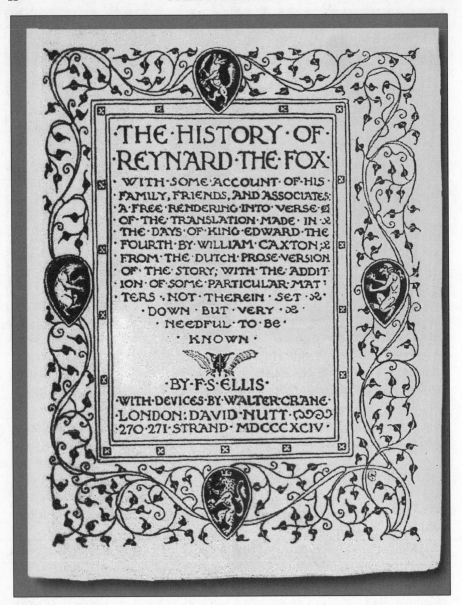

A page with a woodcut illustration from The History of Raynard the Fox, *printed in 1894 by David Nutt, London. It in included in Special Collections at the Bailey, Howe Library, University of Vermont.*

Digital enhancement by Jonathan Draudt, Tamarac Arts

However, the Frank Baum Oz books, Uncle Wiggily, Mary Frances, Palmer Cox's Brownies, The Teenie Weenies, Arthur Ransom, and Volland Publishing still have special appeal for collectors and nostalgia buffs.

If you are thinking into the future or you're making a list for your children to collect, keep these authors in mind: Brian Jacques, James Marshall,

Gary Paulsen, Daniel Pinkwater, Madeline L'Engle, Betsy Byar and the inimitable Chris Van Allsburg, to mention just a few.

The children's book market is a very active sector in the out-of-print book world, and shows no sign of declining.

The world of children's books is wide and varied and contains many subdivisions–picture books, series, chapter, pop-up, toy, fiction, non-fiction, illustrated, and more. One of the best ways to educate yourself is to read catalogues offered by dealers who specialize in them. We have space only to skim the surface of this delightful collecting category. So, if your interest in collecting or selling leans toward the whimsical, but you find yourself in a tangled forest with lurking goblins and roads to nowhere, look for a knowledgeable bookseller who can set you on the right path.

SCIENCE FICTION, HORROR, FANTASY

Occasionally, books that fall within these genres may also be included in mystery and even modern first edition genres. Some have even achieved the status of literary classics—witness the likes of Robert Heinlein's *Stranger in a Strange Land*, Arthur C. Clarke's *2001*, and works by Theodore Sturgeon, Ray Bradbury, Jules Verne, Edgar Rice Burroughs, H. P. Lovecraft, August Derleth, Edgar Allan Poe, Ambrose Bierce, Isaac Asimov, and Kurt Vonnegut.

Frank Herbert's books about the planet Dune enjoy a mystique that lures fans and book collectors. And horror-master Stephen King is said to be the most collected living author, especially his early books, including *Carrie,* which was his first novel and the first among many to become a major motion picture. First editions in excellent condition with dust jackets of his other early books, *Salem's Lot, The Shining, Night Shift* and *The Stand,* are also prized by collectors of his work.

Though incredibly popular with movie fans, Star Wars books have been issued in such great numbers that they have not yet achieved high prices on the collectible market. The same can be said for most Star Trek titles, except those published by Bantam Paperbacks in the 1970s, written by established science fiction writers. These are currently selling at prices ranging from $15 to $35.

MILITARY AND THE CIVIL WAR

Some people categorize wars and subjects relating to the military as militaria, but the major conflicts of the United States such as the Revolution, Civil War, and World Wars I and II are also collected as individual genres, the most popular being the Civil War. Diaries, memoirs, biographies of noted officers, and battles are all grist for the collector's mill. Anything pertaining to the Confederacy is highly sought after and commands good prices.

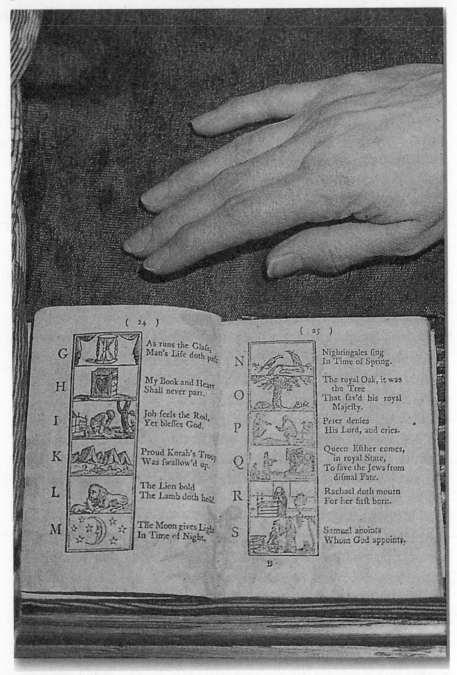

Two pages of The Boston Primer, *a popular chapbook (this one printed in 1811, with engravings to illustrate the alphabet for young learners), are typical examples of the style used on these popular little books.*

Courtesy of the Trustees of the Boston Public Library.

Photo by Marilyn Green.

Two references that include lengthy bibliographies of Civil War collectible books as well as information about the genre are by Tom Broadfoot and Ronald Seagrave. They're both listed in the chapter on Periodicals and Research Resources.

WESTERN AMERICANA

Stories about the winning of the west, from the arduous journeys of pioneering families to the lawlessness of men like Jesse James and his gang have always interested the American public. Memoirs of early gold miners are important research items that show the development of California. Anything on cowboys, homesteading, native Americans, the Rocky Mountains, relations with Mexico in border state conflicts, explorations and discoveries, these and many more subjects whet the appetite for collectors of Western Americana.

Collectible topics, titles and authors in this genre are listed in the Index of Authors and Titles by Popular Genre.

FINE BINDINGS

Fine bindings—that is, leather-bound books with gold-tooled cover decorations, gilt lettering, high quality paper, color plates and wood engravings—all have an audience who prize them not only as decorative pieces but also as investments. Fine Press books from publishers such as The Ashendene Press, Albion, Kelmscott Press, Golden Cockerel, Clarendon and Nonesuch, and others are sought after for their unique treatment and superior quality, and they are generally sold at the high end of the price scale, often in the thousands of dollars.

ILLUSTRATION

Here is one genre that people can't get enough of, especially books with color plates. Of course those most in demand are famous illustrators, the likes of Arthur Rackham, who brought a finely detailed and whimsical style to children's books, and Edmund Dulac, another artist who decorated books with enchanting illustrations. The list is so large we could not do justice to the collectible artists who make this genre so much fun. To name just a few, W. W. Denslow characterized the Oz books, and N. C. Wyeth, Howard Pyle, and Maxfield Parrish brought the Scribner's Classics to life. Then of course, you have books on horticulture, natural history and medicine, illustrated by John Gould, Audubon, and others, not to mention engravings and chromolithographs by a host of anonymous artists. When you come across one of these books, you have a prize item.

FANSHAWE,

A TALE.

"Wilt thou go on with me?"-- Southey.

BOSTON:
MARSH & CAPEN, 362 WASHINGTON STREET.

PRESS OF PUTNAM AND HUNT.

1828.

Facsimile Title Page

T A M E R L A N E

AND

OTHER POEMS

BY A BOSTONIAN

Young heads are giddy and young hearts are warm
and make mistakes for manhood to reform.

Cowper

BOSTON:

CALVIN F. S. THOMAS . . PRINTER

1827

Facsimile Title Page

Some illustrations, such as color plates from an early Audubon book, can be framed and sold individually and some people will break a book with that in mind. We disagree with the practice unless the illustration has been salvaged from an already damaged book.

SCIENCE AND MEDICINE

A highly specialized genre is science and medicine. Some of the most exciting books in this field are rare and hard to find, especially those with handsome woodcut illustrations. Nineteenth-century books on medicine during the Civil War have a ready audience in both the science and medicine and the Civil War genres, and books by men such as Sir William Osler and William Harvey are valued in any collection. Early discoveries, inventions, and biographies of inventors and scientists round out a collection. Look for those books on early rockets, communications, medical cures, technological firsts, anything vintage on airships, planes, the atom bomb, parachutes, windmills, and other scientific pursuits.

SPORTING AND SPELUNKING

A highly specialized field, sporting books are based in the English tradition of field sports such as riding, angling, and hunting. Cave exploration is also a popular subject. If you tread onto the baseball diamond or a golf course, you're in another genre. Sporting collections are currently enjoying considerable popularity and trade in books on these topics is brisk.

The Captain's Angling and Sporting Books of Homosassa Springs, Florida, recommends some newer authors to keep an eye on, including Tom McGuane, Charles Waterman, John Cole, and Jeffrey Cardenas. Also look for limited editions by Meadowood Press. Among currently popular collectible authors, seek out Havilah Babcock, Corey Ford, Gordon McQuarrie, A. J. McClane, Philip Wylie, Tom McNally, Kip Farrington, and others.

To learn more, several books listed below will help the novice gather a list of books for a collection. These resources, recommended by bookman and sporting specialist Ken Andersen of Ken Andersen Books in Middlebury, Vermont, will also benefit booksellers, broadening their knowledge in this fun field.

American Fishing Books. Charles M. Wetzel, copyright 1950, reprinted 1997. Contains more than 2,000 titles.

Catalogue of the Collection of Books on Angling. Dean Sage, 1886 first edition, reprinted 1995. More than 2,000 titles with annotations.

Bibliotheca Piscatoria: A Catalogue of Books on Angling, Fisheries and Fish-Culture. T. Westwood and T. Satchell. Originally printed 1883 and 1901.

Hunting, Hawking, Shooting. C. F. G. R. Schwerdt. Four volumes, illustrated and comprehensively annotated.

THE CARE AND REPAIR
OF BOOKS

A few strong instincts, and a few plain rules.
—WILLIAM WORDSWORTH

Though paper may be fragile, books are surprisingly durable if they are treated well. Proof of this is in the considerable number of incunabula that have survived from the Middle Ages in sturdy enough shape to delight collectors and continue serving as reference materials for serious scholars today.

Our own examination of a 300-year-old Eliot's *"Natick Indian" Bible* at the Boston Public Library revealed a book with pages solid enough to withstand the careful attentions of readers and researchers for many more years.

Even ignored and uncared for, an ancient tome left undisturbed and dry may survive without serious damage. A leather binding will certainly dry out and crack without proper dressing, but the pages of old books are stubbornly durable.

AVOIDING DAMAGE

Unfortunately, newer books may not last so long. Modern paper manufacture produces a lot of paper fast, but the quality of the paper has been inferior and it has a far shorter lifespan. The common product today has a high acid content that causes it to degrade, discolor, become brittle and fall apart over a few decades. Pulp paper used in newspapers and cheap magazines shows this defect in the extreme, as newspapers yellow and become brittle after a mere few days. Unless the industry corrects this problem, older books will be in better shape a hundred years from now than books printed last year. Happily, the publishing world is beginning to take note of this.

Some chief enemies of books are:

Fire. Fire has totally or partially destroyed many important libraries, often during war (for example, the burning of the Alexandrian Library by Caesar's troops, and the destruction of the Library of Congress in Washington by the British in the War of 1812), and sometimes by accident. The Jenkins Company of Austin, Texas, lost an extensive inventory to fire in December, 1985. Fortunately some of the more valuable items—many acquired from other collection dispersal sales through the years—were stored in a large walk-in vault and survived the blaze.

Light or moderate fire damage to a book may be repaired. The binding can be replaced and page ends, if scorched, may be trimmed. If a badly scorched book is still worth the trouble, the leaves may be unbound and mounted by a professional bookbinder.

Some precautions can be taken to minimize the threat of fire damage to a collection. A book room should have fire retardant carpets; draperies and curtains should be kept at a minimum; upholstered and overstuffed furniture should be avoided. Glass enclosed bookshelves are safer than open shelves where fires are a risk. A fire extinguisher should be kept handy and the door kept shut when the room is not in use.

Water. Books can be water-damaged by floods, fire fighting efforts, plumbing problems, storms, any occasion when water comes into contact with covers and leaves.

Whether or not a soaked book can be salvaged depends on the paper quality. Vellum can often take a soaking and be reconditioned. A good rag paper has the best chance, but the book must be dismantled and each leaf dried separately. Modern books on coated paper, such as art books, however, are a loss. The coating disintegrates and you're left with sticky goo and incomplete images on the pages. Newspapers, too, cannot take moisture. They absorb water and return to the pulp they started from.

Properly drying out a book is a delicate process and should be done by a professional. Restoration is an expensive procedure, so a book should be evaluated carefully to determine whether it is worth the cost.

Some steps to take to guard against water damage include avoiding rooms with overhead water pipes for book rooms. (Be aware of kitchens and bathrooms on the floor above. Those pipes are not always visible, but they can still leak down onto your books if they burst.) Avoid basement rooms that may leak or be damp at best. Cover books carefully when transporting them.

Excessive Humidity or Excessive Dryness. Dry air damages leather bindings. Humid air breeds mold and mildew, curls paper, and loosens bindings. The ideal humidity for books is around 50%, give or take ten points. In a

The English were masters of panel binding. It is symmetrical and orderly. The material is black morocco, the tooling is in gold, and the spine has extra embellishing, c. 1690.

Digital enhancement by Jonathan Draudt, Tamarac Arts.

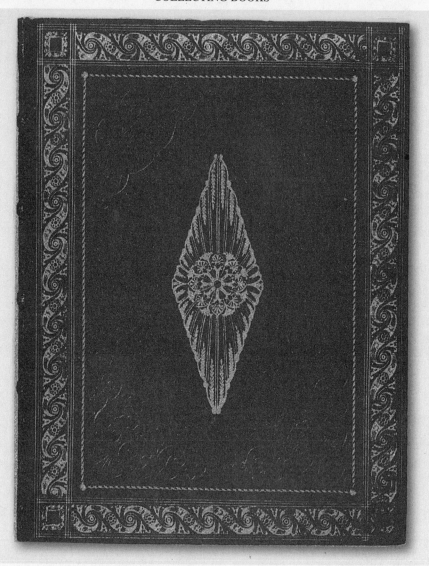

*This French binding features blindstamping and gilt tooling. It dates from
the second quarter of the 19th century.*
                    Digital enhancement by Jonathan Draudt, Tamarac Arts

humid environment, without a dehumidifier, it's best to store books on open
shelves rather than in glass cases where moisture can build up inside.

To help leather remain supple in all environments, but especially in dry
air, treat regularly with a leather dressing. This will be taken up at greater
length when we discuss leather care.

Rough Handling. Be gentle when handling all books, not just those that
appear fragile. Even a big, brawny folio can be easily damaged—sometimes
by the weight of its own pages pulling on the spine—if it's not handled well.

Don't open any book too wide or press it flat on a table to copy from it. This cracks the hinges.

Older books with metal clasps require special handling. If the clasps are tight, don't tug at them to open them. Instead, gently squeeze the outer edges of the book until the clasps pop open easily. To close them, squeeze again and gently fit the clasps in place. If they won't close, don't force them. Over time these books, especially vellum, may have swelled and the clasps no longer fit. Leave them open or risk damaging the binding with too much squeezing.

Improper Storage. A book can be damaged by improper shelving, though the harm is often done over time, almost imperceptibly, so you may not notice it's happening until it's too late. Common mistakes are wedging books too tightly on a shelf or letting books flop about on unfilled shelves, stacking books flat on their sides, one atop another, or shelving books on the fore-edge.

Most spine problems of folio books and larger are caused by shelving on the fore-edge, causing the books to develop loose sections or covers, bent edges and corners, and possibly damaged pages. While it's tempting to place a book that's too large for the shelf on its edge, you should resist the impulse. The weight of the pages will pull them away from the spine and you'll end up with a broken book.

If you can, stand large books on top of the bookcase supported by book-ends. If you can't do this, place them flat on the bookshelf, but don't put other books on top of them.

Light. The ultraviolet component of direct sunlight degrades many kinds of paper and fades the color—or "mellows" the bindings—of books that stand for long periods in the sun. Nothing is more discouraging than to see a table full of books at a flea market warping and wilting unprotected from a hot summer sun.

Bookcases shouldn't receive direct sunlight if it can be avoided, though indirect sunlight to brighten a room is okay. Interior lighting should be incandescent. Fluorescent light damages books.

Insects and Pests. A particularly nasty enemy of books is the bookworm. Not the bookish person devoted to reading, but insect larvae that feast on the binding and paste of books. Bugs, too, can wreak havoc on books. Some bugs, like silverfish, love a meal of sizing and starches used in the manufacture of paper. Some like the dyes and materials used in bindings like buckram.

The best recourse, if worms or insects are attacking your collection, is to call in a professional and have the entire house treated, but don't spray insecticide directly on your volumes. You may cause more damage than the bugs.

DISPLAYING YOUR BOOKS

Bookshelves. You'd think it would be simple to figure out how to store and display your books. Put them on a bookshelf, of course. But, it's not so simple

Miniature and micro books are displayed by Isaiah Thomas Booksellers of Massachusetts at the Vermont Antiquarian Booksellers Fair in Pomfret, Vermont.

Photo by Ilan Fisher

as it sounds. Many book enthusiasts think that old books belong in old book-cases and they will go out to an antique shop or an auction and buy the first old bookcase they see. Wrong.

It's important to look past the brass trimming and the darling, carved gar-goyles to see how the bookcase is constructed. Are the shelves adjustable in height? Are they sagging, cracked or splintered? Are all the shelf supports present? Are they sturdy enough to carry the weight of heavy books?

Whether or not your bookcase should have glass doors depends on several factors. Do you want the books handled? Are there children in the house too young to appreciate the delicacy of your treasures? Do you have pets who like to sit on top of a shelf of books? (Cats do.)

Glass doors are a great protection from dust and they cut down on the work you must do, as well as wear and tear on your books, keeping the books clean. But they are bulky and stand between you and your collection in a way that open, inviting shelves don't.

Bookends. Many bookends are collectible, such as from the Art Nouveau and the Arts and Crafts movements, stunning in brass, copper and bronze. But do they do the job?

Bookends should keep your books from tumbling around and should sup-port heavy volumes. If you find you're constantly repositioning and straight-

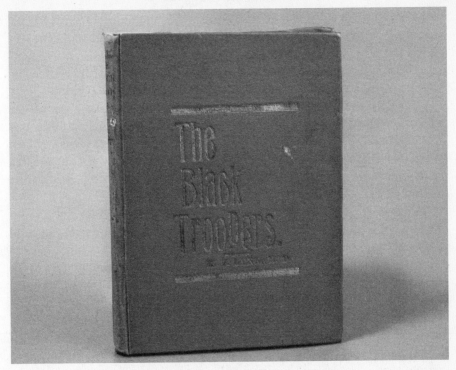

The Black Troopers, *a rare book, written by African American physician M. L. Lynk of Tennessee in 1898, contains biographies of Black American soldiers who fought in the Spanish American War.*

Photo and digital enhancement by Jonathan Draudt, Tamarac Arts

ening or tightening them up, they aren't working and should be replaced. For the best service, and at a fraction of the cost of the fancy bookend, we recommend the metal L-shaped or t-shaped models in which the lower portion slides beneath the first several books. Be sure they're tall enough to support your books and that the edges are smooth and won't scuff the covers and pages.

BOOK REPAIR

We cannot emphasize too strongly leaving the repair of a rare book to a competent bookbinder. For those more common or moderately priced books, learning a few pointers on how to repair them yourself is worthwhile.

Professional Bookbinding. A good bookbinder is a valuable resource, and anyone interested in used and old books should know one. He's first-aid for books, rescuing broken and defective volumes from oblivion, making suggestions and offering alternatives you may not realize you had.

Do not order a complete new binding if the old, loose one is in fairly sound condition. A loose cover can be rehinged, and missing leather can be replaced. New bindings can be created in which usable portions of the old leather are inlaid into a leather of similar grain and color. The old spine—or what's left of it—can be reset into a new spine.

These procedures are expensive and probably not worth the cost unless your book has some special appeal or is particularly ancient or rare.

When pages or gatherings are loose, the book may need resewing. If the paper is too fragile to permit this, the book can be dismantled and the inner edges of the leaves can be attached to guards which are then sewn together. When guards are used, it is generally not possible to recase the volume—that is, return it to the original binding—because the page ends will protrude from the fore-edge. A new binding is necessary.

Home Repair. You may try some home repair on mildly damaged books that are not so rare or expensive that a mistake would be a disaster. Some of the more common repairs are:

•Loose bindings. Loose cloth bindings can usually be repaired by opening the book midway, laying it face downward, and brushing glue along the inner side of the spine. Do not use cement-type glues; polyvinyl acetate, such as Elmer's Glue-All, does the job best. Use it sparingly. When completed, place rubber bands around the book and allow it to dry for several hours.

•Cracked Inner Hinges. Inner hinges can be strengthened by folding a narrow strip of paper and pasting it along the hinge. The paper should be about as heavy as an index card for best results. Make sure it is neither too long nor too short.

•Torn Spines. Spines are best treated by simply brushing a small quantity of glue on the torn sections, pressing them firmly into place, and allowing them to dry under the pressure of a rubber band.

•Notations or Underlinings. Markings done in pencil are easily—but gently!—erased. When the marks are in ink, nothing removes them satisfactorily, and it is probably wise not to make the effort. The paper could be damaged by using strong cleansers or by scraping. At times, the notations might be of interest and could even provide evidence of the book's previous ownership (called provenance).

•Moisture. Treat the book before the pages dry. Once stains are set by drying, they won't come out. Now the treatment we recommend may seem a little strange, but, if the book doesn't warrant professional attention, try this anyway.

First, mop any surface water by patting gently with soft paper towels. Place an oversized sheet of wax paper between all leaves that have gotten wet. In a wooden box about twice the size of the book, place an inch-thick layer of pipe tobacco and lay the book in it. Sprinkle a few more tobacco leaves over the book and seal the box tightly. Store the box in a dry place for several weeks. Some stains will probably remain, but they'll be less visible than if treatment had not been tried.

CARE OF LEATHER BOOKBINDINGS

Leather bindings, though more attractive than cloth, require more upkeep. Leather, an animal substance, has natural oils when new. As it grows old the oil dries out and the leather becomes brittle. Red dust on your bookshelves is a sure sign that your bindings are dry. At that point, emergency treatment is necessary. It won't cure damage that has already occurred but it will halt further deterioration.

Leather bindings must be dressed. This may not be the most pleasant chore, but it can be rewarding. Be sure to get a good leather care preparation, and use it intelligently. Too much will leave the binding sticky.

For best results, use a dressing made expressly for bindings such as the British Museum Leather Dressing. This old stand-by was once hard to get in America and collectors sent to London for it and paid the price. Today, it can generally be purchased in the states. Abide by the directions and don't be disappointed if the leather doesn't look polished. The aim in dressing leather is to give it a drink, not a shine.

Most old leathers will not polish and should not be expected to.

Give your leather-bound books a dressing about every six months. With regular care, any leather binding bought in good condition should remain so. But don't buy a shabby binding in the belief that it can be easily refurbished as this is impossible.

HOW TO USE
THIS BOOK

Books are part of man's prerogative.
—SIR THOMAS OVERBURY

The books in this listing are arranged alphabetically by author's last name, or, if no author, by the title, without reference to category or genre such as Americana, travel, sporting, etc. We believe this system is simple and "user friendly."

We discuss genres and categories in the glossary, in our sections on the book business and on popular collectible genres, and in the index, which is a listing of authors and titles cross-referenced by genre. A careful reader will soon be able to determine the proper categories for whatever book is in question.

In most of the listings, the author's name is followed by the title, place of publication and/or a date. Dates have been taken from the title page or the copyright page. In preferred bibliographic format, which we endorse and use in our own business, dates taken from the copyright page are in parentheses. We have endeavored to adhere to this style as closely as possible.

We have not limited ourselves to listing first editions, but we have identified first editions in the majority of cases. Where a question remains as to whether or not you have a first edition in hand, further research in reference bibliographies is called for. Several excellent research sources are listed at the back of this book.

In most cases, the number of pages in a volume is not given, but where we considered it helpful, or where identification of a work requires it, we have included page counts. Similarly, where illustrations include colored or engraved plates, we have included the number of plates in many cases, especially when identification of an important book is dependent on that information. (Note: When examining any volume, check the table of contents or list of illustrations against the plates present to be sure they are all accounted for, since some people remove plates from old books to frame and sell them separately.)

Readers will notice that many books listed are not first editions. Some titles are rare and valuable in whatever editions they appear. Later editions may contain signatures, provenance, or other attributes of note or may be illustrated by artists of great renown, making those editions more valuable than the first.

Unless otherwise stated, the prices given are for books in their original bindings, except for those dating to the 17th century or earlier, in which case a good period binding is assumed.

Our prices reflect fair retail value based on a concensus of asking prices and realized prices of books on the open market over the past three years.

Dealers typically offer a 10–20% discount to other bookmen. A dealer may pay about 50% of retail for a book bought from a private individual if a customer is waiting in the wings for that book. For stock, a dealer will offer from 20% to 35% of a book's retail value.

If you should offer a dealer an extremely rare and sought-after book, the dealer may act as an agent to market the book and take only a commission on the sale. This happened to us recently when we discovered Professor Albert Einstein's signature on a dinner menu and program from a 1930's TransAtlantic Ocean Liner. Prof. Einstein was on the program to entertain that evening playing his violin.We informed the owner of the menu, who was not aware of the signature, and with her permission sent the document to a New York auction house. We're not only thrilled to be the agents in this case, but discovering the signature was great fun.

Settling on prices for this guide, we used the tools available to us—auction records, dealer catalogues, the Internet, conversations with booksellers, and more than twenty years experience in the trade—to give you the best estimates on the retail value of the books listed.

At times, the variation in our price listings reflects slight differences in the condition of books offered by different dealers. At times, it reflects the vicissitudes of the market where a book may fetch a smart price in the mountains of New England but go far more cheaply in the deserts of Arizona. Or a dealer may offer a book at one price in his shop, while patrons of an auction house bought it at a far different price. And if you go to the Internet, you may find an even wider range of prices. We have not shied away from listing these broad ranges so the reader can see clearly the idiosyncrasies of the antiquarian book trade.

In all cases, books are assumed to be in at least very good condition, and where modern first editions are concerned, excellent condition. To realize their best price, modern firsts must have their dust jackets intact, but some listings clearly do not state dust jacket. These books have been offered or sold for a lower price than they would have fetched with the jacket. Still, many modern firsts, even without their jackets, are worth more than the $.50 charged at library sales, so we've included them here.

At all times, remember that this is a guide and not a guarantee of prices. The marketplace, forever in flux, determines the real value of used and collectible books.

We have endeavored to verify statistics for each listing, but no book of this type can guarantee freedom from error. The serious bibliophile will not depend on any one source, but will use multiple research tools to verify data on important books.

LIST OF ABBREVIATIONS

Albany	Alb
All edges gilt	aeg
American Museum of Natural History	AMNH
Association copy	asso copy
Atlanta	Atl
Backed	bkd
Baltimore	Balt
Boards	bds
Boston	Bos
California	Ca
Cambridge	Camb
Catalogue	cat
Chicago	Chi
Chromolithographs	chromos
Cincinnatti	Cinc
Cleveland	Cleve
Color	clr
Connecticut	Conn
Copies	cc
Dublin	Dub
Dust jacket	dj

Edinburgh	Edin
Edition, edited	ed
Editor.	(ed.)
English	Eng
Engravings.	engr
Ex libris, ex library	xlib
Facsimile	facs
First edition	1st ed
Folding	fldg
Government Printing Office	GPO
Hand colored	hand-clr
Illinois	Ill
Illustrated.	illus
Impression	imp
Indianapolis	Ind
Inscribed	inscrb
Leather	lea
Limited edition	ltd
Marbled	marb
Milwaukee	Milw
Morocco	mor
Original	ori
Pages	pp
Philadelphia	Phila
Pictorial	pict
Pictorial cloth.	pict cl
Pittsburgh.	Pitts
Providence	Prov
Rebound	rbnd
Reprint.	rprnt
Revised edition	rev ed
San Francisco.	SF
Signed	sgn
Softcover	softcvr
Top edge gilt	teg
Toronto	Tor
United Kingdom	UK
United States	US
University	Univ
Volume	vol
Wrapper.	wrpr

COLLECTIBLE
BOOK LISTINGS

The University of these days
is a Collection of Books.
—THOMAS CARLYLE

A Week at the Fair Illustrating the Exhibits and Wonders of the World's Columbian Exposition. Chi. Rand, McNally. 1893. 1st ed. illus. maps, plans, red cl over flexible bds. . . . . *$50.00–$75.00*

Abbatt, William. *Battle of Pell's Point.* NY. 1901. illus. map ports, 500 cc. . . . .
. . . . *$50.00–$75.00*

Abbey, Lynn. *Daughter of the Bright Moon.* NY. Ace Books. (1979). 1st ed. cl-backed bds, dj. . . . . *$35.00–$40.00*

Abbott, John S. C. *History of Hernando Cortez.* NY. Harper. 1855. 1st ed. illus. lea, marbled bds. . . . . *$130.00–$160.00*

Abbott, Wilbur. *Bibliography of Oliver Cromwell.* Harvard Pub Pr. 1929. illus. 2 portraits. . . . . *$50.00–$95.00*

Abe, Kobo. *Woman in the Dunes.* NY. Knopf. 1964. 1st UK ed. dj. . *$55.00–$95.00*

Abel, Ernest L. *Scientific Study of Marihuana.* Chi. Nelson-Hall. 1976. 1st ed. dj.
. . . . *$15.00–$25.00*

Abercrombie, John. *Pathological & Practical Researches on Diseases of the Brain.* Phil. 1843. . . . . *$100.00–$200.00*

Abernethy, John. *Surgical Works.* Lon. 1816. 2 vols. new ed. 1 plate, calf. . . . . . .
. . . . *$100.00–$200.00*

Abrahams, Peter. *The Path of Thunder.* NY. Harper. 1948. 1st ed. dj. . . . .
. . . . *$20.00–$40.00*

Achatenere, Romulo. *Oh, Mio Yemeya.* Cuba. Editorial Ed Arte. 1938. wrps. graphic by Hernadez Cardenas. . . . . *$75.00–$100.00*

Ackley, Edith. *Doll Shop of Your Own.* NY & Tor. Frederick A Stokes. (1941). 1st ed. sgn, dj. . . . . *$25.00–$40.00*

Ackroyd, Peter. *Chatterton.* Lon. Hamish Hamilton. (1987). 1st ed. sgn, bds, dj.. .
. . . . *$75.00–$80.00*

Ackroyd, Peter. *First Light.* Lon. Hamish Hamilton. (1989). 1st ed. bds, dj. . . . . .
. . . . *$35.00–$40.00*

Act for the Making of Bread. Lon. 1758. *$50.00–$75.00*

Activities of Ku Klux Klan Organizations in the United States. DC. GPO. 1966. wrps. . . . . *$75.00–$250.00*

Adair, J. *Navajo & Pueblo Silversmiths.* Norman, OK. 1946. maps, charts, plates, dj.
. . . . *$30.00–$40.00*

Adamic, Louis. *My Native Land.* NY. Harper. 1943. sgn. . . . . *$12.00–$35.00*

Adamic. Louis. *A Nation of Nations.* NY. Harper. 1945. 1st ed. sgn. dj. . . . .
. . . . *$20.00–$35.00*

Adams, A. L. *Field and Forest Rambles....* Lon. 1873. illus. . . . . . *$75.00–$100.00*

Adams, Ansel. *Born Free and Equal.* NY. U S Camera. 1944. 1st ed. illus. scarce in dj. . . . . *$1,500.00–$1,800.00*

Adams, Ansel. *My Camera in the National Parks.* Yosemite National Park. Virginia Adams. 1950. illus. 97 pp, spiral bound bds. sgn.. . . . . *$275.00–$450.00*

Adams, Ansel. *Polaroid Land Photography.* Bos. New York Graphic Society. (1978). rev. ed. illus. sgn. dj. . . . . *$70.00–$100.00*

Adams, Ansel. *Polaroid Land Photography Manual.* NY. Morgan & Morgan. (1963). 1st ed. illus. sgn, cl, dj. . . . . *$75.00–$140.00*

Adams, Ansel. *Yosemite Valley.* SF. 1959. 1st ed. pict wrps. . . . . . *$45.00–$100.00*

Adams, Ansel and Nancy Newhall. *This Is the American Earth.* SF. Sierra Club. 1960. 1st ed. illus. 89 pp. dj. . . . . *$45.00–$200.00*

Adams, Arthur G. *The Hudson Through the Years.* Westwood. Lind. 1983. 3rd prtg. dj. . . . . *$25.00–$35.00*

Adams, Charles. *Lee At Appomattox and Other Papers.* Bos. Houghton Mifflin. 1902. 1st ed. . . . . *$25.00–$45.00*

Adams, Charles Francis. *Confederacy and the Transvaal.* Bos. Houghton Mifflin. 1901. . . . . *$25.00–$50.00*

Adams, Charles Francis, Jr. *Notes on Railroad Accidents.* NY. 1879. cl. . . . .
. . . . *$50.00–$100.00*

Adams, D. *Hitchhiker's Guide to the Galaxy.* 1979. 1st ed. dj. . . . . *$25.00–$65.00*

Adams, Douglas. *Dirk Gently's Holistic Detective Agency.* NY. Simon and Schuster. (1987). 1st US ed. dj.. . . . . *$15.00–$20.00*

Adams, Douglas. *The Long Dark Tea-time of the Soul.* Lon. Heinemann. (1988). 1st ed. bds, dj.. . . . . *$25.00–$30.00*

Adams, Elizabeth Laura. *Dark Symphony.* NY. Sheed & Ward. 1942. 1st ed. dj. . .
. . . . *$65.00–$100.00*

Adams, Frank Davis. *Life and Times of Buckshot South.* NY. Dutton. 1959. 1st ed. dj. . . . . *$15.00–$35.00*

Adams, George. *Doctors in Blue.* NY. Schuman. (1952). 1st ed. . . *$30.00–$65.00*

Adams, George. *Treatise Describing the Construction, and Explaining the Use, of New Celestial and Terrestrial Globes.* Lon. pub by author. 1782. 5th ed. plates. . . .
. . . . *$300.00–$500.00*

Adams, Hannah. *Analysis of the Controversy between the Rev. Jedediah Moore....* Bos. 1814. wrps. . . . . *$125.00–$250.00*

Adams, John. *Message from the President of the United States....* Phila. Fenno. 1799. 1st ed. scarce.. . . . . *$250.00–$300.00*

Adams, John D. *Arts-Crafts Lamps: How to Make Them.* Chi. 1911. illus. . . . . . .
. . . . *$65.00–$85.00*

Adams, Joseph. *Salmon and Trout Angling.* NY. Dutton. 1923. 1st Amer ed. 288 pp.
. . . . *$25.00–$65.00*

Adams, Nehemiah. *South Side View of Slavery.* Bos. Marvin. 1854. . . . .
. . . . *$1,135.00–$350.00*

Adams, Ramon F. (comp.). *The Rampaging Herd: A Bibliography of Books and Pamphlets... in the Cattle Industry.* Norman. Univ of Oklahoma Press. (1959). 1st ed. cl, dj.. . . . . *$80.00–$100.00*

Adams, Rev. William M. A. *Sacred Allegories.* Phila. Butler. 1858. new ed. illus. blue cl.. . . . . *$100.00–$150.00*

Adams, Richard. *Tales from Watership Down.* Lon. (1996). 1st ed. dj. . *$15.00–$30.00*

Adams, Richard. *The Girl in a Swing.* Lon. Allen Lane. (1980). 1st ed. bds, dj. . . .
. . . . *$100.00–$150.00*

Adams, Richard. *Traveller*. NY. Knopf. 1988. 1st ed. dj. . . . . *$25.00–$60.00*

Adcock, Thomas. *Sea of Green*. NY. Mysterious Press. 1989. 1st ed. dj. . . . .
. . . . *$15.00–$40.00*

Addams, Charles. *Favorite Haunts*. NY. Simon & Schuster. (1976). 1st ed. dj. . . .
. . . . *$45.00–*

Addams, Charles. *Homebodies*. NY. Simon & Schuster. 1954. 1st ed. cl-backed bds,
dj. *$85.00–*

Addington, Sarah. *Boy Who Lived in Pudding Lane*. Bos. (1922). illus. . . . .
. . . . *$30.00–$40.00*

Addison, Joseph. *Works of....* Lon. Cadell Y W Davis. 1811. 6 vols. . . . .
. . . . *$375.00–$500.00*

Ade, George. *Breaking Into Society*. NY. 1904. 1st ed. . . . . *$10.00–$25.00*

Ade, George. *Old Time Saloon*. NY. 1931. 1st ed. . . . . *$15.00–$50.00*

Adney, Edwin Tappan. *Klondike Stampede*. WA. 1968. illus. rprnt. ltd ed. . . . . . .
. . . . *$50.00–$85.00*

Agassiz, L. *Lake Superior*. Bos. Ticknor & Fields. 1850. 15 plates, map. . . . .
. . . . *$350.00–$525.00*

Agassiz, Louis. *Journal in Brazil*. Bos. Ticknor & Fields. 1868. . . *$50.00–$75.00*

Agassiz, Louis. *Structure of Animal Life: Six Lectures*. Scribner, Armstrong. 1866.
. . . . *$65.00–$125.00*

Agatha, Sister M. *Texas Prose Writings*. Dallas. (1936). illus. frontis, cl, scarce. . .
. . . . *$25.00–$35.00*

Agee, James. *Death in the Family*. Obolensky. (1957). 1st ed. dj. . *$60.00–$100.00*

Agricultural Implements and Machines. Bos. Ames Plow Company. 1901. illus.
pict wrps.. . . . . *$25.00–$30.00*

Aguilar, Grace. *The Days of Bruce*. Lon. 1900. . . . . *$25.00–$35.00*

Aguilar, Grace. *The Mother's Recompense*. NY. 1851. . . . . *$25.00–$35.00*

Aickman, Robert. *Wine Dark Sea*. NY. Arbor House. (1988). 1st ed. dj. . . . .
. . . . *$25.00–$35.00*

Aiken, Conrad. *Jig of Forslin*. Bos. 1916. 1st ed. . . . . *$50.00–$100.00*

Ainsworth, Ed. *Cowboy Art*. NY. World Pub. (1968). 1st ed. illus. ltd 1000 cc, slipcase. . . . . *$180.00–$250.00*

Akers, Floyd. *Boy Fortune Hunters in Alaska.* Chi. Reilly & Britton. (1908). 1st ed. decal frontis. . . . . *$75.00–$150.00*

Albee, Edward. *Everything in the Garden.* NY. Atheneum. 1968. 1st ed. sgn, dj.. . . . . *$125.00–$150.00*

Albee, Edward. *The American Dream.* NY. Coward McCann. 1961. 1st ed. sgn, dj. . . . . *$200.00–$225.00*

Albert, Lillian. *Complete Button Book.* NY. Doubleday. 1949. 1st ed. dj. . . . . *$65.00–$100.00*

Alcoholics Anonymous. NY. World Services. 1954. dj. . . . . *$400.00–$550.00*

Alcoholics Anonymous. NY. World Services. 1939. 1st ed. red cl, dj.. . . . . *$2,000.00–$6,800.00*

Alcott, Louisa May. *An Old Fashioned Girl.* Bos. Roberts Bros. 1870. 1st ed. ads on copyright page, 2 plates. . . . . *$65.00–$150.00*

Alcott, Louisa May. *Aunt Jo's Scrap Bag.* Bos. Roberts. 1873. . . . *$35.00–$45.00*

Alcott, Louisa May. *Little Men.* Bos. Roberts. 1871. 1st ed. 1st issue, green cl.. . . . . *$250.00–$275.00*

Alcott, Louisa May. *Jo's Boys.* Grosset & Dunlap. 1948. . . . . *$8.00–$14.00*

Alcott, Louia May. *Little Men.* Grosset & Dunalp. 1973. . . . . *$10.00–$15.00*

Aldrich, Herbert L. *Arctic Alaska and Siberia.* Chi/NY. Rand McNally. 1899. illus. photos, maps, blue cl. . . . . *$145.00–$200.00*

Alegra, Claribel and Darwin J. Flakoll. *Ashes of Izalco.* Willimantic. Curbstone. (1989). 1st ed. wrps, sgn.. . . . . *$20.00–$25.00*

Alexander, David. *Most Men Don't Kill.* NY. Random House. 1951. 1st ed. author's first novel, dj. . . . . *$35.00–$65.00*

Alexander, E. P. *Military Memoirs of a Confederate.* NY. Scribner's. 1907. 1st ed. illus. fldg map.. . . . . *$100.00–$275.00*

Alexander, William. *History of Women.* Bristol. 1995. rprnt.. . . . *$125.00–$150.00*

Alexander, William. *History of Women.* Lon. Strahan and Cadell. 1779. 2 vols. 1st ed. scarce. . . . . *$400.00–$700.00*

Alexie, Sherman. *Lone Ranger and Tonto Fistfight in Heaven.* NY. Atlantic Monthly. 1993. wrps. 1st US ed.. . . . . *$50.00–$75.00*

Alfred Stieglitz: Photographs & Writings. DC. National Gallery of Art. (1983). 1st ed. photo plates, folio, dj. . . . . *$60.00–$70.00*

Alger, Horatio. *Adrift in the City*. Phila. John Winston. nd. . . . . . . *$17.00–$50.00*

Alger, Horatio. *Brave and Bold*. Cleve. World Pub. nd.. . . . . *$14.00–$16.00*

Alger, Horatio. *Erie Train Boy*. Whitman Small. paper over cardboard, blue cl spine. . . . . *$12.00–$20.00*

Alger, Horatio. *From Canal Bay to President*. NY. 1881. red with lettering in gold. . . . . *$35.00–$75.00*

Alger, Horatio. *Paul the Peddler*. Chi. Donohue. nd. pict green cl, 242 pp plus ads. . . . . *$12.00–$20.00*

Alger, Horatio. *Silas Snobden's Office Boy*. Garden City. Doubleday. 1973. dj. . . . . *$14.00–$25.00*

Alger, Horatio. *Wait and Hope*. Phila. Winston. 1905. red cl, 352 pp plus ads. . . . . *$10.00–$30.00*

Alger, Horatio. *Young Outlaw*. NY. Hurst &Co. decorated bds.. . . . *$15.00–$20.00*

Alger, Horatio Jr. *Luke Walton or The Chicago Newsboy*. Phila. Coates. nd. taupe cl, 346 pp, frontis. . . . . *$60.00–$100.00*

Alger, William Rounseville. *Life of Edwin Forrest*. Phila. Lippincott. 1877. 2 vols. large 8vo, pict cl, 864 pp, plates. . . . . *$85.00–$100.00*

Algren, Nelson. *Walk on the Wild Side*. Farrar, Straus & Cudahy. (1956). 1st ed. dj. . . . . *$35.00–$90.00*

Ali Baba and the Forty Thieves. Houghton Mifflin. 1950. 6 pop-ups. . . . . *$75.00–$100.00*

Alken, Henry. *Scraps from the Sketch Book*. Lon. 1823. illus. hand-clr plates, folio. . . . . *$500.00–$650.00*

Allan, William. *Army of Northern Virginia in 1862*. Bos/NY. 1892. 1st ed. maps. . . . . *$300.00–$500.00*

Alldredge, Charles. *Some Quick and Some Dead: Poems*. NY. Cooper Square. 1964. 1st ed. . . . . *$75.00–$115.00*

Allen, Charles Dexter. *American Book-Plates*. NY. Macmillan. 1894. 1st ed. illus. . . . . *$85.00–$100.00*

Allen, Grant. *The Cruise of the Albatross*. Bos. Lothrop. (1898). 1st US ed. illus.. . . . . *$25.00–$50.00*

Allen, Harvey. *The Forest and the Fort*. 1943. 1st ed. bds, dj. . . . . . *$20.00–$30.00*

Allen, Henry T. *Report of an Expedition of the Copper, Tana, and Koyukuk Rivers, in the Territory of Alaska.... 1885.* DC. GPO. 1887. 1st ed. illus. 5 fldg maps, plates, 172 pp, marbled wrps. . . . . *$95.00–$125.00*

Allen, Miss A. J. *Ten Years in Oregon.* Ithaca. 1848. 1st ed. 2nd issue. . . . .
. . . . *$125.00–$250.00*

Allen, Steve. *Funny Men.* NY. Simon & Schuster. 1956. dj. . . . . . . *$15.00–$30.00*

Allende, Isabel. *Of Love and Shadows.* NY. Knopf. 1987. 1st ed. dj. . . . .
. . . . *$10.00–$20.00*

Allison, Willie (ed.). *First Golf Review.* Lon. Bonar. (1950). 1st ed. dj. . . . .
. . . . *$25.00–$50.00*

Alliss, Percy. *Better Golf.* Lon. Black. 1926. 1st ed. illus. photos. . . . .
. . . . *$70.00–$100.00*

Almon W. Babbit, Delegate from Deseret. DC. 1850. . . . . *$85.00–$65.00*

Alvarez, Julia. *How the Garcia Girls Lost Their Accents.* Chapel Hill. Algonquin. 1991. 1st ed. dj. . . . . *$35.00–$125.00*

Alvarez, Julia. *In the Time of the Butterfly.* Chapel Hill. Algonquin Books. 1994. 1st ed. sgn, dj. . . . . *$35.00–$50.00*

Ambler, Charles Henry. *History of Transportation in the Ohio Valley.* CA. 1932. 1st ed. illus. . . . . *$100.00–$200.00*

Ambler, Eric. *Night-Comers.* Lon. Heinemann. 1956. 1st ed. dj. . . . *$45.00–$60.00*

Ambler, Eric. *Story So Far: Memories and Other Fictions.* Lon. Weidenfeld & Nocolson. 1993. 1st ed. dj. . . . . *$15.00–$30.00*

Ambler, Louis. *Old Halls & Manor Houses of Yorkshire.* Lon. nd. illus. . . . .
. . . . *$100.00–$235.00*

American Book Prices Current 1970-1975. NY. Bankcroft-Parkman. 1976. 2 vols. red cl. . . . . *$50.00–$85.00*

American Boy's Book of Sports and Games.... NY. (1864). illus. . *$150.00–$425.00*

American Car and Foundry Company in Khaki; Its Production Achievements in the Great War. NY. 1919. 95 pp. . . . . *$50.00–$75.00*

American Jack Stock Stud Book. Nashville. American Breeders Association of Jacks and Jennets. 1891. Vol. I. . . . . *$100.00–$125.00*

American Jack Stock Stud Book. Nashville. American Breeders Association of Jacks and Jennets. 1891. Vol. III. . . . . *$100.00–$125.00*

American Line Type. Jersey City. American Type Founders. 1903. large 4to, 292 pp. . . . . *$100.00–$200.00*

American Pioneer in Science, William James Beal. Amherst, MA. 1925. 1st ed. illus. . . . . *$50.00–$75.00*

American Type Founders Company, Specimen Book and Catalogue, 1923. Jersey City. American Type Founders. (1923). cl bds. . . . . *$100.00–$200.00*

Ames, Nathaniel. *An Astronomical Diary of an Almanack...1760, 1761, 1762, 1763, 1764.* Bos. John Draper. (1759-1763). 5 almanacs bound together, cl, lea label. . . . . *$375.00–$500.00*

Amherst, Alicia. *History of Gardening in England.* Lon. Bernard Tuaritch.1896. illus. . . . . *$90.00–$150.00*

Amis, Martin. *London Fields.* Tor. Lester & Orpen Denny. (1989). 1st Canadian ed, inscr, dj. . . . . *$25.00–$75.00*

Amsden, Charles Avery. *Navaho Weaving....* CA. Santa Ana. 1934. 1st ed. illus. . . . . *$275.00–$400.00*

Amundsen, Roald. *First Crossing of the Polar Sea.* NY. Doran. 1928. dj. . . . . *$45.00–$60.00*

Amundsen, Roald. *South Pole.* NY. 1912. 2 vols. 1st ed. maps. *$850.00–$2,000.00*

Andersen, Hans Christian. *Dulac's The Snow Queen and Other Stories by Hans Christian Andersen.* Garden City. Doubledy Doran. 1976. 1st ed. illus. by Edmund Dulac. dj. . . . . *$30.00–$40.00*

Andersen, Hans Christian. *Ice Maiden....* Lon. (1889). green cl, gilt lettering, clr frontis. . . . . *$65.00–$100.00*

Andersen, Hans Christian. *Kate Greenaway's Original Drawings for The Snow Queen.* NY. Schocken Books. 1st ed. illus. by Kate Greenaway. dj. . *$15.00–$25.00*

Andersen, Hans Christian. *Nightingale and Other Stories.* NY/Lon. Hodder & Stoughton. nd. 1st ed. illus. by Edmund Dulac, tip-in clr plates.. . *$150.00–$200.00*

Andersen, Hans Christian. *Picture Book Without Pictures.* NY. 1848. 1st US ed.. . . . . *$50.00–$60.00*

Andersen, Hans Christian. *Tumble Bug and Other Tales.* NY. Harcourt, Brace. 1940. illus. by Hertha List. red cl over bds, dj. . . . . *$45.00–$100.00*

Anderson, Charles C. *Fighting by Southern Federals.* NY. Neale. 1912. 1st ed. blue cl. . . . . *$85.00–$175.00*

Anderson, Christopher. *Annals of the English Bible.* NY. Carter. 1849. new cl. . . . . *$50.00–$85.00*

Anderson, Eva Greenslit. *Chief Seattle.* Caldwell, IN. Caxton Press. 1943. 1st ed. map. . . . . *$75.00–$115.00*

Anderson, John. *American Theatre & Motion Picture in America.* NY. Dial Press. 1938. illus.. . . . . *$30.00–$70.00*

Anderson, Kenneth. *Nine Man-eaters and One Rogue.* NY. Dutton. 1955. illus. b/w photos, dj. . . . . *$45.00–$65.00*

Anderson, Kent. *Sympathy for the Devil.* Garden City. Doubleday. 1987. 1st ed. author's first novel, sgn, dj. . . . . *$100.00–$200.00*

Anderson, Lawrence. *Art of the Silversmith in Mexico.* NY. Oxford Univ Press. 1975. 2 vols in one. rprnt. . . . . *$30.00–$45.00*

Anderson, Martha Jane. *Social Life and Vegetarianism.* Mt. Lebanon. (Chicago: Guiding Star Printing House). 1893. 27 pp. . . . . *$50.00–$80.00*

Anderson, Mary. *Scenes in Hawaiian Islands & Calif.* Bos. American Tract Society. 1865. illus. . . . . *$75.00–$100.00*

Anderson, Nels. *The Hobo....* Chi. Univ of Chi Press. 1923. 1st ed. illus. photos, cl, scarce. . . . . *$70.00–$85.00*

Anderson, Poul. *Flandry of Terra.* Phila. Chilton Books. 1965. 1st ed. dj. . . . . *$25.00–$35.00*

Anderson, Poul. *Guardians of Time.* Lon. Gollancz. 1961. 1st ed. dj. . . . . *$80.00–$125.00*

Anderson, Poul. *Perish the Sword.* NY. Macmillan. 1959. 1st ed. dj. . *$50.00–$100.00*

Anderson, R. C. *Rigging of the Ships in the Days of the Spritsail Topmast....* Salem. Marine Research Society. 1927. illus. plates, dj.. . . . . *$65.00–$110.00*

Anderson, Rufus. *Hawaiian Islands.* Bos. Gould & Lincoln. 1864. 1st ed. illus. plates, maps. . . . . *$125.00–$375.00*

Anderson, Sherwood. *A Story Teller's Story.* NY. Huebsch. 1924. 1st ed. dj missing. . . . . *$15.00–$30.00*

Anderson, Sherwood. *Anderson, Poor White.* NY. Huebsch. 1920. 1st ed. dj. . . . . *$160.00–$175.00*

Anderson, Sherwood. *Horses and Men.* NY. Huebsch. 1923. 1st ed. orange cl. . . . . *$20.00–$75.00*

Anderson, Sherwood. *Perhaps Women.* NY. Liveright. 1931. 1st ed. dj. . . . . *$125.00–$175.00*

Anderson, Sherwood. *Tar, A Midwest Childhood.* 1926. 1st ed. dj.. *$60.00–$70.00*

Anderson, Sherwood. *Winesburg, Ohio.* NY. Huebsch. 1919. 1st ed. . . . .
. . . . *$125.00–$200.00*

Anderson, William. *Japanese Wood Engravings.* Lon. Seely. 1895. 1st ed. illus. .
. . . . *$55.00–$70.00*

Andrews, Eliza Frances. *War-Time Journal of a Georgia Girl 1864-1865.* NY.
1908. 1st ed. . . . . *$55.00–$85.00*

Andrews, Roy Chapman. *On the Trail of Ancient Man....* NY. Putnam. 1926. illus.
photos. 3rd print. . . . . *$35.00–$40.00*

Angelou, Maya. *Gather Together In My Name.* NY. Random House. 1974. 1st Amer
ed. sgn, dj. . . . . *$75.00–$100.00*

Angelou, Maya. *Just Give Me a Cool Drink of Water 'Fore I Die.* NY. Random
House. 1971. 1st ed. dj. . . . . *$35.00–$100.00*

Angelou, Maya. *Now Sheba Sings the Song.* NY. Dutton. 1987. 1st ed. illus. dj. . . .
. . . . *$15.00–$30.00*

Angelou, Maya. *On the Pulse of Morning.* NY. Random House. 1993. 1st ed. wrps.
inaugural. . . . . *$25.00–$50.00*

Angelou, Maya. *Singin' and Swingin' and Gettin' Merry Like Christmas.* NY.
Random House. 1976. 1st ed. dj. . . . . *$20.00–$50.00*

Angione, Genevieve. *All-Bisque and Half-Bisque Dolls.* Thomas Nelson. (1969). .
. . . . *$30.00–$45.00*

Animated Picture Book of Alice in Wonderland. NY. Grosset & Dunlap. (1945).
illus and animated by Julian Wehr. 4 moveable clr plates. spiral-bound. . . . .
. . . . *$200.00–$300.00*

Annesley, George. *Voyages and Travels to India, Ceylon, The Red Sea, Abyssinia
and Egypt.* Lon. William Miller. 1809. 3 vols. 1st ed. illus. calf maps. . . . .
. . . . *$1,300.00–$1,500.00*

Anno, Mitsumasa. *Anno's Flea Market.* Philomel Books. 1984. 1st US ed. dj. . . . .
. . . . *$15.00–$20.00*

Anno, Mitsumasa. *Anno's Italy.* 1980. 1st ed. dj. . . . . *$20.00–$30.00*

**Annual Report of the Board of Regents of the Smithsonian...Years Ending June
30, 1901.** DC. GPO. 1903. illus. plates, photos. . . . . *$50.00–$90.00*

Anson, Margaret. *Merry Order of St. Bridget: Personal Recollections of the Use of
the Rod.* York. private printing. 1857. . . . . *$60.00–$90.00*

Ansted and Latham. *Channel Islands.* Lon. Allen. 1865. 2nd ed. illus. . . . .
. . . . *$50.00–$80.00*

Anthon, Charles. *Classical Dictionary.* NY. Harper. 1852. 1st ed. *$60.00–$115.00*

Anthony, Gordon. *Russian Ballet.* Lon. Geoffrey Bles. (1939). 1st ed. illus. . . . .
. . . .*$50.00–$80.00*

Apes, William. *Son of the Forest.* NY. William Apes. 1831. 2nd rev. ed. . . . .
. . . .*$70.00–$100.00*

Apperley, C. J. *Horse & the Hound, their various uses & treatment including prac-tical....* Edinburgh. 1863. frontis plates. . . . .*$60.00–$100.00*

Apperley, C. J. *Hunting Reminiscences.* Lon. Rudolph Ackerman. 1843. 1st ed. illus. b/w plates. . . . .*$200.00–$500.00*

Apperley, C. J. *Memoirs of the Life of the Late John Mytton.* Lon. 1851. illus. 18 clr plates by Henry Alken. . . . .*$800.00–$1,000.00*

Applegate, Frank G. *Indian Stories from Pueblos.* Phila. 1929. illus. in clr. . . . . .
. . . .*$50.00–$75.00*

Appleton, L. H. *Indian Art of the Americas.* NY. (1950). illus. . . . *$75.00–$150.00*

Appleton, Victor. *Don Sturdy, The Desert of Mystery.* NY. Grosset & Dunlap. 1925. #1, dj. . . . .*$50.00–$75.00*

Appleton, Victor. *Moving Picture Boys.* NY. Grosset & Dunlap. 1913. #1, dj. . . . . .
. . . .*$15.00–$30.00*

Appleton, Victor. *Tom Swift Among the Fire Fighters.* NY. Grosset & Dunlap. 1921. #24, dj. . . . .*$85.00–$115.00*

Appleton, Victor. *Tom Swift and His Air Glider.* NY. Grosset & Dunlap. 1912. . .
. . . .*$12.00–$15.00*

Appleton, Victor. *Tom Swift and His Air Scout.* NY. Grosset & Dunlap. 1910. no dj.
. . . .*$8.00–$20.00*

Appleton, Victor. *Tom Swift and His Electric Runabout.* NY. Grosset & Dunlap. (1910). 1st ed. # 5, dj. . . . .*$50.00–$125.00*

Appleton, Victor. *Tom Swift and His Giant Cannon.* NY. Grosset & Dunlap. 1913.
. . . .*$14.00–$18.00*

Appleton, Victor. *Tom Swift and His Great Oil Gusher.* NY. Grosset & Dunlap. 1924.
. . . .*$15.00–$20.00*

Appleton, Victor. *Tom Swift and His Ocean Airport.* Whitman. 1934. #37, dj. . . . . .
. . . .*$45.00–$90.00*

Appleton, Victor. *Tom Swift and His Submarine Boat.* NY. Grosset & Dunlap. 1910.
. . . .*$10.00–$12.00*

Appleton, Victor. *Tom Swift Circling the Globe.* NY. Grosset & Dunlap. 1927. dj..
. . . . *$15.00–$18.00*

Appleton, Victor. *Tom Swift in the Caves of Ice.* NY. Grosset & Dunlap. 1911. . .
. . . . *$15.00–$18.00*

Appleton, Victor. *Tom Swift in the City of Gold.* NY. Grosset & Dunlap. 1912. . .
. . . . *$12.00–$15.00*

Appleton, Victor II. *Tom Swift and His G-Force Inverter.* NY. Grosset & Dunlap.
1968. #30 in Tom Swift Jr. series, dj. . . . . *$75.00–$150.00*

Appleton, Victor II. *Tom Swift and, His Repelatron Skyway.* NY. Grosset & Dunlap.
1963. #22 in Tom Swift Jr. series. . . . . *$12.00–$20.00*

Appleton, Victor II. *Tom Swift and His Spectromarine Selector.* NY. Grosset &
Dunlap. 1960. #15 in Tom Swift Jr. series. . . . . *$12.00–$25.00*

Appleton, Victor II. *Tom Swift and, The Asteroid Pirates.* NY. Grosset & Dunlap.
1963. #21 in Tom Swift Jr. series. . . . . *$10.00–$24.00*

Appleton, Victor II. *Tom Swift and, The Race to the Moon.* NY. Grosset & Dunlap.
1958. #12 in Tom Swift Jr. series. . . . . *$12.00–$17.00*

Appleton, Victor II. *Tom Swift and His Electronic Retroscope.* NY. Grosset &
Dunlap. 1959. 1st ed. dj, #14 in Tom Swift Jr. series. . . . . *$15.00–$22.00*

Appleton, Victor II. *Tom Swift and His Jetmarine.* NY. Grosset & Dunlap. 1954. dj.
. . . . *$15.00–$25.00*

Appleton, Victor II. *Tom Swift and His Ultrasonic Cycloplane.* NY. Grosset &
Dunlap. 1957. dj, #10 in Tom Swift Jr. series. . . . . *$15.00–$30.00*

Aptheker, Herbert. *Labor Movement in the South During Slavery....* NY.
International Publishers. wrps. . . . . *$25.00–$40.00*

Aptheker, Herbert (ed.). *Documentary History of the Negro People in the United
States: 1910-1932.* Secaucus. Citadel Press. 1951. 1st ed. dj. . . . . *$35.00–$50.00*

Arabian Stud Book. Arabian Horse Club. 1959. . . . . *$20.00–$30.00*

Arbona, Fred. *Mayflies, the Angler and the Trout.* NY. 1980. 1st ed. illus. dj, photos, charts. . . . . *$45.00–$60.00*

Arbuckle. *Arbuckle's Album of Illustrated Natural History.* np. lithos, 11 plates,
chromolitho wrappers. . . . . *$40.00–$80.00*

Arbuthnot, John. *An Essay Concerning the Effects of Air on Human Bodies.* Lon.
1751. bds paper on spine.. . . . . *$150.00–$200.00*

Archer, Jeffrey. *First Among Equals.* NY. Simon & Schuster. 1984. 1st ed. dj. . . .
. . . . *$15.00–$25.00*

Archer, T. A. and Charles Lethbridge Kingsford. *Crusades; the Story of the Latin Kingdom of Jerusalem.* Lon. T. Fisher Unwin. 1894. illus. calf marbled endpapers maps.. . . . . *$50.00–$60.00*

Arizona. NY. Hastings House. 1940. tan cl.. . . . . *$25.00–$35.00*

Armor, William. *Lives of the Governors of Pennsylvania....* Phila. James K Simon. 1872. illus. . . . . *$45.00–$55.00*

Armstrong, Benjamin G. *Early Life Among the Indians.* Ashland, WI. 1892. 1st ed. illus. 15 plates.. . . . . *$175.00–$225.00*

Armstrong, Harry G. *Principles and Practice of Aviation Medicine.* Balt. Williams & Wilkins. 1939. illus. charts, dj.. . . . . *$100.00–$125.00*

Armstrong, John. *Young Woman's Guide to Virtue, Economy and Happiness....* Newcastle. nd. illus. . . . . *$100.00–$140.00*

Armstrong, John M.D. *Art of Preserving Health: A Poem in Four Books.* Lon. 1744. 1st ed. . . . . *$185.00–$250.00*

Armstrong, Margaret. *Blue Santo Murder Mystery.* NY.Random House. (1941). 1st ed. slipcase, dj. . . . . *$30.00–$75.00*

Army Regulations Adopted for the Use of the Army of the Confederate States. New Orleans. 1861. 198 pp.. . . . . *$400.00–$600.00*

Arnaud de Ronsil, Georges. *Dissertation on Hernias, or Ruptures.* Lon. A Millar. 1748. . . . . *$200.00–$275.00*

Arnold, Sir Edwin. *The Light of Asia.* Lon. Bodley Head. 1926. new ed. illus. clr plates, cl.. . . . . *$45.00–$80.00*

Arnold, Edwin. *Seas & Lands.* NY. Longmans, Green. 1891. illus. clr plates. . . . . *$60.00–$90.00*

Arnold, Isaac N. *History of the Life of Abraham Lincoln and the Overthrow of Slavery.* Chi. 1866. 1st ed. illus. . . . . *$75.00–$95.00*

Arnold, Matthew. *Essays in Criticism.* Lon. 1865. 1st ed. . . . . . . *$95.00–$145.00*

Art Work of the Mohawk River and Valley, Its Cities & Towns. Chi. 1902. 9 vols.. . . . . *$75.00–$90.00*

Arthur Rackham Fairy Book. Phila. Lippincott. 1933. illus. by author, 7 clr plates. . . . . *$125.00–$350.00*

Arthur Rackham Fairy Book. Lon. 1933. 1st ed. illus. by author, 8 clr plates. . . . . *$200.00–$395.00*

Arthur Rackham Fairy Book. NY. Weathervane. 1978. illus. dj. . . . . *$15.00–$25.00*

Arthur, Sir George. *Life of Lord Kitchener: a Great British Life in the Middle East...* Lon. MacMillan. 1920. 3 vols. 1st ed. illus. 3/4 green calf, maps and photos......
.... *$80.00–$100.00*

Artists and Writers Golf Association 1948. np. 1948. spiral-bound bds..........
.... *$100.00–$200.00*

Artzybasheff, Boris. *Poor Shaydullah.* NY. Macmillan. 1931. 1st ed. scarce, dj. . . .
.... *$50.00–$125.00*

Asbury, Herbert. *Ye Olde Fire Laddies.* Ny. Knopf. 1930. 1st ed. pict bds. illus. dj.
.... *$50.00–$75.00*

Ashburner, Charles A. *The Bradford Oil District of Pennsylvania.* Phila. Transcript of Amer. Inst. of Mining Eng. 1879. fldg map.................. *$25.00–$30.00*

Ashby, Thomas. *Valley Campaigns.* NY. Neale. 1914. 1st ed. . . . *$50.00–$100.00*

Ashley, Clifford. *Ashley Book of Knots.* NY. Doubleday: (1944). 1st ed. illus. over-sized blue cl, pict dj, pict endpapers......................... *$50.00–$95.00*

Ashley, Frederick W. *Vollbehr Incunabula and the Book of Books....* DC. Library of Congress. 1932. 420 cc, slipcase on hand made paper........... *$35.00–$50.00*

Ashton, Dorothy Hemenway. *Sheldon Vermont, The People who Lived and Worked There.* privately printed. 1979. red cl over brown wrps. sgn. ...... *$40.00–$50.00*

Ashton, J. *Curious Creatures in Zoology.* Lon. John C. Nimmo. 1890. 1st ed. illus. pict cov.. *$75.00–$100.00*

Ashton, John. *Chap-Books of the Eighteenth Century.* Lon. Chatto & windus. 1882.
.... *$48.00–$55.00*

Asimov, Isaac. *Asimov's Biographical Encyclopedia of Science & Technology.* Doubleday. 1964. 662 pp, dj.............................. *$75.00–$200.00*

Asimov, Isaac. *Currents of Space.* NY. Doubleday. 1952. 1st ed. 217 pp, sgn, dj. .
.... *$175.00–$300.00*

Asimov, Isaac. *Death Dealers.* NY. Avon. 1958. 1st ed. wrps. paperback original..
.... *$30.00–$75.00*

Asimov, Isaac. *End of Eternity.*NY.. Doubleday. 1955. 1st ed. dj. *$165.00–$225.00*

Asimov, Isaac. *Foundation and Earth.* NY. Doubleday. 1986. 1st ed. dj. ....
.... *$15.00–$20.00*

Asimov, Isaac. *I, Robot.* NY. Gnome Press. 1950. 1st ed. dj..... *$350.00–$450.00*

Asimov, Isaac (Paul French). *Lucky Starr and the Moons of Jupiter.* Gregg Press. (1978). dj.. *$20.00–$30.00*

Asimov, Isaac. *Tales of the Black Widow*. Doubleday. 1974. 1st ed. dj. . . . .
. . . .*$75.00–$100.00*

Asimov, Isaac. *The Disappearing Man and Other Mysteries*. NY. Walker. 1985. 1st
ed. illus. dj. . . . .*$75.00–$200.00*

Asimov, Isaac. *The Intelligent Man's Guide to Science*. NY. Basic Books. 1960. 1st
ed. illus. photos, dj. . . . .*$20.00–$30.00*

Asimov, Isaac. *The Ugly Little Boy*. NY. Doubleday. 1992. . . . . . . *$10.00–$30.00*

Askins, Charles. *Game Bird Shooting*. NY. Macmillan. 1931. 1st ed. dj. . . . .
. . . .*$37.00–$55.00*

Asquith, Cynthia. *Ghost Book*. NY. Scribner's. 1927. 1st ed. . . . . *$25.00–$40.00*

Assoc. of Edison Illuminating Co. *Edisonia*. 1904. 1st ed. illus. . . *$55.00–$75.00*

Astaire, Fred. *Steps in Time*. NY. Harper & Bros. 1959. 1st ed. dj. . *$25.00–$85.00*

Astaire, Fred. *Steps in Time*. NY. Harper & Bros. 1959. 1st ed. sgn, dj. . . . .
. . . .*$325.00–$425.00*

Astor, Gerald. *Operation Iceberg*. NY. 1995. 1st ed. illus. dj. . . . . . *$20.00–$25.00*

Atherton, Gertrude. *Rulers of Kings*. NY. 1904. 1st ed. brown cl. . *$20.00–$50.00*

Atherton, Gertrude. *The White Morning*. NY. (1918). 1st ed. cl. . . *$10.00–$25.00*

Atil, Esin. *Art of the Arab World*. DC. Smithsonian. 1975. 1st ed. stiff wrps. . . . . .
. . . .*$20.00–$40.00*

Atkinson, Joseph. *History of Newark, N. J.* Newark. 1878. 1st ed. illus. by Moran
334 pp, plates. . . . .*$60.00–$150.00*

Atkinson, Thomas Witlam. *Travels in the Regions of the Upper and Lower Amoor
and the Russian Acquisitions on the Confines of India and China*. Lon. Hurst and
Blackett. 1860. 1st ed. illus. map, lavender cl, gilt on cvr. . . . . . . *$275.00–$375.00*

Atlas of Ashtabula County, Ohio. Phila. 1874. illus. . . . . *$500.00–$750.00*

Atlas of Cuyahoga County, Ohio. Phil. Titus Simmons & Titus. 1874. folio, cl cvr
bds & lea, plates, maps. . . . .*$400.00–$500.00*

Atomic Energy Commission. *Effects of Atomic Weapons*. DC. GPO. 1950. wrps. rev.
. . . .*$30.00–$45.00*

Attaway, William. *Let Me Breathe Thunder*. NY. Doubleday, Doran. 1939. 1st ed.
author's first book. . . . .*$50.00–$100.00*

Atwater, Caleb. *History of the State of Ohio*. Cinc. (1838). 2nd ed. lea. . . . .
. . . .*$85.00–$150.00*

Atwater, Caleb. *Remarks Made on a Tour to Prairie Du Chien.* Columbus. Jenkins and Glover. 1831. 1st ed. .... *$600.00–$700.00*

Atwater, Mary Meigs. *Shuttle-Craft Book of American Hand-Weaving.* NY. Macmillan. 1937. illus. cl. .... *$25.00–$35.00*

Atwood, Margaret. *Bodily Harm.* McClelland & Steward. 1981. 1st ed. dj. .....
.... *$30.00–$50.00*

Auchincloss, Louis. *Dark Lady.* Bos. Houghton Mifflin. 1977. 1st ed. dj. ....
.... *$15.00–$20.00*

Auchincloss, Louis. *Injustice Collectors.* Bos. 1950. 1st ed. dj.. . . *$50.00–$150.00*

Auden, W. H. *About the House.* NY. Random House. (1965). 1st ed. dj. ....
.... *$35.00–$75.00*

Auden, W. H. *City Without Walls and Other Poems.* NY. Random House. 1969. 1st ed. dj.. .... *$30.00–$55.00*

Auden, W. H. *Collected Poetry of W. H. Auden.* NY. Random House. 1945. 1st ed. dj. .... *$100.00–$250.00*

Auden, W. H. *Dance of Death.* Lon. Faber & Faber. (1933). 1st ed. dj. ....
.... *$165.00–$295.00*

Auden, W. H. *Poems.* Lon. Faber & Faber. (1930). 1st ed. blue wrps,. ....
.... *$340.00–$400.00*

Auden, W. H. *Secondary Works: Essays.* NY. Random House. 1968. 1st Amer ed. dj.
.... *$15.00–$20.00*

Audsley, George A. *Artistic & Decorative Stencilling.* Lon. 1911. *$95.00–$145.00*

Audsley, W. and G. Audsley. *Polychromatic Decoration as applied to Buildings in the Medieval Styles.* Lon. Sotheran. 1882. illus. tall folio 36 plates in gold and clrs.
.... *$600.00–$975.00*

Audubon, John J. *Birds of America.* NY. Macmillan. 1937. illus. clr plates. ......
.... *$30.00–$75.00*

Audubon, John James. *Quadrupeds of North America.* NY. 1849-51-54. 3 vols. 1st 8vo ed. 155 hand-clr plates, fine binding. .... *$9,000.00–$12,000.00*

Audubon, John W. *Audubon's Western Journal 1849-1850.* Cleve. Arthur H. Clark Co. 1906. 1st ed. fldg map, rprnt.. .... *$200.00–$325.00*

Audubon, Maria. *Audubon and His Journals.* Lon. John C. Nimmo. 1898. 2 vols.. illus. 35 plates, olive cl. .... *$400.00–$500.00*

Auel, Jean. *Clan of the Cave Bear.* NY. Crown. 1980. 1st ed. author's first book, dj
.... *$50.00–$75.00*

Aurthur, R. A. *Third Marine Division*. DC. 1948. 1st ed. . . . . *$50.00–$75.00*

Austen, Jane. *Pride and Prejudice*. Lon. T. Egerton. 1813. 2nd ed. . . . .
. . . . *$5,000.00–$6,000.00*

Auster, Paul. *Ghosts*. LA. Sun and Moon Press. 1986. 1st ed. dj. . . *$40.00–$55.00*

Austin, Mary. *American Rhythm*. NY. Harcourt, Brace. (1923). 1st ed. 155 pp, dj.
. . . . *$150.00–$175.00*

Austin, Mary. *Arrow Maker*. Duffield & Co. 1911. 128 pp. . . . . . *$75.00–$100.00*

Austin, Mary. *Land of Little Rain*. Bos/NY. Houghton Mifflin. 1903. 1st ed. author's
first book. . . . . *$125.00–$250.00*

Avary, Myrta Lockett. *Dixie After the War*. NY. Doubleday. 1906. 1st ed. illus. . .
. . . . *$45.00–$125.00*

Avedon, Richard and Truman Capote. *Observations*. NY. Simon & Schuster. 1959.
1st ed. illus. photos. . . . . *$80.00–$120.00*

Averill, Charles. *Short Treatise on Operative Surgery, describing the principal operations as they are practised in England and France*. Phil. 1823. 1st Amer ed. 4 fldg
plates. . . . . *$150.00–$200.00*

Avery, Al. *Yankee Flyer with the RAF*. NY. Grosset & Dunlap. 1941. Air Combat
Stories #8, dj. . . . . *$15.00–$24.00*

Ayling, Augustus D. *Revised Register of the Soldiers and Sailors of New Hampshire
in the War of the Rebellion 1861–1866*. Concord. 1895. rev ed. folio, half lea. . . . .
. . . . *$150.00–$300.00*

Ayton, Laurie, et al. *Golf as Champions Play it*. Chi. Associated Editors. 1925. 1st
ed. wrps. illus. . . . . *$30.00–$50.00*

Babault, Guy. *Chasses et Recherches Zoologiques en Afrique...1913*. Paris. Librairie
Plon. 1917. 1st ed. illus. photos. . . . . *$80.00–$120.00*

Babbitt, Bruce. *Grand Canyon*. 1st ed. sgn. . . . . *$60.00–$80.00*

Babcock, Philip H. *Falling Leaves*. NY. Derrydale. (1937). 1st ed. review copy, ltd
950 cc.. . . . . *$70.00–$100.00*

Back, Captain. *Narrative of the Arctic Land Expedition to the Mouth of the Great
Fish River... 1833, 1834, and 1835*. Phila. Carey & Hart. 1836. 1st Amer ed. rbnd, fldg
map, 456 pp. . . . . *$325.00–$650.00*

Bacom, G. *New Large Scale Ordnance Atlas of the British Isles*. 1884. hand-clr maps,
full lea. . . . . *$175.00–$225.00*

Bacon, Edgar Mayhew. *Narragansett Bay, Its Historic and Romantic Associations
and Picturesque Setting*. Putnam. 1904. 1st ed. illus. by author, map. *$50.00–$65.00*

Baden-Powell, Capt. R. S. *Pigsticking or Hog-Hunting.* Lon. Harrison & Sons. 1889. . . . . *$700.00–$900.00*

Baden-Powell, Lord. *Handbook for Brownies or Bluebirds.* Lon. Arthur Pearson. (1920). wrps.. . . . . *$30.00–$45.00*

Baedeker, Karl. *Belgien und Holland.* Leipzig. 1900. . . . . *$20.00–$30.00*

Baedeker, Karl. *Belgium and Holland.* Lon. Dulau and Co. 1891. illus. 10th ed. rev. . . . . *$40.00–$50.00*

Baedeker, Karl. *Belgium and Holland.* Leipzig. 1910. 15th ed. rev. *$40.00–$60.00*

Baedeker, Karl. *Belgium and Holland including the Grand-Duchy of Luxembourg.* Leipsic. 1897. illus. 12th ed. rev. . . . . *$25.00–$45.00*

Baedeker, Karl. *Belgium and Holland including the Grand-Duchy of Luxembourg.* Leipsic. 1894. illus. 11th ed. rev. . . . . *$30.00–$60.00*

Baedeker, Karl. *Berlin and Its Environs.* Leipzig. 1908. 3rd ed. . . *$95.00–$125.00*

Baedeker, Karl. *Berlin and Umgebung.* Leipsic. 1921. German ed. . *$70.00–$110.00*

Baedeker, Karl. *Dominion of Canada.* Leipzig. 1894. 254 pp. . . . *$95.00–$150.00*

Baedeker, Karl. *Dominion of Canada with Newfoundland and an excursion to Alaska.* Leipzig. 1900. 2nd rev. ed. . . . . *$95.00–$135.00*

Baedeker, Karl. *Egypt.* Leipzig. 1914. 4th ed. 442 pp. maps, plans, drawings.. . . . . *$100.00–$150.00*

Baedeker, Karl. *Egypt and the Sudan.* Leipzig. 1914. 7th ed. 458 pp. maps, plans, red cl. . . . . *$95.00–$125.00*

Baedeker, Karl. *Etats-Unis.* 1894. *$35.00–$50.00*

Baedeker, Karl. *Italy from the Alps to Naples.* Leipzig. 1909. wrps. 2nd ed. . . . . *$20.00–$30.00*

Baedeker, Karl. *Italy. First Part.* Leipsic. 1879. 5th ed. . . . . *$45.00–$65.00*

Baedeker, Karl. *Italy. Second Part.* Coblenz. 1869. 2nd ed. rev. maps, plans. . . . . *$125.00–$225.00*

Baedeker, Karl. *Italy. Third Part: Southern Italy and Sicily.* Leipsic. 1887. 9th ed. rev. maps, plans. . . . . *$60.00–$85.00*

Baedeker, Karl. *Les Bords du Rhin, la Foret-Noire, Les Vosges.* Leipsic. 1910. 18th ed. . . . . *$30.00–$45.00*

Baedeker, Karl. *Northern France from Belgium and the English Channel to the Loire excluding Paris and its environs.* Lon. Dulau. 1899. 3rd ed. illus. . . . . *$25.00–$45.00*

Baedeker, Karl. *Northern France from Belgium and the English Channel to the Loire excluding Paris and its Environs.* Lon. Dulau. 1899. 3rd ed. illus. . . *$25.00–$45.00*

Baedeker, Karl. *Northern Germany.* Leipzig. 1910. 15th ed. . . . . . *$65.00–$75.00*

Baedeker, Karl. *Northern Germany.* Lon. Dulau. 1886. 9th ed. rev. *$45.00–$60.00*

Baedeker, Karl. *Northern Germany as far as the Bavarian and Austrian Frontiers with excursions to Cophenhagen and the Danish Islands.* Lon. Dulau. 1890. 10th ed. rev. . . . . *$50.00–$60.00*

Baedeker, Karl. *Palatina Und Syrien.* 1900. . . . . *$125.00–$150.00*

Baedeker, Karl. *Palestine and Syria.* Leipzig. 1912. 5th ed. . . . . *$125.00–$225.00*

Baedeker, Karl. *Palestine and Syria.* Leipzig. 1894. 2nd ed. . . . . *$125.00–$200.00*

Baedeker, Karl. *Palestine and Syria with the Chief Routes Through Mesopotamia and Babylonia.* Leipzig. 1906. 4th ed. red cl-cvred wrps. . . . . *$150.00–$250.00*

Baedeker, Karl. *Palestine et Syrie.* Leipzig. 1912. 21 maps, 56 plans, panorama of Jerusalem. . . . . *$185.00–$225.00*

Baedeker, Karl. *Paris and Environs with Routes from London to Paris.* Leipsic. 1891. 10th ed. rev. . . . . *$25.00–$45.00*

Baedeker, Karl. *Paris and Environs with Routes from London to Paris.* Leipsic. 1896. 12th ed. rev. . . . . *$25.00–$45.00*

Baedeker, Karl. *Paris and Its Environs.* Leipzig. 1891. 10th ed, red cl. . . . . *$35.00–$45.00*

Baedeker, Karl. *Russia.* NY. Arno/Random House. 1971. facs, dj. *$75.00–$100.00*

Baedeker, Karl. *Russia with Teheran, Port Arthur and Peking.* Leipzig. 1914. 1st ed. 40 maps, 78 plans. . . . . *$800.00–$1,000.00*

Baedeker, Karl. *Southern France.* Lon. 1905. . . . . *$35.00–$65.00*

Baedeker, Karl. *Southern Germany.* Leipzig. 1914. 12th ed. rev. . . . *$40.00–$50.00*

Baedeker, Karl. *Southern Germany including Wurtemberg and Bavaria.* Leipsic. 1895. 8th ed. rev. . . . . *$25.00–$50.00*

Baedeker, Karl. *Spain and Portugal.* Leipzig. 1913. lea. . . . . *$25.00–$60.00*

Baedeker, Karl. *Switzerland.* 1907. . . . . *$22.00–$45.00*

Baedeker, Karl. *The Dominion of Canada with Newfoundland and an Excursion to Alaska.* NY. Scribner's. 1900. illus. 2nd ed. rev. . . . . *$70.00–$90.00*

Baedeker, Karl. *The Traveler's Manual of Conversation.* Leipsic. nd. Stereotype ed. . . . . *$45.00–$60.00*

Baedeker, Karl. *The United States with an Excursion into Mexico.* Leipsic. 1904. 3rd ed. rev. maps, plans. . . . . *$50.00–$175.00*

Baedeker, Karl. *United States With An Excursion Into Mexico.* Leipzig. 1893. 1st ed. red cl, 516 pp, 17 maps, 22 plans. . . . . *$150.00–$300.00*

Baedeker, Karl. *United States with Excursions into Mexico, Cuba, Puerto Rico, and Alaska.* Leipzig. 1909. 4th ed. soft cvr, 33 maps, 44 plans. . . . . . *$145.00–$200.00*

Bagg, Aaron and Samuel Eliot. *Birds of the Connecticut Valley in Massachusetts.* MA. 1937. illus. clr frontis, b/w plates. . . . . *$150.00–$200.00*

Bailey, C. W. *Brain and Golf: Some Hints.* Lon. Mills & Boon. (1924). 2nd ed. . . . . *$80.00–$100.00*

Bailey, C. W. *Professor on the Golf Links.* Lon. Silas Birch. (1925). 1st ed. . . . . *$100.00–$200.00*

Bailey, Carolyn Sherwin. *Little Reader Series No. 3.* Springfield. (1934). 4 vols. illus. by Ruth Hallock. original box, scarce. . . . . *$50.00–$65.00*

Bailey, F. M. *Birds of New Mexico.* DC. 1928. illus. . . . . *$100.00–$150.00*

Bailey, L. H. *Cylopedia of American Horticulture.* NY. 1900-1902. 4 vols. . . . . *$100.00–$195.00*

Bailey, L. H. *Standard Cyclopedia of Horticulture.* NY. Macmillan. 1935. 3 vols. illus. 24 clr & 96 b/w. . . . . *$60.00–$90.00*

Baines, Anthony. *European and American Musical Instruments.* NY. Viking. (1966). 1st ed. illus. b/w photos. . . . . *$40.00–$60.00*

Baird, Bill. *Art of the Puppet.* NY. Macmillan. 1965. 1st ed. dj. . . *$70.00–$100.00*

Baker, Gen L. C. *History of the U.S. Secret Service.* Phila. 1867. 1st ed. . . . . *$40.00–$75.00*

Baker, Marcus. *Geographic Dictionary of Alaska.* GPO. 1906. 2nd ed. . . . . *$60.00–$80.00*

Baker, Roger. *Dolls & Dolls' Houses....* Crescent Books. (1973). illus. dj. . . . . *$15.00–$20.00*

Baker, Samuel W. *Ismailia.* NY. Harper. 1875. 1st Amer ed. Illus, plates, 542 pp. . . . . *$100.00–$150.00*

Baker, Samuel W. *Nile Tributaries of Abyssinia.* Lon. Macmillan. 1894. maps. . . . . *$50.00–$60.00*

Bakst, Leon. *Designs of Leon Bakst for the Sleeping Princess.* Lon. Benn Bros. 1923. ltd ed. . . . . *$550.00–$1,200.00*

Baldwin, James. *Blues for Mister Charlie*. NY. Dial 1964. 1st ed. sgn, dj. . . . .
. . . . *$200.00–$400.00*

Baldwin, James. *Fire Next Time*. NY. Dial. 1963. 1st ed. dj. . . . . . . *$30.00–$50.00*

Baldwin, James. *Go Tell It On the Mountain*. Franklin. Center. Franklin Library.
1979. 1st ed. ltd. sgn, red lea.. . . . . *$175.00–$300.00*

Baldwin, James. *Going to Meet the Man*. Dial. 1965. 1st ed. dj.. . . *$25.00–$50.00*

Baldwin, James. *If Beale Street Could Talk*. NY. Dial. 1974. 1st ed. ltd 250 cc, sgn,
slipcase.. . . . . *$200.00–$250.00*

Baldwin, James. *If Beale Street Could Talk*. NY. Dial. 1974. 1st ed. dj.. . . . .
. . . . *$50.00–$75.00*

Baldwin, James. *Just Above My Head*. NY. Dial. (1979). 1st ed. ltd 500 cc, sgn, slipcase. . . . . *$125.00–$200.00*

Baldwin, James. *Just Above My Head*. NY. Dial Press. (1979). 1st ed. dj.. . . . . . .
. . . . *$40.00–$50.00*

Baldwin, James. *Little Man, Little Man*. NY. Dial. (1976). 1st US prtg. illus by Yoran
Cazac. dj.. . . . . *$40.00–$100.00*

Baldwin, James. *Native Son*. Bos. Beacon Press. 1955. 1st ed. sgn, dj. . . . .
. . . . *$350.00–$700.00*

Baldwin, James. *Nobody Knows My Name, more notes of a native son*. NY. Dial
Press. 1961.. 1st ed. dj. . . . . *$75.00–$150.00*

Baldwin, James. *Tell Me How Long the Train's Been Gone*. NY. Dial Press. 1968. 1st
ed. dj. . . . . *$30.00–$65.00*

Baldwin, James. *Un Altro Mondo: Romanzo*. Milan. Feltrinelli. 1963. 1st Italian ed.
dj. . . . . *$30.00–$50.00*

Baldwin, William C. *African Hunting from Natal to the Zambesi*. Harper. NY. 1863.
illus. fldg map. . . . . *$80.00–$125.00*

Balfour, William. *Illustrations of the Power of Emetic Tartar...in Preventing C and
Consumption and Apoplexy*. Lexington. Palmer. 1823. . . . . *$150.00–$200.00*

Ball, Charles. *History of the Indian Mutiny*. Lon. London Printing & Publ. 1880. 1st
ed. illus. 3/4 dark brown calf steel engr.. . . . . *$150.00–$200.00*

Ball, Col. T. A. *Le Golf*. Paris. Editions Paris-Vendome. (1950). 1st ed. illus. in
French. . . . . *$60.00–$70.00*

Balzac, Honoré de. *Droll Stories*. NY. Boni & Liveright. 1928. 2 vols. illus. . . . .
. . . . *$20.00–$45.00*

Bambara, Toni Cade. *The Salt Eaters*. NY. Random House. 1980. 1st ed. dj. . . . .
. . . . *$10.00–$25.00*

Bamford, Georgia Loring. *Mystery of Jack London*. Oakland. 1931. 1st ed. dj. . .
. . . . *$95.00–$125.00*

Bancroft, Hubert Howe. *History of Alaska, 1730-1886*. SF. A. K. Bancroft.. 1886.
map. . . . . *$150.00–$225.00*

Bancroft, Hubert Howe. *History of the Northwest Coast*. SF. The History Co. 1886.
2 vols.. . . . . *$50.00–$75.00*

Bancroft, Hubert Howe. *History of Utah*. SF. The History Co. 1890. 1st ed. illus.
col plates. . . . . *$100.00–$250.00*

Bancroft, Laura (L. Frank Baum). *Bandit Jim Crow*. Chi. Reilly & Lee. nd. illus.
by Enright, pict cvr.. . . . . *$100.00–$200.00*

Bancroft, Laura (L. Frank Baum). *Mr. Woodchuck*. Chi. Reilly & Lee. (1906).
14 clr illus.. . . . . *$250.00–$425.00*

Bancroft, Laura. *Sugar-Loaf Mountain*. Chi. Reilly & Britton. (1906). 1st ed. illus.
16 clr plates. an L. Frank Baum pseudonym book.. . . . . *$275.00–$350.00*

Bancroft, Laura. *Prairie Dog Town*. Chi. Reilly & Britton. (1906). 1st ed. illus.
16 clr plates, an L. Frank Baum pseudonym book.. . . . . *$350.00–$500.00*

Bangay, R. D. *Wireless Telephony*. Lon. 1924. 1st ed. illus. . . . . . . *$18.00–$25.00*

Bangs John Kendrick. *Bicyclers and Three Other Forces*. NY. Harper & Bros. 1896.
1st ed.. . . . . *$30.00–$50.00*

Bangs, John Kendrick. *Foothills of Parnassus*. NY. 1914. review copy, dj.. . . . . . .
. . . . *$50.00–$75.00*

Bangs, John Kendrick. *Ghosts I Have Met*. NY. Harper & Bros. 1898. 1st ed. illus.
. . . . *$50.00–$125.00*

Bangs, John Kendrick. *A House-Boat on the Styx*. NY. Harper & Bros. 1896. 1st ed.
illus. . . . . *$35.00–$75.00*

Bangs, John Kendrick. *Mr. Munchausen*. Bos. Noyes, Platt & Co. 1901. 1st ed.
illus. by Peter Newell.. . . . . *$40.00–$60.00*

Bangs, John Kendrick. *Mrs. Raffles*. NY. Harper & Bros. 1905. 1st ed. illus. . . .
. . . . *$75.00–$150.00*

Bangs, John Kendrick. *Olympian Nights*. NY. Harper & Bros. 1902. 1st ed. illus.
. . . . *$20.00–$35.00*

Bangs, John Kendrick. *Peeps at People*. NY. Harper & Bros. 1899. 1st ed. illus. by
Penfield. presentation copy.. . . . . *$120.00–$150.00*

Bangs, John Kendrick. *Pursuit of the House-Boat.* NY. Harper & Bros. 1897. 1st ed. no dj. . . . . *$50.00–$100.00*

Bangs, John Kendrick. *Songs of Cheer.* Bos. 1910. 1st ed. dj. . . . *$95.00–$125.00*

Bangs, John Kendrick. *The Dreamers.* NY. 1899. 1st ed. illus. by Penfield. . . . . *$60.00–$95.00*

Bangs, John Kendrick. *Three Weeks In Politics.* NY. 1894. 1st ed. illus. . . . . *$30.00–$45.00*

Bangs, John Kendrick. *Water Ghost and Athens.* NY. 1894. 1st ed. illus. . . . . *$25.00–$65.00*

Banks, Nathaniel P. *Purchase of Alaska.* Wash. 1868. 1st ed. . . . . *$50.00–$75.00*

Banks, Russell. *Relation of My Imprisonment.* Wash. Sun & Moon Press. 1983. 1st trade ed. dj. . . . . *$30.00–$65.00*

Banks, Russell. *Cloudsplitter.* NY. Harper Flamingo. 1998. 1st ed. wrps. advance reading copy. . . . . *$38.00–$45.00*

Banks, Russell. *Rule of the Bone.* NY. Harper Collins. 1995. 1st ed. sgn, dj. . . . . *$30.00–$75.00*

Bannerman, Helen. *A New Story of Little Black Sambo.* Racine Whitman. (1932). pict wrps. . . . . *$50.00–$65.00*

Bannerman, Helen. *Histoire du Petit Negre Sambo.* NY. Stokes. (1921). 1st ed. in French, dj. . . . . *$125.00–$185.00*

Bannerman, Helen. *Little Black Sambo.* Racine Whitman. illus. by Cobb and Shinn, 64 pp, dark brown cl bds. . . . . *$75.00–$100.00*

Bannerman, Helen. *Little Black Sambo.* NY. Platt & Monk. 1972. illus. by Eulalie Hardcvr. rprnt, dj. . . . . *$100.00–$150.00*

Bannerman, Helen. *Little Black Sambo.* NY. Little Golden Book. 1948. *$40.00–$55.00*

Bannerman, Helen. *Little Black Sambo.* NY. Platt & Munk. 1935. dj. . . . . *$165.00–$320.00*

Bannerman, Helen. *Little Black Sambo.* Akron. 1933. illus. by Peat. *$80.00–$130.00*

Bannerman, Helen. *Little Black Sambo Animated.* DueneWold Printing Corp. (1949). illus. paper bds, 4 moveable plates. . . . . *$150.00–$350.00*

Bannerman, Helen. *Little Black Sambo Animated.* NY. Dutton. 1943. spiral bound. . . . . *$150.00–$225.00*

Bannerman, Helen. *Sambo and the Twins.* Phila. 1946. illus. by Helen Bannerman. . . . . *$45.00–$60.00*

Bannerman, Helen. *Story of Little Black Sambo*. Lon. 1899. 1st ed. green cl with dark stripes and lettering. . . . . *$5,000.00–$10,000.00*

Bannerman, Helen. *The Story of Little Black Mingo by the Author of 'The Story of Little Black Sambo'*. NY. Stokes. nd. red cl. . . . . *$100.00–$150.00*

Bannerman, Helen. *The Story of Little Black Sambo*. Phila. Lippincott. nd. full red cl, illus cvr, dj. . . . .·. . . *$50.00–$100.00*

Bannerman, Helen. *The Story of Little Black Sambo*. David McKay. 1931. . . . . *$90.00–$250.00*

Baraka, Amiri. *Home: Social Essays, by LeRoi Jones*. NY. William Morrow. 1966. 1st ed. dj. . . . . *$55.00–$75.00*

Barbeau, M. *Haida Myths Illustrated in Argillite Carvings*. Ottawa. 1953. 1st ed. wrps. . . . . *$90.00–$185.00*

Barbeau, Marius. *Haida Carvers in Argillite*. Ottawa. National Museum of Canada. 1957. illus. Bulletin No. 139, pict gray bds.. . . . . *$75.00–$100.00*

Barbeau, Marius. *La Rossignol y Chante*. Ottawa. National Museum of Canada. 1962. stiff wraps. . . . . *$25.00–$35.00*

Barbeau, Marius. *Medicine Men on the North Pacific Coast*. Ottawa. National Museum of Canada. 1958. 1st paperback ed. stiff wrps. . . . . *$35.00–$40.00*

Barbeau, Marius. *Totem Poles*. Ottawa. National Museum of Canada. 1950. 2 vols. 1st ed. wrps. illus. . . . . *$150.00–$225.00*

Barbeau, Marius. *Totem Poles of the Gitksan, Upper Skeena River, British Columbia*. Ottawa. National Museum of Canada. 1929. wrps. 275 pp. . . . . *$175.00–$225.00*

Barbeau, Marius. *Tsimsyan Myths*. Ottawa. National Museum of Canada. 1st ed. Bulletin No. 174.. . . . . *$50.00–$75.00*

Barbeau, Marius and Michael Hornyansky. *The Golden Phoenix and Other French-Canadian Fairy Tales*. NY. Scholastic. 1965. illus. . . . . *$5.00–$20.00*

Barber, Joel. *Wild Fowl Decoys*. NY. 1934. illus. dj. . . . . *$75.00–$150.00*

Barber, John (ed.). *History of the Amistad Captives*. New Haven. E. L. & J.W. Barber. 1840. 1st ed. 32 pp, plamphlet, fldg plate. . . . . *$150.00–$250.00*

Barclay, J.T. *City of the Great King....* Phil. W H Thompson. 1883. 1st ed. illus. maps, engr. . . . . *$45.00–$75.00*

Baring-Gould, S. *Family Names & Their Story*. Lon. Seeley & Co. 1910. blue cl.. . . . . *$40.00–$50.00*

Barker, Clive. *In the Flesh*. NY. Poseidon. 1986. 1st ed. inscr. dj.. . *$25.00–$35.00*

Barker, Clive. *The Damnation Game.* Lon. Weidenfeld & Nicolson. 1985. 1st ed. sgn, dj.. *$40.00–$125.00*

Barker, Clive. *The Great and Secret Show.* NY. Harper & Row. 1989. 1st ed. quarter cl, sgn, dj.. *$35.00–$60.00*

Barker, Clive. *Weave World.* NY. Poseidon. 1987. 1st ed. sgn, dj... *$35.00–$40.00*

Barnard, Charles. *First Steps in Electricity.* NY. 1888. 1st ed. illus. *$40.00–$60.00*

Barnard, George. *The Theory and Practice of Landscape Painting in Water Colours.* Lon. William S. Orr. 1855. 1st ed. illus. mor, aeg............. *$145.00–$175.00*

Barnard, Harry. *Tattered Volunteers: the 27th Alabama Infantry Regiment.* Northport, AL. 1965. scarce, dj............................ *$75.00–$85.00*

Barnard, Lady Anne. *South Africa a Century Ago.* Lon. Smith, Elder. 1901. 2nd impression. original cl. .... *$30.00–$40.00*

Barneby, Henry W. *Life and Labour in the Far, Far West....* Lon. Cassell. 1884. 1st ed. map... *$80.00–$175.00*

Barnes, A. R. *South African Household Guide.* Capetown. 1907. 4th ed......... .... *$25.00–$55.00*

Barnes, Henry. *Guerilla Bride.* Bellefontaine, OH. privately printed. 1858. cl, scarce... *$225.00–$300.00*

Barnes, James M. *My Picture Analysis of Gold Strokes.* Phil. 1919. 1st ed. illus. . ... *$85.00–$250.00*

Barnes, Linda. *Bitter Finish.* NY. St. Martin's. 1983. 1st ed. dj.... *$65.00–$85.00*

Barnes, Will C. *Western Grazing Grounds... A History of the Live-Stock Industry as Conducted on Open Ranges....* Chi. Breeder's Gazette. 1913. 1st ed. illus. 390 pp.. .... *$150.00–$300.00*

Barnum, P. T. *Struggles and Triumphs.* Buffalo. Johnson & Co. 1873. illus. author's ed.. *$40.00–$55.00*

Barol, B. H. *Treatise on the Marine Boilers of the United States.* Phila. Barnard & Sons. 1851. drawings, embossed cl........................ *$240.00–$300.00*

Baroni, George (ed.). *The Pyramiders.* np. nd. 300 pp, photos..... *$60.00–$75.00*

Barrett, Edwin S. *What I Saw at Bull Run.* Bos. Beacon Press. 1886. frontis, 48pp. .... *$125.00–$185.00*

Barrie, J. M. *Margaret Ogilvy.* NY. Scribner's. 1896. 1st Amer ed. gray bds. .... *$20.00–$30.00*

Barrie, J. M. *Peter Pan.* NJ. Unicorn Publishing. 1987.......... *$7.00–$10.00*

Barrie, J. M. *Quality Street/The Plays of J. M. Barrie.* NY. Scribner's. 1918. 1st ed.
. . . . *$8.00–$10.00*

Barrie, J. M. *The Little Minister.* Lon. Cassell & Co. 1891. 3 vols. 1st ed. quarter mor slipcase.. . . . . *$750.00–$1,500.00*

Barrie, J. M. *The Little Minister.* NY. Grosset & Dunlap. Photoplay ed. dj.. . . . . .
. . . . *$150.00–$200.00*

Barrie, J. M. *Tommy and Grizel.* NY. Scribner's. 1912. illus. by Bernard Partridge.
. . . . *$10.00–$20.00*

Barrie, J.M. *Peter and Wendy.* NY. Scribner's. 1911. 1st Amer ed, green cl. . . . . .
. . . . *$100.00–$225.00*

Barrie, J.M. *Peter Pan.* NY. Grosset & Dunlap. Photoplay ed. dj. *$125.00–$200.00*

Barrie, J.M. *Tommy and Grizel.* Scribner's. 1900. 1st ed. illus. by Partridge.. . . . .
. . . . *$20.00–$35.00*

Barrie, Robert. *Early Days of the Corinthian Yacht Club of Philadelphia.* Phila. private printing. 1940. illus. photos.. . . . . *$30.00–$40.00*

Barringer, Paul B., J. M. Garnett & Rosewell Page. *University of Virginia....* Lewis Pub. 1904. 2 vols. illus. b/w, aeg, half lea.. . . . . *$75.00–$100.00*

Barron, Archibald F. *Vines and Vine Culture.* Lon. 1900. 4th ed. illus. . . . .
. . . . *$90.00–$150.00*

Barrows, W. B. *Michigan Bird Life.* Lansing. 1912. illus. . . . . *$45.00–$75.00*

Barth, Henry. *Travels and Discoveries in North Central Africa.* NY. Harper & Bros. 1857. 3 vols. 1st Amer ed. illus. maps.. *$250.00–$500.00*

Barth, John. *Chimera.* Lon. Andre Deutsch. (1974). 1st ed. dj.. . . . *$50.00–$65.00*

Barth, John. *End of the Road.* Lon. 1962. 1st UK ed. dj. . . . . *$90.00–$125.00*

Barth, John. *End of the Road.* Garden City. Doubleday. 1958. 1st ed. dj. . . . .
. . . . *$250.00–$500.00*

Barth, John. *Floating Opera.* Garden City. Doubleday. (1956). 1st ed. dj author's first book. . . . . *$225.00–$300.00*

Barth, John. *Giles Goat-Boy.* Garden City. Doubleday. 1966. dj. . . *$30.00–$65.00*

Barth, John. *Lost in the Funhouse.* Garden City. Doubleday. 1968. 1st ed. dj.. . . . .
. . . . *$15.00–$25.00*

Barth, John. *Sot-Weed Factor.* Garden City. Doubleday. 1960. 1st ed. dj. . . . .
. . . . *$50.00–$200.00*

Barthelme, Donald. *Come Back, Dr. Caligari.* Bos. Little, Brown. 1964. 1st ed. author's first book, dj. . . . . *$150.00–$175.00*

Barthelme, Donald. *Guilty Pleasures.* NY. Farrar, Straus & Giroux. (1974). 1st ed. dj. . . . . *$25.00–$40.00*

Barthelme, Donald. *Sixty Stories.* NY. Putnam's n. (1979). 1st ed. sgn, dj. . . . . *$24.00–$60.00*

Barthelme, Donald. *Snow White.* NY. Atheneum. 1967. 1st ed. sgn, dj. . . . . *$135.00–$175.00*

Barthelme, Roland. *Rangoon.* NY. Winter House. 1970. stiff wrps. illus. photos., author's first book. . . . . *$50.00–$100.00*

Bartholomew, Ed. *Wild Bill Longley, a Texas Hard-case.* Houston. 1953. illus. . . . . *$30.00–$40.00*

Bartholow, Roberts. *Practical Treatise on Materia Medica and Therapeutics.* NY. Appleton. 1884. 5th ed. . . . . *$25.00–$50.00*

Bartlett, W. *An Elementary Treatise on Optics.* NY. 1839. 1st ed. illus. fldg plates. . . . . *$30.00–$40.00*

Bartlett, W. H. *Forty Days in the Desert, on the Track of the Israelites.* Lon. Hall & Co. nd. 5th ed. decorated bds, engr, fldg map. . . . . *$150.00–$250.00*

Bartlett, W. H. *Walks About the City and Environs of Jerusalem.* Lon. 1842. frontis 3/4 mor aeg. . . . . *$175.00–$225.00*

Barton, Clara. *Red Cross in Peace and War.* DC. American Historical Press. 1899. 1st ed. . . . . *$50.00–$100.00*

Barton, Lucy. *Historic Costume for the Stage.* Lon. A & C Black. 1935. illus.b/w. . . . . *$50.00–$65.00*

Barton, Lucy. *Historic Costume for the Stage.* Bos. Baker. 1935. 1st ed. illus. . . . . *$50.00–$125.00*

Bass, W. W. *Adventures in the Canyons of Colorado... Grand Canyon.* 1920. wrps. 38 pp. . . . . *$95.00–$200.00*

Batchelor, D. *Jack Johnson & His Times.* Lon. Sportsmans Book Club. 1957. illus. 190 pp, dj. . . . . *$30.00–$45.00*

Bates, H. W. *Naturalist on the River Amazons.* Lon. John Murray. 1873. 3rd ed. illus. . . . . *$75.00–$150.00*

Bates, Joseph D., Jr. *Atlantic Salmon Flies & Fishing.* Harrisburg. Stackpole. 1970. 1st ed. dj. . . . . *$50.00–$120.00*

Bates, Joseph D., Jr. *Streamers & Bucktails*. NY. Knopf. 1979. dj.. *$40.00–$75.00*

Battersby, Col. J. C. *Bridle Bits, a Treatise on Practical Horsemanship*. NY. Orange Judd. 1886. 1st ed. . . . . *$140.00–$185.00*

Battleground Korea: The Story of the 25th Infantry Division. Arlington. 1951. 1st ed. dj. . . . . *$50.00–$85.00*

Baughman, A. J. *History of Huron County, Ohio*. Chi. Clarke. 1909. 2 vols. 1st ed. illus. . . . . *$80.00–$100.00*

Baum, Frank. *Land of Oz*. Chi. Reilley & Lee. (1904). red cl, pict pastedown, b/w illus. . . . . *$40.00–$60.00*

Baum, Frank. *New Wizard of Oz*. Indianapolis. Bobbs-Merrill. (1903). illus. by W. W. Denslow, green cl, pict pastedown, clr plates. . . . . *$45.00–$60.00*

Baum, Frank. *The Emerald City*. Chi. Reilly & Lee. (1910). . . . . . *$35.00–$95.00*

Baum, Frank. *The Scarecrow*. Chi. Reilly & Lee. (1915). illus. 12 clr plates. . . . . *$75.00–$300.00*

Baum, Frank L. *The Land of Oz*. Chi. Reilly & Lee. 1932. illus. by Neill. . . . . *$22.00–$25.00*

Baum, Frank L. *TheWizard of Oz*. Ind. Bobbs Merrill. 1944. . . . . *$18.00–$20.00*

Baum, L. Frank. *Dorothy and the Wizard of Oz*. Chi. Reilly & Lee. illus. by John R. Neill, rprnt of 1908 ed, b/w drawings, four clr paste-on cvr. . . . . . . *$60.00–$75.00*

Baum, L. Frank. *John Dough and the Cherub*. Chi. Reilly & Britton. (1906). 1st ed. illus. by John R Neill. rare contest blank present.. . . . . *$425.00–$850.00*

Baum, L. Frank. *Land of Oz - A Sequel to the Wizard*. Chi. (1925). clr frontis. . . . . *$40.00–$65.00*

Baum, L. Frank. *Lost Princess of Oz*. Chi. 1939. illus. by J Neill, junior ed.. . . . . *$18.00–$27.00*

Baum, L. Frank. *Marvelous Land of Oz*. Reilly & Britton. 1904. 1st ed. illus. by J. Neill, 2nd state. . . . . *$245.00–$575.00*

Baum, L. Frank. *Ozma of Oz*. Chi. Reilly & Briton. 1907. 1st ed. illus. tan cl. . . . . *$400.00–$575.00*

Baum, L. Frank. *Patchwork Girl of Oz*. Reilly & Britton. (1913). 1st ed. illus. by Neill, 1st state.. . . . . *$375.00–$425.00*

Baum, L. Frank. *Rinkitink in Oz*. Reilly & Briton. (1916). 1st ed. illus. by J Neill, clr plates.. . . . . *$675.00–$800.00*

Baum, L. Frank. *Sky Island*. Chi. Reilly & Britton. (1912). 1st ed. illus. by John R. Neill. 12 clr plates, red cl. . . . . *$385.00–$500.00*

Baum, L. Frank. *The Yellow Hen and Other Stories*. Chi. Reilly & Britton. (1916). 1st ed. 2nd state. illus. by John R. Neill. 4 clr plates, dj. . . . . *$400.00–$650.00*

Baum, L. Frank. *Wizard of Oz Illustrated*. NY. Grosset & Dunlap. 1936. illus. by Labeck. . . . . *$75.00–$100.00*

Baumbach, Werner. *Life and Death of the Luftwaffe*. NY. 1960. 1st Amer ed. photos. . . . . *$18.00–$25.00*

Baxter, Charles. *South Dakota Guidebook*. NY. Rivers Press. 1974. 1st ed. hardcvr, scarce, sgn, dj. . . . . *$250.00–$450.00*

Bayard, Samuel J. *Sketch of the Life of Commodore Robert F. Stockton*. NY. 1856. . . . . *$35.00–$50.00*

Beach, Frank A. *Hormones and Behavior*. NY. Cooper Square. 1961. 2nd e.. . . . . *$40.00–$60.00*

Beach, S. A. *Apples of New York*. Albany. 1905. 2 vols. illus. 130 clr plates. . . . . *$150.00–$375.00*

Beadle, J. H. *Life in Utah*. Phila. 1870. 1st ed. map, plates. . . . . . *$50.00–$125.00*

Beale, R. L. T. *History of the Ninth Virginia Cavalry in the War Between the States*. Richmond. B. F. Johnson Pub. 1899. 1st ed. 192 pp. . . . . *$1,250.00–$1,500.00*

Beale, Reginald. *Practical Greenkeeper*. Lon. Carter. 1936. new ed. illus. green wrps. . . . . *$80.00–$125.00*

Beals, Ralph L. *Cheran: A Sierra Tarascan Village*. DC. Washington Printing Office. 1946. wrps. illus. . . . . *$10.00–$45.00*

Bear, Greg. *Eon*. NY. Bluejay. 1985. 1st ed. dj sgn. . . . . *$85.00–$100.00*

Beard, D. C. *The American Boy's Handy Book*. NY. 1882. . . . . . . *$50.00–$65.00*

Beard, James. *Delights and Prejudices*. NY. 1964. 1st ed. dj. . . . . . *$18.00–$25.00*

Beard, James B., Harriet J. Beard and David Martin, (eds.). *Turfgrass Bibliography from 1672 to 1972*. np. Michigan State Univ 1977. 1st ed. . . . . *$70.00–$130.00*

Beatty, Clyde & Earl Wilson. *Jungle Performers*. NY. 1941. 1st ed. sgn, dj.. . . . . *$25.00–$90.00*

Beaty, John. *Iron Curtain Over America*. Dallas. Wilkinson Pub. 1952. cl. . . . . *$50.00–$85.00*

Beauvallet, Leon. *Rachel and the New World.* NY. Dix, Edwards. 1856. 1st ed. embossed cl. . . . . *$15.00–$30.00*

Beck, Alfred. *Hints on Golf for Everyone.* York. private printing. 1st ed. printed red wrps. . . . . *$50.00–$80.00*

Beck, Henry. *Bridge Busters: The 39th Bomb Group (M).* Cleve. Howard Printers. 1946. photos, map. . . . . *$175.00–$300.00*

Becker, Friedrich. *Breed of the Racehorse.* Lon. British Bloodstock Agency. 1935. 1st ed. . . . . *$50.00–$85.00*

Beckwith, Edward Griffin. *Reports of Explorations and Surveys... for a Railroad from the Mississippi River to the Pacific Ocean.* DC. House of Representatives. 1855. vol. II. illus. hand-tinted plates. . . . . *$225.00–$300.00*

Bedford-Jones, H. B. *Mardi Gras Mystery.* NY. Doubleday Page. 1921. 1st ed. . . . . *$18.00–$25.00*

Bedford-Jones, H. B. *Saint Michael's Gold.* NY. Putnam. 1926. 1st ed. . . . . *$14.00–$17.00*

Beebe, Lucius. *American West.* Dutton. 1955. 1st ed. . . . . *$30.00–$40.00*

Beebe, William. *A Naturalist's Life of New York.* Lon. Bodley Head. 1954. 1st UK ed. . . . . *$15.00–$27.00*

Beebe, William. *Galapagos, World's End.* Putnam. 1924. . . . . *$25.00–$45.00*

Beebe, William. *Jungle Days.* NY. Putnam. 1925. 1st ed. dj. . . . . . . *$10.00–$40.00*

Beebe, William. *Pheasant Jungles.* NY. Putnam. 1927. 1st ed. cl, plates. . . . . *$15.00–$20.00*

Beebe, William. *The Arcturus Adventure.* NY. Putnam. 1926. 1st ed. illus. photos, maps. . . . . *$70.00–$150.00*

Beebe, William. *The Log of the Sun, A Chronicle of Nature's Year.* NY. Holt. 1906. 1st ed. illus. by Walter King Stone. pict cl, teg. . . . . *$50.00–$80.00*

Beebe, William. *Two Bird-Lovers in Mexico.* Bos. Houghton Mifflin. 1905. 1st ed. illus. photos. author's first book. decorated cl, teg. . . . . *$95.00–$115.00*

Beecher, Catherine. *Physiology and Calisthenics for schools and families.* NY. Harper. 1856. brown cl. . . . . *$50.00–$65.00*

Beecher, Catherine E. *Miss Beecher's Domestic Receipt Book.* NY. Harper. 1872. 5th ed. . . . . *$30.00–$45.00*

Beecher, Catherine E. *Treatise on Domestic Economy.* NY. Harper. 1850. illus. rev ed. . . . . *$35.00–$65.00*

Beecher, Catherine E. and Harriet Beecher Stowe. *American Woman's Home.* NY. Ford. 1869. 1st ed. illus. 3/4 mor.. . . . . *$80.00–$120.00*

Beecher, Henry W. *Norwood.* NY. Scribner's. 1868. 1st ed. . . . . . . *$35.00–$75.00*

Beecher, John. *All Brave Sailors....* NY. Eischer. 1945. dj. . . . . *$75.00–$90.00*

Beede, A. McG. *Sitting Bull-Custer.* Bismark, ND. 1913. 1st ed. illus. . . . .
. . . . *$125.00–$150.00*

Beehler, B. M., T. K. Pratt, and D. A. Zimmerman. *Birds of New Guinea.* Princeton University Press. 1986. illus. 56 clr plates, dj. . . . . *$50.00–$75.00*

Beehler, W. H. *Cruise of the Brooklyn.* Phila. Lippincott. 1885. illus. maps plates..
. . . . *$95.00–$150.00*

Beerbohm, Max. *A Survey.* Lon. (1921). 1st ed. ltd 225 cc. sgn.. *$200.00–$300.00*

Beerbohm, Max. *A Survey.* Lon. Heinemann. 1921. 1st ed. plates, dj. . . . .
. . . . *$125.00–$450.00*

Beerbohm, Max. *Letters to Reggie Turner.* Lon. 1964. 1st ed. edited by Rupert Hart-Davis. cl, dj. . . . . *$45.00–$60.00*

Beerbohm, Max. *Mainly On the Air.* NY. Knopf. 1947. 1st ed. dj. . *$18.00–$50.00*

Beerbohm, Max. *Rossetti and His Circle.* Lon. Heinemann. 1922. 1st ed. illus. 20 clr plates. . . . . *$135.00–$225.00*

Beerbohm, Max. *Rossetti and His Circle.* Lon. Heinemann. 1922. 1st ed. blue cl..
. . . . *$100.00–$150.00*

Beerbohm, Max. *Things New and Old.* .Lon. Heinemann. 1923. 1st ed. dj. . . . . . .
. . . . *$50.00–$85.00*

Beerbohm, Max. *Yet Again.* NY. Knopf. 1923. 1st ed. . . . . *$30.00–$35.00*

Beerbohm, Max. *Zuleika Dobson: An Oxford Love Story.* Lon. Heinemann. 1911. 1st ed. . . . . *$225.00–$300.00*

Beerhohm, Max. *A Survey.* NY. Doubledy Page. 1921. 1st Amer ed.. . . . .
. . . . *$25.00–$100.00*

Beers, D. B. *Atlas of Luzerne County, Pa.* Phila. Beers & Co. 1873. illus. hand-clr maps.. . . . . *$300.00–$750.00*

Beers, F. W. *Atlas of Delaware County, NY.* Beers & Co. 1869. illus. gilt lettering, maps.. . . . . *$125.00–$175.00*

Beers, F. W. *Combination Atlas of Saratoga and Ballston.* NY. Beers. 1876. 1st ed. illus. hand-clr maps.. . . . . *$275.00–$350.00*

Beers, F. W. *History of Montgomery and Fulton Counties, NY.* NY. Beers. 1878. illus. litho, maps, folio. . . . .*$200.00–$250.00*

Beeton, Isabella. *Book of Household Management.* Lon. S. O. Beeton. 1861. 1st ed. 1/2 lea.. . . . .*$400.00–$800.00*

Beever, John. *Practical Fly Fishing.* Lon. 1893. . . . .*$45.00–$65.00*

Begin, Menachem. *White Nights, the Story of a Prisoner in Russia.* NY. Harper & Row. 1977. 1st US ed. dj. . . . .*$35.00–$45.00*

Behan, Brendan. *Brendan Behan's Island.* NY. Bernard Geiss. 1962. 1st Amer ed. sgn. . . . .*$85.00–$100.00*

Behan, Brendan. *Confessions of an Irish Rebel.* Lon. 1965. 1st ed. dj. . . . .*$25.00–$35.00*

Behan, Brendan. *Hold Your Hour And Have Another.* Bos. Little Brown. 1954. 1st Amer ed. dj. . . . .*$25.00–$30.00*

Beldam, George W. *Golfing Illustrated.* Lon. Gowans & Gray. 1908. 1st ed. pict wrps. . . . .*$120.00–$250.00*

Belknap, Jeremy. *Foresters, An American Tale.* Exeter. S. Hardy. 1831. lea. . . . .*$40.00–$100.00*

Belknap, Jeremy. *Sermon Preached at the Installation of Rev. Jedidiah Morse.* Bos. Samuel Hall. 1789. 1st ed. wrps. sewn. . . . .*$75.00–$100.00*

Bell, Charles Dent. *Winter on the Nile in Egypt and in Nubia.* Lon. Hodder & Stoughton. 1889. illus. fold out map. . . . .*$80.00–$95.00*

Bell, Gertrude. *Letters of Gertrude Bell.* Lon. Ernest Benn. 1927. 2 vols. 1st ed. illus. green cl, 32 photos, map of Persia. . . . .*$75.00–$100.00*

Bell, Landon Covington. *Old Free State.* Richmond. Byrd. 1927. 2 vols. illus. maps. . . . .*$60.00–$125.00*

Bell, Louis. *The Telescope.* NY/Lon. 1922. 1st ed. illus. . . . .*$35.00–$50.00*

Bell, Louise Price. *Kitchen Fun.* Cleve. Harter. (1932). 1st ed. illus. by Jessie Willcox Smith. . . . .*$50.00–$85.00*

Bell, Sir Charles. *Portrait of the Dalai Lama.* Lon. Collins. 1946. 1st ed. illus. . . . .*$50.00–$85.00*

Bell Telephone Laboratories. *History of Engineering and Science In The Bell System.* 1975. 1st ed. illus. dj. . . . .*$30.00–$45.00*

Bell, W. D. M. *Karomojo Safari.* NY. Harcourt Brace. 1949. 1st ed. dj. *$90.00–$150.00*

Bellerive Country Club. St. Louis. B.C.C. 1910. 1st ed. . . . .*$80.00–$100.00*

Belloc, Hilaire. *Mr Clutterbuck's Election*. Lon. 1908. . . . . *$75.00–$125.00*

Bellow, Saul. *Adventures of Augie March*.NY. Viking. 1953. 1st ed. dj. . . . .
. . . . *$90.00–$150.00*

Bellow, Saul. *Dean's December*. NY. Harper & Row. (1982). ltd 500 cc, sgn, slipcase. . . . . *$100.00–$135.00*

Bellow, Saul. *Dean's December*. NY. Harper & Row. 1982. 1st ed. wrps. dj. . . . . .
. . . . *$25.00–$35.00*

Bellow, Saul. *Herzog*. NY. Viking. 1964. 1st ed. dj photo on back of jacket. . . . . .
. . . . *$40.00–$55.00*

Bellow, Saul. *Last Analysis*. NY. Viking. 1965. 1st ed. dj. . . . . *$40.00–$54.00*

Bellow, Saul. *Mr. Sammler's Planet*. NY. Viking. (1970). 1st ed. dj. *$45.00–$85.00*

Bellow, Saul. *Seize the Day*. NY. Viking. (1956). 1st ed. dj. . . . . . . *$20.00–$75.00*

Bellow, Saul. *The Victim*. NY. Vanguard Press. 1947. 1st ed. dj. . . *$60.00–$250.00*

Bellow, Saul. *To Jeruselem and Back*. NY. 1976. 1st ed. dj.. . . . . . . *$20.00–$60.00*

Belmont, Perry. *An American Democrat*. NY. Columbia University Press. 1940. 1st
ed. . . . . *$65.00–$115.00*

Bemelmans, Ludwig. *Hansi*. NY. Viking. 1934. 1st ed. . . . . *$85.00–$175.00*

Bemelmans, Ludwig. *Madeline and the Gypsies*. NY. Viking. 1959. 1st ed. . . . . .
. . . . *$50.00–$65.00*

Bemelmans, Ludwig. *My War With the United States*. NY. Viking. 1937. 1st ed. dj.
. . . . *$25.00–$75.00*

Bemelmans, Ludwig. *Now I Lay Me Down to Sleep*. NY. Viking. 1945. illus. ltd 400
cc, sgn, slipcase. . . . . *$95.00–$125.00*

Bemelmans, Ludwig. *Parsley*. NY. Harper. 1955. 1st ed. illus. . . . .
. . . . *$75.00–$125.00*

Benedict, George Grenville. *Vermont In The Civil War....* Burlington, VT. Free Press.
1886-88. 2 vols.. 1st ed. . . . . *$75.00–$125.00*

Benet, Stephen Vincent. *John Brown's Body*. NY. Doubleday, Doran. 1928. 3/4 red
mor, teg. . . . . *$40.00–$75.00*

Bennett, Colin N. *Guide to Kinematography*. Lon. Heron. 1917. 1st ed. illus. . . .
. . . . *$75.00–$85.00*

Bennett, Frank M. *Monitor & the Navy Under Steam*. Bos. Houghton Mifflin. 1900.
1st ed. illus. . . . . *$50.00–$100.00*

Bennett, Ian (ed.). *Complete Illustrated Rugs and Carpets of the World.* NY. A&W. (1977). 1st Amer ed.. *$35.00–$50.00*

Bennett, Ira C. *History of the Panama Canal....* DC. Historical Pub. 1915. 1st ed. illus. plates.. *$95.00–$185.00*

Bennett, James. *Overland Journey To California....* NY. Eberstadt. 1932. wrps. ltd 200 cc,j... *$45.00–$125.00*

Bennett, Russell H. *Complete Rancher.* NY. 1946. 1st ed. illus. by Ross Santee, dj. .... *$120.00–$150.00*

Bennett, William P. *First Baby in Camp.* Salt Lake. Rancher. 1893. 1st ed. printed pink wraps... *$50.00–$75.00*

Benson E. F. *Colin.* NY. Doran. (1923). 1st Amer ed. 334 pp.... *$115.00–$150.00*

Benson, A. C. & Weaver, Sir Lawrence (eds.). *Everybody's Book of the Queen's Dolls' House.* Lon. Daily Telegraph & Meuthen. (1924). 2 vols. illus. .... *$60.00–$75.00*

Bent, Arthur Cleveland. *Life Histories of North American Thrushes.* DC. Smithsonian. 1949. wrps. plates........................... *$28.00–$35.00*

Bentley, E. C. *Trent's Own Case.* NY. Knopf. 1936. 1st ed. ...... *$35.00–$60.00*

Benton, Frank. *Cowboy Life on the Sidetrack.* Denver. Cowboy Stories Syndicate. (1903). 1st ed. .... *$60.00–$125.00*

Benton, Josiah Hart. *Voting in the Field.* Bos. privately printed. .. *$75.00–$95.00*

Benton, Thomas Hart. *An Artist in America.* McBride. 1937. 1st ed. illus. blue cl, dj. .... *$50.00–$75.00*

Berkeley, Earl of. *Sound Golf by Applying Principles to Practice.* Lon. Seely, Service. (1936). 1st ed. .... *$100.00–$120.00*

Berkeley, Edmund Callis. *Giant Brains or Machines That Think.* NY. (1949). 1st ed. 270 pp, dj... *$100.00–$150.00*

Bermann, Richard A. *Mahdi of Allah....* NY. Macmillan. 1932. illus. 1st US ed red cl maps.. *$40.00–$50.00*

Berndt, R. M. (ed.). *Australian Aboriginal Art.* Sidney. (1964). .... *$250.00–$350.00*

Berners, Dame Juliana. *Treatyse of Fysshynge wyth an Angle.* NY. 1875. 1st Amer ed. brown cl... *$200.00–$250.00*

Berryman, John. *Poems.* Norfolk. New Directions. (1942). ltd 1500 cc, stapled wrps, sgn, dj, scarce. .... *$375.00–$475.00*

Berton, Ralph. *Remembering Bix.* Lon. Allen. 1974. 1st UK ed. dj. . *$45.00–$65.00*

Best Short Stories of 1923. Bos. 1924. . . . . *$45.00–$60.00*

Bester, Alfred. *Demolished Man.* Chi. Shasta. 1953. dj. . . . . *$125.00–$175.00*

Betten, H. L. *Upland Game Shooting.* Phila. 1940. 1st ed. illus. by Lynn Bogue Hunt.
. . . . *$40.00–$60.00*

Betts, Doris. *Gentle Insurrection.* NY. Putnam. 1954. 1st ed. author's first book, dj.
. . . . *$60.00–$150.00*

Beuchner, Thomas S. *Norman Rockwell: Artist and Illustrator.* NY. Abrams. (1970).
1st ed. illus. . . . . *$40.00–$100.00*

Beveridge, Albert J. *Life of John Marshall.* Bos/NY. Houghton Mifflin Co. 1916-
1919. 4 vols. green cl. . . . . *$175.00–$225.00*

Bhushan, Jamila Brij. *Indian Jewelry, Ornaments and Decorative Designs.*
Bombay. nd. 1st ed. illus. . . . . *$75.00–$140.00*

Bianco, Margery Williams. *The Candlestick.* Garden City. Doubleday. 1929. 1st ed.
illus. cl. . . . . *$20.00–$30.00*

Bianco, Margery Williams. *The Velveteen Rabbit, or How Toys Become Real.* NY.
Henry Holt. 1983. illus. dj. . . . . *$10.00–$20.00*

Bible. *Holy Bible.* Newburyport. William B Allen & Co. 1815. . . . *$50.00–$75.00*

Bible. *New Testament.* NH. Justin Hinds. 1825. . . . . *$25.00–$35.00*

Bible. *Holy Scriptures, Translated and Corrected by the Spirit of Revelation, By
Joseph Smith, Jr., The Seer.* Plano. 1867. . . . . *$300.00–$500.00*

***Bible, das ist: die gantze Heilige Schrifft Alten un Newen Testament . . . Martin
Luther.*** Tubingen. 1769. folio, tooled pigskin over wooden bds, metal clasps, wood-
cut text illus. . . . . *$220.00–$300.00*

Bible Atlas.... Phila. American Sunday School Union. 1827. wrps. illus. clred maps,
9 leaves, 135 x 11 cm. . . . . *$95.00–$115.00*

Bickersteth, Rev. Edward. *Scripture Help....* Bos. S H Parker. 1817. 4 maps lea. .
. . . . *$40.00–$50.00*

Bickerstaff. *Boston Almanac.* Providence. 1810. . . . . *$20.00–$50.00*

Biddle, Ellen. *Reminiscences of a Soldier's Wife.* Phila. Lippincott. 1907. . . . . . .
. . . . *$125.00–$150.00*

Biddle, Major Charles. *Way of the Eagle.* NY. Scribner's. 1919. 1st ed. illus. photos.
. . . . *$60.00–$80.00*

Biddulph, John (Colonel). *Pirates of Malabar*. Lon. Smith, Elder. 1907. . . . .
. . . . *$50.00–$75.00*

Bidwel, Percy Wells and John I. Falconer. *History of Agriculture in the Northern United States*. DC. Carnegie. 1925. 1st ed. illus. . . . . *$60.00–$90.00*

Bidwell, O. B. *Missionary Map of Africa*. NY. 1851. wall map. *$800.00–$1,000.00*

Bierce, Ambrose. *A Vision of Doom*. RI, Grant. 1980. dj. . . . . *$15.00–$25.00*

Bierce, Ambrose. *Shapes of Clay*. SF. W. E. Wood. 1903. . . . . . *$400.00–$700.00*

Bierce, Ambrose. *Ten Tales*. Lon. First Editions Club. 1925. . . . . . *$50.00–$75.00*

Bierce, Ambrose. *The Ambrose Bierce Satanic Reader*. NY. Doubleday. 1968. Jerome Hopkins (ed.), dj.. . . . . *$30.00–$35.00*

Bierce, Ambrose. *The Monk and the Hangman's Daughter*. Heritage. 1967. 1st thus. dj. . . . . *$10.00–$20.00*

Bierce, Ambrose. *The Shadow on the Dial*. SF. Robertson. 1909. 1st ed. no dj. . . .
. . . . *$75.00–$100.00*

Bierce, Ambrose. *The Shadow on the Dial*. SF. Robertsoon. 1909. 1st ed. green buckram, dj.. . . . . *$300.00–$325.00*

Bierce, Ambrose. *Write It Right. A Little Blacklist of Literary Faults*. NY. Union Library. 1934. dj.. . . . . *$10.00–$45.00*

Bierstadt, Edward Hale. *Satan Was a Man*. Garden City. Doubleday, Doran. 1935. 1st ed. dj.. . . . . *$80.00–$100.00*

Bigelow, Jacob. *Useful Arts...with the applications of science*. Bos. Webb & Co. 1842. 396 pp, illus. . . . . *$60.00–$75.00*

Bigelow, John. *Memoir of the Life & Public Services of John Charles Fremont*. NY. 1856. . . . . *$40.00–$60.00*

Bigelow, John. *Peach Orchard*. Minn. 1910. 1st ed. illus. fldg maps.*$55.00–$75.00*

Bigelow, Poultney. *Borderland of Czar & Kaiser*. NY. 1895. 1st ed. illus. by F Remington. . . . . *$80.00–$100.00*

Bigelow, Poultney. *White Man's Africa*. NY. Harper. 1898. . . . . . . *$20.00–$25.00*

Biggers, Earl Derr. *Behind That Curtain*. NY. Pocket Books. 1942. 1st paperback ed.. . . . . *$10.00–$12.00*

Biggers, Earl Derr. *Celebrated Cases of Charlie Chan*. Lon. Cassell. 1933. 1st ed. . . . . *$20.00–$35.00*

Biggers, Earl Derr. *Charlie Chan Carries On*. NY. Grosset & Dunlap. 1920. rprnt, dj. . . . . *$20.00–$30.00*

Biggers, Earl Derr. *Charlie Chan Carries On.* Ind. Bobbs-Merrill. (1930). 1st ed. yellow cl, dj. . . . . *$150.00–$350.00*

Biggers, Earl Derr. *Keeper of the Keys.* Ind. Bobbs-Merrill. 1932. 1st ed. dj. . . . . *$275.00–$350.00*

Biggers, Earl Derr. *Love Insurance.* Ind. Bobbs-Merrill. 1914. 1st ed. . . . . *$50.00–$125.00*

Biggers, Earl Derr. *Seven Keys to Baldpate.* Ind. Bobbs-Merrill. 1913. 1st ed. . . . . *$25.00–$100.00*

Biggers, Earl Derr. *Seven Keys to Baldpate.* Ind. Bobbs-merrill. 1913. 1st ed. illus. decorative cl. . . . . *$25.00–$40.00*

Biggers, Earl Derr. *The Agony Column.* Ind. Bobbs-Merrill. (1916). 1st ed. brown cl. . . . . *$15.00–$40.00*

Biggers, Earl Derr. *The Chinese Parrot.* Bobbs-Merrill. 1926. 1st US ed. cl. . . . . *$50.00–$175.00*

Biggers, Earl Derr. *The Chinese Parrot.* NY. Grosset & Dunlap. 1926. dj. . . . . *$25.00–$75.00*

Bigsby, John J. *The Shoe and Canoe* Lon. 1850. 2 vols. illus. . *$500.00–$2,000.00*

Billiards Simplified, or How to Make Breaks. Lon. Burroughs & Watts. nd. illus. diagrams, 1889 cat of billiards accessories, blue cl. . . . . *$75.00–$175.00*

Billings, John D. *Hardtack and Coffee or the Unwritten Story of Army Life.* Bos. George M. Smith. 1887. 1st ed. illus. plates. . . . . *$125.00–$375.00*

Billings, John D. *Hardtack and Coffee, or the Unwritten Story of Army Life.* Alexandria. Time-Life Books. 1982. illus. . . . . *$25.00–$35.00*

Billington, Elizabeth. *Randolph Caldecott Treasury.* NY. Frederick Warne. 1978. 1st ed. dj. . . . . *$35.00–$60.00*

Bindloss, Harold. *In the Niger Country.* Edin. Blackwood. 1898. cl. . . . . *$100.00–$150.00*

Bingham, Capt. *The Bastille.* NY. James Pott & Co. 1901. 2 vols. illus. . . . . *$75.00–$100.00*

Bingham, Hiram. *Residence of Twenty-One Years in the Sandwich Islands.* Hartford. Hezekiah Huntington. 1847. 1st ed. illus. fldg map. . . . . *$250.00–$500.00*

Bingham, John. *Trial of Conspirators... Assassination of President Lincoln.* DC. GPO. 1865. 1st ed. wrps. . . . . *$200.00–$400.00*

Binkerd, Adam D. *Mammoth Cave And Its Denizens.* Cinc. 1869. 1st ed. wrps. . . . . *$65.00–$90.00*

Bird, Isabella. *A Lady's Life in the Rocky Mountains.* Lon. Murray 1885. illus. 5th ed. . . . . *$65.00–$75.00*

Bird, Isabella. *Hawaiian Archipelago.* Lon. Murray. 1875. 1st ed. green cl.. . . . . *$150.00–$175.00-*

Bird, Isabella. *Hawaiian Archipelago.* NY. (1882). 5th ed. . . . . *$60.00–$80.00*

Bird, Isabella. *Unbeaten Tracks in Japan.* Lon. Murray. 1911. 2nd ed. illus. . . . . *$90.00–$140.00*

Bird, Isabella. *Unbeaten Tracks in Japan.* NY. Putnam. 1881. 2 vols. illus. fldg map. . . . . *$135.00–$180.00*

Bird, Isabella L. *A Lady's Life in the Rocky Mountains.* OK. University of Oklahoma. 1960. rprnt. dj. . . . . *$15.00–$30.00*

Bird, Isabella L. *Six months Among the Palm Groves, Coral Reefs, and Volcanoes of the Sandwich Islands.* NY. Putnam. 1882. 5th ed. illus. maps. . . . *$150.00–$200.00*

Bird, Isabella L. *Six Months Among the Palm Groves, Coral Reefs, and Volcanoes of the Sandwich Islands.* NY. Scribner's & Welford. 1881. 4th ed. fldg map. . . . . *$75.00–$195.00*

Bird, Isabella L. *Six Months Among the Palm Groves, Coral Reefs, and Volcanoes of the Sandwich Islands.* Lon. John Murray. 1880. 3rd ed. gilt cl, fdg map, illus. . . . . *$65.00–$80.00*

Bird, Isabella L. *The Golden Chersonese and the Way Theater.* Putnam. 1883. frontis, fldg map, gilt pict cl. . . . . *$300.00–$350.00*

Birds of New York. The State of New York. 1910-1914. clr plates.. *$60.00–$125.00*

Birket-Smith, Kaj. *The Eskimos.* NY. Crown. 1971. illus. 1st Amer ed, dj. . . . . *$40.00–$60.00*

Bishop Harriet E. *Floral Home.* NY. Sheldon, Blakeman. 1857. 1st ed. illus. 10 plates, 342 pp. . . . . *$150.00–$225.00*

Bishop, Isabella Bird. *Korea and Her Neighbors.* NY. Revell. 1898. illus. maps. . . . . *$160.00–$200.00*

Bishop, Mrs. J. F. (Isabella Bird). *Yangtze Valley and Beyond.* Lon. Murray. 1899. 1st ed. illus. map. . . . . *$250.00–$650.00*

Bishop, Nathaniel H. *Pampas and Andes: A Thousand Miles' Walk Across South America.* Bos. Lee & Shepard. 1869. 1 vol. illus. 14 plates, pict gilt orange cl.. . . . . *$110.00–$120.00*

Bishop, Richard E. *Bishop's Wildfowl.* St Paul. Brown & Bigelow. 1948. 1st ed. lea. . . . . *$100.00–$200.00*

Biss, Gerald. *Door of the Unreal.* NY. Putnam. 1920. 1st Amer ed. . . . .
. . . . *$125.00–$150.00*

Bissel, E. *Map of Manchester, Conn..* Hartford. 1849. wall map. *$750.00*

Bjist, Robert. *American Flower Garden Directory.* Phila. 1841. . . *$50.00–$75.00*

Black Anti-Semitism and Jewish Racism. NY. Baron. 1969. intro by Nat Hentoff, dj.
. . . . *$25.00–$20.00*

Black Book: The Nazi Crime Against the Jewish People. NY. Duell Sloan & Pearce.
1946. 1st ed. . . . . *$60.00–$85.00*

Black, A. P. *End of the Longhorn Trail.* ND. nd. illus. . . . . *$60.00–$75.00*

Blackburn, I. *Illus. of Gross Morbid Anatomy of the Brain in the Insane.* DC. GPO.
1908. 1st ed. tall book photos. . . . . *$125.00–$150.00*

Blackford, William Willis. *War Years with Jeb Stuart.* NY. 1945. 1st ed. dj. . . . . .
. . . . *$35.00–$50.00*

Blackman, William Fremont. *Making of Hawaii....* NY/Lon. Macmillan Co. 1899.
. . . . *$65.00–$85.00*

Blackwell, Sarah Ellen. *Military Genius...Life of Anna Ella Carroll of Maryland.*
DC. 1891. 1st ed. . . . . *$40.00–$50.00*

Blackwood, Algernon. *Day and Night Stories.* NY. Dutton. (1917). 1st Amer ed. 228
pp. . . . . *$75.00–$125.00*

Blackwood, Algernon. *Doll and One Other.* Sauk City. Arkham House. 1946. 1st ed.
dj. . . . . *$40.00–$90.00*

Blackwood, Algernon. *Incredible Adventures.* NY. Macmillan. 1914. 1st Amer ed.
green cl, 368 pp. . . . . *$70.00–$80.00*

Blackwood, Algernon. *The Listener.* NY. Vaughn & Gomme. 1914. 1st US ed, ltd.
. . . . *$75.00–$175.00*

Blackwood, Algernon. *The Wave.* NY. Dutton. (1916). 1st ed. . . . . *$25.00–$50.00*

Blades, William F. *Fishing Flies & Fly Tying.* Harrisburg. Stackpole. 1962. 2nd ed.
dj. . . . . *$35.00–$60.00*

Blaine, John. *Rocket's Shadow.* NY. Grosset & Dunlap. 1947. Rick Brant #1, dj. .
. . . . *$20.00–$30.00*

Blaine, John. *Stairway to Danger.* NY. Grosset & Dunlap. 1952. dj. . . . .
. . . . *$15.00–$30.00*

Blaine, John. *The Caves of Fear.* NY. Grosset & Dunlap. 1951. dj. . *$8.00–$35.00*

Blaine, John. *Veiled Raiders.* NY. Grosset & Dunlap. 1965. #20, map endpapers. .
. . . . *$45.00–$150.00*

Blake, Sir Henry Arthur. *China.* Lon. A & C. 1909. 1st ed. illus. dark blue cl, clr
plates. . . . . *$60.00–$70.00*

Blake, John L. *Geographical Chronological and Historical Atlas.* NY. Cook & Co.
1826. illus. charts, engr.. . . . . *$75.00–$200.00*

Blake, W. O. *History of Slavery and the Slave Trade.* Columbus. J & H Miller. 1858.
engr. . . . . *$75.00–$125.00*

Blanch, Lesley. *Sabres of Paradise.* Lon. John Murray. 1960. 1st ed. illus. dj, maps.
. . . . *$75.00–$85.00*

Blanchan, Neltje. *Bird Neighbors.* NY. Doubleday & McClure. 1899. . . . .
. . . . *$20.00–$35.00*

Blanchan, Neltje. *Birds that Hunt and are Hunted.* NY. Doubleday & McClure.
1898. 1st ed. illus. . . . . *$30.00–$40.00*

Blanchan, Neltje. *Nature Library.* NY. Nelson Doubleday. 1926. 5 vols.. illus. . . . .
. . . . *$30.00–$50.00*

Blanchan, Neltje. *Nature's Garden.* NY. Doubleday Page. 1900. 1st prtg, photos. .
. . . . *$25.00–$32.00*

Blanchard, Elizabeth, Amis Cameron and Manly Wade Wellman. *Life and Times
of Sir Archie 1805-1833.* Chapel Hill. Univ of N.C. Press. 1958. 1st ed. dj. . . . . . .
. . . . *$48.00–$200.00*

Blanchard, Rufus. *Discovery and Conquests of the Northwest.* Wheaton. R.
Blanchard & Co. 1880. small. . . . . *$125.00–$200.00*

Blanchard, Rufus. *History of Illinois to Accompany an Historical Map of the State.*
Chi. Nat'l School. 1883. 1st ed. 128 pp, fldg map mounted on linen. . . . .
. . . . *$125.00–$200.00*

Blanck, Jacob. *Bibliography of American Literature.* New Haven. Yale Univ Press.
(1968). 7 vols. illus. . . . . *$300.00–$350.00*

Bland, J. O. & E. Backhouse. *China Under the Empress Dowager.* Phila/Lon. 1912.
. . . . *$25.00–$65.00*

Blatty, William. *The Exorcist.* NY. Harper & Row. 1971. 1st ed. scarce, dj. . . . . . .
. . . . *$75.00–$125.00*

Blavatsky, Helena Petrovna. *From the Caves and Jungles of Hindostan.* Lon.
Theosophical Society. 1908. 1st ed. . . . . *$50.00–$75.00*

Blesh, Rudi. *Combo USA.* Phila. Chilton. 1971. 1st ed. dj. . . . . *$20.00–$50.00*

Blesh, Rudi. *This is Jazz.* SF. private printing. 1943. 1st ed. wrps. inscr. . . . .
. . . . *$100.00–$475.00*

Blew, W. C. *A History of Steeple-Chasing.* Lon. John C. Nemmo. 1901. . . . .
. . . . *$125.00–$272.00*

Blinn, Henry Clay. *Life and Gospel Experience of Mother Ann Lee.* Canterbury.
Shakers. 1901. . . . . *$140.00–$160.00*

Bloch, Robert. *Lori.* NY. Doherty. 1989. 1st ed. cl, dj. . . . . *$35.00–$45.00*

Bloch, Robert. *Night of the Ripper.* NY. Doubleday. 1981. 1st ed. inscr & sgn, dj.
. . . . *$50.00–$70.00*

Bloch, Robert. *Psycho.* NY. Simon & Schuster. 1959. 1st ed. sgn, dj. . . . .
. . . . *$250.00–$300.00*

Block, Lawrence. *Burglar Who Liked to Quote Kipling.* NY. Random House. 1979.
1st ed. dj, presentation copy, sgn.. . . . . *$125.00–$150.00*

Block, Lawrence. *Burglar Who Painted Like Mondrian.* NY. (1983). 1st ed. dj.. . .
. . . . *$50.00–$135.00*

Block, Lawrence. *Burglar Who Studied Spinoza.* NY. Random House. 1980. 1st ed.
dj. . . . . *$35.00–$50.00*

Block, Lawrence. *Dance at the Slaughter House.* NY. (1991). 1st ed. dj.. . . . .
. . . . *$20.00–$40.00*

Block, Lawrence. *Even the Wicked.* Lon. (1996). 1st ed. ltd, dj. . *$150.00–$250.00*

Block, Lawrence. *Even the Wicked.* NY. (1997). 1st US ed. sgn, dj. *$20.00–$40.00*

Block, Lawrence. *Random Wall.* NY. (1988). 1st ed. dj. . . . . *$30.00–$35.00*

Block, Lawrence. *Ronald Rabbit Is a Dirty Old Man.* Chi. Bernard Geis. 1971. 1st
ed. dj. . . . . *$150.00–$250.00*

Block, Lawrence. *Sins of the Father.* Arlington Hts. Dark Harvest. 1992. 1st hardcvr
ed. intro by Stephen King, dj. . . . . *$50.00–$65.00*

Block, Lawrence. *Ticket to the Boneyard.* NY. William Morrow. 1990. 1st ed. inscr,
dj. . . . . *$40.00–$50.00*

Block, Lawrence. *Two for Tanner.* Greenwich, CT. (1968). 1st ed. wrps. sgn, dj.. .
. . . . *$45.00–$65.00*

Block, Lawrence. *When the Sacred Ginmill Closes.* NY. Arbor House. 1986. 1st ed.
dj. . . . . *$35.00–$50.00*

Block, Robert. *Dead Beat.* NY. Simon & Schuster. 1960. 1st ed. dj.*$60.00–$75.00*

Blot, Pierre. *Hand-Book of Practical Cookery*. NY. Appleton. 1868. . . . . **$125.00–$195.00**

Bly, Robert. *Jumping Out of Bed*. MA. Barre Publishers. 1973. 1st ed. wrps. sgn. . . . . **$30.00–$45.00**

Bly, Robert. *Light Around the Body*. Lon. Rapp & Whiting. 1968. sgn. dj. . . . . **$50.00–$85.00**

Bly, Robert. *Man in the Black Coat Turns*. NY. Dial. 1981. 1st ed. dj. . . . . **$20.00–$35.00**

Bly, Robert. *Morning Gloria*. SF. 1969. wrps. illus. by Tommie De Paola, ltd 800 cc. . . . . **$25.00–$30.00**

Bly, Robert. *Silence In the Snowy Fields*..... Lon. Jonathan Cape. 1967. dj. . . . . **$40.00–$60.00**

Bly, Robert. *Teeth Mother Naked At Last*. S. F. San Francisco City Lights. 1970. sgn by author, dj. . . . . **$35.00–$50.00**

Bly, Robert. *The Loon*. Minnesota. Ox Head Press. (1977). ltd 500 cc, wrps.. . . . . **$30.00–$40.00**

Boas, Franz. *Kathlamet Texts*. DC. GPO. 1901. 1st ed. Bulletin 26. 261pp. . . . . **$55.00–$125.00**

Boas, Franz (ed.). *Folk-Tales of Salishan and Sahaptin Tribes*. NY. American Folklore Society. 1917. 1st ed. 201pp. . . . . **$60.00–$75.00**

Boerhaave, Hermann. *De Viribus Medicamentorum, The Virtue and Energy of Medicines*. Venice. Thomas Bettinelli. 1774. 3rd ed. illus. . . . . . . **$150.00–$200.00**

Bogardus. *Field, Cover, and Trap Shooting*. NY. Orange Judd. 1881. frontis.. . . . . **$50.00–$80.00**

Bohn, Henry. *Bohn's New Hand Book of Games*. Bos. 1850. . . . **$100.00–$125.00**

Bohr, Neils. *Theory of Spectra and Atomic Constitution*. Lon. 1922. **$35.00–$45.00**

Bolton, Reginald Pelham. *Washington Heights, Manhattan*. NY. privately printed. 1924. illus. red cl, photos. . . . . **$60.00–$75.00**

Bond, Carrie Jacobs. *A Perfect Day and Other Poems*. Joliet. Volland. (1926). illus. silhouettes, boxed. . . . . **$35.00–$50.00**

Bond, Horace Mann. *Education of the Negro in the American Social Order*. NY. Prentice-Hall. 1934. 1st prtg, ex lib.. . . . . **$80.00–$95.00**

Bond, J. Wesley. *Minnesota and Its Resources*. NY. Redfield. 1854. 1st ed. illus. cl lithographs. . . . . **$65.00–$75.00**

Bondy, Louis W. *Miniature Books: Their History....* Lon. Sheppard Press. 1981. 1st ed. dj. . . . . *$50.00–$150.00*

Bonner, Mary Graham. *Sir Noble, the Police Horse.* NY. Knopf. 1940. 1st ed. illus. dj. . . . . *$35.00–$45.00*

Bonney, Edward. *Banditti Of The Prairies....* Chi. 1850. wrps. illus. plates. . . . . *$3,000.00–$5,000.00*

Bontemps, Arna Wendell and Jack Conroy. *They Seek a City.* Garden City. Doubleday, Doran. 1945. 1st ed. dj. . . . . *$100.00–$125.00*

Bontemps, Arna Wendell and Jack Conroy. *They Seek a City.* Garden City. Doubleday, Doran. 1945. 1st ed. . . . . *$30.00–$60.00*

Bonwick, James. *Mormons and the Silver Mines.* Lon. 1872. . . . *$95.00–$125.00*

Book of Baseball. NY. 1911. . . . . *$150.00–$300.00*

Book of Kalushin. Tel Aviv. 1961. 570 pp, Yiddish, photos. . . . . . . *$80.00–$50.00*

Book of Kells. Lon/NY. 1933. illus. 4th ed. tip-in clr plate. . . . . *$50.00–$65.00*

Boomer & Boschert. *Cider & Wine Presses.* Syracuse, NY. 1876. wrps. . . . . *$65.00–$90.00*

Booth, Mary. *History of the City of New York.* NY. 1867. 2 vols.. lea. . . . . *$50.00–$85.00*

Booth, Maud Ballington. *After Prison–What?* NY. 1903. rprnt sgn. *$28.00–$45.00*

Borden, Mary. *Forbidden Zone.* NY. Doubleday. 1930. 1st US ed. . *$25.00–$45.00*

Borden, Mrs. John. *Cruise of the "Northern Light."* NY. Macmillan. 1928. 1st ed. illus. map, end papers. . . . . *$35.00–$75.00*

Borden, W. *Use of the Roentgen Ray by the Medical Dept of the US Army in War with Spain.* DC. GPO. 1900. illus. plates and text illus. . . . . *$250.00–$350.00*

Borges, Jorge Luis. *Atlas.* NY. Dutton. (1985). 1st Amer dj. . . . . . . *$45.00–$55.00*

Borges, Jorge Luis. *Book of Imaginary Beings.* NY. Dutton. 1969. 1st ed. dj. . . . . *$55.00–$75.00*

Borges, Jorge Luis. *Irish Strategies.* Dublin. Dolmen Press. 1975. ltd 350 cc slipcase. . . . . *$50.00–$75.00*

Borges, Jorge Luis. *Personal Anthology.* NY. Grove Press. (1967). 1st ed. dj. . . . . *$40.00–$60.00*

Borland, Robert. *Border Raids and Reivers.* Thomas Fraser. 1898. *$30.00–$50.00*

Born, Max. *La Constitution de la Matiere.* Paris. 1922. wrps. illus. Nobel Prize winning author. . . . . *$37.00–$45.00*

Bostock, Frank C. *Training of Wild Animals.* NY. 1903. illus. . . . . *$37.00–$45.00*

Botkin, Benjamin Albert. *Civil War Treasury of Tales, Legends and Folklore.* NY. Random House. (1960). 1st ed. dj. . . . . *$25.00–$35.00*

Botkin, Benjamin Albert. *Treasury of Southern Folklore.* 1949. . . *$20.00–$30.00*

Botta, Charles. *History of the War of Independence of the U.S.A.* New Haven. Nathan Whiting. 1834. 2 vols.. . . . . *$100.00–$250.00*

Boucher, Jonathan. *Reminiscences of an American Loyalist 1783-1789.* Bos. 1925. bds, 575 cc, boxed. . . . . *$50.00–$100.00*

Boule, Pierre. *Bridge Over the River Kwai.* NY. Vanguard. 1954. 1st Amer ed. adv copy, wrps. . . . . *$85.00–$100.00*

Bourke, John. *On the Border With Crook.* NY. 1891. 1st ed. bds. *$300.00–$600.00*

Bourke, John. *Urine Dance of the Zuni Indians of New Mexico.* Ann Arbor. 1885. 1st ed. wrps. . . . . *$300.00–$400.00*

Bourke, John G. *An Apache Campaign.* NY. Scribner's. (1958). dj. *$18.00–$22.00*

Bourke, John G. *Scatologic Rites of All Nations.* DC. Lowdermilk. 1891. teg, brown cl. . . . . *$125.00–$675.00*

Bourke, John G. *Snake Dance of the Moquis of Arizona.* Tucson. 1984. illus. rprnt. . . . . *$15.00–$22.00*

Bourke-White, M. *Dear Fatherland, Rest Quietly.* NY. 1946. 1st ed. sgn. . . . . *$200.00–$300.00*

Bourke-White, M. *Say, Is This the USA.* NY. Duell, Sloan. 1941. 1st ed. . . . . *$90.00–$145.00*

Bourke-White, M. *Shooting the Russian War.* NY. Simon & Schuster. 1942. dj. . . . . *$30.00–$60.00*

Bourke-White, Margaret. *One Thing Leads to Another.* Bos/NY. Houghton Mifflin. 1936. 1st ed. blue cl, dj. . . . . *$30.00–$40.00*

Bourke-White, Margaret. *They Called it "Purple Heart Valley." A Combat Chronicle....* NY. 1944. illus. 2nd prtg. . . . . *$20.00–$30.00*

Bouton, Elizabeth Gladwin. *Grandmother's Doll.* NY. 1931. inscr. . . . . *$75.00–$90.00*

Bouton, Nathaniel. *Mr. Bouton's Centennial Discourses.* Concord. 1830. wrps. fldg map. . . . . *$35.00–$50.00*

Bouvier, Jacqueline and Lee. *One Special Summer.* NY. Delacorte Press. 1974. 1st ed. illus. . . . . *$80.00–$120.00*

Bovey, Martin. *Saga of the Waterfowl.* DC. 1949. 1st ed. illus. presentation copy, dj. . . . . *$40.00–$50.00*

Bowditch, Henry I. *Life and Correspondence of Henry I. Bowditch.* Bos. Houghton Mifflin. 1902. 2 vols. 1st ed. . . . . *$75.00–$100.00*

Bowditch, Nathaniel. *American Practical Navigator.* DC. Defense Mapping Agency. 1984. 2 vols. . . . . *$20.00–$35.00*

Bowditch, Nathaniel. *New American Practical Navigator.* Newburyport. 1802. 1st ed. illus. 7 plates, diagrams, fldg map. . . . . *$900.00–$1,200.00*

Bowen, Elizabeth. *Death of a Heart.* Lon. Victor Gollancz. 1938. 1st ed. dj. . . . . *$150.00–$200.00*

Bowen, Elizabeth. *Eva Trout.* Lon. Cape. 1968. 1st ed. sgn, dj. . . *$75.00–$100.00*

Bowen, Elizabeth. *House in Paris.* NY. Knopf. 1936. 1st Amer ed. . . . . *$150.00–$175.00*

Bowen, Elizabeth. *House in Paris.* Lon. Victor Gollancz. 1935. 1st UK ed. dj. . . . . *$125.00–$150.00*

Bowen, Elizabeth. *Ivy Gripped the Steps and Other Stories.* NY. Knopf. 1946. 1st ed. dj. . . . . *$31.00–$45.00*

Bowen, Elizabeth. *Look at All Those Roses.* NY. Knopf. 1941. 1st ed. dj. . . . . *$90.00–$125.00*

Bowen, Frank C. *Sea, It's History and Romance.* Eng. McBride. 1927. 4 vols. illus. charts, red cl, scarce. . . . . *$145.00–$195.00*

Bowen, J. J. *The Strategy of Robert E. Lee.* NY. Neale. 1914. illus. *$50.00–$85.00*

Bowles, Paul. *Little Stone.* Lon. Lehmann. 1950. 1st ed. gilt, dj. . *$100.00–$150.00*

Bowles, Paul. *Spider's House.* NY. Random House. 1955. 1st ed. dj. . . . . *$120.00–$150.00*

Bowles, Samuel. *Across the Continent: A Summer's Journey to the Rocky Mountains.* Springfield, MA. Bowles. 1865. fldg map. . . . . *$100.00–$125.00*

Bowlker, Charles. *The Art of Angling.* Lon. Ludlow. 1854. . . . . *$150.00–$175.00*

Bowring, John. *Specimens of the Russian Poets.* Bos. Cummings & Hillard. 1822. 3/4 lea, marbled bds. . . . . *$50.00–$125.00*

Boy Scouts of America: Handbook for Boys. Boy Scouts of America. 1928. wrps. Norman Rockwell cvr. . . . . *$20.00–$35.00*

Boy's Treasury of Sports, Pastimes and Recreations. NY. Clark, Austin, Maynard. 1850. pict cl. . . . . *$100.00–$125.00*

Boyd, James. *Drums.* NY. Scribner's. (1925). 1st ed. author's first book. . . . . *$45.00–$60.00*

Boyd, James. *Drums.* NY. Scribner's. 1928. illus. by N. C. Wyeth. . *$35.00–$45.00*

Boyd, James P. *Story of the Crusades.* Phila. Ziegler. (1892). 1st ed. illus. Dore engr. . . . . *$120.00–$175.00*

Boyd, William. *An Ice Cream War.* NY. William Morrow. 1983. 1st ed. dj. . . . . *$20.00–$45.00*

Boyd, William. *School Ties.* NY. William Morrow. 1985. 1st Amer ed, dj. . . . . *$40.00–$50.00*

Boyle, Frederick. *Culture of Greenhouse Orchids.* Lon. Chapman. 1902. . . . . *$55.00–$65.00*

Boyle, Kay. *Year Before Last.* NY. Harrison Smith. 1932. 1st ed. dj. *$75.00–$100.00*

Boyle, Ray. *Nothing Ever Breaks Except the Heart.* Garden City. Doubleday. 1966. 1st ed. dj. . . . . *$30.00–$40.00*

Boyle, T. Coraghessan. *Descent of Man.* Bos. Little, Brown. 1979. 1st ed. author's first book, dj. . . . . *$400.00–$475.00*

Boyle, T. Coraghessan. *Water Music.* Bos. Little, Brown. (1981). 1st ed. sgn and dated, dj. . . . . *$60.00–$100.00*

Boylston, Helen Dore. *Sue Barton, Senior Nurse.* Bos. Little, Brown. 1946. dj. . . . . *$65.00–$75.00*

Boys, William F. A. *Practical Treatise on Office & Duties of Coroners.* Tor. 1864. 3/4 calf. . . . . *$75.00–$125.00*

Brace, Charles Loring. *Short Sermons to News Boys....* NY. Scribner's. 1866. inscr by author. . . . . *$35.00–$65.00*

Brackenridge, Henry M. *History of the Late War Between the U.S and Great Britain.* Balt. Cushing & Jewett. 1817. illus. . . . . *$100.00–$250.00*

Bradbury, Ray. *Dandelion Wine.* Garden City. Doubleday. 1957. 1st ed. scarce, dj. . . . . *$360.00–$450.00*

Bradbury, Ray. *Dark Carnival.* Sauk City. Arkham House. 1947. ltd 3000 cc, sgn. . . . . *$600.00–$900.00*

Bradbury, Ray. *Dark Carnival.* Lon. Hamish Hamilton. 1948. 1st UK ed. dj. . . . . *$250.00–$450.00*

Bradbury, Ray. *Day It Rained Forever.* Lon. Rupert Hart-Davis. 1959. 1st UK ed. 254 pp, dj. . . . . *$60.00–$75.00*

Bradbury, Ray. *Halloween Tree.* NY. Knopf. (1972). 1st ed. dj. . . *$75.00–$150.00*

Bradbury, Ray. *Long After Midnight.* NY. Knopf. 1976. 1st ed. dj.. *$30.00–$35.00*

Bradbury, Ray. *Martian Chronicles.* Garden City. Doubleday. 1950. 1st ed. dj. . . . . *$275.00–$325.00*

Bradbury, Ray. *Medicine for Melancholy.* Garden City. Doubleday. 1959. 1st ed. sgn, dj. . . . . *$140.00–$175.00*

Bradbury, Ray. *October Country.* Lon. Rupert Davis. 1956. dj. . . *$90.00–$100.00*

Bradbury, Ray. *R is For Rocket.* NY. Doubleday. (1962). 1st ed. dj. . . . . *$125.00–$175.00*

Bradbury, Ray. *S is for Space.* NY. Doubleday. 1966. 1st ed. dj. . . *$50.00–$75.00*

Bradbury, Ray. *Toynbee Convector.* NY. Knopf. 1988. 1st ed. trade state, dj. . . . . *$25.00–$35.00*

Bradbury, Ray. *Toynbee Convector.* NY. Knopf. (1988). 1st ed. sgn, dj. . . . . *$40.00–$50.00*

Bradbury, Ray. *Where Robot Mice and Robot Men Run Round in Robot Towns.* NY. Knopf. 1977. sgn, dj. . . . . *$30.00–$50.00*

Bradbury, Ray. *Zen and the Art of Writing.* Santa Barbara. Capra Press. 1989 1st ed. sgn. . . . . *$50.00–$150.00*

Bradford, Richard. *Red Sky at Morning.* Phila. Lippincott. (1968). wrps. advance reading copy. . . . . *$40.00–$65.00*

Bradford, Roark. *This Side of Jordan.* NY/Lon. Harper. 1929. dj.. . . . . *$85.00–$125.00*

Bradley, Marion Zimmer. *House Between the Worlds.* Garden City. Doubleday. 1980. 1st ed. sgn, dj. . . . . *$35.00–$45.00*

Bradley, Will. *Peter Poodle.* NY. Dodd, Mead. 1906. 1st ed. illus. oversize grey pict bds. . . . . *$300.00–$500.00*

Bradley, Will. *Will Bradley, His Chap Book an Account in the words of dean of American....* NY. The Typophiles. 1955. 650cc. . . . . *$45.00–$95.00*

Brady, Edwin. *Australia Unlimited.* Melbourne. Geo. Robertson. c 1915. . . . . *$100.00–$275.00*

Brady, Joseph P. *Trial of Aaron Burr.* NY. 1913. 89 pp. . . . . *$28.00–$35.00*

Braid, James & Harry Vardon. *How to Play Golf.* NY. American Sports. nd. illus. . . . . *$45.00–$58.00*

Brake, Hezekiah. *On Two Continents.* Kansas. 1896. 1st ed. . . . . *$85.00–$100.00*

Brand Book for the Montana Grower's Association for 1910. Helena. Independent Pub. (1910). red lea. . . . . *$800.00–$1,000.00*

Brand Book of Wyoming. Laramie. Laramie Republican Co. 1919. . . . . *$300.00–$600.00*

Brand, Max. *Dr. Kildare Takes Charge.* Ny. Dodd, Mead. 1941. 1st ed. dj. . . . . *$450.00–$500.00*

Brand, Max. *Hunted Riders.* NY. Dodd, Mead. 1935. 1st ed. dj. . . . . *$75.00–$125.00*

Brand, Max. *Seventh Man.* NY. Putnam. 1921. 1st ed. dj. . . . . *$25.00–$35.00*

Brand, Max. *Streak.* NY. Dodd, Mead.1937. dj. . . . . *$75.00–$125.00*

Brand, Max. *Timbal Gulch Trail.* NY. Dodd, Mead. 1934. 1st ed. dj. . . . . *$400.00–$450.00*

Brand, Max. *Valley of Vanishing Men.* NY. Dodd, Mead. 1947. 1st ed. dj. . . . . *$50.00–$75.00*

Brand, Max. *Valley Thieves.* NY. Dodd, Mead. 1946. 1st ed. dj. . *$200.00–$250.00*

Brandt, H. *Alaska Bird Trails.* Cleve. Bird Research Foundation. 1943. . . . . *$140.00–$170.00*

Brandt, Herbert. *Arizona and It's Bird Life.* Cleve. Bird Research Foundation. 1951. illus. col plates, pict green cl. . . . . *$60.00–$90.00*

Braugtigan, Richard. *In Watermelon Sugar.* SF. Four Seasons Foundation. (1968). 1st ed. ltd 50 cc, sgn. . . . . *$100.00–$200.00*

Braun, Susan Roger. *Miniature Vignettes.* NY. Scribner's. (1975). 1st ed. illus. dj. . . . . *$15.00–$25.00*

Brazeal, Brailsford R. *Brotherhood of Sleeping Car Porters.* NY. Harper & Bros. 1946. dj. . . . . *$75.00–$125.00*

Brazer, Esther Stevens. *Early American Decoration.* Springfield. Pond-Ekbert Cp. 1961. illus. 4th ed. dj. . . . . *$35.00–$50.00*

Brehm, Alfred E. *From the North Pole to the Equator.* Lon. Blackie & Son. 1896. text illus. . . . . *$70.00–$85.00*

Brennan, Joseph Payne. *Nine Horrors and a Dream.* Arkham House. 1958. 1st ed. dj. . . . . *$100.00–$200.00*

Bresson, Henri Cartier. *People of Moscow.* NY. Simon & Schuster. 1955. 1st ed. dj. .... *$50.00–$135.00*

Breton, Andre, et al. *Yves Tanguy: Une Recueill des ses Oeuvre.* NY. Pierre Matisse. 1963. illus. drawings.. .... *$600.00–$750.00*

Brewer, A. T. *History Sixty-first Regiment, Pennsylvania Volunteers, 1861-65.* Pitts. Art Engraving and Printing Co. 1911. .... *$100.00–$150.00*

Brewer, Samuel Child. *Every Man His own Brewer: A Small Treatise....* Lon. nd. 3rd ed. half calf.. .... *$75.00–$115.00*

Brewster, Charles W. *Rambles About Portsmouth.* Portsmouth. Brewster. 1859. 1st ed. .... *$75.00–$95.00*

Brewster, David. *The Stereoscope.* NY. Morgan & Morgan. (1971). facs, dj. .... *$35.00–$45.00*

Brice, Tony. *So Long.* Chi. Rand McNally. 1937. 1st ed. illus. bds... *$5.00–$12.00*

Brice, Tony. *Tony Brice Picture Book.* Chi. Rand McNally. 1944. illus. clr, b/w. .. .. *$30.00–$45.00*

Bricker, Charles. *Landmarks of Mapmaking.* NY. Thomas Croswell. (1976). illus. maps, dj. .... *$55.00–$100.00*

Bridgman, E. C. *New Rail Road, Township and Post Office Map of Vermont and New Hampshire.* NY. 1881. fldg map. .... *$350.00–$450.00*

Brief Exposition of the Established Principles and Regulations of the United Society of Believers Called Shakers. NY. Jenkins. 1851. 30pp.... *$150.00–$95.00*

Briggs, Richard. *English Art of Cookery....* Lon. 1794. illus. 3rd ed. engr plates. .. .. *$95.00–$150.00*

Bright, Charles. *Story of the Atlantic Cable.* NY. Appleton. 1903. 1st ed. illus. .. .. *$20.00–$30.00*

Brin, David. *The Postman.* NY. Bantam. (1985). 1st ed. sgn, dj.... *$55.00–$80.00*

Brine, Vice-Admiral Lindesay. *Travels Amongst American Indians, Their Ancient Earthworks and Temples....* Lon. Sampson Low, Marston. 1894. 1st ed. illus. 429 pp, fldg map.. .... *$150.00–$225.00*

Brininstool, E. A. *Fighting Red Cloud's Warriors: True Tales of Indian Days....* NY. Cooper Square. 1975. illus. .... *$30.00–$55.00*

Brininstool, E. A. *Trooper with Custer and... Battle of the Little Bighorn.* Columbus, OH. Hunter, Trader, Trapper. 1925. 1st ed. illus. .... *$100.00–$140.00*

Brisbin, Gen. James. *Belden, the White Chief... Among the Wild Indians of the Plains.* Cinn. C. F. Vent. 1870. .... *$50.00–$85.00*

Bristol, Sherlock. *Pioneer Preacher, An Autobiography*. Revell. (1887). 1st ed. . .
. . . . *$40.00–$50.00*

Brock, Alan St. H. *History of Fireworks*. Lon. Harrap. 1949. 1st ed. dj. *$70.00–$100.00*

Brockelhurst, Thomas Unett. *Mexico To-Day*. Lon. John Murray. 1883. maroon cl.
. . . . *$70.00–$125.00*

Broder, Patricia. *Bronzes of the American West*. NY. Abrams. (1974). 1st ed. cl, dj.
. . . . *$100.00–$250.00*

Broder, Patricia Janis. *Bronzes of the American West*. NY. Abrams. (1974). illus. dj.
. . . . *$75.00–$125.00*

Bronte, Charlotte. *Jane Eyre: An Autobiography*. Lon. Smith, Elder & Co. 1848. 3
vols. by Currer Bell. 3rd ed. near fine, original cl. . . . . *$9,500.00–$10,000.00*

Bronte, Charlotte. *The Professor*. Lon. 1857. 2 vols. . . . . . . *$1,000.00–$2,000.00*

Bronte, Emily. *Wuthering Heights*. Franklin Library. 1945. . . . . . . *$30.00–$40.00*

Brooke, Henry K. *Book of Pirates....* Phila. 1847. illus. . . . . . . *$100.00–$175.00*

Brooke, Jocelyn. *Wild Orchids of Britain*. Lon. The Bodley Head. 1950. ltd 1100 cc
40 clr plates dj slipcase. . . . . *$125.00–$175.00*

Brooke, Leslie. *Johnny Crow's Party*. Lon. 1930. illus. by Brooke, 8 clr plates, b/w.
drawings. . . . . *$35.00–$45.00*

Brooke, Rupert. *Democracy and the Arts*. Lon. Rupert Hart-Davis. 1946. 1st ed. dj.
. . . . *$50.00–$65.00*

Brooks, E. S. *Under the Allied Flags: A Boy's Adventures... against the Boxers in
China*. Bos. 1901. 1st ed. illus. . . . . *$30.00–$45.00*

Brooks, Juanita. *Mountain Meadows Massacre*. Stanford. 1950. 1st ed. illus. map,
sgn. . . . . *$100.00–$150.00*

Brooks, Terry. *Sword of Shannara*. NY. Random House. (1977). 1st ed. so stated.
illus. by the Brothers Hilldebrandt. brown cl, black cl spine, map frontis, pict dj. . .
. . . . *$100.00–$250.00*

Broomhall, Marshall (ed.). *Martyred Missionaries of the China Inland Mission*.
Lon. nd. illus. fldg maps, photos. . . . . *$30.00–$50.00*

Brough, Charles Hillman. *Irrigation in Utah*. Balt. Johns Hopkins Press. 1898. 1st
ed. illus. photos, scarce. . . . . *$25.00–$50.00*

Brown, D. W. *Salt Dishes*. MA. Brown. 1937. illus. . . . . *$30.00–$45.00*

Brown, Dee. *Bury My Heart at Wounded Knee*. NY. Holt. (1970). 1st ed. dj. . . . . . .
. . . . *$50.00–$100.00*

Brown, Dee. *Trail Driving Days, The Golden Days of the Old Trail Driving Cattlemen.* NY. Scribner's. 1952. 1st ed. 264 pp, folio, dj......... *$40.00–$90.00*

Brown, Frederic. *Bloody Moonlight.* NY. Dutton. 1949. 1st ed. dj............
.... *$125.00–$265.00*

Brown, Frederic. *Deep End.* NY. Dutton. 1952. 1st ed. dj...... *$200.00–$275.00*

Brown, Frederic. *Far Cry.* NY. Dutton. 1951. 1st ed. dj........ *$150.00–$150.00*

Brown, Frederic. *Knock Three-One-Two.* Lon. Boardman. (1959). 1st Brit ed. cl, dj.
.... *$125.00–$150.00*

Brown, Frederic. *Knock Three-One-Two.* NY. Dutton. 1959. 1st ed. dj..........
.... *$2,275.00–$400.00*

Brown, Frederic. *Mind Thing.* NY. (1961). 1st ed. pict wrps...... *$20.00–$35.00*

Brown, Frederic. *Paradox Lost.* Lon. Robert Hale. 1975. 1st ed. dj............
.... *$30.00–$35.00*

Brown, Frederic. *Screaming Mimi.* NY. Dutton. 1949. 1st ed. dj.............
.... *$250.00–$300.00*

Brown, Frederic. *Space On My Hands.* Chi. Shasta. (1951). 1st ed. sgn, presentation copy to Fritz Leiber, Leiber's ownership signature, dj.......... *$650.00–$850.00*

Brown, Frederic. *The Pickled Punks.* Hilo. Dennis McMillan. 1991. 1st ed. ltd 450 numbered cc. dj. .... *$75.00–$85.00*

Brown, Fredric. *Carnival of Crime.* Carbondale. Southern Illinois Univ 1985. 1st ed. dj... *$40.00–$55.00*

Brown, G. S. *First Steps to Golf.* Bos. Small Maynard. nd. ...... *$60.00–$75.00*

Brown, Helen E. *Good Catch; or, Mrs. Emerson's Whaling Cruise.* Phila. 1884. 1st ed. illus. .... *$75.00–$125.00*

Brown, Hugh Victor. *History of the Education of Negroes in North Carolina.* Raleigh. Irving Swain Press. 1961. 1st ed. sgn. .... *$60.00–$90.00*

Brown, Innis (ed.). *How to Play Golf.* NY. 1930. illus. Spalding's Athletic lib. ....
.... *$45.00–$50.00*

Brown, Jennie Broughton. *Fort Hall on the Oregon Trail....* Caldwell. Caxton Printers. 1934. illus. drawings, maps, dj. .... *$45.00–$65.00*

Brown, John Henry. *History of Texas from 1685-1892.* St Louis. (1892-93. 2 vols.
.... *$350.00–$700.00*

Brown, L. and D. Amadon. *Eagles, Hawks, and Falcons of the World.* NY. McGraw Hill. 1968. 2. 1st Amer ed. slipcase....................... *$140.00–$200.00*

Brown, Lloyd A. *Story of Maps.* Bos. Little, Brown. 1949. 1st ed. illus. bibliography, dj. . . . . *$20.00–$28.00*

Brown, Margaret Wise. *Noisy Book.* NY. Harper & Row. 1939. . . *$20.00–$30.00*

Brown, Margaret Wise. *Wait Till the Moon Is Full.* NY. Harper & Row. 1948. illus. by Garth Williams, dj. . . . . *$30.00–$60.00*

Brown, Paul. *Crazy Quilt Circus Pony.* NY. Scribner's. 1934. rprnt, dj. . . . . *$50.00–$65.00*

Brown, Paul. *Hits and Misses.* NY. Derrydale. 1935. ltd 950 cc, sgn, tissue dj. . . . . *$350.00–$450.00*

Brown, Thomas. *Elements of Conchology.* Lon. 1816. 1st ed. illus. 9 engr plates. . . . . *$150.00–$250.00*

Brown, Thomas. *Lectures on the Philosophy of the Human Mind.* Phil. 1824. 3 vols. . . . . *$225.00–$300.00*

Brown, Warren. *Chicago Cubs.* NY. 1946. illus. . . . . *$30.00–$40.00*

Brown, William Harvey. *On the South African Frontier.* NY. Scribner's. 1899. fldg maps. . . . . *$30.00–$125.00*

Brown, William Symington. *Capability of Women to Practice the Healing Art.* Bos. Ripley. 1859. 1st ed. illus. 15 pp. . . . . *$58.00–$85.00*

Browne, Bellmore H. *Guns and Gunning.* Chicopee Falls. Stevens Arms & Tool. (1908). illus. . . . . *$70.00–$100.00*

Browne, Halbot K. *Sketches of Young Gentlemen.* Lon. 1838. 1st ed. 6 etched plates by "Phiz," 3/4 crimson mor. . . . . *$95.00–$120.00*

Browne, J. Ross. *Adventures in Apache Country.* NY. Harper & Co. 1869. illus. . . . . *$275.00–$3,325.00*

Brownell, Clarence. *Heart of Japan.* NY. 1903. 1st ed. illus. . . . . . *$40.00–$65.00*

Browning, Elizabeth Barrett. *An Essay on Mind.* Lon. Duncan. 1826. 1st ed. bound by Sangorski & Sutcliffe, tan calf, aeg. . . . . *$700.00–$1,000.00*

Browning, Robert. *History of Golf.* NY. Dutton. (1955). 1st ed. illus. clr plates. . . . . *$50.00–$100.00*

Browning, Robert. *Pied Piper of Hamelin.* Phila. (1934). 1st Amer ed. illus by Arthur Rackham. dj. . . . . *$145.00–$175.00*

Browning, Robert. *Saul.* Bos. Prang. 1890. 1st ed. illus. aeg, rare. . . . . *$150.00–$350.00*

Brownlow, W. G. *Sketches of the Rise, Progress & Decline of Secession*. Phila. 1862. 1st ed. illus. . . . . *$50.00–$175.00*

Bruccoli, Matthew. *F. Scott Fitzgerald: A Descriptive Biography*. Pitt. Univ Pittsburg Press. 1987. rev ed. illus.. . . . . *$80.00–$100.00*

Bruce, Lenny. *How to Talk Dirty and Influence People*. Chi. Playboy Press. 1965. 1st ed. cl, dj. . . . . *$35.00–$50.00*

Bruce, Philip A. *Virginia Plutarch*. Chapel Hill. Univ of N.C. Press. 1929. 2. ltd 200 cc. sgn. . . . . *$45.00–$65.00*

Bruette, William. *American Duck, Goose & Brant Shooting*. NY. 1943. . . . . *$25.00–$40.00*

Bruette, William. *Cocker Spaniel, Breeding, Breaking & Handling*. NY. Stackpole. 1937. 1st ed. . . . . *$25.00–$40.00*

Brummitt, Stella W. *Brother Van*. NY. Missionary Education Movement. 1919. 1st ed. . . . . *$50.00–$75.00*

Bryan, John (ed.). *Notes From Underground*. SF. Underground Press. (1964). wrps. illus. decorated black and grey cvr. . . . . *$35.00–$50.00*

Bryan, Thomas Conn. *Confederate Georgia*. Athens. Univ of Georgia Press. 1953. 1st ed. . . . . *$48.00–$65.00*

Bryan, W. A. *Key to the Birds of the Hawaiian Group*. Honolulu. Museum Memoirs no 3. 1901. wrps. . . . . *$35.00–$50.00*

Bryant, W. C. *Picturesque America*. NY. Appleton. (1872-74). 2 vols. plates. . . . . *$350.00–$500.00*

Bryant, William Cullen. *Flood of Years*. NY. Putnam. 1878. 1st ed. full mor, raised bands. . . . . *$100.00–$145.00*

Bryce, James. *Impressions of South Africa*. Lon. Macmillan. 1897. 1st ed. illus. fldg maps. . . . . *$45.00–$55.00*

Bryce, Viscount. *Treatment of Armenians in the Ottoman Empire 1915-16*. Lon. Hodder & Stoughton. 1916. 1st ed. fldg map. . . . . *$50.00–$75.00*

Bryk, Felix. *Voodoo-Eros*. NY. private printing. 1933. illus. photos, ltd 500 cc. . . . . *$65.00–$100.00*

Brynner, Irena. *Modern Jewelry: Design and Technique*. NY. Van Nostrand. 1968. illus. . . . . *$45.00–$60.00*

Buber, Martin. *Israel and Palestine*. Lon. East & West Lib. 1952. dj. . . . . *$25.00–$45.00*

Buchan, John. *Blanket of the Dark.* Lon. Hodder & Stoughton. 1931. 1st ed. dj.. .
. . . . *$200.00–$300.00*

Buchan, John. *Castle Gay.* Lon. Hodder & Stoughton. 1930. 1st ed. dj. . . . .
. . . . *$100.00–$350.00*

Buchan, John. *Gap in the Curtain....* Bos/NY. Houghton Mifflin. 1932. 1st US ed.
. . . . *$35.00–$75.00*

Buchan, John. *Gordon at Khartoum.* Lon. Peter Davies. 1934. 1st UK ed. . . . . . .
. . . . *$16.00–$45.00*

Buchan, John. *Island of Sheep.* Lon. Hodder & Stoughton. 1936. 1st ed. dj. . . . . .
. . . . *$85.00–$175.00*

Buchan, John. *Power-House.* Lon. Blackwood. 1916. 1st ed. . . . . *$55.00–$100.00*

Buchan, John. *Witch Wood.* Bos. Houghton Mifflin. 1927. 1st Amer ed. dj.. . . . . .
. . . . *$45.00–$75.00*

Buchanan, Edna. *Nobody Lives Forever.* NY. Random House. 1990. 1st ed. first
mystery, dj. . . . . *$20.00–$50.00*

Buchanan, Frederick Stewart. *Emigration of Scottish Mormons to Utah, 1949-
1900.* Salt Lake. 1961. sgn. . . . . *$60.00–$75.00*

Buchanan, James. *Message of the Pres. of the US... Massacre at Mountain
Meadows.* DC. 1860. softbound. . . . . *$75.00–$100.00*

Buchanan, Joseph R. *Story of a Labor Agitator.* NY. Outlook. 1903. 1st ed. cl. . .
. . . . *$40.00–$50.00*

Buchanan, Robert Williams. *Saint Abe and His Seven Wives: A Tale of Salt Lake
City.* Lon. Strahan. 1872. 1st Brit ed. . . . . *$50.00–$80.00*

Buck, Frank. *All in a Lifetime.* NY. McBride. 1941. 1st ed. sgn.. . *$65.00–$150.00*

Buck, Frank. *Bring 'em Back Alive.* NY. Garden City Pub. 1930. 1st ed. illus. photos. . . . . *$30.00–$45.00*

Buck, Franklin. *Yankee Trader in the Gold Rush.* Bos. Houghton Mifflin. 1930. dj.
. . . . *$50.00–$65.00*

Buck, Pearl. *China in Black & White.* NY. John Day. 1944-5. 1st ed. illus. woodcuts,
95 pp, dj.. . . . . *$45.00–$95.00*

Buck, Pearl. *Death in the Castle.* NY. Joh Day. (1965). 1st ed. dj. . *$30.00–$50.00*

Buck, Pearl. *Fighting Angel.* Reynal & Hitchcock. 1936. 1st ed. dj. *$24.00–$30.00*

Buck, Pearl S. *Kennedy Women.* NY. John Day. 1970. 1st ed. illus. dj, sgn. . . . . . .
. . . . *$16.00–$20.00*

Buckingham, J. S. *Slave States of America.* Lon. Fisher. (1842). 2 vols. 1st ed. scarce. . . . . *$250.00–$350.00*

Buckingham, J. S. *Slave States of America.* Negro University Press. 1968. reprnt. . . . . *$30.00–$45.00*

Buckingham, Nash. *De Shootinest Gent'man.* NY. Scribner's. 1941. 1st ed. dj. . . . . *$45.00–$55.00*

Buckingham, Nash. *Game Bag.* NY. 1945. 1st ed. illus. by Hoecker, dj 1250 cc sgn. . . . . *$120.00–$170.00*

Buckingham, Nash. *Mark Right!.* Derrydale Press. (1936). ltd 1250 cc, inscr. . . . . *$300.00–$450.00*

Buckingham, Nash. *Tattered Coat.* NY. Putnam. 1944. dj. . . . . *$45.00–$55.00*

Buckingham, Nash. *Tattered Coat.* NY. Putnam. 1944. ltd 995, sgn. . . . . *$160.00–$300.00*

Buckley, James. *Wrong and Peril of Woman Suffrage.* NY. Revell. 1909. . . . . *$30.00–$35.00*

Bucknall, Rixon. *Boats, Trains and Channel Packets.* Lon. Stuart. 1957. illus. photos, maps, dj. . . . . *$50.00–$60.00*

Budge, E. A. Wallis. *The Mummy.* Camb Univ Press. 1894. 2nd ed. illus. . . . . *$75.00–$90.00*

Budge, E. A. Wallis. *The Nile: Notes for Travelers in Egypt.* Lon. Cook & Son. 1901. 7th ed. limp brown cl, blindstamped on rear cvr. . . . . *$45.00–$60.00*

Buechner, Thomas S. *Norman Rockwell Artist and Illustrator.* NY. 1970. illus. folio dj. . . . . *$70.00–$100.00*

Buel, J. W. *Heroes of the Plains.* St Louis. 1883. illus. clr frontis, pict cl. . . . . *$40.00–$60.00*

Buell, Augustus. *Paul Jones Founder of the American Navy.* NY. Scribner's. 1905. 2 vols. . . . . *$30.00–$60.00*

Bugbee, Lester. *Slavery in Early Texas.* Political Science Quarterly. 1898. 22pp. . . . . *$65.00–$100.00*

Bugbee, Lester Gladstone. *Texas Frontier.* Pa. 1900. . . . . *$40.00–$65.00*

Builders of Steam Fire Engines, Hose Carriages, Tenders, Etc. Hudson, NY. Clapp & Jones Mfg Co. 1872. purple printed wrps, illus, 60 pp. . . . . . . *$225.00–$300.00*

Buist, Robert. *Family Kitchen Gardener.* NY. Saxton. 1855. illus. *$70.00–$115.00*

Buist, Robert. *Rose Manual.* Phila. 1847. 7th ed. . . . . *$25.00–$35.00*

Bujold, Lois McMaster. *Vor Game*. Norwalk. Easton Press. (1990). 1st ed. full lea, aeg, ribbon bookmark, laid-in Easton bookplate as issued, sgn (not issued in dj). . . . . *$165.00–$185.00*

Buley, R. Carlyle. *Old Northwest*. Ind. Indiana Univ Press. 1951. 2 vols. illus. maps, plates, slipcase. . . . . *$30.00–$45.00*

Bulfinch, Thomas. *Age of Chivalry*. Bos. 1859. brown cl.. . . . . . *$175.00–$200.00*

Bulfinch, Thomas. *Oregon and Eldorado*. Bos. J E Tilton. 1866. 1st ed. . . . . *$60.00–$90.00*

Bull, J. *Birds of New York State*. NY. Doubleday. 1974. illus. . . . . . *$45.00–$60.00*

Bull, Rice C. *Soldiering, The Civil War Diary of Rice C. Bull, 123rd Vol. Infantry....* CA. San Rafael Presidio. 1978. dj.. . . . . *$25.00–$35.00*

Bullard, Robert L. *Personalities and Reminiscences of the War*. NY. Doubleday Page. 1925. 1st ed. . . . . *$45.00–$50.00*

Bullen, F. T. *Deep-Sea Plunderings*. NY. Appleton. 1902. 8 illus. . . *$15.00–$25.00*

Bullen, F. T. *Idylls of the Sea*. NY. Appleton. 1899. (authorized ed). *$20.00–$25.00*

Bullen, F. T. *Deep Sea Plunderings*. Smith Elder. 1901. blue cl. . . *$75.00–$100.00*

Bullen, Frank. *Back to Sunny Seas*. Lon. Smith Elder. 1905. 1st ed. illus. clr plates. . . . . *$25.00–$50.00*

Bullen, Frank. *Cruise of the Cachalot*. NY. Dodd, Mead 1926. illus. by Mead Schaeffer. . . . . *$20.00–$35.00*

Bullen, Frank. *Log of a Sea Wolf....* NY. Appleton. 1899. illus. 1st Amer ed. pict cl. . . . . *$125.00–$175.00*

Bullock, James D. *Secret Service of the Confederate States in Europe*. NY/Lon. Thomas Yoseloff. 1959. slipcase rprnt.. . . . . *$45.00–$60.00*

Bullock, W. *Mexico*. Lon. John Murray. 1824. 1st ed. illus. plates, maps, half-calf with mor spine labels. . . . . *$600.00–$800.00*

Bulpin, T. V. *Hunter is Death*. Johannesburg. Thomas Nelson. 1962. 1st ed. illus. . . . . *$22.00–$30.00*

Bumstead, John. *On The Wing*. Bos. Fields Osgood. 1869. illus. . . *$30.00–$50.00*

Bunyan, John. *Pilgrim's Progress*. NY. 1928. . . . . *$25.00–$40.00*

Bunyan, John. *Pilgrim's Progress*. NY. Century. 1898. folio, 184 pp. . . . . *$100.00–$105.00*

Bunyan, John. *Pilgrim's Progress..., by the Rev. Robert Philip*. Lon. James S. Virtue. 1861. illus. 3/4 lea. . . . . *$50.00–$75.00*

Burbank, Nelson L. *House Construction Details*. NY. Simmons Boardman. 1942. 2nd. . . . . *$22.00–$30.00*

Burch, E. S. and W. Forman. *The Eskimos*. Norman. 1988. dj. . . . *$25.00–$40.00*

Burch, John P. & Charles W. Burch. *Quantrell: A True History of His Guerrilla Warfare*.... Texas. pub by author. (1923). 1st ed. illus. dj. . . . . *$50.00–$150.00*

Burckhardt, John Lewis. *Notes on the Bedouins and Wahabys*. Cinc. 1968. rprnt. . . . . *$20.00–$35.00*

Burder, George. *Welch Indians*. NY. 1922. softbound. . . . . *$24.00–$35.00*

Burdett, Charles. *Life and Adventures of Christopher Carson*. Phila. Evans. 1861. . . . . *$28.00–$35.00*

Burdett, Charles. *Life of Kit Carson*. NY. Grosset & Dunlap. 1902. *$8.00–$15.00*

Burdick, Usher. *Last Battle of the Sioux Nation*. Stevens Point. Warzalla. 1929. 1st ed. dj. . . . . *$100.00–$150.00*

Burgess, Anthony. *Clockwork Orange*. Lon. Heinemann. 1962. 1st UK ed. dj. . . . . *$400.00–$1,200.00*

Burgess, Anthony. *Clockwork Orange*. W.W. Norton. (1963). 1st Amer ed. purple bds, dj. . . . . *$265.00–$400.00*

Burgess, Anthony. *Devil of a State*. Norton. 1962. 1st Amer ed. . . . *$35.00–$70.00*

Burgess, Anthony. *Devil of a State*. Lon. Heinemann. (1961). 1st ed. dj. . . . . *$35.00–$100.00*

Burgess, Anthony. *Ninety-Nine Novels*. Lon. Allison & Busby. 1984. dj 1st UK ed. . . . . *$60.00–$75.00*

Burgess, Gelett. *Bayside Bohemia, Fin de siècle San Francisco & its Little Magazines*. SF. Book Club of California. 1954. 1st ed. Ltd 375 cc. *$65.00–$100.00*

Burgess, Gelett. *Goop Directory*. Stokes. 1913. 1st ed. illus. paper over bds. . . . . *$100.00–$200.00*

Burgess, Gelett. *Goops and How to Be Them*. Stokes. 1900. illus. . *$50.00–$60.00*

Burgess, Gelett. *Maxims of Methusaleh*. Stokes. (1907). . . . . *$25.00–$40.00*

Burgess, Gelett. *More Goops and How Not to Be Them*. NY. Lippincott. 1931. illus. yellow cl. . . . . *$25.00–$50.00*

Burgess, Gelett. *Purple Cow and Other Nonsense*. NY. Dover. 1961. illus. . . . . *$25.00–$45.00*

Burgess, Thornton. *Adventures of Bobby Coon*. Canada. 1943. 1st ed. illus. by Harrison Cady. blue cl. . . . . *$12.00–$18.00*

Burgess, Thornton. *Adventures of Reddy Fox*. Bos. Little, Brown. 1923. illus. by Harrison Cady.. . . . . *$25.00–$50.00*

Burgess, Thornton. *Bedtime Stories*. NY. Grosset & Dunlap. 1974. illus. by Carl and Mary Hauge. . . . . *$25.00–$50.00*

Burgess, Thornton. *Billy Mink*. Bos. Little, Brown. 1924. 1st ed. illus. by Cady, dj. . . . . *$50.00–$105.00*

Burgess, Thornton. *Book of Nature Lore*. NY. 1965. dj. . . . . *$25.00–$450.00*

Burgess, Thornton. *Bowser The Hound*. Bos. Little, Brown. 1920. 1st ed. illus. by Harrison Cady.. . . . . *$55.00–$175.00*

Burgess, Thornton. *Neatness of Bobby Coon*. Stoll and Edwards. 1927. illus. by Harrison Cady.. . . . . *$50.00–$100.00*

Burgess, Thornton. *Tales From the Storyteller's House*. Little, Brown. 1937. 1st ed. illus. clr plates by Lemuel Palmer. . . . . *$85.00–$150.00*

Burgess, Thornton. *While the Story Log Burns*. Bos. 1938. 1st ed. illus. by Lemuel Palmer, green cl, red lettering, frontis. . . . . *$50.00–$125.00*

Burgess, Thornton W. *Old Mother Westwind*. Bos. Little, Brown. 1910. 1st ed. illus. by Kerr, 169 pp, 7 plates. . . . . *$100.00–$150.00*

Burke, Emma Maxwell. *Perfect Course in Millinery*. NY. 1925. illus. . . . . *$30.00–$40.00*

Burke, James Lee. *Neon Rain*. NY. Holt. 1987. 1st ed. dj. . . . . . . *$95.00–$140.00*

Burke, James Lee. *Neon Rain*. NY. Henry Holt. 1987. 1st ed. sgn, dj.. . . . . *$200.00–$250.00*

Burleigh, T. D. *Georgia Birds*. Univ of Oklahoma Press. 1958. dj. .*$50.00–$100.00*

Burley, W. J. *Wycliffe and the Cycle of Death*. Gollancz. 1990. 1st UK ed.. . . . . *$32.00–$40.00*

Burnaby, Fred. *Ride to Kiva*. NY. Harper. 1877. 1st ed. illus. fldg maps.. . . . . *$100.00–$200.00*

Burnet, J. A. *Treatise on Painting*. Lon. 1850. plates. . . . . *$85.00–$100.00*

Burnett, Frances Hodgson. *Editha's Burgler*. J Marsh. 1888. blue cl, 13 plates, 64 pp, illus by Sandham. . . . . *$40.00–$50.00*

Burnett, Frances Hodgson. *Giovanni and the Other*. NY. Scribner's. 1892. 1st ed. . . . . *$50.00–$60.00*

Burnett, Frances Hodgson. *In the Closed Room*. McClure. 1904. 1st ed. illus. by Jessie Wilcox Smith. . . . . *$30.00–$80.00*

Burnett, Frances Hodgson. *Sara Crewe or What Happened at Miss Minchin's.* NY. 1888. illus. . . . . *$30.00–$45.00*

Burnett, Frances Hodgson. *Secret Garden.* NY. Stokes. 1911. illus. by Maria Kirk. . . . . *$20.00–$50.00*

Burnett, Frances Hodgson. *T. Tembarom.* NY. Century. 1913. 1st ed. illus. by Chapman. . . . . *$25.00–$30.00*

Burnett, Frances. *Little Lord Fauntleroy.* NY. Scribner's. 1925. . . *$15.00–$22.00*

Burnham, Major Frederick. *Scouting on Two Continents.* Garden City. Doubleday. 1926. 1st ed. sgn.. . . . . *$25.00–$40.00*

Burns, Eugene. *Advanced Fly Fishing.* Harrisburg. Stackpole. 1953. illus. . . . . *$120.00–$150.00*

Burns, Robert. *The Songs.* Lon. Hodder & Stoughton. 1903. 1st ed. 536 pp, 4 plates. . . . . *$50.00–$75.00*

Burns, Walter Noble. *Robin Hood of El Dorado.* NY. Coward McCann. (1932). dj. . . . . *$20.00–$60.00*

Burns, Walter Noble. *Saga of Billy the Kid.* Garden City. Garden City Pub. (1925-6). dj. . . . . *$22.00–$40.00*

Burns, Walter Noble. *Tombstone. An Illiad of the Southwest.* NY. 1927. . . . . *$30.00–$45.00*

Burns, Walter Noble. *Year With a Whaler.* NY. Macmillan. 1919. . *$30.00–$45.00*

Burns, Walter Noble. *Year With a Whaler.* NY. Outing Pub. 1913. 1st ed. illus. . . . . *$50.00–$85.00*

Burpee, Lawrence J. *Search for the Western Sea....* Lon. 1908. 1st ed. illus. 6 maps, 51 plates.. . . . . *$125.00–$200.00*

Burris-Meyer, Elizabeth. *Decorating Livable Houses.* NY. Prentice-Hall. 1937. 1st ed. illus. . . . . *$20.00–$25.00*

Burritt, Elijah H. *Geography of the Heavens and Class Book of Astronomy.* NY. Mason Bros. 1860. 345 pp. . . . . *$75.00–$85.00*

Burritt, Elijah Hinsdale. *Logarithmick Arithmetick Containing a New... Table of Logarithms....* Williamsburgh, MA. Ephraim Whitman. 1818. lea, fldg plates, 251 pp. . . . . *$100.00–$150.00*

Burroughs, Edgar Rice. *Apache Devil.* Tarzana. Burroughts. (1933). 1st ed. dj. . . . . *$700.00–$1,000.00*

Burroughs, Edgar Rice. *At the Earth's Core.* Lon. Methuen. 1938. 1st UK ed.. . . . . *$35.00–$45.00*

Burroughs, Edgar Rice. *Bandit of Hell's Bend.* Lon. Methuen. 1926. 1st ed. . . . .
. . . . *$35.00–$50.00*

Burroughs, Edgar Rice. *Beasts of Tarzan.* McClurg. 1916. 1st ed. illus. by Allen St
John, cl. . . . . *$250.00–$500.00*

Burroughs, Edgar Rice. *Beasts of Tarzan.* NY. A. L. Burt. (1917). dj. *$50.00–$75.00*

Burroughs, Edgar Rice. *Beyond Thirty and the Man Eater.* NY. 1957. 1st ed. dj. .
. . . . *$65.00–$85.00*

Burroughs, Edgar Rice. *Carson of Venus.* Tarzana. Burroughs. (1939). 1st ed. fine,
dj. . . . . *$250.00–$600.00*

Burroughs, Edgar Rice. *Cave Girl.* NY. Grosset & Dunlap. 1927. *$15.00–$25.00*

Burroughs, Edgar Rice. *Escape on Venus.* Tarzana. Burroughs. (1946). 1st ed. dj.
. . . . *$90.00–$150.00*

Burroughs, Edgar Rice. *Gods of Mars.* Chi. McClurg. 1918. 1st ed. red cl, dj. . . .
. . . . *$230.00–$600.00*

Burroughs, Edgar Rice. *Jungle Tales of Tarzan.* Chi. McClurg. 1919. 1st ed. illus.
cl. . . . . *$45.00–$60.00*

Burroughs, Edgar Rice. *Land That Time Forgot.* NY. Grosset & Dunlap. 1925. dj.
. . . . *$25.00–$30.00*

Burroughs, Edgar Rice. *Llana of Gathol.* CA. Burroughs. (1948). 1st ed. dj. . . . .
. . . . *$95.00–$150.00*

Burroughs, Edgar Rice. *Llana of Gathol.* Tarzana. Burroughs, Inc. (1948). 1st ed.
fine, dj. . . . . *$150.00–$400.00*

Burroughs, Edgar Rice. *Monster Men.* NY. Canaveral Press. 1962. new ed. illus. dj.
. . . . *$30.00–$50.00*

Burroughs, Edgar Rice. *New Adventures of Tarzan "Pop-Up".* Chi. Pleasure
Books. (1935). illus. . . . . *$300.00–$500.00*

Burroughs, Edgar Rice. *Oakdale Affair and the Rider.* Tarzana. Burroughs. 1937.
1st ed. blue cl, dj. . . . . *$70.00–$125.00*

Burroughs, Edgar Rice. *Return of Tarzan.* Burt. dj. . . . . *$45.00–$65.00*

Burroughs, Edgar Rice. *Savage Pellucidar.* NY. Canaveral Press. 1963. 1st thus. dj.
. . . . *$75.00–$85.00*

Burroughs, Edgar Rice. *Tarzan and the Ant Men.* Chi. McClurg. 1924. 1st ed. illus.
. . . . *$75.00–$110.00*

Burroughs, Edgar Rice. *Tarzan and the Forbidden City*. NY. Burroughs. 1938. 1st ed. illus. by John Coleman Burroughs. clr frontis. . . . . *$125.00–$450.00*

Burroughs, Edgar Rice. *Tarzan and the Foreign Legion*. Tarzana. Burroughs. 1947. 1st ed. dj. . . . . *$100.00–$125.00*

Burroughs, Edgar Rice. *Tarzan and the Golden Lion*. NY. Grosset & Dunlap. 1923. rprnt. . . . . *$45.00–$85.00*

Burroughs, Edgar Rice. *Tarzan and the Jewels of Opar*. NY. Grosset & Dunlap. 1918. reprnt. . . . . *$30.00–$75.00*

Burroughs, Edgar Rice. *Tarzan and the Lost Empire*. NY. Metropolitan Books. (1929). 1st ed. orange cl. . . . . *$50.00–$75.00*

Burroughs, Edgar Rice. *Tarzan at the Earth's Core*. NY. Metropolitan Books. 1930. 1st ed. red cl, dj. . . . . *$175.00–$225.00*

Burroughs, Edgar Rice. *Tarzan Lord of the Jungle*. NY. Grosset & Dunlap. 1928. illus. . . . . *$30.00–$100.00*

Burroughs, Edgar Rice. *Tarzan of the Apes*. NY. Grosset & Dunlap. 1914. rprnt. . . . . *$10.00–$25.00*

Burroughs, Edgar Rice. *Tarzan of the Apes*. NY. A. L. Burt. 1915. . . . . *$25.00–$70.00*

Burroughs, Edgar Rice. *Tarzan the Invincible*. Tarzana. Edgar Rice Burroughs, Inc. 1931. 1st ed. pict dj. . . . . *$525.00–$700.00*

Burroughs, Edgar Rice. *Tarzan the Terrible*. NY. Grosset & Dunlap. (c1940). dj, later ed. . . . . *$20.00–$35.00*

Burroughs, Edgar Rice. *Tarzan the Untamed*. NY. Grosset & Dunlap. 1920. rprnt. *$45.00–*

Burroughs, Edgar Rice. *Tarzan-The Lost Adventure*. OR. Dark Horse Books. 1995. 1st ed. dj. . . . . *$10.00–$30.00*

Burroughs, Edgar Rice. *The Lad and the Lion*. Tarzana. Burroughs. 1938. 1st ed. dj. . . . . *$300.00–$400.00*

Burroughs, Edgar Rice. *The Warlord of Mars*. NY. Grosset & Dunlap. 1919. . . . . *$40.00–$60.00*

Burroughs, John. *Bird Stories*. Bos. 1911. 1st ed. illus. by L. A. Fuertes. . . . . *$18.00–$25.00*

Burroughs, John. *Camping & Tramping with Roosevelt*. Bos. 1907. 1st ed. illus. photos. . . . . *$24.00–$35.00*

Burroughs, John. *In the Catskills.* Bos. Houghton. 1910. 1st ed. 1st prtg. illus.. . . . . *$48.00–$60.00*

Burroughs, Wiliam S. *Exterminator!.* NY. Viking Press. 1973. 1st ed. dj sgn. . . . . *$225.00–$400.00*

Burroughs, William S. *Naked Lunch.* NY. Grove Press. (1959). dj. . . . . *$150.00–$225.00*

Burroughs, William S. *Soft Machine.* NY. Grove Press. 1966. 1st ed. dj.. . . . . *$85.00–$95.00*

Burroughs, William S. *Soft Machine.* Lon. 1968. 1st UK ed. . . . . . *$45.00–$65.00*

Burroughs, William S. *Third Mind.* NY. 1978. dj. . . . . *$35.00–$40.00*

Burroughs, William S. *Tornado Alley.* Cherry Valley Editions. 1989. 1st ed. ltd 100 cc. . . . . *$75.00–$150.00*

Burroughs, William S. *Western Lands.* NY. Viking. (1987). 1st ed. dj. *$20.00–$35.00*

Burton, Frederick R. *American Primitive Music...Songs of the Ojibways.* NY. Moffat. 1909. . . . . *$55.00–$65.00*

Burton, Miles. *Early Morning Murder.* Lon. Collins Crime Club. 1945. 1st ed. dj. . . . . *$200.00–$250.00*

Burton, R. *Anatomy of Melancholy....* Lon. 1898. . . . . *$35.00–$75.00*

Burton, Richard. *Lake Regions of Central Africa.* Lon. The Folio Society. 1993. illus. . . . . *$60.00–$65.00*

Burton, Richard. *Lake Regions of Central Africa.* NY. Horizon Press. 1961. 2 vols. illus. new ed. dj. . . . . *$110.00–$150.00*

Burton, Richard F. *City of Saints and Across the Rocky Mts. to California.* Lon. 1861. illus. maps, plan. . . . . *$250.00–$500.00*

Burton, Richard F. *City of Saints, and Across the Rocky Mts. to California.* NY. Harper. 1862. 1st Amer ed. maps, plates. . . . . *$125.00–$275.00*

Burton, Richard F. *Vikram and the Vampire.* Lon. Longmans, Green. 1870. 1st ed. illus. . . . . *$650.00–$750.00*

Burton, Richard Francis. *Etruscan Bologna: A Study.* Lon. Smith, Elder. 1876. blue-grey cl, fldg frontis. . . . . *$225.00–$500.00*

Burton, Richard Francis. *Wanderings in Three Continents.* Lon. Hutchingson & Co. 1901. 1st ed. edited by W. H. Wilkins, plates. . . . . *$125.00–$200.00*

Burton, Sir Richard Francis. *Etruscan Bologna, a Study.* Lon. Smith, Elder. 1876. 1st ed. rec mor. . . . . *$100.00–$400.00*

Burton, Sir Richard Francis. *Personal Narrative of a Pilgrimage to Al-Madinah & Mecca....* Lon. Tylstone and Edwards. 1893. 2 vols. illus. ...... *$500.00–$750.00*

Burton, Sir Richard Francis. *The Lake Regions of Central Africa.* Lon. Longmans Green. 1860. illus. chromolithographs, woodcuts, 1/2 lea. ...... *$500.00–$900.00*

Burton, Sir Richard Francis (ed.). *The Book of a Thousand Nights and a Night.* Lon. Nichols. 1897. 12 vols. illus. 'Kamashastra' ed. 3/4 lea. ... *$600.00–$1,000.00*

Burton, Sir Richard Francis (ed.). *The Kasidah of Haji Adbu El-Yezoi.* Chi. Reilly & Lee. nd. .... *$10.00–$20.00*

Burton, Sir Richard Francis (ed.). *The Land of Midian (Revisited).* Lon. 1879. Kegan Paul. 2 vols. 1st ed. illus. chromolithographs, fldg map.................
.... *$1,500.00–$2,000.00*

Burton, Sir Richard Francis (ed.). *The Lands of Cazembe.* Lon. John Murray. 1873. 1st ed. fldg map. .... *$300.00–$400.00*

Busch, W. *Max Und Moritz.* NY. Frederick Unger. nd. illus. b/w in German......
.... *$30.00–$40.00*

Busch, Wilhelm. *Max & Moritz.* Munich. 1939. illus. .... *$25.00–$45.00*

Busch, Wilhelm. *Neues Wilhelm Busch Album.* Leipzig. Weise. nd. 1st ed. dj, slipcase. .... *$100.00–$150.00*

Bushnan, J. S. *Naturalist's Library, Ichthyology.* Edin. 1840. vol. II. illus. ......
.... *$58.00–$75.00*

Bushnell, Charles I. *Narrative of the Life and Adventures of Levi Hanford....* NY. private printing. (1863). 1st ed. illus. bds. .... *$95.00–$150.00*

Busk, Hans. *Navies of the World.* Lon. Warnes & Routledge. 1859. ....
.... *$55.00–$68.00*

Butler, A. G. *Foreign Finches in Captivity.* Lon. Brumby and Clark. 1899. 2nd ed. 60 clr plates.. *$300.00–$425.00*

Butler, Charles. *American Lady.* Phila. Hogan & Thompson. 1836. 1st ed. .....
.... *$85.00–$100.00*

Butler, Ellis Parker. *Philo Gubb.* Bos. Houghton Mifflin. 1918. 1st ed. ....
.... *$150.00–$200.00*

Butler, Robert Olen. *Alleys of Eden.* NY. Horizon. (1981). 1st ed. author's first book, dj, sgn.. *$100.00–$150.00*

Butler, Robin. *The Philoenic Antiquary.* Honiton. 1978. illus. cat. . *$45.00–$50.00*

Butler, Robin and Gilliam Walking. *The Book of Wine Antiques.* Woodbridge. Antique Collector's Club. 1987. 2nd prtg. illus................. *$40.00–$65.00*

Butler, Samuel. *An Atlas of Ancient Geography*. Phila. Carey, Lee & Blanchard. 1838. hand clr maps. . . . .*$175.00–$200.00*

Butler, Winifred. *Dolls' Dressmaking*. NJ. D Van Nostrand Co. (1962). 1st ed. dj. . . . .*$12.00–$20.00*

Buttree, Julia M. *Rhythm of the Redman*. NY. (1930). intro and illus by E Thomson Seton. . . . .*$35.00–$45.00*

Butts, I. R. *Merchant and Shipmaster's Manual....* Bos. 1867. illus. 4th ed. plates. . . . .*$95.00–$135.00*

Butts, I. R. *Tinman's Manual*. Bos. 1861. 205 pp.. . . . . *$50.00–$85.00*

By a Free-Will Baptist. *Church Member's Book... In Three Parts*. NH. 1847. . . . .*$28.00–$30.00*

By a Gentleman About Town. *Imortalia: An Anthology of American Ballads...For the First Time Brought Together in Book Form*. np. private printing. 1927. ltd 100 cc. selections by James Joyce.. . . . .*$70.00–$150.00*

By A Lady. *Art of Cookery Made Plain and Easy*. Lon. 1770. new addition. . . . .*$550.00–$725.00*

By a Lady. *New System of Domestic Cookery....* Edin. 1843. illus. rbnd, 3/4 calf, marbled bds. . . . .*$95.00–$110.00*

By A Lady of Boston. *Stories of Gen. Warren*. 1835. lea. . . . .*$20.00–$30.00*

By a Practical Housekeeper. *Good Cook*. NY. 1853. . . . .*$55.00–$65.00*

By-Laws of the Orphan House of Charleston, South Carolina, 4th April 1861. Charleston. Steam Power Press. 1861. 1st ed. wrps. 40 pp. . . . .*$50.00–$55.00*

Byington, Cyrus. *A Dictionary of the Choctaw Language*. DC. GPO. 1915. Smithsonian bulletin No. 46. green silk.. . . . .*$30.00–$75.00*

Byrd, Martha. *Chennault: Giving Wings to the Tiger*. Tuscaloosa. University of Alabama Press. 1987. 1st ed. illus. photos, dj.. . . . .*$20.00–$35.00*

Byrd, Admiral Richard E. *Discovery: The Story of the Second Byrd Anarctic Expedition*. NY. Putnam. 1935. 1st ed. photos, dj. . . . .*$35.50–$65.00*

Byrd, Admiral Richard E. *Discovery*. NY. Putnam. 1935. 1st ed. illus. cl, dj.. . . . .*$30.00–$60.00*

Byrd,l Richard E. *Skyward*. Chi. Lakeside. 1981. teg. . . . .*$20.00–$25.00*

Byrd, Richard E. *Alone*. NY. Putnam. 1938. blue cl, dj.. . . . .*$30.00–$95.00*

Byrd, Richard E. *Little America*. NY. 1930. 1st ed. illus. sgn, dj. . . . .*$65.00–$100.00*

Byrd, Richard Evelyn. *Little America...the Flight to the South Pole.* NY/Lon. Putnam. 1930. 4th impr. illus. maps. . . . .*$20.00–$80.00*

Byrd, Richard Evelyn. *Little America: Aerial Exploration in the Antarctic.* NY. Putnam. 1930. 2nd impr. blue cl, sgn. . . . .*$40.00–$60.00*

Byrd, Richard Evelyn. *Skyward, Man's Mastery of the Air....* NY/Lon. Putnam. 1928. 1st ed. illus. plates, maps. *$160.00*

Cabell, James Branch. *Ballades of the Hidden Way.* NY. Crosby Gaige. 1928. 1st ed. designs by W. A. Dwiggins, 831cc sgn. . . . .*$60.00–$100.00*

Cabell, James Branch. *Jurgen and the Censor.* NY. Emergency Committee. 1920. 77 pp. ltd. sgn.. . . . .*$100.00–$150.00*

Cable, George. *Old Creole Days.* NY. 1879. 1st ed. no ads in rear. *$150.00–$175.00*

Cable, George. *The Negro Question.* NY. 1888. illus. . . . .*$45.00–$60.00*

Cable, George W. *Creoles of Louisiana.* NY. 1884. 1st ed. sgn, slipcase. . . . .*$200.00–$300.00*

Cable, George W. *Gideon's Band.* NY. 1914. 1st ed. . . . .*$30.00–$40.00*

Cable, George W. *Negro Question.* NY. Doubleday Anchor. 1958. . *$20.00–$30.00*

Cable, George Washington. *'Posson Jone' and Pere Raphael.* NY. Scribner's. 1909. decorative blue cl. . . . .*$45.00–$85.00*

Cabot, W. B. *In Northern Labrador.* Bos. 1912. 1st ed. . . . .*$40.00–$80.00*

Cady, Harrison. *School Opens on Butternut Hill.* Racine, WI. Whitman. 1929. 1st ed. illus by author. dj. . . . .*$75.00–$100.00*

Caiger, G. *Dolls on Display.* Tokyo. Hokuseido Press. nd. illus. silk brocade w/silk ties, boxed. . . . .*$95.00–$150.00*

Cain, James M. *Institute.* NY. Mason/Charter. 1976. 1st ed. dj. . . . *$25.00–$50.00*

Cain, James M. *Mildred Pierce.* Cleve. World Pub. 1945. 1st Motion Picture ed. illus.. . . . .*$40.00–$50.00*

Cain, James M. *Our Government.* NY. Knopf. 1930. 1st ed. author's first book. . . . .*$100.00–$175.00*

Cain, James M. *The Moth.* NY. Knopf. 1948. 1st ed. dj. . . . .*$60.00–$110.00*

Cain, Julien. *Lithographs of Chagall.* Bos. Boston Book and Art Shop. (1969). 2 original lithos by Chagall, dj. . . . .*$350.00–$800.00*

Cairns, Huntington. *The Limits of Art.* NY. Pantheon/Bollingen. (1966). 5th prtg. soft bds.. . . . .*$15.00–$25.00*

Calasanctius, M J. *Voice of Alaska. A Missioner's Memories.* Quebec. Lachine. 1935. illus. 1st UK ed. marbled bds. . . . . *$40.00–$50.00*

Caldecott, Randolph. *Last Graphic Pictures.* Lon. 1888. 1st ed. illus. . . . .
. . . . *$85.00–$150.00*

Caldecott, Randolph. *Ride a-Cock Horse to Banbury Cross.* Lon. Routledge. 1884. illus. 6 clr plates. . . . . *$100.00–$150.00*

Caldecott, Randolph. *Sketchbook of Randolph Caldecott.* Lon/NY. 1883. illus. . .
. . . . *$70.00–$125.00*

Calderwood, W. L. *Life of the Salmon.* Lon. Edward Arnold. 1907. illus. . . . .
. . . . *$40.00–$50.00*

Caldwell, E. N. *Alaska Trail Dogs.* NY. Richard Smith. 1945. illus. *$35.00–$90.00*

Caldwell, Erskine. *A House in the Uplands.* NY. Duell Sloane & Pearce. 1946. 1st ed. dj.. . . . . *$65.00–$80.00*

Caldwell, Erskine. *A Place Called Estherville.* NY. Duell Sloan & Pearce. (1949). 1st ed. inscr. dj. . . . . *$175.00–$300.00*

Caldwell, Erskine. *A Place Called Estherville.* NY. (1949). 1st ed. dj. . . . .
. . . . *$15.00–$40.00*

Caldwell, Erskine. *Afternoons in Mid-America.* NY. Dodd, Mead. 1976. 1st ed. dj.
. . . . *$15.00–$35.00*

Caldwell, Erskine. *American Earth.* NY. Scribner's. 1931. 1st ed. dj. . . . .
. . . . *$75.00–$300.00*

Caldwell, Erskine. *Claudelle Inglish.* Bos. 1958. 1st ed. dj. . . . . . . *$20.00–$30.00*

Caldwell, Erskine. *Erskine Caldwell's Gulf Coast Stories.* Bos. Little, Brown. 1956. 1st ed. dj.. . . . . *$30.00–$40.00*

Caldwell, Erskine. *God's Little Acre.* NY. Viking. 1933. 1st ed. dj.*$400.00–$850.00*

Caldwell, Erskine. *God's Little Acre.* Franklin Center. Franklin Library. 1979. ltd, sgn. . . . . *$85.00–$100.00*

Caldwell, Erskine. *God's Little Acre.* NY. 1933. 1st ed. . . . . . *$800.00–$1,500.00*

Caldwell, Erskine. *Journeyman.* NY. 1938. 1st trade ed. dj. . . . . . *$45.00–$100.00*

Caldwell, Erskine. *Some American People.* NY. McBride. (1935). 1st ed. dj. . . . .
. . . . *$35.00–$50.00*

Caldwell, Erskine. *Southways.* NY. 1938. 1st ed. . . . . *$25.00–$35.00*

Caldwell, Erskine. *Tenant Farmer.* NY. Phalanx Press. 1935. 1st ed. green wrps. .
. . . . *$125.00–$150.00*

Caldwell, Erskine. *The Bastard.* NY. Heron Press. c1929. 1st ed. illus. by Ty Mahon, ltd 1100 cc, author's first book. . . . . *$150.00–$200.00*

Caldwell, Erskine. *The Weather Shelter.* NY. World Pub. 1969. 1st ed. dj.. . . . . *$15.00–$20.00*

Caldwell, Erskine. *This Very Earth.* NY. Duell Sloane & Pearce. 1948. 1st ed. dj.. . . . . *$25.00–$40.00*

Caldwell, Erskine. *Tobacco Road.* NY. Scribner's. 1932. 1st ed. dj.. . . . . *$150.00–$600.00*

Caldwell, Erskine. *Tobacco Road.* NY. Grosset & Dunlap. (1932). illus. . . . . *$10.00–$20.00*

Caldwell, Erskine. *Tobacco Road.* NY. 1940. wrps. illus. by Fredenthal, boxed. . . . . *$45.00–$65.00*

Caldwell, Erskine and Margaret Bourke-White. *Say, Is This the USA.* NY. Duell, Sloane & Pearce. (1941). 1st ed. illus. . . . . *$50.00–$150.00*

Caldwell, H. R. and J. C. Caldwell. *South China Birds.* Hester May Vanderbufgh. 1931. . . . . *$95.00–$120.00*

Calendar of the American Fur Company's Papers. DC. GPO. 1945. 2 vols. 1st ed. . . . . *$85.00–$170.00*

California and the Far West. SF. Grabhorn Press. 1948. 1st ed. 217 pp, large folio, plates, ltd 500 cc. . . . . *$100.01–$100.00*

Calisher, Hortense. *In the Absence of Angelo.* Bos. 1951. 1st ed. dj. . . . . *$30.00–$75.00*

Callahan, James Morton. *American Foreign Policy in Mexican Relations.* NY. Cooper Square. 1967. rprnt. . . . . *$25.00–$45.00*

Callaway, Nicholas (ed.). *Georgia O'Keeffe: 100 Flowers.* NY. 1987. 1st ed. clr plates, folio, dj. . . . . *$75.00–$100.00*

Calthrop, Dion Clayton. *Charm of Gardens.* Lon. Black. 1910. 1st ed. illus. . . . . *$80.00–$100.00*

Calvin, Verplanck. *Report of the Superintendant of the State Land Survey....* Albany. 1896. 1st ed. maps, photos. . . . . *$145.00–$200.00*

Calvino, Italo. *Mr. Palomar.* San Diego. Harcourt Brace Jovanovich. 1985. 1st Amer ed. dj. . . . . *$10.00–$20.00*

Calvino, Italo. *Silent Mr. Palomar.* NY. Targ Editions. 1981. 1st ed. 250cc. sgn. . . . . *$150.00–$250.00*

Camehl, A. W. *Blue China Book.* NY. Halcyon House. 1916. . . . . . . *$20.00–$30.00*

Camp, David. *History of New Britain.* New Britain, CT. Thompson & Co. 1889. illus. brown cl.. . . . . *$35.00–$45.00*

Camp, John. *Fools Run.* NY. Henry Holt. 1989. 1st ed. sgn, dj. . . . *$45.00–$90.00*

Camp, R. *Duck Boats: Blinds, Decoys.* NY. Knopf. 1952. 1st ed. . . *$40.00–$50.00*

Camp, R. *Game Cookery.* NY. Coward-McCann. 1958. 1st ed. . . . *$20.00–$30.00*

Camp, Samuel G. *Fine Art of Fishing.* NY. Macmillan. (1911). . . . *$50.00–$65.00*

Camp, Samuel G. *Fishing Kits and Equipment.* NY. Outing Publishing. 1910. 1st ed. . . . . *$30.00–$40.00*

Campbell, C. A. R. *Bats, Mosquitoes and Dollars.* Bos. 1925. illus. *$30.00–$47.00*

Campbell, Dugald. *Wanderings in Central Africa.* Phila. Lippincott. 1st ed. illus. photo plates. . . . . *$50.00–$80.00*

Campbell, Mary Emily. *Attitude of Tennesseans Toward the Union 1847-1861.* NY. 1961. 1st ed. . . . . *$30.00–$45.00*

Campbell, Patrick. *Travels in the Interior Inhabited Parts of North America.* Tor. 1937. ltd 550cc. . . . . *$150.00–$300.00*

Campbell, Ruth. *Small Fry and Winged Horse.* Chi. Volland. (1927). illus. . . . . *$55.00–$85.00*

Campbell, T. *Isaac Jogues, Discoverer of Lake George.* NY. 1911. wrps. illus. . . . . *$25.00–$40.00*

Campbell, T. J. *Isaac Jogues Discoverer of Lake George.* NY. The America Press. 1911. 1st ed. illus. soft brown wrps.. . . . . *$45.00–$75.00*

Campbell, Wilfred. *Canada.* Lon. A & C Black. 1907. 1st ed. illus. *$75.00–$125.00*

Camus, Albert. *Exile and the Kingdom.* NY. Knopf. 1958. 1st Amer ed., dj. . . . . *$40.00–$60.00*

Camus, Albert. *Myth of Sisyphus.* NY. Knopf. 1955. 1st Amer ed. dj. *$85.00–$150.00*

Camus, Albert. *Resistance, Rebellion and Death.* Hamish Hamilton. 1961. 1st UK ed., dj. . . . . *$45.00–$50.00*

Camus, Albert. *The Fall.* Kentfield, CA. The Allen Press. 1960. folio. ltd 140 cc. tan grey and black bds, dj.. . . . . *$400.00–$650.00*

Camus, Albert. *The Stranger.* NY. (1946). 1st US ed. dj. . . . . *$75.00–$125.00*

Candee, Helen C. *Weaves and Draperies.* NY. Stokes. 1930. 1st ed. illus. . . . . *$40.00–$55.00*

Canfield, William W. *The Sign Above the Door*. Phila. Jewish Publication Society. 1912. 1st ed. . . . . *$25.00–$50.00*

Cannon, Donald J., (ed.). *Heritage of Flames*. NY. Artisan Books. 1977. 1st ed. illus. hist of early Amer firefighting, dj. . . . . *$60.00–$100.00*

Cannon, George Q. *Delegate From Utah*. DC. GPO. 1872. wrps. . *$45.00–$60.00*

Cannon, George Q. *Physiology of Common Life*. Edin. 1865. vol. 2. illus. sgn. . . . . *$100.00–$175.00*

Cannon, George Q. *Writings from the "Western Standard." Published in San Francisco, California*. Liverpool. 1864. 1st ed. . . . . *$300.00–$650.00*

Canot, Capt. Theodore. *Adventures of an African Slaver*. NY. Albert & Charles Boni. 1928. 1st ed. illus. . . . . *$80.00–$120.00*

Canton, Frank M. *Frontier Trails*. Bos. Houghton Mifflin. 1930. dj. . . . . *$100.00–$150.00*

Cantwell, J. C. *Report of the Operations of the US Steamer Nunivak, 1899-1902*. DC. GPO. 1902. 1st ed. illus. 153 photos, green cl. . . . . *$150.00–$275.00*

Cantwell, Lieut. *Report of the Operations of the U S Revenue Steamer Nunivak*. DC. GPO. 1902. 1st ed. illus. green cl. . . . . *$150.00–$250.00*

Capa, R. *Images of War*. NY. (1964). 1st ed. dj. . . . . *$75.00–$95.00*

Capa, Robert. *Death in the Making*. NY. Covici-Friede. (1938). 1st ed. dj. . . . . *$650.00–$750.00*

Capote, Truman. *A Christmas Memory*. NY. (1966). 1st ed. slipcase. . . . . *$80.00–$100.00*

Capote, Truman. *Answered Prayers: The Unfinished Novel*. NY. Random House. 1987. 1st ed. dj. . . . . *$20.00–$35.00*

Capote, Truman. *Breakfast at Tiffany's*. NY. Random House. (1958). wrps. dj. . . . . *$175.00–$300.00*

Capote, Truman. *Grass Harp, A Play*. NY. Random House. (1951). 1st ed. dj. . . . . *$100.00–$300.00*

Capote, Truman. *In Cold Blood*. NY. Random House. (1965). 1st ed. dj. . . . . *$25.00–$30.00*

Capote, Truman. *Muses Are Heard*. NY. Random House. (1956). 1st ed. dj. . . . . *$75.00–$125.00*

Capote, Truman. *Music for Chameleons*. NY. Random House. 1980. 1st ed. dj. . . . . *$25.00–$30.00*

Capote, Truman. *Other Voice, Other Rooms*. NY. Random House. 1948. 1st ed. dj. . . . . *$350.00–$500.00*

Capote, Truman. *Thanksgiving Visitor*. NY. Random House. 1967. *$24.00–$35.00*

Capote, Truman. *The Dogs Bark: Public People and Private Places*. NY. Random House. 1973. 1st ed. red cl, bds, dj. . . . . *$60.00–$100.00*

Capp, Al. *Hardhat's Bedtime Story Book*. NY. Harper & Row. 1971. 1st ed. . . . . *$20.00–$30.00*

Capp, Al. *Return of the Schmoo*. NY. 1959. 1st ed. wrps. . . . . *$28.00–$35.00*

Caputo, Philip. *Rumor of War*. NY. Rinehart & Winston. (1977). 1st ed. dj. . . . . *$20.00–$30.00*

Card, Orson Scott. *Ender's Game*. NY/Tor. 1985. 1st ed. scarce, dj. *$500.00–$675.00*

***Care and Operation of Plows and Cultivators*.** Moline, IL. John Deere & Co. nd. 1st ed. wrps. illus. . . . . *$50.00–$65.00*

Carleton, William. *Traits and Stories of the Irish Peasantry*. Dublin. 1843-4. 2 vols.. . . . . *$115.00–$150.00*

Carlisle, D. *Belvedere Hounds*. Derrydale Press. 1935. ltd 1250cc, pict bds, glassine wrps. . . . . *$75.00–$125.00*

Carlisle, Lillian Baker. *Vermont Clock and Watch Makers*. VT. 1970. 1st ed. ltd 1000 cc, dj. . . . . *$40.00–$50.00*

Carmen, Carl. *French Town*. New Orleans. Pelican Pub. (1968). wrps. illus. pres copy to Ralph Hill, VT writer. . . . . *$20.00–$40.00*

Carmer, Carl. *Deep South*. NY. Farrar & Rinehart. 1930. 1st ed. sgn. . *$25.00–$50.00*

Carmer, Carl. *Rivers of America: The Hudson*. NY. Farrar & Rinehart. 1939. illus. sgn. . . . . *$40.00–$100.00*

Carnegie, Andrew. *An American Four-in-Hand in Britain*. NY. Scribner's. 1883. 1st ed. decorative cl. . . . . *$25.00–$40.00*

Carnegie, Andrew. *Round the World*. NY. Scribner's. 1884. 1st Amer trade ed. . . . . *$35.00–$65.00*

Caron, Pierre. *French Dishes for American Tables*. NY. Appleton. 1886. 1st ed. . . . . *$25.00–$35.00*

Carpenter, Don. *Hard Rain Falling*. NY. Harcourt, Brace & World. (1966). author's first book, dj. . . . . *$25.00–$40.00*

Carpenter, Frank. *Alaska Our Northern Wonderland*. NY. 1928. illus. photos, 2 fldg maps. . . . . *$25.00–$70.00*

Carpenter, Frank. *Mexico.* NY. Doubleday. 1928. illus. photos.... *$25.00–$45.00*

Carpenter, R. *Game Trails from Alaska to Africa 1938.* private printing. 1938. ltd 850 cc, sgn. . . . . *$125.00–$200.00*

Carpenter, W. *Microscope and Its Revelations.* Phila. Blakiston's. 1901. illus. . . . . *$85.00–$150.00*

Carpenter, W. *Microscope: and its Revelations.* Phila. 1856. illus. 1st Amer ed. . . . . *$125.00–$150.00*

Carpenter, W. *Principles of Human Physiology.* Phila. Blanchard and Lee. 1853. 5th Amer ed. . . . . *$35.00–$45.00*

Carpenter, William. *Microscope & Its Revelations.* NY. Wood. 1883. 2 vols. . . . . *$90.00–$130.00*

Carr, Harry. *West is Still Wild.* Bos. Houghton Mifflin. 1932. 1st ed. illus. . . . . *$25.00–$35.00*

Carr, James F. *Mantle Fielding's Dictionary of American Painters, Sculptors and Engravers.* NY. Carr. 1965. rev. . . . . *$80.00–$120.00*

Carr, John. *Pioneer Days in California: Historical and Personal Sketches.* Eureka. Times Publishing Co. 1891. 1st ed. . . . . *$125.00–$150.00*

Carr, John Dickson. *Arabian Nights Murder.* NY. Harper & Bros. 1936. 1st ed. . . . . *$45.00–$75.00*

Carr, John Dickson. *Death Turns the Tables.* NY. Harper & Bros. 1941. 1st ed. dj. . . . . *$200.00–$400.00*

Carr, John Dickson. *The Man Who Could Not Shudder.* NY. Harper. 1940. 1st ed. . . . . *$300.00–$350.00*

Carr, John Dickson. *Third Bullet and Other Stories.* NY. Harper. 1954. 1st ed. 231pp, dj. . . . . *$30.00–$50.00*

Carrick, Alice Van Leer. *History of American Silhouettes... 1790-1840.* Rutland. (1968). dj. . . . . *$30.00–$50.00*

Carriker, M. A., Jr. *An Annotated List of the Birds of Costa Rica.* Carnegie Museum of Natural History. 1910. wrps. . . . . *$45.00–$60.00*

Carrington, Frances C. *Army Life on the Plains.* Phila. Washington Square Press. 1911. 2nd ed. . . . . *$45.00–$65.00*

Carrington, Herny B. *Indian Question.* Bos. 1884. maps. . . . . . *$225.00–$300.00*

Carroll, Jim. *Basketball Diaries.* CA. Bolinas. (1978). 1st ed. wrps. *$280.00–$350.00*

Carroll, Jim. *Book of Nods.* NY. Viking. (1986). 1st ed. scarce, dj. . *$70.00–$85.00*

Carroll, Jim. *Living at the Movies.* NY. Grossman. 1973. 1st ed. sgn, dj.. . . . .
. . . . **$175.00–$250.00**

Carroll, Lewis. *Alice in Wonderland.* Lon. Raphael Tuck & Sons. (1910). illus. by
Mabel Lucie. 1st thus. scarce, green and gilt binding. . . . . **$720.00–$800.00**

Carroll, Lewis. *Alice's Adventures in Wonderland.* NY/Lon. Harpers. 1901. illus. by
Peter Newell. 1st thus.. . . . . **$130.00–$200.00**

Carroll, Lewis. *Alice's Adventures in Wonderland.* Bos. Lee and Shepard. 1869. 1st
ed. illus. printed in America, 192 pp, green cl, scarce. . . . . **$300.00–$500.00**

Carroll, Lewis. *Alice's Adventures in Wonderland.* Chi. Rand McNally. (1916). illus.
. . . . **$55.00–$80.00**

Carroll, Lewis. *Alice's Adventures in Wonderland...in Pitman's Shorthand.* Lon.
Guilbert Pitman. nd. printed wrps, 64 pp.. . . . . **$75.00–$115.00**

Carroll, Lewis. *Annotated Alice.* NY. Bramhall House. (1970). illus. rust and buff
cvr pict dj.. . . . . **$25.00–$30.00**

Carroll, Lewis. *Doublets: A Word-Puzzle.* Lon. Macmillan. 1879. 1st ed. red cl. . .
. . . . **$150.00–$200.00**

Carroll, Lewis. *Further Nonsense: Verse and Prose.* NY. Appleton. 1926. 1st ed. .
. . . . **$40.00–$50.00**

Carroll, Lewis. *Hunting of the Snark.* Lon. Macmillan. 1876. 1st ed. illus. by Henry
Holiday pict tan cl. . . . . **$125.00–$375.00**

Carroll, Lewis. *Sylvie and Bruno.* Lon. 1893. 1st ed. illus. by Harry Furnise. . . . .
. . . . **$100.00–$150.00**

Carroll, Lewis. *The Letters of Lewis Carroll, edited by Mortonn N. Cohen....* NY.
Oxford University Press. 1979. 2 vols. 1st ed. illus. blue cl, slipcase. . **$65.00–$75.00**

Carroll, Lewis. *Through the Looking Glass.* Phila. Lippincott. (1929). illus. by M
Kirk. . . . . **$50.00–$85.00**

Carroll, Lewis. *Through the Looking Glass.* NY. Harper. 1902. illus. by Newell, 40
plates. . . . . **$120.00–$130.00**

Carruth, Hayden. *Adventures of Jones.* NY. Harper. 1895. 1st ed. illus. **$25.00–$35.00**

Carruth, Hayden. *Contra Mortem.* VT. Crow's Mark Press. (1967). 1st ed. wrps. ltd
250 cc, sgn.. . . . . **$85.00–$120.00**

Carruth, Hayden. *Crow And the Heart.* NY. Macmillan. 1959. 1st ed. dj.. . . . . . .
. . . . **$30.00–$45.00**

Carry, John. *Life of George Washington.* NY. 1807. . . . . **$95.00–$250.00**

Carson, Rachel. *Edge of the Sea.* Bos. 1955. 1st ed. dj. . . . . *$30.00–$75.00*

Carson, Rachel. *Silent Spring..* Bos. Houghton Mifflin. 1962. 1st ed. dj. . . . .
. . . . *$55.00–$75.00*

Carson, Rachel. *Under the Sea Wind.* NY. 1941. 1st ed. dj. . . . . *$100.00–$150.00*

Carter, Jimmy & Rosalynn Carter. *Everything to Gain.* NY. Random House. (1987). 1st ed. 2nd prntg. sgn by both.. . . . . *$50.00–$100.00*

Cartier-Bresson, Henri. *From One China to Another.* NY. (1956). 1st ed. dj. . . . .
. . . . *$100.00–$125.00*

Cartier-Bresson, Henri. *Henri Cartier-Bresson Photographer.* Bos/NY. Graphics Society. 1979. 1st ed. dj. . . . . *$85.00–$150.00*

Cartier-Bresson, Henri. *People of Moscow.* NY. Simon & Schuster. 1955. 1st ed. illus. dj. . . . . *$75.00–$350.00*

Cartier-Bresson, Henri. *The Europeans.* NY. Simon & Schuster. (1955). folio pict bds. . . . . *$275.00–$500.00*

Carvalho, S. N. *Incidents of Travel and Adventure in the Far West.* NY. 1857. . . .
. . . . *$95.00–$250.00*

Carver, Jonathan. *Travels through Interior Parts of No. America...1766, '67, '68..* Lon. 1781. 3rd ed. lea, mor-bkd clamshell case, hand-clr maps and plates. . . . .
. . . . *$900.00–$2,000.00*

Carver, Raymond. *A New Path to the Water: Poems.* Lon. Collins Harvill. 1989. 1st End ed. dj. . . . . *$60.00–$100.00*

Carver, Raymond. *Cathedral.* NY. Knopf. 1983. 1st ed. dj. . . . . . *$65.00–$125.00*

Carver, Raymond. *Fires.* Santa Barbara. Capra Press. (1983). wrps. *$45.00–$55.00*

Carver, Raymond. *New Path to the Waterfall.* NY. Atlantic Monthly Press. 1989. 1st ed. dj. . . . . *$30.00–$40.00*

Carver, Raymond. *No Heroics, Please.* Lon. Harvill. 1991. 1st ed. dj. . . . .
. . . . *$85.00–$125.00*

Carver, Raymond. *Put Yourself in My Shoes.* NY. 1981. 1st ed. dj. *$150.00–$200.00*

Carver, Raymond. *The Toes.* Ewert. 1988. 1st ed. wrps. wrps 26cc.*$175.00–$125.00*

Carver, Raymond. *This Water.* Concord. Ewert. 1985. wrps. ltd ed. sgn.. . . . .
. . . . *$135.00–$200.00*

Carver, Raymond. *Ultramarine.* NY. Random House. 1986. 1st ed. dj, sgn. . . . . .
. . . . *$200.00–$300.00*

Carver, Raymond. *Ultramarine.* NY. Random House. 1986. 1st ed. dj. . . . .
. . . . *$45.00–$65.00*

Carver, Raymond. *Water Comes Together With Other Water.* NY. Random House.
1st ed. dj. . . . . *$35.00–$75.00*

Carver, Raymond. *What We Talk About When We Talk About Love.* NY. Knopf.
1981. 1st ed. dj. . . . . *$150.00–$250.00*

Carver, Raymond. *Where I'm Calling From.* NY. Atlantic Monthly Press. 1988. 1st
ed. cl, dj. . . . . *$25.00–$90.00*

Carver, Raymond. *Where I'm Calling From.* Franklin Center. Franklin Library.
(1987). 1st ed. ltd. sgn. . . . . *$150.00–$350.00*

Carver, Raymond. *Will You Please Be Quiet, Please?* NY. McGraw Hill. 1976. 1st
ed. dj. . . . . *$300.00–$600.00*

Cassidy, Carl (compiler). *History of the 775th Bombardment Squadron.* Iowa. 1982.
illus. rprnt, 300 cc, sgn. . . . . *$95.00–$125.00*

Casson, Herbert N. *Romance of the Reaper.* NY. Doubleday, Page. 1908. 1st ed.
illus. *$45.00*

Castenada, Carlos. *Teachings of Don Juan.* Berkeley. 1968. 1st ed. dj. . . . .
. . . . *$90.00–$150.00*

Castle, Henry A. *Army Mule And Other War Sketches.* Ind. Bowen Merrill. 1898.
illus. . . . . *$50.00–$75.00*

Castleman, Alfred. *Army of the Potomac.* Milw. Strockland & Co. 1863. . . . .
. . . . *$100.00–$175.00*

Caswell, J. *Sporting Rifles & Rifle Shooting.* NY. Appleton. 1920. 1st ed. illus. photos. . . . . *$24.00–$35.00*

Catalogue No. 16. Havana, IL. Havana Metal Wheel Co. nd. wrps. illus. . . . .
. . . . *$50.00–$65.00*

Catalogue No. R-52, Rosettes, Ornaments.... Akron, OH. The Enterprise Mfg. Co.
1932. wrps. illus. . . . . *$30.00–$45.00*

*Catalogue of Drugs Chemicals, Dye Stuffs, Druggists' Sundries, Proprietary
Medicines, Oils, Paints....* Burlington, VT. Wells, Richardon & Co. 1878. pebbled cl,
200 pp. . . . . *$95.00–$125.00*

Catalogue of Hardy Fruit Trees and Plants.... Sioux Falls, Dak Terr. E DeBell.
1884. illus. self-printed wrps, 8 pp. . . . . *$75.00–$100.00*

*Catalogue of Microscopes and Accessories. Microtomes. Bacteriological
Apparatus. Laboratory Supplies....* Phila. Charles Lentz & Sons. 1899. printed wrps,
illus, 136 pp. . . . . *$125.00–$175.00*

Catalogue of Weathervanes, No 9. Waltham, MA. L W Cushing & Sons. 1883. decorative wrps, illus, 20 pp.................................. *$500.00–$750.00*

Catalogues of Birds, Eggs.... Nat'l Museum of Rhodesia. 1970. stiff wrps scarce.. .... *$50.00–$60.00*

Cate, Wirt Armistead. *Lucius Q.C. Lamar: Secession and Reunion.* Chapel Hill. 1935. 1st ed. illus. .... *$30.00–$50.00*

Cather, Willa. *A Lost Lady.* NY. Knopf. 1923. 1st ed. .... *$30.00–$45.00*

Cather, Willa. *April Twilights.* Bos. Richard G Badger/The Gorham Press. 1903. 1st ed. author's first book, paper-cvred bds, paper spine label, uncut, sgn. .... *$1,500.00–$2,500.00*

Cather, Willa. *Death Comes for the Archbishop.* NY. Knopf. 1927. 1st ed. dj..... .... *$125.00–$200.00*

Cather, Willa. *Death Comes for the Archbishop.* NY. Knopf. 1927. 1st trade, dj, inscr.. *$800.00–$1,000.00*

Cather, Willa. *Lucy Gayheart.* NY. Knopf. 1935. ltd 749 cc sgn. dj. *$300.00–$400.00*

Cather, Willa. *Lucy Gayheart.* NY. Knopf. 1935. 1st ed. green cl, dj. .... *$225.00–$300.00*

Cather, Willa. *Lost Lady.* NY. Knopf. 1923. 1st ed. .... *$30.00–$40.00*

Cather, Willa. *My Mortal Enemy.* NY. Knopf. 1926. 1st ed. chipped dj. .... *$125.00–$350.00*

Cather, Willa. *Obscure Destiny.* NY. 1932. 1st ed. dj........... *$40.00–$50.00*

Cather, Willa. *Old Beauty and Others.* NY. Knopf. 1948. 1st ed. dj. .... *$35.00–$65.00*

Cather, Willa. *On Writing.* NY. Knopf. 1949. 1st ed. green cl, dj.. *$85.00–$100.00*

Cather, Willa. *Professor's House.* NY. Knopf. 1925. 1st ed. .... *$100.00–$200.00*

Cather, Willa. *Sapphira and the Slavegirl.* NY. Knopf. 1940. 1st ed. dj. .... *$40.00–$60.00*

Cather, Willa. *Shadows on the Rock.* NY. Knopf. 1931. 1st ed. ltd. inscr. dj. .... *$400.00–$1,000.00*

Cather, Willa. *Shadows on the Rock.* NY. Knopf. 1931. 1st ed. dj. sgn.......... .... *$350.00–$500.00*

Cather, Willa. *Shadows on the Rock.* NY. Knopf. 1931. 1st ed. dj.*$100.00–$125.00*

Cather, Willa. *Song of the Lark.* Bos. Houghton Mifflin. 1915. 1st ed. .... *$225.00–$500.00*

Cather, Willa. *The Old Beauty and Others.* NY. Knopf. 1948. 1st ed. dj. . . . .
. . . . *$35.00–$75.00*

Cather, Willa. *Willa Cather in Europe.* NY. Knopf. 1956. 1st ed. dj. *$25.00–$30.00*

Cather, Willa. *Youth and the Bright Medusa.* NY. Knopf. 1920. 1st ed. green cl. . .
. . . . *$75.00–$100.00*

Cather, Willa. *Youth and the Bright Medusa.* NY. Knopf. 1920. 1st ed. dj. . . . . . .
. . . . *$100.00–$250.00*

Catholic Encyclopedia. NY. Appleton-Encylopedia Press. 1907-14. 10 vols. 3/4 lea.
. . . . *$475.00–$525.00*

Catlin, George. *Illustrations of the Manners, Customs and Condition of the North American Indians: In a Series of Letters and Notes....* Lon. Henry G Bohn. 1845. 2 vols. illus. 5th ed. . . . . *$750.00–$1,250.00*

Catlin, George. *Letters and Notes on the North American Indians.* NY. (1965). 2 vols. illus. . . . . *$50.00–$75.00*

Catlin, George. *Life Amongst the Indians.* Lon. 1861. 14 plates. . . *$50.00–$125.00*

Catlin, George. *North American Indian Portfolio.* Chi. Swallow Press. (1970). folio, rprnt of earlier ed. . . . . *$700.00–$1,400.00*

Catlin, George. *North American Indians.* Edin. John Grant. 1926. 2 vols. . . . . . .
. . . . *$1,200.00–$1,400.00*

Catlin, George. *North American Indians.* Phil. Leary, Stuart & Co. 1913. 2 vols. illus. ex lib, red cl. . . . . *$80.00–$100.00*

Catlin, George. *North American Indians: Being Letters and Notes on their Manners, Customs, and Conditions.* NY. Dover Pub. 1973. 2 vols. illus. . . . . *$35.00–$80.00*

Catlin, George. *Story of the Political Philosophers.* NY. McGraw Hill. 1939. dj. . .
. . . . *$30.00–$35.00*

Catton, Bruce. *Banners of Shenandoah.* Garden City. Doubleday. 1955. illus. dj. .
. . . . *$30.00–$40.00*

Catton, Bruce. *Grant Moves South..* Bos/Tor. Little, Brown. 1960. 1st ed. illus. presentation copy, sgn, dj. . . . . *$30.00–$40.00*

Caverly, A. M. *History of the Town of Pittsford, Vermont.* Rutland. 1872. illus. rbnd,.
. . . . *$80.00–$95.00*

Ce Camoens, Luis. *Poems from the Portuguese.* Lon. James Carpenter and Son. 1824. cl. . . . . *$60.00–$75.00*

Centennial History of Lemhi County, Idaho. Salmon. Lemhi County History Committee. 1992. vols 1-3. 1st ed. illus. photos. . . . . *$60.00–$75.00*

Century Company War Book. *Battles and Leaders of the Civil War.* NY. 1884-1887. 4 vols.. . . . . *$75.00–$100.00*

Cervantes, Miguel de. *History of Don Quixote.* Lon. Gustav Dore. illus. lea bnd. . . . . *$100.00–$150.00*

Cescinsky, Herbert and Ernest Gribble. *Early English Furniture and Woodwork.* Lon. 1927. 2 vols. illus. folio, lea. . . . . *$135.00–$200.00*

Chadwick, Lee. *Lighthouses and Lightships.* Lon. Dobson. 1971. illus. photos, dj. . . . . *$25.00–$33.00*

Chagall, Marc. *Drawings and Watercolors for the Ballet.* NY. Tudor Pub. (1969). 1st ed. 1 orig litho, dj, slipcase. . . . . *$200.00–$250.00*

Chagall, Marc. *Jerusalem Windows.* NY. George Braziller. (1962). 2 orig lithos by Chagall, red cl, gilt, dj.. . . . . *$1,200.00–$1,500.00*

Chagall, Marc. *Lithographs V. 1974–1979.* NY. Crown. 1984. 1st Amer ed. . . . . *$40.00–$60.00*

Chalfant, W. A. *Gold Guns & Ghost Towns.* Stanford. 1947. . . . . . *$25.00–$35.00*

Chamberlain, George A. *African Hunting Among the Thongas.* NY. 1923. 1st ed. illus. . . . . *$45.00–$65.00*

Chamberlain, Samuel. *Rockefeller Center.* 1947. photos, dj. . . . . . *$10.00–$18.00*

Chamberlain, Samuel, and Narcissa Chamberlain. *Southern Interiors of Charleston, South Carolina.* NY. Hastings House. (1956). illus. . . . . . . *$30.00–$40.00*

Chamberlayne, Churchill Gibson, (ed.). *Vestry Book of Bristol Parish....* Richmond. private printing. 1892. #251/500 cc inscr. . . . . *$90.00–$100.00*

Chamberlin, Lt. Col. Harry D. *Training Hunters, Jumpers and Hacks.* NY. Derrydale. 1937. ltd 950 cc.. . . . . *$65.00–$130.00*

Chambers, E. T. D. *Ouananiche and Its Canadian Environment.* NY. Harper & Bros. 1896. 1st ed. . . . . *$85.00–$120.00*

Chambers, Thomas King. *Renewal of Life.* Phil. Lindsay & Blakiston. 1866. . . . . *$40.00–$50.00*

Chandler, Raymond. *Backfire: Story for the Screen.* CA. 1984. 1st ed. ltd 200 cc, softcvr, sgn, presentation. . . . . *$85.00–$125.00*

Chandler, Raymond. *Big Sleep.* NY. Knopf. 1939. 1st ed. dj, cl box. . . . . *$3,500.00–$7,500.00*

Chandler, Raymond. *Big Sleep.* 1946. movie ed. . . . . *$15.00–$25.00*

Chandler, Raymond. *Big Sleep.* NY. Knopf. 1939. 1st ed. no dj. *$215.00–$250.00*

Chandler, Raymond. *Big Sleep*.NY. Avon. 1943. pbk. #38. . . . . . . *$50.00–$65.00*

Chandler, Raymond. *Farewell My Lovely*. NY. Knopf. 1940. 1st ed. no dj. . . . . . .
. . . . *$250.00–$375.00*

Chandler, Raymond. *Farewell My Lovely*. NY. Knopf. 1940. 1st ed. dj. . . . .
. . . . *$1,500.00–$2,000.00*

Chandler, Raymond. *High Window*. NY. Knopf. 1942. 1st ed. dj. . . . .
. . . . *$85.00–$100.00*

Chandler, Raymond. *Killer in the Rain*. Bos. Houghton Mifflin. 1964. 1st US ed.
dj. . . . . *$375.00–$450.00*

Chandler, Raymond. *Killer in the Rain*. Lon. Hamish Hamilton. (1964). 1st ed. dj.
. . . . *$150.00–$350.00*

Chandler, Raymond. *Lady in the Lake*. NY. Knopf. 1943. 1st ed. dj. . . . .
. . . . *$700.00–$1,500.00*

Chandler, Raymond. *Little Sister*. Bos. Houghton Mifflin. 1949. 1st Amer ed. dj..
. . . . *$150.00–$350.00*

Chandler, Raymond. *Long Goodbye*. Bos. Houghton Mifflin. 1954. 1st ed. dj. . . . .
. . . . *$275.00–$500.00*

Chandler, Raymond. *Playback*. Lon. Hamish Hamilton. 1958. 1st ed. dj. . . . .
. . . . *$250.00–$300.00*

Chandler, Raymond. *Red Wind*. Cleve. World Pub. 1946. 1st ed. dj. . . . .
. . . . *$50.00–$100.00*

Chandler, Raymond. *Simple Art of Murder*. NY. W. W. Norton. 1968. 1st ed. dj. . .
. . . . *$50.00–$100.00*

Chandler, Raymond. *Smell of Fear*. Lon. Hamish Hamilton. 1965. 1st ed. dj. . . . .
. . . . *$200.00–$300.00*

Chandler, Raymond. *Spanish Blood*. NY. World Pub. 1946. 1st ed. dj. . . . .
. . . . *$75.00–$100.00*

Chandler, Raymond. *The Big Sleep*. Pocket Books. 1950. 1st prtg. . .*$15.00–$25.00*

Chandler, Raymond. *The Blue Dahlia*. Illinois. Carbondale. 1976. 1st ed. dj. . . . .
. . . . *$150.00–$200.00*

Channing, William. *Slavery*. Bos. 1835. 1st ed. . . . . *$75.00–$125.00*

Chanslor, Torrey. *Our First Murder*. NY. Stokes. 1940. 1st ed. dj. . *$50.00–$75.00*

Chapelle, Howard I. *History of American Sailing Ships*. NY. W. W. Norton. 1935.
1st trade ed. illus, plates, photos, ship drawings. . . . . *$30.00–$50.00*

Chaplin, R. *Wobbly*. Chi. (1948). presentation copy, dj. . . . . *$30.00–$50.00*

Chapman, A. *On Safari*. Lon. 1908. illus. photos. . . . . *$150.00–$300.00*

Chapman, Allen. *Bound to Succeed or Mail Order Franks Chances*. OH. Goldsmith. 1907. cl. . . . . *$12.00–$17.00*

Chapman, Allen. *Radio Boys First Wireless*. NY. Grosset & Dunlap. (1922). series #1, dj. . . . . *$27.00–$35.00*

Chapman, Allen. *Radio Boys Trailing a Voice*. NY. Grosset & Dunlap. 1922. 1st ed. series #5. . . . . *$15.00–$35.00*

Chapman, Allen. *Radio Boys with the Flood Fighters*. NY. Grosset & Dunlap. 1925. 1st ed. series #8. . . . . *$25.00–$30.00*

Chapman, Allen. *Radio Boys with the Forest Rangers*. NY. Grosset & Dunlap. 1923. 1st ed. series #6. . . . . *$20.00–$25.00*

Chapman, Allen. *Radio Boys with the Iceberg Patrol*. NY. Grosset & Dunlap. 1924. 1st ed. Radio Boys #7, dj. . . . . *$28.00–$35.00*

Chapman, Charles E. *History of California: the Spanish Period*. NY. 1921. illus. maps. . . . . *$40.00–$50.00*

Chapman, F. Spencer. *Northern Lights*. NY. 1933. illus. 1st Amer ed. fldg map. . . . . *$60.00–$75.00*

Chapman, F. M. *Distribution of Bird Life in Ecuador*. NY. 1926. 29 plates, fldg map (Bulletin Amer Museum of Natural History, vol. 55). . . . . *$140.00–$170.00*

Chapman, Frank. *Bird Life*. NY. Appleton. 1898. illus. by E. S. Thompson. pict cl. . . . . *$60.00–$70.00*

Chapman, Frank. *Warblers of North America*. NY. Appleton. 1907. *$30.00–$45.00*

Chapman, Olive Murray. *Across Iceland the Land of Frost and Fire*. Lon/NY. 1930. 1st ed. illus. . . . . *$40.00–$95.00*

Chapman, Priscilla. *Hindoo Female Education*. Lon. Seeley & Burnside. 1839. 1st ed. illus. 4 engr. . . . . *$100.00–$150.00*

Chapone, Mary. *Letters on the Improvement of the Mind*. NY. Richard Scott. 1819. small frontis. . . . . *$50.00–$125.00*

Chappell, Fred. *Dagon*. NY. Harcourt, Brace & World. (1968). 1st ed. 177 pp, dj. . . . . *$35.00–$45.00*

Chapple, H. Barton. *Popular Television*. 1935. 1st ed. illus. dj. . . . *$45.00–$60.00*

Chaptal, M. F. A. *Elements of Chemistry*. Buckingham. 1806. 3 vols in. 3rd Amer ed. 612 pp, calf. . . . . *$100.00–$135.00*

Chardin, Sir John. *Travels in Persia.* Lon. 1927. illus. ltd 975 cc. . *$125.00–$225.00*

Charney, Desire. *Ancient Cities of the New World.* NY. Harper & Bros. 1887. 1st US ed. illus. fldg map, 35 plates, cl, red lea label. . . . . *$125.00–$200.00*

Charteris, Leslie. *Call for the Saint.* Garden City. Doubleday Crime Club. (1948). 1st ed. dj.. . . . . *$50.00–$75.00*

Charteris, Leslie. *Last Hero.* Garden City. Doubleday. 1930. 1st ed. dj. . . . .
. . . . *$25.00–$50.00*

Charteris, Leslie. *Saint Goes West.* Garden City. Doubleday. 1943. 1st ed. pict dj.
. . . . *$60.00–$85.00*

Charteris, Leslie. *Saint In Miami.* Garden City. Doubleday. 1940. 1st ed. dj.. . . . .
. . . . *$100.00–$175.00*

Charteris, Leslie. *Saint Overboard.* NY. Triangle. 1936. dj. . . . . . . *$15.00–$45.00*

Charteris, Leslie. *Saint Sees It Through.* Garden City. Doubleday. 1946. 1st ed. dj.
. . . . *$60.00–$75.00*

Charteris, Leslie. *Saint Steps In.* Triangle Books. 1943. . . . . *$9.00–$15.00*

Charteris, Leslie. *Saint to the Rescue.* Hodder & Stoughton. 1961. 1st UK ed. dj.. .
. . . . *$50.00–$75.00*

Charteris, Leslie. *Tar Baby.* NY. Holt, Rinehart & Winston. 1973. 1st ed. dj. . . . .
. . . . *$40.00–$55.00*

Charteris, Leslie. *Thanks to the Saint.* Lon. Hodder & Stoughton. 1958. 1st ed. dj.
. . . . *$30.00–$125.00*

Charteris, Leslie. *Trust The Saint.* Hodder & Stoughton. 1st UK ed. dj. . . . .
. . . . *$50.00–$75.00*

Charteris, Leslie. *Trust the Saint.* Lon. Hodder & Stoughton. 1962. 1st ed. red cl, dj.
. . . . *$95.00–$150.00*

Charteris, Leslie. *Vendetta for the Saint.* Lon. Hodder & Stoughton. 1965. 1st UK ed. dj. . . . . *$60.00–$65.00*

Charteris, Leslie. *Vendetta for the Saint.* Lon. Hodder & Stoughton. 1965. 1st UK ed. no dj.. . . . . *$15.00–$30.00*

Charteris, Leslie. *Vendetta for the Saint.* Garden City. Doubleday Crime Club. 1964. 1st ed. dj.. . . . . *$40.00–$90.00*

Charters, Ann. *Kerouac.* (1974). 1st UK ed. wrps, dj. . . . . *$30.00–$50.00*

Chase, A. *Dr. Chase's Recipes.* Ann Arbor. 1866. . . . . *$30.00–$45.00*

Chase, Edward. *Memorial Life of General William Tecumseh Sherman.* Chi. 1891. 1st ed. . . . . *$40.00–$85.00*

Chase, J. Smeaton. *Yosemite Trails. Camp & Pack-train in the Yosemite Region....* Bos. Houghton Mifflin. 1911. 16 plates, map. . . . . *$50.00–$65.00*

Chase, Mary. *Benjamin Lee, 2d: A Record Gathered from Letters, Notebooks, and Narratives of Friends.* Bos. 1920. photos. . . . . *$45.00–$65.00*

Chase, Mary Ellen. *Fishing Fleets of New England.* Bos. 1961. illus. . . . . *$22.00–$35.00*

Chase, Peter S. *Reunion Greeting...Complete Description List of the Members of C1 2nd Regt, Vt Vols.* Brattleboro. 1891. . . . . *$45.00–$80.00*

Chastellux, Francois J. (Marquis de). *Travels in North America in the Years 1780, 1781, and 1782.* Lon. Robinson. 1787. 2 vols. 1st UK ed. 2 fldg maps, 3 plates, new 1/4 bown calf, marbled bds, red labels. *$600.00–$725.00*

Chastellux, Marquis de. *Travels in North America in the Years 1780, 1781, and 1782.* Chapel Hill. Univ N. C. Press. 1963. 2 vols. slipcase. . . . . *$65.00–$85.00*

Chatelain, Verne. *Defenses of Spanish Florida, 1565 to 1763.* DC. Carnegie Institution of Washington. 1941. 1st ed. illus. fldg maps & plates. . *$50.00–$75.00*

Chatham, Russell. *Angler's Coast.* Doubleday. 1976. 1st ed. dj. . . . . *$25.00–$40.00*

Chatterton, E. Keble. *Brotherhood of the Sea.* Lon. Longmans, Green. 1927. 1st ed. illus. endpaper maps. . . . . *$45.00–$60.00*

Chatterton, E. Keble. *Sailing Models Ancient and Modern.* Lon. Hurst B lockett. 1934. 1st ed. . . . . *$75.00–$125.00*

Chatwin, Bruce. *On the Black Hills.* NY. Viking. 1983. 1st ed. dj. . . . . *$30.00–$35.00*

Chavez, Fray Angelico. *Clothed with the Sun.* Santa Fe. Writer's Editons. 1939. 1st ed. sgn, dj. . . . . *$125.00–$150.00*

Chavez, Fray Angelico. *Eleven Lady-Lyrics and Other Poems.* Paterson, NJ. 1945. 1st ed. sgn presentation copy, dj. . . . . *$65.00–$75.00*

Chavez, Fray Angelico. *Song of Frances.* Flagstaff. (1973). 1st ed. illus. sgn, dj. . . . . *$30.00–$40.00*

Chayefsky, Paddy. *Altered States.* NY. Harper. 1978. 1st ed. dj. . . . . *$28.00–$35.00*

Cheever, John. *Bridgadier and the Golf Widow.* NY. Harper & Row. (1964). 1st ed. sgn, dj. . . . . *$95.00–$125.00*

Cheever, John. *Brigadier and the Golf Widow*. NY Harper & Row. (1964). 1st ed. dj. . . . . *$35.00–$80.00*

Cheever, John. *Bullet Park*. NY. Knopf. 1969. 1st ed. sgn, dj. . . . *$85.00–$100.00*

Cheever, John. *Enormous Radio*. NY. Funk & Wagnalls. 1953. 1st ed. "1" on copyright page, dj. . . . . *$75.00–$200.00*

Cheever, John. *Falconer*. NY. Knopf. 1977. 1st ed. sgn, dj. . . . . . *$65.00–$175.00*

Cheever, John. *Leaves, the Lion-Fish & the Bear*. LA. Sylvester & Orphanos. 1980. ltd 300 cc. sgn. . . . . *$90.00–$130.00*

Cheever, John. *Oh What a Paradise It Seems*. NY. Knopf. 1982. 1st ed. dj. . . . . *$20.00–$25.00*

Cheever, John. *The Day the Pig Fell Into the Well*. Northridge, CA. Lord John Press. 1978. 1st ed. ltd 275 numbered cc, sgn. . . . . *$100.00–$150.00*

Cheever, John. *Wapshot Chronicle*. Franklin Center. The Franklin Library. (1978). 1st ed. sgn. . . . . *$45.00–$125.00*

Cheever, John. *Wapshot Chronicle*. Lon. Gollancz. 1957. 1st ed. dj. . . . . *$75.00–$100.00*

Cheever, John. *Way Some People Live*. NY. Random House. (1943). 1st ed. author's first book. . . . . *$850.00–$925.00*

Cheever, John. *World of Apples*. NY. Knopf. 1973. 1st ed. dj. . . . . *$25.00–$35.00*

Chekov, Anton. *Cherry Orchard*. Brentanos. 1923. black red and beige cvr. . . . . *$75.00–$95.00*

Chekov, Anton. *Two Plays: The Cherry Orchard, Three Sisters*. NY. Ltd Ed Club. 1966. illus. ltd 1500 cc, sgn by Szalay, slipcase. . . . . *$40.00–$50.00*

Chekov, Anton. *Uncle Vanya*. NY. Covici Friede. 1930. 1st ed. . . . . *$75.00–$100.00*

Chennault, Anna. *Chennault and The Flying Tigers*. NY. Paul S. Erikson. 1963. photos, maps. . . . . *$25.00–$35.00*

Chennault, Claire. *Way of a Fighter: Memoirs of Claire Lee Chennault*. NY. Putnam. 1949. photos. . . . . *$30.00–$40.00*

Chenu, Charles Maurice. *My Canoe*. Lon. Partridge. 1931. 1st ed. sgn. . . . . *$80.00–$160.00*

Chenu, J. C. *Manuel Conchyliogie et de Paleontologie Conchyliogique*. Paris. 1859-62. 1 vol. illus. 1/2 mor. . . . . *$150.00–$210.00*

Chesteron, G. K. *Five Types*. Lon. Arthur L. Humphries. 1910. wrps. . *$30.00–$40.00*

Chesterton, G. K. *The Man Who Knew Too Much.* Lon. Cassell & Co. 1922. . . . .
. . . . *$25.00–$50.00*

Chicago School of Architecture. NY. Random House. 1964. dj. . . . *$25.00–$45.00*

Chichester, Francis. *Lonely Sea and the Sky.* Lon. Hodder & Stoughton. 1967. illus.
352 pp, dj. . . . . *$25.00–$35.00*

Chief Standing Bear. *My People, the Sioux.* Bos. Houghton Mifflin. 1928. 2nd prtg,
dj. . . . . *$35.00–$40.00*

Child, Hamilton. *Gazeteer and Business Directory of Sullivan County, NY.* Syracuse.
1872. illus. fldg map. . . . . *$75.00–$115.00*

Child, Hamilton. *Gazeteer and Business Directory of Bennington County, VT for
1880-1881.* Syracuse. 1880. fldg map, cl. . . . . *$100.00–$125.00*

Child, Hamilton. *Gazeteer and Business Directory of Cattaraugus County, NY for
1874-1875.* Syracuse. 1874. 1st ed. . . . . *$60.00–$75.00*

Child, Hamilton. *Gazeteer and Business Directory of Crawford County, PA for 1874.*
Syracuse. 1874. rbnd. . . . . *$110.00–$125.00*

Child, Hamilton. *Gazeteer and Business Directory of Lamoille and Orleans
Counties, Vt..* Syracuse. 1883. cvr off. . . . . *$25.00–$35.00*

Child, Hamilton. *Gazeteer and Business Directory of Wyoming County, NY.*
Syracuse. 1870. illus. original cvrs, fldg map. . . . . *$100.00–$135.00*

Child, Hamilton. *Gazette, Orange County, Vermont -1762-1888.* June, 1888. . . . . .
. . . . *$50.00–$125.00*

Child, Hamilton. *Gazetteer and Bus. Directory of Rensselaer County, NY, 1870-71..*
. . . . *$120.00–$150.00*

Child, Hamilton. *Gazetteer and Business Directory of Alleghany County, NY for
1875.* Syracuse. Journal Office. 1875. fldg map. . . . . *$50.00–$60.00*

Child, Hamilton. *Gazetteer and Business Directory of Orange County, VT 1762-
1888.* Syracuse. 1888. illus. spine replaced. . . . . *$75.00–$85.00*

Child, Hamilton. *Gazetteer and Business Directory of Windham County, VT.*
Syracuse. 1884. illus. 624 pp. . . . . *$75.00–$125.00*

Child, L. Maria. *American Frugal Housewife.* NY. Samuel & William Wood. 1836.
20th ed. bds. . . . . *$185.00–$200.00*

Child, L. Maria. *Letters from New York.* NY/Bos. Francis. 1843. 1st ed. 288 pp, ltd
1500 cc. . . . . *$75.00–$125.00*

Child, L. Maria. *New Flowers for Children.* NY. Francis & Co. 1856. 1st ed. cl. . .
. . . . *$200.00–$300.00*

Child, L. Maria. *Freedman's Book.* Bos. 1865. 1st ed. green stamped cl. . . . .
. . . . *$250.00–$350.00*

Child, Mrs. *American Frugal Housewife.* NY. Wood. 1847. . . . . . . *$45.00–$60.00*

Child, Mrs. Lydia M. *An Appeal in Favor of That Class of Americans Called Africans.* NY. John S. Taylor. 1836. . . . . *$90.00–$115.00*

Child, William. *A History of the Fifth Regiment, New Hampshire....* Bristol. R. W. Musgrove, Printer. 1893. . . . . *$125.00–$200.00*

Children and Animals. Racinem, WI. Whitman Pub. (1935). 1st ed. illus. oblong pict wrps desgn by Lotte Schmeil School of Emmy Zweybruck Vienna - art deco. . . . .
. . . . *$45.00–$125.00*

Children of God: An American Epic. NY. 1939. 1st ed. map endsheets, dj. . . . . .
. . . . *$45.00–$50.00*

Children's Picture Book of Birds. NY. Harper. 1861. 1st ed. illus. engr, blue pebbled cl. . . . . *$65.00–$85.00*

Childress, Alice. *A Hero Ain't Nothin' But a Sandwich.* NY. Coward McCann & Geoghegan. 1973. sgn. . . . . *$45.00–$50.00*

Childress, Alice. *Like One of the Family.* Brooklyn. Independence Pub. (1956). 1st ed. dj. . . . . *$75.00–$100.00*

Childs, Harold. *Child's Book of Abridged Wisdom.* SF. Paul Elder. (1905). illus. pict bds, exposed spine. . . . . *$75.00–$150.00*

Chilton Automotive Directory. Oct, 1918. clr ads, 770 pp. . . . . *$45.00–$65.00*

Chiniquy, Father (Charles). *Priest, a Woman, and the Confessional.* Chi. Craig. 1888. 296 pp. . . . . *$22.00–$35.00*

Chipman, N P. *Tragedy of Andersonville, Trial of Captain Henry Wirz....* Sacramento. 1911. 2nd ed. . . . . *$50.00–$65.00*

Chittenden, Hiram. *Yellowstone National Park.* Stanford. 1933. rev. *$60.00–$70.00*

Chittenden, Hiram M. *American Fur Trade of the Far West.* NY. Harper. 1902. 3 vols. map plates. . . . . *$575.00–$900.00*

Chittenden, Hiram M. *History of Early Steamboat Navigation on the Missouri River....* NY. 1903. 2 vols. ltd 950 cc. . . . . *$350.00–$500.00*

Chittenden, Hiram M. *History of the American Fur Trade of the Far West.* Stanford. CA Academic Reprints. (1954). 2 vols. rprnt, maps, dj. . . . . *$75.00–$125.00*

Chittenden, Hiram M. & A. T Richardson. *Life, Letters and Travels of Father Pierre-Jean De Smet.* NY. Francis Harper. 1905. 4 vols. . . . . *$400.00–$850.00*

Cholmondeley-Pennel, H., et al. *Fishing.* Lon. Longmans Green. 1895 &1896. 2. illus. blue mor, teg. . . . . *$125.00–$200.00*

Cholmondeley-Pennell, H. *The Sporting Fish of Great Britain, with Notes in Ichthyology.* Lon. Sampson, Low. 1886. 1st ed. illus. ltd 150 cc. 16 chromolith plates. . . . . *$400.00–$600.00*

Cholmondeley-Pennell, H. (ed.). *Fishing Gossip, or Stray Leaves from the Note-Books of Several Anglers.* Edin. Adam & Charles Black. 1866. 1st ed. illus. steel-engr plates, 3/4 mor and cl, raised bands, marbled endpapers. . . . . *$55.00–$150.00*

Cholmondeley-Pennell, H. (ed.). *The Modern Practical Angler.* Lon. Frederick Warne. 1870. 1st ed. illus. plates, engr, 3/4 mor & cl, marbled endpapers, teg. . . . . *$85.00–$150.00*

Chopin, Kate. *Bayou Folk.* Bos. Houghton, Mifflin. 1894. 1st ed. scarce. . . . . *$300.00–$950.00*

Chopin, Kate. *The Awakening.* Chi/NY. Herbert S. Stone. 1899. ex lib, scarce. . . . . *$500.00–$1,000.00*

Chopin, Kate. *The Awakening.* Chi. Herbert S. Stone. 1899. 1st ed. decorated cl, scarce. . . . . *$700.00–$1,500.00*

Christie, Agatha. *Absent in the Spring.* Lon. Collins. 1944. 1st UK ed. dj. . . . . *$150.00–$250.00*

Christie, Agatha. *Adventures of the Christmas Pudding.* Lon. Collins Crime Club. 1960. dj. . . . . *$25.00–$35.00*

Christie, Agatha. *And Then There Were None.* NY. Grosset & Dunlap. Photoplay ed. dj. . . . . *$50.00–$75.00*

Christie, Agatha. *At Bertram's Hotel.* Lon. 1965. 1st ed. dj. . . . . *$35.00–$55.00*

Christie, Agatha. *At Bertram's Hotel.* NY. Dodd, Mead. 1966. 1st Us ed. dj. . . . . *$20.00–$30.00*

Christie, Agatha. *Big Four.* NY. 1927. 1st Amer ed. dj. . . . . *$100.00–$125.00*

Christie, Agatha. *By the Pricking of My Thumbs.* NY. Dodd, Mead & Co. 1968. 1st ed. dj. . . . . *$25.00–$35.00*

Christie, Agatha. *Cards on the Table.* Lon. 1936. 1st ed. . . . . . . *$200.00–$300.00*

Christie, Agatha. *Cards on the Table.* NY. Dodd, Mead. 1937. 1st Amer ed. dj. . . . . *$300.00–$375.00*

Christie, Agatha. *Caribbean Mystery.* NY. Dodd, Mead. 1965. 1st Amer ed. dj. . . . . *$20.00–$35.00*

Christie, Agatha. *Cat Among the Pigeons.* Lon. Collins. (1959). 1st ed. dj. . . . . .
. . . . *$20.00–$50.00*

Christie, Agatha. *Come, Tell Me How You Live.* Lon. Collins. 1946. 1st UK ed. red
cl, dj. . . . . *$40.00–$95.00*

Christie, Agatha. *Dead Man's Folly.* Lon. Collins Crime club. 1956. 1st ed. dj. . .
. . . . *$10.00–$30.00*

Christie, Agatha. *Death Comes As the End.* Lon. Collins. 1945. 1st ed. dj. . . . . . .
. . . . *$125.00–$175.00*

Christie, Agatha. *Easy to Kill.* NY. Dodd, Mead. 1939. 1st ed. dj. *$250.00*

Christie, Agatha. *Mirror Crack'd From Side to Side.* Lon. Collins Crime Club.
(1962). 1st ed. fine, dj. . . . . *$75.00–$125.00*

Christie, Agatha. *Miss Marple's Final Cases.* Lon. Collins. 1979. 1st ed. dj. . . . .
. . . . *$35.00–$45.00*

Christie, Agatha. *Murder in Mesopotamia.* Lon. 1936. 1st ed. . . *$100.00–$400.00*

Christie, Agatha. *Pale Horse.* NY. 1962. 1st ed. 1st US ed. dj. . . . *$20.00–$30.00*

Christie, Agatha. *Partners In Crime.* NY. Dodd, Mead. 1929. 1st ed. dj. . . . .
. . . . *$60.00–$85.00*

Christie, Agatha. *Sleeping Murder.* NY. Dodd, Mead. 1976. 1st US ed. dj. . . . . .
. . . . *$15.00–$25.00*

Christie, Agatha. *Sleeping Murder.* NY. Dodd, Mead. 1976. 1st ed. dj. . . . .
. . . . *$10.00–$15.00*

Christie, Agatha. *They Do It With Mirrors.* Lon. Collins Crime Club. 1952. 1st ed.
dj. . . . . *$75.00–$100.00*

Christie, Agatha. *Thirteen at Dinner.* NY. Dodd, Mead. 1933. 1st ed. dj. . . . .
. . . . *$350.00–$375.00*

Christie, Agatha. *Towards Zero.* Lon. Collins Crime Club. (1944). 1st ed. fine,
scarce, dj. . . . . *$350.00–$400.00*

Christmas Carols. Akron. (1937). illus. by Fern Bisel Peat. scarce dj. . . . .
. . . . *$95.00–$125.00*

Christmas on Stage. NY. Polygraphic Company of America. 1950. 5 pop-ups, spiral
bound. . . . . *$35.00–$55.00*

Christy, Howard Chandler. *Christy Girl.* Ind. Bobbs Merrill. (1906). illus. decorative binding, clr plates. . . . . *$50.00–$85.00*

Church, James R. *University Football.* NY. 1893. illus. . . . . *$150.00–$175.00*

Churchill, Frank G. *Practical and Scientific Horseshoeing*. Missouri. Franklin Hudson. 1912. 1st ed. . . . . *$85.00–$100.00*

Churchill, Winston. *Great Contemporaries*. NY. 1937. 1st US ed. . . . .
. . . . *$50.00–$85.00*

Churchill, Winston. *History of the English-Speaking Peoples*. Lon. Cassell. 1956–58. 4 vols. 1st ed. dj. . . . . *$175.00–$200.00*

Churchill, Winston. *Liberalism & the Social Problems*. Lon. 1909. 1st UK ed. . .
. . . . *$400.00–$800.00*

Churchill, Winston. *Second World War*. Lon. 1948–54. 6 vols.. 1st ed. djs. . . . . .
. . . . *$125.00–$275.00*

Churchill, Winston. *While England Slept*. NY. 1938. 1st Amer ed. dj. . . . .
. . . . *$60.00–$75.00*

Churchill, Winston. *World Crisis*. NY. 1931. 1. illus. 1st Amer ed. charts, maps and text illus.. . . . . *$70.00–$125.00*

Churchill, Winston S. *Sinews of Peace*. Lon. Cassell. 1948. 1st ed. dj. . . . .
. . . . *$75.00–$125.00*

Churchill, Winston Spencer. *Ian Hamilton's March*. Lon/NY/Bombay. Longman's Green 1900. 1st ed. illus. red mor, maps & photos. . . . . *$400.00–$600.00*

Chute, Carolyn. *Beans of Egypt Maine*. Lon. (1985). 1st UK ed. dj . . . .
. . . . *$45.00–$80.00*

Cist, Charles. *Cincinnati in 1841....* Cin. private printing. 1841. illus. 8 plates, brown cl. . . . . *$80.00–$120.00*

Clarke, Asia Booth. *Unlocked Book....* NY. Putnam's. 1938. illus. dj . . . .
. . . . *$35.00–$50.00*

Clancy, P. A. *Birds of Natal and Zululand*. Edin. 1964. illus. . . . . *$85.00–$135.00*

Clancy, P. A. *Gamebirds of Southern Africa*. NY. 1967. illus. . . . . *$55.00–$110.00*

Clancy, Tom. *Hunt for Red October*. Annapolis: Naval Institute Press. (1984). 1st ed. author's first book, dj. . . . . *$350.00–$700.00*

Clancy, Tom. *Red Storm Rising*. Putnam. (1986). 1st ed. dj. . . . . . . *$30.00–$50.00*

Clapham, R.. *Foxhounds and Fox Hunting*. Lon. (1922). . . . . *$40.00–$60.00*

Clark, A. *Lectures on Diseases of the Heart*. Birmingham Medical Library. 1884. 1st ed. . . . . *$25.00–$50.00*

Clark, Dick. *Murder on Tour: A Rock 'n' Roll Mystery*. NY. Mysterious Press. 1989. 1st ed. with Paul Francis (sgn by Francis). *$20.00–$35.00*

Clark, Emmons. *History of the Seventh Regiment of New York.* NY. 1890. 2 vols.. 1st ed. . . . . *$125.00–$300.00*

Clark, James. *Shoeing and Balancing the Light Harness Horse.* Buffalo. The Horse World Company. 1916. 1st ed. . . . . *$125.00–$150.00*

Clark, Mary Higgins. *Cradle Will Fall.* NY. Simon & Schuster. 1980. 1st ed. dj. . . . . *$35.00–$60.00*

Clark, Mary Higgins. *Cry in the Night.* NY. Simon & Schuster. 1982. 1st ed. dj. . . . . *$25.00–$30.00*

Clark, W. P. *Indian Sign Language.* Phila. 1885. 443 pp, map. . . . . *$100.00–$150.00*

Clark, Walter Van Tilburg. *Track of the Cat.* NY. (1949). 1st ed. dj. . . . . *$75.00–$100.00*

Clarke, Arthur. *Exploration of the Moon.* Lon. Frederick Muller. (1954). 1st ed. black cl.. . . . . *$25.00–$70.00*

Clarke, Arthur C. *2001: A Space Odyssey.* NY. New American Library. 1968. 1st ed. scarce, dj. . . . . *$300.00–$500.00*

Clarke, Arthur C. *2001: A Space Odyssey.* Lon. 1968. 1st UK ed. dj. . . . . *$95.00–$115.00*

Clarke, Arthur C. *2061: Odyssey Three.* NY. Del Rey. 1987. 1st Us ed. dj. . . . . *$25.00–$30.00*

Clarke, Arthur C. *Childhood's End.* NY. (1953). 1st ed. pict wrps, sgn. . . . . *$50.00–$75.00*

Clarke, Arthur C. *Expedition to Earth.* Ballantine. (1953). 1st ed. printed wrps. . . . . *$30.00–$40.00*

Clarke, Arthur C. *Sands of Mars.* NY. Gnome Press. (1952). 1st Us ed. dj. . . . . *$90.00–$125.00*

Clarke, H. T. *Chemistry of Penicillin.* Princeton Univ 1949. 1st ed. *75.00–$125.00*

Clarke, John Henry. *Dictionary of Practical Materia Medica.* Sussex. 1962. 3 vols. . . . . *$100.00–$125.00*

Clarke, Lewis. *Narr. of the Sufferings of Lewis and Milton Clarke....* Bos. 1846. wrps. . . . . *$60.00–$100.00*

Clarke, T. Wood. *Bloody Mohawk.* NY. Macmillan. 1940. 1st ed. dj. . *$40.00–$65.00*

Clay, John. *My Life on the Range.* NY. Antiquarian Press. 1961. rprnt. . . . . *$45.00–$75.00*

Clay, R. S. & T. H. Court. *History of the Microscope.* Lon. 1975. rprnt, dj. . . . . .
. . . . *$60.00–$70.00*

Clay, R. S. and T. H. Court. *History of the Microscope.* Lon. 1932. . . . .
. . . . *$150.00–$200.00*

Clayton, Victoria V. *White and Black Under the Old Regime.* Milw. (1899). 1st ed.
. . . . *$125.00–$150.00*

Cleater, P. E. *Rockets Through Space.* NY. 1936. illus. 1st Amer ed. . . . .
. . . . *$100.00–$150.00*

Cleaver, Eldridge. *Eldridge Cleaver: Post Prison Writings and Speeches.* NY.
(1969). 1st ed. dj. . . . . *$25.00–$35.00*

Cleaver, Eldridge. *Idi and the Sultan.* Stanford. C. P. Times Press. 1984. 1st ed. wrps.
. . . . *$50.00–$65.00*

Cleaver, Eldridge. *Soul on Ice.* NY. McGraw-Hill. 1968. 1st ed. dj. *$75.00–$105.00*

Clemens, Samuel. *Dog's Tale.* NY/Lon. Harper & Bros. 1904. 1st ed. . . . .
. . . . *$75.00–$150.00*

Clemens, Samuel. *Following the Equator.* Hartford. Amer Pub Co. 1897. 1st ed.
illus. frontis photo. . . . . *$175.00–$225.00*

Clemens, Samuel. *Life On the Mississippi.* Bos. Osgood. 1883. 1st ed. illus. . . . .
. . . . *$125.00–$300.00*

Clement, Arthur W. *Our Pioneer Potters.* NY. Maple Press. 1947. illus. ltd 500 cc,
slipcase. . . . . *$45.00–$100.00*

Clerk, Dugald. *Gas Engine.* Lon. 1887. . . . . *$35.00–$60.00*

Cleveland, Grover. *Fishing & Shooting.* NY. Outing Pub. 1906. 1st ed. . . . .
. . . . *$45.00–$60.00*

Cliffe, John Henry. *Notes and Recollections of an Angler.* Lon. Hamilton, Adams.
1860. 1st ed. brown mor, marbled bds, teg. . . . . *$95.00–$125.00*

Clifford, F. *Romance of Perfume Lands.* Bos. 1881. . . . . *$32.00–$45.00*

Clift, Virgil A. (ed.). *Negro Education in America, Its Adequacy, Problems and
Needs.* NY. 1962. 1st ed. . . . . *$28.00–$37.00*

Clougher, T. R. (ed.). *Golf Clubs of the Empire: the Golfing Annual.* Lon. 1931. 5th
issue. . . . . *$45.00–$50.00*

Coan, T. *Life in Hawaii, an Autobiographic Sketch.* NY. 1882. . . . . . *$30.00–$50.00*

Coates, Robert. *Outlaw Years.* NY. 1930. 1st ed. . . . . *$20.00–$30.00*

Coatsworth, Elizabeth. *Cricket and the Emperor's Son*. NY. Macmillan. 1932. 1st ed. illus. by Weda Yap, dj. . . . . *$35.00–$40.00*

Coatsworth, Elizabeth. *Golden Horshoe*. NY. 1935. 1st ed. illus. by Lawson. . . . . *$35.00–$50.00*

Cobb, Sanford H. *Story of the Palatines*. NY. Putnam. 1897. brown cl. . . . . *$25.00–$65.00*

Cobb, Sanford H. *The Story of the Palatines, an Episode in Colonial History*. NY. Putnam. 1897. . . . . *$25.00–$40.00*

Cobb, Ty. *My Life in Baseball*. NY. 1961. 1st ed. dj. . . . . *$30.00–$40.00*

Cobb, W. Mantague. *First Negro Medical Society...Dist. of Columbia, 1884-1939*. DC. Associated Publishers. 1939. . . . . *$35.00–$45.00*

Cobbett, William. *Cottage Economy*. NY. Gould & Son. 1824. 1st Amer ed. . . . . *$65.00–$100.00*

Cobbett, William. *Letters on The Late War*. NY. J. Belden. 1815. 1st ed. bds. . . . . *$40.00–$60.00*

Coblentz, Stanton A. *Into Plutonian Depths*. NY. (1950). 1st ed. pict wrps. . . . . *$50.00–$65.00*

Coblentz, Stanton A. *Villains and Vigilantes*. NY. 1936. 1st ed. dj. . . . . *$35.00–$65.00*

Coburn, Silas. *Across the Ferry*. Mass. 1886. illus. brown cl, frontis. . . . . *$30.00–$60.00*

Cochin, Augustin. *Results of Slavery*. Bos. Walker, Wise & Co. 1863. 1st ed. . . . . *$40.00–$85.00*

Cochran, D. M. *Frogs of Southeastern Brazil*. DC. 1955. illus. . . . *$25.00–$45.00*

Cochran, D. M & C. J. Goin. *Frogs of Columbia*. DC. 1970. illus. . . . . *$30.00–$45.00*

Cochran, Doris M. *Poisonous Reptiles of the World*. DC. 1943. wrps. *$40.00–$50.00*

Cock, the Mouse, and the Little Red Hen. Akron. Saalfield. (1931). 1st ed. illus. by Fern Bissel Peat.. . . . . *$95.00–$125.00*

Cody, William. *Adventures of Buffalo Bill*. Harper Bros. 1904. 1st ed. red cl. . . . . *$20.00–$30.00*

Cody, William. *Buffalo Bill's Life Story*. NY. 1920. . . . . *$25.00–$40.00*

Cody, William F. *Story of the Wild West & Camp Fire Chats by Buffalo Bill*. Phila. 1889. illus. . . . . *$35.00–$60.00*

Cody, William F. *True Tales of the Plains*. NY. Empire. 1908. . . . *$30.00–$100.00*

Coello De Portugal y Queseda, Francisco. *Isla de Cuba Medias Hojas Estremas Oriental y Occidental*. Madrid. 1851. large folio, map. . . . . *$350.00–$400.00*

Coffin, Albert Isaiah. *Treatise on Midwifery*. Manchester. Medico-Botanic Press. 1849. 184 pp. . . . . *$100.00–$165.00*

Coffin, Charles C. *Boys of 1861*. Bos. 1885. . . . . *$30.00–$65.00*

Coffin, Charles C. *Life of Abraham Lincoln*. NY. 1893. . . . . *$40.00–$50.00*

Coffin, Joshua. *Sketch of the History of Newbury, Newburyport, and West Newbury*. Bos. Sanuel Drake. 1845. . . . . *$40.00–$60.00*

Cohen, Octavus Roy. *Bigger and Blacker*. Bos. Little, Brown. 1925. 1st ed. sgn. . . . . *$50.00–$85.00*

Cohen, Octavus Roy. *Transient Lady*. NY. Appleton-Century. 1934. 1st ed. dj. . . . . *$40.00–$75.00*

Cohn, Albert M. *George Cruikshank: A Catalogue....* Lon. 1924. ltd 500 cc, brown cl, mounted facs, erratum. . . . . *$200.00–$270.00*

Coigney, Rodolphe L. *Isaak Walton: A New Bibliography, 1653–1987*. NY. 1989. ltd 540 cc, sgn. . . . . *$80.00–$100.00*

Colbert, E. *Chicago and the Great Conflagration*. Cinc. Vent. 1872. 1st ed. illus. maps. . . . . *$28.00–$45.00*

Colcord, Joanna C. *Songs of American Sailormen*. NY. Norton. 1938. illus. . . . . *$35.00–$60.00*

Cole, George E. *Early Oregon Jottings... of a Pioneer, 1850*. np. (1905). 1st ed. . . . . *$50.00–$60.00*

Cole, Ralph. *The Young Angler's Pocket Companion*. Lon. R. Bassam. 1795. 1st ed. marbled bds backed with sheep. . . . . *$500.00–$800.00*

Cole, S. W. *American Fruit Book....* Bos. 1849. 1st ed. . . . . *$40.00–$50.00*

Coleman, Elizabeth. *Dolls Makers and Marks vol 1*. WA. Hobby House Press. 1966. illus. rev 2nd ed. . . . . *$15.00–$20.00*

Colenso, John W. *Ten Weeks in Natal*. Camb. Macmillan. 1855. fldg map, plates, original cl, rbkd. . . . . *$165.00–$225.00*

Colenso, John W. *Ten Weeks in Natal*. Camb. Macmillan. 1855. fldg map, plates. . . . . *$275.00–$325.00*

Coleridge, S. T. *Friend: A Series of Essays*. Burlington. Chauncey Goodridge. 1831. 1st Amer ed 1 vol. . . . . *$85.00–$150.00*

Colleen Moore's Doll House The Story of the Most Exquisite Toy in the World.
Garden City. 1935. illus. pamphlet. . . . . *$15.00–$25.00*

Collier's Photographic History of the European War. NY. Collier. (1916). oblong
folio, 144 pp, photos. . . . . *$30.00–$40.00*

Collingwood, R. G. *Speculum Mentis for the Map of Knowledge.* Oxford.
Clarendon. (1924). dj. . . . . *$20.00–$30.00*

Collins, A. Frederick. *Experimental Television.* 1932. 1st ed. illus. dj. . . . .
. . . . *$95.00–$175.00*

Collins, Hubert E. *Warpath and Cattle Trail.* NY. William Morrow. 1928. 1st ed.
. . . . *$65.00–$95.00*

Collins, John S. *Across the Plains in '64.* Omaha. Nat'l Printing Co. 1904. 1st ed.
. . . . *$50.00–$100.00*

Collins, Wilkie. *No Name.* NY. Harper& Bros. 1863. 1st ed. illus. purple cl. . . . .
. . . . *$100.00–$200.00*

Collins, Wilkie. *Armadale.* NY. Harper& Bros. 1866. lst Amer ed. . . . .
. . . . *$100.00–$300.00*

Collins, Wilkie. *Man and Wife.* NY. Harper & Bros. 1870. 1st Amer ed. illus. lavender pebbled cl. . . . . *$95.00–$125.00*

Collins, Wilkie. *The Moonstone.* NY. Harper & Bros. 1868. illus. 1st Amer ed. . .
. . . . *$100.00–$225.00*

Collis, Septima M. *Woman's Trip to Alaska.* NY. Cassell. (1890). 1st ed. teg. . . . . .
. . . . *$75.00–$125.00*

Collodi, Carlo. *Pinnochio.* Phila. (1920). illus. by Maria Kirk. deluxe ed. 14 mounted
clr plates, pict endpapers, scarce in box. . . . . *$85.00–$100.00*

Collodi, Carlo. *Pinnochio.* NY. A. L. Burt. 1930. illus. . . . . *$20.00–$25.00*

Collodi, Carlo. *Pinocchio.* Phila. Winston. nd. illus. by Richardson. pict label on cvr.
. . . . *$20.00–$35.00*

Collodi, D. *Pinocchio.* Akron. (1924). illus. by Frances Brundage, pict cvr paste-on.
. . . . *$25.00–$35.00*

Colorado. NY. Hastings House. 1941. tan cl. . . . . *$20.00–$30.00*

Colquhoun, John. *Rocks and Rivers.* Lon. John Murray. 1849. 1st ed. green cl. . .
. . . . *$100.00–$150.00*

Colquhoun, John. *The Moor and the Lock.* Lon. John Murray. 1841. 2nd ed. illus.
plates, cl. . . . . *$125.00–$150.00*

Colt, Mrs. S. S. *Tourist Guide Through the Empire State.. ..* Albany. 1871. 1st ed.. . . . . *$50.00–$60.00*

Colton, Calvin. *Lecture on the Railroad to the Pacific.* NY. 1850. . *$35.00–$45.00*

Colton, Harold S. *Hopi Kachina Dolls with a Key to the Identification.* Albuquerque. Univ of New Mexico Press. 1949. 1st ed. dj. . . . . *$50.00–$80.00*

Colton, J. Ferrell. *Last of the Square-Rigged Ships.* NY. Putnam. 1937. 1st ed. illus. dj. . . . . *$80.00–$100.00*

Colton, J. H. *Colton's United States Showing the Military Stations....* NY. Putnam. 1862. . . . . *$95.00–$120.00*

Colton, J. H. *Map of South Carolina.* NY. 1856. in clr. . . . . *$75.00–$115.00*

Colton, J. H. *Traveler and Tourist's Guide Book Through the United States and the Canadas.* NY. 1850. 2 maps. . . . . *$100.00–$250.00*

Colton, Walter. *Deck and Port.* NY. Barnes. 1854. . . . . *$75.00–$155.00*

Colton, Walter. *Three Years in California.* NY. 1850. 1st ed. . . . . *$95.00–$150.00*

Colum, Padraic. *Creatures.* NY. 1927. 1st ed. illus. by Artzybashoff. . . . . *$30.00–$50.00*

Colum, Padraic. *Frenzied Prince.* Phila. (1943). 1st ed. illus. by Pogany in clr and b/w. decorated endpapers, dj. . . . . *$75.00–$100.00*

Colum, Padraic. *Girl Who Sat by the Ashes.* NY. 1919. 1st ed. illus. by Dugald Walker. . . . . *$40.00–$50.00*

Colum, Padraic, (ed.). *Arabian Nights.* NY. Macmillan. 1923. illus. *$25.00–$30.00*

Combat Digest: 33rd Fighter Group. np. nd. 48 pp, photos, scarce. *$125.00–$195.00*

Combat History of 2nd Infantry Division. Baton Rouge. 1946. . . . *$55.00–$65.00*

Combe, Andrew. *Principles of Physiology Applied to Preservation of Health.* Edin. 1835. 3rd ed. . . . . *$25.00–$40.00*

Comly, John. *New Spelling Book.* Phila. Solomon W. Conrad. 1818. bds. . . . . *$25.00–$45.00*

Comstock, J. L. *An Introduction to the Study of Botany.* NY. Robinson Pratt & Co. 1843. full lea. . . . . *$30.00–$40.00*

Comstock, J. L. *Elements of Chemistry.* NY. Pratt Woodford & Co. 1853. revised ed. lea. . . . . *$24.00–$35.00*

Comstock, John H. *Spider Book.* Garden City. Doubleday. 1913. . . . . *$50.00–$65.00*

Conder, Claude Reignier. *Syrian Stone-Lore.* Lon. Palestine Exploration Fund. 1896. illus. fldg maps. .... *$30.00–$45.00*

Condon, E. U. & G. H. Shortly. *Theory of Atomic Spectra.* Cambridge Univ Press. 1935. 1st ed. .... *$45.00–$65.00*

Condon, R. *Manchurian Candidate.* NY. McGraw-Hill. 1959. 1st ed. dj. .... *$75.00–$110.00*

Cone, Mary. *Two Years in California.* Chi. Griggs. 1876. 1st ed. illus. 238 pp. .... *$95.00–$125.00*

Conklin, E. *Picturesque Arizona.* NY Mining Record Printing Establishment 1878. .... *$250.00–$300.00*

Conn, Granville. *History of the New Hampshire Surgeons in the War of Rebellion.* Concord. New Hampshire Assn of Military Surgeons. 1906. 1st ed. 558 pp....... .... *$100.00–$150.00*

Connelley, William. *Wild Bill and His Era. The Life and Adventures of James Hickok.* NY. Press of the Pioneers. 1933. .... *$125.00–$225.00*

Connelley, William E. *Quantrill and the Border Wars.* Iowa. Torch Press. 1910. 1st ed. illus. maps. .... *$125.00–$250.00*

Connett, E. *Wildfowling in the Mississippi Flyway.* NY. Van Nostrand. 1949. 1st ed. illus. .... *$125.00–$195.00*

Connett, Eugene V. *My Friend the Trout.* NY. Van Nostrand. (1961). 1st ed. dj. .. .. *$50.00–$70.00*

Conrad, Howard. *Uncle Dick Wootton and the Pioneer Frontiersman.* (Time-Life Books 1980). rprnt of the 1890 ed. .... *$20.00–$35.00*

Conrad, Howard. *Uncle Dick Wootton, the Pioneer Frontiersman of the Rocky Mountain Region.* Chi. 1890. 1st ed. .... *$200.00–$300.00*

Conrad, Joseph. *Conrad Argosy.* NY. Doubleday Doran. 1942. illus. woodcuts, dj. .... *$35.00–$50.00*

Conrad, Joseph. *Lord Jim.* Edin/Lon. William Blackwood. 1900. 1st ed. scarce. . ... *$600.00–$1,000.00*

Conrad, Joseph. *Lord Jim.* Tor. Gage. 1909. 1st Candadian ed. . *$150.00–$225.00*

Conrad, Joseph. *Nigger of the Narcissus.* Lon. Heinemann. 1898. 1st ed. .... *$200.00–$450.00*

Conrad, Joseph. *Nigger of the Narcissus: A Tale of the Forecastle.* Garden City. Doubleday, Page. 1914. gray cl. .... *$200.00–$500.00*

Conrad, Joseph. *Tales of Hearsay.* NY. (1925). 1st Amer ed. dj. .. *$50.00–$70.00*

Conrad, Joseph. *Tales of Unrest*. NY. Scribner's. 1898. 1st ed. . *$125.00–$450.00*

Conrad, Joseph. *The Rover*. Doubleday. 1923. 1st ed. dj. . . . . . *$125.00–$150.00*

Conrad, Joseph. *The Rover*. Garden City. Doubleday, Page. 1923. 1st ed. ltd 377, sgn, tissue guard, dj, original box. . . . . *$500.00–$875.00*

Conrad, Joseph. *The Sisters*. NY. 1928. marbled bds ltd 926 cc. . *$75.00–$100.00*

Conrad, Joseph. *Typhoon and Other Stories*. Lon. Heinemann. 1903. 1st ed. . . . . *$250.00–$500.00*

Conrad, Joseph. *Youth: A Narrative*. Edin & Lon. Blackwood. 1902. 1st ed. cl. . . . . *$300.00–$850.00*

Conroy, Frank. *Stop-time*. NY. Viking. (1967). 1st ed. author's first book, dj. . . . . *$45.00–$100.00*

Conroy, Jack. *The Disinherited*. Lon. (1934). 1st UK ed. rust cl. *$150.00–$200.00*

Conroy, Jack. *Worker - Writer In America*. Chi. (1944). blue cl, dj. *$20.00–$25.00*

Conroy, Jack. *World to Win*. Covici Friede. 1935. 1st Amer ed. dj. *$20.00–$35.00*

Conroy, Jack. *Writers in Revolt: the Anvil Anthology*. NY. Lawrence Hill. (1973). 1st ed. dj. . . . . *$25.00–$35.00*

Conroy, Pat. *Beach Music*. NY. Doubleday. 1995. 1st ed. sgn, dj. . *$40.00–$50.00*

Conroy, Pat. *Great Santini*. Bos. Houghton Mifflin. 1976. 1st ed. sgn, dj. . . . . *$150.00–$200.00*

Conroy, Pat. *Lords of Discipline*. Bos. Houghton Mifflin. 1980. 1st ed. sgn, dj. . . . . *$100.00–$225.00*

Conroy, Pat. *Prince of Tides*. Bos. Houghton Mifflin. 1986. 1st ed. dj. . . . . *$35.00–$45.00*

Constitution of the State of Deseret . . . Adopted March 2, 1872. Salt Lake. 1872. wrps. 21pp, scarce. . . . . *$75.00–$120.00*

Contributions to Medical and Biological Research. NY. 1919. 2 vols. illus. ltd 1600 cc. . . . . *$75.00–$125.00*

Conway, W Martin. *The Alps*. Lon. Adam & Charles Black. 1904. 1st ed. illus. by A D McCormick, 70 clr plates, pict blue cl, teg. . . . . *$90.00–$110.00*

Cook, C. *Observations of Fox Hunting and Management of Hounds*. Lon. William Nicol. 1826. . . . . *$175.00–$250.00*

Cook, C. H. *Among the Pimas*. Albany. 1893. . . . . *$50.00–$100.00*

Cook, Capt. James. *Captain Cook's Australia*. 1969. dj. . . . . *$10.00–$25.00*

Cook, Capt. James. *The Life of Captain James Cook.* Stanford University Press. (1974). 44 plates, 5 maps. . . . . *$145.00–$200.00*

Cook, Capt. James. *Voyages Around theWorld.* Lon. Robins. 1822. frontis, engr. . . . . *$1,750.00–$2,000.00*

Cook, Frederick A. *My Attainment of the Pole.* NY. Polar Pub. 1911. 1st ed. . . . . *$200.00–$1,000.00*

Cook, Frederick A. *To the Top of the Continent.* NY. 1908. 1st ed. . . . . *$75.00–$100.00*

Cook, John A. *Pursuing the Whale.* Bos. Houghton Mifflin. 1926. 1st ed. grey cl. . . . . *$20.00–$80.00*

Cook, Roy Bird. *Family and Early Life of Stonewall Jackson.* VA. 1925. 1st ed. . . . . *$50.00–$75.00*

Cooke, Philip St. George. *Scenes and Adventures in the Army.* Phila. 1859. 2nd ed. . . . . *$100.00–$250.00*

Cooke, Philip St. George. *Scenes and Adventures in the Army.* Phila. Lindsay. 1857. . . . . *$250.00–$500.00*

Coolidge, Susan. *What Katy Did.* Bos. 1872. . . . . *$45.00–$65.00*

Cooper, A. *Complete Distiller....* Lon. 1757. . . . . *$225.00–$300.00*

Cooper, Alonzo. *In and Out of Rebel Prisons.* Oswego, NY. Oliphant. 1888. . . . . *$75.00–$125.00*

Cooper, Frederic Tabor. *An Argosy of Fables.* NY. Stoles. (1921). 1st ed. illus. clr plates. . . . . *$70.00–$100.00*

Cooper, J. W. *Experienced Botanist or Indian Physician.* PA. 1840. . . . . *$175.00–$215.00*

Cooper, James Fenimore. *The Deerslayer.* NY. Scribner's. 1925. 1st ed. illus. by N.C. Wyeth, dj. . . . . *$425.00–$500.00*

Cooper, James Fennimore. *Last of the Mohicans.* NY. Scribner's. 1919. illus. by N. C. Wyeth. 1st Wyeth ed. . . . . *$75.00–$140.00*

Cooper, James Fennimore. *The Deerslayer.* Phila. 1841. 1st ed. purple cl. . . . . *$150.00–$350.00*

Cooper, James Fennimore. *The Pathfinder.* Lon. Bentley. 1840. 3 vols. 1st UK ed. . . . . *$500.00–$2,000.00*

Cooper, James Fennimore. *The Pathfinder.* Phila. Lea & Blanchard. 1840. 1st ed. . . . . *$500.00–$1,200.00*

Cooper, James Fennimore. *The Prairie.* Phila. 1832. 2 vols. 5th ed. . . . .
. . . . *$40.00–$60.00*

Cooper, James Fennimore. *The Water-Witch, or the Skimmer of the Sea. A Tale.*
Phila. Carey & Lea. 1831. 1st Amer ed. 2 vols. in 1, half calf & marbled bds. . . . .
. . . . *$250.00–$500.00*

Cooper, John M. *Analytical & Critical Biblio. of Tribes of Tierra Del Fuego.* DC.
GPO. 1917. fldg map. . . . . *$35.00–$50.00*

Coover, Robert. *Universal Baseball Association, Inc.* Lon. Hart Davis. 1970. 1st ed.
dj. . . . . *$45.00–$65.00*

Coppard, A. E. *Fearful Pleasures.* Racine, WI. Arkham House. 1946. 1st US ed. dj.
. . . . *$80.00–$100.00*

Coppinger, Joseph. *American Practical Brewer and Tanner.* NY. 1815. 1st ed.
plates. . . . . *$300.00–$450.00*

Copway, George. *Life, History and Travels of Kah-Ge-Ga-Gak-Bowk... Ojibway....*
PA. Hormstead. 1847. 2nd ed. presentation copy, sgn. . . . . *$200.00–$225.00*

Corbett, Jim. *Man-Eating Leopard of Rudrapravag.* NY. Oxford University Press.
1948. 1st Amer ed. rust cl. . . . . *$25.00–$100.00*

Corder, E M. *Deer Hunter.* NY. Exeter. (1979). 1st ed. dj. . . . . *$25.00–$30.00*

Cornelius, Mrs. *Young Housekeeper's Friend.* Bos/NY. 1859. rev ed.*$20.00–$30.00*

Cornish, Dudley Taylor. *Sable Arm, Negro Troops in the Union Army, 1861–1865.*
NY. 1956. 1st ed. . . . . *$40.00–$65.00*

Cornwallis, Caroline Francis. *An Introduction to Practical Organic Chemistry.*
Lon. Pickering. 1843. . . . . *$100.00–$170.00*

Cornwell, Bernard. *Sharpe's Eagle.* NY. Viking. (1981). 1st ed. dj. . . . .
. . . . *$45.00–$65.00*

Correll & Gosden. *All About Amos 'n' Andy and Their Creators Correll & Gosden.*
NY. Rand McNally. 1930. illus. 2nd ed. *$22.00–$35.00*

Correspondence between the rev Samuel H Cox of Brooklyn.... NY. Office of the
American Anti-Slavery Society. 1846. wrps. . . . . *$50.00–$75.00*

Corso, Gregory. *Bomb.* SF. City Lights. 1958. . . . . *$85.00–$100.00*

Corso, Gregory. *Happy Birthday of Death.* NY. New Directions. (1960). 1st ed.
wrps. . . . . *$35.00–$45.00*

Cory, David. *Iceberg Express.* NY. Grosset & Dunlap. (1922). 1st ed. illus. by P H
Webb. scarce dj. . . . . *$25.00–$35.00*

Cossley-Batt, Jill. *Last of the California Rangers.* NY/Lon. Funk & Wagnalls. (1928). illus. 2nd prtg. . . . . ***$25.00–$75.00***

Cossley-Batt, Jill. *Last of the California Rangers.* NY/Lon. Funk & Wagnalls. 1928. 1st ed. . . . . ***$90.00–$120.00***

Catton, Bruce. *Reflections on the Civil War.* CT. Doubleday. 1981. . . ***$35.00–$45.00***

Cotton, Charles. *The Compleat Angler, Being Instructions how to Angle for Trout or Grayling in a Clear Stream.* Lon. Marriott & Brome. 1676. 1st ed. mor, aeg. . . . . ***$2,000.00–$3,000.00***

Couch, Jonathan. *A History of the Fishes of the British Islands.* Lon. Groombridge & Son. 1862-1865. 1st ed. illus. wood-engr plates. . . . . ***$1,250.00–$2,000.00***

Couch, Jonathan F. L. S. *History of the Fishes of the British Isles.* Lon. George Bell & sons. 1879. 4 vols. illus. with 252 tissue-guarded full-clr chromoliths, pict design of fish on front cvr. . . . . ***$900.00–$1,000.00***

Coues, Elliott. *Birds of the Northwest.* Bos. 1877. . . . . ***$50.00–$80.00***

Coues, Elliott. *Expeditions of Zebulon Montgomery Pike to Headwaters....* Minn. 1965. 3 vols. rprnt, ltd 2000 cc. . . . . ***$100.00–$200.00***

Coues, Elliott. *Key to North American Birds.* Bos. Estes & Lauriat. 1890. 4th ed. illus. 1 clr plate, cl. . . . . ***$50.00–$75.00***

Coues, Elliott. *Key to North American Birds.* Salem. Dodd, Mead. 1972. illus. 6 plates. . . . . ***$30.00–$40.00***

Coues, Elliott, (ed.). *New Light on the Early History of the Greater Northwest....* NY. 1895. 3 vols. maps, ltd 500 cc. . . . . ***$250.00–$300.00***

Coulter, Ellis Merton. *Civil War and Readjustment in Kentucky.* Chapel Hill. Univ N. C. Press. 1926. 1st ed. . . . . ***$65.00–$90.00***

Coulter, Ellis Merton. *William G. Brownlow, Fighting Parson of The Southern Highlands.* Chapel Hill. Univ N. C. Press. 1937. 1st ed. . . . . ***$30.00–$60.00***

Courlander, Harold. *Negro Folk Music, USA.* NY. Columbia Univ Press. 1963. dj. . . . . ***$30.00–$45.00***

Couture, Richard T. *Powhatan A Bicentennial History.* Dietz. Richmond, VA. 1980. illus. b/w, inscr, dj. . . . . ***$40.00–$50.00***

Covarrubias, Miguel. *Island of Bali.* NY. Knopf. 1937. 1st ed. illus. by Covarrubias, photos, pict cl, dj. . . . . ***$75.00–$90.00***

Coward, Noel. *Bitter Sweet and Other Plays.* NY. Doubleday, Doran. 1929. 1st Amer ed. ltd 1000 cc, nbr, sgn. . . . . ***$200.00–$250.00***

Coward, Noel. *Private Lives.* Lon. Heinemann. 1930. dj. . . . . . . ***$100.00–$300.00***

Coward, Noel. *Quadrille, a Play in Three Acts.* Lon. Heinemann. 1952. dj. . . . . .
. . . .*$25.00–$40.00*

Cox, Earnest Sevier. *White America.* Richmond, VA. White American Society. 1923.
1st ed. dj, scarce. . . . .*$75.00–$500.00*

Cox, Ernest. *White America.* Richmond, VA. White American Society. 1925).
Congress ed, dj. . . . .*$35.00–$75.00*

Cox, Jacob D. *Military Reminiscences of the Civil War.* NY. 1900. 2 vols. . . . . . .
. . . .*$195.00–$250.00*

Cox, Palmer. *Brownies at Home.* NY. Century. 1893. illus. b/w. . . *$75.00–$200.00*

Cox, Palmer. *Brownies. Their Book.* NY. (1887). 1st ed. illus. bds. *$200.00–$300.00*

Cox, Palmer. *Rhyme & Reason.* Clark's O.N.T.Thread. illus. booklet. pict clr paper
wrps. . . . .*$50.00–$75.00*

Crafts, W. A. *Southern Rebellion.* Bos. Walker. 1862. 1st ed. illus. steel engr. . . . .
. . . .*$200.00–$350.00*

Craig, David. *Message Ends.* Lon. Jonathan Cape. 1971. 1st ed. dj. *$40.00–$45.00*

Craig, David. *The Alias Man.* Lon. Jonathan Cape. 1968. 1st ed. dj. *$60.00–$65.00*

Craig, Maurice. *Irish Book Bindings 1600-1800.* Lon. Cassell. (1954). illus. dj. .
. . . .*$275.00–$350.00*

Craig, Maurice. *Psychological Medicine.* Lon. 1905. plates. . . . . . *$20.00–$27.00*

Craighead, John J., Jay Sumner and John A. Mitchell. *Grizzly Bears of
Yellowstone.* DC. Island Press. 1995. 1st ed. 1st prtg. illus. with clr and b/w photos.
grey cl, dj. . . . .*$90.00–$115.00*

Cram's Universal Atlas. Chi. 1889. 3/4 lea. . . . .*$95.00–$125.00*

Cram's Unrivaled Family Atlas. Rochester. W. H. Stewart. 1891. *$130.00–$300.00*

Cramer, Zadok. *Navigator, containing directions for navigating The Monongahela,
Allegheny, Ohio and Mississippi Rivers.* Pitt. 1817. 9th ed. maps. . *$280.00–$1,000*

Crane, Frances. *Coral Princess Murders.* NY. Random House. (1954). 1st ed. dj.
. . . .*$20.00–$30.00*

Crane, Frances. *Murder on the Purple Water.* NY. Random House. (1947). 1st ed.
dj. . . . .*$40.00–$75.00*

Crane, Hart. *Seven Lyrics.* Camb. The Ibex Press. (c1966). 1st ed. ltd 250 cc . . . .
. . . .*$75.00–$125.00*

Crane, Stephen. *Monster and Other Stories.* NY/Lon. Harper & Bros. 1899. 1st ed.
. . . .*$150.00–$200.00*

Crane, Stephen. *O'Ruddy.* NY. Stokes. 1903. 1st ed. . . . . *$45.00–$125.00*

Crane, Stephen. *Open Boat and Other Stories.* Lon. 1898. 1st ed. green cl. . . . . .
. . . . *$195.00–$225.00*

Crane, Stephen. *Red Badge of Courage.* NY. Appleton. 1896. 1st ed. . . . .
. . . . *$125.00–$200.00*

Crane, Stephen. *The Little Regiment.* NY. 1896. . . . . *$100.00–$125.00*

Crane, Stephen. *Work of Stephen Crane.* NY. Knopf. 1925. 12. limited ed, boxed.
. . . . *$250.00–$300.00*

Crane, Walter. *Absurd ABC.* Lon. Routledge & Sons. 1st ed. red lea. *$350.00*

Crane, Walter. *Flora's Feast of Flowers.* Lon. 1889. 1st ed. illus. 40 pp, pict bds..
. . . . *$90.00–$150.00*

Crane, Walter. *Masque of Days.* Lon/Paris/NY/Melbourne. Cassell & Co. 1901.
illus. by Crane. pict bds. . . . . *$120.00–$180.00*

Crane, Walter. *Queen Summer.* Lon/Paris/Melbourne. Cassell & Co. 1891. 1st ed.
pict bds. . . . . *$120.00–$180.00*

Crane, Walter. *Walter Crane's Picture Book.* Lon. (1874). 1st ed. 64 clr plates, aeg.
. . . . *$600.00*

Crapo, Capt Thomas and Wife. *Strange But True.* New Bedford. 1893. 1st ed.
brown cl. . . . . *$25.00–$65.00*

Craven, Avery. *Edmund Ruffin Southerner.* NY. Appleton. 1932. . . . . *$45.00*

Crawford, Samuel W. *Genesis of the Civil War. The Story of Sumter, 1860–1861.*
NY. 1887. . . . . *$100.00–$125.00*

Crawfurd, Oswald (ed.). *A Year of Sport and Natural History.* Lon. Chapman &
Hall. 1895. 1st ed. illus. red cl, teg. . . . . *$45.00–$125.00*

Crawhall, Joseph (ed.). *A Collection of Right Merrie Garlands for North Country
Anglers.* Newcastle-on-Tyne. Rutland. 1864. illus. ltd 50 cc. half mor & cl, teg. . .
. . . . *$400.00–$600.00*

Creighton, Helen. *Maritime Folk Songs.* NY. Folklorica. 1979. dj. . . . .
. . . . *$25.00–$35.00*

Creole Cookery Book. New Orleans. T. H. Thomason. 1885. 1st ed. by Christian
Woman's Exchange. . . . . *$100.00–$150.00*

Crews, Harry. *A Childhood....* NY. Harper. 1978. 1st ed. dj. . . . . *$75.00–$200.00*

Crews, Harry. *All We Need of Hell.* NY. Harper. 1987. 1st ed. dj. . *$40.00–$50.00*

Crews, Harry. *Blood and Grits*. NY. Harper & Row. (1979). 1st ed. dj. . . . .
. . . . *$40.00–$50.00*

Crews, Harry. *Feast of Snakes*. Lon. Atheneum. (1977). 1st UK ed dj. . . . .
. . . . *$75.00–$125.00*

Crews, Harry. *Gospel Singer*. NY. Morrow. (1968). 1st ed. author's first book, dj.
. . . . *$400.00–$900.00*

Crews, Harry. *Gypsie's Curse*. NY. Knopf. (1974). 1st ed. dj. . . . *$80.00–$125.00*

Crews, Harry. *Karate is a Thing of the Spirit*. NY. Morrow. 1971. 1st ed. dj. . . . .
. . . . *$100.00–$150.00*

Crews, Harry. *Knockout Artist*. NY. Harper & Row. (1988). 1st ed. dj. . . . .
. . . . *$25.00–$40.00*

Crews, Harry. *Madonna at Ringside*. Lord John. 1992. ltd 275 cc, sgn. . . . *$75.00*

Crews, Harry. *Naked in Garden Hills*. NY. Morrow. 1969. 1st ed. dj. . . . .
. . . . *$75.00–$200.00*

Crews, Harry. *Scar Lover*. NY. Poseidon. (1992). dj. . . . . *$20.00–$30.00*

Crews, Harry. *This Thing Don't Lead to Heaven*. NY. William Morrow.1970. 1st ed.
dj. . . . . *$125.00–$250.00*

Crichton, Michael. *Andromeda Strain*. NY. Knopf. 1969. 1st ed. dj. *$50.00–$65.00*

Crichton, Michael. *Andromeda Strain*. NY. Knopf. 1969. 1st ed. sgn. dj. . . . .
. . . . *$200.00–$275.00*

Crichton, Michael. *Great Train Robbery*. NY. Knopf. 1975. 1st ed. dj. . . . .
. . . . *$35.00–$65.00*

Crichton, Michael. *Jurassic Park*. NY. 1990. 1st ed.stn. dj. . . . *$200.00–$450.00*

Crichton, Michael. *Jurassic Park*. NY. Knopf. 1990. 1st trade ed. dj. *$35.00–$60.00*

Crichton, Michael. *Rising Sun*. NY. Knopf. 1992. 1st ed. sgn, dj. . *$70.00–$85.00*

Crichton, Michael. *Rising Sun*. NY. Knopf. 1992. sgn, dj. . . . . *$25.00–$40.00*

Crichton, Michael. *Sphere*. NY. Knopf. 1987. 1st ed. dj. . . . . *$20.00–$40.00*

Crichton, Michael. *Terminal Man*. NY. 1972. 1st ed. dj. . . . . *$45.00–$60.00*

Crichton, Michael (Michael Douglas). *Dealing or the Berkeley-to-Boston Forty-Brick Lost-Bag Blues*. NY. Knopf. 1971. 1st ed. scarce, dj. . . . . . *$140.00–$150.00*

Crichton, Michael (Michael Douglas). *Eaters of the Dead*. NY. Knopf. 1976. 1st ed.
dj. . . . . *$35.00–$45.00*

Crockett, Walter Hill. *History of Lake Champlain.* Burlington, VT. Hobart & Shanley. 1909. illus. . . . . *$95.00–$120.00*

Croff, G. B. *Progressive American Architecture.* DC. 1875. illus. folio, plates.. . . . . *$1,200.00–$1,450.00*

Croffut, W. A., et al. *Military and Civil History of Conn... During War of 1861–65.* NY. 1868. . . . . *$75.00–$150.00*

Croly, Mrs. J. C. *Jennie June's American Cookery Book.* NY. 1870. . *$45.00–$62.00*

Cromie, R. *Dillinger, A Short & Violent Life.* NY. McGraw Hill. 1962. 1st ed. sgn, dj. . . . . *$22.00–$28.00*

Cron, Gretchen. *Roaring Veldt.* NY. Putnam. 1930. 1st Amer ed. illus. plates.. . . . . *$30.00–$50.00*

Cronau, Rudolf. *Amerika.* Leipzig. 1892. 2 vols. illus. photos, maps. . . . . *$125.00–$375.00*

Cronin, A. J. *Grand Canary.* Lon. Victor Gollancz. 1933. dj. . . . . . *$25.00–$40.00*

Cronyn, George W. (ed.). *Path of the Rainbow.* NY. Boni and Liveright. 1918. 1st ed. 2nd prtg. rare. . . . . *$50.00–$110.00*

Cross, Robert. *Auvergne: Its Thermo-Mineral Springs....* Lon. Robert Hardwicke. 1867. 1st ed. illus. clr litho plates,. . . . . *$40.00–$50.00*

Cross, Wilbur. *History of Henry Fielding.* Yale. 1918. 3 vols. 1st ed. *$50.00–$75.00*

Crossman, E. C. *Military & Sporting Rifle Shooting.* NC. (1932). . *$30.00–$40.00*

Crosswaith, Frank B. *Negro and Socialism.* NY. United Colored Socialists of America. 4pp, brochure. . . . . *$45.00–$65.00*

Crosswaith, Frank R. and Alfred B. Lewis. *True Freedom for Negro and White Labor.* NY. Negro Labor News Service. nd. wrps. . . . . *$30.00–$65.00*

Crothers, Samuel McChord. *Children of Dickens.* NY. Scribner's. 1925. 1st ed. illus. by Jessie Willcox Smith. scarce dj. . . . . *$200.00–$350.00*

Crowe, Philip K. *Sport Is Where You Find It.* NY. Van Nostrand. (1953). 1st ed. sgn. . . . . *$30.00–$50.00*

Crowninshield, Mary Bradford. *All Among the Lighthouses.* Bos. 1886. . . . . *$42.00–$50.00*

Cruise of the Revenue Steamer Corwin in Alaska. DC. GPO. 1883. illus. clr & b/w plates. . . . . *$300.00–$135.00*

Crump, Paul. *Grille, Assassin, Grille!* Paris. Presses de la Cite. 1963. 1st French ed. dj. . . . . *$15.00–$25.00*

Culff, Robert. *World of Toys.* Lon. Paul Hamlyn. (1969). 1st ed. illus. b/w photos.
. . . . *$20.00–$35.00*

Cullen, Countee. *Black Christ.* NY. Harper. 1929. 1st ed. illus. by Charles Cullen.
. . . . *$50.00–$325.00*

Cullen, Countee. *Color.* NY. Harper. (1925). illus. by author. . . *$125.00–$300.00*

Cullen, Countee. *Color.* NY. Harper. 1925. 1st ed. 1st imp. author's first book. sgn.
dj. . . . . *$600.00–$1,200.00*

Cullen, Countee. *Copper Sun.* NY. 1927. 1st ed. marbled bds, dj. *$75.00–$300.00*

Cullen, William. *Synopsis of Methodical Nosology, ... with the Synonimous of Those from Savages.* Phila. Parry Hall. 1793. enlarged, translated by Henry Wilkins, (8) pp,
bds. . . . . *$350.00–$500.00*

Culmsee, Carlton. *Utah's Black Hawk War.* Logan. 1973. 1st ed. wrps. scarce. . . .
. . . . *$35.00–$40.00*

Culver, Henry B. *Book of Old Ships.* NY. 1928. illus. drawings, mor, mar bds. . .
. . . . *$35.00–$55.00*

Culverwell, Robert J. *How To Live 100 Years.* Lon. 1847. stiff paper. *$30.00–$45.00*

Cummings, Byron. *First Inhabitants of Arizona and the Southwest.* Tucson. 1953. wrps. pict dj, map endpapers, clr photos, fldg map. . . . . *$70.00–$85.00*

cummings, e. e. *eimi.* NY. Covici Friede. 1933. ltd 1381 cc, sgn. *$175.00–$250.00*

cummings, e. e. *Him.* NY. Boni & Liveright. 1927. 1st ed. dj. . . *$150.00–$175.00*

cummings, e. e. *Tulips and Chimneys.* NY. Thomas Seltzer. 1923. 1st ed. . . . .
. . . . *$300.00–$500.00*

cummings, e. e. *W.* NY. Liveright. 1931. 1st ed. brown paper bds. . *$125.00–$200.00*

Cuneo, John. *Winged Mars: Volume 1, The German Air Weapon 1870-1914.* Harrisburg. Military Service Pub. 1942. illus. . . . . *$60.00–$100.00*

Cunningham, Albert B. *Old Black Bass.* NY/Chi. (1922). illus. dj. *$22.00–$32.00*

Cunningham, Eugene. *Famous in the West.* El Paso. 1926. wrps. illus. 25 pp, scarce.
. . . . *$275.00–$450.00*

Cunningham, Peter. *Hand-Book of London.* Lon. John Murray. 1850. . . . .
. . . . *$60.00–$200.00*

Curie, Madam Marie. *Radioactivite.* Paris. 1935. wrps. . . . . . . *$125.00–$135.00*

Currey, L. W. *Science Fiction and Fantasy Authors....* Bos. Hall. (1979). 1st ed. dj.
. . . . *$100.00–$125.00*

Currier & Ives Prints. The Red Indian. Lon/NY. The Studio. 1931. intro by WS Hall, sgn by Hall, dj. . . . . *$35.00–$45.00*

Currier, John J. *History of Newbury, Mass. 1635-1902.* Bos. 1902. cl. *$30.00–$40.00*

Currier, N. *The Battery, New York. By Moonlight.* NY. 1852. clr litho scene. . . . . *$600–$750.00*

Curry, Manfred. *Yacht Racing....* NY. Henry Holt. 1927. . . . . *$25.00–$45.00*

Curtis, Edward S. *Portraits from North American Indian Life.* NY. Promontory Press. (1972). 1st ed. thus, oblong folio, sepia portraits. . . . . *$60.00–$100.00*

Curtis, George W. *Horses, Cattle, Sheep and Swine.* NY. Rural Publishing. 1893. 2nd rev ed. illus. . . . . *$50.00–$65.00*

Curtis, George William. *Howadji in Syria.* NY. 1856. 1st ed. maps. *$30.00–$45.00*

Curtis,George William. *Washington Irving: A Sketch.* NY. Grolier. 1891. 1st ed. red mor, teg, slipcase. . . . . *$195.00–$225.00*

Curtis, John. *Harvey's Views on the Circulation of the Blood.* NY. Columbia Univ Press. 1915. . . . . *$30.00–$60.00*

Curtis, John H. *An Essay on the Deaf and Dumb.* Lon. 1834. 2nd ed. 2 plates. . . . . *$50.00–$250.00*

Curtis, Mattoon. *Book of Snuff and Snuff Boxes.* NY. 1935. illus. dj. . *$15.00–$45.00*

Curtis, N. M. *From Bull Run to Chancellorsville.* NY. 1906. illus. . *$40.00–$75.00*

Curtis, Natalie (editor and compiler). *Indians' Book.* NY. Harper & Bros. 1907. 1st ed. illus. . . . . *$235.00–$260.00*

Curtis, Newton. *From Bull Run to Chancellorsville.* NY. 1906. . . . *$85.00–$95.00*

Curtis, Paul A. *Sportsmen All.* Derrydale Press. (1938). ltd 950, illus. . *$80.00–$95.00*

Curtis, Paul A., Jr. *American Game Shooting.* NY. 1927. dj. . . . . . *$48.00–$62.00*

Curtis, W. H. *Elements of Wood Ship Construction.* NY. 1919. 1st ed. illus. . . . . *$65.00–$95.00*

Curtis, William E. *Children of the Sun.* Chi. 1833. inscr. . . . . . . *$175.00–$225.00*

Curwood, James. *Danger Trail.* Bobbs Merrill. (1910). 1st ed. . . . *$20.00–$30.00*

Curwood, James. *Plains of Abraham.* NY. 1928. 1st ed. dj. . . . . . . *$20.00–$25.00*

Cushing, Caleb. *Reminiscences of Spain.* Bos. 1833. 2 vols. in one. *$35.00–$45.00*

Cushing, Caleb](. *Reply to the Letter of J Fenimore Cooper....* Bos. 1834. 1st ed. printed wrps, sewn, 76 pp, inscr. . . . . *$95.00–$125.00*

Cushing, Harvey. *Consecratio Medici.* 1928. 1st ed. . . . . *$40.00–$150.00*

Cushing, Harvey. *From A Surgeon's Journal 1915–1918.* Bos. 1936. 1st ed. . . . .
. . . . *$50.00–$75.00*

Cushing, Harvey. *Harvey Cushing's Seventieth Birthday Party, April 8, 1939.* np.
Thomas. 1939. 1st ed. illus. dj. . . . . *$60.00–$100.00*

Cushing, Harvey. *Life of Sir William Osler.* Oxford. Clarendon Press. 1925. 2 vols.
1st ed. illus. 4th impression. . . . . *$90.00–$375.00*

Cushing, Harvey. *Life of Sir William Osler.* Ox. 1940. . . . . *$30.00–$40.00*

Cushman, H B. *History of the Choctaw, Chickasaw and Natchez Indians.* Greenville.
Headlight Printing House. 1899. . . . . *$160.00–$250.00*

Cussans, John E. *Handbook of Heraldry.* Lon. Chatto & Windus. 1893. 4th ed. . .
. . . . *$30.00–$45.00*

Cussler, Clive. *Night Probe!.* NY. Bantam. 1981. 1st ed. dj. . . . . . . *$80.00–$90.00*

Custead, E. Rose and Elza Custead. *Songs and Stories of Bygone Days in Fayette
County.* NY. 1882. 1st ed. . . . . *$20.00–$30.00*

Custer, Carl. *Story of the American Clipper.* NY. (1930). illus. . . . *$40.00–$55.00*

Custer, Elizabeth. *Boots and Saddles.* NY. Harper & Bros. 1885. 1st ed. 2nd issue,
map and portrait. . . . . *$45.00–$85.00*

Custer, Elizabeth. *Following the Guidon.* NY. Harper & Bros. 1890. 1st ed. . . . .
. . . . *$45.00–$85.00*

Custer, Elizabeth. *Tenting On the Plains.* Norman, OK. Univ OK Press. (1971). 3
vols. new ed. boxed. . . . . *$45.00–$60.00*

Custer, Gen. G. A. *Life on the Plains.* NY. 1874. 1st ed. illus. . . *$100.00–$300.00*

Cutcliffe, H. C. *The Art of Trout Fishing on Rapid Streams... with Detailed
Instructions in the Art of Fishing with the Artificial Fly....* South Molton. Tucker,
Square. 1863. 1st ed. brown mor, marbled bds, teg. . . . . *$500.00–$800.00*

Cutler, Carl C. *Greyhounds of the Sea.* NY. Halcyon. 1930. . . . . *$50.00–$100.00*

Cutler, Carl C. *Queens of the Western Ocean.* Annapolis, MD. US Naval Institute.
1967. illus. . . . . *$30.00–$40.00*

D'Aulaire, Ingri and Edgar Parin. *Leif the Lucky.* NY. Doubleday. (1941). illus. pict
bds, map endpapers, dj. . . . . *$25.00–$35.00*

D'Ewes, J. *Sporting in Both Hemispheres.* Lon. 1858. 2nd ed. . . . *$95.00–$125.00*

Dabney, R. L. *Life & Campaigns of Lieut-Gen. T. J. Jackson.* NY. 1866. 1st ed. fldg
map. . . . . *$75.00–$125.00*

Dahl, Roald. *Ah, Sweet Mysteries of Life*. NY. Knopf. 1989. illus. 1st US ed. dj. .
. . . . *$30.00–$40.00*

Dahl, Roald. *Charlie and the Chocolate Factory*. NY. Knopf. 1964. 1st ed. 6 lines of printing info on back page, dj. . . . . *$2,000.00–$4,000.00*

Dahl, Roald. *Fantastic Mr. Fox*. NY. Knopf. 1970. 1st ed. dj. . . . *$150.00–$300.00*

Dahl, Roald. *Gremlins*. NY. Random House. (1943). 1st US ed. author' first book.
. . . . *$975.00–$4000.00*

Dahl, Roald. *Switch Bitch*. NY. Knopf. 1974. 1st ed. dj. . . . . *$50.00–$100.00*

Daiken, Leslie. *World of Toys*. Lon. Lambarde Press. 1963. 1st UK ed. b/w photos.
. . . . *$15.00–$30.00*

Dale, Harrison C. (ed.). *Ashley-Smith Explor. & Disc. of Route to Pacific 1822–1829*. Cleve. 1918. 1st ed. maps, plates. . . . . *$175.00–$250.00*

Dalgliesh, Alice. *Enchanted Book*. NY. Scribner's. 1947. 1st ed. dj. *$20.00–$50.00*

Dalgliesh, Alice. *Long Live the King*. NY. Scribner's.1937. illus. 77 pp, pict endpapers. . . . . *$25.00–$35.00*

Dali, Salvador. *Hidden Faces*. Dial Press. 1944. illus. 1st US ed. dj. *$65.00–$75.00*

Dali, Salvador. *Les Diners de Gala*. NY. Felicie. (1973). illus. pict cl, gold foil, pict dj. . . . . *$60.00–$90.00*

Dali, Salvador. *Secret Life of Salvador Dali*. NY. Dial Press. 1942. 1st Amer ed. dj.
. . . . *$125.00–$250.00*

Dana, Charles. *Eastern Journeys*. NY. Appleton. 1898. teg. . . . . *$30.00–$50.00*

Dana, Charles. *Life of Ulysses S. Grant*. Gurdon Bell & Co. 1868. . *$25.00–$40.00*

Dana, Charles L. *Peaks of Medical History:Outline of Evolution of Medicine*. NY. Hoeber. 1926. 1st ed. illus. plates. . . . . *$75.00–$100.00*

Dana, E. S. *Textbook of Mineralogy*. NY. 1926. 4th revised ed. . . . *$25.00–$35.00*

Dana, James D. *Manual of Mineralogy and Lithology Containing the Elements of the Science of Minerals and Rocks*. Lon. 1882. 4th ed. . . . . *$40.00–$60.00*

Dana James D. *Manual of Mineralogy*. New Haven. Durrie & Peck. 1855. 7th ed.
. . . . *$25.00–$40.0*

Dana, Richard Henry. *To Cuba and Back*. Bos. 1859. 1st ed. 288 pp. . . . .
. . . . *$100.00–$125.00*

Dana, Richard Henry, Jr. *Two Years Before the Mast*. Chi. Lakeside. 1930. slipcase.
. . . . *$60.00–$80.00*

Dance of the Hours. NY. Disney. (1940). 1st ed. stiff pict paper bds, illus, dj. . . .
. . . . *$80.00–$95.00*

Daniel, William Barker. *Rural Sports.* Lon. Longman, Hurst.. 1812 & 1813. 3vols.
illus. copper-engr plates, brown mor, marbled bds. . . . . *$300.00–$800.00*

Daniele, Joseph. *Building Colonial Furnishings Miniatures & Folk Art.* Pa.
Stackpole Books. (1976). 1st ed. . . . . *$25.00–$30.00*

Daniels, Elam. *An Exposure of Father Divine....* Fairfield. 1946. wrps. illus. . . . . .
. . . . *$25.00–$45.00*

Darby, Charles. *Bacchanalia. Or, A Description of a Drunken Club.* Lon. 1680.
folio, calf. . . . . *$325.00–$425.00*

Darr, Patrick T. *A Guide to Art and Pattern Glass.* Springfield. Pilgrim House. 1960.
1st ed. illus. b/w and clr plates, sgn. *$65.00*

Darrow, Clarence. *Open Shop.* Chi. Charles H Kerr. nd, c1920. wrps. 32pp, rprnt.
. . . . *$40.00–$45.00*

Darrow, Clarence. *Story of My Life.* NY. Scribner's. 1932. 1st ed. sgn, dj. . . . . . .
. . . . *$400.00–$700.00*

Darwin, Charles. *Descent of Man.* Lon. Murray. 1871. 2 vols. 1st ed. 1st issue. illus.
. . . . *$2,750.00–$3,800.00*

Darwin, Charles. *Descent of Man.* Lon. Murray. 1871. 2 vols. 1st ed. 2nd issue. illus.
. . . . *$400.00–$800.00*

Darwin, Charles. *Descent of Man.* NY. Appleton. 1871. 2 vols. 1st Amer ed. . . . .
. . . . *$280.00–$600.00*

Darwin, Charles. *Effects of Cross and Self Fertilization....* NY. 1889. *$45.00–$80.00*

Darwin, Charles. *Expression of the Emotions: Man & Animals.* Appleton. 1873. .
. . . . *$125.00–$300.00*

Darwin, Charles. *Insectivorous Plants.* NY. Appleton. 1875. 1st US ed. . . . .
. . . . *$125.00–$175.00*

Darwin, Charles. *Journal of Researches...Countries Visited by HMS Beagle.* NY.
Hafner. (1901). 26 plates. . . . . *$40.00–$50.00*

Darwin, Charles. *Naturalist's Voyage...of HMS Beagle.* Lon. John Murray. 1890.
500 pp. . . . . *$60.00–$75.00*

Darwin, Charles. *On the Origin of Species by Means of Natural Selection.* Lon.
1859. 3rd issue. . . . . *$8,000.00–$10,000.00*

Darwin, Charles. *On the Origin of Species by Means of Natural Selection.* NY.
Appleton. 1871. 5th ed. . . . . *$90.00–$150.00*

Darwin, Charles. *On the Origin of Species by Means of Natural Slection.* NY. 1860. 1st Amer ed. fldg diagram, brown cl. . . . . *$1,000.00–$2,500.00*

Darwin, Charles. *Various Contrivances by Which Orchids Are Fertilized.* Chi. Univ of Chi Press. 1984. wrps. facs of 1877 ed. . . . . *$25.00–$35.00*

Darwin, Charles. *Works.* NY. Appleton. 1873–1883. 11 vols. . . *$150.00–$250.00*

Darwin, G. H. *Evolution of Satellites.* DC. GPO. 1898. pamphlet. . *$20.00–$35.00*

Das Plakat. *Mitteilungen des Vereins der Plakat-Freunde.* Berlin. 1910-1921. Vols 1-12. wrps. clr, b& w illus. . . . . *$900.00–$2,500.00*

Daumas, M. *Scientific Instruments of the 17th &18th Centuries.* Lon. 1972. dj. . . . . *$30.00–$50.00*

Davenport, Alfred. *Camp and Field Life of the Fifth New York Volunteer Infantry.* NY. 1879. . . . . *$175.00–$250.00*

Davenport, Cyril. *Royal English Book Bindings.* Lon. Seeley. 1896. 1st ed. illus. . . . . *$45.00–$65.00*

Davenport, John. *Aphrodisiacs and Anti-Aphrodisiacs.* Lon. private printing. 1869. 1st ed. illus. . . . . *$75.00–$125.00*

Davenport-Hill, Florence. *Children of the State.* Lon. Macmillan. 1889. 2nd ed. . . . . *$46.00–$100.00*

David Livingstone and the Victorian Encounter with Africa. Lon. National Portrait Gallery. 1996. 1st ed. illus. dj. . . . . *$35.00–$75.00*

Davidson, Ellis. *Practical Manual of House Painting.* Lon. 1884. . . . . *$50.00–$100.00*

Davidson, Gordon Charles. *North West Company.* Berkeley. Univ of CA Pub. 1918. 1st ed. illus. maps, plates. . . . . *$145.00–$300.00*

Davidson, J. N. *Muh-he-ka-ne-ok. A History of the Stockbridge Nation.* Milwaukee. 1893. . . . . *$45.00–$55.00*

Davie, Oliver. *Nests and Eggs of North American Birds.* OH. Landon Press. 1898. illus. . . . . *$45.00–$60.00*

Davie, Oliver. *Reveries and Recollections of a Naturalist.* Columbus. private printing. 1898. 1st ed. illus. plates, teg, ltd 200 cc. . . . . *$60.00–$90.00*

Davies, Thomas. *Preparation and Mounting of Microscopic Objects.* Lon. 1864. 1st ed. . . . . *$100.00–$140.00*

Davis, Angela Y. *Women, Culture, and Politics.* NY. Random House. 1989. 1st ed. . . . . *$15.00–$25.00*

Davis, Burke. *Grey Fox: Robert E. Lee and The Civil War.* NY. New York Wings Books. 1956. illus. maps, dj. . . . . *$25.00–$35.00*

Davis, Daniel. *An Address to Inhabitants...Maine....* Portland. 1791. *$50.00–$100.00*

Davis, Henry P. *Training Your Own Bird Dog.* NY Putnam's. 1948. 1st ed. dj. . . . . *$10.00–$30.00*

Davis, Jefferson. *Purchase of Camels for Military Transportation.* DC. 1857. illus. . . . . *$150.00–$200.00*

Davis, Jefferson. *Rise and Fall of the Confederate Government.* NY. Appleton. 1881. 2 vols. 1st ed. 808 pp. . . . . *$150.00–$275.00*

Davis, Jerome. *Capitalism and Its Culture.* NY. Farrar & Rinehart. 1941. 3rd ed. cl, inscr. . . . . *$30.00–$45.00*

Davis, M. L. *Memoirs of Aaron Burr.* NY. 1836. 2 vols. . . . . *$100.00–$300.00*

Davis, Mary Lee. *Uncle Sam's Attic, the Intimate Story of Alaska.* Bos. 1930. 1st ed. . . . . *$35.00–$50.00*

Davis, Ossie. *Escape to Freedom.* NY. Viking. 1976. 2nd prtg. sgn,dj. . *$75.00–$100.00*

Davis, Paris M. *An Authentick History of the Late War Between the United States and Great Britain.* Ithaca. Davis & Saunders. 1829. 1st ed. original sheep, black label. . . . . *$65.00–$100.00*

Davis, Rear-Admiral C. H. (ed.). *Narrative of the North Polar Expedition. US Ship Polaris.* DC. GPO. 1878. 2nd prtg, engr, lithos, maps, decorative red cl. *$60.00–$75.00*

Davis, Reg S. & Steiner. *Mona Lisa Philippine Orchids.* NY. 1952. *$50.00–$65.00*

Davis, Richard Harding. *About Paris.* NY. Harper. 1895. 1st ed. illus. by Dana Gibson. . . . . *$20.00–$35.00*

Davis, Richard Harding. *Bar Sinister.* NY. 1903. 1st ed. . . . . *$30.00–$50.00*

Davis, Richard Harding. *Cuban and Porto Rican Campaigns.* NY. 1898. 1st ed. illus. . . . . *$30.00–$75.00*

Davis, Richard Harding. *Van Bibber and Others.* NY. 1892. 1st ed. *$35.00–$40.00*

Davis, Richard Harding. *Vera the Medium.* Scribner's. 1908. 1st ed. purple binding. . . . . *$25.00–$40.00*

Davis, Richard Harding. *West From a Car Window.* NY/Lon. 1892. 1st ed. illus. by Frederick Remington. . . . . *$50.00–$65.00*

Davis, Susan Lawrence. *Authentic History of the Ku Klux Klan 1865–1877.* NY. Private printing. 1924. . . . . *$140.00–$225.00*

Davis, W. W. H. *El Gringo, or New Mexico and Her People*. NY. 1857. . . . .
. . . . *$225.00–$350.00*

Davis, W. W. H. *History of Doylestown, Old and New*. Doylestown. 1900. 1st ed.
illus. green cl, gold lettering on front cvr and spine. . . . . *$100.00–$175.00*

Davis, W. W. H. *Spanish Conquest of New Mexico*. Doylestown, PA. private prtg.
1886. 1st ed. inscr, pullout map. . . . . *$350.00–$600.00*

Davis, William W. *History of Bucks County Pennsylvania*. NY/Chi. Lewis Pub Co.
1905. 3. illus. 2nd ed, rev and enlarged, lea, marbled bds, marbled endpapers, pres
copy sgn by author. . . . . *$200.00–$300.00*

Davy, Humphry. *Salmonia*. Lon. John Murray. 1851. 4th ed. illus. *$125.00–$150.00*

Davy, John. *The Angler and His Friend*. Lon. Longman, Brown. 1855. 1st ed. mor
and cl. . . . . *$75.00–$125.00*

Dawson, Mrs. Nelson (Edith B.). *Enamels*. Chi. 1910. illus. . . . . . *$25.00–$35.00*

Dawson, Sarah M. *Confederate Girl's Diary*. Bos. 1913. 1st ed. . . . .
. . . . *$75.00–$125.00*

Dawson, Simon J. *Report of the Exploration of the Country Between Lake Superior
and the Red River Settlement....* Tor. John Lovell. Legislative Assembly. 1859. 3 lg
fldg maps. . . . . *$285.00–$300.00*

Dawson, W. F. *Christmas: Its Origin and Associations*. Lon. Stock. 1902. 1st ed.
illus. teg. . . . . *$100.00–$150.00*

Day, Francis. *The Fishes of Great Britain and Ireland*. Lon. Williams & Norgate.
1880-1884. 2 vols. 1st ed. illus. litho plates, teg. . . . . *$450.00–$700.00*

Day, Jeremiah. *Introducton to Algebra*. New Haven. 1814. 1st ed. . . . .
. . . . *$45.00–$65.00*

Day, L. W. *Story of the One Hundred and First Ohio Infantry*. Cleve. 1894. 1st ed.
illus. . . . . *$150.00–$250.00*

Day, Lal Behari. *Bengal Peasant Life*. Lon. Macmillan.1892. . . . . *$22.00–$30.00*

Day, Mrs. C. M. *History of the Eastern Townships*. Montreal. 1869. . . . .
. . . . *$75.00–$125.00*

Dayan, Moshe. *Story of My Life*. NY. 1976. 1st ed. illus. photos, sgn, dj. . . . .
. . . . *$30.00–$45.00*

Dayton, Fred Erving. *Steamboat Days*. NY. 1925. 1st ed. illus. by John Wolcott
Adams. . . . . *$40.00–$60.00*

De Angel, Marguerite. *Book of Nursery & Mother Goose Rhymes*. Garden City.
Doubleday. 1954. illus. Caldecott Honor book, dj. . . . . *$35.00–$50.00*

De Beauvoir, Simone. *Long March.* Cleve/NY. World Pub. 1958. 1st ed. dj. . . . . .
. . . . *$47.00–$60.00*

De Beauvoir, Simone. *The Mandarins.* NY. 1956. 1st Amer ed. dj. *$22.00–$30.00*

De Bothezat, George. *Back to Newton.* NY. 1936. 1st ed. 152 pp, dj. *$30.00–$35.00*

De Brunhoff, Jean. *Babar and Father Christmas.* NY. Random House. (1940). 1st
ed. illus. dj. . . . . *$80.00–$90.00*

De Brunhoff, Jean. *Babar and His Children.* NY. (1938). 1st Amer ed. illus, folio.
. . . . *$100.00–$175.00*

De Brunhoff, Jean. *Babar and His Children.* Random House. (1938). 1st Amer ed.
illus. . . . . *$225.00–$325.00*

De Brunhoff, Jean. *Babar the King.* NY. Smith/Haas. 1935. 1st Amer, folio. . . . .
. . . . *$125.00–$150.00*

De Brunhoff, Jean. *Babar the King.* NY. Random House. 1986. folio, printed in
France, dj. . . . . *$35.00–$50.00*

De Brunhoff, Jean. *Travels of Babar.* NY. Smith/Haas. 1934. 1st ed. illus. . . . . . .
. . . . *$250.00–$300.00*

De Camp, Etta. *Return of Frank Stockton.* NY. 1913. 1st ed. . . . . . *$75.00–$85.00*

De Chastellux, Marquis. *Travels in North America in the Years 1780, 1781,1782.*
Lon. G. G. J and J. Robinson. 1788. 2 vols. contemporary calf binding, raised bands,
black and red labels on spine, 2 fldg maps. . . . . *$750.00–$850.00*

De Clifford, N. F. *Egypt the Cradle of Ancient Masonry.* NY. 1907. 2 vols. . . . . .
. . . . *$65.00–$85.00*

De Fontelle, M. *Conversations on the Plurality of Worlds.* Dublin. Wilson. 1761.
illus. . . . . *$50.00–$100.00*

De Groat, Robert W. *Totem Poles—A Happy Hobby for Boys.* NY. Boy Scouts of
America. 1930. 1st ed. wrps. illus. . . . . *$28.00–$35.00*

De La Mare, Walter. *Eight Tales.* Sauk City. Arkham House. 1971. 1st ed. 2992 cc,
dj. . . . . *$35.00–$45.00*

De La Mare, Walter. *Memoirs of a Midget.* Lon. (1921). 1st ed. dj. *$35.00–$50.00*

De La Mare, Walter. *Mr. Bumps and His Monkey.* Chi. 1942. 1st ed. illus. . . . . . .
. . . . *$95.00–$135.00*

De La Mare, Walter. *Riddle and Other Stories.* Lon. (1923). 1st ed. blue cl, dj. . . .
. . . . *$120.00–$150.00*

De Leon, T. C. (ed.). *South Songs: From the Lays of Later Days.* NY. 1866. 1st ed.
. . . . *$95.00–$125.00*

De Maupassant, Guy. *Odd Number*. Lon. 1891. 1st Eng. ed. . . . . . *$50.00–$75.00*

De Poncins, Gontran. *From a Chinese City*. Garden City. 1957. 1st ed. dj. . . . . .
. . . . *$50.00–$65.00*

De Quille, Dan. *History of the Big Bonanza*. Hartford. 1876. . . . *$100.00–$250.00*

De Quille, Dan. *History of the Comstock Silver Lode*. Nev. (1889). wrps. . . . .
. . . . *$100.00–$250.00*

De Quincey, Thomas. *Essays on the Poets and Other English Writers*. Bos. Ticknor
& Fields. 1859. . . . . *$50.00–$80.00*

De Roos, Frederick. *Personal Narrative of Travels in the U.S. and Canada in 1826.*
Lon. 1827. illus. 2nd ed. lithos, maps. . . . . *$165.00–$250.00*

De Segur, Philip. *History of the Expedition to Russia*. Lon. Treuttel & Wurtz. 1825.
2 vols. in one. fldg map, rev and corrected. . . . . *$60.00–$90.00*

De Shields, James T. *Border Wars of Texas*. Tioga, TX. 1912. 1st ed. illus. . . . . . .
. . . . *$175.00–$250.00*

De Smet, P. J. *Western Missions and Missionaries*. NY. Kennedy. 1859. 1st ed. . .
. . . . *$105.00–$195.00*

De Smet, Pierre-Jean. *Oregon Missions and Travels Over the Rocky Mountains.*
NY. 1847. 1st ed. wrps. plates, fldg map. . . . . *$350.00–$900.00*

De Voto, Bernard. *Across the Wide Missouri*. Bos. 1947. illus. . . . *$40.00–$90.00*

De Voto, Bernard. *Mark Twain at Work*. 1942. 1st ed. dj. . . . . *$22.00–$35.00*

De Voto, Bernard. *Year of Decision 1846*. Bos. Little, Brown. 1943. 1st ed. dj. . .
. . . . *$24.00–$32.00*

De Vries, Hugo. *Species and Varieties. Their Origin by Mutation*. Chi. 1906. 2nd ed.
. . . . *$75.00–$95.00*

De Vries, Peter. *I Hear America Singing.*Bos. Little, Brown. 1976. 1st ed. dj. . . . .
. . . . *$24.00–$30.00*

De Vries, Peter. *Into Your Tent I'll Creep*. Bos. Little, Brown. 1971. 1st Amer ed. dj.
. . . . *$20.00–$30.00*

De Vries, Peter. *Slouching Towards Kalamazoo*. Bos. (1983). 1st ed. sgn, dj. . . . .
. . . . *$20.00–$30.00*

De Vries, Peter. *Vale of Laughter*. Bos. 1967. sgn, presentation copy, dj. . . . .
. . . . *$35.00–$45.00*

Deane, Samuel. *History of Scituate, Massachusetts*. Bos. 1831. 1st ed. 406 pp. . .
. . . . *$200.00–$225.00*

Dearborn, R. F. *Saratoga Illustrated.* Troy, NY. 1872. 1st ed. illus. fldg map, clr lithos. . . . . *$96.00–$125.00*

Death, J. *Beer of the Bible with a Visit to an Arab Brewery.* Lon. 1887. 179 pp. . . . . *$90.00–$120.00*

Debs, Eugene. *His Life, Writings and Speeches.* Chi. Girard. 1908. sgn. . . . . *$100.00–$135.00*

Decker, Amelia Stickney. *That Ancient Trail.* pub by author. 1942). illus. 3rd ed. . . . . *$20.00–$30.00*

Decker, John W. *Cheese Making.* WI. 1909. . . . . *$30.00–$45.00*

Decter, Midge. *Liberated Woman and Other Americans.* NY. Coward McCann. (1971). 256 pp, dj. *$30.00*

Deere, John & Co. *How To Keep Your Farm Equipment in the Fight.* illus. . . . . *$15.00–$25.00*

Deere, John & Co. *Operation, Care and Repair of Farm Machinery.* 1957. illus. . . . . *$25.00–$45.00*

Deering Ideals. Chi. Deering Harvester Co. 1902. illus. pict wrps. . . *$40.00–$50.00*

Defoe, Daniel. *Adventures of Robinson Crusoe.* Lon. (1867). illus. gilt cl. . . . . *$90.00–$115.00*

Defoe, Daniel. *Journal of the Plague Year.* Limited Edition Club. 1968. illus. ltd 1500 cc. sgn, dj, glassine slipcase. . . . . *$50.00–$85.00*

Defoe, Daniel. *Life and Strange Surprising Adventures of Robinson Crusoe.* NY/Lon. Harper & Bros. (1900). illus. by Louis and Frederick Rhead. black cl, pict pastedown. . . . . *$20.00–$30.00*

Defoe, Daniel. *Memoirs of a Cavalier.* Lon. (1720). 1st ed. calf. *$175.00–$250.00*

Defoe, Daniel. *Moll Flanders.* John Lane. The Bodley Head. 1929. illus. . . . . *$40.00–$75.00*

Defoe, Daniel. *Robinson Crusoe.* NY. Cosmo. 1920. illus. w/clr plate by N C Wyeth. . . . . *$90.00–$190.00*

Defoe, Daniel. *Robinson Crusoe.* Worcester, MA. 1795. illus. wood-engr frontis. . . . . *$60.00–$90.00*

Deighton, Len. *Bomber.* NY. Harper & Row. 1970. 1st ed. dj. . . . . *$44.00–$55.00*

Deighton, Len. *Funeral in Berlin.* Putnam's. 1965. 1st Us ed. dj. *$60.00*

Deighton, Len. *Ipcress File.* NY. Simon & Schuster. 1963. 1st US ed. dj. . . . . *$75.00–$140.00*

Deighton, Len. *Only When I Laugh.* NY. 1987. ltd 250cc, sgn, slipcase. . . . .
. . . . *$95.00–$125.00*

Deite, C. *Practical Treatise on Manufacture of Perfumery.* Phila. 1892. illus. 1st
Amer ed. . . . . *$40.00–$55.00*

Del Rey, Lester. *Attack from Atlantis.* Phila. Winston. (1953). 207 pp, dj. . . . .
. . . . *$50.00–$65.00*

Delany, Samuel R. *Dhalgren.* NY. Bantam Books. (1975). 1st ed. pict wrps. . . . .
. . . . *$20.00–$25.00*

Dellenbaugh, Frederick S. *Romance of the Colorado River.* NY. Putnam's. 1903.
2nd prtg. illus. photos, drawings. . . . . *$80.00–$100.00*

Dellenbaugh, Frederick S. *Romance of the Colorado River.* NY. Putnam's Sons.
1903. illus. . . . . *$75.00–$90.00*

Dempsey, Hugh. *History In Their Blood, The Indian Portraits of N. Grandmaison.*
Hudson Hills, NY. 1982. 1st Amer ed. dj. *$40.00–$50.00*

Dempsey, Jack. *Dempsey: By the Man Himself.* 1960. 1st ed. sgn. . *$50.00–$65.00*

Dempsey, Jack. *Round by Round.* 1940. 1st ed. wrps. . . . . *$28.00–$35.00*

Denham, Major Dixon. *Narrative of Travels & Discoveries in Northern & Central
Africa.* 1826. . . . . *$500.00–$650.00*

Denhardt, Robert Moorman. *King Ranch Quarter Horses.* Norman. Univ
Oklahoma Press. 1970. 1st ed. dj. . . . . *$50.00–$65.00*

Denhardt, Robert Moorman. *Quarter Horses.* Norman. Univ Oklahoma Press.
1967. 1st ed. sgn, dj. . . . . *$40.00–$65.00*

Denliger, Milo. *Complete Cocker Spaniel.* DC. Denliger. 1946. 1st ed. *$25.00–$35.00*

Dennis, Morgan. *Morgan Dennis Dog Book.* NY. 1946. 1st ed. illus. dj. *$25.00–$35.00*

Denslow, W. W. *Denslow's Scarecrow and the Tin Man.* 1903. 1st ed. illus. linen.
. . . . *$300.00–$600.00*

Denslow, W. W. *Mother Goose.* NY. McClure. 1901. illus. paper bds. . . . .
. . . . *$100.00–$500.00*

Denslow, W. W. *Pearl and the Pumpkin.* NY. Dillingham. 1904. 1st ed. illus. green
cl. . . . . *$100.00–$200.00*

Denslow, W. W. *Scarecrow and the Tin-Man.* Dillingham. (1904). *$150.00–$300.00*

Denslow, W. W. *When I Grow Up.* Century. 1909. 1st ed. illus. 24 clr plates. . . . .
. . . . *$100.00–$150.00*

Denslow, William. *Freemasonry & the American Indian.* Missouri Lodge of Research. 1972. illus. photos. . . . . *$25.00–$45.00*

Densmore, Frances. *Chippewa Music II.* DC. GPO. 1913. 1st ed. 341 pp. Bulletin 53. . . . . *$50.00–$90.00*

Densmore, Frances. *Papago Music.* DC. GPO. 1929. illus. . . . . . . *$35.00–$60.00*

Derby, W. L. A. *Tall Ships.* NY. Scribner's. 1937. 1st ed. illus. photos, plates. . . . . *$50.00–$100.00*

Derleth, August. *Bright Journey.* NY. Scribner's. 1940. 1st ed. inscr. . . . . *$50.00–$65.00*

Derleth, August. *Casebook of Solar Pons.* Sauk City. 1965. 1st ed. dj. *$35.00–$45.00*

Derleth, August. *Dark Mind, Dark Heart.* Sauk City. Arkham House. 1962. dj inscr and sgn. . . . . *$80.00–$120.00*

Derleth, August. *Fell Purpose.* NY. Arcadia House. 1953. 1st ed. dj. *$35.00–$45.00*

Derleth, August. *Not Long For This World.* Sauk City. Arkham House. 1948. 1st ed. ltd, dj. . . . . *$50.00–$150.00*

Derleth, August. *Over the Edge.* Sauk City. Arkham House. 1964. 1st ed. dj sgn. . . . . *$50.00–$75.00*

Derleth, August. *Over the Edge.* Sauk City. Arkham House. 1964. 1st ed. dj. . . . . *$30.00–$45.00*

Derleth, August. *Restless Is the River.* NY. Scribner's. 1939. 1st ed. dj. . . . . *$50.00–$100.00*

Derleth, August. *Something Near.* Sauk City. Arkham House. 1945. 1st ed. 274 pp, inscr. . . . . *$75.00–$95.00*

Derleth, August. *Thirty Years of Arkham House.* Sauk City. Arkham House. 1970. 1st ed. dj. . . . . *$50.00–$85.00*

Derry, Joseph. *Story of the Confederate States.* Richmond. 1895. 1st ed. illus. . . . . *$50.00–$100.00*

Descharnes, Robert. *World of Salvador Dali.* Atide Books. nd. dj. . *$50.00–$80.00*

Description of the New York Central Park. NY. 1869. . . . . *$250.00–$700.00*

Descriptive Catalogue of School Supplies. Chi. Central School Supply House. c1897-98. illus. pict wrps, 88 pp. . . . . *$95.00–$125.00*

Desmond, Kay. *All Color Book of Dolls.* Lon. Octopus Books Ltd. 1974. 1st ed. illus. photos. . . . . *$10.00–$25.00*

Desmond, Ray. *Bibliography of British Gardens*. London. St. Paul's Bibliographies. (1988). 1st ed. illus. . . . . *$50.00–$80.00*

Deutsch, Babette. *Take Them, Stranger*. NY. (1944). 1st ed. sgn. . . *$44.00–$60.00*

Development of the Locomotive. OH. Central Steel Co. (1925). illus. buff and brown cl. . . . . *$15.00–$20.00*

Devries, Juliana. *The Campfire Girls on Caliban Island*. Cleve. 1933. 1st ed. dj. . . . . *$8.00–$15.00*

Dewar, George A. B. *The Book of the Dry Fly*. Lon. Lawrence & Bullen. 1897. 1st ed. illus. plates, teg. . . . . *$100.00–$150.00*

Dewees, F. P. *Molly Maguires*. Phila. 1877. map. . . . . *$95.00–$150.00*

Dewees, William. *Compendious System of Midwifery*. Phila. Carey & Lea. 1832. 5th ed. engr, 636 pp. . . . . *$130.00–$150.00*

Dewees, William. *Compendious System of Midwifery*. Phila. 1847. illus. lea. . . . . *$75.00–$120.00*

Dewees, William. *Treatise on the Diseases of Females*. Phila. 1840. illus. 7th ed. calf, steel plates. . . . . *$75.00–$125.00*

Dewey, John. *Experience and Education*. 1938. 1st ed. sgn. . . . . . *$55.00–$75.00*

Dewitt, David Miller. *Judicial Murder of Mary E. Surratt*. Balt. 1895. 1st ed. . . . . *$185.00–$250.00*

Dexte, Colin. *The Remorseful Day*. Lon. Macmillan. 1999. 1st ed. sgn, dj. . . . . *$55.00–$65.00*

Dexte, Colin. *The Riddle of the Third Mile*. Lon. Macmillan. 1983. 1st ed. sgn, dj. . . . . *$450.00–$500.00*

Dexte, Colin. *The Secret of Annexe 3*. Lon. Macmillan. 1986. 1st ed. sgn, dj. . . . . *$600.00–$650.00*

Dick & Jane: Our New Friends. 1946. . . . . *$65.00–$70.00*

Dick and Jane: Before We Read. Scott Forsman. 1962. softcvr. . . . *$40.00–$80.00*

Dick and Jane: Fun Wherever We Are. 1962. softcvr. . . . . *$35.00–$85.00*

Dick and Jane: Fun With Dick & Jane. 1946. . . . . *$150.00–$180.00*

Dick and Jane: Fun With Dick & Jane. 1946. . . . . *$100.00–$180.00*

Dick and Jane: Now We Read. 1965. softcvr. . . . . *$75.00–$165.00*

Dick and Jane: We Look and See. 1946-47. softcvr. . . . . *$120.00–$120.00*

Dick and Jane: We Talk, Spell and Write. 1951. softcvr. . . . . *$75.00–$195.00*

Dick, Philip. *Counter Clock World.* NY. Berkley. (1967). wrps. . . . *$40.00–$50.00*

Dick, Philip. *Game Players of Titan.* Ace Pub. (1963). wrps. . . . . . *$20.00–$25.00*

Dick, Philip. *Time Out of Joint.* Lon. 1961. 1st UK ed. blue cl.. . *$120.00–$150.00*

Dick, Philip K. *Broken Bubble.* NY. Arbor House. (1988). 1st ed. dj. . . . .
. . . . *$30.00–$40.00*

Dick, Philip K. *Cosmic Puppets.* Severn House. (1986). 1st ed. dj. . *$35.00–$45.00*

Dick, Philip K. *Crack in Space.* (Wallington). Severn House. (1989). 1st separate hardcvr ed. dj. . . . . *$25.00–$45.00*

Dick, Philip K. *Golden Man.* Berkeley. (1980). 1st ed. paperback. . . . .
. . . . *$30.00–$35.00*

Dick, Philip K. *I Hope I Shall Arrive Soon.* NY. 1985. dj. . . . . *$25.00–$35.00*

Dick, Philip K. *Our Friends from Frolix 8.* Lon. Kinnell. 1989. 1st hardcvr ed. dj.
. . . . *$25.00–$65.00*

Dick, Philip K. *Scanner Darkly.* Garden City. 1977. 1st ed. dj. . . *$75.00–$125.00*

Dick, William B. *Dick's Hand Book of Cribbage.* NY. 1885. . . . . . *$18.00–$25.00*

Dickens, Charles. *A Christmas Carol.* Lon. Chapman & Hall. 1843. 1st ed. reddish-brown ribbed cl. . . . . *$5,750.00–$20,000.00*

Dickens, Charles. *A Christmas Carol.* Phila. 1844. illus. by John Leech 4 clr plates, 4 woodcuts, dark blue binding 158 pp. *$600.00–$900.00*

Dickens, Charles. *Battle of Life.* Lon. Bradbury and Evans. 1846. 30 vols. 1st ed. cl aeg. . . . . *$200.00–$350.00*

Dickens, Charles. *Dombey & Son.* NY. 1847. wrps. . . . . *$100.00–$210.00*

Dickens, Charles. *Life and Adventures of Martin Chuzzlewit.* Lon. Chapman and Hall. 1844. 1st ed. illus. original bds. . . . . *$75.00–$150.00*

Dickens, Charles. *Life and Adventures of Nicholas Nickelby.* Chapman & Hall. 1839. 1st ed in book form. . . . . *$150.00–$200.00*

Dickens, Charles. *Little Dorrit.* Lon. 1857. illus. 1st ed in book form, engr, 1/2 calf, mar bds. . . . . *$185.00–$300.00*

Dickens, Charles. *Martin Chuzzlewit.* Ticknor & Fields. 1867. illus. *$40.00–$65.00*

Dickens, Charles. *Our Mutual Friend.* Lon. 1865. 2 vols. 1st ed. in book form. . .
. . . . *$150.00–$250.00*

Dickens, Charles. *The Chimes.* Lon. Limited Ed Club. 1931. 1st thus. ltd 1500cc. sgn by Arthur Rackham, cvr design by Rackham, teg, illus.. . . . . *$400.00–$500.00*

Dickens, Charles. *Works of....* NY. Scribner's. 1899. 36 vols. illus. . . . .
. . . . *$1,000.00–$3,000.00*

Dickens, Charles. *Works of....* Lon. Folio Society. 1981-88. 16 vols. illus. cl backed bds, slipcases. . . . . *$200.00–$300.00*

Dickey, James. *Deliverance.* Bos. 1970. 1st ed. 1st prtg, dj. . . . . . . *$35.00–$55.00*

Dickey, James. *To the White Sea.* Bos. Houghton Mifflin. 1993. 1st ed. sgn, dj. . .
. . . . *$45.00–$50.00*

Dickey, James. *Tucky the Hunter.* NY. Crown.. 1978. 1st ed. . . . . . *$25.00–$35.00*

Dickinson, Emily. *Bolts of Melody.* NY. 1945. 1st ed. Todd & Bingham (eds). . . .
. . . . *$25.00–$40.00*

Dickinson, Emily. *Poems.* Bos. Roberts Bros. 1892. 9th ed. dec cl. *$90.00–$120.00*

Dickinson, Emily. *Poems.* Bos. Roberts. 1891. 1st ed. edited by TW Higginson and Mabel Loomis Todd, second series, 8vo, 230 pp, teg, gray-green cl. *$350.00–$800.00*

Dickinson, Emily. *Single Hound.* Bos. 1914. . . . . *$200.00–$400.00*

Dickinson, S. N. *Boston Almanac for the year 1843.* Bos. illus. . . . *$45.00–$75.00*

Dickson, Walter. *Japan.* Peter Fenelon Collier. 1898. illus. red cl. . . . .
. . . . *$22.00–$30.00*

Didion, Joan. *Run River.* Obolensky. 1963. 1st ed. dj. . . . . *$75.00–$125.00*

Didion, Joan. *Slouching Towards Bethlehem.* NY. Farrar, Straus & Giroux. 1968. dj.
. . . . *$40.00–$60.00*

Dietz, August. *Postal Service of the Confederate States of America.* Richmond. Dietz. 1929. 1st ed. sgn. . . . . *$200.00–$350.00*

Dietz, William. *Star Wars Dark Forces.* Putnam's. 1997. 1st ed. dj. . . . .
. . . . *$14.00–$20.00*

Digges, Jeremiah. *Cape Cod Pilot.* Provincetown/NY. WPA. 1937. 2nd prtg, dj. . .
. . . . *$25.00–$35.00*

Dillard, Annie. *An American Childhood.* Harper. 1987. 1st ed. dj. . *$25.00–$35.00*

Dillard, Annie. *Holy the Firm.* NY. Harper & Row. (1977). 1st ed. dj. . . . .
. . . . *$30.00–$75.00*

Dillin, Capt. John. *The Kentucky Rifle.* DC. National Rifle Association. 1924. . . .
. . . . *$125.00–$250.00*

Dillon, Richard. *Images of Chinatown: Louis J. Stellman's Chinatown Photographs.* SF. Book Club of California. 1976. 1st ed. . . . . *$75.00–$140.00*

Dimsdale, Thomas J. *Vigilantes of Montana.* Helena. nd. 4th ed. . *$50.00–$75.00*

Dinesen, Isak. *Anecdotes of Destiny.* NY. Random House. (1958). 1st ed. dj. . . . . *$30.00–$60.00*

Dinesen, Isak. *Out of Africa.* NY. 1938. 1st ed. dj. . . . . *$45.00–$250.00*

Dinesen, Isak. *Seven Gothic Tales.* NY. 1934. 1st ed. dj. . . . . *$35.00–$85.00*

Directory of the City of New Brunswick 1855–56. J. Terhune. 1855. *$100.00–$135.00*

Dirigibles Captifs Spheriques; Parachutes; Treuils & Tenders D'Aerostation. Paris. Zodiac, Anciens Establissements Aeronautiques. 1918. illus. pict wrps, 32 pp. . . . . *$175.00–$250.00*

Dismond, Binga. *We Who Would Die.* NY. Wendell Malliet and Co. 1943. 1st ed. illus. by E. Simms Campbell. inscr, dj. *$100.00–$300.00*

Disney. *Mickey Mouse Story Book.* Phila. (1931). orange pict cl. . . . . *$140.00–$750.00*

Disney. *Mickey Mouse Waddle Book.* NY. 1934. bds. . . . . *$300.00–$800.00*

Disney. *Pop-up Mickey Mouse.* Blue Ribbon Books. 1933. illus. 3 pop-ups. . . . . *$125.00–$600.00*

Disney. *Pop-Up Minnie Mouse.* 1933. illus. 3 pop-ups. . . . . *$200.00–$350.00*

Disney, Alfred N. *Origin and Devlopment of the Microscope.* Lon. 1928. illus. plates. . . . . *$140.00–$150.00*

Disney, Walt. *Bambi.* NY. Grosset & Dunlap. (1942). illus. yellow pict bds, dj. . . . . *$65.00–$85.00*

Disney, Walt. *Fantasia Program.* 1940. 1st ed. wrps. illus. clr. . . . *$40.00–$200.00*

Disney, Walt. *Life of Donald Duck.* NY. Random House. (1941). 1st ed. pict bds. . . . . *$75.00–$125.00*

Disney, Walt. *Mickey Mouse Club Annual.* Racine. Whitman. 1957. *$25.00–$50.00*

Disney, Walt. *Mickey Mouse Stories, Book #2.* Phila. David McKay. 1934. wrps. illus. . . . . *$100.00–$175.00*

Disney, Walt. *Snow White and the Seven Dwarfs.* Walt Disney Enterprises. 1938. 1st ed. wrps. illus. clr pictures from the movie. . . . . *$75.00–$100.00*

Disney, Walt. *Stories from Fantasia.* NY. Random House. (1940). 1st ed. dj. . . . . *$75.00–$100.00*

Disney, Walt. *Three Little Pigs.* NY. Blue Ribbon. (1933). illus. dj. *$200.00–$250.00*

Ditmars, R. L. *Snakes of the World.* NY. (1931). . . . . *$25.00–$35.00*

Diving...Attempt to Describe Method of Supplying Diver With Air. Hartford. 1813. 1st ed. wrps. pamphlet. . . . . *$200.00–$375.00*

Dix, Dorothea. *Memorial to the Legislature of Massachusetts.* Salem. Gazette Office. 1843. 1st ed. wrps. unopened, 15 pp. . . . . *$200.00–$375.00*

Dixon, Franklin. *Brushing The Mountain Top.* NY. Grosset & Dunlap. 1934. . . . . *$10.00–$15.00*

Dixon, Franklin. *Hardy Boys A Figure in Hiding.* NY. Grosset & Dunlap. 1937. . . . . *$15.00–$18.00*

Dixon, Franklin. *Hidden Harbor Mystery.* NY. Grosset & Dunlap. 1935. Hardy Boys #14. . . . . *$14.00–$16.00*

Dixon, Franklin. *Hooded Hawk Mystery.* NY. Grosset & Dunlap. 1971. Hardy Boys #34 dj. . . . . *$25.00–$35.00*

Dixon, Franklin. *House on the Cliff.* NY. Grosset & Dunlap. 1927. Hardy Boys #2, dj. . . . . *$20.00–$25.00*

Dixon, Franklin. *House on the Cliff.* NY. Grosset & Dunlap. (1959). Hardy Boys #2 dj. . . . . *$15.00–$20.00*

Dixon, Franklin. *Hunting for Hidden Gold.* NY. Grosset & Dunlap. illus. . . . . *$12.00–$15.00*

Dixon, Franklin. *Mark On The Door.* NY. Grosset & Dunlap. dj. . *$15.00–$18.00*

Dixon, Franklin. *Missing Chums.* NY. Grosset & Dunlap. (1957). dj. *$15.00–$18.00*

Dixon, Franklin. *Missing Chums.* NY. Grosset & Dunlap. (1957). Hardy Boys, dj. . . . . *$12.00–$15.00*

Dixon, Franklin. *Mystery of Cabin Island.* NY. Grosset & Dunlap. 1929. Hardy Boys #8 dj. . . . . *$19.00–$21.00*

Dixon, Franklin. *Mystery of Cabin Island.* NY. Grosset & Dunlap. 1929. Hardy Boys #8. . . . . *$9.00–$12.00*

Dixon, Franklin. *Shore Road Mystery.* NY. Grosset & Dunlap. 1928. . . . . *$15.00–$35.00*

Dixon, Franklin. *Short Wave Mystery.* NY. Grosset & Dunlap. (1945). Hardy Boys #24, dj. . . . . *$18.00–$25.00*

Dixon, Franklin. *Sign of the Crooked Arrow.* NY. Grosset & Dunlap. (1934). Hardy Boys #28, dj. . . . . *$18.00–$20.00*

Dixon, Franklin. *While The Clock Ticked.* NY. Grosset & Dunlap. 1941. tan cl. . .
. . . . *$15.00–$30.00*

Dixon, Franklin W. *Danger Trails of the Sky.* NY. Grosset & Dunlap. 1931. 1st ed.
Ted Scott #14, dj. . . . . *$50.00–$65.00*

Dixon, Franklin W. *The Hardy Boys: the Hidden Harbor Mystery.* NY. Grosset &
Dunlap. (1935). #14, tan bds with brown lettering. . . . . *$15.00–$20.00*

Dixon, Franklin W. *The Hardy Boys: the Secret of the Lost Tunnel.* NY. Grosset &
Dunlap. 1950. 1st ed. #29, cl, dj. . . . . *$15.00–$20.00*

Dixon, Franklin W. *The Hardy Boys: the Tower Treasure.* NY. Grosset & Dunlap.
1959. dj. . . . . *$15.00–$22.00*

Dixon, Joseph K. *Vanishing Race, The Last Great Indian Council....* NY. 1914. illus.
. . . . *$85.00–$125.00*

Dixon, Peter. *Bobby Benson in the Tunnel of Gold.* Buffalo Hecker HO Co. 1936. 1st
ed. wrps. illus. . . . . *$12.00–$25.00*

Dobie, Frank. *Tales of Old Time Texas.* Bos. Little, Brown. 1955. dj. . . . .
. . . . *$45.00–$55.00*

Dobie, J Frank. *Man Bird and Beast.* Austin. 1930. 1st ed. cl. . . . . *$35.00–$75.00*

Dobie, J. Frank. *Apache Gold & Yanqui Silver.* Bos. Little, Brown. 1939. 1st ed. dj.
. . . . *$30.00–$75.00*

Dobie, J. Frank. *As the Moving Finger Writ.* np. 1955). wrps. 12 pp. *$25.00–$40.00*

Dobie, J. Frank. *Ben Lilly Legend.* Little, Brown. 1950. 1st ed. dj. *$30.00–$60.00*

Dobie, J. Frank. *Life and Literature of the South West.* Austin. Univ of Texas Press.
1943. 1st ed. illus. by Peter Hurd. . . . . *$50.00–$90.00*

Dobie, J. Frank. *The Longhorns.* Bos. Little, Brown. 1941. 1st ed. dj. . . . .
. . . . *$40.00–$50.00*

Dobie, J. Frank. *The Mustangs.* Bos. Little, Brown. (1952). 1st ed. dj. . . . .
. . . . *$40.00–$70.00*

Dobie, J. Frank. *The Mustangs.* Bos. Little, Brown. (1952). 1st ed. *$25.00–$40.00*

Dobie, J. Frank. *Voice of the Coyote.* Little, Brown. 1949. 1st ed. dj. . . . .
. . . . *$50.00–$90.00*

Dobie, J. Frank. *Wild and Wily.* Flagstaff. Northland Press. 1980. 1st ed. dj. . . . .
. . . . *$30.00–$45.00*

Dobson, William. *Kunopaedia, a Practical Essay on Breaking or Training the
English Spaniel or Pointer.* Lon. 1817. 2nd ed. . . . . *$100.00–$200.00*

Doctorow, E. L. *Billy Bathgate*. NY. Random House. (1989). 1st ed. ltd 300 cc, sgn, slipcase. . . . . *$85.00–$125.00*

Doctorow, E. L. *Lives of the Poets*. NY. Random House. (1984). 1st ed. dj. . . . . .
. . . . *$25.00–$30.00*

Doctorow, E. L. *Loon Lake*. NY. Random House. 1980. 1st ed. dj. *$20.00–$30.00*

Doctorow, E. L. *Loon Lake*. NY. Random House. (1980). 1st ed. 1/350 cc, sgn, slip-case. . . . . *$100.000–$125.00*

Doctorow, E. L. *Ragtime*. NY. Random House. (1975). 1st ed. sgn, dj. . . . .
. . . . *$50.00–$65.00*

Doctorow, E. L. *Welcome to Hard Times*. NY. Simon & Schuster. 1960. 1st ed. dj, author's first book. . . . . *$300.00–$700.00*

Dodge, Col. Richard I. *Our Wild Indians*. Hartford. Worthington. 1882. . . . .
. . . . *$50.00–$75.00*

Dodge, Grenville. *Battle of Atlanta and Other Campaign Addresses, etc.* Council Bluff, IA. Monarch. 1910. 1st ed. illus. *$65.00–$175.00*

Dodge, Mary M. *Hans Brinker*. NY. Scribner's. 1926. illus. clr plates. . . . .
. . . . *$22.00–$30.00*

Dodge, Mary M. *When Life is Young*. Century. 1894. 1st ed. illus. . . . .
. . . . *$30.00–$40.00*

Dodge, Mary Mape. *Hans Brinker and the Silver Skates*. NY. Scribner's.1915. illus.
. . . . *$35.00–$50.00*

Dodge, Richard I. *Plains of the Great West & Their Inhabitants*. NY. 1877. 1st ed. illus. fldg map. . . . . *$95.00–$125.00*

Dolbear, A. E. *The Telephone*. 1877. 1st ed. illus. cl. . . . . *$95.00–$150.00*

Doll's House. Viking Press & Kestrel Books. 1981. oblong, facs of antique Pop-up book, illus by Meggendorfer. . . . . *$30.00–$40.00*

Domenech, Emmanuel. *Seven Years' Residence in the Great Deserts of North America*. Lon. Longman, Green, Logman and Roberts. 1860. 2 vols. 1st ed. illus. fldg map, plates. . . . . *$600.00–$850.00*

Donaldson, Alfred L. *History of the Adirondacks*. NY. 1921. 2 vols. 1st ed. . . . . .
. . . . *$110.00–$200.00*

Donne, John. *The Sermons*. Berkeley. Univ of CA. 1962. 10 vols. . . . .
. . . . *195.00–$250.00*

Donnelly, Ned. *Self-Defense; or, The Art of Boxing*. Lon. Weldon. 1879. 1st ed. . .
. . . . *$150.00–$250.00*

Donnovan, Dick. *In the Face of the Night.* Lon. Long. 1908. 1st ed. . . . .
. . . . *$8,000.00–$100.00*

Dore Bible Gallery. Phila. 1883. illus. . . . . *$45.00–$65.00*

Dorsett, Helen. *Cabinetmaker's Guide for Dollhouse Furniture.* privately printed. 1964. spiral bound, pamphlet. . . . . *$20.00–$25.00*

Dorsey, James Owen and John R. Swanton. *Dictionary of the Biloxi and Ofo Languages.* DC. GPO. 1912. 1st ed. . . . . *$50.00–$125.00*

Dorsey, Sarah A. *Recollections of Henry Watkins Allen...Confederate Army.* NY. 1866. 1st ed. lea. . . . . *$125.00–$200.00*

Dos Passos John. *State of the Nation.* NY. Houghton Mifflin. 1944. 1st ed. dj. . . .
. . . . *$25.00–$45.00*

Dossenbach, Monique and Hans. *Great Stud Farms of the World.* NY. William Morrow. 1978. 1st US ed. illus. dj. . . . . *$95.00–$150.00*

Douet, Valerie Jackson. *Dollhouses the Collector's Guide.* Chartwell Books. (1994). folio. . . . . *$10.00–$15.00*

Doughty, Charles M. *Wanderings in Arabia.* Lon. Duckworth & Co. (1923). 2 vols. maps. . . . . *$60.00–$75.00*

Douglas, Norman. *In the Beginning.* NY. 1928. 1st Amer ed. dj. . . *$50.00–$80.00*

Douglass, Frederick. *Life and Times.* Hartford. 1881. 1st ed. illus. *$350.00–$700.00*

Douglass, Frederick. *My Bondage and My Freedom.* NY/Auburn. 1855. 1st ed. . . .
. . . . *$130.00–$250.00*

Dow, George Francis. *Slave Ships and Slaving.* Salem. Marine Research Society. 1927. 1st ed. . . . . *$145.00–$250.00*

Downing, A. G. *Architectural Heritage of Newport, RI.* NY. 1967. 2nd ed. dj. . . .
. . . . *$50.00–$75.00*

Downing, A. J. *A treatise on the theory and practice of landscape gardening adapted to North America....* NY. 1849. 4th ed. illus.. . . . . *$250.00–$550.00*

Downing, A. J. *Fruit and Fruit Trees of America.* NY. John Wiley. 1866. illus. . . .
. . . . *$60.00–$100.00*

Downing, A. J. *Fruits and Fruit Trees of America.* NY. 1846. cl. *$125.00–$300.00*

Downing, A. J. *Fruits and Fruit Trees of America....* NY. 1858. illus. . . . .
. . . . *$100.00–$200.00*

Downing, A. J. *Rural Essays.* NY. 1853. illus. . . . . *$75.00–$150.00*

Downing, A. J. *The Horticulturist.* Albany. July, 1846. 1st ed. . . *$100.00–$125.00*

Downing, A. J. *Treatise on the Theory and Practice of Landscape Gardening.* NY. 1859. 6th ed. illus. . . . . *$125.00–$150.00*

Downing, A. J. *Treatise on the Theory and Practice of Landscape Gardening.* NY. Putnam. 1854. illus. . . . . *$100.00–$300.00*

Downing, Andrew Jackson. *The Architecture of Country Houses.* NY/Lon. Appleton. 1850. 1st ed. pict cl. . . . . *$275.00–$325.00*

Downing, Andrew Jackson. *The Fruits and Fruit Trees of America.* NY/Lon. Wiley & Putnam. 1845. illus. . . . . *$200.00–$300.00*

Dowsett, H. M. *Wireless Telephony and Broadcasting.* 1924. 1st ed. illus. . . . . *$75.00–$100.00*

Doyle, A. Conan. *The Croxley Master.* NY. Doran. (1925). 1st Amer ed.. . . . . *$100.00–$125.00*

Doyle, A. Conan. *The Return of Sherlock Holmes.* Lon. Newnes. 1905. 1st ed. . . . . *$800.00–$900.00*

Doyle, Arthur Conan. *Adventures of Sherlock Holmes.* NY. (1892). 1st Amer ed. . . . . *$300.00–$500.00*

Doyle, Arthur Conan. *Adventures of Sherlock Holmes.* Lon. 1892. 1st ed. blue cl. . . . . *,750.00–$2,000.00*

Doyle, Arthur Conan. *Case-book of Sherlock Holmes.* Lon. Murray. 1927. 1st ed. *$300.00*

Doyle, Arthur Conan. *Croxley Master.* NY. Doran. (1925). 1st Amer ed. dj. . . . . *$80.00–$150.00*

Doyle, Arthur Conan. *Danger and Other Stories.* Lon. 1918. 1st ed. brown cl. . . . . *$60.00–$195.00*

Doyle, Arthur Conan. *Desert Drama.* Phil. 1898. illus. by Paget . 1st US ed. . . . . *$100.00–$125.00*

Doyle, Arthur Conan. *Green Flag.* NY. 1900. 1st Amer ed. . . . . *$65.00–$125.00*

Doyle, Arthur Conan. *Hound of the Baskervilles.* Lon. 1927. rprnt dj. . . . . *$60.00–$75.00*

Doyle, Arthur Conan. *Hound of the Baskervilles.* Lon. Newnes. 1902. 1st ed. 1st state with "you" for "your" on page 13, line 3. . . . . *$1,200.00–$2,000.00*

Doyle, Arthur Conan. *Hound of the Baskervilles.* NY. 1902. 1st Amer ed. 249 pp. 8 pp of ads. . . . . *$600.00–$1,000.00*

Doyle, Arthur Conan. *Lost World.* Lon. Hodder & Stoughton. (1912). 1st ed. illus. 319 pp. . . . . *$150.00–$225.00*

Doyle, Arthur Conan. *Lost World.* NY. Doran. (1912). 1st Amer ed. . . . .
. . . . *$65.00–$75.00*

Doyle, Arthur Conan. *New Revelation.* NY. Doran. (1918). . . . . . *$35.00–$45.00*

Doyle, Arthur Conan. *Sign of Four.* Lon. George Newnes. 1893. 3rd ed. red pict cvrs,. . . . . *$250.00–$375.00*

Doyle, Arthur Conan. *Sir Nigel.* Lon. Smith, Elder. 1906. . . . . . . *$40.00–$65.00*

Doyle, Arthur Conan. *The Parasite.* Lon. Constable. 1894. 1st ed. *$65.00–$150.00*

Doyle, Arthur Conan. *Through the Magic Door.* Lon. 1907. illus. *$65.00–$135.00*

Doyle, Arthur Conan. *Valley of Fear.* NY. Doran. 1914. 1st ed. . . . .
. . . . *$140.00–$175.00*

Doyle, Arthur Conan. *White Company.* NY. Cosmopolitan Book Co. 1922. illus. by N. C. Wyeth, dj. . . . . *$60.00–$100.00*

Drake, A. W. *Notable Collection of Brass and Copper Formed by Mr. A. W. Drake.* NY. American Art Galleries. 1907. wrps. illus. . . . . *$30.00–$40.00*

Drake, Benjamin. *Life of Tecumseh and of his Brother the Prophet....* Cinc. 1856.
. . . . *$90.00–$200.00*

Drake, D. *Dr. Daniel Drake's Letters on Slavery.* NY. 1940. 1st ed. ltd 250 cc, dj.
. . . . *$65.00–$75.00*

Drake, Ensg. Robert. *Boy Allies Under the Sea, or the Vanishing Submarine.* NY. A.L. Burt. 1916. illus. . . . . *$25.00–$45.00*

Drake, Francis. *Indian History for Young Folks.* NY/Lon. Harper & Bros. 1919. illus. red dec cl. . . . . *$20.00–$35.00*

Drake, Samuel. *Indian Biography.* Bos. Drake. 1832. 1st ed. . . . . *$85.00–$125.00*

Drake, Samuel Adams. *A Book of New England Legends and Folk Lore.* Bos. 1902.
. . . . *$12.00–$20.00*

Drane, Maude Johnston. *History of Henry County, Kentucky.* 1948. 1st ed. . . . . . .
. . . . *$50.00–$60.00*

Draper, John William. *Intellectual Development of Europe.* NY. Harper & Bros. 1876. 2 vols. rev ed. . . . . *$40.00–$50.00*

Dreiser, Theodore. *Gallery of Women.* NY. Liveright. 1929. 2 vols. 1st ed. djs. . .
. . . . *$150.00–$300.00*

Driggs, Howard R. *Pony Express Goes Through.* NY. 1935. . . . . . *$35.00–$45.00*

Drinker, Frederick E. and James G. Lewis. *Radio, Miracle of the 20th Century.* 1922. 1st ed. illus. . . . . *$20.00–$25.00*

Droeger, Joe. *Here's Who in Horses of the Pacific Coast.* Encino. 1945. vol. I. . . .
. . . . *$30.00–$40.00*

Drummond, H. *Tropical Africa.* John B. Alden. NY. 1890. . . . . . . *$50.00–$60.00*

Drury, Clifford. *Marcus and Narcissa Whitmen and the Opening of the Old Oregon.*
Glendale. Clark. 1973. 2 vols. 1st ed. illus. blue cl, inscr, sgn. . . . *$80.00–$115.00*

Drury, John. *Old Illinois Houses.* Illinois State Historical Society. 1948. 1st ed.
illus. 21 plates. . . . . *$75.00–$125.00*

Dryden, Adam. *Hints to Anglers.* Edin. Black. 1862. 1st ed. fldg maps, half mor &
cl. . . . . *$100.00–$175.00*

Du Bois, W. E. B. *Color and Democracy: Colonies and Peace.* NY. Harcourt, Brace.
1945. 1st ed. . . . . *$30.00–$45.00*

Du Bois, W. E. B. *Darkwater.* NY. Harcourt, Brace and Howe. 1920. 1st ed. dark
blue cl. . . . . *$100.00–$125.00*

Du Bois, W. E. B. *In Battle for Peace.* NY. Masses & Mainstream. 952. 1st ed. dj.
. . . . *$30.00–$40.00*

Du Bois, W. E. B. *The Autobiography of W. E. B. Du Bois.* NY. International
Publishers. 1968. 1st ed. dj. . . . . *$22.00–$32.00*

Du Bois, W. E. B. *World and Africa.* NY. (1947). . . . . *$35.00–$50.00*

Du Bois, W. E. B. *Writings.* NY. Library of America. 1986. 1st prtg. dark red cl, dj.
. . . . *$35.00–$60.00*

Du Chaillu, Paul. *Land of the Midnight Sun.* NY. Harper. (1881). 2 vols. illus. wood
engrs. pocket map. . . . . *$40.00–$60.00*

Du Chaillu, Paul. *Lost in the Jungle.* NY. 1869. 1st ed. . . . . *$40.00–$50.00*

Du Chaillu, Paul. *Midnight Sun.* NY. 1881. 2 vols. illus. fldg map. . . . .
. . . . *$100.00–$200.00*

Du Chaillu, Paul. *Stories of the Gorilla Country.* NY. 1868. 1st ed. illus. . . . .
. . . . *$275.00–$350.00*

Du Maurier, Daphne. *Scapegoat.* NY. 1957. 1st ed. dj. . . . . *$18.00–$25.00*

Du Puy, William Atherton. *Hawaii and Its Race Problem.* DC. GPO. 1932. illus.
. . . . *$20.00–$40.00*

Dubois, Abbe J. *Hindu Manner, Customs & Ceremonies.* Oxford. Clarendon. 1899.
2nd revised, corrected and enlarged ed. 732 pp. . . . . *$60.00–$75.00*

Dubois, Donald. *Fisherman's Handbook of Trout Flies.* NY. 1960. 1st ed. illus. clr
plates dj. . . . . *$45.00–$55.00*

Dubois, W. E. B. *Dark Princess*. NY. Harcourt. 1928. 1st ed. near fine. . . . .
. . . . *$135.00–$150.00*

Dubose, Heyward. *The Half Pint Flask*. NY. Farrar & Rinehart. 1929. 1st ed. illus.
. . . . *$15.00–$40.00*

Dubourg, George. *The Violin*. Lon. 1852. 4th ed. . . . . *$30.00–$40.00*

Dubus, Andre. *All the Time in the World*. NY. Knopf. 1996. 1st ed. *$35.00–$45.00*

Dubus, Andre. *Finding a Girl in America*. Bos. Godine. 1980. 1st ed. inscr, dj. . .
. . . . *$150.00–$200.00*

Dubus, Andre. *The Lieutenant*. NY. Dial. 1967. 1st ed. author's first book, dj. . . .
. . . . *$65.00–$175.00*

Duchaussois, P. *Mid Snow and Ice: The Apostles of the North-West*. Lon. 1923. 1st
ed. illus. . . . . *$60.00–$85.00*

Duckworth, C. L. D. and G. E. Langmuir. *West Highland Steamers*. Lon. 1935.
illus. 239 pp with index, pict bds. . . . . *$60.00–$100.00*

Dufur, S. M. *Over the Deadline or Tracked by Bloodlines*. Burlington, VT. 1902. .
. . . . *$75.00–$125.00*

Duke, Basil. *History of Morgan's Cavalry*. Cinn. 1867. . . . . *$75.00–$300.00*

Dulac, Edmund. *Daughters of the Stars*. Lon. 1939. dj. . . . . *$35.00–$50.00*

Dulac, Edmund. *Edmund Dulac's Fairy Book*. Doran. (1916). 1st ed. illus. . . . . .
. . . . *$160.00–$230.00*

Dulac, Edmund. *Edmund Dulac's Picture Book*. Lon. Hodder & Stoughton. 1915.
1st ed. wrps. illus. 19 plates. . . . . *$125.00–$150.00*

Dulac, Edmund. *Stories for the Arabian Nights*. Lon. Hodder & Stoughton. nd. illus.
by Dulac. . . . . *$75.00–$160.00*

Dulac, Edmund. *Stories from Hans Anderson*. Doran. nd. 1st ed. illus. by Dulac, clr
plates. . . . . *$100.00–$135.00*

Dulac, Edmund. *Stories from the Arabian Nights*. NY. Hodder & Stoughton. 1907.
illus. clr plates. . . . . *$850.00–$1,000.00*

Dulles, Allen. *Germany's Underground*. NY. Macmillan. 1947. 1st ed. sgn, dj. . . .
. . . . *$50.00–$75.00*

Dumas, Lt-Gen. M. *Memoirs of His Own Time Including the Revolution*. Phila.
1839. 2 vols.. . . . . *$175.00–$250.00*

Dumond, Dwight L. *Secession Movement*. NY. Macmillan. 1931. 1st ed. dj. . . . .
. . . . *$30.00–$50.00*

Dumont Henrietta. *Lady's Oracle*. Phila. Peck & Bliss. 1853. 270 pp, aeg. .... *$60.00–$70.0*

Dunaway, W. F. *Reminiscences of a Rebel*. Neale. NY. 1913. .... *$175.00–$250.00*

Dunbar, Alice Moore. *Masterpieces of Negro Eloquence*. NY. 1914. .... *$140.00–$180.00*

Dunbar, Lawrence. *When Malindy Sings*. NY. Dodd, Mead. 1903. 1st thus. illus. photos, green cl, teg,. .... *$125.00–$250.00*

Dunbar, Paul Laurence. *Candle-Lightin' Time*. NY. Dodd, Mead. 1901. 1st ed. photos by Hampton Camera Club, 127 pp. .... *$125.00–$200.00*

Dunbar, Paul Laurence. *Folks From Dixie*. NY. Dodd, Mead. 1926. illus. by Kemble. .... *$45.00–$55.00*

Dunbar, Paul Laurence. *Howdy Honey Howdy*. NY. Dodd, Mead. 1905. 1st ed. illus. photos. .... *$175.00–$375.00*

Dunbar, Paul Laurence. *Li'l Gal*. NY. 1904. 1st ed. photos. ... *$100.00–$150.00*

Dunbar, Paul Laurence. *Lyrics of Love and Laughter*. NY. Dodd, Mead. 1903. 1st ed. .... *$40.00–$115.00*

Dunbar, Paul Laurence. *Lyrics of Lowly Life*. NY. Dodd, Mead. 1896. 1st ed. author's first book published by major company. .... *$195.00–$300.00*

Dunbar, Paul Laurence. *Lyrics of Lowly Life*. NY. 1909. .... *$65.00–$80.00*

Dunbar, Paul Laurence. *Poems of Cabin and Field*. NY. Dodd, Mead. 1902. illus. photos, decorative cvr. .... *$125.00–$150.00*

Dunbar, Paul Laurence. *Poems of Cabin and Field*. NY. Dodd, Mead. 1899. 1st ed. illus. by Hampton Institute. .... *$125.00–$250.00*

Dunbar, Paul Laurence. *When Malindy Sings*. NY. Dodd, Mead & Co. 1903. illus. photos, brown decorated cl, frontis. .... *$175.00–$250.00*

Duncan Brothers. *United States Homeopathic Pharmacopoeia*. Chi. 1878. 1st ed. 281 pp. .... *$50.00–$60.00*

Duncan, Isadore. *My Life*. NY. 1927. illus. ltd 650cc. .... *$30.00–$50.00*

Dunlop, William. *History of the American Theatre*. NY. 1832. ... *$200.00–$350.00*

Dunn, Finley Peter. *Mr. Dooley in Peace and in War*. Bos. Small, Maynard. 1898. 1st ed. green cl. .... *$65.00–$75.00*

Dunn, Robert W. *Labor and Automobiles*. NY. International. 1929. 1st ed. dj. ... . *$30.00–$40.00*

Dunn, Robert W. (ed.). *Palmer Raids.* NY. International. 1948. 1st ed. wrps. . . . .
. . . . *$20.00–$30.00*

Dunn, William Edward. *Spanish and French Rivalry in the Gulf Region of the United States 1678-1702.* Austin. 1917. wrps. 238pp, 5 maps (1fldg). . . . .
. . . . *$95.00–$125.00*

Dunne, Peter M. *Early Jesuit Missions in Tarahumara.* Berkeley. 1948. 1st ed. illus. fldg map. . . . . *$40.00–$75.00*

Dunning, John. *Booked To Die.* NY. Scribner's. 1992. 1st ed. sgn, dj. . . . .
. . . . *$750.00–$900.00*

Dunning, John. *Booked To Die.* NY. Scribner's. 1992. 1st ed. dj. *$450.00–$600.00*

Dunning, John. *Bookman's Wake.* NY. Scribner's. 1995. 1st ed. dj. *$40.00–$65.00*

Dunning, John. *Bookman's Wake.* NY. Scribner's. 1995. 1st ed. sgn, dj. . . . .
. . . . *$85.00–$100.00*

Dunning, John. *Deadline.* Huntington Beach. Cahill. 1995. 1st Amer hardcvr ed. sgn. . . . . *$80.00–$100.00*

Dunning, John. *Deadline.* Huntington Beach. Cahill. 1995. 1st Amer ed. sgn, dj. . .
. . . . *$75.00–$100.00*

Dunning, John. *Deadline.* NY. Fawcett. 1981. 1st ed. wrps. . . . . . *$70.00–$85.00*

Dunsany, Lord. *Blessing of Pan.* NY. Putnam. 1928. 1st Amer ed. 277 pp. . . . . . .
. . . . *$30.00–$40.00*

Dunsany, Lord. *Chronicles of Rodriquez.* NY. Putnam. 1922. 1st ed. *$10.00–$35.00*

Dunsany, Lord. *Fourth Book of Jorkens.* Arkham House. 1948. 1st ed. dj. . . . . . .
. . . . *$80.00–$100.00*

Dunsany, Lord. *His Fellow Man.* Lon. 1952. 1st ed. dj. . . . . *$65.00–$85.00*

Dunsany, Lord. *Rory and Bran.* Putnam. 1937. 1st ed. green cl. . . *$25.00–$75.00*

Dunsany, Lord. *Selections from the Writings.* Churchtown, Dundrum. Cuala Press. 1912. 1st ed. 1/250 cc. . . . . *$125.00–$200.00*

Dunsany, Lord. *Sword of Welleran.* Lon. 1908. 1st ed. illus. by Sidney Sime. . . .
. . . . *$95.00–$150.00*

Dunsany, Lord. *Sword of Welleran.* Bos. 1916. 1st Amer. . . . . *$25.00–$45.00*

Dunsany, Lord. *Tales of War.* Dub. Talbot. 1918. 1st ed. dj. . . . . . *$50.00–$225.00*

Dunsany, Lord. *Time and the Gods.* Lon. Heinemann. 1906. 1st ed. 1st issue, 179 pp, illus. . . . . *$100.00–$150.00*

Dunton, W Herbert. *Rigging of a Texan.* Austin. The Texas State Historical Asso. 1943. illus. . . . . *$25.00–$40.00*

DuPont, J. E. *Philippine Birds.* Delaware Museum of Natural History. 1971. dj. . . . . *$35.00–$45.00*

Durant, Will. *Philosophy and the Social Problem.* NY. 1917. . . . . *$35.00–$45.00*

Durrell, Lawrence. *Clea.* NY. Dutton. 1960. 1st ed. dj. . . . . *$20.00–$30.00*

Durrell, Lawrence. *Livia.* Lon. Faber & Faber. (1978). 1st ed. dj. . *$25.00–$40.00*

Durrell, Lawrence. *Numquam.* Lon. Faber. (1970). 1st ed. dj. . . . . *$25.00–$45.00*

Durrell, Lawrence. *Prospero's Cell and Reflections on a Marine Venus.* Dutton. 1960. 1st ed. dj. . . . . *$35.00–$45.00*

Durrell, Lawrence. *Zero & Asylum in the Snow; Two Excursions Into Reality.* Berkeley. Circle Editions. 1947. 1st ed. dj. . . . . *$30.00–$75.00*

Dussauce, H. *General Treatise on the Manufacture of Vinegar.* Phila. 1871. 1st ed. . . . . *$35.00–$45.00*

Dustin, Fred. *Custer Tragedy.* Ann Arbor. 1939. 200 cc, maps. . . . . *$150.00–$250.00*

Dustin, Fred. *Saginaw Treaty of 1819 between Gen. Louis Cass and Chippewa Indians.* Saginaw. 1919. . . . . *$50.00–$75.00*

Dwiggins, W A. *Technique for Dealing with Artists.* NY. Press of the Woolly Whale. 1941. wrps. illus. 954cc. . . . . *$30.00–$40.00*

Dwight, N. *Lives of the Signers of the Declaration of Independence.* NY. 1851. 1st ed. . . . . *$35.00–$60.00*

Dwight, S. E. *Hebrew Wife.* Glasgow. Gallie. 1837. 1st Glasgow ed. 148 pp. . . . . *$150.00–$160.00*

Dwight, Theodore. *History of the Hartford Convention.* NY. White. 1833. 1st ed. original cl & paper label. . . . . *$100.00–$120.00*

Dyke, A. L. *Dyke's Automobile & Gasoline Engine Encyclopedia.* Chi. 1924. illus. dj. . . . . *$45.00–$85.00*

Eames, Wilberforce. *Early New England Catechisms.* Worcester. Hamilton. 1898. 1st ed. wrps. presentation copy. . . . . *$75.00–$115.00*

Earhart, Amelia. *Last Flight.* NY. 1937. 1st ed. illus. dj. . . . . *$40.00–$65.00*

Earle, Alice Morse. *Child Life in the Colonial Days.* NY. Macmillan. 1899. 1st ed. illus. . . . . *$40.00–$55.00*

Earle, Alice Morse. *Sun Dials and Roses of Yesterday*. NY. 1902. 1st ed. illus. . . .
. . . .*$75.00–$120.00*

Earle, Alice Morse. *Two Centuries of Costume in America*. NY. 1903. 2 vols. 1st ed.
illus. . . . .*$40.00–$125.00*

East of Antelope Island. Bountiful. Daughters of Utah Pioneers. 1961. 1st ed.. . . .
. . . .*$35.00–$50.00*

East of the Sun and West of the Moon. NY. 1922. illus. by Kay Nielsen, tip-in clr
plates, dj. . . . .*$150.00–$300.00*

Eastlake, William. *Child's Garden of Verses for the Revolution*. NY. Grove Press.
1970. 1st ed. dj. . . . .*$25.00–$40.00*

Eastlake, William. *Go in Beauty*. NY. (1956). 1st ed. author's first book, dj. . . . .
. . . .*$100.00–$200.00*

Eastman, Charles A. *Indian Boyhood*. NY. 1902. illus. . . . .*$70.00–$85.00*

Eastman, Charles G. *Poems of....* Montpelier. 1848. . . . .*$45.00–$55.00*

Eastman, F. *History of the State of New York*. NY. 1830. lea. . . . . .*$55.00–$65.00*

Eastman, M. E. *East of the White Hills*. N Conway, NH. (1900). 1st ed. illus. . . .
. . . .*$40.00–$60.00*

Eastman, Mrs Mary H. *Aunt Phillis's Cabin or Southern Life as it is*. Phil.
Lippincott. 1852. . . . .*$75.00–$125.00*

Eastman, Mrs. Mary. *American Aboriginal Portfolio*. Phila. 1853. 84 pp, 26 engr,
large 4to, aeg, gold stamped bds, rare. . . . .*$750.00–$1,500.00*

Eastman, Mrs. Mary. *Aunt Phillis's Cabin*. Phila. 1852. . . . .*$50.00–$100.00*

Eaton, Allen H. *Beauty for the Sighted and the Blind*. NY. St. Martin's Press. 1959.
1st ed. foreword by Helen Keller, dj. . . . .*$8.00–$15.00*

Eaton, Allen H. *Handicrafts of New England*. NY. Harper. (1949). 1st ed. dj. . . . .
. . . .*$6.00–$25.00*

Eaton, Allen H. *Handicrafts of the Southern Highlanders*. illus. 2nd prtg, dj. . . . .
. . . .*$50.00–$65.00*

Eaton, Elon Howard. *Birds of New York*. Albany. 1914. 2nd ed. ex lib. *$40.00–$50.00*

Eaton, Elon Howard. *Birds of New York*. Albany. 1910. 2 vols. illus. clr plates. . .
. . . .*$100.00–$200.00*

Eaton, Faith. *Classic Dollls' Houses*. Lon. Artus Books. (1994). reprnt, dj. . . . . .
. . . .*$15.00–$30.00*

Eaton, Faith. *Dolls in Color*. NY. Macmillan Pub. (1975). illus. 1st US ed, clr photos. . . . . *$15.00–$25.00*

Eaton, Faith. *Miniature House*. NY. Harry H Abrams. (1991). illus. 1st US ed. . . . . *$45.00–$65.00*

Eaton, John H. *Life of Andrew Jackson*. Phila. 1824. 2nd ed. . . . . *$50.00–$100.00*

Eaton, John P. & Charles A. Haas. *Titanic*. NY. 1986. illus. dj. . . *$30.00–$45.00*

Eaton, Seymour. *Traveling Bears in Outdoor Sports*. Barse & Hopkins. 1915. illus. . . . . *$135.00–$185.00*

Eaton, Walter P. *Skyline Camps*. Wilde. 1922. pict paste label. . . . *$25.00–$35.00*

Eckert, A. and Karalus. *Owls of North America*. Doubleday. 1974. 1st ed. illus. dj. . . . . *$35.00–$55.00*

Eckert, Allan W. *Great Auk*. Bos. Little, Brown & Co. 1963. dj. . . *$50.00–$75.00*

Economy Cream Separator. Chi. Sears, Roebuck & Co. 1907. illus. pict wrps. . . . . *$35.00–$45.00*

Eddington, A. S. *Space Time & Gravitation*. Camb. 1921. 1st ed. . *$40.00–$60.00*

Eddy, Clyde. *Down the World's Most Dangerous River*. NY. Stoke. 1929. illus. . . . . *$170.00–$230.00*

Eddy, Richmond. *History of the 60th Regiment, New York State Volunteers*. Phila. 1864. . . . . *$100.00–$200.00*

Edison Swan Co. *Pageant of the Lamp*. 1948. 1st ed. illus. . . . . . . *$50.00–$65.00*

Edison, Judith. *Dolls From Kewpie to Barbie and Beyond*. NY. Smithmark. (1994). 1st ed. illus. clr and b/w, dj. . . . . *$20.00–$30.00*

Edmonds, Harfield H. *Brook and River Trouting*. Orange Partridge Press. 1980. illus. slipcase. . . . . *$50.00–$75.00*

Edmonds, Harfield H. and Norman N. Lee. *Brook and River Trouting: A Manual....* Bradford. pub by authors. (1916). 1st ed. ltd 1000 cc. illus. clr plates, buckram. . . . . *$175.00–$300.00*

Edmonds, Walter. *Chad Hanna*. Bos. Little, Brown. (1940). 1st ed. dj. . . . . *$25.00–$50.00*

Edmonds, Walter. *Drums Along the Mohawk*. Bos. 1936. 1st ed. . . *$25.00–$50.00*

Edmonds, Walter. *In the Hands of the Senecas*. Bos. Little, Brown. (1947). 1st ed. dj. . . . . *$30.00–$50.00*

Education of a French Model. NY. Boar's Head Books. 1950. 186 pp, illus, photos by Man Ray, rprnt, dj. . . . . *$75.00–$100.00*

Edward and Miriam A Tale of Iceland. Phila. American Sunday School Union. 1836. illus. frontis lea and bds woodcuts. . . . . ***$14.00–$20.00***

Edward, Ruth Dudley. *Victor Gollancz: A Biography.* Lon. Gollancz. 1987. 1st ed. dj. . . . . ***$30.00–$40.00***

Edwards, Amelia. *Pharaohs, Fellahs and Explorers.* NY. Harper & Bros. 1891. 1st Amer ed. illus. . . . . ***$50.00–$70.00***

Edwards, Amelia. *Thousand Miles Up the Nile.* NY. 2nd ed. cl cvr. ***$30.00–$85.00***

Edwards, E. and J. Rattray. *Whale Off.* NY. 1932. 1st ed. illus. . . ***$27.00–$40.00***

Edwards, E. I. *The Enduring Desert.* LA. Warc Ritchie Press. 1969. 1st ed. cl, slipcase. . . . . ***$80.00–$100.00***

Edwards, E. I. *The Valley Whose Name is Death.* Pasadena. San Pasqual Press. 1940. 1st ed. ltd.. . . . . ***$40.00–$69.00***

Edwards, Gladys Brown. *Anatomy and Conformation of the Horse.* Croton-on-Hudson. Dreenan. 1980. wrps. illus. photos & drawings. . . . . ***$30.00–$35.00***

Edwards, John E. *Life of Rev. John Wesley Childs....* Early. 1852. 1st ed. . . . . ***$90.00–$125.00***

Edwards, Jonathan. *Freedom of the Will.* NY. 1858. . . . . ***$35.00–$50.00***

Edwards, Lionel. *Getting to Know Your Pony.* NY. (1948). 1st US ed. illus. . . . . ***$35.00–$40.00***

Edwards, Lionel. *The Fox.* NY. Scribner's. nd. illus. . . . . ***$50.00–$150.00***

Edwards, Philip Leget. *Diary of Philip Leget Edwards: the Great Cattle Drive....* SF. Grabhorn. 1932. illus. ltd 500 cc.. . . . . ***$50.00–$75.00***

Edwards, William B. *Civil War Guns.* Harrisburg. 1962. illus. dj. . . . . ***$35.00–$75.00***

Edwards, William B. *Story of Colts Revolver.* 1953. 1st ed. dj. . . ***$65.00–$100.00***

Ehwa, Carl Jr. *The Book of Pipes and Tobacco.* NY. Random House/Ridge Press. 1978. 1st ed. illus. dj. . . . . ***$50.00–$65.00***

Eickemeyer, Carl. *Among the Pueblo Indians.* NY. 1895. . . . . ***$50.00–$65.00***

Eidinoff, Maxwell Leigh and Hyman Ruchlis. *Atomics for the Millions.* NY/Lon. 1947. 1st ed. illus. by Maurice Sendak. . . . . ***$100.00–$120.00***

Einstein, Albert. *Relativity, The Special And General Theory.* Lon. (1920). . . . . ***$75.00–$150.00***

Einstein, Albert. *Uber Die Spezielle Und Die Allgemeine Relativitatstheorie.* wrps. 4th ed. . . . . ***$50.00–$65.00***

Einstein, Albert & Leopold Infeld. *Evolution of Physics.* NY. Simon & Schuster. 1938. 1st ed. . . . . *$55.00–$100.00*

Einstein, Albert & Leopold Infeld. *New Physics.* Palestine. 1947. 1st Hebrew ed. sgn, dj. . . . . *$85.00–$125.00*

Einstein, Milton D. and Max Goldstein (eds.). *Collectors Marks.* St. Louis. Laryngoscope Press. 1918. ltd 300 cc. illus. red cl. . . . . *$300.00–$350.00*

Eisenschiml, Otto. *Story of Shiloh.* Chi. 1946. . . . . *$40.00–$50.00*

Elder, Frank. *The Book of the Hackle.* Edin. Scottish Academic Press. 1979. 1st ed. illus. ltd 85 cc. clr plates, red mor, aeg, slipcase. . . . . *$300.00–$500.00*

Elder, Paul. *California the Beautiful.* SF. 1911. . . . . *$50.00–$75.00*

Elder, Paul. *Old Spanish Missions of California.* SF. Elder. 1913. 50 illus. 1/4 buckram, pict paste label. . . . . *$40.00–$65.00*

Eldridge, Charlotte. *Godey Lady Doll Book.* NY. Hastings House. (1953). illus. . . . . *$15.00–$25.00*

Eldridge, Eleanor. *Slave Narrative.* Prov. 1842. . . . . *$125.00–$150.00*

Eldridge, S. *Heroic Life of U S Grant.* Bos. (1902). illus. 4 chromo, b/w illus. . . . . *$35.00–$50.00*

Electric Gas Lighting. Bos. Boston Electric Co. 1880. illus. 12 pp. *$40.00–$50.00*

Electric Railway Dictionary. CA. 1972. rprnt of 1911 ed. dj. . . . *$125.00–$250.00*

Electric Signals for Passenger and Freight Elevators.... NY. Elevator Supply and Repair Co. 1913. 48 pp. . . . . *$90.00–$100.00*

Eliot, George. *Mill On The Floss.* Phil. 1860. purple cl. . . . . *$75.00–$100.00*

Eliot, George. *Mill on the Floss.* Edin/Lon. William Blackwood. 1869. 3 vols. 1st ed. . . . . *$500.00–$550.00*

Eliot, George. *Romola.* NY. 1863. 1st Amer ed.. . . . . *$115.00–$275.00*

Eliot, George. *Romola.* Lon. 1863. 3 vols. 1st ed. . . . . *$450.00–$500.00*

Eliot, George. *Silas Marner.* Edin/Lon. 1861. 1st ed. . . . . *$600.00–$1,200.00*

Eliot, George. *The Works.* Edin. 1878-80. 20 vols. . . . . *$95.00–$125.00*

Eliot, T. S. *Confidential Clerk.* NY. (1954). 1st ed. dj. . . . . *$25.00–$50.00*

Eliot, T. S. *Dante.* Lon. Faber & Faber. (1929). 1st ed. dj. . . . . . *$100.00–$250.00*

Eliot, T. S. *Elder Statesman.* NY. 1959. 1st Amer ed. dj. . . . . *$55.00–$65.00*

Eliot, T. S. *Film of Murder in the Cathedral.* NY. Harcourt. 1952. 1st US ed. dj. . .
. . . . *$25.00–$35.00*

Eliot, T. S. *Four Quartets.* Lon. Faber & Faber. (1944). 1st Brit ed. dj. . . . *$200.00*

Eliot, T. S. *Old Possum's Book of Practical Cats.* Lon. 1939. 1st ed. dj. . . . .
. . . . *$350.00–$400.00*

Elkins, Aaron. *Deceptive Clarity.* Walker. 1987. 1st ed. dj. *$125.00*

Elkins, Aaron. *Murder in the Queen's Armes.* Walker. 1985. 1st ed. dj. . . *$225.00*

Ellett, Charles, Jr. *Mississippi and the Ohio Rivers.* Phila. 1853. inscr, illus, 366 pp.
. . . . *$125.00–$175.00*

Elliot, Daniel Giraud. *North American Shore Birds.* NY. Harper. 1895. illus. . . . .
. . . . *$40.00–$75.00*

Elliot, William. *Washington Guide.* Wash. Franck Taylor. 1837. illus. fldg maps. .
. . . . *$60.00–$90.00*

Elliotson, John. *Numerous Cases of Surgical Operations Without Pain in the Mesmeric State.* Phila. Lea and Blanchard. 1843. 1st Amer ed.. *$750.00–$1,500.00*

Elliott, Henry W. *Report upon the Condition of Affairs in the Territory of Alaska.* DC. GPO. 1875. 277 pp. . . . . *$85.00–$100.00*

Ellis, Edward S. *Thomas Jefferson.* Milwaukee. Campbell. 1898. . *$30.00–$45.00*

Ellis, Havelock. *Study in the Psychology of Sex.* Phila. 1928. 7 vols. *$75.00–$125.00*

Ellis, Havelock. *World of Dreams.* Bos. 1915. . . . . *$35.00–$85.00*

Ellis, R. A. *Spiderland.* Lon. 1912. clr pl. *$25.00–$35.00*

Ellison, Harlan. *Alone Against Tomorrow.* NY. 1971. 1st ed. sgn, dj. *$35.00–$60.00*

Ellison, Harlan. *Approaching Oblivion.* NY. 1974. 1st ed. sgn, dj. . *$40.00–$75.00*

Ellison, Harlan. *Spider Kiss.* NY. Armchair Detective Library. (1991). 1st ed. ltd 26 lettered and sgn cc, slipcase. . . . . *$225.00–$300.00*

Ellison, Harlan. *Stalking the Nightmare.* Phantasia Press. 1st trade ed.. . . . .
. . . . *$25.00–$35.00*

Ellison, Harlan. *Stalking the Nightmare.* Phantasia Press. 1982. 1st ed. ltd 750cc, sgn. . . . . *$75.00–$90.00*

Ellison, Harlan. *Strange Wine.* NY. Harper & Row. (1978). 1st ed. dj. . . . .
. . . . *$55.00–$85.00*

Ellison, Ralph. *Going To The Territory.* NY. 1986. 1st ed. dj. . . . . *$45.00–$75.00*

Ellison, Ralph. *Invisible Man*. NY. 1952. 1st ed. dj. . . . . *$650.00–$750.00*

Ellison, Ralph. *Shadow and Act*. Lon. 1967. 1st UK black paper cvred bds, dj. . . . . *$25.00–$90.00*

Ellwanger, George H. *In Gold and Silver*. NY. Appleton. 1892. 1st ed. illus. ltd 200 cc. . . . . *$70.00–$100.00*

Ellwanger, H. B. *The Rose*. Lon. Heinemann. 1893. rev, 310 pp. . . *$65.00–$85.00*

Ellyson's Business Directory and Almanac for the year 1845. H K Ellyson. . . . . *$125.00–$200.00*

Elwes, H. J. *Memoirs of Travel, Sport and Natural History*. Lon. 1930. 317 pp. . . . . *$22.00–$35.00*

Elzas, Barnett. *Jews of South Carolina*. Phila. 1905. ltd 175 cc. . . *$55.00–$65.00*

Emanuel, Walter. *Dog's Day*. Lon. Heinemann. 1902. illus. by Cecil Aldin. . . . . *$250.00–$275.00*

Embick, Milton. *Military History of the Third Division, 9th Corp. Army Potomac.* np. 1913. 1st ed. illus. . . . . *$48.00–$60.00*

Emerson, Adaline E. *Ralph Emerson, Jr.: Life and Letters. Edited by his Mother.* Rockford, Il. 1891. 1st ed. illus. . . . . *$90.00–$125.00*

Emerson, Alice B. *Ruth Fielding at Snow Camp*. Cupples & Leon. 1913. Fielding #3, dj. . . . . *$12.00–$15.00*

Emerson, Jill. *I Am Curious*. NY. (1970). 1st ed. wrps. sgn. . . . . *$150.00–$200.00*

Emerson, Ralph Waldo. *Complete Works of....* Bos. Houghton Mifflin. 1903. 12 vols. illus. Concord ed. . . . . *$70.00–$100.00*

Emerson, Ralph Waldo. *Essays*. Bos. 1844. 1st ed. 2nd series. . *$200.00–$500.00*

Emerson, Ralph Waldo. *Letters and Social Aims*. Bos. Osgood. 1876. 1st ed.. . . . . *$195.00–$225.00*

Emerson, Ralph Waldo. *Society and Solitude*. Bos. 1870. 1st ed. sm 8vo. . . . . *$50.00–$75.00*

Emory, William. *Lieutenant Emory Reports*. Albuquerque. Univ of New Mexico Press. (1951). illus. rprnt of 1848 ed. . . . . *$50.00–$80.00*

Emory, William. *Report on the United States and Mexican Boundary Survey*. Austin. Texas State Historical Assoc. (1987). facs. copiously illus. . *$150.00–$200.00*

Emory, William H. *Report on the United States and Mexican Boundary Survey*. Austin. Texas State Historical Assoc.. (1987). 3 vols. facs of 1859 version, maps. . . . . *$100.00–$175.00*

Encyclopaedia Britannica - Facsimile of First Edition Printed in 1768 to 1771. 3 vols. illus. 160 copperplates. . . . . *$150.00–$175.00*

Encyclopaedia Britannica, 11th Edition. NY. 1910. 20 vols. . . . .
. . . . *$200.00–$600.00*

Endell, Fritz. *Old Tavern Signs.* Bos. Houghton Mifflin. 1916. illus. ltd 550cc. . .
. . . . *$40.00–$65.00*

Endicott, Wendell. *Adventures in Alaska and Along the Trail.* NY. Stokes. 1928. illus. green cl, decorated cvr, frontis, map endpapers. . . . . *$50.00–$60.00*

Endicott, Wendell. *Adventures with Rod and Harpoon Along the Florida Keys.* NY. Stokes. 1925. 1st ed. 1st prtg. illus.. . . . . *$65.00–$125.00*

Endicott, William. *Wrecked Among Cannibals in the Fijis.* Marine Research Soc. 1923. . . . . *$50.00–$95.00*

Engineers, Architects and Builders in Iron and Steel. East Berlin, CT. The Berlin Iron Bridge Co. c 1890-95. printed wrps, illus, 302 pp. . . . . *$125.00–$250.00*

English, L. E. F. *Newfoundland Past and Present.* Tor. Thomas Nelson & Sons. nd. illus. red stiff wrps. . . . . *$15.00–$20.00*

Ensigns & Thayer. *Seat of War & Battles.* NY. 1847. broadside. small map. . . . . .
. . . . *$1,750.00–$1,850.00*

Ensko, Stephen. *American Silversmiths.* (1989). 1st ed. illus. dj. . . *$35.00–$40.00*

Epstein, Geo. J. *Strabismus, A Clinical Handbook.* Phila. 1948. illus. . . . .
. . . . *$35.00–$48.00*

EROS Magazine, Vol 1, #1. . . . . *$50.00–$75.00*

Erskine, Albert Russel. *History of the Studebaker Corporation.* The Studebaker Corporation. 1924. . . . . *$35.00–$65.00*

Erskine, Laurie York. *Renfrew Rides North.* NY. Grosset & Dunlap. 1931. Renfrew Books #3, dj. . . . . *$22.00–$25.00*

Esdaile, James. *Mesmerism in India.* (1902). Amer ed.. . . . . *$55.00–$200.00*

Esposito, Colonel Vincent, Jr. *West Point Atlas of American Wars.* NY. Praeger. 1960. 2 vols. 1st ed. illus. maps, oblong. . . . . *$100.00–$150.00*

Esquirel, Laura. *Like Water for Chocolate.* NY. Doubleday. 1989. 1st ed. dj. . . . . .
. . . . *$35.00–$60.00*

Eustis, Celestine. *Cooking in Old Creole Days.* NY. 1903. 1st ed. . *$25.00–$40.00*

Eustis, Helen. *Fool Killer.* Garden City. Doubleday. 1954. 1st ed. dj. . . . .
. . . . *$85.00–$100.00*

Euwe, Max. *Judgment and Planning in Chess.* NY. Scribner's. 1955. . . . .
. . . . *$35.00–$45.00*

Evangelical Lutheran Church: a Liturgy . . .. *Evangelical Lutheran Church: a Liturgy....* Balt. Lutheran Church. 1847. . . . . *$100.00–$125.00*

Evans, Augusta Inez. *Tale of the Alamo.* NY. 1888. . . . . *$55.00–$68.00*

Evans, C. S. *Sleeping Beauty.* Lon. (1920). 1st ed. illus. by Arthur Rackham. dj. .
. . . . *$1,250.00–$375.00*

Evans, Clement Anselm, ed. *Confederate Military History.* Atlanta. Confederate Publishing Co. 1899. 12 vols. 1st ed. illus. plates, maps. . . . . *$485.00–$800.00*

Evans, Eli N. *Provincials: a Personal History of Jews in the South.* Atheneum,. 1973. 2nd print dj. . . . . *$25.00–$35.00*

Evans, Frederick William. *Egyptian Sphinx.* Mt Lebanon. nd. wrps. . . . .
. . . . : *$87.00–$110.00*

Evans, Joan. *History of Jewelry, 1100-1870.* NY. (1953). illus. dj. . . . .
. . . . *$100.00–$125.00*

Evans, John. *Ancient Bronze Implements, Weapons... Great Britain & Ireland.* NY. 1881. . . . . *$65.00–$85.00*

Evans, John. *Ancient Stone Implements....* NY. 1872. 1st ed. 640 pp. . *$75.00–$100.00*

Evans, Nicholas. *Horse Whisperer.* Delacorte. 1995. 1st ed. author's first book, sgn, dj. . . . . *$125.00–$135.00*

Evarts, Jeremiah, et al. *Essays on the Present Crisis in the Condition of the American Indians.* Bos. (1829). 1st ed. . . . . *$125.00–$225.00*

Everett, Fred. *Fun With Trout.* Harrisburg. Stackpole. 1952. 1st ed. illus. . . . .
. . . . *$70.00–$100.00*

Everitt, Graham. *English Caricaturists and Graphic Humanists of the Nineteenth Century.* 1886. illus. platees, 3/4 mor & cl. . . . . *$110.00–$130.00*

Ewards, A. Cecil. *Persian Carpet.* Lon. Duckworth. (1967). 3rd ed. illus. dj. . . . .
. . . . *$60.00–$90.00*

Ewart, John S. *Kingdom of Canada: Imperial Federation: Colonial Conferences: Alaska Boundary and Other Essays.* Tor. 1908. 1st ed. illus. 2 maps, sgn. . . . .
. . . . *$35.00–$45.00*

Examples of Church Furnishings. NY. J & R Lamb Co. 1886. stiff wrps, illus, 72 pp. . . . . *$75.00–$100.00*

Eyre, John. *European Stranger in America.* NY. 1839. 1st ed. 84 pp. . . . .
. . . . *$75.00–$100.00*

Faber, Eduard. *Nobel Prize Winners In Chemistry 1901-1961.* Abelard-Schuman. 1963. rev. . . . . *$25.00–$35.00*

Faber, J. Henri. *Life of the Grasshopper.* NY. 1917. dj. . . . . *$35.00–$50.00*

Fabre, H. *Fabre's Book of Insects.* NY. 1935. . . . . *$30.00–$45.00*

Fagg, William P. *Afro-Portuguese Ivories.* Lon. dj. . . . . *$65.00–$90.00*

Fahnestock, W. P. *Artificial Somnambulism, Called Mesmerism; or Animal Magnetism.* Phila. 1869. . . . . *$95.00–$125.00*

Fairbridge, Dorothea. *Historic Farms of South Africa.* Lon. 1931. 1st ed. illus. dj. . . . . *$125.00–$150.00*

Fairchild, David. *Garden Islands of the Great East.* NY. Scribner's. 1943. illus. end paper maps. . . . . *$25.00–$30.00*

Fairchild, David. *World Was My Garden.* Scribner's. 1938. 1st ed. illus. . . . . *$35.00–$45.00*

Fairchild, David and Marian. *Book of Monsters.* DC. 1914. . . . *$100.00–$150.00*

Fairchild, T. B. *History of The Town of Cuyahoga Falls, Summit County, Ohio.* Cleve. 1876. 1st ed. . . . . *$65.00–$75.00*

Fairy Garland. Lon. Cassell. 1928. illus. by Edmund Dulac, 12 clr pl. teg, vellum & bds, ltd 1000 cc, sgn by Dulac. . . . . *$100.00–$150.00*

Fairy Tales of Charles Perrault. Dodge. illus. by Harry Clarke, intro by Bodkin. . . . . *$150.00–$250.00*

Faithfull, Emily. *Three Visits to America.* NY. Fowler & Wells. (1884). 1st US ed. 400 pp. . . . . *$95.00–$125.00*

Falk, Kathryn. *Miniature Needlepoint and Sewing Projects for Dollhouses.* NY. Hawthorn Books. (1977). 1st ed. dj. . . . . *$18.00–$30.00*

Fall, Bernard. *Hell In a Very Small Place.* Phila. 1966. 1st ed. dj. . *$40.00–$50.00*

Fall, Bernard. *Street Without Joy.* Harrisburg. Stackpole. (1964). 4th ed. dj. . . . . *$30.00–$35.00*

Fall, Bernard. *Street Without Joy.* Harrisburg. Stackpole. 1961. 1st ed. dj. . . . . *$425.00–$500.00*

Fall, Bernard. *Vietnam in the Balance.* 1966. wrps. . . . . *$25.00–$35.00*

Family Cabinet Atlas. Phila. Carey & Lea. 1932. 1st Amer ed. rev, clr maps, bds. . . . . *$60.00–$100.00*

Family Circle's Guide to Trout Flies & How to Tie Them. (1954). illus. 48 pp, boxed. . . . . *$25.00–$45.00*

Faris, John T. *Roaming the Rockies....* NY. Farrar & Rinehart. 1930. illus. . . . . . .
. . . . *$35.00–$45.00*

Farley, Walter. *Son of the Black Stallion.* 1947. 1st ed. dj. . . . . *$25.00–$35.00*

Farlie, Barbara. *All About Doll Houses.* IN. Bobbs Merrill. 1st ed. illus. 2nd prntg,
dj. . . . . *$15.00–$25.00*

Farm Receipt Book of John and Jane Longstreth of Phoenixville, Pennsylvania,
1764-1811. folio, parchment, 272pp. . . . . *$525.00–$35.00*

Farmer's and Horsemen's True Guide. Rochester, NY. Fisher & Co. 1841. illus. .
. . . . *$125.00–$150.00*

Farmer, Fannie Merritt. *Chafing Dish Possibilities.* Bos. Little, Brown. 1898. 1st
ed. . . . . *$50.00–$80.00*

Farmer, Philip Jose. *Dare.* NY. (1965). 1st ed. pict wrps. . . . . *$15.00–$25.00*

Farmer, Philip Jose. *Day World Breakup.* NY. (1990). 1st ed. dj. . *$20.00–$25.00*

Farmer, Philip Jose. *Feast Unknown.* Essex House. (1969). 1st ed. . . . .
. . . . *$50.00–$100.00*

Farmer, Philip Jose. *Love Song.* Macmillan. 1983. 1st ed. ltd 500 cc, dj. . . . .
. . . . *$65.00–$75.00*

Farmer, Philip Jose. *Magic Labyrinth.* Berkley Putnam. 1980. 1st ed. sgn, dj. . . .
. . . . *$20.00–$30.00*

Farmer, Philip Jose. *Tarzan Alive.* Garden City. 1972. 1st ed. dj. . . . .
. . . . *$65.00–$100.00*

Farnham, Eliza. *Life In Prairie Land.* NY. 1847. . . . . *$65.00–$85.00*

Farnol, Jeffrey. *The Shadow.* Bos. Little, Brown. 1929. 1st Amer ed. 306 pp. . . . .
. . . . *$25.00–$35.00*

Farquhar, Roger Brooke. *Historic Montgomery County Old Homes & History.*
1952. sgn. . . . . *$35.00–$50.00*

Farrar, Emmie Ferguson & Emilee Hines. *Old Virginia Houses.* Delmar. illus. b/w
photos dj. . . . . *$40.00–$55.00*

Farrel, James T. *Tutto, Ma Non Un Cuore.* Arnoldo Mondadori Editore. 1957. 1st
Italian ed of Gas-House McGinty, inscr, dj. . . . . *$75.00–$100.00*

Farrell, James T. *Father and Son.* Vanguard. 1940. 1st ed. dj. . . *$125.00–$150.00*

Farrell, James T. *My Baseball Diary.* NY. (1957). 1st ed. dj. . . . . . *$45.00–$55.00*

Farrell, James T. *My Days of Anger.* Vanguard. 1943. 1st ed. dj. *$100.00–$125.00*

Farrell, James T. *Yet Other Waters.* Vanguard. 1952. 1st ed. dj. . . . *$50.00–$75.00*

Farrington, S. Kip. *Atlantic Game Fishing.* 1939. . . . . *$28.00–$35.00*

Farrington, S. Kip. *Atlantic Game Fishing.* NY. 1937. illus. sgn. *$145.00–$185.00*

Farrington, S. Kip, Jr. *Ducks Came Back.* NY. Coward McCann. 1945. 1st ed. illus. by Lynne Bogue Hunt, 138 pp. . . . . *$30.00–$40.00*

Fast, Howard. *Passion of Sacco and Vanzetti.* Lon. 1954. 1st ed. dj. *$20.00–$30.00*

Faubion, Nina Lane. *Some Edible Mushrooms and How To Know Them.* OR. 1938. illus. . . . . *$14.00–$20.00*

Faulkner, Georgene. *White Elephant.* Volland. 1929. illus. by Richardson. . . . . . .
. . . . *$25.00–$45.00*

Faulkner, William. *A Fable.* NY. Random House. (1954). 1st ed. dj. . . . .
. . . . *$100.00–$150.00*

Faulkner, William. *A Green Bough.* NY. Harrison Smith & Robert Haas. 1933. 1st trade ed. dj. . . . . *$550.00–$650.00*

Faulkner, William. *Absalom, Absalom.* NY. Random House. 1936. 1st trade ed. cl, dj. . . . . *$1,500.00–$4,750.00*

Faulkner, William. *As I Lay Dying.* Lon. Jonathan Cape. 1935. 1st ed. dj. . . . . . .
. . . . *$360.00–$650.00*

Faulkner, William. *Big Woods.* Random House. 1955. 1st ed. . . . *$95.00–$110.00*

Faulkner, William. *Doctor Martino and Other Stories.* NY. Harrison Smith & Robert Haas. (1934). dj. . . . . *$350.00–$1,300.00*

Faulkner, William. *Faulkner Reader.* NY. 1959. . . . . *$30.00–$45.00*

Faulkner, William. *Go Down Moses and Other Stories.* NY. Random House. (c1942). 1st ed. dj. . . . . *$700.00–$900.00*

Faulkner, William. *Idyll in the Desert.* NY. Random House. 1931. 1st ed. ltd 400 cc. sgn, marbled bds. . . . . *$1,350.00–$3,000.00*

Faulkner, William. *Intruder In The Dust.* NY. (1948). 1st ed. dj. *$125.00–$225.00*

Faulkner, William. *Light in August.* NY. The Modern Library. (1950). dj. . . . . . .
. . . . *$12.00–$20.00*

Faulkner, William. *Light in August.* NY. Smith & Haas. (1932). 1st ed. dj. . . . . .
. . . . *$200.00–$900.00*

Faulkner, William. *Mosquitoes.* NY. Boni & Liveright. 1927. 1st ed. 1st prtg. blue cl, dj. . . . . *$800.00–$1,200.00*

Faulkner, William. *Pylon*. NY. Smith & Haas. 1935. 1st ed. dj. . *$400.00–$500.00*

Faulkner, William. *Requiem for a Nun*. Chatto & Windus. 1953. 1st UK ed. dj. . . .
.... *$35.00–$65.00*

Faulkner, William. *Requiem for a Nun*. NY. Random House. (1951). 1st ed. dj. . . .
.... *$125.00–$200.00*

Faulkner, William. *Salmagundi, and a Poem by Ernest M. Hemingway*. Milwaukee. Casonova Press. 1932. 1st ed. wrps. ltd 525 cc, slipcase. ..... *$650.00–$1,100.00*

Faulkner, William. *Sanctuary*. NY. Jonathan Cape & Harrison Smith. (1931). 1st ed. 1st prtg. cl bds, dj. .... *$900.00–$4,950.00*

Faulkner, William. *Sartoris*. NY. (1929). 1st ed. dj. .... *$1,300.00–$2,600.00*

Faulkner, William. *Soldier's Pay*. NY. Boni & Liveright. 1926. 1st ed. cl. ......
.... *$200.00–$750.00*

Faulkner, William. *The Hamlet*. NY. Random House. 1940. 1st trade ed. dj. ....
.... *$900.00–$4,500.00*

Faulkner, William. *The Mansion*. NY. Random House. (1959). 1st ed. cl dj. ....
.... *$95.00–$200.00*

Faulkner, William. *The Reivers*. NY. Random House. 1962. 1st ed. dj. ....
.... *$75.00–$100.00*

Faulkner, William. *The Town*. NY. Random House. (1957). 1st ed. dj. *$65.00–$100.00*

Faulkner, William. *The Town*. Chatto & Windus. 1958. 1st UK ed. dj. *$50.00–$75.00*

Faulkner, William. *The Unvanquished*. NY. Random House. (1938). 1st ed. illus. by Edward Shenton. cl, dj. .... *$800.00–$1,000.00*

Faulkner, William. *The Wild Palms*. NY. Random House. 1939. 1st ed. 1st prtg. cl, dj. .... *$400.00–$100.00*

Faulkner, William. *The Wild Palms*. NY. Random House. (1939). 1st trade ed. 2nd issue. cl, dj. .... *$550.00–$750.00*

Faulkner, William. *These 13*. NY. Cape & Smith. (1931). 1st ed. 1st prtg. cl, dj. . .
.... *$175.00–$12,500.00*

Fawcett, Clara Hallard. *Dolls A Guide for Collectors*. NY. Lindquist Pub. (1947). 1st ed. .... *$25.00–$65.00*

Fawcett, Clara Hallard. *On Making & Dressing Dolls*. DC. Hobby House Press. (1963). reissue ed. .... *$25.00–$35.00*

Fawcett, Col. P. H. *Lost Trails, Lost Cities*. Funk & Wagnalls. 1953. illus. green cvr, dj. .... *$15.00–$25.00*

Feagans, Raymond. *Railroad That Ran by the Tide*. Howell-North Berkeley. 1972. illus. dj, scarce. . . . . *$60.00–$80.00*

Feather, Leonard. *Pleasures of Jazz*. NY. Horizon. 1976. 1st ed. dj. . . . . *$30.00–$40.00*

Federal Writers' Project. *New Hampshire*. 1st ed. . . . . *$20.00–$40.00*

Federal Writers' Project. *New Jersey*. 1st ed. map. . . . . *$35.00–$40.00*

Fedo, Michael W. *They Was Just Niggers*. Ontario, CA. Brasch & Brasch. 1979. wrps. . . . . *$25.00–$60.00*

Feek, Andrew J. *Every Man His Own Trainer or How To Develop... Trotter or Pacer*. NY. 1889. 1st ed. . . . . *$68.00–$85.00*

Feiffer, Jules. *Little Murders*. NY. 1968. 1st ed. dj. . . . . *$50.00–$75.00*

Feiffer, Jules. *Sick Sick Sick*. NY. McGraw-Hill. (1958). 1st ed. author's first book, paperback, inscr, dj. . . . . *$100.00–$125.00*

Feiffer, Jules. *The Explainers*. NY. McGraw-Hill. (1960). wrps. inscr. . . . . *$85.00–$100.00*

***Felix S. Cohen's Handbook of Federal Indian Law*.** Albuquerque. 1958. . . . . *$28.00–$35.00*

Fellows, M. H. *Land of Little Rain*. Chi. 1946. illus. dj. . . . . *$45.00–$65.00*

Felt, E. P. *Insects Affecting Park and Woodland Trees*. Albany. 1905. illus. . . . . *$45.00–$60.00*

Ferber, Edna. *Giant*. Garden City. 1952. 1st ed. dj. . . . . *$35.00–$45.00*

Ferber, Edna. *Saratoga Trunk*. Garden City. 1941. 1st ed. dj. . . . . *$18.00–$25.00*

Ferguson, William. *On the Poisonous Fishes of the Caribee Islands*. Edin. Neill. 1819. 1st ed. presentation copy, half mor & marbled bds. . . . . . *$700.00–$1,000.00*

Ferlinghetti, Lawrence. *A Coney Island of the Mind*. New Directions. 1968. 1st ed. green cl. . . . . *$50.00–$75.00*

Ferlinghetti, Lawrence. *Mexican Night*. New Directions. 1970. 1st ed. wrps. . . . . *$25.00–$45.00*

Ferlinghetti, Lawrence. *Secret Meaning of Things*. 1968. dj. . . . . . . *$30.00–$40.00*

Ferlinghetti, Lawrence. *Trip to Italy and France*. 1979. ltd 250 cc, sgn. . . . . *$75.00–$100.00*

Fermi, Enrico. *Thermodynamics*. Prentice-Hall. 1937. 1st ed. . . *$300.00–$500.00*

Ferris, Benjamin G. *Utah and the Mormons*. NY. 1854. illus. . . *$100.00–$250.00*

Ferris, Warren Angus. *Life in the Rocky Mountains 1830-1825.* Salt Lake. 1940. 1st ed. fldg map. . . . . *$150.00–$250.00*

Fessenden, T. *New American Gardener.* NY. 1828. 1st ed. lea. . . . *$75.00–$100.00*

Fessenden, Thomas G. *Complete Farmer.* Bos. Russell, Odiorne. 1825. . . . . *$65.00–$75.00*

Fessenden, Thomas (ed.). *New England Farmer.* Bos. 1833-35. vol. XI-XIII. . . . . *$175.00–$200.00*

Fewkes, Jesse Walter. *Preliminary Report on a Visit to the Navaho National Monument Arizona.* DC. GPO. 1911. 1st ed. . . . . *$50.00–$125.00*

Ficklen, Bessie A. *Handbook of Fist Puppets.* Phila. Lippincott. (1935). 1st ed. dj. . . . . *$20.00–$35.00*

Ficklen, John Rose. *History of Reconstruction in Louisiana.* Balt. 1910. 1st ed. wrps. . . . . *$55.00–$100.00*

Field, Eugene. *Echoes From the Sabine Farm.* Chi. 1893. 1st ed. ltd 500 cc. . . . . *$50.00–$75.00*

Field, Eugene. *Florence Bardsley's Story.* Chi. W. Irving Way. 1897. 1st ed. green cl. . . . . *$50.00–$75.00*

Field, Eugene. *Gingham Dog and the Calico Cat.* Newark. (1926). dj. . . . . *$100.00–$150.00*

Field, Eugene. *Little Willie.* np. nd. wrps. . . . . *$25.00–$40.00*

Field, Eugene. *Lullaby-Land.* Scribner's. 1897. 1st ed. illus. by Charles Robinson. . . . . *$50.00–$125.00*

Field, Eugene. *Poems of Childhood.* NY. Scribner's. 1904. illus. by Maxfield Parrish. . . . . *$90.00–$150.00*

Field, Eugene. *Songs of Childhood.* Scribner's. 1895. blue cl. . . . . *$25.00–$50.00*

Field, Eugene. *Winken, Blynken and Nod.* Saalfield. 1930. illus. . . *$25.00–$45.00*

Field, Eugene. *Writings In Prose and Verse.* NY. Scribner's. 1896. 10 vols. 1st ed. gray green cl aeg. . . . . *$60.00–$80.00*

Field, Henry M. *Bright Skies and Dark Shadows.* NY. 1890. 1st ed. maps, sgn. . . . . *$20.00–$35.00*

Field, Henry M. *History of the Atlantic Telegraph.* NY. 1866. 1st ed. illus. . . . . *$55.00–$90.00*

Field, M. *City Architecture: or, Designs for Dwellings, Houses, Stores, Hotels, etc.* NY. Putnam. 1853. 1st ed. illus. . . . . *$80.00–$120.00*

Field, Rachel. *Calico Bush.* NY. Macmillan. 1931.. 1st ed. 213 pp, inscr. . . . .
. . . . *$60.00–$80.00*

Fielde, Adele. *A Corner of Cathay.* NY. Macmillan. 1894. 11 clr plates, pict cl, teg.
. . . . *$30.00–$45.00*

Fielde, Adele M. *Pagoda Shadows, Studies from Life in China.* Bos. Corthell. 1884.
illus. frontis. . . . . *$45.00–$80.00*

Fielding, Mantle. *Gilbert Stuarts Portraits of George Washington.* Phila. 1923. 350 cc
sgn by author. . . . . *$75.00–$95.00*

Fifth Over the Southwest Pacific. LA. AAF Publications (Fifth Air Force). nd. wrps.
illus. . . . . *$95.00–$125.00*

Fifth Report of Senate Fact Finding Comm. on Un-American Activities. Sac. 1949.
wrps. illus. . . . . *$15.00–$25.00*

Figuier. *Mammalia, Popularly Described by Typical Species.* Lon. 1870. illus. . . .
. . . . *$35.00–$45.00*

Figuier, Louis. *Human Race.* NY. Appleton. 1872. 1st Amer ed. illus.. . . . .
. . . . *$150.00–$250.00*

Findlay, Frederick Roderick Noble. *Big Game Shooting and Travel in South East
Africa.* Camden. 1990. rprnt of 1903 ed. illus.. . . . . *$50.00–$140.00*

Findlay, Palmer. *Story of Childbirth.* NY. 1934. 1st ed. . . . . *$50.00–$75.00*

Findley, Palmer. *Priests of Lucina: Story of Obstetrics.* Bos. 1939. 1st ed. . . . . . .
. . . . *$22.00–$35.00*

Finger, Charles J. *Frontier Ballads Heard and Gathered By.* NY. 1927. 1st ed. illus.
woodcuts, ltd 201 cc, sgn. . . . . *$25.00–$45.00*

Finger, Charles J. *Romantic Rascals.* NY. McBride. 1927. illus. black cl. . . . . . .
. . . . *$20.00–$25.00*

Finley, Rev. James B. *History of the Wyandott Missions.* OH. 1840. 1st ed. 432 pp.
. . . . *$200.00–$300.00*

Finley, Ruth. *Old Patchwork Quilts and the Women Who Made Them.* Phila. 1929.
1st ed. . . . . *$60.00–$75.00*

Firbank, Ronald. *Inclinations.* Lon. Grant Richards. 1916. illus. by Albert
Rutherston. dj. . . . . *$250.00–$275.00*

Firebough, Ellen. *Physician's Wife and the Things That Pertain to Her Life.* Phila.
1894. 1st ed. 186 pp. . . . . *$75.00–$125.00*

Fireman, Janet. *Spanish Royal Corps of Engineers....* Glendale. Arthur H Clark.
1977. 1st ed. illus. fac maps & plans. . . . . *$35.00–$50.00*

First Annual Report of the Board of Pharmacy of the State of Washington.
Olympia. 1892. 1st ed. wrps. . . . . *$40.00–$50.00*

First Annual Sports and Bicycle Races. PA. 1896. wrps. 8 pp. . . . *$19.00–$30.00*

Fish, Hamilton. *Challenge of World Communism.* Milwaukee. 1946. 1st ed. cl. . .
. . . . *$30.00–$50.00*

Fishbein, M., et al. *Bibliography of Infantile Paralysis, 1789-1944.* Phila. 1946. 1st
ed. . . . . *$50.00–$65.00*

Fisher, A. K. *Hawks and Owls of the United States.* U S Dept of Agriculture. 1893.
illus. 25 clr lithos. . . . . *$140.00–$160.00*

Fisher, Angela. *Africa Adorned.* NY. Abrams. (1984). 1st ed. illus. clr plates. . . . .
. . . . *$80.00–$120.00*

Fisher, Dorothy Canfield. *Vermont Tradition.* Bos. 1953. 1st ed. . . *$18.00–$25.00*

Fisher, Harrison. *American Beauties.* Ind. (1909). 1st ed. illus. by Fisher. . . . . . .
. . . . *$400.00–$575.00*

Fisher, Harrison. *Dream of Fair Women.* NY. 1907. illus. . . . . . *$140.00–$225.00*

Fisher, Harrison. *Harrison Fisher Book.* NY. Scribner's. 1907. 1st ed. intro by
James Carrington. . . . . *$80.00–$120.00*

Fisher, Harrison. *Harrison Fisher's American Girls in Miniature.* NY. 1912. illus.
clr plates. . . . . *$75.00–$125.00*

Fisher, Harrison. *Hiawatha.* Ind. 1906. 1st ed. . . . . *$50.00–$150.00*

Fisher, Harrison. *Little Gift Book.* Ind. 1913. 1st ed. original box. . . . .
. . . . *$100.00–$125.00*

Fisher, James. *Spring day.* NY. George Lindsay. 1813. illus. 4 woodcuts. . . . .
. . . . *$40.00–$75.00*

Fisher, Rev. H. D. *Gun and the Gospel.* Chi. 1896. 1st ed. . . . . *$50.00–$75.00*

Fisher, Rudolph. *Walls of Jericho.* NY. Knopf. 1928. 1st ed. . . . . . *$45.00–$90.00*

Fisher, Vardis. *Darkness and the Deep.* NY. (1943). dj. . . . . *$40.00–$50.00*

Fiske. *Dutch & Quaker Colonies in America.* Bos. 1899. 2 vols. . . *$30.00–$40.00*

Fiske, John. *American Revolution.* Bos/NY. 1896. 2 vols. green cl. *$100.00–$125.00*

Fiske, John. *John Fiske's Historical Writings.* Bos. 1902. 12 vols. . . . .
. . . . *$50.00–$65.00*

Fite, Emerson D. *Book of Old Maps.* Camb. 1926. 1st ed. folio, maps. . . . .
. . . . *$150.00–$195.00*

Fitz-Adam, Adam. *The World.* Lon. Dodsley. 1772. 4 vols. 1st ed. copper engr, rare.
. . . . *$300.00–$350.00*

Fitzgerald, F Scott. *Flappers and Philosophers.* NY. Scribner's. 1920. 1st ed. green cl. . . . . *$125.00–$450.00*

Fitzgerald, F. Scott. *All the Sad Young Men.* NY. 1926. 1st ed. no dj. *$50.00–$75.00*

Fitzgerald, F. Scott. *All the Sad Young Men.* NY. Scribner's. 1926. 1st ed. rare with dj. . . . . *$600.00–$1,500.00*

Fitzgerald, F. Scott. *Beautiful and the Damned.* Scribner's. 1922. 1st ed. 1st state.
. . . . *$4,000.00–$6,000.00*

Fitzgerald, F. Scott. *Great Gatsby.* NY. Scribner's. 1925. 1st ed. 1st prtg. . . . . . .
. . . . *$800.00–$2,000.00*

Fitzgerald, F. Scott. *Stories of F. Scott Fitzgerald.* NY. Scribner's. 1951. 1st ed. dj.
. . . . *$75.00–$85.00*

Fitzgerald, F. Scott. *Tales of the Jazz Age.* Tor. Copp Clark. 1922. 1st Canadian ed.
. . . . *$350.00–$400.00*

Fitzgerald, F. Scott. *Tales of the Jazz Age.* NY. 1922. no dj. . . . . *$75.00–$100.00*

Fitzgerald, F. Scott. *Tender is the Night.* NY. Scribner's. 1932. 1st ed. . . . .
. . . . *$200.00–$300.00*

Fitzgerald, Rugh Coder. *A Different Story.* Unicorn. illus. . . . . . . *$50.00–$65.00*

Fitzgerald, Zelda. *Save Me the Waltz.* Scribner's. 1932. Zelda's first book. dj. . . .
. . . . *$2,000.00–$2,500.00*

Fitzgerald, Zelda. *Save Me the Waltz.* London. 1953. Zelda's first book. dj missing.
. . . . *$125.00–$135.00*

Flagg, Fannie. *Fried Green Tomatoes at the Whistlestop Cafe.* NY. Random House. 1987. 1st ed. sgn, dj. . . . . *$50.00–$60.00*

Flagg, Wilson. *Birds and Seasons of New England.* Bos. Osgood. 1875. 1st ed. illus. aeg. . . . . *$55.00–$80.00*

Flags of Army of U.S. During the War of Rebellion 1861-65. Phila. 1887. 1st ed. illus. clr lithos, folio. . . . . *$275.00–$450.00*

Flammarion, Camille. *Death and Its Mystery.* Century. 1922. 1st US ed cl. . . . . .
. . . . *$50.00–$60.00*

Flammarion, Camille. *The Atmosphere.* NY. 1873. illus. lithos woodcuts. . . . . . .
. . . . *$75.00–$90.00*

Flammarion, Camille. *Wonders of the Heavens.* NY. Scribner's. 1907. illus. cl. . .
. . . . *$40.00–$50.00*

Fleischer, Nat. *50 Years at Ringside.* NY. 1958. 1st ed. wrps. . . . . . *$35.00–$50.00*

Fleischman, Sid. *Whipping Boy.* NY. Greenwillow Books. (1986). dj. . . . .
. . . . *$18.00–$45.00*

Fleming, Alexander (ed.). *Penicillin, Its Practical Application.* Lon. Butterworth.
1946. 1st ed. . . . . *$55.00–$65.00*

Fleming, Ian. *Chitty Chitty Bang Bang.* NY. Random House. (1964). 1st ed. illus.
red cvr, dj. . . . . *$20.00–$25.00*

Fleming, Ian. *Diamond Smugglers.* Lon. (1957). 1st ed. black cl, dj. . . . .
. . . . *$150.00–$175.00*

Fleming, Ian. *Dr. No.* Lon. Jonathan Cape. 1958. 1st ed. dj. . . *$500.00–$1,300.00*

Fleming, Ian. *From Russia With Love.* Lon. Jonathan Cape. 1957. 1st ed. dj. . . . .
. . . . *$1,500.00–$1,750.00*

Fleming, Ian. *Goldfinger.* Lon. 1959. 1st ed. dj. . . . . *$500.00–$625.00*

Fleming, Ian. *Goldfinger.* NY. Macmillan. 1959. 1st Amer ed. dj. *$90.00–$250.00*

Fleming, Ian. *Ian Fleming Introduces Jamaica.* Lon. Deutsch. 1965. 1st Amer ed.
dj. . . . . *$70.00–$75.00*

Fleming, Ian. *Man with the Golden Gun.* NY. New American Library. 1965. 1st
Amer ed. dj. . . . . *$70.00–$75.00*

Fleming, Ian. *Man with the Golden Gun.* Lon. Jonathan Cape. (1965). 1st ed. dj. .
. . . . *$100.00–$125.00*

Fleming, Ian. *Octopussy and The Living Daylights.* Lon. Jonathan Cape. 1966. 1st
ed. dj. . . . . *$50.00–$100.00*

Fleming, Ian. *Spy Who Loved Me.* Lon. Jonathan Cape. (1962). 1st ed. cl, dj. . . . .
. . . . *$125.00–$230.00*

Fleming, Ian. *Thunderball.* Lon. Jonathan Cape. 1961. 1st ed. dj. *$200.00–$250.00*

Fleming, Ian. *You Only Live Twice.* Lon. Jonathan Cape. (1964). 1st ed. dj. . . . . .
. . . . *$90.00–$125.00*

Fleming, John Ambrose. *Electrons, Electric Waves and Wireless Telephony.* 1923.
1st ed. illus. . . . . *$45.00–$65.00*

Fleming, Thomas. *Now We Are Enemies.* NY. St Martin's Press. 1960. 1st ed. dj,
black cl & red paper-cvr bds. . . . . *$25.00–$50.00*

Fletcher, J. S. *Safe Number Sixty-Nine.* Bos. International Pocket Library. (1931).
1st ed. wrps. . . . . *$60.00–$65.00*

Flint, Austin. *Medical Ethics and Etiquette.* NY. Appleton. 1883. 1st ed. 97 pp. . . .
. . . . *$60.00–$95.00*

Flint, Austin. *Physical Exploration and Diagnosis of Diseases Affecting Respiratory Organs.* Phila. 1856. 1st ed. 636 pp. . . . . : . . . . *$75.00–$100.00*

Flint, Sir William Russell. *Drawings.* Lon. Collins. (1950). 1st ed. illus. . . . .
. . . . *$100.00–$150.00*

Flint, Timothy. *Life and Adventures of Daniel Boone.* Cinc. 1868. maps, illus. . . .
. . . . *$100.00–$250.00*

Flint, Timothy. *Recollections of the Last Ten Years...Journeys in the Valley of the Mississippi....* Bos. Cummings, Hilliard. 1826. 1st ed. . . . . *$125.00–$225.00*

Floyd, William. *Hints on Dog Breeding.* Lon. 1882. . . . . *$25.00–$40.00*

Fluge, Friederich. *Der Seekrieg: The German Navy's Story, 1939-1945.* Annap. Naval Inst. 1965. maps, dj. . . . . *$15.00–$20.00*

Foley, Dan. *Toys Through the Ages.* Phil/NY. Chilton Books. 1962. 1st ed. illus. dj.
. . . . *$20.00–$45.00*

Foley, Edwin. *Book of Decorative Furniture.* NY. 1911. 2 vols. 1st ed. 100 tip-in clr plates. . . . . *$175.00–$250.00*

Foley, Rae. *Back Door to Death.* NY. Dodd, Mead. 1963. 1st ed. inscr, dj. . . . . . .
. . . . *$35.00–$45.00*

Folig, Fred. *Lucy Boston on Women's Rights and Spiritualism.* NY. 1855. 1st ed. illus. . . . . *$50.00–$65.00*

Follett, Ken. *Man From St. Petersburg.* Lon. Hamish Hamilton. 1982. 1st ed. dj. .
. . . . *$50.00–$65.00*

Foran, W. *Kill or Be Killed.* NY. 1988. 1st ed. dj. . . . . *$25.00–$35.00*

Forbes, Alexander. *California, a History of Upper and Lower California.* Lon. 1839. 1st ed. illus. map. . . . . *$925.00–$1,200.00*

Forbes, Allan and Ralph E. Eastman. *Yankee Sailing Cards.* Bos. State Street Trust. (1948-1952). 3 vols. wrps. illus. . . . . *$45.00–$80.00*

Forbes, Esther. *America's Paul Revere.* Bos. 1946. 1st ed. illus. by Lynd Ward. dj.
. . . . *$45.00–$60.00*

Forbes, Esther. *Johnny Tremain.* Bos. Houghton Mifflin. (1943). dec green cl. . . .
. . . . *$20.00–$30.00*

Forbes-Lindsay, C. H. *India Past and Present.* Phila. 1903. 2 vols. illus. fldg map.
. . . . *$50.00–$75.00*

Forbush, Edward Howe. *Birds of Massachusetts....* 1929. 3 vols. illus. folio col plates by Fuertes et al. . . . . *$100.00–$150.00*

Forbush, Edward Howe. *Domestic Cat.* Bos. 1916. 1st ed. wrps. illus. . . . . *$65.00–$75.00*

Forbush, Edward Howe. *Game Birds, Wild Fowl & Shore Birds.* 1912. illus. . . . . *$45.00–$60.00*

Forbush, Edward Howe. *History of Game Birds...of Massachusetts.* 1912. illus. plates. . . . . *$45.00–$50.00*

Forbush, Edward Howe. *Portraits of New England Birds.* MA. 1932. illus. . . . . *$50.00–$75.00*

Force, Manning Ferguson. *General Sherman.* NY. 1899. 1st ed. . *$50.00–$125.00*

Ford, Ford Maddox. *Great Trade Routes.* Unwin. 1937. 1st ed. wrps. . . . . *$30.00–$45.00*

Ford, Paul. *Great K. & A. Train Robbery.* Dodd, Mead. 1897. 1st ed. *$20.00–$30.00*

Ford, Richard. *Piece of My Heart.* NY. Harper & Row. (1976). 1st ed. author's first book, sgn, dj. . . . . *$225.00–$450.00*

Ford, Richard. *Rock Springs.* NY. Atlantic Monthly. (1987). 1st ed. sgn, dj. . . . . *$30.00–$75.00*

Ford, Robert. *Thistledown.* Paisley. Gardner. 1913. 1st ed. illus. by John Duncan. teg. . . . . *$60.00–$90.00*

Forder, Nick. *Victorian Dollhouses.* NJ. Chartwell Books. (1966). dj. . . . . *$14.00–$18.00*

Foreman, Grant. *Indian Justice: a Cherokee Murder Trial at Tahlequah in 1840.* Oklahoma City. 1934. . . . . *$75.00–$85.00*

Forester, C. S. *Sky and the Forest.* Lon. Michael Joseph. (1948). 1st UK ed dj. . . . . *$16.00–$40.00*

Forester, C. S. *The Gun.* Bos. Little, Brown. 1933. . . . . *$125.00–$155.00*

Forester, C. S. *The Ship.* Bos. Little, Brown. (1943). red cl bds. . . *$20.00–$30.00*

Forester, C. S. *To the Indies.* Bos. Little, Brown. 1940. dj. . . . . *$60.00–$85.00*

Forester, C. S. *African Queen.* Bos. 1935. 1st Amer, dj. . . . . *$375.00–$500.00*

Forester, C. S. *Captain from Connecticut.* Bos. Little, Brown. 1942. dj. . . . . *$30.00–$35.00*

Forester, C. S. *Captain Horatio Hornblower.* Bos. 1939. 1st Amer ed. illus by Wyeth, dj. . . . . *$440.00–$50.00*

Forester, C. S. *Hornblower Companion.* Bos. Little, Brown. (1964). 1st ed. red cl, bds, dj. . . . . *$170.00–$350.00*

Forester, C. S. *Lord Hornblower.* Bos. Little, Brown. 1946. 1st ed. *$20.00–$30.00*

Forester, C. S. *Randall and the River of Time.* Bos. Little, Brown. 1950. 1st ed. dj. . . . . *$30.00–$38.00*

Forester, C. S. *The Commodore.* Lon. Michael Joseph LTD. (1945). 1st UK ed. dj. . . . . *$25.00–$100.00*

Forester, C. S. *The African Queen.* NY. Modern Library. (1940). 1st Modern lib ed. cl, dj. . . . . *$50.00–$75.00*

Forester, Frank. *Fishing with Hook and Line.* Hurst & Co. 1858. illus. *$50.00–$60.00*

Forester, Frank. *Hints to Horse-Keepers.* NY. 1859. . . . . *$48.00–$75.00*

Forman, Samuel Engle. *Life and Writings of Thomas Jefferson....* Bowen Merrill. . . . . *$50.00–$65.00*

Formby, John. *American Civil War....* NY. 1910. 2 vols. illus. maps. *$95.00–$125.00*

Forster, E. M. *Passage to India.* Arnold. 1924. 1st ed. dj. . . . . . *$600.00–$800.00*

Forster, E. M. *Room With A View.* Lon. 1908. . . . . *$150.00–$250.00*

Forster, Frank J. *Country Houses.* NY. 1931. 1st ed. . . . . *$125.00–$175.00*

Forsyth, Frederick. *Biafra Story.* Lon. Penguin. 1969. 1st ed. paperback original. . . . . *$125.00–$150.00*

Forsyth, William. *An Epitome of Mr. Forsyth's Treatise on the Culture and Management of Fruit-Trees.* Phila. Poyntell. 1804. illus. . . . . *$50.00–$100.00*

Forsythe, Frederick. *Odessa File.* Viking. 1972. 1st Us ed. dj. . . . *$20.00–$30.00*

Fossett, Frank. *Colorado: Its Gold and Silver Mines.* NY. 1879. 1st thus. illus. maps, plates. . . . . *$100.00–$300.00*

Fossett, Frank. *Colorado: Its Gold and Silver Mines.* NY. 1880. illus. 2nd ed. fldg maps. . . . . *$75.00–$125.00*

Foster, David. *The Scientific Angler.* Lon. Bemrose. (1886). 3rd Eng ed. illus. litho plates. . . . . *$75.00–$200.00*

Foster, Sophie Lee. *Revolutionary Reader, Reminiscences and Indian Legends.* Atlanta, GA. Byrd. 1913. illus. red cl, gilt lettering. . . . . *$30.00–$50.00*

Four Gospels of the Lord Jesus Christ/According to the Authorized Version of King James. Waltham St Laurence. The Golden Cockerel Press. 1931. illus. with 65 wood engrs by Eric Gill, ltd 500 cc, tan cl, white pigskin spine and corner, teg, by Sangorski and Sutcliffe, slipcase. . . . . *$2,000.00–$7,500.00*

Fourth Report on Un-American Activities in California. Sacramento. 1948. 1st ed.
.... *$60.00–$75.00*

Fowke, Gerard. *Archaeological History of Ohio....*Columbus. Ohio State Archaeological & Hist Society. (1902). illus. fldg plate. .... *$75.00–$100.00*

Fowler, H. W. *Dictionary of Modern English Usage.* Ox. 1926. 1st ed. ....
.... *$50.00–$75.00*

Fowler, Harlan D. *Camels to California.* Stanford Univ Pr. 1950. illus. dj. ......
.... *$25.00–$35.00*

Fowler, Jacob. *Journal of Jacob Fowler....* NY. Francis P. Harper. 1898. 1st ed. ltd 950 cc, blue cl. .... *$100.00–$135.00*

Fowler, L. N. *Principles of Phrenology & Physiology....* NY. 1842. 1st ed. ......
.... *$55.00–$65.00*

Fowler, O. S. *A Home for All. Or the Gravel Wall & Octagon Mode of Building.* NY. 1877. illus. .... *$45.00–$60.00*

Fowles, J. *The Aristos.* Bos. Little, Brown. (1964). 1st ed. dj. ... *$135.00–$150.00*

Fowles, John. *A Maggot.* Lon. Jonathan Cape. 1985. ltd 500 cc, sgn. ....
.... *$125.00–$150.00*

Fowles, John. *The Collector.* 1963. 1st ed. 1st state, author's first book. ....
.... *$100.00–$150.00*

Fox, Carl. *The Doll.* NY. Harry N. Abrams. 1974. illus. dj, col and b/w plates. ...
.... *$100.00–$225.00*

Fox, Carl. *The Doll New Shorter Edition.* NY. Harry N Abrams. wrps. ....
.... *$20.00–$35.00*

Fox, John R. *In Happy Valley.* Scribner's. 1917. illus. .... *$20.00–$30.00*

Foxcraft, Thomas. *Observations, Historical and Practical, on the Rise and Primitive State of New-England ...: A Sermon.* Bos. S Kneeland and T Green, for S Gerrish. 1730. 1st ed. 46 pp. .... *$600.00–$1,500.00*

Frame, Janet. *Face in the Water.* NY. 1961. 1st ed. dj. .... *$30.00–$40.00*

France, Anatole. *Gods are Athirst.* Lon. (1927). dj. .... *$35.00–$45.00*

Franchere, Gabriel. *Narr. of a Voyage to the Northwest Coast of America 1811, 1812, 1813, 1814.* NY. 1854. 1st ed. in Eng. .... *$250.00–$350.00*

Francis, Dick. *10-lb. Penalty.* Lon. Michael Joseph. 1997. 1st ed. sgn, dj. ....
.... *$55.00–$85.00*

Francis, Dick. *Bolt.* Lon. Michael Joseph. 1986. 1st ed. dj. ...... *$50.00–$60.00*

Francis, Dick. *Driving Force.* Lon. Michael Joseph. 1992. 1st ed. dj. *$35.00–$50.00*

Francis, Dick. *Enquiry.* Lon. Michael Joseph. 1969. 1st ed. dj. . *$125.00–$175.00*

Francis, Dick. *Flying Finish.* Lon. Michael Joseph. 1966. 1st ed. dj. . . . .
. . . . *$145.00–$400.00*

Francis, Dick. *For Kicks.* Lon. Michael Joseph. 1965. 1st ed. dj. . . . .
. . . . *$1,250.00–$2,000.00*

Francis, Dick. *High Stakes.* NY. 1975. 1st Amer ed. dj. . . . . *$30.00–$40.00*

Francis, Dick. *High Stakes.* Lon. Michael Joseph. 1975. 1st ed. dj. . *$85.00–$100.00*

Francis, Dick. *Hot Money.* Lon. Michael Joseph. 1987. 1st ed. dj. . *$35.00–$45.00*

Francis, Dick. *In the Frame.* Lon. Michael Joseph. 1976. 1st ed. dj. *$50.00–$65.00*

Francis, Dick. *In the Frame.* NY. 1977. 1st Amer ed. dj. . . . . *$30.00–$40.00*

Francis, Dick. *Knock Down.* Lon. Michael Joseph. 1974. 1st ed. dj. . . . .
. . . . *$125.00–$300.00*

Francis, Dick. *Lester, the Official Biography.* Lon. Michael Joseph. 1986. 1st ed. dj.
. . . . *$60.00–$70.00*

Francis, Dick. *Proof.* Lon. Michael Joseph. 1984. 1st ed. dj.. . . . . . *$50.00–$65.00*

Francis, Dick. *Reflex.* Lon. Michael Joseph. 1980. 1st ed. sgn, dj. . *$80.00–$90.00*

Francis, Dick. *Straight.* Lon. Michael Joseph. 1989. 1st ed. dj. . . . *$40.00–$50.00*

Francis, Dick. *The Danger.* Lon. Michael Joseph. 1983. 1st ed. dj.. *$50.00–$65.00*

Francis, Francis. *By Lake and River.* Lon. The Field Office. 1874. 1st ed. 1/2 mor &
marbled bds, raised bands. . . . . *$250.00–$350.00*

Francis, Francis and A. W. Cooper. *Sporting Sketches with Pen and Pencil.* Lon.
The Field Office. 1879. 1st ed. illus. wood-engr plates, mor and cl, aeg. . . . .
. . . . *$150.00–$250.00*

Francis, Jean. *Dolls I Have Known and Loved.* Canada. privately printed. 1980. illus.
pict bds, ltd 1000 cc. sgn by author. . . . . *$25.00–$40.00*

Francis, John W. *Old New York or Reminiscences of the Past Sixty Years.* NY. 1858.
1st ed. . . . . *$30.00–$50.00*

Francis, Peter. *I Worked in a Soviet Factory.* Lon. Jarrolds. 1939. illus. *$10.00–$20.00*

Frank Leslie's Illustrated History of the Civil War. NY. 1895. 1st ed. small folio.
. . . . *$60.00–$125.00*

Frank, Larry. *Indian Silver Jewelry.1868–1930.* Bos. 1978. 1st ed. *$45.00–$75.00*

Frank, P. *Alas, Babylon.* Phila. Lippincott. 1959. 1st ed. scarce, dj. . . . .
. . . . *$250.00–$275.00*

Franklin, Colin and Charlotte. *Catalogue of Early Colour Printing....* Oxford.
1977. illus. clr plates. . . . . *$50.00–$70.00*

Franklin, John. *Narrative of a Journey to the Shores of the Polar Sea, 1819-22.* Lon.
John Murray. 1823. 1st ed. illus. maps, plates. . . . . *$1,500.00–$2,000.00*

Fraser, Antonia. *History of Toys.* Delacorte Press. (1966). illus. dj,. *$30.00–$45.00*

Fraser, Chelsea. *Heroes of the Air.* Crowell. 1928. illus. rev, 550 pp. . . . .
. . . . *$25.00–$35.00*

Fraser, George MacDonald. *Flashman and the Angel of the Lord.* NY. Knopf.
(1994). 1st ed. dj. . . . . *$35.00–$50.00*

Fraser, George MacDonald. *Flashman and the Dragon.* NY. Knopf. (1986). 1st
Amer ed. dj. . . . . *$35.00–$75.00*

Fraser, George MacDonald. *Flashman and the Mountain of Light.* Lon. Collins
Harvill. (1990). 1st UK ed. dj. . . . . *$50.00–$90.00*

Fraser, George MacDonald. *Flashman and the Redskins.* NY. Knopf. (1982). 1st
US ed. dj. . . . . *$35.00–$50.00*

Fraser, George MacDonald. *General Danced at Dawn.* NY. Knopf. (1973). 1st US
ed. white cl-cvr bds, dj, scarce. . . . . *$75.00–$100.00*

Fraser, George MacDonald. *The Pyrates.* NY. Knopf. (1984). dj. . . . .
. . . . *$25.00–$45.00*

Fraser, J. Baillie. *Mesopotamia and Assyria, from the Earliest Ages to the Present.*
NY. Harper. 1842. 1st Amer ed. fldg map frontis, 336 pp. . . . . *$30.00–$40.00*

Frazier, Charles. *Cold Mountain.* NY. Atlantic Monthly Press. (1997). 1st ed. 1st
state. cl & bds, dj. . . . . *$150.00–$250.00*

Frazier, Don. *Recognizing Derrydale Press Books.* np. privately printed. 1983. illus.
22 clr plates, ltd 347cc, brown lea. . . . . *$210.00–$250.00*

Frederick Remington: The American West. Kent, OH. Volair Ltd. 1978. ed by Philip
St Claire, plates, boxed. . . . . *$80.00–$120.00*

Freece, Hans P. *Letters of An Apostate Mormon to His Son.* NY. private printing.
1908. . . . . *$65.00–$85.00*

Freeman, Douglas Southall. *Lee's Lieutenants: a Study in Command.* Scribner's.
3 vols. illus. b/w illus maps. . . . . *$100.00–$125.00*

Freeman, Douglas Southall. *Robert E. Lee, A Biography.* NY. 1934-5. 4 vols. illus.
. . . . *$95.00–$250.00*

Freeman, Harry C. *Brief History of Butte, Montana*. Shepard. 1900. 1st ed. . . . .
. . . . *$75.00–$125.00*

Freeman, Joseph. *Discourse on the Proper Training of Children*. Ludlow, VT. 1862.
wrps. . . . . *$25.00–$40.00*

Freeman, Larry and Jane Beaumont. *Early American Plated Silver*. Watkins Glen.
Century House. 1947. 1st ed. . . . . *$50.00–$65.00*

Freligh, Martin. *Homeopathic Practice of Medicine*. NY. Lamport, Blakeman &
Law. 1854. 2nd ed. . . . . *$90.00–$150.00*

Fremont, Capt. J. C. *Report of the Exploring Expedition to the Rocky Mountains*....
DC. 1842. maps. . . . . *$125.00–$250.00*

Fremont, John. *Life of Col Fremont*. (NY). 1856. 1st ed. 32 pp, sewn, portrait, two
full-page illus. . . . . *$85.00–$100.00*

French, John C. *Passenger Pidgeon in Pennsylvania*. Altoona. Altoona Tribune.
1919. 1st ed. wrps. illus. . . . . *$100.00–$150.00*

Freud, Sigmund. *Interpretation of Dreams*. NY. 1937. dj. . . . . *$30.00–$40.00*

Freud, Sigmund. *Introductory Lectures on Psycho-Analysis*. Lon. 1929. . . . .
. . . . *$50.00–$80.00*

Freud, Sigmund. *Modern Sexual Morality and Modern Nervousness*. NY. Eugenics
Pub Co. 1931. bds. . . . . *$50.00–$75.00*

Freud, Sigmund. *Note on the Unconscious in PsychoAnalysis*. Lon. 1912. wrps. .
. . . . *$25.00–$35.00*

Freud, Sigmund. *Problem of Lay-Analyses*. NY. 1927. 1st Amer ed. dj. . . . .
. . . . *$65.00–$85.00*

Friedan, Betty. *Feminine Mystique*. NY. 1963. 1st ed. dj. . . . . . . *$100.00–$150.00*

Friedman, Bruce Jay. *Black Angels*. NY. (1966). 1st ed. dj. . . . . . *$35.00–$45.00*

Friedman, Bruce Jay. *Stern*. NY. 1962. 1st ed. dj. . . . . *$50.00–$60.00*

Friedmann, H. *The Cowbirds*. Charles C Thomas. 1929. dj, presentation copy. . .
. . . . *$45.00–$60.00*

Frignet, Ernest. *La Californie: Histoire des Progres de l'un Etats-Unis*.... Paris.
Schlesinger Freres. 1867. printed wrps, 2nd ed,. . . . . *$50.00–$75.00*

Froiseth, Jennie Anderson. *Women of Mormonism*. Detroit. 1887. illus. . . . .
. . . . *$90.00–$100.00*

Frost, A. B. *Stuff and Nonsense*. NY. Scribner's. (1884). illus. orig pict bds. . . . . .
. . . . *$60.00–$110.00*

Frost, John. *American Naval Biography*. Phila. 1844. illus. 3/4 mor . . . .
. . . . *$87.00–$185.00*

Frost, John. *Book of Travels in Africa*. NY/Phila. 1848. illus. . . . . *$50.00–$85.00*

Frost, John. *Pictorial History of Mexico and the Mexican War*. Phila. 1849. maps.
. . . . *$35.00–$50.00*

Frost, Robert. *A Boy's Will*. Lon. Nutt. 1913. 1st ed. 1st issue with points. author's
first book, cream paper wrps with 8-petaled flower ornament. *$1,000.00–$3,000.00*

Frost, Robert. *A Further Range*. NY. Holt. 1936. 1st ed. dj. . . . . *$40.00–$100.00*

Frost, Robert. *A Masque of Mercy*. NY. Holt. 1947. 1st ed. 39 pp. *$30.00–$75.00*

Frost, Robert. *A Masque of Reason*. NY. Holt. 1945. 1st trade ed. dj. *$50.00–$75.00*

Frost, Robert. *Collected Poems of Robert Frost*. NY. Henry Holt. 1939. sgn and
dated, dj. . . . . *$450.00–$750.00*

Frost, Robert. *Complete Poems*. NY. Holt, Rinehart & Winston. (1962). 1st ed. dj.
. . . . *$25.00–$45.00*

Frost, Robert. *Complete Poems of Robert Frost*. Lon. (1951). dj. . . *$40.00–$50.00*

Frost, Robert. *Further Range*. NY. 1936. ltd 803 cc, sgn. . . . . . *$275.00–$500.00*

Frost, Robert. *In The Clearing*. NY. (1962). 1st ed. dj. . . . . *$45.00–$75.00*

Frost, Robert. *New Hampshire*. NY. 1923. 1st ed. . . . . *$100.00–$150.00*

Frost, Robert. *Steeple Bush*. NY. Henry Holt. 1947. 1st ed. ltd 750 cc, sgn, dj. . .
. . . . *$125.00–$350.00*

Frost, Robert. *West Running Brook*. NY. Henry Holt. 1928. 1st ed. no dj. . . . . . .
. . . . *$65.00–$95.00*

Frost, Robert. *Witness Tree*. NY. Henry Holt. 1942. 1st ed. ltd, sgn. . . . .
. . . . *$475.00–$500.00*

Frost, Robert. *Witness Tree*. NY. (1942). 1st ed. dj. . . . . *$35.00–$100.00*

Frost, Stanley. *Challenge of the Klan*. Ind. 1924. 1st ed. . . . . *$40.00–$55.00*

Frothingham, Alice Wilson. *Hispanic Glass*. NY. Hispanic Society. 1941. 1st ed.
illus. . . . . *$75.00–$100.00*

Fry, Christopher. *Lady's Not for Burning*. Lon. 1949. dj. . . . . *$30.00–$40.00*

Fry, J. Reese. *Life of Gen. Zachary Taylor*. Phila. 1848. illus. . . . . *$37.00–$45.00*

Fryer, Jane E. *Mary Frances Cook Book*. Phil. Winston. 1912. 1st ed. illus. . . . . .
. . . . *$95.00–$185.00*

Fryer, Jane E. *Mary Frances Sewing Book*. Phila. 1913. 1st ed. illus. patterns. . . .
. . . . *$150.00–$225.00*

Fryer, Mary Ann. *John Fryer of the Bounty*. Lon. Golden Cockerel Press. 1939. illus.
ltd #226/300 cc, sgn, colophon. . . . . *$325.00–$375.00*

Fuentes, Carlos. *Aura*. NY. 1965. 1st UK ed. dj. . . . . *$75.00–$100.00*

Fuentes, Carlos. *Old Gringo*. NY. 1985. 1st ed. 2nd prtg, dj. . . . . . *$20.00–$45.00*

Fuentes, Carlos. *Where the Air is Clear*. NY. Ivan Obolensky. 1960. 1st ed. dj. . .
. . . . *$20.00–$35.00*

***Fugitives. The Story of Clyde Barrow and Bonnie Parker*.** Dallas. 1934. 1st ed. .
. . . . *$47.00–$65.00*

Fuhrer, Charles. *Mysteries of Montreal....* Montreal. 1881. 245 pp. *$85.00–$100.00*

Fulghum, David. *Vietnam Experience*. Boston Pub. (1981-1988). 21 vols. . . . . . .
. . . . *$150.00–$200.00*

Fuller, Claud E. and Richard D. Steuart. *Firearms of the Confederacy, the Shoulder Arms, Pistols and Revolvers of the Confederate Soldier*. Huntington, W Va. Standard Publications. 1944. 1st ed. scarce dj. . . . . *$200.00–$350.00*

Fuller, J. F. C. *Generalship of Ulysses S. Grant*. NY. 1929. . . . . . . *$37.00–$45.00*

Fuller, Metta. *Fresh Leaves From Western Woods*. Buffalo. 1852. 2 vols. 1st ed. . .
. . . . *$15.00–$25.00*

Fuller, R. Buckminster. *Nine Chains to the Moon*. Phila. 1938. 1st ed. authors first
book, dj. . . . . *$75.00–$95.00*

Fuller, R. Buckminster. *Utopia or Oblivion*. Penguin Press. 1970. 1st UK ed. dj.
. . . . *$30.00–$50.00*

Fulton, Frances. *To and Through Nebraska*. Lincoln. 1884. 1st ed. 273 pp. . . . . .
. . . . *$100.00–$145.00*

Fulton, James A. *Peach Culture*. NY. 1905. . . . . *$25.00–$50.00*

Furlong, Charles W. *Let 'Er Buck*. NY. 1921. 1st ed. sgn. . . . . *$55.00–$65.00*

Furneaux, W. *British Butterflies and Moths*. Lon. 1911. plates. . . . *$45.00–$55.00*

Furst, Peter T. and Jill L. Furst. *North American Indian Art*. NY. Rizzoli. illus. photos, dj. . . . . *$40.00–$65.00*

Fuzzlebug, Fritz (John J. Dunkle). *Prison Life During the Rebellion*. Singer's Glen,
VA. 1869. 1st ed. wrps. . . . . *$125.00–$150.00*

Gabler, James M. *Wine into Words*. Baltimore. Bacchus Press. 1985. 1st ed. dj. . .
. . . . *$35.00–$50.00*

Gade, John A. *Book Plates—Old and New*. NY. 1898. illus. . . . . . *$25.00–$30.00*

Gaelic Fairy Tales. Glasgow. 1908. illus. by Katherine Cameron. . . *$30.00–$40.00*

Gage, S. H. *The Microscope*. Ithaca. Comstock Publishing. 1936. . *$40.00–$50.00*

Gage, W. L. *Palestine: Historical and Descriptive*. Bos. 1883. illus. . . . .
. . . . *$55.00–$95.00*

Gallant, Mavis. *Across the Bridge*. NY. (1993). 1st ed. dj. . . . . *$18.00–$25.00*

Gallant, Mavis. *Other Paris*. Bos. Houghton Mifflin. 1956. 1st ed. author's first
book, dj. . . . . *$75.00–$85.00*

Gallaudet, Thomas. *Plan of a Seminary for the Education of Instructers of Youth*.
Bos. Cummings, Hilliard & Co. 1825. 1st ed. illus. 39 pp. . . . . *$50.00–$75.00*

*A **Gallery of Famous English and American Poets***. Phila. Butler. 1860. illus. brown
mor, embossed in gilt and black, aeg.. . . . . *$75.00–$125.00*

Gallico, Paul. *Snow Goose*. 1941. 1st ed. dj. . . . . *$225.00–$250.00*

Galsworthy, John. *Forsythe Saga*. Lon. Heinemann. 1922. 1st ed. lea, aeg. . . . . .
. . . . *$200.00–$400.00*

Galsworthy, John. *Loyalties*. Scribner's. 1922. 1st US ed. dj. . . . . *$60.00–$70.00*

Galsworthy, John. *Maid in Waiting*. Lon. 1931. 1st ed. dj.. . . . . . . *$25.00–$50.00*

Galsworthy, John. *Memories*. NY. 1914. illus. . . . . *$30.00–$40.00*

Galsworthy, John. *Swan Song*. NY. Scribner's. 1928. 1st US ed. dj.*$40.00–$50.00*

Galsworthy, John. *Swan Song*. Lon. 1928. . . . . *$50.00–$75.00*

Galsworthy, John. *Works*. NY. Scribner's. 1930. mor and cl, teg. *$100.00–$150.00*

Gambling World by Rouge et Noir. Dodd, Mead. 1898. . . . . *$50.00–$65.00*

Gambling, Gaming Supplies. Chi. H. C. Evans Co. 1929. wrps. . . . .
. . . . *$85.00–$125.00*

Gammons, Rev. John G. *Third Massachusetts Regiment Volunteer... 1861-1863*.
Prov. 1906. 1st ed. illus. . . . . *$75.00–$100.00*

Gandhi, Mahatma. *My Appeal to the British*. NY. John Day. (1942). 1st Amer ed.
cl, dj.. . . . . *$75.00–$185.00*

Garces, Francisco. *Record of Travels in Arizona and California, 1175-1776*. SF.
John Howell-Books. trans by John Galvin. ltd 1250 cc.. . . . . *$50.00–$80.00*

Garcia Marquez, Gabriel. *In Evil Hour*. NY. Harper & Row. (1979). 1st Amer ed,
dj. . . . . *$60.00–$100.00*

Gard, Wayne. *Rawhide Texas.* Norman. 1965. 1st ed. illus. cl, dj.. . *$22.00–$30.00*

Gardiner, Howard C. *In Pursuit of the Golden Dream: Reminiscences of San Francisco....* MA. Western Hemisphere. 1970. 1st ed. illus. 8 plates 2 maps, 1 fldg. . . . . *$60.00–$90.00*

Gardner, Erle Stanley. *Case of the Careless Cupid.* NY. William Morrow. 1968. 1st ed. dj. . . . . *$45.00–$60.00*

Gardner, Erle Stanley. *Case of the Ice-Cold Hands.* NY. William Morrow. 1962. 1st ed. dj. . . . . *$50.00–$60.00*

Gardner, Erle Stanley. *Case of the Grinning Gorilla.* NY. William. Morrow. 1952. 1st ed. dj.. . . . . *$25.00–$35.00*

Gardner, Erle Stanley. *Case of the Screaming Woman.* NY. 1957. 1st ed. dj.. . . . . *$35.00–$45.00*

Gardner, Erle Stanley. *Case of the Substitute Face.* NY. William Morrow. 1938. 1st ed. dj. . . . . *$350.00–$400.00*

Gardner, Erle Stanley. *DA Breaks an Egg.* NY. William Morrow. 1949. 1st ed. dj. . . . . *$40.00–$50.00*

Gardner, John. *In the Suicide Mountains.* NY. Knopf. 1977. 1st ed. dj. . . . . *$30.00–$35.00*

Gardner, John. *King's Indian: Stories and Tales.* NY. Knopf. 19174. 1st ed. dj. . . . . *$35.00–$60.00*

Gardner, John. *Life and Times of Chaucer.* NY. Knopf. 1977. 1st ed. dj.. . . . . *$35.00–$45.00*

Gardner, John. *October Light.* NY. Knopf. 1976. 1st ed. dj.. . . . . . *$45.00–$50.00*

Gardner, John. *Sunlight Dialogues.* NY. 1972. 1st ed. dj.. . . . . *$60.00–$70.00*

Garfield, James R. *Report of the Commissioner of Corporations on the Beef Industry.* DC. GPO. 1905. . . . . *$75.00–$100.00*

Garis, Howard. *Uncle Wiggily on the Farm.* NY. Platt & Munk Co. 1939. illus. green cl dj. . . . . *$15.00–$25.00*

Garland, H. *Life of John Randolph of Roanoke.* NY. 1851. 2 vols. . *$30.00–$40.00*

Garland, Hamlin. *Trail-makers of the Middle Border.* Macmillan. 1926. 1st ed. dj. . . . . *$25.00–$35.00*

Garner, Elvira. *Ezekiel.* Henry Holt. illus. paper over bds. . . . . *$50.00–$65.00*

Garner, T. and A. Stratton. *Domestic Architecture of England during the Tudor Period.* NY. (1929). 2 vols. 2nd ed. 210 plates. . . . . *$150.00–$300.00*

Garnett, David. *First "Hippy" Revolution.* Cerrillos, NM. 1970. 1st ed. wrps. sgn.
. . . . *$40.00–$50.00*

Garnett, Porter (ed.). *Papers of San Francisco Vigilance Committee of 1851.* Berkeley. Univ of Calif Press. 1910. wrps. . . . . *$40.00–$70.00*

Garnett, Theodore Stanford. *J E B Stuart (Major General) Commander of the Cavalry Corps.* NY/DC. Neale Publishing Co. 1907. 1st ed. illus. plates. . . . .
. . . . *$200.00–$250.00*

Garrard, Lewis H. *Wah-To-Yah and the Taos Trail.* SF. Grabhorn Press. 1936. illus. ltd 550 cc. . . . . *$125.00–$140.00*

Garrison, Fielding H. *An Introduction to the History of Medicine.* Saunders. 1914. 763 pp. . . . . *$75.00–$100.00*

Garwood, Darrell. *Artist in Iowa: A Life of Grant Wood.* NY. W.W. Norton. 1944. 1st ed. illus. photos, dj. . . . . *$25.00–$30.00*

Gask, Norman. *Old Silver Spoons of England.* Lon. 1926. illus. rbnd, 1/4 leather..
. . . . *$75.00–$125.00*

Gass, Patrick. *Gass's Journal of the Lewis & Clark Expedition.* Chi. McClurg. 1904. illus. two-tone cl, sp lettered in gilt, teg. . . . . *$350.00–$500.00*

Gass, Patrick. *Journal of the Voyages and Travels of a Corps of Discovery under the Command of Capt Lewis....* Minn. Ross & Haines. 1958. illus. photos, fldg endpaper map, cl. ltd 2000 cc. . . . . *$50.00–$100.00*

Gass, William. *Omensetter's Luck.* (NY). New American Library. (1966). 1st ed. author's first novel, dj. . . . . *$60.00–$125.00*

Gass, William. *The Tunnel.* NY. Knopf. 1995. 1st ed. dj. . . . . *$35.00–$45.00*

Gass, William. *World Within the World.* NY. Knopf. 1978. 1st ed. dj.. . . . .
. . . . *$34.00–$45.00*

Gaster, M. *Hebrew Illuminated Bibles of the 9th and 10th Centuries.* Lon. 1901. folio, plates.. . . . . *$85.00–$125.00*

Gasthoff's Parade Floats & Decorations. Tampa, FL. Gastoff's Display Service, Inc. 1937–38. pict wrps, illus, 24 pp.. . . . . *$40.00–$50.00*

Gatty, Mrs. A. *Book of Sun Dials.* Lon. 1872. 1st ed. illus. plates. *$100.00–$200.00*

Gay, John. *Beggar's Opera.* Paris. 1937. illus. ltd 1500 cc, slipcase.*$65.00–$75.00*

Gay, Joseph R. *Progress and Achievements of the Colored People....* DC. 1913. 1st ed. 434 pp.. . . . . *$50.00–$60.00*

Gay, Wanda. *Growing Pains.* Coward. 1940. 1st ed. illus. author's first book, 15 pp, dj. . . . . *$200.00–$300.00*

Gay, Wanda. *Millions of Cats.* Coward. 1928. 1st ed. illus. by author, 15 pp, dj. . . .
. . . . *$200.00–$300.00*

Gee, Ernest R. *Early American Sporting Books 1734-1844.* NY. Derrydale Press.
1928. illus. 500 cc, sgn. . . . . *$85.00–$100.00*

Gee, Hugh & Sally Gee. *Belinda and the Magic Journey.* NY. Chanticleer Press.
1948. dj. . . . . *$35.00–$45.00*

Geer, John. *Beyond the Lines: or a Yankee Prisoner Loose in Dixie.* Phila. 1863. 1st
ed. illus. . . . . *$50.00–$125.00*

Geer, Walter. *Campaigns of the Civil War.* 1926. 1st ed. . . . . *$75.00–$130.00*

***General Catalogue and Price List No. 10: The Hill-Brunner Foundry Supply
Company.*** Cinc. 1916. illus. cl. . . . . *$20.00–$30.00*

Genet, Jean. *Book of the Dance.* Bos. 1920. dj. . . . . *$40.00–$55.00*

Genthe, Arnold. *Old Chinatown.* NY. 1908. 2nd ed. . . . . *$80.00–$100.00*

Genthe, Arnold. *Pictures of Old Chinatown.* NY. 1908. 1st ed. illus. scarce. . . . . . .
. . . . *$200.00–$259.00*

Georgia Scenes by a Native Georgian. NY. 1840. illus. 2nd ed. . *$100.00–$195.00*

Gerard, Max (ed.). *Dali.* NY. Abradale/Abrams. 1968. 1st ed. illus. trans by Eleanor
Morse. . . . . *$75.00–$85.00*

Gerhard, Peter. *Pirates on the West Coast of New Spain.* Glendale. Arthur H Clark.
1960. 1st ed. illus. repro maps and engrs. *$35.00–$45.00*

Gerken, Jo Elizabeth. *Wonderful Dolls of War.* NE. Doll Research Asso. (1964).
illus. sgn. . . . . *$30.00–$60.00*

Gernsbach, Hugo. *Radio for All.* 1922. 1st ed. illus. . . . . *$30.00–$40.00*

Gernsbach, Hugo. *Ralph 124C41+ A Romance Of The Year 2660.* 1925. 1st ed. . .
. . . . *$175.00–$245.00*

Gersheim, Helmut. *Origins of Photography.* NY. (1982). 1st Amer ed. illus. dj, slipcase. . . . . *$40.00–$50.00*

Gershwin, George. *George Gershwin's Song-book.* NY. New World Music. (1932).
1st trade ed. illus. cl. . . . . *$125.00–$300.00*

Gerstaecker, Frederick. *Wanderings and Fortunes of Some German Immigrants.*
NY. 1948. . . . . *$95.00–$250.00*

Gerstaecker, Frederick. *Wild Sports of the Far West.* NY. 1884. . . *$35.00–$55.00*

Gibbon, J. M. *Melody and the Lyrics from Chaucer to Cavaliers.* Lon. 1930. . . . . . .
. . . . *$25.00–$60.00*

Gibran, Kahlil. *The Prophet.* NY. Knopf. 1923. 1st ed. dj. . . . . *$40.00–$95.00*

Gibson, Charles Dana. *Gibson Book.* NY. 1907. 2 vols. . . . . . . *$125.00–$175.00*

Gibson, Charles Dana. *Pictures of People.* NY. Russell. 1901. 1st ed. illus. oblong folio. . . . . *$80.00–$105.00*

Gibson, W. B. *Book of Secrets.* 1927. 1st ed. dj. . . . . *$175.00–$200.00*

Gibson, W. H. *Our Edible Toadstools and Mushrooms.* NY. 1895. illus. . . . .
. . . . *$85.00–$125.00*

Gibson, William Hamilton. *Our Native Orchids.* NY. 1905. . . . . . *$50.00–$65.00*

Gide, Charles. *Communist and Co-Operative Colonies.* NY. Crowell. 1930. dj. . . .
. . . . *$50.00–$75.00*

Gielow, Martha S. *Mammy's Reminiscences and Other Sketches.* NY. A. S. Barnes. (1898). illus. blue green decorated cl. . . . . *$85.00–$125.00*

Gilbert, William. *On the Magnet.* NY. (1958). rprnt, illus. . . . . *$75.00–$95.00*

Giles, Herbert A. *Chinese English Dictionary.* 1912. 2nd ed. revised. . . . .
. . . . *$120.00–$160.00*

Giles, Rosean A. *Shasta County California.* CA. 1949. 1st ed. illus. map, ltd 1000 cc. . . . . *$50.00–$60.00*

Gilham, Major William. *Manual of Instruction for the Volunteers and Militia of the United States.* Phila. De Silver. 1861. . . . . *$225.00–$30.00*

Gill, Evan. *Eric Gill: A Bibliography.* Winchester/Detroit. St. Paul's Bibliographies. 1991. revised ed. illus. . . . . *$80.00–$120.00*

Gill, Sir William. *Pompeiana: The Topography, Edifices & Ornaments of Pompeii.* Lon. 1835. 2 vols. illus. . . . . *$300.00–$400.00*

Gillespie, W. Bro. Nelson. *History of Apollo Lodge No.13...Troy, N.Y.* NY. 1886. illus. plates. . . . . *$30.00–$40.00*

Gillette, Mrs. F. L. *White House Cook Book.* Chi. 1889. . . . . *$65.00–$85.00*

Gillian, Arthur J. *Menace of Chemical Warfare to Civilian Populations.* Lon. Chemical Workers Union. 1932. wrps. 20 pp, pict cvr. . . . . *$25.00–$35.00*

Gillies, Rev. John. *Memoirs of the Life and Character of the Late George Whitefield.* Bos. Samuel Armstrong. 1813. lea. . . . . *$18.00–$25.00*

Gillis, Charles J. *Another Summer.* NY. Little & Co. 1893. blue cl. *$60.00–$80.00*

Gillmore, Parker. *Prairie and Forest.* Lon. Chapman & Hall. 1874. 1st ed. illus. wood-engr. plates. . . . . *$50.00–$80.00*

Gilman, Caroline. *Recollections of a Southern Matron*. NY. Harper. 1838. 272 pp .
. . . . *$125.00–$200.00*

Gilmore, Parker. *Accessible Field Sports*. Lon. Chapman & Hall. 1869. 1st ed. illus.
. . . . *$45.00–$80.00*

Ginsberg, Allen. *Bixby Canyon, Ocean Path, Word Breeze*. Botham. 1972. 1st ed.
wrps. . . . . *$35.00–$40.00*

Ginsberg, Allen. *Fall of America*. SF. 1972. wrps. . . . . *$20.00–$45.00*

Ginsberg, Allen. *Journals Mid-fifties, 1954-1958*. NY. Harper Collins. (1995). 1st ed.
wrps. . . . . *$18.00–$45.00*

Ginsberg, Allen. *Planet News*. CA. City Lights. 1968. wrps. 1st US ed. dj. . . . .
. . . . *$25.00–$35.00*

Ginsberg, Allen. *Reality Sandwiches*. (1963). 1st ed. wrps. . . . . . . *$35.00–$45.00*

Ginsberg, Allen. *White Shroud: Poems 1980-1985*. NY. Harper. (1986). 1st ed. ltd
200 cc. sgn, dj, boxed. . . . . *$150.00–$225.00*

Ginzburg, R. *An Unhurried View of Erotica*. NY. 1958. slipcase. . . *$10.00–$25.00*

Giovanni, Nikki. *Cotton Candy on a Rainy Day*. NY. Morrow. 1978. 1st ed. sgn, dj.
. . . . *$45.00–$90.00*

Glacier National Park Montana.... 1920. illus. 32pp pict wrps, brochure. . . . .
. . . . *$75.00–$100.00*

Gladstone, J. H. *Michael Farada*. Lon. 1874. 2nd ed. repairs. . . . . *$22.00–$35.00*

Glasfurd, A. *Musings of an Old Shikari*. Lon. John Lane. (1928). illus. green cl. . . .
. . . . *$75.00–$100.00*

Glasgow, Ellen. *Descendant*. NY. Harper. 1897. 1st ed. author's first book. . . . .
. . . . *$150.00–$200.00*

Glasgow, Ellen. *Freeman and Other Poems*. NY. Doubleday, Page. 1902. 1st ed. . .
. . . . *$225.00–$245.00*

Glasgow, Ellen. *Phases of an Inferior Planet*. NY. Harper. 1898. 1st ed. cl. . . . .
. . . . *$75.00–$100.00*

Glaspell, Susan. *A Jury of Her Peers*. Lon. Benn. 1927. 1st ed. wrps. ltd 250 cc. sgn.
. . . . *$350.00–$400.00*

Glasse, Hannah. *Art of Cookery, made Plain and Easy*. Lon. Prospect. 1983. facs. . .
. . . . *$25.00–$30.00*

Glasse, Hannah. *Art of Cookery, made Plain and Easy*. Lon. Straham. 1784. calf,
fldg table. . . . . *$500.00–$600.00*

Glasser, Otto. *Dr. Wilhelm C. Roentgen.* 1934. 1st UK ed. dj...... *$45.00–$60.00*

Glazier, Capt. Willard. *Down the Great River.* Phila. 1893. ..... *$25.00–$35.00*

Glazier, Capt. Willard. *Headwaters of the Mississippi.* NY. 1893. *$35.00–$50.00*

Gleason, Prof. Oscar R. F. *Gleason's Horse Book.* Chi. Donohue. 1892. .... *$65.00–$75.00*

Glenfin (pseud). *The Fishing-rod; and How to Use It.* Lon. Bailey. 1861. cl, gilt on spine...................................... *$135.00–$150.00*

Glenister, A. G. *Birds of the Malay Peninsula.* Oxford Univ Press. 1951. illus. dj.. .... *$35.00–$55.00*

Gloucester Directory 1899-1900. MA. 1899. bds............... *$45.00–$55.00*

Goaman, Muriel. *Judy's & Andrew's Puppet Book.* Bos. Plays, Inc. (1967). 1st US ed.. *$15.00–$20.00*

Goddard, Henry Herbert. *Kallikak Family.* NY. 1916. .... *$25.00–$35.00*

Godman, John D. *American Natural History.* Phil. Stoddart & Atherton. 1831. 3 vols. .... *$140.00–$250.00*

Godwin, Gail. *Glass People.* NY. 1972. 1st ed. dj. .... *$45.00–$60.00*

Goebbels, Joseph. *Kampf um Berlin.* Munchen. 1938. illus. ..... *$24.00–$30.00*

Goff, Kenneth. *Strange Fire.* Col. 1954. 1st ed. illus. cl......... *$20.00–$30.00*

Goines, Donald. *Black Gangster.* LA. Holloway House. 1972. 1st ed. paperback original... *$15.00–$35.00*

Gold, Herbert. *Fathers.* NY. 1966. 1st ed. dj................. *$18.00–$28.00*

Gold, Herbert. *Love & Like.* NY. 1960. 1st ed. sgn, presentation copy, dj........ .... *$40.00–$65.00*

Goldberg, R. *Rube Goldberg's Guide to Europe.* NY. 1954. 1st ed. presentation copy, sgn. .... *$30.00–$45.00*

Golden, Arthur. *Memoirs of a Geisha.* NY. Knopf. 1997. 1st ed. 1st state. author's first novel. dj. .... *$50.00–$60.00*

Goldenberg, Samuel. *Lace: Its Origin and History.* NY. 1904. 1st ed. illus. presentation copy. .... *$50.00–$85.00*

Golding, William. *An Egyptian Journal.* Faber. 1985. 1st ed. dj.... *$30.00–$40.00*

Golding, William. *Lord of the Flies.* NY. Coward-McCann. 1955. 1st ed. dj...... .... *$300.00–$1,100.00*

Golding, William. *Lord of the Flies*. Lon. Faber & Faber. (1954). dj, red cl. . . . . . .
. . . . *$100.00–$150.00*

Golding, William. *Lord of the Flies*. Lon. Faber & Faber. (1954). 1st ed. 1st UK ed.
dj. . . . . *$1,500.00–$2,000.00*

Golding, William. *The Pyramid*. Lon. Faber & Faber. (1967). 1st ed. sgn, dj. . . . . .
. . . . *$240.00–$300.00*

Goldman, Emma. *My Dissillusionment in Russia*. Lon. 1925. 1st UK ed. 263 pp, red
cl, paper label, sgn. . . . . *$150.00–$250.00*

Goldman, Emma. *Place of the Individual in Society*. Chi. Free Society Forum. nd.
wrps. . . . . *$35.00–$45.00*

Goldman, Emma. *Social Significance of the Modern Drama*. Bos. 1914. . . . .
. . . . *$30.00–$67.00*

Goldman, William. *Marathon Man*. NY. Delacorte. 1974. 1st ed. dj. *$25.00–$65.00*

Goldschmidt, Lucien: naef, J. Weston. *Truthful Lens...1844-1914*. NY. Grolier
Club. 1980. 1st ed. illus. ltd 1,000cc, slipcase. . . . . *$300.00–$350.00*

Goldsmith, Alfred N. *Radio Telephony*. NY. Wireless Press. (1918). 1st ed. 247 pp,
illus. . . . . *$50.00–$75.00*

Goldsmith, Oliver. *History of the Earth and Animated Nature*. Lon. Blackie and Son.
1854. vol 11 only. . . . . *$40.00–$50.00*

Goldsmith, Oliver. *Vicar of Wakefield*. Lon. J M Dent. c1910. illus. aeg, bound by
Sangorski & Sutcliffe. . . . . *$100.00–$150.00*

Goldsmith, Oliver. *Vicar of Wakefield*. Lon. Harrap. (1929). 1st ed thus. illus by
Arthur Rackham. . . . . *$100.00–$150.00*

Goldsmith, Oliver. *Vicar of Wakefield*. McKay. 1929. illus. by Arthur Rackham, clr
plates. . . . . *$75.00–$125.00*

Goldstrom, John. *Narrative History of Aviation*. NY. 1930. 1st ed. illus. . . . .
. . . . *$65.00–$85.00*

Goldwater, Barry. *Arizona*. 1978. 1st ed. dj.. . . . . *$28.00–$35.00*

Goldwater, Barry. *Face of Arizona*. np. 1964. 1st ed. ltd 1000 cc, sgn. . . . .
. . . . *$125.00–$180.00*

Goldwater, Barry. *Journey Down The Green & Colorado Rivers*. Tempe. 1970. illus.
photos, dj. . . . . *$35.00–$45.00*

Gommez, R. *Cake Decoration: Flower and Classic Piping*. Lon. 1899. . . . .
. . . . *$65.00–$90.00*

Goode, George Brown. *Smithsonian Institution 1846-1896 A History....* DC. 1897.
.... *$50.00–$75.00*

Goodison, N. *English Barometers 1680-1860....* Lon. 1969. illus. 1st UK ed. plates.
.... *$50.00–$60.00*

Goodman, Paul. *Compulsory Mis-Education.* NY. 1964. dj. ...... *$20.00–$25.00*

Goodman, Paul. *Growing Up Absurd....* NY. Random House. 1960. 1st ed. dj cl. .
.... *$40.00–$50.00*

Goodman, Richard M. *Genetic Disorders Among The Jewish People.* Balt. Johns
Hopkins. 1979. 1st ed. dj cl. .... *$85.00–$100.00*

Goodrich, Charles A. *History of the United States of America.* Bos. American
Stationers. (1834). .... *$20.00–$30.00*

Goodrich, Samuel. *Second Book of History....* Bos. Hendee. 1836. sheep-backed
printed bds 16 maps. .... *$50.00–$75.00*

Goodrich, Samuel Griswold. *History of the Indians of North & South America.* NY.
1844. 1st ed. illus. .... *$45.00–$60.00*

Goodrich, Samuel Griswold. *Recollections of a Lifetime.* NY. 1851. 2 vols. ....
.... *$95.00–$250.00*

Goodrich, Ward L. *Modern Clock.* Chi. 1905. 1st ed. illus. ...... *$40.00–$55.00*

Goodrich-Freer, A. *Things Seen in Palestine.* NY. 1913. .... *$45.00–$65.00*

Goodspeed, Charles. *Yankee Bookseller.* Bos. Houghton Mifflin. 1937. 1st ed. ltd
310 cc sgn slipcase. .... *$125.00–$175.00*

Goodspeed, Charles. *Yankee Bookseller.* Bos. Houghton Mifflin. 1937. 1st ed. dj.
.... *$35.00–$75.00*

Goodwin, C. C. *Wedge of Gold.* Salt Lake City. 1893. 1st ed. .... *$50.00–$65.00*

Goodwin, D. *Pigeons and Doves of the World.* Cornell University. 1983. dj. .....
.... *$40.00–$55.00*

Goodwin, Grace Duffield. *Anti-Suffrage.* NY. 1913. .... *$14.00–$35.00*

Goodyear, W. A. *Coal Mines of the Western Coast of the United States.* SF. 1877. 1st
ed. 153 pp. .... *$75.00–$125.00*

Gorbachev, Mikhail. *Perestroika Is The Concern of All Soviet Peoples.* Moscow.
1989. wrps. 1st UK ed. .... *$40.00–$50.00*

Gordeon, William S. *Recollections of the old Quarter.* Lynchburg. Moose Bros.
1902. 1st ed. illus. b/w photos. .... *$75.00–$100.00*

Gordimer, Nadine. *House Gun.* Lon. Bloomsbury. (1998). 1st Brit ed. sgn, dj. . . . .
. . . . *$75.00–$85.00*

Gordimer, Nadine. *Lying Days.* NY. Simon and Schuster. 1953. 1st ed. author's first
novel, dj. . . . . *$50.00–$65.00*

Gordimer, Nadine. *Occasion for Loving.* NY. (1963). 1st Amer ed. dj. . . . .
. . : . . . . *$25.00–$35.00*

Gordimer, Nadine. *Soft Voice of the Serpent.* NY. Simon & Schuster. 1952. 1st Amer
ed. author's first book, dj. . . . . *$55.00–$100.00*

Gordimer, Nadine. *Something Out There.* NY. Viking. 1984. 1st Us ed. sgn, dj. . . .
. . . . *$50.00–$65.00*

Gordon, A. C. & Page Thomas Nelson. *Befo' De War - Echoes in Negro Dialect.*
NY. 1888. . . . . *$40.00–$50.00*

Gordon, Armistead Churchill. *Jefferson Davis.* NY. Scribner's. 1918. 1st ed. . . . .
. . . . *$40.00–$50.00*

Gordon, Elizabeth. *Bird Children.* Volland. (1912). illus. . . . . *$85.00–$95.00*

Gordon, Elizabeth. *Buddy Jim.* NY. Wise-Parslow Co. (1935). illus. pict cl cvr. . . .
. . . . *$15.00–$40.00*

Gordon, Elizabeth. *Flower Children.* Volland. (1910). illus. bds. . . *$75.00–$95.00*

Gordon, Elizabeth. *I Wonder Why?.* Chi. (1916). 1st ed. illus. in clr and b/w. . . . . .
. . . . *$15.00–$25.00*

Gordon, Elizabeth. *Loraine and the Little People of the Ocean.* Chi/NY. (1922). 1st
ed. illus. in clr and b/w. . . . . *$35.00–$40.00*

Gordon, Elizabeth. *Really-So Stories.* Joliet. (1924). 1st ed. illus. . *$40.00–$50.00*

Gordon, John B. *Reminiscences of the Civil War.* NY. 1904. illus. . *$150.00–$200.00*

Gordon, Mary. *Company of Women.* NY. 1980. 1st ed. dj, sgn. . . . . *$30.00–$40.00*

Gordon, Sarah. *Hitler, Germans, and The Jewish Question.* Princeton. Princeton
Univ Press. 1984. 1st ed. dj. . . . . *$20.00–$30.00*

Gordon, T. *Gazetteer of the State of Pennsylvania.* Phila. 1832. 1st ed. lea. . . . .
. . . . *$65.00–$85.00*

Gordon, T. F. *Gazetteer of the State of New Jersey.* Trenton. 1834. 2 vols in one. map.
. . . . *$175.00–$250.00*

Goren, Charles. *Sports Illustrated Book of Bridge.* NY. 1961. illus. dj, slipcase. . . .
. . . . *$50.00–$70.00*

Gorey, Edward. *Black Doll*. NY. Gotham Book Mart. 1973. 1st ed. black wrps. . .
. . . . *$60.00–$125.00*

Gorey, Edward. *Blue Aspic*. Meredith Press. 1968. 1st ed. dj.. . . . *$65.00–$100.00*

Gorey, Edward. *Broken Spoke*. NY. Dodd. 1976. 1st ed. dj. . . . . . . *$45.00–$65.00*

Gorey, Edward. *Dancing Cats & Neglected Murderesses*. NY. Workman Publishing. (1980). 1st trade ed. pict glossy wrps, sgn.. *$45.00–$65.00*

Gorey, Edward. *Doubtful Guest*. Lon. (1958). 1st Brit ed dj. . . . . *$75.00–$125.00*

Gorey, Edward. *Dracula. A Toy Theatre*. NY. Scribner's. 1979. folio, spiral bound.
. . . . *$150.00–$200.00*

Gorey, Edward. *Eclectic Abecedarium*. NY. Adams. (1983). 1st trade ed. glossy bds, sgn. . . . . *$100.00–$125.00*

Gorey, Edward. *Epileptic Bicycle*. NY. Dodd, Mead. (1969). 5th printing dj. . . . .
. . . . *$20.00–$30.00*

Gorey, Edward. *Fatal Lozenge*. Ivan Oblelinsky 1960. wrps. . . . . . *$40.00–$65.00*

Gorey, Edward. *Gilded Bat*. NY. Simon & Shcuster. (1966). 1st ed. dj. *$75.00–$100.00*

Gorey, Edward. *Listing Attic*. NY. Duell, Sloan & Pearce. (1954). 1st ed. dj. . . . .
. . . . *$75.00–$400.00*

Gorey, Edward. *The Dwindling Party*. NY. Random House. 1982. 1st ed. illus. by Gorey. pop-up book. . . . . *$65.00–$140.00*

Gorey, Edward. *The Glorious Nosebleed Fifth Alphabet*. NY. Dodd, Mead. 1974. 1st ed. illus. by Gorey. pict paper over bds. *$30.00–$40.00*

Gorey, Edward. *The Haunted Tea-Cosy*. Harcourt. 1997. 1st ed. illus. by Gorey. dj.
. . . . *$10.00–$40.00*

Gorey, Edward. *The Loathsome Couple*. Dodd, Mead. 1977. 1st ed. illus. by Gorey.dj. . . . . *$40.00–$75.00*

Gorey, Edward. *Unstrung Harp*. Duell, Sloan & Pearce. 1953. 1st ed. author's first book, dj. . . . . *$150.00–$300.00*

Gorey, Edward. *Utter Zoo Alphabet*. NY. Meredith Press. (1967). 1st ed. dj.. . . . .
. . . . *$40.00–$65.00*

Gorey, Edward. *Vinegar Works*. NY. 1963. 3 vols. 1st ed. . . . . . *$135.00–$250.00*

Gorey, Edward. *Water Flowers*. NY. Congdon and Weed. (1982). 1st ed. sgn, dj. . .
. . . . *$35.00–$50.00*

Gorey, Edward. *Willowdale Handcar*. NY. Dodd, Mead. (1979). 1st hardcvr ed. dj.
. . . . *$25.00–$45.00*

Gorky, Maxim. *The Judge.* McBride. 1924. 1st ed. . . . . *$30.00–$40.00*

Gosse, P. H. *Birds of Jamaica.* Lon. 1847. . . . . *$300.00–$400.00*

Gotham's Pageant of Games and Toys. NY. Gotham Pressed Steel Corp. illus. pict wrps, 36 pp.. . . . .*$75.00–$100.00*

Goudy, Frederic W. *Italian Old Style....* Phil. 1924. black bds.. . . . *$35.00–$50.00*

Goulart, Ron. *Skyrocket Steele Conquers the Universe and Other Media Tale.* Eugene, OR. (1990). 1st ed. 300 cc, sgn, dj. . . . . *$20.00–$30.00*

Gould, J. *Birds of Great Britian.* Lon. 1873. 5 vols. illus. large folio, 367 clr plates. . . . . *$50,000.00–$75,000.00*

Gould, J. *Century of Birds from the Himalaya Mountains.* Lon. 1832. 1st ed. illus. large folio, 80 hand-clr plates. . . . . *$7,800.00–$10,000.00*

Gould, J. *Handbook of the Birds of Australia.* Melbourne. Landsdowne Press. 1972. rprnt.. . . . . *$30.00–$70.00*

Gould, J. *Handbook to the Birds of Australia.* Lon. 1865. 2 vols. . . . . *$200.00–$300.00*

Gould, Jean. *Young Mariner Melville.* NY. Dodd, Mead. 1956. 1st ed. dj.. . . . . *$25.00–$35.00*

Gould, John. *Budytes Fava.* Lon. c. 1870. illus. lithographs.. . . . . . *$40.00–$55.00*

Gould, John. *Chlorostilbona Prastina (Braziliam Emerald).* Lon. c. 1850-60. illus. lithographs. . . . . *$200.00–$300.00*

Gould, John. *Toucans.* Lon. 1852-54. folio, 51 hand-clr plates. . . . . *$25,000.00–$30,000.00*

Gould, L. McKinley. *Cold. The record of an Antarctic sledge journey.* NY. Brewer, Warren & Putnam. 1931. 1st ed. illus. clr frontis, plates, fldg map, inscr. . . . . *$75.00–$85.00*

Gould, Marcus. *Report of the Trial of Friends.* Phila. 1829. 1/4 mor.. . . . . *$95.00–$150.00*

Gould, R. T. *Case For the Sea Serpent.* Lon. 1930. illus. . . . . *$55.00–$95.00*

Grady, James. *Six Days of the Condor.* NY. Norton. 1974. 1st ed. dj. . . . . *$75.00–$250.00*

Graebner, Theodore. *Church Bells in the Forest, A Story of Lutheran Pioneer Work on the Michigan Frontier, 1840-1850.* St Louis. Concordia. 1944. wrps. illus. 98 pp. . . . . *$28.00–$40.00*

Graffagnino, J. K. *Shaping of Vermont.* Rutland. 1983. illus. 147 pp, dj.. . . . . *$40.00–$50.00*

Grafton, C C The Right Rev. *Lineage from Apostolic Times of the American Catholic Church....* Milwaukee. The Young Churchman Co. (1911). 1st ed. illus. pict cvr. . . . . *$25.00–$35.00*

Grafton, Sue. *"A" Is For Alibi.* NY. Bantam. 1987. illus. wrps. 1st paperback ed. . . . . *$3.00–$7.00*

Grafton, Sue. *"A" Is For Alibi.* Lon. Macmillan. 1982. 1st UK ed. dj.. . . . . *$300.00–$400.00*

Grafton, Sue. *"A" Is For Alibi.* NY. Holt, Rinehart &Winston. 1982. 1st ed. sgn, dj. . . . . *$1,000.00–$3,000.00*

Grafton, Sue. *"B" is for Burglar.* Lon. Macmillan. 1986. 1st ed. iscr, dj. . . . . *$200.00–$250.00*

Grafton, Sue. *"C" is for Corpse.* NY. 1986. 1st ed. dj. . . . . *$625.00–$700.00*

Grafton, Sue. *"E" is for Evidence.* NY. Holt. 1988. 1st ed. dj. . . . *$75.00–$150.00*

Grafton, Sue. *"E" is for Evidence.* NY. Holt. 1988. 1st ed. sgn, dj. . . . . *$175.00–$250.00*

Grafton, Sue. *"F" is for Fugitive.* NY. Holt. 1989. 1st ed. dj.. . . . . *$45.00–$60.00*

Grafton, Sue. *"F" is for Fugitive.* NY. Holt. 1989. 1st ed. sgn, dj. *$75.00–$125.00*

Grafton, Sue. *"G" Is For Gumshoe.* NY. Holt. 1990. 1st ed. dj. . . . *$15.00–$45.00*

Grafton, Sue. *"H" is for Homicide.* NY. Holt. 1991. 1st ed. dj. . . . *$15.00–$50.00*

Grafton, Sue. *"H" is for Homicide.* NY. Holt. 1991. 1st ed. inscr, dj. . . . . *$35.00–$70.00*

Grafton, Sue. *"I" is for Innocent.* NY. Holt. 1993. 1st ed. sgn, dj.. . . . . *$35.00–$75.00*

Grafton, Sue. *"J" is for Judgment.* NY. Holt. [1993]. 1st ed. dj.. . . . *$15.00–$25.00*

Grafton, Sue. *"J" is for Judgment.* NY. Holt. 1993. 1st ed. inscr, dj. . *$40.00–$50.00*

Grafton, Sue. *"K" is for Killer.* NY. Holt. [1994]. 1st ed. dj. . . . . . *$14.00–$28.00*

Grafton, Sue. *"L" Is For Lawless.* NY. 1995. 1st ed. dj.. . . . . *$5.00–$20.00*

Grafton, Sue. *Keziah Dane.* NY. Macmillan. 1967. 1st ed. author's 1st non-mystery, dj.. . . . . *$300.00–$1,000.00*

Graham, Col. W. A. *Custer Myth.* Harrisburg. (1953). 1st ed. illus. dj. . . . . *$50.00–$65.00*

Graham, Frank. *Brooklyn Dodgers.* NY. Putnam' s Series. 1947. illus. dj. . . . . *$32.00–$40.00*

Graham, Kenneth. *Dream Days.* Lon. nd. 1st ed. . . . . *$35.00–$50.00*

Graham, Stephen. *Through Russian Central Asia.* Lon. 1916. illus. fldg map, photos. . . . . *$30.00–$40.00*

Grahame, Kenneth. *Dream Days.* Lon. 1902. illus. by Maxfield Parrish, 2228 pp. . . . . *$95.00–$130.00*

Grahame, Kenneth. *Golden Age.* Lon/NY. 1900. illus. by Maxfield Parrish. . . . . *$85.00–$100.00*

Grahame, Kenneth. *Wind in the Willows.* Lon. Methuen. (1908). 1st ed. 1/4 mor, slipcase. . . . . *$3,000.00–$10,000.00*

Grahame, Kenneth. *Wind in the Willows.* Scribner's. 1908. 1st Amer ed. . . . . *$150.00–$250.00*

Grainge, William. *Daemonologia. Discourse on Witchcraft.* Harrogate. 1882. . . . . *$30.00–$40.00*

Grand Union Grille Works. Chi. 1911. wrps. architectural cat. . . . . *$38.00–$45.00*

Grand, Gordon. *Old Man and Other Colonel Weatherford Stories.* Derrydale. 1934. 1st Amer ed. . . . . *$45.00–$60.00*

Grand, Gordon. *Silver Horn.* NY. 1932. illus. 1/950cc. . . . . *$75.00–$130.00*

Grant, B. C. *Taos Today.* Taos. 1925. photos. . . . . *$75.00–$150.00*

Grant, Blanche C. (ed.). *Kit Carson's Own Story of His Life.* Taos. 1926. softbound. . . . . *$75.00–$125.00*

Grant, Douglas. *Fortunate Slave, An Illustration of African Slavery....* Lon. 1968. 1st ed. dj. . . . . *$33.00–$45.00*

Grant, George Monro (ed). *Picturesque Canada: The Country As It Was and Is.* Tor. 1882. 1st ed. mor, engr. . . . . *$125.00–$200.00*

Grant, James J. *Single Shot Rifles.* NY. 1947. illus. photos, plates. *$30.00–$40.00*

Grant, Madison. *Passing of the Great Race or Racial Basis of European History.* Scribner's. 1923. 4th rev ed. 476 pp. . . . . *$35.00–$50.00*

Grant, T. M. *Mt. Cook. Its Glaciers and Lakes.* Wellington. 1888. fldg map. . . . . *$150.00–$200.00*

Grant, Ulysses S. *Personal Memoirs of U.S. Grant.* NY. 1885. 2 vols. 1st ed. . . . . *$50.00–$85.00*

Grant, Ulysses S. *Report of Lt-General U.S. Grant...1864–65.* NY. 1865. wrps. . . . . *$100.00–$150.00*

Gras, Gunter. *Dog Years.* NY. 1965. 1st ed. dj. . . . . *$25.00–$35.00*

Grau, Shirley Ann. *Black Prince*. NY. Knopf. 1955. 1st ed. author's first book, sgn, dj. . . . . *$75.00–$100.00*

Graumont, Raoul and John Hensel. *Encyclopedia of Knots and Fancy Rope Work*. Cambridge. Cornell Maritime Press. 1972. 4th ed. illus. dj. . . . . *$35.00–$40.00*

Graves, Jackson A. *My Seventy Years in California 1857-1927*. LA. Times-Mirror. 1927. . . . . *$60.00–$85.00*

Graves, John. *Frontier Guns*. Fort Worth. 1964. illus. photos, wrps. *$15.00–$25.00*

Graves, Robert. *Islands of Unwisdom*. Garden City. Doubleday. 1949. 1st ed. dj. . . . . *$50.00–$75.00*

Graves, Robert. *Lawrence and the Arabian Adventure*. Garden City. Doubleday, Doran. 1928. 1st Amer ed. illus.. . . . . *$40.00–$65.00*

Graves, Robert. *On English Poetry*. Lon. Heinemann. 1922. 1st ed. . . . . *$150.00–$175.00*

Graves, Robert. *Sergeant Lamb's America*. NY. Random House. (1940). 1st ed. dj red cl. . . . . *$90.00–$125.00*

Graves, Robert. *The Shout*. Lon. Elkin Matthews & Marrot. 1929. 1st ed. ltd 530 cc, dj. . . . . *$225.00–$250.00*

Graves, Robert J. *Clinical Lectures on the Practice of Medicine*. Lon. 1884. 2 vols. . . . . *$20.00–$35.00*

Gray, Asa. *First Lessons in Botany & Vegetable Physiology*. Ivison & Phinney. 1857. 236 pp. . . . . *$100.00–$135.00*

Gray, Asa. *Gray's Botanical Text-Book (6th Ed)*. American Book Co. 1879. 2 vols. . . . . *$60.00–$85.00*

Gray, Asa. *Introduction to Structural and Systematic Botany and Vegetable Physiology*. NY. Ivison & Phinney. 1862. 5th rev ed.. . . . . *$30.00–$60.00*

Gray, Harold. *Little Orphan Annie and Jumbo the Circus Elephant*. Chi. Pleasure Books. (1935). 1st ed. 3 pop-ups.. . . . . *$150.00–$500.00*

Gray, Harold. *Little Orphan Annie and Sandy*. Racine. Whitman. 1933. 1st ed. pict bds.. . . . . *$35.00–$45.00*

Gray, W. H. *History of Oregon, 1792-1849*. Portland. 1870. 1st ed. . . . . *$175.00–$225.00*

Gray, William C. *Camp-Fire Musings*. NY. Randolph. 1894. 1st ed. illus. . . . . *$40.00–$60.00*

Great Northwest: A Guide Book And Itinerary. St Paul. 1889. illus. fldg map, engr. . . . . *$37.00–$45.00*

Greco, James. *Story of Englewood Cliffs*. NJ. (1964). tan and brown cvr pict dj. . . .
. . . . *$20.00–$25.00*

Greeley, Horace. *History of the Struggles for Slavery*. NY. 1856. 1st ed. wrps. . . . .
. . . . *$75.00–$100.00*

Greely, Adolphus W. *Three Years of Arctic Service*. NY. Scribner's. 1886. 2 vols. 1st
ed. illus. 428 pp, illus, pocket maps, frontis, full lea. . . . . *$175.00–$250.00*

Green, Anna Katharine. *Leavenworth Case*. NY. Putnam. 1878. 1st ed. cl. . . . . . .
. . . . *$450.00–$500.00*

Green, Anna Katherine. *A Difficult Problem*. NY. Lupton. 1900. 1st ed. green clo. .
. . . . *$100.00–$150.00*

Green, Arthur R. *Sundials, Incised Dials, Or Mass Clocks*. NY/Tor. 1926. 1st ed.
illus. . . . . *$35.00–$45.00*

Green, Ben K. *Thousand Miles of Mustangin'*. Flagstaff. Northland Press. 1972. 1st
ed. brown cl dj sgn. . . . . *$100.00–$150.00*

Green, Calvin and Seth Y. Wells. *Brief Exposition of...the Shakers*. NY. 1851. . . .
. . . . *$115.00–$150.00*

Green, Edwin L. *Indians of South Carolina*. Columbia, SC. (1904). 1st ed. . . . . . .
. . . . *$55.00–$75.00*

Green, Gil. *Portugal's Revolution*. NY. International. 1976. wrps. sgn. . . . .
. . . . *$45.00–$55.00*

Green, Gil. *Young Communists and Unity of the Youth*. NY. Youth Publishers. 1935.
wrps. sgn. . . . . *$50.00–$65.00*

Green, Nelson Winch. *Fifteen Years Among the Mormons: Being the Narrative of
Mrs. Mary Ettie V. Smith, late of Great Salt Lake City*. NY. 1858. . *$60.00–$145.00*

Green, Richard Lancelyn. *Bibliography of A Conan Doyle*. Oxford. Clarendon
Press. 1983. illus. dj. . . . . *$70.00–$80.00*

Greenaway, Kate. *A Apple Pie*. Lon. Routledge. 1886. . . . . *$95.00–$300.00*

Greenaway, Kate. *Greenaway's Babies*. Akron, Ohio. Saalfield. 1907. illus. full clr.
limp cl. . . . . *$100.00–$250.00*

Greenaway, Kate. *Kate Greenaway's Painting Book*. Lon/NY. Frederick Warne. nd.
1st ed. full clr pict wrps. . . . . *$200.00–$300.00*

Greenaway, Kate. *Mother Goose*. Lon. Frederick Warne. (1881). *$100.00–$200.00*

Greene, Graham. *Human Factor*. Lon. 1978. 1st UK ed. . . . . *$35.00–$65.00*

Greene, Graham. *Our Man in Havana*. Lon. 1958. dj. . . . . *$85.00–$100.00*

Greene, Graham. *Our Man in Havana.* NY. 1958. 1st US ed. dj. . . *$45.00–$75.00*

Greene, Graham. *Potting Shed.* Lon. 1958. dj. . . . . *$27.00–$100.00*

Greene, Graham. *Third Man and The Fallen Idol.* Lon. Heinemann. 1950. dj. . . . . *$50.00–$60.00*

Greene, Graham. *This Gun is for Hire.* NY. Doubleday Doran. 1936. 1st Amer ed. no dj. . . . . *$100.00–$125.00*

Greene, Graham. *Travels With My Aunt.* NY. 1970. 1st ed. 1st Amer ed dj. . . . . *$25.00–$35.00*

Greene, Graham. *Travels With My Aunt.* 1969. 1st UK ed. dj. . . . . *$20.00–$30.00*

Greene, Vivien. *English Dolls' Houses of the Eighteenth and Nineteenth Centuries.* Lon. B T Batsford Ltd. (1955). 1st ed. illus. . . . . *$80.00–$100.00*

Greenhowe, Jean. *Making a Victorian Dolls' House.* NY. Taplinger Pub. (1979). 1st ed. dj. . . . . *$15.00–$20.00*

Greenough, Ruth Hornblower. *Bible for My Grandchildren.* Bos. private prtg. 1950. 2 vols. illus. ltd 1,000 sets. . . . . *$85.00–$175.00*

Greenwood, Grace. *New Life in New Lands: Notes of Travel.* NY. J B Ford & Co. 1873. . . . . *$75.00–$140.00*

Greer, James K. *Texas Ranger and frontiersman....* Dallas. 1932. sgn by author. . . . . *$100.00–$300.00*

Gregory, Dick. *Shadow That Scares Me.* Garden City. Doubleday. 1968. 1st ed. sgn, dj. . . . . *$45.00–$60.00*

Gregory, Samuel. *Gregory's History of Mexico.* Bos. 1847. illus. rbnd, 100 pp. . . . . *$275.00–$300.00*

Gregory, W. K. and H. C. Raven. *In Quest of Gorillas.* New Bedford. 1937. illus. with b/w photos, map. . . . . *$35.00–$60.00*

Gregson, J. M. *Murder at the Nineteenth.* Lon. Collins Crime Club. 1989. 1st ed. dj. . . . . *$50.00–$65.00*

Gremillion, Nelson. *Company G, 1st Regiment, Louisiana Cavalry, CSA.* np. private printing. 1986. 1st ed. . . . . *$35.00–$65.00*

Grenfell, Wilfred. *40 Years For Labrador.* NY. 1932. presentation copy, sgn, dj. . . . . *$45.00–$60.00*

Grenfell, Wilfred. *Adrift on an Ice-Pan.* Bos. [1909]. 1st ed. . . . . . *$20.00–$40.00*

Grenfell, Wilfred. *Down North on Labrador.* Chi. 1911. 1st ed. illus. . . . . *$20.00–$30.00*

Grenfell, Wilfred. *Labrador*. NY. 1922. . . . . *$35.00–$45.00*

Grenfell, Wilfred. *Labrador Doctor*. NY. 1919. illus. original sketch on flyleaf by author. . . . . *$65.00–$95.00*

Grenfell, Wilfred. *Labrador Doctor The Autobiography*. Bos/NY. Houghton Mifflin. (1910). 1st ed. illus. green cl, photos, an original drawing and signature by Grenfell on front endpaper. . . . . *$75.00–$125.00*

Grew, Joseph. *Report From Tokyo*. NY. Simon & Schuster. 1942. dj.*$15.00–$30.00*

Grey, Edward. *Fly Fishing*. Lon. J. M. Dent. 1899. illus. 1st trade issue. green mor, raised bands, teg. . . . . *$125.00–$250.00*

Grey, Zane. *Arizona Ames*. NY. Grosset & Dunlap. 1932. rprnt, dj. *$12.00–$15.00*

Grey, Zane. *Black Mesa*. NY. Harper & Bros. 1955. 1st ed. dj. . . . *$65.00–$175.00*

Grey, Zane. *Border Legion*. NY. Harper & Bros. 1916. illus. dark green cl. . . . .
. . . . *$40.00–$50.00*

Grey, Zane. *Desert of Wheat*. NY. Grosset & Dunlap. 1919. rprnt, dj. . . . .
. . . . *$10.00–$15.00*

Grey, Zane. *Don: the Story of a Lion Dog*. NY/Lon. Harper & Bros. 1928. 1st ed. illus. by Kurt Wiese in b/w. clr frontis. pict green cl. . . . . *$500.00–$650.00*

Grey, Zane. *Forlorn River*. NY. Grosset & Dunlap. 1927. rprnt, dj.. *$20.00–$35.00*

Grey, Zane. *Horse Heaven Hill*. NY. Harper & Bros. 1959. 1st ed. dj. . . . .
. . . . *$30.00–$75.00*

Grey, Zane. *Knights of the Range*. NY/Lon. Harper. 1939. 1st ed. dj. . . . .
. . . . *$175.00–$250.00*

Grey, Zane. *Knights of the Range*. NY. Grosset & Dunlap. 1936. dj. *$15.00–$40.00*

Grey, Zane. *Lost Wagon Train*. NY. Harper & Bros. 1936. 1st ed. dj. . . . .
. . . . *$250.00–$400.00*

Grey, Zane. *Rainbow Trail*. NY. Harper. 1915. green cl. . . . . *$20.00–$35.00*

Grey, Zane. *Red Headed Outfield*. NY. 1915. dj. . . . . *$14.00–$18.00*

Grey, Zane. *Riders of the Purple Sage*. NY. Grosset & Dunlap. 1940. rprnt, dj. . . . . .
. . . . *$10.00–$14.00*

Grey, Zane. *Roping Lions in the Grand Canyon*. NY. G & D. 1924. illus. rprnt, pict dj. . . . . *$20.00–$45.00*

Grey, Zane. *Roping Lions in the Grand Canyon*. NY. Harper & Bros. 1924. 1st ed. .
. . . . *$250.00–$300.00*

Grey, Zane. *Shepherd of Guadaloupe.* NY. Harper. 1930. 1st ed. dj. . . . .
. . . . *$100.00–$200.00*

Grey, Zane. *Spirit of the Border.* NY. A. L. Burt. 1906. 1st ed. dj. *$75.00–$100.00*

Grey, Zane. *Sunset Pass.* NY/Lon. Harper & Bros. 1931. 1st ed. rust cvr with blue lettering, dec endpapers. . . . . *$35.00–$60.00*

Grey, Zane. *Tales of Fishing Virgin Seas.* Harper. (1925). 1st ed. illus. . . . .
. . . . *$175.00–$250.00*

Grey, Zane. *Tales of Fresh-Water Fishing.* NY. 1928. 1st ed. . . . *$125.00–$200.00*

Grey, Zane. *Tales of Southern Rivers.* NY. Harper. 1924. 1st ed. green cl, 249 pp.. . . . . *$125.00–$200.00*

Grey, Zane. *Tales of Swordfish and Tuna.* NY. Harper. 1927. 1st ed. dj. . . . .
. . . . *$300.00–$400.00*

Grey, Zane. *Tales of the Angler's Eldorado.* NY. Grosset & Dunlap. 1926. illus. photos, dj. . . . . *$45.00–$75.00*

Grey, Zane. *The Call of the Canyon.* NY. Grosset & Dunlap. 1924. rprnt, dj. . . . .
. . . . *$8.00–$35.00*

Grey, Zane. *The Drift Fence.* NY. Grosset & Dunlap. 1933. rprnt. . . . *$4.00–$8.00*

Grey, Zane. *Thundering Herd.* NY. 1925. 1st ed. dj. . . . . *$35.00–$100.00*

Grey, Zane. *Vanishing American.* NY/Lon. Harper. 1925. 1st ed. dj. . . . .
. . . . *$150.00–$200.00*

Grey, Zane. *West of the Pecos.* NY. Harper. 1937. 1st ed. dj. . . . . . . *$75.00–$85.00*

Grey, Zane. *Wild Horse Mesa.* NY/Lon. Harper. 1928. 1st ed. blue cl dj. . . . .
. . . . *$50.00–$75.00*

Grey, Zane. *Wildfire.* NY. Grosset & Dunlap. 1945. dj. . . . . *$10.00–$20.00*

Gridley, A. D. *History of the Town of Kirkland.* NY. 1874. sgn. . . . *$45.00–$55.00*

Griffin, J. H. *Church and the Black Man.* 1969. wrps. illus. . . . . . . *$20.00–$25.00*

Griffin, S. G. *History of the Town of Keene from 1732 to 1874.* Keene. 1904. half lea, 3 fldg maps, plates. . . . . *$50.00–$70.00*

Griffis, William Elliot. *Corea the Hermit Nation.* NY. 1882. illus. map. . . . .
. . . . *$75.00–$150.00*

Grimble, Augustus. *Salmon Rivers of England and Wales.* Lon. Kegan Paul. 1913. 2nd ed. illus.. . . . . *$100.00–$115.00*

Grimble, Augustus. *The Salmon and Sea Trout Rivers of England and Wales.* Lon. Kegan Paul. 1904. 2 vols. 1st ed. illus. ltd 350 cc. fldg frontis, map, mor & cl, raised bands. . . . . *$500.00–$800.00*

Grimes, Martha. *Help the Poor Struggler.* Bos. (1985). 1st ed. dj. . *$30.00–$40.00*

Grimes, Martha. *Man with a Load of Mischief.* Bos. Little, Brown. (1981). 1st ed. map frontis, scarce, dj. . . . . *$150.00–$250.00*

Grimm Brothers. *Little Brother & Little Sister.* Lon. (1917). 1st ed. illus. by Arthur Rackham. scarce dj. . . . . *$500.00–$900.00*

Grimm, Herbert L. & Paul L. Roy. *Human Interest Stories of... At Gettysburg.* Times & News Pub. 1927. illus. b/w photos wrps. . . . . *$45.00–$65.00*

Grimm, Wilhelm. *Dear Mili.* NY. Farrar, Straus and Giroux. (1988). 1st ed. illus. green cl pict dj. . . . . *$20.00–$35.00*

Grimwood, V. R. *American Ship Models....* NY. W. W. Norton. (1942). illus. pull-out plans. . . . . *$35.00–$40.00*

Grinnel, J. , H. C. Bryant and T. I. Storer. *Game Birds of California.* Berkeley. 1918. illus. dj. . . . . *$175.00–$350.00*

Grinnell, G. *American Duck Shooting.* NY. 1901. . . . . *$45.00–$65.00*

Grinnell, George Bird. *Blackfoot Lodge Tales.* NY. 1892. 1st ed. . . *$50.00–$85.00*

Grinnell, George Bird. *Blackfoot Lodge Tales.* NY. 1913. . . . . *$30.00–$45.00*

Grinnell, George Bird. *Indians of Today.* NY. 1915. 3rd prtg, plates. . . . . *$45.00–$75.00*

Griscom, John H. *Use of Tobacco and the Evils, Physical, Mental, Moral and Social Resulting Therefrom.* NY. Putnam. 1868. 1st ed. wrps. 37 pp, scarce. . . . . *$80.00–$100.00*

Grisham, John. *Chamber.* NY. Doubleday. 1994. 1st ed. dj. . . . . . . *$20.00–$25.00*

Grisham, John. *Chamber.* NY. Doubleday. (1994). ltd 350 cc, sgn, nbr, slipcase. . . . . *$100.00–$150.00*

Grisham, John. *Pelican Brief.* NY. Doubleday. (1992). 1st ed. dj. . . *$15.00–$50.00*

Grisham, John. *Rainmaker.* NY. Doubleday. 1995. 1st ed. dj. . . . . *$15.00–$30.00*

Grisham, John. *The Client.* NY. Doubleday. (1993). 1st ed. dj. . . . . *$25.00–$35.00*

Grisham, John. *The Firm.* NY. Doubleday. 1991. 1st ed. sgn, dj. *$175.00–$250.00*

Grisham, John. *The Firm.* NY. Doubleday. 1991. 1st ed. dj. . . . . . . *$75.00–$100.00*

Grisham, John. *Time to Kill.* Tarrytown. Wynwood Press. 1989. 1st ed. author's first book, dj.. . . . . *$1,200.00–$1,500.00*

Grocer's Companion. Bos. New England Grocer Office. (1883). brown cl. . . . . *$20.00–$50.00*

Gromme, O. J. *Birds of Wisconsin.* University of Wisconsin. 1963. d j. . . . . *$45.00–$60.00*

Gross, H. I. *Antique & Classic Cameras.* NY. 1965. 1st ed. illus. dj . *$35.00–$50.00*

Grover, Eulalie Osgood. *Overall Boys.* Chi. Rand McNally. (1905). 1st ed. illus. . .. . *$60.00–$80.00*

Grover, Eulalie Osgood. *Sunbonnet Babies Book.* NY. 1902. . . . . . *$50.00–$70.00*

Grover, Eulalie Osgood. *Sunbonnet Babies Book.* Rand McNally. 1928. illus. . . . . *$25.00–$35.00*

Gruelle, Johnny. *Friendly Fairies.* NY. Johnny Gruelle Co. 1949. dj. *$25.00–$30.00*

Gruelle, Johnny. *Friendly Fairies.* Volland. (1919). illus. by author. *$50.00–$75.00*

Gruelle, Johnny. *Little Sunny Stories.* Chi. Volland. 1919. illus. in clr by Gruelle. dj. . . . . *$100.00–$200.00*

Gruelle, Johnny. *Marcella Stories.* NY. Volland. (1929). 1st ed. illus. by Gruelle. black pict bds. . . . . *$45.00–$90.00*

Gruelle, Johnny. *Raggedy Ann and Andy and the Camel with the Wrinkled Knees.* Chi. Donohue. 1924. pict endpapers, unpaginated. . . . . *$50.00–$125.00*

Gruelle, Johnny. *Raggedy Ann and Andy and the Nice Fat Policeman.* NY. Johnny Gruelle Co. 1942. illus. clr and b/w. . . . . *$85.00–$150.00*

Gruelle, Johnny. *Raggedy Ann and the Golden Butterfly.* NY. Johnny Gruelle Co. (1940). illus. by Justin Gruelle. dj. . . . . *$75.00–$85.00*

Gruelle, Johnny. *Raggedy Ann In Cookie Land.* Donohue. 1931. 1st ed. dj. . . . . *$65.00–$130.00*

Gruelle, Johnny. *Raggedy Ann in the Magic Book.* NY. Johnny Gruelle Co. 1939. dj. . . . . *$25.00–$90.00*

Gruelle, Johnny. *Raggedy Ann Stories.* Volland. (1918). 1st ed. illus. . . . . *$50.00–$70.00*

Gruelle, Johnny. *Raggedy Ann's Alphabet Book.* NY. Volland. 1925. illus. by Gruelle. . . . . *$45.00–$50.00*

Gruelle, Johnny. *Raggedy Ann's Magical Wishes.* Chi. Donohue. 1928. illus. 1st thus. full clr. . . . . *$35.00–$45.00*

Guide to the Birds of South America. Wynnewood. 1970. dj. . . . .
. . . . *$75.00–$100.00*

Guide To The City of Moscow.... Moscow. Cooperative Pub Society of Foreign
Workers. 1937. 1st ed. cl. . . . . *$35.00–$45.00*

Guillaume, Paul & Thomas Munro. *Primitive Negro Sculpture.* NY. Harcourt
Brace. (1926). 1st ed. illus. cl-backed batik bds, dj. . . . . *$50.00–$85.00*

Guillemin, Amedee. *Heavens: An Illustrated Handbook of Popular Astronomy.* Lon.
Bently. 1868. 3rd ed. 503 pp, clr litho. . . . . *$60.00–$85.00*

Guillet, Edwin. *Early Life in Upper Canada.* Tor. 1933. illus. b/w and clr. . . . .
. . . . *$65.00–$75.00*

Guinn, J. M. *History of the State of California...Record of San Joaquin
Valley...Biographies of Well-Known Citiizens....* Chi. Chapman. 1905. 1st ed. illus.
gilt-lettered mor. . . . . *$100.00–$150.00*

Gulley, F. A. *Cattle and Stock Feeding.* Tucson. 1893. illus. . . . . *$250.00–$400.00*

Gumsey, Charles A. *Wyoming Cowboy Days.* NY. 1936. . . . . . . *$145.00–$160.00*

Gun Cotton and its Uses. Lon. illus. . . . . *$25.00–$45.00*

Gun, Rod, and Saddle: Personal Experiences. NY. 1869. 1st Amer ed. 275 pp. pict
cl. . . . . *$50.00–$75.00*

Gunnison, J. W. *The Mormons.* Phila. 1852. 1st ed. . . . . *$150.00–$200.00*

Gunther, R. T. *Historic Instruments for the Advancement of Science.* Humphrey
Milford. 1925. glassine wrapper. . . . . *$25.00–$45.00*

Gurganus, Allan. *Oldest Living Confederate Widow Tells All.* NY. Knopf. [1989]. 1st
ed. dj. . . . . *$65.00–$75.00*

Gussow, H. T. & W. S. Odell. *Mushrooms and Toadstools.* Ottawa. 1927. 1st ed.
illus. . . . . *$27.00–$38.00*

Guthrie, A. B. *Blue Hen's Chick.* (1965). 1st ed. dj. . . . . *$25.00–$35.00*

Guthrie, A. B., Jr. *These Thousand Hills.* Bos. Houghton Mifflin. (1956). 1st ed. dj,
red orange cl. . . . . *$35.00–$75.00*

Gutman, Israel. *Encyclopedia of The Holocaust.* NY. Yad Vashem/Macmillan. 1990.
4 vols. 1st ed. djs photos. . . . . *$150.00–$250.00*

Gutstein, Morris. *Story of the Jews of Newport.* NY. Block Pub Co. 1936. 1st ed.
illus. blue cl. . . . . *$50.00–$65.00*

H.L.R. and M.L.R. *Talks on Graphology.* Bos. Lee and Shepard Pub. 1900. gray
oblong bds. . . . . *$20.00–$40.00*

Hadassah, The Jewish Orphan. Phil. American Sunday School Union. (1834). marbled bds, lea-backed. . . . . *$50.00–$75.00*

Haddock, J. *Souvenir of the Thousand Islands on the St. Lawrence River.* NY. 1896. illus. . . . . *$30.00–$50.00*

Hafen, LeRoy and Ann W. *Handcarts to Zion.* Glendale. 1960. "Pioneers" ed. illus. maps, photos, dj. . . . . *$50.00–$85.00*

Hafen, Leroy R. (ed.). *Mountain Men....* Glendale. Arthur H Clark. 1965–1972. 10 vols. 1st ed. illus. photos, paintings, brown cl. . . . . *$1,000.00–$1,600.00*

Haggard, H. Rider. *Ayesha.* NY. 1905. 1st Amer ed. . . . . *$35.00–$125.00*

Haggard, H. Rider. *Lysbeth: A Tale of the Dutch.* NY/Lon/Bombay. 1901. illus. . . . . *$65.00–$125.00*

Haggard, H. Rider. *Regeneration.* Lon. Longmans, Green & Co. 1910. 1st ed. scarce. . . . . *$100.00–$150.00*

Haggard, H. Rider. *Stella Fregulius, a Tale of Three Destinies.* Longmans, Green. 1904. blue cl. . . . . *$65.00–$150.00*

Haggard, H. Rider. *Virgin of the Sun.* NY. Doubleday. 1922. 1st ed. *$40.00–$50.00*

Haggard, H. Rider. *When the World Shook.* Longmans, Green. 1919. 1st ed. 1st Amer ed.. . . . . *$40.00–$65.00*

Haig-Brown, Roderick. *Western Angler.* William Morrow. 1947. . *$25.00–$35.00*

Haight, Austin D. *Biography of a Sportsman.* NY. Crowell. 1939. 1st ed. illus. slipcase. . . . . *$30.00–$50.00*

Haines, Elijah M. *American Indian (Uh-Nish-In-Na-Ba).* Chi. The Ma-sin-na'-gan Company. 1888. 1st ed. illus. . . . . *$100.00–$150.00*

Haines, Francis. *Nez Perces.* Univ of Ok Press. (1955). 1st ed. dj. . *$40.00–$75.00*

Hakluyt, Richard. *Principal Navigations, Voyages, Traffiques and Discoveries of the English Nation.* Lon. Dutton. 1927. 8 vols. cl. . . . . *$300.00–$750.00*

Hale, Edward Everett. *Man Without a Country.* Bos. Roberts Bros. 1889. illus. by F. T. Merrill. . . . . *$35.00–$50.00*

Hale, Edward Everett. *Memoirs of a Hundred Years.* NY. Macmillan. 1902. 2 vols. 1st ed. decorative cl. . . . . *$40.00–$60.00*

Hale, Edwin M. *Systematic Treatise on Abortion.* Chi. 1866. illus. clr plates. . . . . *$65.00–$95.00*

Haley, Alex. *Roots.* Doubleday. 1976. 1st ed. dj. . . . . *$40.00–$100.00*

Halford, Frederic M. *Dry-Fly Entomology: Leading Types of Natural Insects Serving as Food for Trout and Grayling.* Lon. Vinton. 1902. 2nd ed. illus. plates, fldg tables, blue cl. . . . . *$125.00–$250.00*

Hall, Albert Neely. *Wonderful Hill.* Chi. Rand McNally. (1914). 1st ed. illus. by Norman Hall. . . . . *$100.00–$135.00*

Hall, Capt. Charles Francis. *Narrative of the North Polar Expedition.* DC. GPO. 1876. 1st ed. illus. maps. . . . . *$150.00–$400.00*

Hall, Charles F. and J. E. Nourse. *Narrative of the Second Arctic Expedition Made by Chas F. Hall.* DC. GPO. 1879. illus. maps. . . . . *$85.00–$225.00*

Hall, Donald. *Life Work.* Bos. Beacon Press. (1993). 1st ed. dj. . . . *$24.00–$30.00*

Hall, Donald. *Yellow Room.* NY. Harper & Row. (1971). 1st ed. sgn, dj. . . . . *$40.00–$50.00*

Hall, Fred S. *Sympathetic Strikes and Sympathetic Lockouts.* NY. 1898. softbound. . . . . *$40.00–$60.00*

Hall, Henry. *Ethan Allen: The Robin Hood of Vermont.* NY. Appleton. 1897. . . . . *$20.00–$35.00*

Hall, Henry Marion. *Woodcock Ways.* NY. Oxford Univ Press. 1946. 1st ed. illus. . . . . *$30.00–$45.00*

Hall, Hiland. *History of Vermont.* Albany. 1868. 1st ed. inscr. . . . *$100.00–$125.00*

Hall, Radclyffe. *Well of Lonliness.* Lon. 1928. 1st ed. dj. . . . . . . *$125.00–$350.00*

Hall, Sharlot M. *Cactus and Pine.* privately printed. 1924. 2nd ed. rev, enlarged, sgn. . . . . *$30.00–$65.00*

Hall, Thomas F. *Has the North Pole Been Discovered?.* Bos. Richard G. Badger. 1st ed. photos, charts, maps, dj. . . . . *$70.00–$125.00*

Halliday, Brett. *Michael Shayne Takes Over.* NY. Henry Holt. 1941. 1st ed. inscr, dj. . . . . *$30.00–$45.00*

Halliday, Brett. *Murder is My Business.* NY. Dodd, Mead. 1945. 1st ed. dj. . . . . *$65.00–$80.00*

Halliday, Brett. *She Woke to Darkness.* NY. Torquil. 1954. 1st ed. dj. . . . . *$45.00–$70.00*

Hallock, Charles. *Camp Life in Florida, A Handbook for Sportsmen and Settlers.* NY. 1876. . . . . *$35.00–$50.00*

Hallowell, A. Irving. *Role of Conjuring in Saulteaux Society.* Univ of Pa Pr. 1942. 1st ed. waxine dj. . . . . *$25.00–$35.00*

Halpin, Warren T. *Hoofbeats: Drawings and Comments.* Phila. Lippincott. 1938. 1st ed. illus. . . . . *$60.00–$150.00*

Halsey, F. W. *Pioneers of Unadilla Village.* Unadilla, NY. 1902. ltd 650 cc. . . . . *$45.00–$55.00*

Halsey, Margaret. *Color Blind: a White Woman Looks at the Negro.* NY. 1946. . . . . *$20.00–$30.00*

Halsey, Rosalie V. *Forgotten books of the American Nursery.…* Bos. Charles E Goodspeed. 1911. 700 cc. . . . . *$60.00–$80.00*

Halstead, W. C. *Brain & Intelligence: A Quantitative Study of Frontal Lobes.* Chi. 1947. 1st ed. dj. . . . . *$100.00–$125.00*

Haluck, Paul. *Harness Making.* Phila. 1904. . . . . *$35.00–$40.00*

Hamerton, Philip G. *A Summer Voyage on the River Saone.* Lon. 1887. illus. maps. . . . . *$50.00–$75.00*

Hamilton, J. Taylor. *The Beginnings of the Moravian Missions in Alaska.* Bethlehem. 1890. wrps. . . . . *$20.00–$45.00*

Hamilton, Robert. *Gospel Among the Redmen.* Nashville. 1930. wrps. . . . . *$50.00–$65.00*

Hamilton, William T. *My Sixty Years on the Plains.* NY. 1905. 1st ed. illus. . . . . *$150.00–$175.00*

Hamley Cowboy Catalogue 32. Oregon. (1932). wrps. illus. . . . . *$175.00–$225.00*

Hammerton, Philip. *Etcher's Handbook.* Lon. 1875. illus. 2nd ed. . . . . *$50.00–$75.00*

Hammett, Dashiell. *Blood Money.* Cleve. World Pub. 1943. 1st ed. dj. . . . . *$75.00–$85.00*

Hammett, Dashiell. *Glass Key.* NY. Grosset & Dunlap. 1931. reprint ed. illus. with pict from motion picture, dj. . . . . *$60.00–$75.00*

Hammett, Dashiell. *Thin Man.* NY. Grosset & Dunlap. rprnt, dj. . . *$18.00–$45.00*

Hammett, Dashiell. *Woman in the Dark.* NY. Knopf. 1988. 1st ed. dj.*$8.00–$50.00*

Hammett, Dashiell. *Woman in the Dark.* Lon. Headline. 1988. 1st UK ed. dj. . . . . *$13.00–$35.00*

Hammett, Dashiell. *Adventures of Sam Spade.* Cleve. World Pub. (1945). 1st ed. dj. . . . . *$50.00–$300.00*

Hammett, Dashiell. *Big Knockover.* NY. Random House. (1966). 1st ed. dj. . . . . *$60.00–$130.00*

Hammett, Dashiell. *Maltese Falcon.* NY. Knopf. 1930. 1st ed. tan cl. . . . .
. . . . *$500.00–$800.00*

Hammett, Dashiell. *Thin Man.* NY. 1934. 1st ed. . . . . *$350.00–$600.00*

Hammett, Dashiell. *Dain Curse.* NY. Knopf. 1929. 1st ed. yellow cvr, skull and
bones stamped in red on cvr. . . . . *$400.00–$600.00*

Hammond, Harriot Milton. *Aunt Bet, the Story of a Long Life.* Winchester. The
Handley Library. (1927). illus. b/wphotos. *$50.00–$75.00*

Hammond, Peter. *The Waters of Marah.* NY. Macmillan. 1956. 1st ed. dj. . . . .
. . . . *$20.00–$40.00*

Hanaford, Mrs. P. A. *Young Captain; a Memorial of Capt. Richard C. Berby....* Bos.
1865. . . . . *$25.00–$35.00*

Hanaford, Phebe. *Daughters of America.* Augusta. True and Co. 1882. illus. . . . . . .
. . . . *$20.00–$30.00*

Handbook for European and Oriental Travelers. United States Express Co. 1896.
traveller's guide, brown cl. . . . . *$15.00–$20.00*

Handbook for Scout Masters-Boy Scouts of America. NY. 1914. 1st ed. illus. . . . .
. . . . *$200.00–$300.00*

Handbook for Travellers to Niagara Falls.... Buffalo/Rochester. Ontario and St
Lawrence Steamboat Co. 1854. 175 pp, fldng map. . . . . *$55.00–$70.00*

Handbook of Information for Passengers and Skippers. Nippon Yuse Kaisha. 1896.
map in pocket. . . . . *$40.00–$65.00*

Handbook of the Benet-Mercie Machine Rifle.... DC. GPO. 1917. 31 plates wrps. .
. . . . *$50.00–$75.00*

Handbook of the Colt Automatic.... DC. GPO. 1917. illus. 16 plates wrps. . . . .
. . . . *$50.00–$75.00*

Handbook of the Gatling Gun.... DC. GPO. 1917. 7 fldg plates wrps. . . . .
. . . . *$50.00–$75.00*

Handbook of the Maxim Automatic Machine Gun.... DC. GPO. 1917. 17 plates
wrps. . . . . *$50.00–$75.00*

Handbook of the Oneida Society. Oneida, NY. Office of Oneida Circular. 1875. 48
pp. . . . . *$65.00–$85.00*

Handbook of the Vickers Machine Gun.... DC. GPO. 1917. 16 plates wrps. . . . . . .
. . . . *$50.00–$75.00*

Handbook of Tobacco Culture for Planters in So. Rhodesia. Salisbury. 1913. 1st ed.
illus. . . . . *$75.00–$115.00*

Handley-Read, Charles. *The Art of Wyndham Lewis.* Lon. Faber and Faber. 1951. 1st ed. 109 pp. dj. . . . . *$50.00–$80.00*

Handy, W. C. *Father of the Blues.* NY. Macmillan. 1941. 1st ed. dj. . . . . *$200.00–$250.00*

Handy, W. C. (ed.). *Blues: An Anthology.* NY. Albert & Charles Boni. 1926. 1st ed. illus. by Covarrubias. 1st prtg of author's first book, intro by Abbe Niles, scarce. . . . . *$150.00–$200.00*

Hann, Julius. *Handbook of Climatology, Pt. I: General Climatology.* Macmillan. 1903. . . . . *$30.00–$65.00*

Hanna, A J. *Flight into Oblivion.* Johnson Pub. Co. 1938. 1st ed.   . *$35.00–$50.00*

Hannah, Barry. *Airships.* NY. Knopf. 1978. 1st ed. dj, sgn. . . . . *$100.00–$135.00*

Hannah, Barry. *Geronimo Rex.* NY. Viking. 1972. 1st ed. dj, sgn.*$150.00–$300.00*

Hannah, Barry. *Nightwatchmen.* NY. Viking. (1973). 1st ed. dj.. *$100.00–$200.00*

Hannay, James. *History of the War of 1812.* New Brunswick. 1901. 9 maps printed in text, original cl. . . . . *$120.00–$125.00*

Hansard, George Agar. *Book of Archery.* Lon. 1840. illus. rbnd. . *$75.00–$125.00*

Hansberry, Lorraine. *Raisin in the Sun.* NY. 1959. wrps. . . . . *$25.00–$35.00*

Hansen, Ron. *Desperadoes.* NY. Knopf. 1979. 1st ed. author's first book, dj. . . . . *$25.00–$35.00*

Hanson, F. A. L. *Counterpoint in Maori Culture.* Lon. 1983. illus. . *$55.00–$70.00*

Harbaugh, H. *Birds of the Bible.* Phila. Lindsay & Blackiston. 1854. 1st ed. illus. aeg. . . . . *$70.00–$100.00*

Hardee, William. *Rifle and Light Infantry Tactics.* Phil. 1861. 2 vols. . . . . *$300.00–$600.00*

Harding, A. *Wolf and Coyote Trapping.* OH. 1939. illus. . . . . *$50.00–$75.00*

Harding, A. R. *Fur Farming.* OH. Harding Pub. 1916. 2nd ed.. . . . *$14.00–$20.00*

Harding, A. R. *Ginseng and Other Medicinal Plants.* Columbus. illus. photos, rev. . . . . *$25.00–$40.00*

Harding, A. R. *Mink Trapping.* Columbus. 1906. illus. . . . . *$20.00–$28.00*

Hardware. NY/New Haven, CT. Sargent & Co. 1888. 1,090 pp. . *$195.00–$250.00*

Hardy, Thomas. *Group of Noble Dames.* Lon. 1891. 1st ed. . . . . *$75.00–$115.00*

Hardy, Thomas. *Jude the Obscure.* NY. 1896. 1st Amer ed. . . . . . *$75.00–$250.00*

Hardy, Thomas. *Selected Poems.* Lon. Medici Society. 1921. ltd 1025 cc. frontis, vellum, teg. . . . . ***$100.00–$200.00***

Hardy, Thomas. *Tess of the D'Urbervilles, A Pure Woman.* NY. Limited Ed Press. 1956. illus. engr by Agnes Miller Parker. pict cl, ltd 1500 cc. sgn by Parker. . . . . ***$50.00–$75.00***

Hardy, Thomas. *Tess of the D'Urbervilles.* NY. Harper. 1892. 3 vols. 1st Amer ed. . . . . ***$300.00–$400.00***

Hardy, Thomas. *Well-Beloved.* Harpers. 1897. 1st Amer ed. . . . . . . ***$75.00–$95.00***

Hardy, Thomas. *Winter Words in Various Moods and Meters.* Lon. Macmillan. 1928. 1st Brit ed. green cl, dj. . . . . ***$75.00–$85.00***

Hardy, Thomas. *Woodlanders.* Lon. Macmillan. 1887. 3 vols. 1st ed. green cl. . . . . ***$800.00–$4,000.00***

Harland, Marion. *Some Colonial Homesteads and Their Stories.* NY. Putnam. 1897. 3rd ed. b/w photos. . . . . ***$30.00–$45.00***

Harlow, Alvin. *Old Waybills.* NY. 1934. dj. . . . . ***$40.00–$60.00***

Harman, Dolly Stearns. *Beach Fires.* Bos. Christopher Pub. 1934. scarce. . . . . ***$25.00–$40.00***

Harold, Childe. *Child's Book of Abridged Wisdom.* SF. Paul Elder. (1905). 1st ed. illus. pict bds, exposed spine, double pages. . . . . ***$75.00–$100.00***

Harpham Brothers Company Catalogue No. 36, Saddlery Accessories. Nebraska. nd. wrps. . . . . ***$30.00–$40.00***

Harrington, W. P. *History of Gove County, Kansas.* Kansas. 1911. wrps. illus. . . . . ***$35.00–$50.00***

Harris, Joel Chandler. *Aaron in the Wildwood.* Bos. 1897. 1st ed. ***$55.00–$95.00***

Harris, Joel Chandler. *Gabriel Tolliver.* NY. 1902. 1st ed. 448 pp. ***$60.00–$180.00***

Harris, Joel Chandler. *Little Union Scout.* NY. McClure. 1904. 1st ed. illus. by Gibbs, green cl. . . . . ***$75.00–$200.00***

Harris, Joel Chandler. *Nights With Uncle Remus Myths and Legends of the Old Plantation.* Bos. 1883. 1st published ed. pict cl, 416 pp. . . . . ***$80.00–$120.00***

Harris, Joel Chandler. *On the Wings of Occasion.* NY. 1900. 1st ed. ***$50.00–$80.00***

Harris, Joel Chandler. *Tar Baby and Other Rhymes of Uncle Remus.* NY. Appleton. 1904. 1st ed. illus. orange cl. . . . . ***$100.00–$250.00***

Harris, Joel Chandler. *Told By Uncle Remus, New Stories of the Old Plantation.* NY. McClure Phillips. 1905. 1st ed. 3rd imp. illus. . . . . ***$175.00–$200.00***

Harris, Joel Chandler. *Uncle Remus Returns*. Bos. Houghton Mifflin. 1918. 1st ed. illus. by Frost and Conde. . . . . *$65.00–$300.00*

Harris, Joel Chandler. *Wally Wanderoon and His Story Telling Machine*. NY. 1903. 1st ed. illus. 294 pp.. . . . . *$40.00–$175.00*

Harris, T. W. *Treatise on Insects Injurious to Vegetation*. Bos. 1862. illus. 640 pp, plates. . . . . *$125.00–$200.00*

Harris, Thomas. *Silence of the Lambs*. NY. 1988. 1st ed. dj. . . . . . *$45.00–$60.00*

Harris, Thomas L. *Lyric of the Golden Age*. NY. 1856. 1st ed. 381 pp. . . . . *$100.00–$150.00*

Harris, W. R. *Catholic Church in Utah*. Salt Lake City. (1909). 1st ed. map. . . . . *$50.00–$75.00*

Harrison, Percival T. *Bungalow Residences: A Handbook*. Lon. Crosby, Lockwood. 1909. pict green cl, plates, 79 pp.. . . . . *$75.00–$135.00*

Hart, B H Liddell. *Sherman....* NY. Dodd, Mead. 1929. 1st ed. dj maps. . . . . *$50.00–$75.00*

Hart, B. H. Liddell. *Tanks*. Lon. Cassell. (1959). 2 vols. 1st ed. illus. cl djs plates and fldg maps.. . . . . *$60.00–$90.00*

Hart, George. *Violin and its Music*. Lon. 1875. illus. . . . . *$50.00–$80.00*

Hart, Gerald. *The fall of New France*. Montreal. 1888. 1st ed. illus. . . . . *$100.00–$175.00*

Harte, Bret. *Bell-Ringer of Angel's and Other Stories*. Bos. Houghton Mifflin. 1894. 1st ed. . . . . *$20.00–$40.00*

Harte, Bret. *Crusade of the Excelsior*. Bos. Houghton Mifflin. 1887. 1st ed. 1/300 cc.. . . . . *$40.00–$60.00*

Harte, Bret. *Maruja*. NY. Houghton Mifflin. 1885. 1st ed. 1st US ed.*$20.00–$50.00*

Harte, Bret. *Poems*. Bos. Fields & Osgood. 1871. 1st ed. brown cl gold lettering.. . . . . *$40.00–$50.00*

Harte, Bret. *Salomy Jane*. Bos. Houghton Mifflin. 1910. 1st ed. dj.*$50.00–$250.00*

Harte, Bret. *The Heathen Chinee*. SF. John Henry Nash. 1934. illus. by Phil Little. bds stitched in oriental fashion, slipcase. . . . . *$50.00–$75.00*

Harting, James Edmund. *Sketches of Bird Life from Twenty Years' Observation of Their Haunts and Habits*. Lon. Allen. 1883. 1st ed. illus. . . . . *$80.00–$120.00*

Hartley, Florence. *Ladies Handbook of Fancy and Ornamental Work*. Phila. 1859. . . . . *$75.00–$95.00*

Hartley, L. P. *The Hireling.* NY. Rinehart. 1957. 1st ed. dj........ *$17.00–$40.00*

Hartshorne, A. *Old English Drinking Glasses.* Lon. 1897. folio, plates, 499 pp. . . .
.... *$150.00–$400.00*

Harwell, Richard. *Colorado Volunteers in New Mexico.* Chi. Lakeside. 1962. rprnt.
.... *$25.00–$35.00*

Haskell, Frank Aretas. *Battle of Gettysburg.* WI. 1908. 1st ed. illus. . . . .
.... *$50.00–$75.00*

Hatcher, Edmund N. *Last Four Weeks of the War.* Columbus. Cooperative Pub. 1892.
illus. .... *$50.00–$80.00*

Haupt, Herman. *General Theory of Bridge Construction.* NY. 1856. . . . .
.... *$45.00–$60.00*

Hauser, Thomas. *Muhammad Ali. His Life and Times.* NY. Simon & Schuster. 1991.
sgn. .... *$65.00–$85.00*

Haviland, Laura S. *Woman's Life Work.* Michigan. 1881. illus. . . . *$50.00–$75.00*

Hawk Eye Camera. Bos. Blair Camera Company. 1889. illus, wrps. *$50.00–$75.00*

Hawker, George. *An English Woman's 25 Years in Tropical Africa.* Lon. 1911. . . .
.... *$75.00–$90.00*

Hawker, P. *Instructions to Young Sportsmen. Guns & Shooting.* 1858. *$45.00–$50.00*

Hawkins, Joseph. *A History of a Voyage to the Coast of Africa.* Phila. 1797. . . . . .
.... *$350.00–$750.00*

Hawley, Walter. *Oriental Rugs, Antique and Modern.* Tudor Publishing. 1937. 11 clr
plates. .... *$60.00–$90.00*

Hawley, Walter A. *Early Days of Santa Barbara, California.* Santa Barbara. 1910.
wrps. plates.. .... *$100.00–$135.00*

Hawthorne, Nathaniel. *Doctor Grimshawe's Secret.* Osgood. 1883. 1st ed. . . . . . .
.... *$35.00–$200.00*

Hawthorne, Nathaniel. *House of Seven Gables.* Bos. Tichnor, Reed & Fields. 1851.
1st ed. brown cl. .... *$600.00–$2,000.00*

Hawthorne, Nathaniel. *Marble Faun.* Bos. 1860. 2 vols. 1st ed. 1st Amer ed.. . . . . .
.... *$400.00–$700.00*

Hawthorne, Nathaniel. *Our Old Home.* Ticknor & Fields. 1863. 1st ed. 1st state.. . .
.... *$150.00–$200.00*

Hawthorne, Nathaniel. *Scarlet Letter.* Bos. Ticknor, Reed, & Fields. 1850. . . . . . .
.... *$450.00–$700.00*

Hawthorne, Nathaniel. *Scarlet Letter*. NY. Grosset & Dunlap. illus. dj, illus from photoplay. . . . . *$30.00–$50.00*

Hawthorne, Nathaniel. *The Complete Writings*. Bos. Houghton Mifflin. (1900). 22 vols. half calf & marbled bds. . . . . *$150.00–$175.00* •

Hawthorne, Nathaniel. *True Stories From History and Biography*. Bos. Ticknor , Reed & Fields. 1851. 1st ed. cl. . . . . *$150.00–$200.00*

Hawthorne, Nathaniel. *Wonder Book*. NY. Doran. (1922). illus. by Arthur Rackham. . . . . *$300.00–$800.00*

Hawthorne, Nathaniel. *Wonderbook for Girls and Boys*. Houghton Mifflin. 1893. 1st ed. illus. by Walter Crane. . . . . *$100.00–$150.00*

Hay, John. *Pike County Ballads*. Bos. Houghton Mifflin. (1912). 1st ed. illus. by N. C. Wyeth, pict paste down on cvr. . . . . *$100.00–$150.00*

Hayden, A. *Spode and His Successors*. Lon. 1925. . . . . *$60.00–$75.00*

Hayden, A. S. *Early History of The Disciples in The Western Reserve, Ohio....* Cinc. 1876. 1st ed. . . . . *$50.00–$125.00*

Hayden, F V. *Report of the US Geological Survey of the Territories*. DC. 1979. clr plates. . . . . *$65.00–$100.00*

Hayden, F. V. *Bulletin of the Geological and Geographical Survey of the Territories, vol II, no 1*. DC. 1876. wrps. 63pp, 29 plates. . . . . *$95.00–$100.00*

Hayes, Albert H. *Medical Treatise on Nervous Affections*. Bos. Peabody Medical Inst. (1870). 137 pp. . . . . *$50.00–$75.00*

Hayes, Isaac. *An Arctic Boat Journey*. Bos. 1860. 1st ed. 375 pp, maps. . . . .
. . . . *$100.00–$250.00*

Haynes, Warden G. *Pictures From Prison Life and Suggestions on Discipline*. 1869.
. . . . *$50.00–$65.00*

Hayward, John. *A Gazeteer of the United States of America*. Hartford. Case, Tiffany. 1853. illus. wood engr, hand-clr fldg map, calf.. . . . . *$150.00–$300.00*

Hayward, John. *Gazetteer of Vermont....* Bos. 1849. illus. 216 pp. . *$65.00–$95.00*

Head, Sir Francis B. *A Narrative*. Lon. Murray. 1839. 2nd ed. 1/2 calf, marbled bds.
. . . . *$95.00–$120.00*

Headland, Isaac T. *Chinese Mother Goose Rhymes*. NY. Fleming Revell. (1900). 1st ed. illus. . . . . *$75.00–$250.00*

Headland, Isaac Taylor. *Court Life in China*. NY. (1909). illus. 2nd ed. phots. . . . .
. . . . *$30.00–$40.00*

Headley, J. T. *Adirondacks or Life in the Woods*. NY. 1849. 1st ed. 288 pp. . . . .
. . . . *$95.00–$115.00*

Headley, Joel Tyler. *Second War with England*. NY. Scribner's. 1853. 2 vols. 10
plates (1 fldg), pict brown cl. . . . . *$135.00–$150.00*

Healy, Capt M. A. *Report of the Cruise of the Revenue Marine Steamer....* DC. 1889.
illus. cl 128pp. . . . . *$150.00–$200.00*

Healy, M. A. *Report of the Cruise of the Revenue Marine Steamer Corwin in the
Arctic Ocean in the Year 1885*. DC. GPO. 1887. 1st ed. illus. 38 wood-engr plates, 4
lithos, 2 fldg charts. . . . . *$125.00–$150.00*

Heaney, Seamus. *Door Into The Dark*. Lon. Faber & Faber. 1969. 1st ed. dj. . . . . .
. . . . *$100.00–$150.00*

Heaney, Seamus. *Poems 1965-1975*. NY. Farrar, Straus & Giroux. (1980). 1st ed. dj.
. . . . *$30.00–$40.00*

Heaney, Seamus. *Station Island*. Lon. 1984. 1st ed. dj. . . . . *$50.00–$75.00*

Hearn, Lafcadio. *Boy Who Drew Cats*. Tokyo. 1898. printed & hand-clr in handmade
crepe paper, 18 pp. . . . . *$120.00–$300.00*

Hearn, Lafcadio. *Chita: A Memory of Last Island*. NY. 1889. 1st ed. 204 pp. . . . . . .
. . . . *$200.00–$300.00*

Hearn, Lafcadio. *In Ghostly Japan*. Bos. 1899. 1st ed. illus. photos, teg, Hearn's last
book. . . . . *$115.00–$150.00*

Hearn, Lafcadio. *Japan*. NY. 1904. 1st ed. 1st issue, teg, dj.. . . . *$175.00–$400.00*

Hearn, Lafcadio. *Karma*. NY. 1918. 1st ed. . . . . *$100.00–$150.00*

Hearn, Lafcadio. *Kokaro*. Bos. 1896. 1st ed. . . . . *$50.00–$75.00*

Hearn, Lafcadio. *Out of the East*. Bos. (1895). 1st ed. . . . . *$75.00–$200.00*

Hearst, Mrs. William Randolph, Jr. *Horses of San Simeon*. San Simeon. San
Simeon Press. 1985. sgn, slipcase. . . . . *$225.00–$295.00*

Heathcote, J. M. *Skating and Figure Skating*. Lon. 1892. illus. . . . *$60.00–$85.00*

Hebert, Frank. *40 Years Prospecting & Mining in the Black Hills of So. Dakota*.
Rapid City. 1921. 1st ed. sgn. . . . . *$35.00–$45.00*

Heckewelder, John. *History, Manners and Customs of the Indian Nations Who Once
Inhabited Pennsylvania and the Neighboring States*. NY. Arno Press. 1971. rprnt. dj.
. . . . *$22.00–$30.00*

Heckewelder, John. *Narr. of United Brethren Among Delaware & Mohegan Indians*.
Cleve. 1907. large paper copy. . . . . *$140.00–$275.00*

Hedges, Isaac A. *Sugar Canes and Their Products, Culture and Manufacture.* St. Louis. 1881. illus. . . . . *$28.00–$35.00*

Hedin, Sven. *A Conquest of Tibet.* Garden City. Halcyon House. 1934. illus. . . . . *$50.00–$75.00*

Hedin, Sven. *Through Asia.* NY. Harper & Bros. 1899. 2 vols. 1st ed. 300 photos and sketches, fldg map at rear, decorative cl, teg. . . . . *$250.00–$400.00*

Hedrick, U. P. *Cherries of New York.* Albany. 1915. clr plates. . . *$125.00–$200.00*

Hedrick, U. P. *Peaches of New York.* Albany. 1917. illus. clr plates. . . . . *$100.00–$175.00*

Hedrick, U. P. *Pears of New York.* Albany. 1921. illus. . . . . *$125.00–$250.00*

Hedrick, U. P. *Plums of New York.* Albany. 1911. clr plates. . . . . *$125.00–$200.00*

Hedrick, U. P. (ed.). *Sturtevant's Notes on Edible Plants.* Albany. Lyon. 1919. 1st ed. . . . . *$60.00–$85.00*

Heffernan, J. W. *New York Fire Department Examination Questions.* NY. Duffield. 1929. vol. 1. pullouts. . . . . *$35.00–$50.00*

Heilman, G. *Origins of Birds.* NY. 1927. 2 clr plates, dj. . . . . *$65.00–$75.00*

Heilner, Van Campen. *Adventures in Angling.* Stewart Kidd. (1922). 1st ed. illus. . . . . *$50.00–$85.00*

Heilner, Van Campen. *Our American Game Birds.* Garden City. Doubleday, Doran. 1941. 1st ed. illus. with clr paintings by Lynn Bogue Hunt, dj. . . . . *$60.00–$85.00*

Heilprin, Angelo. *Alaska and the Klondike.* NY. 1899. illus. inscr. . *$35.00–$45.00*

Heilprin, Angelo. *Town Geology.* Phila. 1885. 1st ed. 142 pp, illus. *$65.00–$75.00*

Heindel, Max. *Astro-Diagnosis: A Guide to Healing.* Lon. (1929). 3rd ed.. . . . . *$15.00–$25.00*

Heiner, Dr. Henry. *Gesundheits Schatzkammer.* (Lancaster, PA. 1831). *$30.00–$40.00*

Heinlein, Robert. *Door Into Summer.* Garden City. Doubleday. 1957. 1st ed. scarce, dj. . . . . *$195.00–$1,000.00*

Heinlein, Robert A. *Assignment in Eternity.* Fantasy Press. (1953). 1st ed. dj. . . . . *$100.00–$350.00*

Heinlein, Robert A. *Cat Who Walks Through Walls.* NY. 1985. 1st ed. dj. . . . . *$20.00–$25.00*

Heinlein, Robert A. *Farmer in the Sky.* NY. Scribner's. 1950. 1st ed. dj. . . . . *$180.00–$400.00*

Heinlein, Robert A. *Job: A Comedy of Justice.* NY. Del Rey. 1984. 1st ed. dj......
.... *$8.00–$12.00*

Heinlein, Robert A. *Number of the Beast.* Lon. 1980. 1st ed. dj.... *$30.00–$50.00*

Heinlein, Robert A. *Waldo and Magic, Inc.* Garden City. 1950. 1st ed. dj.........
.... *$200.00–$300.00*

Heinlein, Robert A. *Farnham's Freehold.* NY. Putnam. 1964. 1st ed. dj.........
.... *$220.00–$600.00*

Heinlein, Robert A. *Grumbles from the Grave.* NY. Del Rey. 1990. 1st ed. ed. by
Virginia Heinlein. dj.................................... *$12.00–$20.00*

Heinlein, Robert A. *Rocket Ship Galileo.* Scribner's. 1947. 1st ed. dj...........
.... *$300.00–$600.00*

Heinlein, Robert A. *Space Cadet.* NY. Scribner's. 1948. 1st ed. illus. by Voter. dj. .
.... *$950.00–$150.00*

Heinlein, Robert A. *Three by Heinlein: The Puppet Masters, Waldo, Magic.* Garden
City. Doubleday. 1965. 1st ed. dj. .... *$200.00–$325.00*

Heisler Automotive Works. *Heisler Geared Locomotives.* Erie. Heisler Locomotive
Works. 1908. wrps. illus. 47 pp, cat. .... *$60.00–$75.00*

Heller, Joseph. *Catch-22.* NY. 1961. 1st ed. author's first book, dj. ....
.... *$2,000.00–$3,000.00*

Heller, Joseph. *God Knows.* NY. 1984. 1st ed. sgn, dj. .... *$35.00–$40.00*

Heller, Joseph. *Good As Gold.* NY. Simon & Schuster. (1979). 1st ed. ....
.... *$35.00–$45.00*

Heller, Joseph. *We Bombed in New Haven.* NY. Knopf. 1968. 1st ed. dj.........
.... *$60.00–$75.00*

Hellman, Lillian. *Children's Hour.* NY. 1934. 1st ed. dj. ...... *$250.00–$300.00*

Hellman, Lillian. *Little Foxes.* NY. 1939. 1st ed. dj. .... *$30.00–$45.00*

Helms, Herman (ed.). *Book of the New York International Chess Tournament 1924.*
NY. American Chess Bulletin. 1925. 1st ed. scarce............. *$85.00–$95.00*

Helper, Hinton Rowan. *Impending Crisis of the South.* NY. 1857. ....
.... *$40.00–$60.00*

Helprin, Mark. *Ellis Island and Other Stories.* NY. Delacorte Press. (1981). 1st ed.
dj. .... *$50.00–$60.00*

Hemenway, Abby M. *Clarke Papers; Mrs. Meech and Her Family....* Burlington.
1878. 312 pp. .... *$42.00–$50.00*

Hemenway, Abby Maria. *Abby Hemenway's Vermont.* VT. Stephen Green Press. 1972. dj. . . . . *$7.00–$1,500.00*

Hemenway, Abby Maria. *Local History of Andover, VT.* NJ. 1921. rprnt. . . . . *$30.00–$40.00*

Hemenway, Abby Maria. *Poets and Poetry of Vermont.* Bos. Brown Taggard & Chase. 1860. lavender cl. . . . . *$25.00–$35.00*

Hemenway, Abby Maria. *The History of the Town of Montpelier, Vermont....* Montpelier. private printing. 1882. 1st ed. illus. . . . . *$135.00–$150.00*

Hemenway, Abby Maria. *Vermont Historical Gazetteer...vol III.* NH. 1877. illus. hard to find. . . . . *$300.00–$425.00*

Hemenway, Abby Maria. *Vermont Historical Gazetteer...vol IV.* Montpelier. 1882. illus. rbnd. . . . . *$130.00–$165.00*

Hemenway, Abby Maria. *Vermont Historical Gazetteer...vol V.* Brandon. 1891. illus. . . . . *$425.00–$475.00*

Hemenway, Abby Maria. *Vermont Historical Gazetteer....vols. I & II.* Burlington. 1867, 1871. illus. . . . . *$200.00–$300.00*

Hemenway, Abby Maria. *Vermont Historical Gazetteer...vol IV.* Monpelier. 1882. illus. 1,200 pp. . . . . *$165.00–$175.00*

Hemingway, Ernest. *A Farewell to Arms.* NY. Scribner's. 1929. 1st ed. 1st issue, dj. . . . . *$300.00–$4,000.00*

Hemingway, Ernest. *Across the River and Into the Trees.* Lon. Jonathan Cape. 1950. 1st ed. dj. . . . . *$60.00–$90.00*

Hemingway, Ernest. *Across the River and Into the Trees.* NY. Scribner's. 1950. 1st Amer ed. black cl, dj. . . . . *$100.00–$350.00*

Hemingway, Ernest. *Death In the Afternoon.* NY. 1932. 1st ed. dj. . . . . *$750.00–$1,250.00*

Hemingway, Ernest. *For Whom the Bell Tolls.* NY. NY. Scribner's. 1940. no dj. . . . . *$34.00–$40.00*

Hemingway, Ernest. *For Whom the Bell Tolls.* NY. Scribner's. 1940. 1st ed. dj. . . . . *$150.00–$450.00*

Hemingway, Ernest. *In Our Time.* NY. Scribner's. 1930. 2nd Amer ed. rev. black cl, dj. . . . . *$300.00–$500.00*

Hemingway, Ernest. *Islands in the Stream.* NY. Scribner's. 1970. 1st ed. dj. . . . . *$50.00–$75.00*

Hemingway, Ernest. *Old Man and the Sea.* NY. Scribner. 1952. 1st ed. . . . .
. . . . *$15.00–$25.00*

Hemingway, Ernest. *Old Man and the Sea.* Lon. Jonathan Cape. (1952). 1st UK ed.
dj. . . . . *$100.00–$225.00*

Hemingway, Ernest. *Old Man and the Sea.* NY. Scribner's. 1952. 1st ed. dj. . . . . . .
. . . . *$180.00–$400.00*

Hemingway, Ernest. *To Have and Have Not.* NY. Scribner's. 1937. 1st ed. . . . . . .
. . . . *$850.00–$1,000.00*

Hemingway, Ernest. *Winner Take Nothing.* NY. Scribner's. 1933. 1st ed. black cl, dj.
. . . . *$450.00–$1,200.00*

Henderson, Alice P. *Rainbow's End: Alaska.* NY. Herbert Stone & Co. 1898. 1st ed.
. . . . *$125.00–$150.00*

Henderson, Mrs. Mary F. *Practical Cooking and Dinner Giving.* NY. Harper. 1881.
1st ed. . . . . *$70.00–$100.00*

Henderson, Peter. *Henderson's Handbook of Plants and General Horticulture.* NY.
1910. 2nd ed. illus. . . . . *$50.00–$65.00*

Henderson, W. A. *Modern Domestic Cookery and Useful Receipt Book.* Bos. 1844.
. . . . *$135.00–$170.00*

Henely, Louise Miller. *Letters from the Yellowstone.* Iowa. 1914. 1st ed. illus. inscr.
. . . . *$50.00–$100.00*

Hening, Mrs. E. F. *History of the African Mission of the Episcopal Church in the
United States.* NY. Stanford & Swords. 1850. 1st ed. fldg map. . . . . *$40.00–$50.00*

Henry, Alice. *Women and the Labor Movement.* NY. Doran. (1923). 1st ed. 241 pp. .
. . . . *$45.00–$65.00*

Henry, Capt. W. S. *Campaign Sketches of the War with Mexico.* NY. 1847. 1st ed.
illus. . . . . *$190.00–$250.00*

Henry, Marguerite. *Album of Horses.* Chi. Rand McNally. 1951. illus. dj. . . . .
. . . . *$32.00–$45.00*

Henry, Marguerite. *Birds at Home.* Chi. Donohue. 1942. 1st ed. illus. scarce, dj. . . .
. . . . *$45.00–$58.00*

Henry, Marguerite. *Black Gold.* Chi. Rand McNally. 1957. illus. by Wesley Dennis,
presentation copy, sgn by Henry and Dennis, dj. . . . . *$65.00–$125.00*

Henry, Marguerite. *Brighty of the Grand Canyon.* Chi. Rand McNally. 1953. 1st ed.
illus. by Wesley Dennis, dj. . . . . *$50.00–$65.00*

Henry, Marguerite. *Justin Morgan Had a Horse*. Chi. Wilcox & Follett. 1945. 1st ed. . . . . *$25.00–$45.00*

Henry, Marguerite. *King of the Wind*. Chi. Rand McNally & Co. (1951). illus. red cl. . . . . , ... *$10.00–$20.00*

Henry, Marguerite. *King of the Wind*. Chi. Rand McNally. 1948. 1st ed. illus. by Wesley Dennis, dj. . . . . : . . . . *$50.00–$95.00*

Henry, Marguerite and Wesley Dennis. *Benjamin West and His Cat Grimalkin*. Indianapolis. Bobb, Merrill. 1947. dj. *$58.00–*

Henry, O. *Cabbages and Kings*. NY. 1904. 1st ed. . . . . *$100.00–$150.00*

Henry, O. *Heart of the West*. McClure. 1907. 1st ed. . . . . *$60.00–$85.00*

Henry, O. *Whirlygigs*. NY. 1910. 1st ed. 1st Amer ed.. . . . . *$60.00–$80.00*

Henry, Robert Mitchell. *Evolution of Sinn Fein*. Dublin. 1920. 1st ed. sgn by Sean Cullen.. . . . . *$35.00–$95.00*

Henry, Robert Selph. *Story of the Confederacy*. Ind. (1931). . . . . *$30.00–$40.00*

Henry, Will. *Alias Butch Cassidy*. NY. (1967). 1st ed. dj. . . . . *$50.00–$75.00*

Henry, Will. *To Follow a Flag*. NY. Random House. (1953). 1st ed. dj. . . . . *$65.00–$100.00*

Henry, Will. *Who Rides With Wyatt*. NY. Random House. (1955). 1st ed. dj. . . . . *$30.00–$40.00*

Henson, Josiah. *Truth Stranger Than Fiction*. MA. Corner House Pub. 1973. dj.. . . . . *$14.00–$20.00*

Hentoff, Nat. *Peace Agitator*. NY. Macmillan. 1963. 1st ed. author's first book, dj. . . . . *$10.00–$20.00*

Henty, G. A. *Beric The Briton*. NY. Scribner's. 1895. illus. by Parkinson 1st US ed brown cl.. . . . . *$30.00–$45.00*

Henty, G. A. *Both Sides of the Border*. Lon. 1899. 1st ed. illus. . . . *$50.00–$70.00*

Henty, G. A. *By Pike & Dyke*. Lon. (1890). *$25.00–$30.00*

Henty, G. A. *In the Irish Brigade*. NY. Scribner's. 1900. 1st ed. . . . *$30.00–$35.00*

Henty, G. A. *Maori and Settler....* Lon. Blackie. nd. . . . . *$15.00–$30.00*

Henty, G. A. *On The Irrawoddy*. NY. Scribner's. 1896. blue decorated cvr. . . . . *$40.00–$45.00*

Henty, G. A. *Out With Garibaldi*. NY. 1900. 1st Amer ed. illus. . . . *$40.00–$75.00*

Henty, G. A. *Redskins and Colonists.* NY. (1905). dj. . . . . *$25.00–$30.00*

Henty, G. A. *Through Russian Snows.* NY. Scribner's. 1895. illus. by Overend maps.
. . . . *$40.00–$60.00*

Henty, G. A. *With Buller in Natal.* Lon. nd. 1st UK ed.. . . . . *$35.00–$55.00*

Henty, G. A. *With Cochrane the Dauntless.* NY. 1896. 1st Amer ed. *$30.00–$45.00*

Henty, G. A. *With Lee In Virginia.* NY. illus. by Gordon Browne. . . *$15.00–$40.00*

Henty, G. A. *With Wolfe In Canada.* Lon. illus. by Gordon Browne, green pict bds. .
. . . . *$20.00–$25.00*

Henty, G. A. *Young Franc-Tireurs and Their Adventures in the Franco-Prussian War.*
The Federal Book Co. nd. illus. . . . . *$15.00–$30.00*

Herbert, Frank. *Charterhouse Dune.* NY. (1985). 1st ed. ltd 750 cc, sgn, dj. . . . . .
. . . . *$50.00–$70.00*

Herbert, Frank. *God Emperor of Dune.* NY. 1981. 1st ed. sgn, dj. . *$50.00–$75.00*

Herbert, Frank. *God Emperor of Dune.* NY. Putnam. 1981. 1st ed. dj. . . . .
. . . . *$25.00–$85.00*

Herbert, Frank. *Heretics of Dune.* NY. (1984). 1st Amer ed. 1500 cc, sgn, slipcase.
. . . . *$50.00–$100.00*

Herbert, Frank. *White Plague.* NY. (1982). 1st ed. ltd 500 cc, sgn. *$40.00–$50.00*

Herbert, George R. *South Sea Bubbles.* Lon. Bentley. 1872. illus. . . . .
. . . . *$40.00–$65.00*

Herbert, H. *First Principles of Evolution.* NY. Appleton. 1896. . . . *$18.00–$25.00*

Herbert, Henry William. *American Game in its Seasons.* NY. Scribner's. 1853. 1st
ed. illus. . . . . *$145.00–$250.00*

Herbert, Henry William. *Frank Forester's Field Sports.* NY. Stringer & Townshend.
1849. 2 vols. illus. 1st Amer ed.. . . . . *$100.00–$195.00*

Herbert, Henry William. *Frank Forester's Fish and Fishing.* NY. Stringer &
Townshend. 1850. 1st ed. illus. . . . . *$75.00–$150.00*

Herbert, Henry William. *Hints to Horsekeepers.* NY. Orange Judd. (1859). 1st ed.
illus. . . . . *$60.00–$100.00*

Herbert, Henry William (Frank Forester). *American Game in its Seasons.* NY.
Scribner's. 1853. 1st ed. . . . . *$125.00–$250.00*

Herbert, William. *Frank Forester's Fugitive Sporting Sketches.* Westfield, WI. 1879.
. . . . *$125.00–$225.00*

Herford, Oliver. *An Alphabet of Celebrities*. Bos. 1899. 1st ed. . . *$50.00–$150.00*

Heriot, George. *Travels Through the Canadas*. Rutland. Chas. E. Tuttle Co. [1971]. rprnt, illus, fldg map, dj. . . . . *$60.00–$75.00*

Herndon, Angelo. *Let Me Live*. NY. Random House. (1937). cl frontis. . . . . *$50.00–$75.00*

Herrick, F H. *American Eagle*. NY. Appleton Century. 1934. . . . . *$30.00–$45.00*

Herrick, F H. *Flower Poems*. Lon. Routledge. illus. by Castle teg. . *$50.00–$80.00*

Herrigel, Eugen. *Zen in the Art of Archery*. [NY]. Pantheon. [1953]. 1st ed. dj. . . . . *$30.00–$40.00*

Hersey, John. *Hiroshima*. NY. Knopf. 1946. 1st ed. dj. . . . . *$10.00–$20.00*

Hersey, John. *Key West Tales*. NY. 1994. 1st ed. dj. . . . . *$18.00–$25.00*

Hersey, John. *The Call*. Franklin Center. Franklin Library. 1985. 1st ed. ltd. sgn, blue lea, aeg. . . . . *$20.00–$35.00*

Hersey, John. *The Wall*. NY. Limited Editions Club. 1957. illus. aquatints and drawings, ltd 1500 cc, sgn by artist. . . . . *$25.00–$40.00,*

Hersey, John. *The Wall*. NY. 1950. 1st ed. dj. . . . . *$25.00–$35.00*

Hersey, John. *War Lover*. Knopf. 1959. 1st ed. dj. . . . . *$15.00–$25.00*

Hertz, Louis. *Handbook of Old American Toys.*. Wetherfield. 1947. 1st ed. . . . . *$25.00–$50.00*

Hervey, A. B. *Beautiful Wild Flowers of America*. Bos. Cassino. 1883. illus. chromolith plates, brown cl. . . . . *$300.00–$400.00*

Hervey, John. *American Trotter*. NY. Cower McCann. 1947. 1st ed. dj. . . . . *$85.00–$150.00*

Hesse, Hermann. *Siddhartha*. [NY. New Directions. 1951]. 1st Amer ed. dj. . . . . *$85.00–$100.00*

Hewitt, Edward R. *Trout and Salmon Fisherman for Seventy-five Years*. Scribner's. 1948. . . . . *$40.00–$65.00*

Hewitt, Abram S. *On the Statistics and Geography of the Production of Iron.*. NY. 1856. wrps. . . . . *$45.00–$70.00*

Hewlett, John. *Harlem Story.*. NY. 1948. 1st ed. dj. . . . . *$50.00–$75.00*

Heydecker, Joe J & J Leeb. *Nuremberg Trial: A History of Nazi Germany*. Cleve. 1962. 1st ed. . . . . *$30.00–$40.00*

Heyer, Georgette. *Charity Girl*. Lon. Bodley Head. 1970. 1st ed. dj. . *$30.00–$40.00*

Heyer, Georgette. *No Wind of Blame.* NY. Doubleday Crime Club. 1939. 1st Amer ed. dj. . . . . *$150.00–$200.00*

Heyer, Georgette. *Pistols for Two & Other Stories.* Lon. Heinemann. 1960. dj. . . . . *$20.00–$25.00*

Heyer, Georgette. *Sylvester or the Wicked Uncle.* Lon. Heinemann. 1957. 1st ed. dj. . . . . *$10.00–$25.00*

Heyerdahl, Thor. *American Indians in the Pacific.* Lon. Allen & Unwin. (1952). 1st UK ed. illus. dj. . . . . *$70.00–$90.00*

Heyward, DuBose. *Half Pint Flask.* NY. 1929. 1st ed. dj. . . . . *$40.00–$60.00*

Hiaasen, Carl. *Stormy Weather.* NY. Knopf. 1995. 1st ed. sgn, dj. . *$30.00–$45.00*

Hiaasen, Carl and William D. Montalbano. *Powder Burns.* NY. Atheneum. 1981. 1st ed. dj. . . . . *$350.00–$425.00*

Hibben, Frank. *Prehistoric Man in Europe.* Univ of Ok Press. 1958. 1st ed. illus. . . . . *$22.00–$27.00*

Hibbert, Shirley. *Field Flowers.* Lon. 1878. illus. . . . . *$35.00–$45.00*

Hibbert, Shirley. *Wild Flower.* Lon. 1878. 2nd ed. illus. . . . . *$25.00–$40.00*

Higbee, Elias & Robert Thompson. *Latter Day Saints, Alias Mormons.* DC. 1840. second oldest US document to mention Mormons, 13 pp. . . . . . . *$350.00–$350.00*

Higgins, Jack. *A Prayer for the Dying.* Lon. Collins. 1973. 1st ed. dj. . . . . *$60.00–$75.00*

Higgins, Jack. *Day of Judgment.* Lon. Collins. 1978. 1st ed. dj. . . . *$25.00–$65.00*

Higgins, Jack. *Eagle Has Landed.* Collins. 1975. 1st UK ed dj. . . . . *$100.00–$250.00*

Higgins, Jack. *Eye of the Storm.* Lon. Chapmans. 1992. 1st ed. dj. . *$15.00–$45.00*

Higgins, Jack. *Last Place God Made.* Lon. Collins. 1971. 1st ed. dj. . . . . *$225.00–$250.00*

Higgins, Jack. *Night Judgement at Sinos.* Lon. Hodder & Stoughton. 1970. 1st ed. dj. . . . . *$70.00–$85.00*

Higgins, Jack. *Savage Day.* Lon. Collins. 1972. 1st ed. dj. . . . . . . *$65.00–$100.00*

Higginson, Ella. *Alaska.* NY. Macmillan Co. 1926. illus. new ed. . . *$20.00–$35.00*

Hildreth, Richard. *White Slave.* Lon. 1852. 1st UK ed. . . . . *$45.00–$65.00*

Hill, B. L. *An Epitome of the Homoeopathic Healing Arts.* Detroit. 1869. . . . . *$45.00–$55.00*

Hill, Charles T. *Fighting a Fire.* NY. 1898. illus. pict red cl. . . . . . . *$50.00–$90.00*

Hill, Frank Pierce. *American Plays Printed 1714-1830.* Stanford Univ Press. (1934). dj. . . . . *$30.00–$50.00*

Hill, Grace Livingston. *Through These Fires..* Phila. 1943. 1st ed. dj. . . . .
. . . . *$35.00–$47.00*

Hill, L. *Meteorological & Chronological Register, 1806 to 1869..* Plymouth, Ma. 1869. 1st ed. . . . . *$30.00–$45.00*

Hill, Ralph Nading. *Sidewheeler Saga.* Rinehart. 1953. 1st ed. illus. dj. . . . .
. . . . *$22.00–$35.00*

Hill, Ralph Nading. *Voyages of Brian Sea Worthy.* Montpelier. Vermont Life Magazine. 1971. 151 pp, dj.. . . . . *$16.00–$25.00*

Hillary, William. *Observations on the Changes of the Air... Yellow Fever.* Lon. 1766. 2nd ed. bds. . . . . *$235.00–$400.00*

Hillerman, Tony. *Talking God.* NY. Harper. (1989). 1st ed. dj. . . . . *$15.00–$35.00*

Hillerman, Tony. *Canyon De Chelly.* CA. Cahill. 1998. 1st ed. ltd 174 numbered cc, sgn. slipcase, no dj issued. . . . . *$175.00–$200.00*

Hillerman, Tony. *Coyote Waits.* NY. (1990). 1st ed. . . . . *$55.00–$75.00*

Hillerman, Tony. *Dance Hall of the Dead.* NY. (1973). 1st ed. 100cc inscr and sgn slipcase. . . . . *$100.00–$125.00*

Hillerman, Tony. *Dark Wind.* NY. (1982). 1st ed. sgn, dj. . . . . . . *$100.00–$175.00*

Hillerman, Tony. *Fly on the Wall.* NY. Harper & Row. 1971. 1st ed. dj.. . . . .
. . . . *$300.00–$500.00*

Hillerman, Tony. *Ghostway.* Lon. Victor Gollancz. 1985. 1st UK ed. dj. . . . .
. . . . *$90.00–$100.00*

Hillerman, Tony. *Ghostway.* NY. Harper & Row. 1985. 1st trade ed. dj. . . . .
. . . . *$150.00–$200.00*

Hillerman, Tony. *Great Taos Bank Robbery and Other Indian Country Affairs.* Albuquerque. (1973). 1st ed. sgn, dj. . . . . *$325.00–$450.00*

Hillerman, Tony. *Listening Woman.* Lon. Macmillan. 1979. 1st ed. dj. . . . .
. . . . *$200.00–$250.00*

Hillerman, Tony. *Listening Woman.* NY. (1978). 1st ed. sgn, dj, slipcase. . . . .
. . . . *$295.00–$375.00*

Hillerman, Tony. *New Mexico, Rio Grande and Other Essays.* Portland. Graphic Arts Center. (1989). 1st ed. dj. . . . . *$35.00–$45.00*

Hillerman, Tony. *People of Darkness*. NY. Harper & Row. 1980. 1st ed. dj. . . . . . .
. . . . *$250.00–$325.00*

Hillerman, Tony. *People of Darkness*. Lon. 1982. 1st UK ed. dj. . . *$60.00–$75.00*

Hillerman, Tony. *Sacred Clowns*. NY. Harper Collins. (1993). wrps. *$30.00–$45.00*

Hillerman, Tony. *Skinwalkers*. Lon. Michael Joseph. 1988. 1st UK ed. dj.. . . . .
. . . . *$40.00–$50.00*

Hillerman, Tony. *The Fallen Man*. Lon. Michael Joseph. 1997. 1st UK ed. dj. . . . .
. . . . *$40.00–$50.00*

Hillerman, Tony. *Thief of Time*. NY. Harper & Row. 1988. 1st ed. dj. *$25.00–$50.00*

Hillerman, Tony. *Thief of Time.*. NY. Harper & Row. 1988. 1st ed. dj, sgn. . . . .
. . . . *$60.00–$75.00*

Hillerman, Tony. *Words, Weather and Wolfmen*. Gallup. Southwesterner. 1989. 1st
ed. ltd 26 numbered cc, lea, sgn, slipcase. . . . . *$500.00–$600.00*

Hilton, James. *Goodbye, Mr. Chips*. Bos. Little, Brown. 1935. 1st illus ed. dj.. . . . .
. . . . *$22.00–$35.00*

Himes, Chester. *Case of Rape*. NY. Targ Editions. (1980). 1st ed. dj.. . . . .
. . . . *$90.00–$125.00*

Himmel, Richard. *I'll Find You*. NY. Fawcett. 1950. 1st ed. wrps. . *$40.00–$50.00*

Hinds, William. *American Communities....* Oneida. Office of the American Socialist.
1878. 176 pp.. . . . . *$100.00–$150.00*

Hinton, S E. *Tex*. NY. Delacorte. (1979). 1st ed. dj. . . . . *$25.00–$50.00*

Hinton, S E. *That Was Then This Is Now.*. NY. (1971). 1st ed. dj. . . *$60.00–$95.00*

Hinton, S E. *The Outsiders*. NY. 1967. 1st ed. dj.. . . . . *$100.00–$250.00*

Hipkins, A J. *Musical Instruments....* Lon. 1945. illus. . . . . *$65.00–$75.00*

Historic Illustrations of the Bible. Lon. Fisher. (1841). illus. 30 engr plates, 3/4 mor.
. . . . *$100.00–$180.00*

History of American Missions to the Heathen. Spooner & Howland. 1840. . . . . . .
. . . . *$45.00–$65.00*

History of Golf in Southern California. (LA). 1925. 1st ed. . . . . *$75.00–$115.00*

History of Kane County. Salt Lake. Daughters of Utah Pioneers. 1970. 1st ed. illus.
photos, maps, scarce.. . . . . *$60.00–$75.00*

History of Los Angeles County. CA. Berkeley. 1959. rprnt map.. . *$95.00–$150.00*

History of Medicine and Surgery and Physicians and Surgeons of Chicago. Chi. 1922. 1st ed. . . . . *$150.00–$200.00*

History of Rock County, Wisconsin. Chi. 1879. 3/4 lea. . . . . *$100.00–$125.00*

History of the 121st Regiment Pennsylvania Volunteers. Phil. 1906. . . . .
. . . . *$50.00–$80.00*

History of the 14th Armored Division. Atlanta. nd. . . . . *$55.00–$65.00*

History of the 157th Infantry Regiment, 4 June, '43 – 8 May, '45. Baton Rouge. 1946. 1st ed. illus. photos, fldg maps. . . . . *$95.00–$130.00*

History of the Connecticut Valley in Massachusetts. Phil. 1879. 2 vols. . . . .
. . . . *$60.00–$80.00*

History of the Fifth Massachusettes Battery. Bos. 1902. . . . . . . *$175.00–$250.00*

History of the Fire & Police Depts of Patterson, N J. Patterson. 1893. 1st ed. illus. plates. . . . . *$48.00–$60.00*

History of the Town of Johnson, VT. Burlington. 1907. . . . . *$20.00–$30.00*

History of the Translations or Rather Versions of the English Bible Anno Domini 1380 to 1611. Alhambra. Braun. 1948. 1st facs ed. . . . . *$50.00–$80.00*

Hitchcock, Edward. *Elementary Geology.* NY. 1845. 3rd ed. . . . . . . *$50.00–$65.00*

Hitchcock, Edward et al. *Report on the Geology of Vermont....* Claremont, NH. 1861. 2 vols. illus. fldng maps. . . . . *$60.00–$100.00*

Hitchens, Robert. *Near East.* Century. 1913. 1st ed. 268 pp, plates. . . . .
. . . . *$60.00–$75.00*

Hitler, Adolf. *My New Order.* NY. (1941). 1st Amer ed dj. . . . . . . *$75.00–$100.00*

Hitt, Thomas. *Treatise on Fruit Trees.* Dublin. 1758. fldg copperplate engr, rbnd. .
. . . . *$250.00–$325.00*

Hobbs, William H. *Characteristics of Existing Glaciers.* NY. Macmillan. 1911. 1st ed. illus. . . . . *$40.00–$60.00*

Hobson, R. L. *Chinese Art.* NY. Macmillan. 1927. illus. clr plates, rbnd, ex lib.. . .
. . . . *$25.00–$50.00*

Hodge, Frederick Webb. *Handbook of American Indians North of Mexico.* DC. GPO. 1907-10. 2 vols. illus. . . . . *$95.00–$150.00*

Hodge, Hirim. *Arizona....* NY. 1877. 1st ed. sgn. . . . . *$175.00–$225.00*

Hoffman, Abbie. *Best of Abbie Hoffman.* NY. Four Walls Eight Windows. 1989. 1st ed. dj. . . . . *$18.00–$30.00*

Hoffman, Abbie. *Square Dancing in the Ice Age.*. NY. Putnam. (1982). 1st ed. . . . .
. . . . *$25.00–$45.00*

Hoffman, Abbie. *Steal This Book.*. NY. Grove Press. 1971. 1st ed. illus. sgn. . . . . .
. . . . *$100.00–$160.00*

Hoffman, Alice. *Property Of.* NY. FSG. (1977). 1st ed. author's first book, inscr, dj.
. . . . *$125.00–$175.00*

Hoffman, E. *The Nutcracker.* NY. 1984. 1st ed. dj. . . . . *$20.00–$45.00*

Hoffman, Heinrich. *Slovenly Peter.* Phila. nd. . . . . *$200.00–$375.00*

Hoffman, Heinrich. *Slovenly Peter.* NY. 1935. ltd 1500 cc. . . . . *$400.00–$600.00*

Hoffman, Professor. *Later Magic.* Routledge. . . . . *$40.00–$64.00*

Hoffman, Professor. *Modern Magic, A Practical Treatise on the Art of Conjuring.*
Phila. nd. illus. 563 pp. . . . . *$60.00–$75.00*

Hoffman, William. *The Monitor.* NY. Carleton Pub. 1863. 1st ed. *$100.00–$125.00*

Hoffman, William. *The Monitor.* NY. 1863. 1st ed. illus. . . . . *$35.00–$100.00*

Holbrook, Florence. *Hiawatha Alphabet.* Chi. Rand McNally & Co. (1910). 1st ed.
illus. by H. D. Pohl, bds, pict pastedown. . . . . *$45.00–$100.00*

Holden, C. F. *Louis Agassiz; His Life and Work.* NY. Putnam. 1893. 1st ed. illus.
plates, cl. . . . . *$40.00–$60.00*

Holden, William Curry. *Spur Ranch.* Bos. (1934). 1st ed. map endpapers. . . . .
. . . . *$200.00–$300.00*

Holder, C. *Life in the Open.* NY. 1906. 1st ed. . . . . *$40.00–$50.00*

Holder, Charles Frederick. *All About Pasadena and Its Vicinity.* Bos. Lee &
Shepard. 1889. 1st ed. illus. . . . . *$90.00–$180.00*

Holder, Charles Frederick. *Along the Forida Reef.* NY. Appleton. 1892. 1st ed. illus.
. . . . *$75.00–$95.00*

Holder, Charles Frederick. *Big Game At Sea.*. Lon. 1908. 1st UK ed. . . . .
. . . . *$200.00–$250.00*

Holder, Charles Frederick. *Cannel Islands of California.* Chi. McClurg. 1910. 1st
ed. illus. . . . . *$90.00–$180.00*

Holder, Charles Frederick. *Game Fishes of the World.* Lon. Hodder & Stoughton.
(1913). illus. . . . . *$165.00–$300.00*

Holder, Charles Frederick. *Santa Catalina, an Isle of Summer.* SF. Murdock. 1895.
1st ed. illus. . . . . *$120.00–$500.00*

Hole, S Reynolds. *Book About Roses.* Lon. Blackwood. 1887. clr frontis. . . . .
. . . .*$35.00–$65.00*

Holiday, Billie. *Lady Sings the Blues.* NY. Doubleday. 1956. 1st ed. 250 pp, dj.. . . .
. . . .*$65.00–$120.00*

Holland, W. J. *Moth Book.* NY. Doubleday Page & Co. 1904. illus. *$45.00–$75.00*

Holley, Marietta. *Samantha on the Race Problem.* NY. Dodd, Mead Co. 1892. illus.
. . . .*$75.00–$100.00*

Holling, H. C. *Book of Indians.* NY. Platt & Munk. (1935). illus. . . *$25.00–$40.00*

Holling, Holling C. *Claws of the Thunderbird.* Joliet. Volland. (1928). illus. by
Holling. . . . .*$40.00–$55.00*

Hollis, A. C. *The Masai.* Oxford. 1905. illus. scarce. . . . .*$125.00–$225.00*

Hollon, W. Eugene. *Beyond the Cross Timbers.* Univ of OK Press. 1955. 1st ed. dj.
. . . .*$30.00–$40.00*

Holloway, Mark. *Heavens on Earth.* Lon. 1951. 1st ed. dj.. . . . . . . *$25.00–$40.00*

Holloway, W. R. *Indiana (Directory).* Ind. 1870. 1st ed. illus. maps, lithos, cl.. . . .
. . . .*$150.00–$175.00*

Holmes, Oliver Wendell. *Autocrat at the Breakfast Table.* Bos. 1894. 2 vols. illus.
by Howard Pyle. . . . .*$25.00–$40.00*

Holmes, Oliver Wendell. *Complete Poetical Works of Oliver Wendell Holmes.* Bos.
Houghton. 1895. illus. teg.. . . . .*$30.00–$65.00*

Holmes, Oliver Wendell. *Grandmother's Story of Bunker Hill.* Bos. 1875. . . . . . .
. . . .*$150.00–$175.00*

Holmes, W. H. *Aboriginal Pottery of the Eastern United States.* DC. GPO. 1903.
dark green cl, clr plates.. . . . .*$90.00–$175.00*

Holmstrom, J. G. *Modern Blacksmithing Rational Horse Shoeing and Waggon
Making.* Lon. 1913. illus. cl. . . . .*$30.00–$50.00*

Holsinger, John B. *Descriptions of Virginia Caves.* VA Div. of Mineral Resources.
1975. illus. b/w photos, maps of caves, 7 fldg maps of cave systems. *$40.00–$50.00*

Holy Bible. NY. American Bible Society. 1838, 1839. 26th ed. . . . . *$30.00–$40.00*

Holy Bible. Hartford. 1845. steel engr, 2 maps. . . . . *$50.00–$75.00*

Holy Bible. Bos. 1812. lea. . . . .*$150.00–$175.00*

Holy Bible. Phila. Berriman & Co. [1796]. folio, calf. . . . .*$100.00–$150.00*

Holy Bible contained in the Old and New Testaments and the Apocrypha. Bos. (1904). 14 vols. illus. full lea. . . . . *$250.00–$300.00*

Holy Bible Explained. Balt. Keatinge. 1808. illus. lea. . . . . *$50.00–$75.00*

Honey, W. B. *German Porcelain.* Lon. Faber & Faber. 1947. 1st ed. folio. . . . .
. . . . *$30.00–$40.00*

Honey, W. B. *Wedgewood Ware.* Lon. Faber & Faber. (1948). dj. . . *$40.00–$50.00*

Hood, Grant. *Modern Methods in Horology.* Bradley Polytechnic Institute. 1944. illus. . . . . *$22.00–$30.00*

Hood, Jennings & Charles J. Young. *American Orders & Societies and Their Decorations..* Phila. 1917. illus. clr plates. *$30.00–$45.00*

Hood, Thomas. *Epping Hunt.* NY. Derrydale Press. 1930. ltd 490 cc, bds.. . . . .
. . . . *$75.00–$100.00*

Hood, Thomas. *Tylney Hall.* Phila. Carey, Lea & Blanchard. 1834. 2. 1st Amer ed. cl-backed bds. . . . . *$200.00–$300.00*

Hook, Sidney. *Reason, Social Myths and Democracy.* NY. 1940. 1st ed. dj.. . . . . . .
. . . . *$25.00–$35.00*

Hooker, William F. *Prairie Schooner.* Chi. 1918. 1st ed. illus. . . . *$60.00–$100.00*

Hooper, Lucy. *Lady's Book of Flowers and Poetry.* Phila. 1863. illus. clr plates. . . .
. . . . *$40.00–$95.00*

Hoover, Herbert. *A Boyhood in Iowa.* NY. 1931. ltd ed. sgn. . . . *$125.00–$150.00*

Hope, Bob. *They Got Me Covered..* Hollywood. 1941. 1st ed. wrps. *$20.00–$30.00*

Hope, Laura Lee. *Bobbsey Twins and Their Schoolmates.* NY. Grosset & Dunlap. 1928. dj. . . . . *$20.00–$30.00*

Hope, Laura Lee. *Bobbsey Twins at Meadowbrook.* NY. Grosset & Dunlap. 1915. Bobbsey Twins #7, dj. . . . . *$22.00–$27.00*

Hope, Laura Lee. *Bobbsey Twins in Cedar Camp.* NY. Grosset & Dunlap. 1921. dj.
. . . . *$20.00–$25.00*

Hope, Laura Lee. *Bobbsey Twins of Lakeport.* NY. Grosset & Dunlap. 1961. #1. . .
. . . . *$7.00–$10.00*

Hope, Laura Lee. *Bobbsey Twins on Blueberry Island.* NY. Grosset & Dunlap. 1917. Bobbsey Twins #10, dj. . . . . *$22.00–$25.00*

Hope, Laura Lee. *Bunny Brown and His Sister Sue Playing Circus.* NY. Grosset & Dunlap. 1916. dj. . . . . *$15.00–$18.00*

Hope, Laura Lee. *In the Land of Cotton.* NY. Grosset & Dunlap. 1942. #35. . . . .
. . . .*$12.00–$22.00*

Hope, Laura Lee. *Outdoor Girls of Cape Cod.* NY. Grosset & Dunlap. 1924. dj. .
. . . .*$25.00–$35.00*

Hope, Laura Lee. *The Bobbsey Twins Camping Out.* NY. Grosset & Dunlap. 1923.
illus. . . . .*$7.00–$23.00*

Hope, Laura Lee. *The Bobbsey Twins on the Deep Blue Sea.* NY. Grosset & Dunlap.
1918. illus. . . . .*$7.00–$10.00*

Hopkins, G. M., Jr. *Map of the Town of Ashburton, Worcester County, Mass.* Phila.
1855. wall map. . . . .*$875.00–$900.00*

Hopkins, John Henry. *Two Discourses on the Second Advent of the Redeemer.*
Burlington, VT. Goodrich. 1843. 3rd ed. wrps.. . . . .*$95.00–$125.00*

Hopkins, Rev. Samuel. *Historical Memoirs Relating to the Housatonic Indians.* NY.
1911. rprnt. . . . .*$60.00–$85.00*

Hopkinson, E. *Records of Birds Bred in Captivity..* Lon. 1926. . . .*$45.00–$60.00*

Hopkinson, F. *Pathetic...Narrative of Miss Perrine.* Phila. 1841. *$900.00–$2,500.00*

Hoppe, Willie. *20 Years of Billiards.* NY. 1925. 1st ed. illus. . . . . .*$30.00–$45.00*

Horan, Jack. *Burnt Leather.* Mon. 1937. wrps. . . . .*$30.00–$40.00*

Horn, Stanley F. *Invisible Empire. The Story of the Ku Klux Klan..* Bos. 1939. 1st
ed. illus. dj. . . . .*$45.00–$60.00*

Hornaday, W. T. *Our Vanishing Wildlife.* NY. Zoological Society. 1913. 1st ed. illus.
. . . .*$20.00–$40.00*

Hornaday, William T. *Campfires in the Canadian Rockies.* NY. Scribner's. 1906. 1st
issue, maps. . . . .*$125.00–$150.00*

Hornbein, Thomas F. *Everest:The West Ridge.* SF. The Sierra Club. 1966. 201 pp,
frontis, clr photos, map. . . . .*$60.00–$75.00*

Horne, Charles F. (ed.) *Great Men and Famous Women.* NY. Selmar Hess Pub.
(1894). 4 vols. 1st ed. illus. 3/4 lea and pebbled cl with gold lettering on cvr and
spine, raised bands, marbled endpapers. . . . .*$90.00–$200.00*

Horne, George. *Pheasant Keeping for Amateurs..* Lon. illus. . . . . .*$55.00–$95.00*

Hornung, Ernest William. *Camera Fiend.* NY. Scribner's. 1911. 1st ed. illus. . . .
. . . .*$90.00–$125.00*

Horst, Claude W. *Model Sail & Power Boats.* NY. Bruce Pub. 1939. illus. photos &
plans (6 fold out), scarce. . . . .*$100.00–$135.00*

Horwich, Frances R. *Ding Dong School Book.* Rand McNally & Co. 1953. 1st ed. illus. pict wrps. . . . . *$15.00–$40.00*

Houdini, Harry. *Miracle Mongers and their Methods.* NY. Dutton. (1920). 1st ed. brown cl. . . . . *$50.00–$60.00*

Hough, Franklin B. *History of Jefferson County in the State of New York....* Albany. 1854. 1st ed. 601 pp, illus. . . . . *$50.00–$100.00*

House, Homer D. *Wildflowers of New York..* Albany. 1918. 2 vols. illus. folio, plates. . . . . *$75.00–$150.00*

Houseman, A. E. *Shropshire Lad.* Lon. (1907). 1st ed. sgn. . . . . *$225.00–$600.00*

Housman, Clemence. *Were-Wolf.* Lon. John Lane. 1896. 1st ed. illus. . . . . *$150.00–$225.00*

Houston, Henry C. *Thirty-second Maine Regiment of Infantry Volunteers.* Portland. Press of the Southworth Bros. 1903. *$35.00–$50.00*

Houston, John W. *Address On The Hist. of the Boundaries of the St. of Delaware..* Wilmington, DE. 1879. 1st ed. wrps. *$35.00–$50.00*

Houston, Julie. *Woman's Day Book of Best Loved Toys & Dolls.* NY. Sedgewood Press. (1982). dj. . . . . *$10.00–$15.00*

Hovey, C. M. *Magazine of Horticulture.* Bos. Hovey. 1893. vol. 29. . . . . *$25.00–$50.00*

Howard, Clark. *Zebra.* NY. Marek. 1979. dj. . . . . *$20.00–$25.00*

Howard, F. E. *English Church Woodwork..* Lon. Batsford. 1917. illus. . . . . *$50.00–$80.85*

Howard, Joseph Kinsey. *Strange Empire.* NY. William Morrow. 1952. illus. dj. . . . . *$15.00–$40.00*

Howard, Maj. Gen. O.O. *Famous Indian Chiefs I Have Known.* Century. 1908. . . . . *$45.00–$55.00*

Howard, Oliver O. *Nez Perce Joseph. An Account of....* Bos. 1881. 1st ed. illus. plates, fldng maps. . . . . *$150.00–$500.00*

Howard, Robert. *Conan the Barbarian.* NY. Gnome Press. 1954. 1st ed. dj. . . . . *$130.00–$400.00*

Howard, Robert. *King Conan.* Gnome Press. (1953). 1st ed. dj.. *$200.00–$300.00*

Howard, Robert. *Singers in the Shadows.* Donald M Grant. 1970. 1st ed. dj. . . . . *$95.00–$150.00*

Howard, Robert. *Sword of Conan.* Gnome Press. 1952. 1st ed. dj. *$65.00–$125.00*

Howe, Julia Ward. *World's Own*. Bos. Ticknor & Fields. 1857. 1st ed. . . . .
. . . . *$175.00–$250.00*

Howell, A. H. *Birds of Alabama*. Montgomery. Dept of Game & Fisheries. 1924.
illus. . . . . *$20.00–$45.00*

Howells, W. D. *Boy's Town*. Harper. 1890. 1st ed. illus. . . . . *$20.00–$30.00*

Hower, Ralph Merle. *History of an Advertising Agency*. Cambridge. 1949. rev ed.
. . . . *$20.00–$45.00*

Howitt, William. *Boy's Adventures in the Wilds of Australia*. Bos. 1855. 1st US ed.
illus. . . . . *$50.00–$65.00*

Howlett, E. *Driving Lessons*. NY. Russell & Son. 1894. 1st ed. illus. . . . .
. . . . *$70.00–$110.00*

Hoyland, John. *Historical Survey of the Customs, Habits & Present State of the
Gypsies*. York. 1816.. 1st ed. 265 pp. . . . . *$225.00–$500.00*

Hrdlicka, Ales. *Tuberculosis Among certain Tribes*. DC. GPO. 1909. wrps. illus. .
. . . . *$25.00–$50.00*

Hrdlicka, Ales. *Early Man in South America*. DC. GPO. 1912. wrps. *$40.00–$50.00*

Hrdlicka, Ales. *Skeletal Remains Suggesting or Attributed to Early Man in North
America*. DC. 1907. illus. bds. . . . . *$28.00–$40.00*

Hubback, T. R. *To Far Western Alaska for Big Game*. Lon. Rowland Ward. 1929. 1st
ed. illus. dec green cl, photos, clr map in pocket. . . . . *$115.00–$250.00*

Hubbard, Clifford L. *Dogs in Britain*. Lon. Macmillan. 1948. 1st ed. illus. dj. . . .
. . . . *$35.00–$65.00*

Hubbard, Elbert. *Little Journeys or the Homes of Great Musicians*. Roycrofters.
1901. ltd 940 cc. sgn. . . . . *$175.00–$200.00*

Hubbard, Henry V., and Theodora Kimball. *An Introduction to the Study of
Landscape Design*. Bos. Hubbard Educatonal Trust. 1967. rev ed. dj. *$22.00–$35.00*

Hubbard, L. Ron. *Battlefield Earth: A Saga of the Year 3000*. St Martin's Press.
(1982). 1st ed. dj. . . . . *$35.00–$45.00*

Hubbard, L. Ron. *Dianetics:The Modern Science of Mental Health*. NY. Hermitage
House. [1950]. 1st ed. dj. . . . . *$125.00–$175.00*

Hubbard, L. Ron. *Slaves of Sleep*. Chi. Shasta Pub. 1948. 1st ed. dj. . . . .
. . . . *$180.00–$400.00*

Hubbard, L. Ron. *The Kingslayer*. LA. Fantasy Publishing Co. 1949. 1st ed. dj. .
. . . . *$85.00–$200.00*

Hubbard, L. Ron. *Triton and Battle of Wizards.* LA. Fantasy Publishing Co. 1949. 1st ed. dj... *$150.00–$200.00*

Hubbard, L. Ron. *Typewriter in the Sky/Fear.* Gnome. 1951. 1st ed. .... *$175.00–$300.00*

Hubbard, W. *Narrative of the Troubles with the Indians in New England....* Bos. 1677. illus. map.................................... *$22,000.00–$45,000.00*

Huddle, David. *Intimates.* Bos. David R. Godine. 1993. 1st ed. dj.. *$20.00–$25.00*

Hudson, Alvin. *Streetcars of Birmingham.* Birmingham. pub by author. wrps. spiral bound, scarce....................................... *$100.00–$135.00*

Hudson, Derek. *Arthur Rackham his life and work.* Lon. Heinemann. 1960. 1st ed. illus. tip-in clr plates.. *$50.00–$75.00*

Hudson, W. H. *Afoot in England.* Lon. 1909. 1st ed. .... *$40.00–$60.00*

Hudson, W. H. *Crystal Age.* NY. Dutton. 1917. .... *$30.00–$35.00*

Hudson, W. H. *Green Mansions.* Phila. 1935. 1500 cc, sgn by illus. *75.00–$100.00*

Hudson, W. H. *Green Mansions.* Lon. Duckworth. 1926. illus. aeg, bound by Bayntun... *$100.00–$150.00*

Huey, Pennock. *True Hist. of the Charge of 8th Pa. Cavalry at Chancelorsville.* Phila. 18851883. 1st ed. illus. .... *$115.00–$145.00*

Huffaker, Clair. *One Time, I Saw Morning Come Home.* NY. 1974. dj, scarce. .... *$25.00–$45.00*

Huffington, Arianna Stassinopoulos. *Picasso Creator and Destroyer.* Franklin Center. Franklin Library. 1988. 1st ed. ltd. sgn, red lea, aeg. ...... *$25.00–$45.00*

Hughes, Dorothy. *Pueblo on the Mesa, the First Fifty Years of the University of New Mexico.* Albuquerque. 1939. 1st ed. illus. photos................ *$50.00–$60.00*

Hughes, Dorothy. *Ride the Pink Horse.* NY. (1946). 1st ed. dj.... *$75.00–$100.00*

Hughes, Elizabeth & Marion Lester. *Big Book of Buttons..* MA. 1991. illus. rprnt. .... *$95.00–$125.00*

Hughes, G. B. *Horse Brasses.* Country Life. 1956. 1st ed. dj...... *$30.00–$40.00*

Hughes, G. B. *Small Antique Silverware.* Batsford. 1957. illus. ... *$25.00–$50.00*

Hughes, Langston. *Book of Negro Humor.* NY. Dodd, Mead. 1966. 1st ed. dj. .... *$40.00–$175.00*

Hughes, Langston. *Fields of Wonder.* NY. Knopf. 1947. 1st ed. dj. *$195.00–$250.00*

Hughes, Langston. *Poems From Black Africa.* Bloomington. 1963. 1st ed. dj. . . . .
. . . .*$35.00–$40.00*

Hughes, Langston. *Simple Stakes of Claim.* NY. Rinehart & Winston. 1957. 1st ed.
dj. . . . .*$75.00–$175.00*

Hughes, Richard B. *Pioneer Years in the Black Hills....* Glendale. Arthur H. Clark.
1957. 1st ed. illus. photos, red cl. . . . .*$75.00–$100.00*

Hult, Ruby E. *Steamboats in the Timber.* Caldwell. Caxton. 1953. 1st ed. illus. photos, dj. . . . .*$35.00–$50.00*

Humphrey Maude. *Babes of the Year.* Stokes. 1888. illus. by author. . . . .
. . . .*$150.00–$250.00*

Humphrey, Maude. *Treasury of Stories, Jingles and Rhymes....* Stokes. 1894. illus.
clr plates. . . . .*$135.00–$160.00*

Humphreys, G. R. *List of Irish Birds.* Dublin. 1939. 5th ed. . . . . . . *$30.00–$45.00*

Humphries, Sydney. *Oriental Carpets.* Lon. Black. 1910. cl, teg, 24 clr plates. . . .
. . . .*$60.00–$80.00*

Hunt, Blanche Seale. *Little Brown Koko.* American Colortype. (1940). 1st ed. . . .
. . . .*$45.00–$65.00*

Hunt, Lynne Bogue. *Our American Game Birds.* NY. Doubleday, Doran. 1941. illus.
dj. . . . .*$35.00–$65.00*

Hunt, Wilson Price. *Overland Diary of Wilson Price Hunt.* Ashland. The Oregon
Book Society. 1973. illus. 600 cc. . . . .*$40.00–$60.00*

Hunter, Alexander. *Women of the Debateable Land.* DC. Corden Publishing. 1912.
1st ed. illus. plates, fldg map, scarce. . . . .*$295.00–$350.00*

Hunter, Dard. *My Life With Paper.* NY. Knopf. 1958. dj. . . . . . . *$100.00–$200.00*

Hunter, Dard. *Papermaking Through Eighteen Centuries.* NY. William Edwin
Rudge. 1930. 1st ed. illus. . . . .*$40.00–$60.00*

Hunter, Dard. *Papermaking: The History and Technique of an Ancient Craft.* NY.
Knopf. 1947. 2nd ed.. . . . .*$90.00–$100.00*

Hunter, George L. *Decorative Furniture.* Phila. 1923. 1st ed. illus. *$75.00–$95.00*

Hunter, J. A and Daniel P. Mannix. *Tales of the African Frontier.* NY. Harper.
(1954). 1st ed. illus. photo plates, dj. . . . .*$45.00–$75.00*

Huntington, Dwight W. *Our Big Game.* NY. Scribner's. 1904. 1st ed.*$40.00–$50.00*

Huntington, Emily. *Cooking Garden.* np. (1885). 1st ed. illus. by Jessie Shepherd.
. . . .*$80.00–$120.00*

Huntington, R. Gen. *Grant's Arabian Horses*. Phil. Lippincott. 1885. 1st ed. illus. plates. . . . . *$225.00–$250.00*

Hurd, D. H. *Town and City Atlas of the State of New Hampshire*. Bos. 1892. Folio. . . . . *$150.00–$250.00*

Hurn, Ethel A. *Wisconsin Women in the War Between the States*. Wisc. (1911). . . . . *$40.00–$60.00*

Huse, Caleb. *Supplies For The Confederate Army*.... Bos. 1904. 1st ed. wrps. . . . . *$150.00–$175.00*

Hussey, John A. (ed.). *Voyage of the Raccoon: A Secret Journal of a Visit to Oregon, California and Hawaii*. SF. Book Club of CA. 1958. illus. drawings, cl-backed marbled bds. . . . . *$50.00–$75.00*

Hutchings, James Mason. *Seeking the Elephant*.... Glendale. Arthur H Clark. 1980. 1st ed. ltd 750 cc, red cl. . . . . *$50.00–$80.00*

Hutchins, Samuel. *Theory Of The Universe*. NY. 1868. . . . . *$60.00–$75.00*

Hutchinson, Francis. *An Historical Essay Concerning Witchcraft*. . Lon. 1718. 1st ed. 3/4 calf. . . . . *$325.00–$400.00*

Hutchinson, Horace G. *Golf*. Lon. 1898. illus. 6th ed. . . . . *$45.00–$50.00*

Hutchinson, Horace G. *Golfing: The Oval Series of Games*. Lon. Rutledge. 1903. 7th ed. . . . . *$60.00–$75.00*

Huxley, Aldous. *Along the Road*. NY. Doran. (1925). bds, lea spine label, ltd 250 cc. sgn. . . . . *$50.00–$75.00*

Huxley, Aldous. *Brave New World*. Lon. Chatto & Windus. 1932. 1st ed. dj. . . . . *$600.00–$1,500.00*

Huxley, Aldous. *Brave New World Revisited*. NY. Harper. 1958. 1st ed. dj. . . . . *$20.00–$50.00*

Huxley, Aldous. *Defeat of Youth & Other Poems*. (Oxford. B. H. Blackwell. 1918). 1st ed. stiff wrps. . . . . *$175.00–$225.00*

Huxley, Aldous. *Eyeless in Gaza*. Lon. Chatto & Windus. 1936. 1st ed. dj. . . . . *$75.00–$150.00*

Huxley, Aldous. *Leda*. NY. Doran. 1920. 1st ed. . . . . *$25.00–$50.00*

Huxley, Aldous. *Point, Counterpoint*. Lon. 1928. 1st UK ed. dj. . . . *$60.00–$90.00*

Huxley, Aldous. *Themes and Variations*. Lon. 1932. 1st ed. dj. . . . *$100.00–$300.00*

Huxley, Aldous. *Time Must Have a Stop*. NY. Harper. 1944. 1st ed. dj. . . . . *$45.00–$150.00*

Huxley, Julian. *Huxley's Diary of the Voyage of H.M.S. Rattlesnake.* NY. Doubleday. 1936. 1st Amer ed. . . . . *$40.00–$50.00*

Huxley, Julian. *Science and Social Needs.* NY. Harper & Brothers. 1935. inscr. . . . . *$30.00–$60.00*

Huxley, Leonard. *Life and Letters of Thomas Henry Huxley.* Lon. 1903. 3 vols. 2nd ed. . . . . *$40.00–$50.00*

Huxley, Thomas. *American Address With a Lecture on the Study of Biology.* NY. 1877. 1st ed. illus. . . . . *$50.00–$75.00*

Huxley, Thomas. *Evidence As To Man's Place in Nature.* Lon. Norgate. 1863. 1st ed. . . . . *$300.00–$600.00*

Huxley, Thomas. *Evidence as to Man's Place in Nature.* NY. Appleton. 1863. 1st Amer ed. . . . . *$120.00–$400.00*

Huxley, Thomas. *Lay Sermons, Addresses & Reviews.* Lon. 1870. . . . . *$30.00–$45.00*

Huxley, Thomas. *Manual of the Anatomy of Invertebrate Animals..* Appleton. 1888. . . . . *$30.00–$50.00*

Huxley, Thomas. *Yoga.* Lon. 1902. 1st ed. wrps. 43 pp. . . . . *$75.00–$100.00*

Hyatt, Arthur H. (ed.). *Book of Sundial Mottoes.* Lon/NY. 1903. 1st ed. aeg. . . . . *$60.00–$90.00*

Hyatt, Rebecca Dougherty. *"Marthy Law's Kiverlid."* pub by author. (1937). . . . . *$25.00–$35.00*

Hyer, J. K., W. Starring, and A. Hann. *Dictionary of the Sioux Language.* New Haven. 1968. ltd 300 cc. . . . . *$75.00–$100.00*

Ibsen, Henrik. *Doll's House.* NY. 1889. 1st Amer. . . . . *$25.00–$35.00*

Ibsen, Henrik. *Peer Gynt.* Garden City. 1929. 1st ed. . . . . *$50.00–$75.00*

Igloo Life. Revillon Freres Fur Co.. 1923. 1st ed. pict bds. . . . . *$25.00–$35.00*

Illustrated Catalogue of Iron Toys. Fullerton, PA. Dent Hardware Co. c 1900. pict wrps, 39 pp.. . . . . *$75.00–$100.00*

Illustrated Catalogue of Lightning Conductors. Nottingham, England. Blackburn, Starling & Co, Ltd. 1924. pict wrps, 8 pp. . . . . *$50.00–$75.00*

Illustrated Catalogue of School Merchandise. Bos. J L Hammett. 1872-73. printed wrps, illus. . . . . *$150.00–$125.00*

Illustrated Catalogue of US Cartridge Company's Collection of Firearms. MA. c1903. illus. 140 pp. . . . . *$50.00–$75.00*

Illustrated List of Bride Cakes. Chester, England. Bolland & Sons. c1893. beige wrps, 44 pp.. . . . . *$50.00–$75.00*

Illustrated Memoir of the World War. CT. National Pub. Co. 1930. 1st ed. illus. folio, presentation copy. . . . . *$12.00–$25.00*

Illustrated Catalogue Of Railway And Contractors Supplies. Buda Foundry & Mfg Co. 1902. illus. cat. . . . . *$75.00–$125.00*

Imray, James. *Sailing Directions for the English Channel, the Bristol Channel, and South & South West Coasts of Ireland.* Lon. Imray. 1850. illus. . . . . . *$50.00–$80.00*

Indian Narratives. *Containing a Correct and Interesting History of the Indian Wars.* Claremont. 1854. . . . . *$55.00–$75.00*

Ingalls, Albert G. (ed.). *Amateur Telescope Making.* NY. Scientific American, Inc. 1970. 3 vols. . . . . *$50.00–$75.00*

Inge, William. *Dark at the Top of the Stairs.* NY. (1958). 1st ed. dj. *$30.00–$40.00*

Inge, William. *Dark at the Top of the Stairs.* NY. Random House. (1958). 1st ed. dj. . . . . *$75.00–$125.00*

Ingersoll, C. J. *Discourse Concerning the Influence of America on the Mind.* Phila. 1823. . . . . *$50.00–$75.00*

Ingersoll, Ernest. *Crest of the Continent.* Chi. 1885. 1st ed. frontis, engr. . . . . *$25.00–$40.00*

Ingersoll, Ernest. *Goldfields of the Klondike and the Wonders of Alaska.* Edgewood. . . . . *$45.00–$60.00*

Ingham, George Thomas. *Digging Gold Among the Rockies.* Phila. 1888. illus. . . . . *$50.00–$90.00*

Ingraham, I. (ed.). *Sunny South or Southerner at Home.* 1860. 1st ed. . . . . *$100.00–$250.00*

Inman, Col. Henry. *Old Santa Fe Trail, Story of a Great Highway.* Topeka. 1916. illus. . . . . *$25.00–$35.00*

Inman, Henry. *Great Salt Lake Trail.* NY. 1898. 1st ed. illus. 529 pp, plates. . . . . *$75.00–$100.00*

Inn, Henry. *Chinese Houses and Gardens.* Honolulu. 1940. illus. ltd 2000 cc, sgn. . . . . *$50.00–$85.00*

Instructions for Voluntary Observers of the Signal Service, United States Army. DC. GPO. 1882. illus. 108 pp.. . . . . *$35.00–$55.00*

Investigation of the Fur-Seal and Other Fisheries of Alaska. DC. GPO. 1889. illus. photos, maps. . . . . *$40.00–$80.00*

Ipsen, Ludvig S. *Book Plates*. Bos. 1904. illus. . . . . *$75.00–$100.00*

Iron Toys. PA. Dent Hardware. wrps. illus. cat. . . . . *$48.00–$55.00*

Irving, John. *158-Pound Marriage*. NY. Random House. (1974). 1st ed. inscr with full-page self-caricature in wrestling mode, dj. . . . . *$350.00–$800.00*

Irving, John. *Hotel New Hampshire*. 1981. 1st ed. dj. . . . . *$35.00–$60.00*

Irving, John. *Widow for One Year*. NY. Randon House. (1998). 1st ed. dj. . . . .
. . . . *$20.00–$40.00*

Irving, John. *World According to Garp*. NY. Dutton. 1978. 1st ed. dj. *$75.00–$200.00*

Irving, John Treat. *Indian Sketches Taken During an Expedition to the Pawnee....* Phila. 1835. 2 vols. 1/2 mor. . . . . *$150.00–$235.00*

Irving, Washington. *A Tour on the Prairies*. Phila. 1835. . . . . . . *$100.00–$400.00*

Irving, Washington. *Astoria or Anecdotes of an Enterprise Beyond Rocky Mountains*. Phila. 1836. 2 vols. 1st Amer ed. . . . . *$350.00–$500.00*

Irving, Washington. *Legends of the Alhambra*. Phil/Lon. Lippincott. 1909. illus. George Hood. blue cl, pict pastedown. . . . . *$25.00–$50.00*

Irving, Washington. *Rip Van Winkle*. David McKay. (1921). illus. by N. C. Wyeth.
. . . . *$75.00–$150.00*

Irving, Washington. *Rip Van Winkle*. Phila. David McKay. (1921). illus. front cvr pastedown by Wyeth, 8 clr plates. . . . . *$100.00–$150.00*

Irving, Washington. *Works of Washington Irving*. NY. Putnam. (1895). 40 vols. lea marbled bds. . . . . *$1,000.00–$2,000.00*

Irwin, W. *Highlights of Manhattan*. NY. (1927). 1st ed. illus. . . . . . *$20.00–$50.00*

Isaacs, Edith J. R. *Negro in the American Theatre*. NY. Theatre Arts, Inc. 1947. illus. photos, 143 pp. . . . . *$35.00–$50.00*

Isadora Duncan, Twenty-four Studies by Arnold Genthe. NY. Mitchell Kennerly. 1929. 1st ed. teg. . . . . *$125.00–$175.00*

Isherwood, Christopher. *Berlin of Sally Bowles*. Lon. Hogarth. 1975. 1st collected ed. dj. . . . . *$50.00–$75.00*

Isherwood, Christopher. *Condor and the Cows*. NY. 1949. 1st Amer ed. . . . .
. . . . *$40.00–$55.00*

Isherwood, Christopher. *Exhumations*. NY. 1966. 1st ed. dj. . . . . . *$25.00–$40.00*

Isherwood, Christopher. *Prater Violet*. Lon. Methuen & Co. 1946. 1st ed. dj. . . .
. . . . *$50.00–$75.00*

Isherwood, Christopher. *Single Man*. NY. 1964. 1st ed. dj. . . . . . . *$25.00–$35.00*

J. S. Lothrop's Champaign County Directory 1870–71.... Chi. 1871. illus. fldg map.
. . . . *$55.00–$75.00*

Jackson, C. *Foreign Bodies in the Air and Food Passages*. MA. 1924. . . . .
. . . . *$50.00–$75.00*

Jackson, Frederick G. *Thousand Days in the Arctic.*. NY. 1899. 1st ed. illus. fldg
maps.. . . . . *$85.00–$140.00*

Jackson, Helen Hunt. *Glimpses of California and the Missions*. Bos. Little, Brown.
1914. plates. . . . . *$35.00–$40.00*

Jackson, Helen Hunt (H. H.). *Ramona*. Roberts Bros. 1884. 1st ed. green cl. . . . . .
. . . . *$150.00–$375.00*

Jackson, Helen Hunt][. *Sonnets & Lyrics*. Bos. 1886. 1st ed. cl. . . *$30.00–$75.00*

Jackson, Jesse. *Tessie*. NY. Harper & Row. 1968. 1st ed. dj. . . . . . . *$25.00–$35.00*

Jackson, Leroy F. *Peter Patter Book*. Chi. Rand McNally. 1918. 1st ed. illus. green
bds with pict pastedown. . . . . *$35.00–$95.00*

Jackson, Sheldon. *Alaska and the Missions on the North Pacific Coast*. NY. 1880.
engr, 400 pp, map.. . . . . *$50.00–$125.00*

Jackson, Shirley. *Bird's Nest*. NY. Farrar, Straus, Young. [1954]. 1st ed. 276 pp, dj..
. . . . *$50.00–$100.00*

Jackson, Shirley. *Haunting of Hill House*. NY. 1959. 1st ed. dj. . . . .
. . . . *$150.00–$475.00*

Jackson, Shirley. *Road Through the Wall*. NY. Farrar, Straus. 1948. 1st ed. dj,
author's scarce first book. . . . . *$200.00–$375.00*

Jackson, Shirley. *The Lottery*. 1949. 1st ed. dj.. . . . . *$150.00–$225.00*

Jackson, Shirley. *The Sundial*. NY. Farrar, Straus & Cudahy. (1958). 1st ed. dj. . . .
. . . . *$65.00–$100.00*

Jackson, Shirley. *We Have Always Lived in the Castle*. NY. Viking. (1962). 1st ed.
dj. . . . . *$65.00–$85.00*

Jacobs, Flora Gill. *Dolls' Houses in America*. NY. Scribner's. (1974). 1st ed. illus.
dj. . . . . *$35.00–$60.00*

Jacobs, Flora Gill. *History of Doll's Houses Four Centuries of the Domestic World
in Miniature*. NY. Scribner's. 1953. 1st ed. dj. . . . . *$40.00–$50.00*

Jacobs, Laura. *Barbie What a Doll!*. NY. Artabras. (1994). 1st ed. illus. dj. . . . . . .
. . . . *$15.00–$25.00*

Jacobs, Michael. *Rebel Invasion of Maryland, Penn. & Battle of Gettysburg.* Gettysburg. 1909. wrps. . . . . *$35.00–$40.00*

Jacobs, T. C. H. *Sinister Quest.* NY. Macaulay. 1934. 1st Amer ed. dj. . . . .
. . . . *$50.00–$65.00*

Jacobsen, Carol L. *Past and Present Portrait of Dolls.* CA. Mandarin Pub. sgn, dj.
. . . . *$20.00–$25.00*

Jacques, Brian. *Castaways of the Flying Dutchman.* NY. 2001. 1st ed. dj. . . . . . .
. . . . *$10.00–$12.00*

Jacques, Brian. *Pearls of Lutra.* Philomel. 1997. 1st ed. dj. . . . . . . *$12.00–$15.00*

James, Cyril Lionel Robert. *History of Negro Revolt.* Lon. Fact. 1938. 1st ed. wrps.
. . . . *$75.00–$125.00*

James, Edgar. *Allen Outlaws and Their Career of Crime....* Balt. 1912. 1st ed. wrps.
illus. . . . . *$45.00–$55.00*

James, G. W. *Practical Basket Making.* Pasadena. nd. illus. . . . . *$100.00–$125.00*

James, George W. *Through Ramona's Country.* Bos. 1909. 1st ed. *$55.00–$65.00*

James, George W. *What the White Race May Learn from the Indian.* Chi. Forbes & Co. 1908. illus. . . . . *$85.00–$100.00*

James, George Wharton. *Grand Canyon of Arizona.* Bos. Little, Brown. 1910. fldg map. . . . . *$65.00–$175.00*

James, George Wharton. *Indian Basketry.* Rio Grande Press. (1970). 3rd ed. . . . .
. . . . *$25.00–$35.00*

James, George Wharton. *Indian Blankets and Their Makers.* NY. 1937. new ed. .
. . . . *$75.00–$100.00*

James, George Wharton. *Utah The Land of Blossoming Valleys.* Bos. 1922. 1st ed. illus. clr. . . . . *$65.00–$115.00*

James, Henry. *Bostonians.* Lon. 1886. 3 vols. boxed.. . . . . *$900.00–$1,500.00*

James, Henry. *Bostonians.* Lon/NY. Macmillan. (1886). 1st Amer ed. 1 vol. . . . . .
. . . . *$150.00–$250.00*

James, Henry. *Daisy Miller.* Lon. Macmillan. 1879. 2 vols. 1st UK ed.. . . . .
. . . . *$300.00–$400.00*

James, Henry. *Ghostly Tales of Henry James.* New Brunswick. Rutgers Univ Press. 1948. dj. . . . . *$35.00–$45.00*

James, Henry. *Letters of Henry James.* NY. Scribner's. 1920. 1st Amer ed. illus. .
. . . . *$25.00–$40.00*

James, Henry. *Notebooks of Henry James*. NY. 1947. 1st ed. cl dj.. *$45.00–$50.00*

James, Henry. *Roderick Hudson*. Bos. Osgood. 1876. 1st ed. green cl. author's first novel. . . . . *$60.00–$90.00*

James, Henry. *Siege of London*. Bos. Osgood. 1883. 1st ed. green cl. . . . .
. . . . *$225.00–$300.00*

James, Henry. *The Ambassadors*. NY. 1903. 1st Amer ed. dj. . . . *$100.00–$300.00*

James, Henry. *Washington Square*. NY. Harper. 1881. 1st ed. illus. by George Du Maurier.. . . . . *$100.00–$275.00*

James, Henry. *What Maisie Knew*. Chi/NY. Herbert S. Stone. 1897. 1st Amer ed.. .
. . . . *$100.00–$200.00*

James, Jesse, Jr. *Jesse James, My Father*.. Missouri. 1899. wrps. *$100.00–$300.00*

James, P. D. *A Certain Justice*. Lon. Faber and Faber. 1997. 1st ed. dj. . . . .
. . . . *$40.00–$45.00*

James, P. D. *A Certain Justice*. NY. Knopf. 1997. 1st ed. sgn, dj. . . *$30.00–$45.00*

James, P. D. *Children of Men*. NY. Knopf. 1993. 1st Amer ed. sgn, dj. . . . .
. . . . *$30.00–$50.00*

James, P. D. *Death of an Expert Witness*. Lon. Faber & Faber. 1977. 1st ed. sgn, dj.
. . . . *$100.00–$150.00*

James, P. D. *Innocent Blood*. Lon. Faber & Faber. 1980. 1st ed. sgn, dj. . . . .
. . . . *$50.00–$125.00*

James, P. D. *Innocent Blood*. NY. Scribner's. 1980. 1st ed. 1st Amer ed. dj.. . . . . .
. . . . *$20.00–$35.00*

James, P. D. *Skull Beneath the Skin*. NY. 1982. 1st ed. dj.. . . . . *$15.00–$30.00*

James, P. D. *Solomon's Vineyard*. Santa Barbara. Neville. 1982. 1st Amer ed. ltd 300 numbered cc, sgn. . . . . *$60.00–$80.00*

James, P. D. *Taste for Death*. Lon. 1986. 1st ed. sgn, dj.. . . . . *$75.00–$100.00*

James, P. D. *The Black Tower*. Lon. Faber & Faber. 1975. 1st ed. dj.. . . . .
. . . . *$100.00–$150.00*

James, P. D. *The Mink-lined Coffin*. Lon. Methuen. 1960. 1st UK ed.dj. . . . .
. . . . *$100.00–$135.00*

James, P. D. *Ticktock*. Lon. Headline. 1996. 1st ed. dj. . . . . *$70.00–$90.00*

James, P. D. and T. A. Critchley. *Maul and the Pear Tree: the Ratcliff Murders 1811*. NY. Mysterious Press. 1986. dj.. . . . . *$15.00–$20.00*

James, Weldon Johnson. *God's Trombones*. NY. Viking. (1927). illus. no dj. . . . .
. . . . *$30.00–$60.00*

James, Will. *Big Enough*. NY. Scribner's. 1931. illus. by author.. . . *$35.00–$50.00*

James, Will. *Cow Country*. NY. Scribner's. 1927. illus. . . . . *$100.00–$185.00*

James, Will. *Dark Horse*. NY. Scribner's. 1939. 1st ed. illus. cl, col frontis.. . . . . .
. . . . *$100.00–$175.00*

James, Will. *Home Ranch*. Cleve. World Pub. (1945). illus. . . . . . . *$20.00–$40.00*

James, Will. *Lone Cowboy*. NY. Scribner's. 1930. illus. by author, frontis. . . . . . .
. . . . *$40.00–$100.00*

James, Will. *Lone Cowboy: My Life Story*. NY. Scribner's. 1930. 1st ed. illus. by
author, dj. . . . . *$150.00–$250.00*

James, Will. *Sand*. NY. Grosset & Dunlap. (1929). . . . . *$10.00–$20.00*

James, Will. *Sun Up*. NY. Scribner's. 1931. illus. . . . . *$24.00–$45.00*

James, Will. *Three Mustangeers*. NY. 1933. 1st ed. . . . . *$45.00–$65.00*

James, William. *Will to Believe*. NY. 1897. 1st ed. . . . . *$200.00–$300.00*

Jane's Fighting Ships. 1971. . . . . *$20.00–$30.00*

Jane's Fighting Ships. 1920. . . . . *$85.00–$100.00*

Jane, Fred T. *Imperial Russian Navy*. Lon. 1899. illus. . . . . *$125.00–$200.00*

Jansen, Murk. *Feebleness of Growth & Congenital Dwarfism....* Lon. 1921. 1st ed.
. . . . *$60.00–$80.00*

Janvier, T. A. *Aztec Treasure-House*. NY. 1890. 1st ed. . . . . *$50.00–$75.00*

Janvier, Thomas A. *In the Sargasso Sea*. NY. Harper. 1898. 1st ed. *$30.00–$45.00*

Japan Imperial Government Railways Guide. Tokyo. 1915. 62 pp, maps, illus.. . . .
. . . . *$40.00–$45.00*

Jarrell, Randall. *Pictures from an Institution*. NY. Knopf. 1954. 1st ed. dj. . . . . . .
. . . . *$35.00–$75.00*

Jarrell, Randall. *Third Book of Criticism*. NY. Farrar, Straus & Giroux. (1969). 1st
ed. dj. . . . . *$45.00–$60.00*

Jay, William. *Inquiry Into Character & Tendency of American Anti-Slavery Soc*.
1838. 6th ed. . . . . *$40.00–$50.00*

Jay, William. *Review of the Causes and Consequences of the Mexican War*. Fos.
Benjamin B Murray & Co. 1849. 1st ed. inscr.. . . . . *$140.00–$200.00*

Jay, William. *View of the Action of the Federal Government, In Behalf of Slavery.* NY. 1839. green cl, 217 pp. . . . . *$75.00–$175.00*

Jeans, James. *New Background of Science.* NY. Macmillan. 1933. . *$15.00–$25.00*

Jeans, James. *Through Space and Time.* NY. Macmillan. 1934. . . . *$15.00–$40.00*

Jeffers, Robinson. *Dear Judas and Other Poems.* NY. Liveright. 1929. 1st ed. ltd 375 cc, sgn, slipcase. . . . . *$250.00–$300.00*

Jeffers, Robinson. *Such Counsels You Gave to Me.* NY. 1937. . . . *$65.00–$150.00*

Jefferson, Joseph. *Autobiography of Joseph Jefferson.* NY. 1890. . *$20.00–$30.00*

Jefferson, Joseph. *Life and Morals of Jesus of Nazareth.* DC. GPO. 1904. facs. . . . . *$70.00–$150.00*

Jeffrey, William H. *Richmond Prisons 1861-62.* St. Johnsbury, VT. nd. 1st ed. . . . . *$75.00–$100.00*

Jeffries, Richard. *Gamekeeper at Home.* Lon. Smith, Elder. 1892. new ed. illus.. . . . . *$35.00–$60.00*

Jeffries, Richard. *Gamekeeper at Home.* Bos. 1880. aeg, illus.. . . . *$40.00–$50.00*

Jehl, Francis. *Menlo Park - Reminiscences.* Dearborn, MI. Edison Insitute. 1937. 3 vols. 1st complete ed. stiff wrps. . . . . *$500.00–$150.00*

Jehl, Francis. *Menlo Park: Reminiscences.* Dearborn, MI. Edison Institute. 1936. 2 parts in one vol, 430 pp, dj. . . . . *$60.00–$85.00*

Jekyll, Gertrude. *Children and Gardens.* Lon. 1908. . . . . *$35.00–$50.00*

Jekyll, Gertrude. *Gardener's Testament.* Lon. Country Life. (1937). 1st ed. illus. . . . . *$75.00–$90.00*

Jekyll, Gertrude. *Home and Garden.* Lon. Longmans, Green. 1901. illus. new ed. . . . . *$50.00–$90.00*

Jekyll, Gertrude. *Lilys for English Gardens.* Covent Garden. 1901. 1st ed. . . . . *$60.00–$75.00*

Jekyll, Gertrude. *Old West Surrey.* Lon. 1904. 1st ed. photos. . . *$100.00–$150.00*

Jekyll, Gertrude. *Wood and Garden.* Lon. Longmans, Green. 1899. illus. 4th impression.. . . . . *$100.00–$150.00*

Jellicoe, Viscount. *Crisis of the Naval War.* NY/Lon. 1920. illus. plates, pocket charts. . . . . *$40.00–$65.00*

Jenkins, C. Francis. *Boyhood of an Inventor.* DC. 1931. inscr.. . . *$85.00–$110.00*

Jenkins, Dan. *Best 18 Golf Holes in America.* NY. 1966. 1st ed. dj. *$22.00–$32.00*

Jenness, Diamond. *Indians of Canada.* Ottawa. Nat'l Museum of Canada. 1955. illus. red cl. . . . . *$35.00–$65.00*

Jennings, John. *Salem Frigate.* NY. Doubleday & Co. (1946). 1st ed. gray green cl dj. . . . . *$15.00–$25.00*

Jennings, John. *Shadow and the Glory.* NY. Reynal & Hitchcock. (1943). 1st ed. blue dec cl dj. . . . . *$15.00–$25.00*

Jennings, N. A. *Texas Ranger.* NY. Scribner's. 1899. 1st ed. 321 pp, glassine dj. . . . . *$150.00–$500.00*

Jennings, Preston J. *Book of Trout Flies.* NY. Crown. 1935. 1st trade ed. . . . . *$20.00–$45.00*

Jennings, Preston J. *Book of Trout Flies.* Derrydale Press. 1935. ltd 850, numbered. . . . . *$250.00–$375.00*

Jennings, Robert. *Horse and His Diseases.* Phila. 1860. 1st ed. illus. . . . . *$25.00–$35.00*

Jensen, Gerald E. *Early American Dollhouse Miniatures.* PA. Chilton Book Co. (1981). 1st ed. dj. . . . . *$20.00–$25.00*

Jenson, Andrew. *Historical Record, a Monthly Periodical.* Salt Lake. vol. 7-9. 1st ed. . . . . *$100.00–$150.00*

Jenyns, Soame. *A View of the Internal Evidence of the Christian Religion.* Phila. Crukshank. 1788. . . . . *$150.00–$190.00*

Jessee, Dean C., (comp. & ed.). *Personal Writings of Joseph Smith.* Salt Lake. 1985. illus. photos, dj. . . . . *$50.00–$65.00*

Jessup, Henry Harris. *Women of the Arabs.* NY. Dodd, Mead. (1973). illus. green dec cl. . . . . *$75.00–$125.00*

Jewett, Charles. *Speeches, Poems and Miscellaneous Writings on...Temperance and Liquor Traffic.* Bos. Jewett. 1849. 1st ed. illus. 200pp. . . . . *$75.00–$100.00*

Jewett, Paul. *New England Farrier.* Exeter. 1826. 4th ed. . . . . . . *$130.00–$165.00*

Jewett, Sarah Orne. *Country By-Ways.* Bos. Houghton, Mifflin. 1881. 1st ed. 249 pp, green cl, 2000 cc printed. . . . . *$125.00–$150.00*

Jewett, Sarah Orne. *Country of the Pointed Firs.* Bos. Houghton Mifflin. 1896. 1st ed. ltd 984 cc. . . . . *$120.00–$155.00*

Jewett, Sarah Orne. *Deephaven.* Bos. 1877. 1st ed. cl. . . . . *$30.00–$45.00*

Jillson, Willard R. *Coal Industry in Kentucky: An Historical Sketch..* Frankfort. 1922. 1st ed. illus. . . . . *$35.00–$50.00*

Jobe, Joseph. *Great Age of Sail.* Switzerland. Lausanne. (1976). illus. trans. by Michael Kelly, slipcase. . . . . *$50.00–$100.00*

Jobe, Joseph. *Great Tapestries.* Lausanne. 1965. large folio, dj, slipcase. . . . .
. . . . *$50.00–$60.00*

Jocelyn, Stephen Perry. *Mostly Alkali: A Biography.* Caldwell. Caxton Printers. 1953. 1st ed. illus. photos, map. . . . . *$35.00–$50.00*

Johl, Janet Pagter. *Still More About Dolls.* NY. H. L Lindquist. (1950). 1st ed. illus. dj. . . . . *$25.00–$75.00*

Johl, Janet Pagter. *Your Dolls and Mine.* NY. H. L. Lindquist. 1952. 1st ed. illus. dj, sgn. . . . . *$45.00–$60.00*

John F Kennedy Memorial Miniature.. . . NY. Random House. (1966). 4 vols. 1st ed. illus. by Jan Menting, cl, slipcase. . . . . *$60.00–$100.00*

Johns, Henry T. *Life with the Forty-ninth Massachusetts Volunteers.* Pittsfield, MA. Alvord. 1864. . . . . *$125.00–$150.00*

Johns, Rowland. *Our Friend the Scottish Terrier.* NY. (1933). 1st ed. dj. . . . .
. . . . *$15.00–$22.00*

Johnson's California, Territories of New Mexico and Utah. 1864. . . . .
. . . . *$160.00–$175.00*

Johnson's Illustrated Family Atlas. NY. 1863. folio. . . . . *$385.00–$425.00*

Johnson's New Illustrated Family Atlas of the World. NY. 1865. folio, mor, maps. .
. . . . *$600.00–$750.00*

Johnson, Audrey. *Furnishing Dolls' Houses.* Long. G Bell & Sons Ltd. 1972. 1st ed. illus. dj. . . . . *$25.00–$50.00*

Johnson, Burges. *Lost Art of Profanity.* Ind. Bobbs-Merrill. 1948. 1st ed. dj. . . . . .
. . . . *$30.00–$40.00*

Johnson, Clifton. *Highways and Byways of the Mississippi Valley.* Macmillan. 1906. 1st ed. . . . . *$35.00–$50.00*

Johnson, Clifton. *Picturesque Hudson.* NY. 1909. 1st ed. illus. . . . *$25.00–$35.00*

Johnson, Edward, M.D. *Hydropathy.* Lon. 1843. illus. . . . . *$60.00–$80.00*

Johnson, G. *Ante-Bellum North Carolina.* 1937. . . . . *$60.00–$75.00*

Johnson, Harold. *Who's Who in the American League.* 1935. . . . . *$27.00–$35.00*

Johnson, Haynes. *Bay of Pigs.* NY. W. W. Norton. 1964. illus. maps, dj. . . . .
. . . . *$20.00–$30.00*

Johnson, Helen Kendrick. *Woman and the Republlic*. NY. 1897. 1st ed. 327 pp. .
. . . . *$65.00–$75.00*

Johnson, Ithiel. *Story of My Life*. Vt. Free Press. 1912. illus. green cl.. . . . .
. . . . *$15.00–$20.00*

Johnson, J. H. *Great Western Gun Works*. 1873. cat.. . . . . *$95.00–$150.00*

Johnson, James R. *Treatise on the Medicinal Leech*. Lon. Longman, Hurst, Rees, Orme, and Brown. 1816. 1st ed. lib stamps, 147 pp, scarce. . . . . . *$225.00–$450.00*

Johnson, James Weldon. *God's Trombones*. NY. 1927. 1st ed. . *$250.00–$300.00*

Johnson, James Weldon (ed.). *Book of American Negro Spirituals*. NY. 1925. . . .
. . . . *$50.00–$70.00*

Johnson, Martin. *Safari*. NY. 1928. illus. . . . . *$35.00–$40.00*

Johnson, Merle. *American First Editions*. NY. 1936. 3rd ed. . . . . . *$25.00–$30.00*

Johnson, Merle. *Bibliography of the Works of Mark Twain*. NY. 1935. rev ed. dj. .
. . . . *$60.00–$80.00*

Johnson, Richard M. *Biographical Sketch of Col Richard M Johnson of Kentucky. By a Kentuckian*. NY. 1843. 1st ed. pict wrps, sewn, 46 pp. . . . . . . *$150.00–$200.00*

Johnson, Samuel. *The Idler*. Lon. Davis. 1767. 2 vols. 3rd ed. 1st ed in book form.
. . . . *$200.00–$250.00*

Johnson, Sir Harry H. & K. C. B. *British Central Africa*. Lon. Methuen & Co. 1897. 1st ed. maps, illus. . . . . *$300.00–$350.00*

Johnson, W. Fletcher. *Life of Sitting Bull and History of the Indian War of 1890-91*. Edgewood Publishing Co. 1891. 1st ed. illus. . . . . *$40.00–$50.00*

Johnson, Walter R. *Report to the Navy Dept. of the U.S. on American Coals....* DC. GPO. 1844. 1st ed. . . . . *$60.00–$75.00*

Johnston, Carol. *Thomas Wolfe: A Descriptive Biography*. Pitts. Univ Pittsburgh Press. 1987. 1st ed. illus. . . . . *$60.00–$75.00*

Johnston, F. B. & T. T. Waterman. *Early Architecture of North Carolina.*. Univ of N.C. 1947. 2nd prtg, folio, plates. . . . . *$150.00–$200.00*

Johnston, Harry H. *Uganda Protectorate*. NY. Dodd, Mead. 1904. 2 vols. 2nd enlarged ed. illus. 48 clr plates, 9 maps, 1/2 red mor, teg. . . . . . . *$300.00–$375.00*

Johnston, Mary. *The Witch.*. Bos. Houghton Mifflin. 1914. dj.. . . . *$30.00–$40.00*

Johnston, Mary. *To Have and To Hold*. Bos. Houghton Mifflin. 1900. 1st ed. illus.
. . . . *$45.00–$60.00*

Johnstone, Annie Fellows. *Ole Mammy's Torment*. Bos. 1897. . . . *$25.00–$45.00*

Jolly Jump-ups and Their New House. MA. McLoughlin Bros. 1939. 6 pop-ups. . .
. . . . *$30.00–$40.00*

Jolly Jump-Ups Favorite Nursery Stories. McLoughlin Bros. 1942. pict bds, pop-up
stories.. . . . . *$45.00–$95.00*

Jolly, Ellen Ryan. *Nuns of the Battlefield.* [Providence, RI]. Providence Visitor Press.
1927. 1st ed. 336 pp.. . . . . *$45.00–$65.00*

Jones, Bobby. *Golf is My Game.* NY. 1960. 1st ed. dj. . . . . *$30.00–$40.00*

Jones, Charles C., Jr. *Negro Myths from the Georgia Coast told in the Vernacular.*
Bos. Houghton Mifflin. 1888. 1st ed. 171 pp. . . . . *$150.00–$250.00*

Jones, Howard. *Key For the Identification of Nests and Eggs of Common Birds.* OH.
1927. wrps. . . . . *$25.00–$30.00*

Jones, J. William. *Christ in The Camp or Religion in Lee's Army.* B F Johnston.
1887. b/w illus. . . . . *$60.00–$75.00*

Jones, James. *From Here to Eternity.* NY. 1951. 1st ed. author's first book, dj. . . . .
. . . . *$130.00–$150.00*

Jones, James. *Some Came Running.* NY. Scribner's. (1957). 1st ed. dj. . . . .
. . . . *$45.00–$85.00*

Jones, Laurence Clifton. *Piney Woods and Its Story.* Revell. 1922. 1st ed. illus. . .
. . . . *$15.00–$35.00*

Jones, LeRoi. *Dutchman and The Stone.* NY. William Morrow. 1964. 1st ed. dj. . . . .
. . . . *$30.00–$50.00*

Jones, LeRoi (aka Imamu Amiri Baraka). *Raise: Essays Since 1965.* NY. Random
House. 1971. 1st ed. dj.. . . . . *$25.00–$35.00*

Jones, N. E. *Squirrel Hunters of Ohio....* Cinc. 1898. 1st ed. illus. . *$70.00–$85.00*

Jones, P. *Annals and Recollections of Oneida County..* Rome, NY. 1851. . . . .
. . . . *$60.00–$80.00*

Jones, Robert Edmond. *Drawings for the Theatre.* NY. 1925. . . . . *$60.00–$80.00*

Jones, Thomas. *Experience of Thomas Jones... a Slave For Forty-Three Years.* Bos.
1850. wrps. 2nd ed.. . . . . *$50.00–$85.00*

Jones, Virgil Carrington. *Ranger Mosby.* Chapel Hill. (1944). 1st ed. . . . .
. . . . *$40.00–$85.00*

Jones, William A. *Report Upon the Reconnaissance of Northwestern Wyoming....*
DC. GPO. 1874. illus. 56 fldg lith plates.. . . . . *$100.00–$140.00*

Jones, Winfield. *Story of the Ku Klux Klan.* DC. (1921). 107 pp.. . . . .
. . . . *$150.00–$175.00*

Jong, Erica. *At The Edge of the Body*. NY. Holt, Rinehart & Winston. 1979. 1st ed. dj. . . . . *$9.00–$20.00*

Jong, Erica. *Fear of Flying*. NY. Holt, Rinehart. 1973. 1st ed. sgn, dj. . . . . *$95.00–$125.00*

Jong, Erica. *Fear of Flying*. NY. 1973. dj. . . . . *$35.00–$45.00*

Jong, Erica. *Loveroot*. NY. 1975. 1st ed. dj. . . . . *$35.00–$45.00*

Jordan, David Starr & Barton Warren Evermann. *American Food and Game Fishes....* NY. Doubleday, Page. 1903. illus. chromo plates. . . . . . . *$40.00–$60.00*

Jordan, J. *Elephants & Ivory*. NY. Rinehart & Co. 1956. 1st ed. illus. dj. . . . . *$30.00–$85.00*

Jordan, Nina. *Homemade Dolls in Foreign Dress*. NY. (1939). 1st ed. illus. by author. dj. . . . . *$45.00–$60.00*

Jordan, Nina R. *Homemade Dolls in Foreign Dress*. NY. Harcourt, Brace & Co. (1939). 1st ed. illus. 2nd prtg, dj. . . . . *$18.00–$30.00*

Jordan, Weymouth T. *Hugh Davis and His Alabama Plantation*. Univ of AL Press. 1948. 1st ed. dj. . . . . *$30.00–$40.00*

Josephus, Ben Gorion. *Wonderful & Most Deplorable History of Latter Times of Jews*. Bellows Falls, Vt. 1819. calf over bds. . . . . *$45.00–$75.00*

Journal of A Prisoner of War in Richmond. NY. 1862. . . . . *$40.00–$50.00*

Journal of a Young Lady of Virginia, 1782. Balt. 1871. . . . . *$20.00–$25.00*

Joyce, James. *Cat and the Devil*. Lon. Faber & Faber. (1965). 1st ed. cl dj. . . . . *$50.00–$60.00*

Joyce, James. *Chamber Music*. NY. 1923. . . . . *$75.00–$95.00*

Joyce, James. *Exiles, a play*. NY. Huebsch. 1918. 1st US ed. . . . *$150.00–$200.00*

Joyce, James. *Haveth Childers Everywhere*. Lon. Faber & Faber. (1931). 1st Eng ed stiff wrps. . . . . *$65.00–$75.00*

Joyce, James. *Portrait of the Artist as a Young Man*. NY. (1948). wrps. . . . . *$40.00–$50.00*

Joyce, James. *Stephen Hero*. np. New Directions. 1944. 1st Amer ed. dj. . . . . *$30.00–$90.00*

Joyce, James. *Ulysses*. Paris. Shakespeare and Company. 1922. 1st ed. ltd 750 cc in handmade paper. . . . . *$5,000.00–$7,000.00*

Joyce, James. *Ulysses*. NY. Random House. (1934). 1sr Amer ed. dj. . . . . *$350.00–$1,500.00*

Judd, Mary. *Wigwam Stories*. Bos. 1901. illus. . . . . *$20.00–$45.00*

Judd, S. D. *Bobwhite & Other Quails of U. S.* DC. 1905. illus. wrps.. . . . .
. . . . *$20.00–$30.00*

Jung, Carl G. *Contributions to Analytical Psychology*. Harcourt. 1928. 1st Amer ed.
. . . . *$50.00–$60.00*

Junkin, D. *Life of Winfield Scott Hancock*. NY. 1880. illus. . . . . . . *$35.00–$48.00*

Kafka, Franz. *Parables*. NY. (1947). 1st ed. dj. . . . . *$35.00–$45.00*

Kahn, David. *Code Breakers*. Lon. Weidenfield & Nicholson. (1966). dj. . . . .
. . . . *$40.00–$55.00*

Kahn, David. *Code Breakers*. NY. Macmillan. (1967). 1st ed. illus. dj. . . . .
. . . . *$60.00–$75.00*

Kalvern, Harry. *Negro and the First Amendment*. 1965. 1st ed. dj cl. . *$30.00–$45.00*

Kane, Elisha Kent. *Arctic Explorations:...in Search of Sir John Franklin*. Phila.
1856. 2 vols. maps. . . . . *$60.00–$150.00*

Kane, Elisha Kent. *US Grinnell Expedition in Search of Sir John Franklin*. NY.
1854. 1st ed. 552 pp, maps, illus. . . . . *$120.00–$300.00*

Kantor, MacKinlay. *Andersonville*. NY. 1955. . . . . *$15.00–$35.00*

Kantor, MacKinlay. *Wicked Water*. NY. (1949). 1st ed. dj. . . . . *$50.00–$60.00*

Kaplan, Sidney. *Black Presence in the Era of the American Revolution, 1770–1800*.
DC. Smithsonian. 1973. dj. . . . . *$35.00–$50.00*

Kargau, F. D. *St. Louis in Fruhren Dahren*. St. Louis, MO. 1893. cl, decorated endpapers, gold on spine. . . . . *$50.00–$60.00*

Karloff, Boris (ed.). *And The Darkness Falls*. Cleve. 1946. 1st ed. . . . .
. . . . *$20.00–$25.00*

Katayev, Valentin. *White Sail Gleams*. Moscow. 1954. illus. . . . . . *$22.00–$35.00*

Katzenbach, Lois and William. *Practical Book of American Wallpaper*. Phila.
(1951). inscr, dj. . . . . *$45.00–$55.00*

Kay, S. *Travels & Researches in Caffaria*. NY. 1834. fldg map. . . . *$30.00–$45.00*

Kearfott, Clarence Baker. *Highland Mills*. Vantage Press. illus. b/w photos map
endpapers dj. . . . . *$50.00–$65.00*

Keene, Caroline. *Haunted Bridge*. NY. Grosset & Dunlap. 1937. dj.*$20.00–$38.00*

Keene, Caroline. *Message in the Hollow Oak*. NY. Grosset & Dunlap. 1935-36. #12.
. . . . *$125.00–$150.00*

Keene, Carolyn. *In The Shadow of the Tower*. NY. Grosset & Dunlap. 1934. illus. dj. . . . . *$20.00–$50.00*

Keene, Carolyn. *Password to Larkspur Lane*. NY. Grosset & Dunlap. Wartime Edition. no dj. . . . . *$25.00–$65.00*

Keene, Carolyn. *Phantom Surfer*. NY. Grosset & Dunlap. 1968. . . . .
. . . . *$15.00–$20.00*

Keene, Carolyn. *Ringmaster's Secret*. NY. Grosset & Dunlap. 1959. Cameo ed. of Nancy Drew #31, dj. . . . . *$25.00–$35.00*

Keene, Carolyn. *Secret of the Old Clock*. NY. Grosset & Dunlap. 1959. Nancy Drew #1, dj. . . . . *$12.00–$25.00*

Keene, Carolyn. *Secret of the Old Clock*. NY. Grosset & Dunlap. 1959. . . . .
. . . . *$9.00–$12.00*

Keene, Carolyn. *Secret of the Golden Pavilion*. NY. Grosset & Dunlap. (1959). . .
. . . . *$8.00–$12.00*

Keene, Carolyn. *Three Cornered Mystery*. NY. Grosset & Dunlap. 1935. Dana Girls, dj. . . . . *$20.00–$35.00*

Keene, Carolyn. *Witch Tree Symbol*. NY. Grosset & Dunlap. 1955. Nancy Drew #33.
. . . . *$10.00–$20.00*

Keillor, Garrison. *Lake Wobegone Days*. NY. Viking. 1985. 1st ed. dj. . . . .
. . . . *$30.00–$50.00*

Keith, Thomas. *New Treatise on the Use of Globes*. Longman, Hurst. 1805. 4 fldg plates, original sheep. . . . . *$75.00–$150.00*

Keithahn, Edward. *Monuments in Cedar*. Ketchikan. 1945. 1st ed. illus. . . . .
. . . . *$40.00–$95.00*

Kelemen, P. *Medieval American Art*. NY. 1943. 2 vols. 1st ed. . . . *$75.00–$150.00*

Kelland, Clarence Budington. *Death Keeps a Secret*. NY. (1953). 1st ed. dj. . . . .
. . . . *$25.00–$40.00*

Keller, Helen. *Our Duties to the Blind*. Bos. 1904. 1st ed. wrps. author's first book.
. . . . *$75.00–$125.00*

Keller, Helen. *Story of My Life*. NY. Doubleday. 1903. 1st ed. 441 pp.. . . . .
. . . . *$35.00–$50.00*

Keller, Keith (ed.). *Mickey Mouse Club Scrapbook*. NY. Grosset &Dunlap. 1975. 5th prtg, dj. . . . . *$35.00–$50.00*

Kellerman, Faye. *Sacred and Profane*. NY. Arbor House. 1987. 1st ed. dj. . . . . . .
. . . . *$35.00–$50.00*

Kellerman, Jonathan. *Butcher's Theater.* NY. Bantam. 1988. 1st ed. dj. . . . .
. . . . *$18.00–$25.00*

Kellerman, Jonathan. *Time Bomb.* NY. Bantam. 1990. 1st ed. dj. . *$10.00–$20.00*

Kellog, Vernon. *Nuova the New Bee.* NY. (1920). illus. by Milo Winter. scarce dj.. .
. . . . *$30.00–$45.00*

Kelly's Hand Forged Bits and Spurs. El Paso, TX. Kelly Bros Mfg. nd. wrps.
cat*$65.00–$95.00*cat**Kelly, Charles.** *Outlaw Trail.* NY. 1959. . . . . . *$30.00–$45.00*

Kelly, Charles. *Outlaw Trail: A History of Butch Cassidy....* Salt Lake City. Printed
by author. 1938. 1st ed. illus. photo plates, brn cl lettered in gilt. . *$150.00–$200.00*

Kelly, Emmet. *Clown.* NY. 1954. 1st ed. wrps. . . . . . . : . . . . *$40.00–$55.00*

Kelly, Fanny. *Narrative of My Captivity Among the Sioux Indians.* Hartford. 1871.
illus. . . . . *$50.00–$125.00*

Kelly, H. *Medical Gynecology.* NY/Lon. 1908. 1st ed. illus. . . . . . *$75.00–$120.00*

Kelly, H. A. *Snakes of Maryland.* Balt. 1936. wrps. illus. . . . . *$15.00–$25.00*

Kelly, L. V. *Range of Men: The Story of the Ranchers and Indians of Alberta.* Tor.
William Briggs. 1913. 1st ed. illus, teg. *$750.00–$800.00*

Kelly, Robert. *Cruise of the Pnyx.* NY. (1979). 1st ed. wrps. ltd 500 cc. . . . .
. . . . *$35.00–$45.00*

Kelly, Walt. *Equal Time for Pogo.* NY. Simon & Schuster. 1968. 1st ed. hardcvr.. . .
. . . . *$80.00–$85.00*

Kelly, Walt. *Incomplete Pogo.* NY. (1954). 1st ed. wrps. . . . . *$18.00–$25.00*

Kelly, Walt. *Pogo.* 1961. wrps. . . . . *$65.00–$75.00*

Kelly, Walt. *Pogo Peek-A-Book.* NY. 1955. 1st ed. wrps. illus. . . . . *$35.00–$60.00*

Kelly, Walt. *Positively Pogo.* NY. 1957. 1st ed. wrps. . . . . *$15.00–$24.00*

Kelly, Walt. *Song of the Pogo.* NY. Simon & Schuster. 1956. 1st ed. illus. . . . .
. . . . *$35.00–$60.00*

Kelly, Walt. *Uncle Pogo So-So Stories.* NY. 1953. 1st ed. wrps. . . . *$18.00–$25.00*

Kelso, Isaac. *Stars and Bars; Or, The Reign of Terror in Missouri.* Bos. 1863. 1st ed.
. . . . *$50.00–$75.00*

Kemelman, Harry. *Nine Mile Walk.* NY. Putnam. 1967. 1st ed. dj. . . . .
. . . . *$55.00–$75.00*

Kemelman, Harry. *One Fine Day the Rabbi Bought a Cross.* NY. William Morrow.
1987. 1st ed. dj. . . . . *$10.00–$20.00*

Kemelman, Harry. *Saturday the Rabbi Went Hungry.* NY. Crown. 1966. Book Club ed. dj. . . . . *$9.00–$15.00*

Kemelman, Harry. *Sunday the Rabbi Stayed Home.* NY. 1969. 1st ed. dj. . . . . *$25.00–$30.00*

Kemelman, Harry. *Tuesday the Rabbi Saw Red.* NY. Arthur Fields. 1973. 1st ed. dj. . . . . *$7.00–$15.00*

Kemelman, Harry. *Wednesday the Rabbi Got Wet.* NY. William Morrow. 1976. 1st ed. dj. . . . . *$30.00–$40.00*

Kemp, John R. *New Orleans.* Preservation Resource Center. [1981]. 1st ed. photos and maps. . . . . *$20.00–$40.00*

Kendall, J. B. *Treatise on the Horse and His Diseases.* VT. 1891. . *$25.00–$40.00*

Kennan, George. *Siberia and the Exile System.* NY. Century. 1891. 2 vols. 1st ed. illus. maps, woodcuts, 409 pp, 575 pp. *$150.00–$200.00*

Kennan, George. *Tent Life in Siberia.* NY. Putnam. 1882. . . . . *$75.00–$90.00*

Kennedy, Edward. *Our Day and Generation.* 1979. sgn, dj. . . . . . . *$30.00–$40.00*

Kennedy, John. *History of Steam Navigation.* Liverpool. 1903. illus. . . . . *$90.00–$110.00*

Kennedy, John F. *Profiles in Courage.* NY. Harper & Row. 1964. memorial ed. dj. . . . . *$15.00–$25.00*

Kennedy, Joseph P. *I'm for Roosevelt.* NY. 1936. . . . . *$95.00–$125.00*

Kennedy, Michael S. (ed.). *Red Man's West....* NY. Hastings House. 1965. 1st ed. illus. ltd 199 cc, buckskin with silkscreen Indian Shield on front cvr. . . . . *$100.00–$130.00*

Kennedy, Sen. John F. *Strategy of Peace.* NY. 1960. 1st ed. . . . . . *$35.00–$40.00*

Kennedy, William. *Quinn's Book.* Lon. Jonathan Cape. 1988. 1st Brit ed. dj, sgn. . . . . *$15.00–$20.00*

Kenrick, William. *American Silk Grower's Guide.* Bos. 1839. 2nd ed. illus. . . . . *$80.00–$95.00*

Kent, Alexander. *Inshore Squadron.* NY. Putnam. 1979. 1st US ed dj. *$30.00–$65.00*

Kent, Rockwell. *N by E.* Brewer & Warren. 1930. 1st ed. illus. dj. . *$25.00–$35.00*

Kent, Rockwell. *Northern Christmas.* NY. (1941). dj. . . . . *$25.00–$65.00*

Kent, Rockwell. *Rockwell Kentiana.* NY. 1933. 1st ed. . . . . *$50.00–$125.00*

Kent, Rockwell. *Salomina.* NY. 1935. 1st ed. dj. . . . . *$35.00–$50.00*

Kephart, Horace. *Camping and Woodcraft.* Outing Pub. 1916–1917. 2 vols. . . . . .
. . . . *$25.00–$35.00*

Kercheville, F. M. *Preliminary Glossary of New Mexican Spanish.* Albuquerque.
1934. wrps. . . . . *$30.00–$45.00*

Kerouac, Jack. *Book of Dreams.* SF. City Lights. (1961). 1st ed. wrps. . . . .
. . . . *$150.00–$200.00*

Kerouac, Jack. *Dharma Bums.* NY. 1958. 1st ed. dj. . . . . *$125.00–$200.00*

Kerouac, Jack. *Lonesome Traveler.* NY. (1960). 1st ed. dj. . . . . . . *$75.00–$225.00*

Kerouac, Jack. *Maggie Cassidy.* NY. Avon. 1959. 1st ed. paperback original. . . . . .
. . . . *$28.00–$35.00*

Kerouac, Jack. *On The Road.* Viking. 1957. 1st ed. dj. . . . . . *$1,250.00–$6,000.00*

Kerouac, Jack. *Pull My Daisy.* NY. Grove Press. (1961). 1st ed. dj. . . . .
. . . . *$200.00–$400.00*

Kerouac, Jack. *Satori in Paris.* NY. Grove Press. (1966). 1st ed. dj. . . . .
. . . . *$200.00–$275.00*

Kerouac, Jack. *Tristessa.* NY. 1960. 1st ed. wrps. . . . . *$40.00–$60.00*

Kerouac, Jack. *Visions of Cody.* NY. McGraw Hill. (1972). 1st ed. dj. . . . .
. . . . *$95.00–$135.00*

Kerouac, John. *Town and the City.* NY. Harcourt. [1950]. 1st ed. dj. . . . .
. . . . *$160.00–$270.00*

Kerr, Donald I. *African Adventure.* Harrisburg. Stackpole. (1957). 1st ed. illus. photos, dj. . . . . *$70.00–$100.00*

Kerr, Evor Samuel, Jr. *United States Coast Guard.* NY. Kelly Pub. 1935. illus. green
pict cl. . . . . *$36.00–$45.00*

Kerr, J. Lennox. *Wilfred Grenfell.* NY. Dodd, Mead. 1959. illus. 259 pp, dj. . . . . . .
. . . . *$22.00–$35.00*

Kerr, Philip. *German Requiem.* Lon. Viking. 1991. 1st ed. dj. . . . . *$50.00–$100.00*

Kerr, Walter. *Silent Clowns.* NY. Knopf. 1975. 1st ed. illus. dj. . . . *$35.00–$50.00*

Kersh, Gerald. *Song of the Flea.* Garden City. 1948. dj. . . . . *$45.00–$55.00*

Kesey, Ken. *Demon Box.* NY. Viking. 1986. 1st ed. dj, sgn. . . . . . . *$45.00–$65.00*

Kesey, Ken. *Kesey's Garage Sale..* NY. Viking. 1973. 1st ed. dj, sgn. . . . .
. . . . *$150.00–$225.00*

Kesey, Ken. *Sometimes a Great Notion.* (1964). 1st ed. dj sgn. . *$900.00–$1,000.00*

Kesey, Ken. *Wavy Gravy.* NY. (1974). wrps. . . . . *$50.00–$75.00*

Ketchum, Milo S. *Designs of Steel Mills Buildings and the Calculation of Stresses in Framed Structures.* NY. 1905. 1st ed. . . . . *$40.00–$60.00*

Khayyam, Omar. *The Rubaiyat.* NY. (1930). illus. by Pogany, 500 cc. . . . . *$200.00–$350.00*

Kidder, Daniel P. *Mormonism and the Mormons.* NY. 1844. 2nd ed. 342 pp.. . . . . *$75.00–$125.00*

Kieran, John W. *American Sporting Scene.* NY. 1941. 1st ed. dj. . . *$30.00–$45.00*

Kiernan, Dr. P. F. *Hints On Horse-Shoeing.* GPO. 1871. 1st ed. 11 pp. . . . . *$75.00–$100.00*

Killikelley, Sarah H. *History of Pittsburgh.* Pitts. 1906. 1st ed. illus. 568 pp. . . . . *$35.00–$45.00*

Kimball, Edward L. and Andrew E. *Spencer W. Kimball, Twelfth President of the Church.* Salt Lake. 1978. illus. photos, sgn, dj.. . . . . *$110.00–$135.00*

Kincaid, Jamaica. *Autobiography of My Mother.* NY. Farrar, Straus & Giroux. 1996. 1st ed. sgn, dj.. . . . . *$30.00–$35.00*

Kincaid, Jamaica. *Small Place.* NY. (1988). 1st ed. dj.. . . . . *$35.00–$45.00*

King, Clarence. *Mountaineering in the Sierra Nevada.* Bos. 1872. 1st ed. . . . . *$125.00–$200.00*

King, Constance Eileen. *Collector's History of Dolls.* Lon. (1983). dj. . . . . *$40.00–$60.00*

King, Coretta Scott. *My Life With Martin Luther King, Jr..* NY. 1969. 1st ed. dj, sgn. . . . . *$50.00–$75.00*

King, Martin Luther. *Triumph of Concience.* NY. (1968). 1st ed. dj. . . . . *$75.00–$50.00*

King, Martin Luther, Jr. *Where Do We Go from Here: Chaos or Community?* NY. (1967). 1st ed. dj.. . . . . *$75.00–$125.00*

King, Stephen. *Christine.* NY. Viking. 1983. 1st ed. red cl, dj. . . . *$65.00–$85.00*

King, Stephen. *Cycle of the Werewolf.* 1985. 1st ed. dj.. . . . . *$65.00–$80.00*

King, Stephen. *Dark Half.* Lon. Hodder & Stoughton. 1989. 1st UK dj. . . . . *$50.00–$65.00*

King, Stephen. *Dark Tower.* RI. Grant. 1982. 1st ed. scarce, dj. . *$350.00–$550.00*

King, Stephen. *Dead Zone.* NY. Viking. 1979. 1st ed. dj. . . . . *$65.00–$75.00*

King, Stephen. *Different Seasons.* NY. Viking. 1982. 1st ed. dj. . . . *$30.00–$45.00*

King, Stephen. *Dolores Claiborne.* Lon. Hodder & Stoughton. 1992. 1st UK ed dj.. . . . . *$15.00–$45.00*

King, Stephen. *Eyes of the Dragon.* NY. Viking. 1987. 1st ed. illus. dj. . . . . *$12.00–$25.00*

King, Stephen. *It.* NY. Viking. 1986. 1st ed. dj. . . . . *$30.00–$45.00*

King, Stephen. *The Shining.* Garden City. Doubleday. 1977. 1st ed. dj. . . . . *$100.00–$150.00*

King, Stephen. *The Stand.* Garden City. Doubleday. 1978. 1st ed. dj. . . . . *$145.00–$275.00*

Kinglsey, Charles. *Water Babies.* NY. nd. illus. by G. Sopher. . . . . *$45.00–$50.00*

Kingsford, Anna Bonus. *Ideal in Diet.* Lon. 1898. . . . . *$24.00–$35.00*

Kingsley, Charles. *Westward Ho!* NY. (1920). illus. by N. C. Wyeth. *$45.00–$65.00*

Kingston, W. H. G. *Henricks the Hunter.* NY. Armstrong. 1880. illus. engr plates. . . . . *$40.00–$60.00*

Kinietz, Vernon. *Chippewa Village.* Bloomfield Hills, MI. Cranbrook. 1947. 1st ed. illus. 259 pp, dj.. . . . . *$35.00–$45.00*

Kinnell, Galway. *Black Light.* Bos. 1966. 1st ed. dj, sgn. . . . . *$85.00–$125.00*

Kinnell, Galway. *What a Kingdom It Was.* Bos. 1960. 3rd prntg, sgn, dj. . . . . *$80.00–$150.00*

Kinnell, Galway and Claire Van Vliet. *Two Poems.* Newark, VT. Janus Press. 1979. 1st ed. ltd ed, 185 cc, sgn by author and artist. . . . . *$100.00–$150.00*

Kinney, Henry W. *Manchuria Today.* Darien. 1930. illus. 100 pp. . *$15.00–$25.00*

Kinsey, A. C. *Gall Wasp Genus Cynips.* Bloomington. 1929. . . . . . *$24.00–$35.00*

Kinsey, Alfred C. et al. *Sexual Behavior in the Human Female.* Phila/Lon. Saunders. 1953. 1st ed. . . . . *$95.00–$125.00*

Kinsey, Alfred C. et al. *Sexual Behavior in the Human Male.* Phila/Lon. Saunders. 1948. 1st ed. . . . . *$95.00–$125.00*

Kip, William I. *Early Jesuit Missions in North America.* NY. 1846. 2 vols. in one, map. . . . . *$150.00–$225.00*

Kipling, Rudyard. *Barrack Room Ballads.* 1892. 1st ed. illus. . . . *$50.00–$125.00*

Kipling, Rudyard. *Brushwood Boy.* NY. 1899. illus. . . . . *$85.00–$100.00*

Kipling, Rudyard. *Captains Courageous.* NY. Century. 1897. 1st Amer ed. green cl, teg. . . . . *$75.00–$100.00*

Kipling, Rudyard. *Collected Dog Stories.* Lon. 1934. lea, teg. . . *$125.00–$200.00*

Kipling, Rudyard. *Just So Stories.* Lon. 1902. 1st ed. . . . . *$300.00–$600.00*

Kipling, Rudyard. *Kim.* NY. 1901. 1st Amer ed. . . . . *$35.00–$120.00*

Kipling, Rudyard. *Kim.* Lon. Macmillan. 1901. 1st UK ed. illus. with plates by J. Lockwood Kipling. red cl. . . . . *$75.00–$100.00*

Kipling, Rudyard. *Many Inventions.* NY. Macmillan. 1893. 1st ed. *$20.00–$30.00*

Kipling, Rudyard. *Puck of Pook's Hill.* NY. 1906. illus. by Arthur Rackham, 4 clr plates, teg. . . . . *$45.00–$75.00*

Kipling, Rudyard. *Second Jungle Book.* Lon. 1895. 1st ed. . . . . . *$75.00–$100.00*

Kipling, Rudyard. *Song of the English.* NY. Doubleday Page. (1909). illus. by W. Heath Robinson. 16 tip-in clr plates. drawings, tissue guards. . . . *$120.00–$150.00*

Kipling, Rudyard. *Songs of the Sea.* Lon. Macmillan. 1927. illus. . . . . *$40.00–$80.00*

Kipling, Rudyard. *Works of Rudyard Kipling.* Doubleday & McClure. 1898. 14 vols. 3/4 lea, bds, teg. . . . . *$150.00–$175.00*

Kirby, Georgiana B. *Years of Experience, An Autobiographical Narrative.* NY. 1887. 1st ed. . . . . *$120.00–$200.00*

Kirby, Percival. *Musical Instruments.* Lon. 1934. . . . . *$100.00–$200.00*

Kirby, Percival R. *Musical Instruments of the Native Races of South Africa.* Johannesburg. 1965. 2nd ed. illus. dj. . . . . *$50.00–$125.00*

Kirby, Percival R. *Musical Instruments of the Native Races of South Africa.* Lon. Oxford Univ Press. 1934. . . . . *$50.00–$75.00*

Kirkland, Jack. *Tobacco Road.* Duell, Sloan & Pearce. (1952). 1st ed. thus. acting script. dj. . . . . *$30.00–$65.00*

Kirkland, Mrs. (Caroline Matilda). *Evening Book: or Fireside Talk on morals and manners.* NY. Scribner's. 1852. 1st ed. red cl, stamped, aeg, 312 pp. . . . . *$150.00–$200.00*

Kirkland, Thomas, and Robert Kennedy. *Historic Camden.* Columbia, SC. The State Co. 1905-26. 2 vols. 1st ed. illus. 486 pp, maps. . . . . *$175.00–$250.00*

Kitchin, Thomas. *Map of New York....* Lon. R Baldwin. 1778. . . . . *$60.00–$80.00*

Kitto, John. *Palestine: Physical Geography, Natural History....* Lon. 1841. illus. 3/4 calf. . . . . *$45.00–$75.00*

Kittredge, George Lyman. *Witchcraft in Old and New England.* Harvard. 1929. 1st ed. . . . . *$105.00–$200.00*

Kittredge, George Lyman. *Witchcraft in Old and New England.* NY. Russell & Russell. [1956]. . . . . *$20.00–$45.00*

Kittredge, Henry. *Shipmasters of Cape Cod.* 1935. 1st ed. dj. . . . . *$25.00–$35.00*

Kitzmiller, Helen H. *One Hundred Years of Western Reserve.* OH. 1926. photos. . . . . *$20.00–$30.00*

Klansman's Manual. Atlanta. 1924. 1st ed. wrps. . . . . *$75.00–$125.00*

Klein, Frederic Shriver (ed.). *Just South of Gettysburg, Carroll County, Md, in the Civil War.* MD. 1963. 1st ed. sgn, dj. . . . . *$42.00–$50.00*

Klein, H. *Mushrooms and Other Fungi.* Garden City. 1962. 1st Amer ed. photos, dj. . . . . *$30.00–$40.00*

Klingberg, Frank. *An Appraisal of the Negro in Colonial S.C.* DC. 1941. 1st ed. . . . . *$35.00–$45.00*

Kluckhohn, C. & K. Spencer. *Bibliography of the Navaho Indians.* NY. 1940. . . . . *$75.00–$100.00*

Knee, Ernest. *Santa Fe, New Mexico.* NY. Hastings House. 1942. 1st ed. photos. . . . . *$20.00–$35.00*

Kneeland, Samuel. *An American in Iceland.* Bos. 1876. map. . . . . *$35.00–$45.00*

Knickerbocker, Diedrich. *A History of New York, from the Beginning of the World to the End of the Dutch Dynasty....* NY. Grolier Club. 1886. 2vols. ltd 175 cc. . . . . *$400.00–$600.00*

Knight, Charles (ed.). *Old England: A Pictorial Museum of Regal....* Lon. James Sangster. c188's. 2 vols. illus. chromo plates, red cl. aeg. . . . . *$80.00–$125.00*

Knight, Damon. *In Search of Wonder: Essays on Modern Science Fiction.* Chi. 1956. 1st ed. dj. . . . . *$20.00–$25.00*

Knight, Mrs. Helen C. *Hannah More....* NY. American Tract Soc. (1862). rev ed. . . . . *$20.00–$125.00*

Knights of the Ku Klux Klan.... Atlanta. 1926. wrps. . . . . *$55.00–$75.00*

Knipe, Emilie Benson. *Story of Old Ironsides.* NY. Dodd, Mead. [1928]. 1st ed. . . . . *$40.00–$65.00*

Knowles, James D. *Memoir of Mrs. Ann H. Judson.* Bos. 1829. fldg map, calf. . . . . *$50.00–$60.00*

Knowlton, Charles. *Fruits of Philosophy....* Mount Vernon. Peter Pauper Press. 1937. rprnt, dj, decorated paper bds. . . . . *$30.00–$40.00*

Knox, Dudley W. *Naval Genius of George Washington.* Bos. 1932. 1st ed. ltd 550 cc. . . . . *$65.00–$85.00*

Knox, Thomas. *Travels of Marco Polo for Boys and Girls.* NY. Putnam. 1885. 1st ed. . . . . *65.00–$85.00*

Knox, Thomas W. *Adventures Of Two Youths In A Journey To Egypt and Holy Land.* NY. 1883. illus. . . . . *$20.00–$30.00*

Koch, Rudolph. *Little ABC Book of Rudolph Koch.* Bos. David R. Godine. 1976. 1st ed thus, ltd 2500 cc.. . . . . *$15.00–$25.00*

Kohlers Medizinal-Pflanzen. G. Pabst. 1887. 2 vol. clr plates. . . *$500.00–$650.00*

Kolb, Ellsworth L. *Through the Grand Canyon from Wyoming to Mexico.* NY. 1958. 1st ed. illus. blue cl.. . . . . *$25.00–$35.00*

Koontz, Dean. *The Mask.* Lon. Headline. 1989. 1st hardcvr ed. dj. . . . . *$90.00–$100.00*

Koontz, Dean. *Trapped.* Forestville. Eclipse. 1993. 1st ed. dj.. . . . . *$40.00–$45.00*

Koontz, Dean R. *Dragon Tears.* NY. Putnam. 1993. 1st ed. dj sgn.. *$35.00–$45.00*

Koontz, Dean R. *Night Chills.* NY. Atheneum. 1976. 334 pp, dj.. . . . . *$185.00–$225.00*

Koontz, Dean R. *Servants of Twilight.* Illinois. 1988. 1st US ed. dj.. . . . . *$35.00–$45.00*

Kopp, Marie. *Birth Control in Practice.* NY. 1934. 1st ed. dj.. . . . . . *$40.00–$50.00*

Korn, Bertram Wallace. *American Jewry and the Civil War.* Phila. 1951. 1st ed. illus. . . . . *$35.00–$125.00*

Kornbluth, C. M. *Mile Beyond the Moon.* Garden City. 1958. 1st ed. dj.. . . . . *$75.00–$85.00*

Kornbluth, Jesse. *Pre-Pop Warhol..* NY. 1988. 1st ed. . . . . *$65.00–$70.00*

Koros, Alexander Cosma De. *Dictionary of Tibetan English.* New Delhi. Cosmo Publications. 1978. rprnt.. . . . . *$30.00–$45.00*

Korson, George (ed.). *Pennsylvania Songs and Legends.* Phila. Univ of PA. 1949. 1st ed. dj.. . . . . *$8.00–$30.00*

Kouwenhoven, John. *Columbia Historical Portrait of New York.* NY. 1953. dj.. . . . . *$40.00–$60.00*

Kovacs, Ernie. *Zoomar.* Doubleday. 1957. 1st ed. dj. . . . . *$45.00–$60.00*

Krauss, Ruth. *A Hole Is To Dig.* NY. 1952. 1st ed. illus. by Maurice Sendak, dj.. . . . . *$125.00–$400.00*

Krauss, Ruth. *Charlotte and The White Horse.* NY. Harper & Brothers. illus. by Maurice Sendak in clr pict bds dj. . . . . *$50.00–$75.00*

Krider, John. *Forty Years Notes of a Field Ornithologist.* Phila. 1879. . . . . *$30.00–$50.00*

Krige, E. J. *Social System of the Zulus.* Lon. 1957. illus. 3rd ed.. . . *$35.00–$45.00*

Kroeber, A. L. *Handbook of the Indians of California.* DC. GPO. 1925. illus. maps plates. . . . . *$200.00–$300.00*

Krug, J A. *Columbia River.* DC. GPO. 1947. illus. folio, pocket maps. . . . . *$50.00–$75.00*

Krug, J. A. *Colorado River.* DC. GPO. 1946. wrps. . . . . *$65.00–$100.00*

Kunitz, Stanley. *Intellectual Things.* NY. Doubleday Doran. 1930. 1st ed. 63 pp, dj, author's first book. . . . . *$125.00–$195.00*

Kunitz, Stanley. *Passport to the War.* NY. Henry Holt. [1944]. 1st ed. 60 pp, dj. . . . . *$40.00–$85.00*

Kunz, George Frederick. *Curious Lore of Precious Stones.* Phila. 1913. illus. . . . . *$125.00–$150.00*

Kuppuram, G. & Kumdamani K. *History and Science and Technology in India.* Delhi. Sundeep Prakashan. 1990. . . . . *$150.00–$185.00*

Kuran, Aptullah. *Mosque in Early Ottoman Architecture.* Chi. 1968. illus. . . . . *$35.00–$50.00*

Kurtz & Erlich. *Art of the Toy Soldier.* NY. 1987. illus. folio. . . . . *$40.00–$60.00*

Kylie, Hieronymus & Hall. *CCC Forestry.* DC. GPO. 1937. 335 pp, photos. . . . . *$18.00–$25.00*

L'Amour, Louis. *Bendigo Shafter.* NY. (1979). 1st ed. dj. . . . . *$75.00–$100.00*

L'Amour, Louis. *Frontier.* NY. Bantam. (1984). 1st ed. photos, dj. . *$40.00–$60.00*

L'Amour, Louis. *Hopalong Cassidy and the Trail to Seven Pines.* Garden City. Doubleday. 1951. 1st ed. author's first Western novel, dj. . . . . *$375.00–$500.00*

L'Amour, Louis. *Last of the Breed.* NY. Bantam. 1986. dj. . . . . *$12.00–$20.00*

L'Amour, Louis. *Lonesome Gods.* NY. Bantam Books. 1983. 1st ed. dj. . . . . *$12.00–$28.00*

L'Amour, Louis. *Over on the Dry Side.* NY. (1975). 1st ed. dj. . . . *$25.00–$100.00*

L'Amour, Louis. *Rivers West.* NY. 1975. 1st ed. dj. . . . . *$50.00–$135.00*

L'Amour, Louis. *Sackett's Land.* NY. 1974. 1st ed. dj. . . . . *$140.00–$165.00*

L'Engle, Madeleine. *A Wrinkle in Time. NY.* (1962) . . . . *$45.00–$65.00*

L'Engle, Madeleine. *Ladder of Angels.* Seabury. 1979. 1st ed. illus. dj. . . . .
. . . . *$25.00–$35.00*

La Farge, Oliver. *As Long as the Grass Shall Grow.* NY. Alliance Book Corp. 1940.
1st ed. sgn. . . . . *$50.00–$65.00*

La Farge, Oliver. *Higher Life in Art.* NY. 1908. 1st ed. . . . . *$45.00–$50.00*

La Farge, Oliver. *Laughing Boy.* Bos. Houghton Mifflin. 1929. 1st ed. dj. . . . . . .
. . . . *$350.00–$500.00*

La Farge, Oliver (ed.). *Changing Indian.* Norman. Univ of OK. 1942. 1st ed. dj. . .
. . . . *$25.00–$35.00*

La Fayette, Gen. *Memoirs of Embracing Details of Public and Private Life.*
Hartford. 1825. 1st ed. lea.. . . . . *$65.00–$100.00*

La Fontaine, Jean de. *Fables in Rhyme.* Volland. (1918). illus. by Rae. . . . .
. . . . *$35.00–$45.00*

La Guerre Recontee par Nos Generaux Commandants de Groupe d'Armees. Paris.
Librarie Schwarz. 1921. 3 vols. illus. full mor.. . . . . *$200.00–$400.00*

La Monte, Francesca. *North American Game Fishes.* NY. 1945. 1st ed. illus. limp
lea, clr plates. . . . . *$25.00–$35.00*

Lacroix, Paul. *Arts in the Middle Ages.* NY. 1875. illus. . . . . *$22.00–$30.00*

***Ladies' Indispensable Assistant. Being a Companion for the Sister, Mother, and
Wife.*** NY. 1851. orig blue cl. . . . . *$75.00–$100.00*

Lafever, Minard. *Beauties of Modern Architecture.* NY. Appleton. 1855. illus. New
ed.. . . . . *$80.00–$120.00*

Lahee, Henry C. *Famous Violinists of To-day and Yesterday.* Bos. 1906. illus. . . .
. . . . *$25.00–$35.00*

Lake, Simon. *Submarine In War And Peace.* Phila. 1918. 1st ed. illus. photos,
presentation copy, sgn.. . . . . *$50.00–$75.00*

Lama Anagarika Govinda. *Foundations of Tibetan Mysticism.* Lon. Rider. (1959).
illus. photos, 1st ed in Eng, sgn. . . . . *$50.00–$70.00*

Lamb, Charles & Mary Lamb. *Tales from Shakespeare..* Lon/NY. 1909. illus. with
12 clr plates by Arthur Rackham, red lea. . . . . *$100.00–$150.00*

Lamb, Frank W. *Indian Baskets of North America..* Riverside, CA. 1972. illus. dj.
. . . . *$45.00–$75.00*

Lamb, M. *Homes of America.* NY. 1879. illus. 256 pp, aeg. . . . . . *$75.00–$150.00*

Lamb, Mrs. Martha. *History of the City of New York; It's Origin, Rise and Progress.* NY. Barnes. 1877. 2 vols. illus. maps, plates.................. *$50.00–$65.00*

Lamb, Wallace E. *Lake Champlain and Lake George Valleys.* NY. 1940. 3 vols. illus. maps... *$125.00–$150.00*

Lamon & Slocum. *Mating and Breeding of Poultry.* NY. 1920. illus. *$40.00–$60.00*

Lamson, David. *Two Years Experience Among the Shakers; Being a Description ....* West Boylston. 1848. 212 pp. .... *$140.00–$185.00*

Landis, T. J. S. *Newark, New Jersey and Suburbs.* Newark. 1916. clr, bird's-eye view of Newark... *$300.00–$350.00*

Landor, A Henry Savage. *In the Forbidden Land.* NY. Harper & Bros. 1899. fldg map, clr plates. .... *$125.00–$200.00*

Landor, A. Henry Savage. *Across Wildest Africa.* Lon. Hurst & Blackett. 1907. 2 vols. illus. .... *$195.00–$260.00*

Landor, A. Henry Savage. *China and Allies.* Lon. Heinemann. 1901. 2 vols. illus. 8 maps, 53 plates, text illusdark blue cl, red lea labels. .... *$175.00–$225.00*

Lands in Alabama.... GPO. 1828. 1st ed. .... *$18.00–$25.00*

Landseer & Herring. *Aunt Louisa's Choice Present....* Lon. Frederick Warne. c1860's. illus. chromos, blue cl.. .... *$100.00–$175.00*

Lane, C K. *Rabbits, Cats and Cavies.* Lon. J. M. Dent. 1903. illus. gilt dec and lettered green cl. .... *$40.00–$60.00*

Lane, Carl D. *American Paddle Steamboats.* NY. Coward McCann. 1943. illus. decorated endpapers, dj. .... *$45.00–$55.00*

Lane, Frank. *Kingdom of the Octopus.* NY. Sheridan House. 1960. dj. .... *$15.00–$30.00*

Lane, Margaret. *Tale of Beatrix Potter, A Biography.* NY. (1946). 1st ed. .... *$35.00–$50.00*

Lang, Andrew. *Animal Story Book.* Lon. 1896. illus. 1st UK ed.. *$100.00–$150.00*

Lang, Andrew. *Blue Poetry Book.* Lon. 1891. 1st UK ed. illus.... *$75.00–$100.00*

Lang, Andrew. *Book of Dreams and Ghosts.* Lon/NY/Bombay. Longmans, Green. 1897. 1st ed. pict cl.................................... *$50.00–$145.00*

Lang, Andrew. *Book of Romance.* Lon. 1902. 1st UK ed. illus..... *$50.00–$80.00*

Lang, Andrew. *Green Fairy Book.* Lon. 1924. illus. .... *$30.00–$40.00*

Lang, Andrew. *True Story Book.* Lon. 1893. illus. 1st UK...... *$100.00–$135.00*

Lanier, Charles D. *We Go Foxhunting Abroad.* np. private printing. 1924. 1st ed. sgn. . . . . *$32.00–$45.00*

Lankes, J. J. *Woodcut Manual.* NY. Crown. 1932. rprnt. . . . . *$12.00–$25.00*

Lardner, Rev. Dionysius. *Cabinet Cyclopaedia.* Phila. 1832. illus. *$50.00–$65.00*

Lardner, Ring. *Bib Ballads.* Chi. [1915]. 1st ed. author's firstbook, illus, ltd 1500 cc, boxed. . . . . *$275.00–$350.00*

Lardner, Ring. *Gullible's Travels.* Ind. (1917). 1st ed. . . . . *$40.00–$150.00*

Lardner, Ring. *My Four Weeks in France.* Ind. (1918). 1st ed. illus. dj. . . . . *$200.00–$400.00*

Lardner, Ring. *You Know Me Al.* NY. (1916). 1st ed. . . . . *$350.00–$450.00*

Larned, Linda H. *New Hostess To-Day.* NY. 1917. . . . . *$14.00–$21.00*

Larsen, Kenneth. *Flying Saucer Designs.* LA. 1965. 1st ed. illus. three-ring binder . . . . *$50.00–$80.00*

Last Journals of David L. Livingstone. Hartford. 1875. illus. maps. *$35.00–$40.00*

Lathrop, Dorothy C. *Sung Under the Umbrella Tree.* NY. 1935. 1st ed. scarce dj. . . . . *$35.00–$50.00*

Lathrop, Elise. *Early American Inns and Taverns.* NY. 1926. 1st ed. . . . . *$25.00–$30.00*

Lathrop, Elise. *Historic Houses of Early America.* NY. 1936. rprnt, 464 pp, photos, dj. . . . . *$15.00–$25.00*

Lathrop, S.K. *Treasures of Ancient America....* Geneva. Albert Skira. illus. cl, dj, wrap-around band. . . . . *$50.00–$80.00*

Latimer, Jonathan. *The Westland Case.* Garden City. Sundial. 1937. Photoplay ed. . . . . *$125.00–$175.00*

Lattimore, Owen. *Inner Asian Frontiers of China.* NY. 1940. illus. *$25.00–$35.00*

Laurie, J. and R. S. Gutteridge. *Homeopathic Domestic Medicine....* Lon. 1888. . . . . *$45.00–$55.00*

Laut, Agnes C. *Blazed Trail of the Old Frontier.* NY. 1926. 1st ed. illus. 271 pp.. . . . . *$60.00–$125.00*

Laut, Agnes C. *Conquest of Our Western Empire.* NY. 1927. 1st ed. dj. . . . . *$40.00–$50.00*

Laut, Agnes C. *Conquest of the Great Northwest....* NY. 1908. 2 vols. 1st ed. illus. . . . . *$100.00–$225.00*

Laut, Agnes C. *Pathfinders of the West*. NY. 1904. 1st ed. . . . . *$40.00–$50.00*

Laut, Agnes C. *Story of the Trapper*. NY. 1902. 1st ed. author's first book. . . . .
. . . . *$35.00–$50.00*

Laut, Agnes C. *Vikings of the Pacific*. NY. Macmillan. 1914 [1905]. illus. maps. . . .
. . . . *$18.00–$25.00*

Lavin, Mary. *House in Clewe Street*. Bos. 1945. 1st ed. dj. . . . . *$50.00–$65.00*

LaWall, Charles H. *Four Thousand Years of Pharmacy*. Phila. Lippincott. 1927. 665 pp, prentation copy. . . . . *$65.00–$85.00*

Lawrence, D. H. *Amores*. NY. 1916. 1st Amer ed.. . . . . *$45.00–$125.00*

Lawrence, D. H. *David*. Knopf. 1926. dj. . . . . *$75.00–$125.00*

Lawrence, D. H. *Lady Chatterley's Lover*. Knopf. 1932. 1st Amer ed. . . . .
. . . . *$75.00–$125.00*

Lawrence, D. H. *Ladybird, the Fox, the Captain's Doll*. Lon. Martin Secker. (1923). 1st ed. dj.. . . . . *$125.00–$350.00*

Lawrence, D. H. *Lovely Lady*. NY. Viking. 1933. 1st US dj. . . . . . *$20.00–$125.00*

Lawrence, D. H. *Mornings in Mexico*. Lon. Martin Secker. 1927. 1st ed. dj. . . . . . .
. . . . $300.00–$500.00*

Lawrence, D. H. *Pansies*. NY. 1929. 1st Amer ed. dj. . . . . *$30.00–$50.00*

Lawrence, D. H. *Pansies: Poems*. np. (1929). pink wrps, sgn. . . . *$125.00–$400.00*

Lawrence, D. H. *Pornography & Obscenity*. Lon. Faber & Faber. 1929. 1st UK ed..
. . . . $100.00–$175.00*

Lawrence, D. H. *Touch and Go: A Play in Three Acts*. Lon. C W Daniel. 1920. 1st ed. wrps. . . . . *$300.00–$400.00*

Lawrence, D. H. *Virgin and the Gypsy*. Lon. Martin Secker. (1930). 1st UK ed. dj. .
. . . . $100.00–$250.00*

Lawrence, D. H. *Women in Love*. Lon. Martin Seeker. 1921. 1st trade ed.. . . . .
. . . . $100.00–$195.00*

Lawrence, Robert M. *Magic of the Horseshoe*. Bos/NY. 1898. 1st ed. . . . .
. . . . $50.00–$75.00*

Lawrence, T. E. *Oriental Assembly*. Lon. Norgate. 1939. 1st ed. illus. dj. . . . .
. . . . $135.00–$185.00*

Lawrence, T. E. *Revolt in the Desert*. NY. 1927. illus. 1st US ed. fldg map, dj. . . . .
. . . . $100.00–$125.00*

Lawson, John. *History of North Carolina.* Raleigh. 1860. 1st ed. *$115.00–$150.00*

Lawson, Robert. *Ben and Me.* Bos. Little, Brown. 1944. dj.. . . . . . *$50.00–$60.00*

Lawson, Robert. *Rabbit Hill.* NY. 1944. 1st ed. dj.. . . . . *$45.00–$125.00*

Layard, Austen H. *Discoveries in the Ruins of Nineveh and Babylon.* NY. 1853. 1st ed. illus. maps, lithos, 686 pp. . . . . *$75.00–$100.00*

Layard, Austen Henry. *Nineveh and its Remains.* NY. Putnam. 1849. 2 vols. illus. 1st Amer ed. litho, map,. . . . . *$195.00–$300.00*

Lazarus, Emma. *Songs of a Semite.* NY. 1882. 1st ed. . . . . *$65.00–$90.00*

Le Blanc, Maurice. *From Midnight to Morning.* Macaulay. 1933. 1st ed. dj.. . . . . .
. . . . *$75.00–$100.00*

Le Blond, Mrs. Aubrey. *True Tales of Mountain Adventure for Non-climbers Young and Old.* NY. Dutton. 1903. illus. gray and white on blue cl.. . . . . . *$50.00–$85.00*

Le Carre, John. *Call For the Dead.* 1962. 1st Amer ed. dj. . . . *$600.00–$2,500.00*

Le Carre, John. *Honourable Schoolboy.* Lon. Hodder & Stoughton. 1977. 1st US ed. dj.. . . . . *$25.00–$45.00*

Le Carre, John. *Little Drummer Girl.* Knopf. 1983. 1st US ed. dj.. *$15.00–$25.00*

Le Carre, John. *Looking-Glass War.* Lon. Heinemann. 1965. 1st ed. dj. . . . .
. . . . *$45.00–$50.00*

Le Carre, John. *Our Game.* Lon. Hodder & Stoughton. 1995. 1st UK ed. dj. . . . .
. . . . *$250.00–$350.00*

Le Carre, John. *Our Game.* Franklin Center. Franklin Library. 1995. 1st ed. ltd. sgn, green lea, aeg.. . . . . *$50.00–$75.00*

Le Carre, John. *Perfect Spy.* NY. Knopf. 1986. 1st Amer ed. sgn, dj. . . . .
. . . . *$50.00–$150.00*

Le Carre, John. *Russia House.* NY. Knopf. 1989. 1st ed. dj. . . . . . *$10.00–$20.00*

Le Carre, John. *Secret Pilgrim.* NY. 1991. 1st Amer ed. sgn, dj. . *$85.00–$100.00*

Le Carre, John. *Small Town in Germany.* NY. Coward-McCann. 1968. 1st Amer ed. dj.. . . . . *$50.00–$80.00*

Le Carre, John. *Smiley's People.* Lon. Hodder & Stoughton. 1979. 1st ed. dj.. . . . .
. . . . *$100.00–$150.00*

Le Carre, John. *Smiley's People.* NY. Knopf. 1980. 1st Amer ed. dj.*$35.00–$65.00*

Le Carre, John. *Spy Who Came In From the Cold.* Lon. Gollancz. 1963. 1st ed. dj.
. . . . *$750.00–$950.00*

Le Carre, John. *The Russia House*. Lon. London Limited Editions. 1989. 1st UK ed. ltd 250 numbered cc, sgn. glassine wrapper.. . . . . *$200.00–$300.00*

Le Carre, John. *Tinker, Tailor, Soldier, Spy*. Lon. 1974. 1st UK ed. dj. . . . . *$25.00–$30.00*

Le Gallienne, Richard. *Romance of Perfume*. NY. 1928. 1st ed. illus. by George Barbier, clr plates, Richard Hudnut brochure in rear pocket, dj. . . *$100.00–$185.00*

Le Guin, Ursula. *Dispossessed*. NY. (1974). 1st ed. dj.. . . . . *$50.00–$60.00*

Le Guin, Ursula. *Lathe of Heaven*. Lon. 1972. 1st UK ed. dj. . . . . *$30.00–$85.00*

Le May, Curtis. *Mission with LeMay: My Story*. NY. 1965. photos. *$15.00–$25.00*

Le Moine, J. M. *Picturesque Quebec*. Montreal. 1882. softcvr.. . . . *$24.00–$30.00*

Le Queux, William. *Rasputin in London*. Lon. Cassell. 1919. 1st ed. dj. . . . . *$80.00–$100.00*

Le Queux, William. *The Elusive Four*. Lon. Cassell. 1921. 1st ed. dj. . . . . *$150.00–$225.00*

Lea, Elizabeth. *Domestic Cookery*. Balt. 1878. . . . . *$60.00–$100.00*

Lea, Tom. *Hands of Cantu*. Bos. Little, Brown. (1964). 1st ed. dj. . . . . *$32.00–$45.00*

Lea, Tom. *King Ranch*. Little, Brown. (1957). 2 vols. 1st ed. . . . . *$75.00–$100.00*

Leach, David G. *Rhododendrons of the World*. NY. Scribner's. 1st ed. illus. fldg clr plates, folio, dj. . . . . *$50.00–$65.00*

Leaf, Munro. *Story of Ferdinand*. Lon. Hamish Hamilton. (1937). illus. by Robert Lawson. 1st UK ed.. . . . . *$40.00–$60.00*

Lederer, William & Eugene Burdick. *Ugly American*. 1958. 1st ed. dj. . . . . *$25.00–$35.00*

Ledger, Edmund. *Sun: Its Planets and their Satellites*. Lon. Edward Stanford. 1882. illus. 3 Woodburytypes, 1 clr litho, wood engrs in text. . . . . *$100.00–$150.00*

Lee, Amy Freeman. *Hobby Horses*. NY. Derrydale. 1940. ltd 250 cc, sgn. . . . . *$125.00–$250.00*

Lee, Art. *Fishing Dry Flies for Trout On Rivers and Streams.*. NY. 1982. 1st ed. dj.. . . . . *$30.00–$50.00*

Lee, Harper. *To Kill a Mockingbird.*. Lon. 1960. 1st Brit ed. dj. . . . . *$200.00–$300.00*

Lee, Irvin H. *Negro Medal of Honor Men*. NY. Dodd, Mead. (1969). dj. . . . . *$14.00–$35.00*

Lee, Mrs. R.. *Anecdotes of the Habits and Instincts of Birds, Reptiles and Fishes.* Bos. 1876. illus. . . . . *$15.00–$25.00*

Lee, Robert. *Clinical Midwifery..* Phila. 1849. 1st Amer ed. . . . . *$125.00–$150.00*

Leeds, Joseph. *Let My People Know....* Pub by Manny's Friends. 1943. wrps. 2nd print. . . . . *$75.00–$100.00*

Lees, Willis T. *Stories in Stone.* NY. Chautauqua Press. 1927. illus. photos, dj. . . . . *$35.00–$40.00*

Leeson, F. *Identification of Snakes of the Gold Coast..* Lon. 1950. illus. . . . . *$65.00–$100.00*

Leffingwell, William Bruce. *Art of Wing Shooting.* Rand McNally. 1895. 1st ed. slipcase. . . . . *$95.00–$175.00*

Leffingwell, William Bruce. *Shooting on Upland, Marsh, and Stream.* Rand McNally. 1890. 1st ed. . . . . *$165.00–$225.00*

Leffingwell, William Bruce. *Wild Fowl Shooting.* Rand McNally. 1890. 1st ed. . . . . *$75.00–$95.00*

Legend of the Shasta Spring of California. SF. nd. 1st ed. wrps. . . *$50.00–$75.00*

Leger, Jacques Nicolas. *Haiti, Her History and Her Detractors.* NY/DC. 1907. 1st ed. . . . . *$95.00–$150.00*

Leiber, Fritz. *Bazaar of the Bizarre.* Kingston. 1st ed. 1300 cc, dj. . *$25.00–$40.00*

Leiber, Fritz. *Heroes and Horrors.* Whispers Press. 1978. 1st ed. dj. . *$25.00–$35.00*

Leiber, Fritz. *Two Sought Adventure.* NY. Gnome. 1957. 1st ed. 1st binding, dj. . . . . *$45.00–$60.00*

Leibovitch, J. *Ancient Egypt.* Cairo. 1938. 1st ed. wrps. illus. . . . . *$25.00–$40.00*

Leighton, Clare. *Four Hedges.* NY. 1935. illus. sgn, dj. . . . . *$75.00–$100.00*

Leighton, Clare. *Growing New Roots: An Essay with Fourteen Wood Engravings.* Book Club of California. 1979. 1st ed. thus, ltd 500 cc, sgn. . . . . . *$50.00–$100.00*

Leighton, Clare. *Southern Harvest.* Macmillan. 1942. 1st ed. 1st ptg, sgn, dj. . . . . *$95.00–$150.00*

Leighton, Clare. *Where Land Meets Sea.* NY. (1954). illus. by Leighton, dj. . . . . *$20.00–$30.00*

Leighton, Clare. *Where Land Meets Sea.* NY. Rinehart & Winston. 1954. 1st ed. illus. dj. . . . . *$25.00–$100.00*

Leland, E H. *Farm Homes.* NY. 1881. illus. . . . . *$30.00–$67.00*

Lennon, John. *In His Own Write*. Lon. 1964. 1st ed. . . . . *$50.00–$60.00*

Lennon, John. *Spaniard in the Works*. Lon. 1965. . . . . *$85.00–$125.00*

Lenski, Lois. *Blue Ridge Billy*. Phila. Lippincott. (1946). illus. by Lenski, dj. . . . . .

Lenski, Lois. *Deer Valley Girl*. Phila. Lippincott. 1968. illus. by Lenski. cl, dj. . . . .
. . . . *$150.00–$175.00*

Lenski, Lois. *Little Fire Engine*. 1946. 1st ed. . . . . *$30.00–$100.00*

Lenski, Lois. *Skipping Village*. NY. 1927. 1st ed. illus. by author. . *$35.00–$100.00*

Lenski, Lois. *Strawberry Girl*. Phila. Lippincott. 1945. 1st ed. illus. *$35.00–$50.00*

Lensky, Lois. *Jack Horner's Pie*. NY. Harper. 1927. 1st ed. illus. . . *$20.00–$35.00*

Lenton, H. T. *Warships of W W II*. Lon. 1968. illus. . . . . *$35.00–$50.00*

Lentz, Harold. *Pop-Up Pinocchio*. NY. 1932. . . . . *$95.00–$125.00*

Leonard, Elmore. *City Primeval*. Lon. W. H. Allen. 1981. 1st UK ed. dj. . . . .
. . . . *$40.00–$50.00*

Leonard, Elmore. *City Primeval*. NY. Arbor House. 1980. 1st ed. dj. *$25.00–$50.00*

Leonard, Elmore. *Gunsights*. NY. Bantam. 1979. 1st ed. wrps. . . . *$80.00–$90.00*

Leonard, Elmore. *Killshot*. NY. Arbor House/William Morrow. 1989. 1st ed. dj.. . .
. . . . *$35.00–$45.00*

Leonard, Elmore. *La Brava*. NY. Arbor House. 1983. 1st ed. sgn, dj. . . . .
. . . . *$50.00–$100.00*

Leonard, Elmore. *Moonshine War*. Garden City. Doubleday. 1969. 1st ed. dj.. . . . .
. . . . *$145.00–$290.00*

Leonard, Elmore. *Mr. Majestyk*. NY. Dell. 1974. 1st ed. wrps. . . . *$50.00–$70.00*

Leonard, Elmore. *Stick*. NY. Arbor House. 1983. 1st ed. dj, sgn. . . *$20.00–$50.00*

Leonard, Elmore. *Swag*. NY. Delacorte. 1976. 1st ed. dj. . . . . . . *$125.00–$150.00*

Leonard, Elmore. *The Switch*. Lon. Secker & Warburg. 1979. 1st hardcover ed. dj.. .
. . . . *$250.00–$250.00*

Leonard, Elmore. *Touch*. NY. Arbor House. 1987. 1st ed. dj. . . . . . *$10.00–$35.00*

Leonhardt, Olive. *New Orleans Drawn and Quartered*. Richmond. The Dale Press.
1938. illus. . . . . *$35.00–$50.00*

Leopold, Aldo. *Report on a Game Survey of the North Central States*. Madison.
American Game Assoc. 1931. 1st ed. illus. . . . . *$35.00–$70.00*

Lerner, Max. *America as a Civilization*. NY. Simon & Shuster. 1957. 3rd printing cl. . . . . *$15.00–$25.00*

Lesley, J. P. *Geological Hand Atlas of the Sixty-Seven Counties of Pennsylvania.. .1874 to 1884*. Harrisburg. 1885. maps. . . . . *$65.00–$85.00*

Leslie, Frank. *Famous Leaders and Battle Scenes of the Civil War.*. NY. 1896. 1st ed. folio. . . . . *$135.00–$150.00*

Leslie, Frank. *Frank Leslie's History of the Civil War*. 1895. . . . *$135.00–$150.00*

Leslie, Frank. *Illustrated History of the Civil War*. NY. (1895). illus. repaired. . . . . *$60.00–$175.00*

Leslie, Frank. *Leslie's Famous War Pictures: Portfolio of War and Nation—Civil War*. DC. War Dept. 1906. illus. 582 pp, rebound, folio. . . . . *$150.00–$175.00*

Leslie, J. et al. *Narrative of Discovery and Adventure in the Polar Seas and Regions*. Edin. Oliver & Boyd. 1830. fldg map, 1/2 lea. . . . . *$65.00–$100.00*

Leslie, Miss. *75 Receipts for Pastry, Cakes, and Sweetmeats*. Bos. nd. . . . . *$145.00–$185.00*

Leslie, Miss. *Directions for Cookery*. Phila. 1839. . . . . *$100.00–$125.00*

Leslie, Miss. *Directions for Cookery*. Phila. 1863. 59th ed. . . . . *$18.00–$30.00*

Leslie, Miss. *Miss Leslie's New Recipes for Cookin.*. Phila. 1854. . . . . *$120.00–$150.00*

Lessing, Doris. *African Stories*. NY. Simon & Schuster. 1965. 1st US ed. dj. . . . . *$25.00–$35.00*

Lessing, Doris. *Fifth Child*. NY. 1988. 1st ed. dj. . . . . *$20.00–$25.00*

Lessing, Doris. *Real Thing*. Harper Collins. [1992]. 1st ed. 214 pp, dj. . . . . *$12.00–$25.00*

Lester, Chadwick. *Baseball Joe Around the World*. Cupples & Leon. 1918. Baseball Joe #8, dj. . . . . *$42.00–$75.00*

Lester, J. C. & D. L Wilson. *Ku Klux Klan*. Nashville. 1884. wrps. . . . . *$700.00–$1,000.00*

Letters of John James Audubon, 1826-1840. 1930. 2 vols. ltd 225 cc, slipcase. . . . . *$250.00–$275.00*

Letts, W. M. and M. F. S. Letts. *Helmet and Cowl*. NY. Stokes. nd. illus. by Stephen Reid... . . . . *$45.00–$50.00*

Lever, John. *Practical Treatise on Organic Diseases of the Uterus*. Newburgh, NY. Proudfit. 1845. 1st Amer ed. . . . . *$100.00–$175.00*

Levi, Wendell M. *The Pigeon.* Sumter, SC. 1963. illus. sgn. . . . . . . *$50.00–$65.00*

Levi-Strauss, Claude. *Introduction to a Science of Mythology: The Raw and the Cooked and From Honey to Ashes.* NY. Harper & Row. 1969. 2 vols. 1st Amer ed. dj. . . . . *$100.00–$133.00*

Levin, Ira. *Rosemary's Baby.* NY. Random House. 1967. 1st ed. dj. . *$75.00–$100.00*

Levine, Philip. *New Season.* WA. Graywolf Press. (1975). 1st ed. 225letterpress copies not sgn. . . . . *$100.00–$145.00*

Levine, Philip. *Walk With Tom Jefferson.* NY. 1988. 1st ed. sgn, dj. *$55.00–$72.00*

Lewis, Alfred Henry. *Wolfville.* NY. Stokes. 1902. 1st ed. . . . . *$50.00–$60.00*

Lewis, G. Griffin. *Practical Book of Oriental Rugs.* Phila. 1920. map, illus. . . . . *$75.00–$95.00*

Lewis, G. Griffin. *Practical Book of Oriental Rugs.* NY. 1945. illus. rev ed. . . . . *$50.00–$65.00*

Lewis, Jan. *Pursuit of Happiness....* Cambridge Univ Press. 1983. dj. *$20.00–$25.00*

Lewis, John. *Printed Ephemera.* Ipswich. (1962). 1st ed. illus. dj. . *$40.00–$60.00*

Lewis, Sinclair. *Ann Vickers.* NY. Doubleday. [1933]. dj. . . . . . . *$150.00–$250.00*

Lewis, Sinclair. *Ann Vickers.* Garden City. Doubleday, Doran. 1933. 1st ed. ltd 2,350 cc. blue cl, dj. . . . . *$200.00–$300.00*

Lewis, Sinclair. *Arrowsmith.* NY. Harcourt, Brace. (1925). 1st ed. sgn, blue bds, teg. . . . . *$400.00–$900.00*

Lewis, Sinclair. *Babbitt.* NY. Harcourt, Brace. (1927). 1st ed. 1st prtg. blue cl, dj.. . . . . *$400.00–$750.00*

Lewis, Sinclair. *Dodsworth.* NY. Grosset & Dunlap. (1929). dj. . . . *$30.00–$75.00*

Lewis, Sinclair. *Dodsworth.* NY. Harcourt, Brace. (1929). 1st ed. blue cl, dj. . . . . *$600.00–$1,400.00*

Lewis, Sinclair. *Elmer Gantry.* NY. Harcourt, Brace. (1927). 4th prtg. presentation copy, sgn, blue cl, dj. . . . . *$400.00–$900.00*

Lewis, Sinclair. *Elmer Gantry.* NY. Harcourt, Brace. (1927). 1st ed. 1st binding. has points, sgn, blue cl, dj. . . . . *$1,500.00–$2,500.00*

Lewis, Sinclair. *Free Air.* NY. Harcourt, Brace. 1919. 1st ed. blue cl. . . . . *$75.00–$100.00*

Lewis, Sinclair. *Main Street.* Chi. Limited Edition Club. 1937. illus. by Grant Wood. ltd 1,500 cc. sgn, cl, slipcase. . . . . *$100.00–$185.00*

Lewis, Sinclair. *Main Street.* NY. Harcourt, Brace. 1921. 17th prtg. presentation copy. sgn, blue cl. . . . . *$500.00–$650.00*

Lewis, Sinclair. *Main Street.* NY. Harcourt, Brace. (1921). 21st prtg. black cl, dj. . . . . *$75.00–$150.00*

Lewis, Sinclair. *Mantrap.* NY. Harcourt, Brace. (1926). 1st ed. blue cl, dj. . . . . *$700.00–$1,500.00*

Lewis, Sinclair. *Our Mr. Wrenn.* NY. Harper. 1914. 1st ed. green cl. . . . . *$300.00–$400.00*

Lewis, Sinclair. *Prodigal Parents.* Doubleday. 1938. 1st ed. dj. . . . . *$45.00–$60.00*

Lewis, Sinclair. *The Innocents.* NY. Harper. (1917). 1st ed. frontis, green cl. . . . . *$75.00–$125.00*

Lewis, Sinclair. *The Man who Knew Coolidge.* NY. Harcourt, Brace. (1928). 1st ed. blue cl, dj. . . . . *$200.00–$325.00*

Lewis, Sinclair. *The Trail of the Hawk.* NY. Harper. (1915). 1st ed. clr frontis by Norman Rockwell, blue cl, presentation coopy, sgn by Rockwell. *$500.00–$950.00*

Lewisohn, Ludwig. *Island Within.* NY. Harper & Bros. 1928. inscr. . . . . *$30.00–$45.00*

Leyner, Mark. *Et Tu, Babe.* NY. Harmony. 1992. 1st ed. dj. . . . . . . *$22.00–$30.00*

Leys, John K. *The Black Terror.* Lon. Sampson, Low, Martson. 1889. 1st ed. pict bds. . . . . *$175.00–$225.00*

Lichten, Frances. *Folk Art of Rural Pennsylvania.* NY. Scribner's. (1946). illus. . . . . *$35.00–$65.00*

Lichtenstein, Gaston. *George Washington's Birthday....* Wm. Byrd. 1924. dj. . . . . *$30.00–$45.00*

Liddle, Hart B. H. *Sherman, The Genius of the Civil War.* Ernest Benn Ltd. 1930. . . . . *$30.00–$45.00*

Lieber, Fritz. *Specter is Hauntin Texas.* NY. Walker. (1968). 1st ed. 245 pp, dj. . . . . *$30.00–$45.00*

Liebetrau, Preben. *Oriental Rugs in Color.* NY. 1963. illus. dj. . . . . *$40.00–$50.00*

Liebig, Justus. *Natural Laws of Husbandry.* Lon. Walton & Maberly. 1863. 416 pp. . . . . *$125.00–$175.00*

Life & Adventures of Sam Bass the Notorious...Train Robber. Dallas. 1878. wrps. . . . . *$75.00–$100.00*

Life of Fremont. NY. 1856. 1st ed. illus. *$32.00–$40.00*

Life of General Putnam. NY. Nofis & Cornish. 1847. illus. with woodcuts small. . .
. . . . *$20.00–$75.00*

Life of Miss Anne Catley: Celebrated Singing Performer.... Lon. 1888. . . . .
. . . . *$30.00–$40.00*

Life of Sergeant I. W. Ambler. Bos. Lea & Shepard. 1883. illus. red brown dec cl gold
lettering on spine. . . . . *$45.00–$50.00*

Likins, W. M. *Patriotism Capitalized or Religion Turned Into Gold.* Pa.
The Watchman Pub Co. 1925. 1st ed. wrps. . . . . *$60.00–$75.00*

Lilienthal, Howard. *Imperative Surgery for the General Practioner....* NY.
Macmillan. 1901. rprnt. . . . . *$50.00–$60.00*

Abraham Lincoln, President of the United States. Worcester. Achille J. St. Onge.
1950. 1st ed. illus. miniature book, 2x3 inches, calf, bound by Sangorski & Sutcliffe
of Lon, ltd 1500 cc. . . . . *$125.00–$175.00*

Lincoln, Almira. *Familiar Lectures on Botany... For the Use of Schools and
Academics.* Hartford. Huntington. 1832. 3rd ed. 440 pp. . . . . *$25.00–$40.00*

Lincoln, Mrs D A. *Boston School Kitchen Text-Book.* Bos. Little, Brown. 1905. . . .
. . . . *$15.00–$30.00*

Lincoln, Mrs. D. A. *Boston School Kitchen Textbook.* Bos. 1887. illus. in b/w. . . . .
. . . . *$225.00–$350.00*

Lind, Andrew W. *Hawaii's Japanese An Experiment in Democracy.* Princeton.
Princeton Univ Press. 1946. 1st ed. . . . . *$35.00–$50.00*

Lindberg, Anne Morrow. *Dearly Beloved.* Harcourt. 1962. sgn, dj. *$35.00–$45.00*

Lindberg, Anne Morrow. *Flower and the Nettle, Diaries and Letters of...1936-39.*
NY. Harcourt Brace. [1976]. 1st ed. dj. . . . . *$10.00–$25.00*

Lindberg, Anne Morrow. *Gift From the Sea.* 1955. 1st ed. illus. slipcase. . . . .
. . . . *$20.00–$35.00*

Lindberg, Anne Morrow. *North to the Orient.* Harcourt Brace. 1935. 1st ed. dj. . . .
. . . . *$25.00–$35.00*

Lindberg in Paris, All the Photos. Paris. Edison Nilsson. wrps. photo pastedown on
cvr. . . . . *$25.00–$40.00*

Lindberg, Charles. *Of Flight and Life.* NY. Scribner's. 1948. 1st ed. dj. . . . .
. . . . *$50.00–$60.00*

Lindberg, Charles. *Spirit of St Louis.* NY. Scribner's. 1953. 1st ed. illus. dec endpapers, blue cl, dj. . . . . *$45.00–$100.00*

Lindbergh, Charles A. *We.* NY. Putnam. 1927. 1st ed. dj. . . . . . . *$40.00–$125.00*

Lindley & Widney. *California of the South.* NY. 1888. 1st ed. illus. . . . .
. . . . *$32.00–$45.00*

Lindsay, David Moore. *Voyage to the Arctic In the Whaler 'Aurora'.* Bos. 1911. 1st
ed. illus. . . . . *$60.00–$75.00*

Lindsay, Maud & Emilie Poulsson. *Joyous Guests.* Bos. Lothrop Lee & Shepard
Co. (1921). illus. pict cvr. . . . . *$40.00–$55.00*

Linsley, D. C. *Morgan Horses.* NY. Saxton. 1857. 1st ed. . . . . . . *$450.00–$535.00*

Lipton, Lawrence. *Holy Barbarians.* NY. 1959. 1st ed. dj. . . . .
. . . . *$45.00–$65.00*

Littauer, Capt. Vladimir. *Common Sense Horsemanship.* NY. Van Nostrand. 1951.
1st ed. dj.. . . . . *$45.00–$58.00*

Littauer, Captain V. S. *Jumping the Horse.* NY. Derrydale. 1931. 1st ed. 48. . . . .
. . . . *$32.00–$48.00*

Little Childs A B C Home Book. NY. McLoughlin Bros. wrps. chromolithos. . . . .
. . . . *$50.00–$75.00*

Littlejohn, F. J. *Legends of Michigan and the Old Northwest.* Mich. 1875. . . . . . .
. . . . *$40.00–$60.00*

Livermore, Mary. *My Story of the War.* Hartford. 1889. illus. . . . .
. . . . *$50.00–$100.00*

Lives of Distinguished Shoemakers. Portland. 1849. 1st ed. brown cl. . . . .
. . . . *$50.00–$100.00*

Lives of the Holy Evangelists, and Apostles, With their Martyrdoms.... Barnard, VT.
1813. 120 pp. . . . . *$20.00–$25.00*

Livingston, John. *Birds of the Northern Forest.* Houghton Mifflin. 1956. 1st ed. dj.
. . . . *$20.00–$35.00*

Livingstone, David. *Missionary Travels and Researches in South Africa.* Lon. John
Murray. 1857. 1st ed. 687 pp, map. . . . . *$400.00–$600.00*

Livingstone, David. *Missionary Travels and Researches in South Africa..* NY. 1858.
illus. 1st Amer ed. maps. . . . . *$300.00–$500.00*

Livingstone, David and Charles Livingstone. *Narrative of an Expedition to the
Zambesi and Its Tributaries; 1858-1864.* Lon. John Murray. 1865. 1st ed. fldg map,
tan cl. . . . . *$250.00–$375.00*

Livingtone, David and Charles Livingstone. *Narrative of an Expedition to the
Zambesi and Its Tributaries; 1858-1864.* NY. Harper & Bros. 1866. 1st Amer ed.
illus, fldg map.. . . . . *$110.00–$125.00*

Llewellyn, Karl. *Cheyenne Way.* Norman. Univ of OK. 1941. 1st ed. illus. scarce. .
....$50.00–$65.00

LLewellyn, Sam. *Blood Orange.* NY. Summit. 1989. 1st ed. dj. . . . *$15.00–$25.00*

Lloyd, A. B. *In Dwarf Land and Cannibal Country.* Lon. Fisher Unwin. 1899. 1st ed.
illus. photos. ....$69.00–$100.00

Lloyd, Freeman. *All Spaniels.* NY. nd. illus. ....*$15.00–$25.00*

Lloyd, James T. *Lloyd's Topographical Railway Map of North America, or the
United States Continent in 1900.* NY. 1867. wall map.......*$1,750.00–$1,900.00*

Lobel, Arnold. *Fables.* Harper Collins (1980). illus. pict dj. ......*$10.00–$15.00*

Lobel, Arnold. *Frog and Toad All Year.* NY. Harper & Row. 1976. 1st ed. sgn with
original Lobel Frog character. ....$48.00–$60.00

Locke, David Ross. *Hannah Jane.* Lon. Lee and Shepard. 1882. 1st ed. ....
....$65.00–$125.00

Locke, David Ross. *Ekkoes from Kentucky by Petroleum B Nasby.* Bos. 1868. 1st ed.
illus. by Thomas Nast.................................$100.00–$150.00

Lockett, Hattie Greene. *Unwritten Literature of the Hopi.* Tucson. 1933. wrps. illus.
photos. Bulletin No. 2, Vol. IV, No. 4...........................$28.00–$40.00

Lockridge, Richard. *One Lady, Two Cats.* Lon. Hutchinson. 1968. 1st UK ed. dj.. .
....$200.00–$300.00

Lockwood, Luke V. *Colonial Furniture in America.* NY. 1926. 2 vols. 3rd ed.......
....$95.00–$125.00

Lodge, Sir Oliver. *Electrons.* Lon. 1907. 2nd ed. ....*$40.00–$65.00*

Lodge, Sir Oliver. *Ether and Reality.* Lon. 1925. 1st ed. ....*$15.00–$30.00*

Loewy, Raymond. *Locomotive.* Lon/NY. The Studio. (1937). 1st ed. illus. tan cl lettering in dark brown..................................$65.00–$100.00

Lofting, Hugh. *Doctor Dolittle and the Secret Lake.* Phila. Lippincott. (1948).
1st ed. illus. dj. ....$75.00–$100.00

Lofting, Hugh. *Doctor Dolittle in the Moon.* NY. Stokes. (1928). 1st ed. illus. by
author. ....$150.00–$200.00

Lofting, Hugh. *Doctor Dolittle's Circus.* NY. (1924). 1st ed. .....*$40.00–$50.00*

Lofting, Hugh. *Doctor Doolittle's Zoo.* NY. Stokes. (1925). 1st ed. *$30.00–$50.00*

Lofting, Hugh. *Voyages of Doctor Dolittle.* NY. Stokes. 1922. illus. 2nd printing. . .
....$60.00–$90.00

Logan, H. and L. C. Cosper. *Orchids Are Easy to Grow*. Englewood Cliffs, NJ. 1949. dj. . . . . *$25.00–$35.00*

Logan, James & R R McIan. *Clans of the Scottish Highlands*. Lon. Ackerman & Co. 1845-47. 2 vols. 1st ed. illus. 72 hand-clr plates, folio, 2 clr armorial frontises. . . . . *$5,000.00–$7,000.00*

Logan, Mrs. John. *Reminiscences of a Soldier's Wife*. NY. Scribner's. 1913. 1st ed. illus. inscr and sgn. . . . . *$40.00–$60.00*

Logan, Mrs. John A. *Thirty Years In Washington*. Hartford. 1901. 1st ed. illus. 3/4 lea and red cl. . . . . *$35.00–$75.00*

Logue, Roscoe. *Tumbleweeds and Barb Wire Fences.*. Amarillo. 1936. 1st ed. illus. . . . . *$30.00–$45.00*

Logue, Roscoe. *Under Texas and Border Skies.*. Amarillo. 1935. wrps. 2nd prtg. . . . . *$45.00–$65.00*

Lomax, Alan. *Folk Songs of North America*. Garden City. (1960). . *$25.00–$35.00*

Lomax, John A. *Adventures of a Ballad Hunter*. NY. 1947. 1st ed. dj. . . . . *$30.00–$60.00*

Lomax, John A. *Cowboy Songs and Other Frontier Ballads*. NY. 1911. 1st ed. 2nd prtg. dj. . . . . *$65.00–$115.00*

Lomax, John A. and Alan Lomax. *American Ballads and Folk Songs*. NY. 1934. 1st ed. . . . . *$90.00–$125.00*

Lommel, A. *Masks, Their Meaning and Function*. Zurich. 1970. photos. . . . . *$100.00–$135.00*

London, Jack. *A Daughter of the Snows*. Phila. Lippincott. 1902. 1st ed. illus. red cl. . . . . *$250.00–$450.00*

London, Jack. *A Son of the Sun*. Garden City. Doubleday, Page. 1912. 1st ed. navy blue cl.. . . . . *$300.00–$500.00*

London, Jack. *Before Adam*. NY. Macmillan. 1907. 1st ed. illus. clr plates, map, buckram. . . . . *$25.00–$75.00*

London, Jack. *Burning Daylight*. NY. Macmillan. 1910. 1st ed. *$100.00–$125.00*

London, Jack. *Children of the Frost*. NY. Macmillan. 1902. 1st ed. blue-gray cl.. . . . . *$350.00–$500.00*

London, Jack. *Dutch Courage and Other Stories*. NY. Macmillan. 1922. 1st ed. 7 plates, red cl, with dj.. . . . . *$950.00–$2,000.00*

London, Jack. *Hearts of Three*. NY. McClure, Phillips. 1920. 1st Amer ed. maroon cl. . . . . *$225.00–$500.00*

London, Jack. *Jerry of the Islands.* NY. Macmillan. 1917. 1st ed. red cl.. . . . .
. . . . *$200.00–$300.00*

London, Jack. *John Barleycorn.* NY. Century. 1913. 1st ed. 1st prtg. plates, green cl.
. . . . *$75.00–$175.00*

London, Jack. *Lost Face.* NY. Macmillan. 1910. 1st ed. illus. plates, blue cl. . . . . .
. . . . *$375.00–$450.00*

London, Jack. *Love of Life and Other Stories.* NY. Macmillan. 1907. 1st ed. blue cl.
. . . . *$150.00–$450.00*

London, Jack. *Martin Eden.* NY. Macmillan. 1909. 1st ed. blue cl. *$100.00–$375.00*

London, Jack. *Michael, Brother of Jerry.* NY. Macmillan. 1917. 1st ed. red cl. . . . .
. . . . *$45.00–$25.00*

London, Jack. *Moon-Face and Other Stories.* NY. Macmillan. 1906. 1st ed. blue cl,
teg. . . . . *$125.00–$250.00*

London, Jack. *On the Maaloa Mat.* NY. Macmillan. 1919. 1st ed. green-blue cl. . .
. . . . *$400.00–$500.00*

London, Jack. *Revolution and Other Essays.* NY. Macmillan. 1910. 1st ed. variant
binding. . . . . *$475.00–$500.00*

London, Jack. *Scorn of Women, In Three Acts.* NY. Macmillan. 1906. 1st ed. 1st
issue. maroon cl, teg. . . . . *$1,300.00–$2,250.00*

London, Jack. *Smoke Bellew.* NY. Century. 1912. 1st ed. illus. plates, blue-gray cl..
. . . . *$90.00–$225.00*

London, Jack. *South Sea Tales.* NY. Macmillan. 1911. 1st ed. blue cl. . . . .
. . . . *$200.00–$350.00*

London, Jack. *Tales of the Fish Patrol.* NY. Macmillan. 1905. 1st ed. illus. map,
plates. blue cl, teg. . . . . *$175.00–$500.00*

London, Jack. *The Abysmal Brute.* NY. Century. 1913. 1st ed. illus. cl stamped in
black & yellow, dj. . . . . *$85.00–$1,500.00*

London, Jack. *The Abysmal Brute.* NY. Century. 1913. 1st ed. later issue, cl stamped
in balck & green, dj. *$1,750.00*

London, Jack. *The Acorn-Planter: A California Forest Play.* NY. Macmillan. 1916.
1st ed. cl, teg. . . . . *$900.00–$1,200.00*

London, Jack. *The Adventure.* NY. Macmillan. 1911. 1st Amer ed. blue cl. . . . .
. . . . *$175.00–$450.00*

London, Jack. *The Call of the Wild.* NY. Macmillan. 1903. 1st ed. 1st issue. illus. by
Godwin & Livingston Bull. green cl, teg, with dust jacket.. . . *$6,000.00–$8,500.00*

London, Jack. *The Cruise of the Dazzler.* NY. Century. 1902. 1st ed. illus. . . . . .
. . . . *$2,000.00–$2,500.00*

London, Jack. *The Cruise of the Snark.* NY. Macmillan. 1911. 1st ed. illus. blue-
green cl, teg. . . . . *$250.00–$500.00*

London, Jack. *The Faith of Men and Other Stories.* NY. Macmillan. 1904. 1st ed.
blue cl, teg. . . . . *$150.00–$475.00*

London, Jack. *The Game.* NY. Macmillan. 1905. 1st ed. illus. by Henry Hutt & T.
C. Lawrence. clr plates, green cl, teg. *$300.00–$1,000.00*

London, Jack. *The God of His Fathers and Other Stories.* NY. McClure, Phillips.
1901. 1st ed. blue cl. . . . . *$350.00–$800.00*

London, Jack. *The House of Pride and Other Tales of Hawaii.* NY. Macmillan.
1912. 1st ed. green cl. . . . . *$250.00–$1,000.00*

London, Jack. *The Human Drift.* NY. Macmillan. 1917. 1st ed. red-brown cl. . . . .
. . . . *$300.00–$600.00*

London, Jack. *The Iron Heel.* NY. Macmillan. 1908. 1st ed. blue cl. . . . .
. . . . *$200.00–$350.00*

London, Jack. *The Iron Heel.* NY. Wilshire Book Co. 1908. blue cl. *$95.00–$300.00*

London, Jack. *The Little Lady of the Big House.* NY. Macmillan. 1916. 1st ed. blue
cl. . . . . *$60.00–$100.00*

London, Jack. *The Night-Born.* NY. Century. 1913. 1st ed. blue cl. . . . .
. . . . *$200.00–$375.00*

London, Jack. *The People of the Abyss.* NY. Macmillan. 1903. 1st ed. illus. plates,
teg. . . . . *$350.00–$650.00*

London, Jack. *The Red One.* NY. Macmillan. 1918. 1st ed. brown bds. . . . .
. . . . *$500.00–$1,000.00*

London, Jack. *The Road.* NY. Macmillan. 1907. 1st ed. illus. photo plates. . . . . . .
. . . . *$300.00–$2,500.00*

London, Jack. *The Scarlet Plague.* NY. Macmillan. 1915. 1st ed. illus. by Plum. red
cl. . . . . *$195.00–$750.00*

London, Jack. *The Sea-Wolf.* NY. Macmillan. 1904. 1st ed. plates, teg, gilt on spine.
. . . . *$500.00–$750.00*

London, Jack. *The Son of the Wolf: Tales of the Far North.* Bos. Houghton Mifflin.
1900. 1st ed. 1st prtg. gray cl. . . . . *$750.00–$950.00*

London, Jack. *The Star Rover.* NY. Macmillan. 1915. 1st Amer ed. blue cl. . . . . .
. . . . *$250.00–$850.00*

London, Jack. *The Strength of the Stron.* NY. Macmillan. 1914. 1st ed. blue cl. . . .
. . . . *$125.00–$375.00*

London, Jack. *The Turtles of Tasman.* NY. Macmillan. 1916. 1st ed. mauve cl. . . . .
. . . . *$75.00–$650.00*

London, Jack. *The Valley of the Moon.* NY. Macmillan. 1913. 1st ed. orange cl. . . .
. . . . *$300.00–$500.00*

London, Jack. *Theft: a Play in Four Acts.* NY. Macmillan. 1910. 1st ed. . . . .
. . . . *$600.00–$900.00*

London, Jack. *War of the Classes.* NY. Macmillan. 1905. 1st ed. maroon cl. . . . . . .
. . . . *$250.00–$350.00*

London, Jack. *When God Laughs and Other Stories.* NY. Macmillan. 1911. 1st ed.
plates. . . . . *$300.00–$500.00*

London, Jack. *White Fang.* NY. Macmillan. 1906. 1st ed. 2nd issue. plates. . . . . . .
. . . . *$30.00–$100.00*

London, Jack. *Wonder of a Woman: A "Smoke Bellew" Story.* NY. International
Magazine Co. (1912). wrps. . . . . *$200.00–$300.00*

Long, E. *History of Pathology.* Balt. 1928. 1st ed. . . . . *$40.00–$50.00*

Long, Haniel. *Children, Students, and a Few Adults.* Santa Fe. 1942. 1st ed. wrps. .
. . . . *$35.00–$75.00*

Long, Haniel. *Grist Mill.* NM. Rydal Press. 1946. 1st ed. dj. . . . . . *$35.00–$50.00*

Long, Haniel. *Interliner to Cabeza de Vaca.* Santa Fe. 1936. 1st ed. dj. . . . .
. . . . *$175.00–$250.00*

Long, Haniel. *Notes for a New Mythology.* Chi. 1926. 1st ed. ltd 450 cc, sgn. . . . . . .
. . . . *$55.00–$175.00*

Long, Haniel. *Pinon Country.* NY. (1941). 1st ed. dj. . . . . *$40.00–$85.00*

Long, Haniel. *Spring Returns.* NY. (1958). 1st ed. dj. . . . . *$15.00–$35.00*

Long, Huey. *My First Days in the White House.* Telegraph Press. 1935. 1st ed. . . . . .
. . . . *$45.00–$50.00*

Long, John Luther. *Billy Boy.* NY. 1906. 1st ed. illus. in clr and b/w by Jesse Willcox
Smith. scarce. . . . . *$95.00–$135.00*

Long, Major A. W. *Irish Sport of Yesterday.* Bos. Houghton Mifflin. 1923. 1st ed.
illus. . . . . *$40.00–$100.00*

Long, William J. *Following the Deer.* Ginn & Co. 1903. 1st ed. . . . .
. . . . *$25.00–$40.00*

Longfellow, Henry Wadsworth. *Courtship of Miles Standish.* Ind. 1903. 1st thus. clr & b/w illus. . . . . *$50.00–$85.00*

Longfellow, Henry Wadsworth. *Courtship of Miles Standish and Other Poems.* Bos. Ticknor & Fields. 1858. 1st ed. . . . . *$80.00–$150.00*

Longfellow, Henry Wadsworth. *Divine Tragedy.* Bos. James R Osgood. 1871. 1st ed. . . . . *$75.00–$175.00*

Longfellow, Henry Wadsworth. *Longfellow's Poetical Works.* Bos. Houghton Mifflin. 1886. 4 vols. . . . . *$60.00–$75.00*

Longfellow, Henry Wadsworth. *Poetical Works.* Lon. illus. 6 mounted albumen photos, mor, aeg. . . . . *$50.00–$90.00*

Longfellow, Henry Wadsworth. *Song of Hiawatha.* Platt & Monk. 1963. 1st ed. thus gold illus cl. . . . . *$35.00–$50.00*

Longfellow, Henry Wadsworth. *Song of Hiawatha.* Bos. Ticknor and Fields. 1855. 1st Amer ed. points of issue include 'Dove' instead of 'Dived' in line 7 page 95. . . . . *$300.00–$500.00*

Longfellow, Henry Wadsworth. *Tales of a Wayside Inn.* Bos. 1863. 1st ed. . . . . *$150.00–$175.00*

Longman, E. D. *Pins & Pincushions.* Lon. Longmans & Green. 1911. 1st ed. illus. cl. . . . . *$45.00–$175.00*

Longstreet, Augustus B. *Georgia Scenes.* NY. 1860. 2nd ed. 214 pp, illus. . . . . *$65.00–$85.00*

Longstreet, Helen D. *Lee and Longstreet At High Tide: Gettysburg....* Gainesville, Ga. 1905. illus. 2nd ed. . . . . *$50.00–$100.00*

Longstreet, Stephen. *Real Jazz Old and New.* Baton Rouge. Louisiana State Univ Press. 1956. 1st ed. illus. dj. . . . . *$50.00–$95.00*

Longstreet, Stephen. *Sportin' House.* LA. Sherbourne Press. 1965. 1st ed. illus. dj. . . . . *$25.00–$65.00*

Longstreth, T. Morris. *Understanding the Weather.* NY. 1953. rev ed, dj, 10 illus, 118 pp. . . . . *$10.00–$14.00*

Lonn, Ella. *Reconstruction in Louisiana After 1868.* NY/Lon. 1918. 1st ed. maps. . . . . *$75.00–$125.00*

Lonn, Ella. *Salt as a Factor in the Confederacy.* NY. 1933. 1st ed. . . . . *$125.00–$175.00*

Loomis, Frederic. *Hunting Extinct Animals in Patagonian Pampas.* NY. 1913. 141 pp, illus. . . . . *$65.00–$85.00*

Loos, Anita. *Gentlemen Prefer Blondes.* NY. 1925. 1st ed. dj...... *$65.00–$95.00*

Lopez, Barry. *Crossing Open Ground.* NY. Scribner's. 1988. 1st ed. dj. ....
.... *$30.00–$40.00*

Lopez, Barry. *Of Wolves and Men.* NY. Scribner's. 1978. 1st ed. dj.*$95.00–$125.00*

Loque, Roscoe. *Tumbleweeds and Barb Wire Fences.* Amarillo. 1936. 1st ed. wrps.
.... *$50.00–$85.00*

Lord, Eliot, John Trenor and Samuel Barrows. *Italian in America.* NY. B.F. Buck
& Co. 1905. illus. red cl, frontis. .... *$40.00–$70.00*

Lorentz, H. A. *Theory of Electrons....* Leipzig. 1916. 2nd ed. ..... *$30.00–$40.00*

Loring, Charles G. *Neutral Relations of England & the United States.* NY. 1863.
wrps. .... *$30.00–$60.00*

Loss of the United States Steamer Oneida. US Gov Doc, HED #236. 1870. fldg map.
.... *$25.00–$35.00*

Lossing, Benson J. *History of the Civil War, 1861-1865.* NY. 1912. illus. ....
.... *$65.00–$90.00*

Lossing, Benson J. *Pictorial Field Book of the American Revolution.* Freeport NY.
1969. 2 vols. rprnt. .... *$35.00–$55.00*

Lossing, Benson J. *Pictorial Field-Book of the War of 1812.* NY. Harper & Bros.
1869. clr frontis, gilt red calf, rbkd. .... *$150.00–$225.00*

Lossing, Benson J. *Pictorial History of the Civil War in the United States....* Phila.
1866. 3 vols. 1/2 lea. .... *$85.00–$100.00*

Lossing, Benson. *A History of the Civil War.* NY. 1912. illus. with photos by Brady,
16 parts. wrps. .... *$100.00–$250.00*

Lothrop, Jason. *Juvenile Philosopher: or, Youth's Manual of Philosophy, Natural
Experimental & Analytical.* Bogert. 1823. 312 pp. .... *$125.00–$150.00*

Love, Robertus. *Rise and Fall of Jesse James.* NY. (1939). ...... *$22.00–$33.00*

Lovecraft, H. P. *At the Mountains of Madness and Other Novels.* Sauk City. Arkham
House. 1964. 1st ed. dj. .... *$125.00–$250.00*

Lovecraft, H. P. *Dagon and Other Macabre Tales.* Sauk City. Arkham House. 1965.
1st ed. dj. .... *$100.00–$125.00*

Lovecraft, H. P. *Dark Brotherwood.* Arkham House. 1966. 1st ed. dj. ....
.... *$95.00–$125.00*

Lovecraft, H. P. *Dunwich Horror & Others.* Sauk City. Arkham House. 1963. 1st ed.
dj. .... *$90.00–$125.00*

Lovecraft, H. P. *Horror in the Museum and Other Revisions.* Sauk City. Arkham House. 1970. 1st ed. dj. . . . . *$50.00–$150.00*

Lovecraft, H. P. *Something About Cats.* Sauk City. Arkham House. 1949. 1st ed. dj. . . . . *$140.00–$175.00*

Lovecraft, H. P and August Derleth. *Lurker at the Threshold.* Sauk City. Arkham House. 1945. 1st ed. dj. . . . . *$85.00–$175.00*

Lovecraft, H. P. and August Derleth. *Watchers Out of Time.* Arkham House. 1974. 1st ed. dj. . . . . *$30.00–$45.00*

Lovecraft, H. P and Diverse Hands. *Dark Brotherhood and Other Pieces.* Sauk City. Arkham House. 1966. 1st ed. dj. . . . . *$50.00–$125.00*

Lovell, Mrs. F. S. and L. C. Lovell. *History of the Town of Rockingham, Vt.* Bellows Falls. 1958. illus. . . . . *$35.00–$45.00*

Lovett, Sarah. *Dangerous Attachments.* NY. (1995). 1st ed. dj. . . . . *$25.00–$35.00*

Lowel, G. *More Small Italian Villas and Farmhouses.* NY. 1920. folio. *$70.00–$85.00*

Lowell, Amy. *John Keats.* Bos. Houghton Mifflin. 1925. 2 vols. 1st ed. illus. cl. . . . . *$35.00–$70.00*

Lowell, James Russell. *Biglow Papers.* Bos. Ticknor & Fields. 1867. 1st Amer ed. . . . . *$75.00–$150.00*

Lowell, James Russell. *The Courtin'.* Bos. 1874. illus. by Winslow Homer. . . . . *$75.00–$125.00*

Lowell, James Russell. *The Rose.* Bos. 1878. . . . . *$24.00–$45.00*

Lowell Offering. Lowell, MA. Misses Curtis & Farley. May, 1845. wrps. rare. . . . . *$35.00–$50.00*

Lowell, Percival. *Mars and Its Canals.* NY. Macmillan. 1906. 1st ed. illus. green cl. . . . . *$180.00–$240.00*

Lowell, Robert. *For the Union Dead.* NY. Farrar, Straus & Giroux. (c1964). 1st ed. dj. . . . . *$35.00–$50.00*

Lowell, Robert. *Mils of the Kavanaughs.* NY. 1951. 1st ed. . . . . *$100.00–$125.00*

Lowell, Robert. *Oresteia of Aeschylus.* NY. Farrar, Straus & Giroux. (1978). 1st ed. dj, blue cl. . . . . *$45.00–$55.00*

Lower Colorado River Land Use Plan. DC. GPO. 1964. wrps. illus. clr maps. . . . . *$35.00–$50.00*

Lowie, Robert H. *Primitive Religion.* Lon. Routledge. 1925. 1st UK ed. . . . . *$95.00–$125.00*

Lubbock, Basil. *Last of the Windjammers.* Bos. Lauriat. 1927. 1st Amer ed. 2 vols. illus. blue cl. . . . . *$75.00–$125.00*

Lubbock, Basil. *Log of the Cutty Sark.* Glasgow. Brownison & Ferguson. 1974. rprnt, dj. . . . . *$25.00–$40.00*

Lubbock, Sir John. *Ants, Bees and Wasps.* NY. 1890. . . . . *$37.00–$40.00*

Lubbock, Sir John. *Origin of Civilisation and the Primitive Condition of Man.* NY. Appleton. 1895. illus. green cl, frontis. . . . . *$35.00–$50.00*

Ludlow, Fitz Hugh. *Heart of the Continent, A Record of Travel Across the Plains....* NY. 1870. . . . . *$100.00–$150.00*

Ludlum, Robert. *Bourne Ultimatum.* NY. Random House. 1990. 1st ed. dj. . . . . *$20.00–$30.00*

Ludlum, Robert. *Icarus Agenda.* NY. Random House. 1988. 1st ed. dj. *$10.00–$30.00*

Ludlum, Robert. *Road to Gandolfo.* NY. DialPress. 1975. 1st ed. 3 dj's. . . . . *$60.00–$100.00*

Ludlum, Robert. *Scarlatti Inheritance.* NY. World Pub. (1971). 1st ed. dj. . . . . *$35.00–$75.00*

Lumholtz, Carl. *Among Cannibals.* NY. 1889. portrait maps, chromolitho, decorative cl, 395 pp. . . . . *$175.00–$300.00*

Lumley, Brian. *Beneath the Moors.* Sauk City.. Arkham House. 1974. 1st ed. dj. . . . . *$30.00–$85.00*

Lummis, Charles F. *King of the Broncos & Other Stories of New Mexico.* NY. 1897. . . . . *$40.00–$55.00*

Lummis, Charles F. *Mesa, Canon and Pueblo.* Century. (1925). illus. *$22.00–$35.00*

Lunn, Arnold. *The Mountains of Youth.* Lon. Oxford Univ Press. 1925. 1st ed. illus. moss green cl. . . . . *$25.00–$45.00*

Lutz, Alma. *Created Equal.* John Day. (1940). 1st ed. sgn, dj. . . . . *$40.00–$50.00*

Lutz, Frank. *Fieldbook of Insects.* NY. 1921. illus. clr plates. . . . . . *$18.00–$25.00*

Lydenberg, Harry. *Care and Repair of Books.* NY. R. R. Bowker Co. 1931. 1st ed. . . . . *$25.00–$40.00*

Lyell, Sir Charles. *Travels in North America, Canada, and Nova Scotia with Geological Observations.* Lon. John Murray. 1855. 2nd ed. fldg map, plates. . . . . *$250.00–$325.00*

Lymon, Henry and Frank Woolner. *Complete Book of Striped Bass Fishing.* NY. (1954). dj. . . . . *$15.00–$25.00*

Lynch Bohun. *Collecting.* Lon. Jarrolds. 1928. 1st ed. presentation copy sgn. . . . .
. . . . *$20.00–$45.00*

Lynch, Jeremiah. *Egyptian Sketches.* Lon. 1890. illus. . . . . *$40.00–$75.00*

Lynk, Miles. *Black Troopers....* Tenn. M. V. Lynk Pub House. 1899. illus. red cl.. .
. . . . *$750.00–$1,000.00*

Lynk, Miles. *Black Troopers....* Tenn. 1971. rprnt.. . . . . *$30.00–$45.00*

Lyons, Nick. *Confessions of a Fly Fishing Addict.* NY. Simon & Schuster. 1989.
1st ed. dj.. . . . . *$25.00–$40.00*

M'Clintock, Capt. *Voyage of the Fox in the Arctic Seas.* Bos. Ticknor & Fields.
1860. illus. 4 maps, 3 fldg. . . . . *$40.00–$60.00*

M'Clintock, Francis L. *Voyage of the 'Fox' in the Arctic Seas.* Bos. Ticknor &
Fields. 1860. author's ed. small 8vo, frontis, illus, fldg maps. . . . *$100.00–$130.00*

Mabie, Hamilton Wright. *Under the Trees & Elsewhere.* NY. Dodd, Mead. 1902.
illus. 1st illus ed.. . . . . *$30.00–$60.00*

MacBeth, R. G. *making of the Canadian West: Being the Reminiscences of an Eye-
Witness.* Tor. Briggs. 1898. 1st ed. gilt-stamped maroon cl. . . . . *$50.00–$80.00*

MacDiarmid, Hugh. *Sangshaw.* Blackwood. 1925. 1st ed. dj. . . *$150.00–$300.00*

MacDonald, Alexander. *Design for Angling, The Dry Fly on Western Trout Streams.*
Bos. 1947. . . . . *$65.00–$100.00*

MacDonald, John D. *Pale Gray for Guilt.* NY. Gold Medal Books. 1968. 1st ed.
wrps.. . . . . *$35.00–$55.00*

MacDonald, John D. *The Girl, the Gold Watch and Everything.* Lon. Robert Hale.
1974. 1st hardcvr ed. dj. . . . . *$80.00–$90.00*

MacDonald, John D. *The Long Lavender Look.* Phila. Lippincott. 1972. 1st hardcvr
ed. dj. . . . . *$250.00–$300.00*

Macdonald, Ross. *The Chill.* NY. Knopf. 1964. 1st ed. cl. . . . . . . *$75.00–$225.00*

MacDonald, Ross. *The Underground Man.* NY. Knopf. 1971. 1st ed. dj.. . . . .
. . . . *$40.00–$60.00*

MacFall, Haldane. *Aubrey Beardsley, The Man and His Work.* Lon. 1928. illus. . .
. . . . *$75.00–$125.00*

MacGillivray, D. *Mandarin-Romanized Dictionary of Chinese.* Shanghai. 1918. 4th
ed.. . . . . *$25.00–$35.00*

MacGillvray. *History of British Quadrapeds.* Edin. 1838. 1st ed. 310 pp. . . . .
. . . . *$100.00–$140.00*

Machen, Arthur. *London Adventure.* Lon. Martin Secker. (1924). dj. . . . .
. . . . *$65.00–$75.00*

Machen, Arthur. *Rose Garden.* NY. 1932. wrps. 50 cc privately printed. . . . .
. . . . *$30.00–$40.00*

Machen, Arthur. *Things Near and Far.* NY. (1923). 1st Amer ed. . *$20.00–$30.00*

Mack, Arthur C. *Palisades of the Hudson.* NJ. The Palisade Press. (1909). 1st ed.
illus. red pict cvr, pull-out map. . . . . *$35.00–$95.00*

Macken, Arthur. *Dog and Duck.* NY. 1924. 1st ed. . . . . *$22.00–$30.00*

Mackenzie, A. L. *Clarence Milton, the Heroic Fireman....* Cleveland. United Printing
Co. 1900. 1st ed. illus. blue cl. . . . . *$50.00–$75.00*

MacKenzie, Alexander. *Voyages from Montreal on the River St. Lawrence.* Tor.
Master Works. 1927. illus. . . . . *$65.00–$125.00*

MacKenzie, Colin. *MacKenzie's Five Thousand Recipes.* Phila. 1825. *$35.00–$100.00*

Mackenzie, Jean Kenyon. *Black Sheep: Adventures in West Africa.* Bos. Houghton
Mifflin. 1916. 1st ed. illus. photos. . . . . *$80.00–$100.00*

MacLean, Alistair. *Guns of Navarone.* NY. Doubleday. 1957. 1st ed. dj. . . . .
. . . . *$50.00–$125.00*

MacLean, Alistair. *HMS Ulysses.* Lon. Collins. [1955]. 1st UK ed. author's first
book, dj. . . . . *$95.00–$250.00*

MacLean, Alistair. *Ice Station Zebra.* Lon. Collins. 1963. 1st ed. dj. . *$30.00–$45.00*

MacLean, Alistair. *Lonely Sea.* Garden City. Doubleday. 1986. 1st ed. green cl dj. .
. . . . *$15.00–$35.00*

Maclean, Alistair. *South by Java Head.* Lon. Collins. 1958. 1st ed. dj. . . . .
. . . . *$50.00–$75.00*

MacLean, Norman. *River Runs Through It.* Chi. 1976. 1st ed. illus. dj. . . . .
. . . . *$35.00–$75.00*

MacLeish, Archibald. *Conquistador.* Bos/NY. Houghton Mifflin. 1932. 1st ed. no
dj. . . . . *$20.00–$35.00*

MacLeish, Archibald. *Herakles.* Bos. 1967. 1st ed. dj. . . . . *$20.00–$25.00*

MacLeish, Archibald. *Irresponsibles.* Duell. 1944. 1st ed. dj. . . . . . *$25.00–$40.00*

MacLeish, Archibald. *Public Speech.* NY. Farrar & Rinhart. (1936). 1st ed. sgn. . . .
. . . . *$80.00–$120.00*

MacLeod, G. *Treatment of Horses by Homeopathy.* Walden, Eng. Daniel Co, Ltd.
1983. dj. . . . . *$18.00–$25.00*

MacManus, Seaumas. *Red Poocher.* 1903. 1st US ed. . . . . *$25.00–$35.00*

Maeterlinck, Maurice. *Blue Bird.* NY. Souvenir Books. 1910. illus. pict cvrs. . . .
. . . . *$30.00–$40.00*

Maeterlinck, Maurice. *Blue Bird.* NY. 1911. illus. with 25 clr plates by Robinson.
. . . . *$125.00–$160.00*

Maeterlinck, Maurice. *Life of the Bee.* Lon. George Allen. (1911). 1st ed. illus. .
. . . . *$150.00–$200.00*

Maeterlinck, Maurice. *Life of the White Ant.* 1939. illus. sgn by von Hagen. . . . .
. . . . *$20.00–$25.00*

Maeterlinck, Maurice. *Intelligence of the Flowers.* NY. (1907). 1st Amer ed.
decorated bds. . . . . *$30.00–$40.00*

Magalever, Jacob. *Death to Traitors.* 1960. 1st ed. dj. . . . . *$20.00–$25.00*

Magician's Own Book.... NY. 1857. 1st ed. . . . . *$150.00–$200.00*

Magner, D. *Standard Horse and Stock Book.* Akron. Standard. 1903. . . . .
. . . . *$100.00–$125.00*

Mahan, A. T. *Gulf and Inland Waters.* NY. Scribner's. 1883. 1st ed. maps and plans.
. . . . *$85.00–$125.00*

Mahan, A. T. *Life of Nelson.* Bos. Little, Brown. 1900. 2 vols. 2nd ed. revised, illus,
20 maps & plans, teg. . . . . *$120.00–$150.00*

Mahan, A. T. *Sea Power In Its Relation to the War of 1812.* Lon. 1905. 2 vols. dj..
. . . . *$78.00–$95.00*

Mahan, A. T. *Types of Naval Officers.* Lon. 1902. illus. plates. . . . . . *$55.00–$74.00*

Maidment, James (ed.). *Scottish Ballads and Songs.* Edin. 1868. 2 vols. . . . .
. . . . *$35.00–$45.00*

Mailer, Norman. *Advertisements For Myself.* NY. Putnam. 1959. 1st ed. dj. . . . . .
. . . . *$35.00–$45.00*

Mailer, Norman. *An American Dream.* NY. Dial Press. 1971. 1st ed. dj. . . . .
. . . . *$28.00–$45.00*

Mailer, Norman. *Barbara Shore.* NY. Rinehart & Co. (1951). 1st ed. dj. . . . .
. . . . *$75.00–$100.00*

Mailer, Norman. *Last Night. A Story of Armageddon.* NY. 1984. ltd 250 cc, sgn. .
. . . . *$95.00–$130.00*

Mailer, Norman. *Marilyn, A Biography.* NY. 1973. 1st ed. dj. . . . . *$35.00–$50.00*

Mailer, Norman. *Naked and the Dead.* NY. Rinehart. (1948). 1st ed. sgn, dj. . . . . .
. . . . *$500.00–$1,700.00*

Mailer, Norman. *Prisoner of Sex.* NY. 1971. dj. . . . . *$20.00–$30.00*

Maine, a Guide Down East. Bos. Houghton Mifflin. 1937. illus. map in rear pocket,
dj. . . . . *$25.00–$35.00*

Major, John (ed.). *Complete Angler.* Lon. D. Bogue. 1844. illus. 12 plates, woodcuts, large paper copy. . . . . *$100.00–$150.00*

Malamud, Bernard. *Dubin's Lives.* NY. 1979. 750 cc. . . . . *$45.00–$60.00*

Malamud, Bernard. *Magic Barrel.* Chatto & Windus. 1979. 1st UK ed dj. . . . .
. . . . *$18.00–$35.00*

Malamud, Bernard. *Magic Barrel.* NY. Farrar, Straus & Giroux. 1958. 1st ed. dj. . .
. . . . *$85.00–$150.00*

Malamud, Bernard. *Pictures of Fidelman.* Farra, Straus & Giroux. 1969. 1st ed. dj.
. . . . *$32.00–$40.00*

Malamud, Bernard. *The Fixer.* NY. 1966. 1st ed. dj. . . . . *$35.00–$50.00*

Malamud, Bernard. *The Natural.* NY. (1952). 1st ed. of author's first book. . . . . . .
. . . . *$125.00–$250.00*

Malamud, Bernard. *The Tenants.* Farrar, Straus & Giroux.. (1971). 1st ed. dj. . . . .
. . . . *$25.00–$50.00*

Malesworth, Mrs. *A Christmas Child.* Lon. 1880. . . . . *$50.00–$100.00*

Malls, Thom E. *People Called Apache.* NJ. 1974. dj. . . . . *$75.00–$125.00*

Mammals of Utah. Univ of KA Pub. wrps 1/50 cc. . . . . *$50.00–$65.00*

**Manfacturers of Military, Sporting, Hunting, and Target Breech-Loading Rifles,
Shotguns and Pistols.** NY. E. Remington & Sons. 1883. printed wrps, 48 pp. . . . . .
. . . . *$175.00–$250.00*

Mann, A. *History of the Forty-Fifth Regiment (Mass.).* 1908. . . . .
. . . . *$100.00–$150.00*

Mann, F. W. *Bullet's Flight from Powder to Target.* Huntington, WV. 1942. illus. photos, 2d ed. . . . . *$130.00–$175.00*

Mann, H. *Historical Annals of Dedham, MA, to 1847.* Dedham, MA. 1847. . . . . . .
. . . . *$65.00–$85.00*

Mann, Horace. *Speech of Hon Horace Mann of Mass on Slavery & the Slave Trade...*
Phila. 1849. 48 pp, unbound. . . . . *$60.00–$85.00*

Mann, Kathleen. *Peasant Costume In Europe*. Lon. 1931. illus. clr plates. . . . . . .
. . . . *$35.00–$80.00*

Mann, Mrs Horace. *Christianity in the Kitchen....* Bos. 1861. . . . . *$50.00–$72.00*

Mann, Thomas. *Joseph and His Brothers*. NY. 1938. 6th prtg of Amer ed. sgn.. . .
. . . . *$125.00–$150.00*

Mann, Thomas. *Magic Mountain*. NY. Knopf. 1927. 2 vols. 1st Amer ed.. . . . . . .
. . . . *$375.00–$900.00*

Mann, Thomas. *Tales of Jacob*. Lon. 1934. 1st ed. dj. . . . . *$130.00–$225.00*

Mann, Thomas. *This War*. NY. 1940. 1st Amer ed. 69 pp, dj. . . . . . *$50.00–$65.00*

Mann, Thomas. *Transposed Heads*. NY. Knopf. 1941. 1st Amer ed. dj.. . . . .
. . . . *$40.00–$65.00*

Manners, Customs, and Antiquities of the Indians of North and South America.
Bos. 1844. 1st ed. . . . . *$125.00–$150.00*

Manni, Pietro. *Manuale Pratico per la Cura degli Apparentemente Morti*. Napoli.
1835. 4th ed. plates.. . . . . *$200.00–$300.00*

Manning, Samuel. *Palestine Illustrated by Pen and Pencil*. NY. Hurst & Co. nd.
illus. folio pict cl. . . . . *$50.00–$75.00*

Mansfield, Katherine. *Doves Nest and Other Stories*. Lon. Constable. (1923). 1st
ed. dj. . . . . *$150.00–$200.00*

Mansfield, Katherine. *Novels and Novelists*. Lon. Constable. 1930. 1st ed. ed by J
Middleton Murray, dj. . . . . *$120.00–$150.00*

Mansfield, Katherine. *Poems*. NY. Knopf. 1924. 1st ed. . . . . *$35.00–$45.00*

Mansfield, Katherine. *Short Stories of....* NY. Knopf. 1937. . . . . . *$25.00–$35.00*

Mansfield, Katherine. *The Aloe*. NY. 1930. 1st Amer ed. 750 cc. . . . .
. . . . *$50.00–$100.00*

Manson, F. L. *Wright to 1910: The First Golden Age*. Reinhold. 1958. dj. . . . . . .
. . . . *$120.00–$150.00*

Mantle, Mickey & Phil Pepe. *My Favorite Summer*. NY. Doubleday. 1991. 1st ed.
dj. . . . . *$20.00–$25.00*

Manual of Homeopathic Veterinary Practice . . . Domestic Animals. NY. 1874. 1/2
lea. . . . . *$50.00–$75.00*

Manual of Pack Transportation. DC. GPO. 1917. illus. . . . . *$30.00–$40.00*

Manuel, Frank. *Portrait of Isaac Newton*. Belknap Press. 1968. dj. *$40.00–$50.00*

Manufacturers of Bells and Toys Catalogue No 40. East Hampton, CT. The N. N. Hill Brass Co. 1921. printed wrps, 31 pp. *$50.00–$75.00*

Manufacturers of Every Description of Aircraft, Balloons, Parachutes, Airships & Aeronautical Apparatus.... Lon. C. G. Spencer & Sons, Ltd. 1919. illus. pict wrps, 12 pp. . . . . *$125.00–$200.00*

Manufacturers of Horse Clothing, Harness and Saddlery. Phila. Blair & Letts. 1888-89. illus. printed wrps, 16 pp. . . . . *$50.00–$75.00*

Manwaring, Christopher. *Essays, Historical, Moral, Political and Agricultural.* New London, Ct. 1829. 1st ed. bds. . . . . *$85.00–$125.00*

March, Joseph. *Mancure.* NY. 1928. 6th prtg. . . . . *$18.00–$22.00*

March, Joseph Moncure. *The Set-Up.* NY. Covici Friede. 1928. . . *$25.00–$60.00*

Marcus, Jacob. *Rise and Destiny of the German Jew.* Cinc. Union of American Hebrew Congregations. 1934. black cl. . . . . *$15.00–$22.00*

Marcy, Randolph. *Prairie Traveler.* NY. Harper. 1859. 1st ed. illus. fldg map. . . . . *$300.00–$700.00*

Marie Burroughs Art Portfolio of Stage Celebrities. Chi. 1894. 14 parts, bound. . . . . *$50.00–$75.00*

Maritime History of New York. NY. WPA Writers Project. 1941. illus. dj. . . . . *$35.00–$50.00*

Marks, David. *Life Of....* Me. 1831. . . . . *$50.00–$100.00*

Marquand, John P. *Stopover: Tokyo.* Bos. 1957. 1st ed. dj. . . . . . . *$27.00–$35.00*

Marquis, Don. *Archy's Life of Mehitabel.* 1933. 1st ed. dj. . . . . . . *$85.00–$150.00*

Marquis, Don. *Danny's Own Story.* Garden City. 1912. 1st ed. . . . *$40.00–$75.00*

Marquis, Don. *Revolt of the Oyster.* NY. 1922. dj. . . . . *$30.00–$45.00*

Marriott, Alice. *Maria, The Potter of San Idelfonso.* Norman. 1948. 1st ed. dj. . . . . *$35.00–$100.00*

Marryat, Capt. *Children of the New Forest.* NY. Harper Bros. 1864. 279 pps. . . . . *$25.00–$35.00*

Marryat, Capt. Frederick. *Settlers in Canada..* Lon. 1844. 2 vols. 1st ed. mor, marbled bds. . . . . *$100.00–$150.00*

Marryatt, Frank. *Mountains and Molehills or Recollections of a Burnt Journal.* NY. Harper & Bros. 1855. 1st Amer ed. illus. . . . . *$100.00–$600.00*

Marsh, Ngaio. *Death of a Peer.* Bos. Little, Brown. 1940. 1st ed. dj. *$75.00–$100.00*

Marsh, Ngaio. *False Scent*. Lon. Collins Crime Club. 1960. 1st ed. dj. . . . .
. . . . *$40.00–$50.00*

Marsh, Ngaio. *Off With His Head*. Lon. Collins Crime Club. 1957. 1st ed. dj. . . . .
. . . . *$50.00–$70.00*

Marsh, Ngaio. *Scales of Justice*. Lon. Collins Crime Club. 1955. 1st ed. dj. . . . . .
. . . . *$35.00–$45.00*

Marsh, Ngaio. *Swing, Brother, Swing*. Lon. Collins Crime Club. 1949. 1st ed. dj. . .
. . . . *$60.00–$75.00*

Marsh, Othniel Charles. *Dinocerata: A Monograph of an Extinct Order of Gigantic Mammals*. DC. GPO. 1886. illus. plates. *$125.00–$175.00*

Marshall, A. J. *Bower Birds*. Clarendon Press. 1954. d j. . . . . *$60.00–$85.00*

Marshall, Albert O. *Army Life from a Soldier's Journal*. Ill. Self published. 1893.
. . . . *$60.00–$90.00*

Marshall, F. H. *Tempting Tours for Cyclists*. Lon. Russell. 1899. dark red cl. . . . .
. . . . *$20.00–$35.00*

Marshall, J. *History of the Colonies Planted by the English*. Phila. 1824. . . . .
. . . . *$40.00–$55.00*

Marshall, John. *Life of George Washington....* Phila. 1836. 2 vols. . . . .
. . . . *$50.00–$90.00*

Marshall, Logan. *Sinking of the Titanic and Great Sea Distasters*. Meyers. 1912. illus. red cl, pict pastedown. . . . . *$125.00–$300.00*

Martin & Martin. *Harness, Sadlery, Horse Clothing*. NY/Phila. 1890s cat. . . . . .
. . . . *$45.00–$60.00*

Martin, Charles-Noel. *The Atom: Friend or Foe*. Franklin Watts. (1962). dj. . . . . .
. . . . *$14.00–$25.00*

Martin, L. C. *Optical Measuring Instruments*. Glasgow. 1924. illus. ex lib, 270 pp.
. . . . *$30.00–$45.00*

Martin, Sadie E. *Life and Professional Career of Emma Abbott..* Minn. 1891. illus. photos. . . . . *$25.00–$35.00*

Martineau, Harriet. *Retrospect of Western Travel*. NY. Harper. 1838. 1st US ed. 276 pp, 239 pp. . . . . *$100.00–$300.00*

Martyn, Charles. *William Ward Genealogy....* NY. Artemus Ward. 1925. illus. . . .
. . . . *$45.00–$65.00*

Martyn, Mrs. S. T. *Women of the Bible*. NY. American Tract Society. 1868. illus.
. . . . *$20.00–$30.00*

Marvin, Edwin E. *Fifth Regiment, Connecticut Volunteers.* Hartford. Wiley, Waterman & Eaton. 1889. 1st ed. . . . . *$200.00–$275.00*

Marx, Karl. *World Without Jews.* NY. Philosophical Lib. 1959. 1st ed. dj. . . . . *$30.00–$40.00*

Marx, Karl & Frederick Engles. *Civil War In the United States.* NY. International Pub Co. 1937. 1st ed. . . . . *$40.00–$55.00*

Mary Rose, Rev. Mother. *Mission Tour in the Southwest Pacific.* (Bos. 1942). illus. . . . . *$15.00–$22.00*

Marzani, Cark. *We Can Be Friends: Origins of the Cold War.* NY. Topical Books. 1952. 1st ed. dj. . . . . *$15.00–$25.00*

Masefield, John. *Midnight Folk.* Lon. 1927. 1st Uk ed. dj. . . . . *$75.00–$95.00*

Masefield, John. *Taking of the Gry.* NY. Macmillan Co. (1934). 1st ed. red cl dj. . . . . *$25.00–$45.00*

Mason, A. E. W. *The Sapphire.* Lon. Hodder & Stoughton. 1933. 1st ed. dj. . . . . *$300.00–$400.00*

Mason, A. E. W. *The Three Gentlemen.* Garden City. Doubleday Doran. 1932. 1st Amer ed. dj. . . . . *$100.00–$150.00*

Mason, Amelia. *The Women of French Salons.* The Century Co. 1891. green cl. . . . . *$35.00–$100.00*

Mason, Amelia. *Women of the French Salons.* The Century Co. 1891. green cl, frontis. . . . . *$35.00–$45.00*

Mason, Bobbie Ann. *In Country.* NY. Harper & Row. [1985]. 1st ed. dj. . . . . *$30.00–$40.00*

Mason, Bobbie Ann. *Shiloh.* NY. Harper & Row. 1982. 1st ed. dj. . *$45.00–$60.00*

Mason, Charles F. *Medical Electricity.* 1887. 1st ed. . . . . *$30.00–$45.00*

Mason, F. Van Wyck. *Our Valiant Few.* Bos. Little, Brown. 1956. 1st ed. gray cl dj. . . . . *$25.00–$55.00*

Mason, F. Van Wyck. *Young Titan.* Garden City. Doubleday. (1959). 1st ed. dj dark blue cl. . . . . *$16.00–$40.00*

Mason, F. Van Wyck. *Rascal's Heaven.* Bos. Little, Brown. [1980]. 1st ed. dj. . . . . *$20.00–$30.00*

Mason, Michael H. *Where the River Runs Dry.* Lon. 1934. illus. dj.*$20.00–$30.00*

Mason, Otis Tufton. *Women's Share in Primitive Culture.* Lon. Macmillan. 1895. illus. dark brown cl. . . . . *$50.00–$85.00*

Massachusetts Atlas, Worcester County. Richards. 1898. . . . . *$300.00*

Masters, Edgar Lee. *Golden Fleece of California.* NY. (1936). 1st ed. . . . .
. . . . *$25.00–$35.00*

Masters, Edgar Lee. *Spoon River Anthology.* NY. 1915. 1st ed.   *$250.00–$350.00*

Matheson, R. *Handbook of the Mosquitoes of North America.* Ithaca. 1944. . . . . .
. . . . *$25.00–$35.00*

Mathews. *Writing Table of the 20th Century.* NY. 1900. illus.   . . . . *$35.00–$40.00*

Matsuo, Kinoaki. *How Japan Plans to Win.* Bos. Little, Brown. 1942. trans by Haan.
. . . . *$35.00–$50.00*

Matthiessen, Peter. *African Silences.* NY. Random House. 1991. 1st ed. dj. . . . . .
. . . . *$15.00–$20.00*

Matthiessen, Peter. *Cloud Forest.* NY. Viking. 1961. 1st ed. dj. . . *$75.00–$150.00*

Matthiessen, Peter. *Indian Country.* NY. Viking. 1984. 1st ed. dj. . *$45.00–$75.00*

Matthiessen, Peter. *Lost Man's River.* NY. Random House. 1997. 1st ed. sgn, dj. .
. . . . *$40.00–$70.00*

Matthiessen, Peter. *Midnight Turning Gray.* Bristol. Ampersand Press. 1984. 1st ed.
wrps. author's first collection, sgn. . . . . *$65.00–$85.00*

Matthiessen, Peter. *Midnight Turning Gray.* Bristol, R.I. Ampersand Press. 1984.
1st ed. wrps. author's first collection. . . . . *$35.00–$40.00*

Matthiessen, Peter. *Oomingmak.* NY. Hastings House. 1967. 1st ed. dj, sgn. . . . . .
. . . . *$85.00–$100.00*

Matthiessen, Peter. *Oomingmak.* NY. Hastings House. 1967. 1st ed. dj. . . . .
. . . . *$45.00–$50.00*

Matthiessen, Peter. *Partisans.* NY. Viking. 1955. 1st ed. sgn, dj.. *$100.00–$450.00*

Matthiessen, Peter. *Sal Si Puedes.* NY. Random House. 1969. 1st ed. deep red dj.
. . . . *$45.00–$65.00*

Matthiessen, Peter. *Shore Birds of North America.* NY. Viking. 1967. 1st ed. dj. . . .
. . . . *$55.00–$75.00*

Matthiessen, Peter. *Under the Mountain Wall.* NY. Viking. 1962. 1st ed. illus. dj..
. . . . *$25.00–$55.00*

Matthiessen, Peter. *Wildlife in America.* NY. (1959(. 1st ed. illus. drawings, dj. . . .
. . . . *$150.00–$175.00*

Matthiessen, Peter. *Wind Birds.* NY. Viking. 1973. 1st ed. dj. . . . . . . *$20.00–$50.00*

Maugham, W. Somerset. *Making of a Saint.* Lon. T. Fisher Unwin. (1898). 1st ed. green bds. . . . . *$90.00–$125.00*

Maugham, W. Somerset. *Moon and Sixpence.* George Doran. 1919. 1st Amer ed. . . . . *$50.00–$75.00*

Maugham, W. Somerset. *Summing Up.* Garden City. Doubleday, Duran. 1938. 1st ed. black cl, dj. . . . . *$25.00–$75.00*

Maugham, W. Somerset. *Theatre.* NY. Doubleday. 1937. 1st ed. dj. . . . . *$125.00–$200.00*

Maugham, W. Somerset. *Then and Now.* Lon. (1946). 1st ed. dj.. . *$10.00–$35.00*

Maugham, W. Somerset. *Writer's Notebook.* Lon. (1949). 1st ed. dj. . . . . *$12.00–$40.00*

Maunsell, Henry. *Dublin Practice of Midwifery.* NY. William LeBlanc. 1842. 1st Amer ed. 292 pp. . . . . *$200.00–$275.00*

Maurice, Sir Frederick. *Statesmen and Soldiers of the Civil War.* Bos. 1926. 1st ed. . . . . *$15.00–$40.00*

Mauriceau, A. M. *Married Woman's Private Medical Companion.* NY. 1848. cl. . . . . *$150.00–$250.00*

Maury, M. F. *Physical Geography of the Sea.* NY. Harper & Bros. 1856. 6th ed. 13 fold-out plates. . . . . *$65.00–$75.00*

Mawson, Sir Douglas. *Home of the Blizzard....* Phila. Lippincott. (1915). 2 vols. illus. 1st Amer ed. blue cl, fldg map in rear pocket. . . . . *$200.00–$300.00*

Maxim, Sir Hiram. *Artificial and Natural Flight.* NY. 1908. 1st ed. illus. . . . . *$50.00–$100.00*

Maxwell, Aymer. *Pheasants & Covert Shooting.* 1913. illus. clr plates. . . . . *$60.00–$85.00*

May, J. B. *Hawks of North America.* NY. 1935. . . . . *$30.00–$60.00*

Maydon, Major H. C. *Big Game Shooting in Africa.* Lon. Seeley, Service. 1951. . . . . *$60.00–$75.00*

Mayer, John. *Sportsman's Director.* Simkin Marshall. 1845. 7th ed.*$45.00–$55.00*

Mayer, Robert. *Super-folks.* NY. 1977. 1st ed. dj.. . . . . *$25.00–$40.00*

Mayer, Tom. *Climbing for the Evening Star.* Bos. 1974. 1st ed. dj.. *$30.00–$40.00*

Mayor, Archer. *Borderlings.* NY. Putnam. 1990. 1st ed. sgn, dj. . . . *$50.00–$75.00*

McAdie, Alexander. *FOG.* Macmillan. 1934. 23 pp, plates. . . . . . *$30.00–$50.00*

McAllester, David P. *Enemy Way Music*. Cambridge, MA. 1954. wrps. 96 pp.. . . .
. . . . *$50.00–$65.00*

McAllister, Agnes. *Lone Woman in Africa*. NY. 1896. illus. . . . . . . *$60.00–$85.00*

McBain, Ed. *Ax*. NY. Simon & Schuster. 1964. 1st ed. dj.. . . . . . *$150.00–$200.00*

McBain, Ed. *Blood Relatives*. NY. Random House. 1975. 1st ed. dj. . *$35.00–$50.00*

McBain, Ed. *Poison*. NY. Arbor House. 1987. 1st ed. dj.. . . . . *$25.00–$45.00*

McBain, Ed. *Sadie When She Died*. Garden City. Doubleday. 1972. 1st ed. dj. . . .
. . . . *$50.00–$60.00*

McCaffrey, Anne. *White Dragon*. Del Rey Books. 1978. 1st ed. dj.. . . . .
. . . . *$45.00–$55.00*

McCarthy, Cormac. *All the Pretty Horses*. NY. 1992. 1st ed. illus. . . . .
. . . . *$150.00–$200.00*

McCarthy, Cormac. *Blood Meridian*. NY. Random House. 1985. 1st ed. dj.. . . . . .
. . . . *$675.00–$975.00*

McCarthy, Cormac. *Stone Mason*. Ecco Preso. 1994. 1st ed. . . . . *$15.00–$20.00*

McCarthy, Cormac. *Stone Mason*. Ecco Press. 1994. 1st ed. dj.. . . . *$50.00–$65.00*

McCarthy, Cormac. *Suttree*. NY. Random House. 1979. 1st ed. dj.. . . . .
. . . . *$500.00–$1,000.00*

McCarthy, Cormac. *The Crossing*. NY. 1994. 1st ed. dj. . . . . *$15.00–$50.00*

McCarthy, John J. *Science of Fighting Fire*. NY. 1943. 1st ed. illus. . . . .
. . . . *$45.00–$55.00*

McClellan, George B. *Report of the Secretary of War*. DC. GPO. 1864. . . . .
. . . . *$85.00–$100.00*

McClellan, George B. *Rept. On The Organization & Campaigns...Army of the
Potomac*. NY. 1864. 1st ed. illus. maps. . . . . *$60.00–$250.00*

McClintock, James H. *Mormon Settlement in Arizona*. Phoenix. 1921. illus. photos,
fldg map, biblio. . . . . *$60.00–$85.00*

McClintock, John S. *Pioneer Days in the Black Hills*. Deadwood. 1939. 1st ed.
. . . . *$100.00–$145.00*

McClure, J. B. *Edison and his Inventions*. 1879. 1st ed. illus. . . . *$65.00–$100.00*

McCracken, H. *Alaska Bear Trails*. NY. 1931. 1st ed. . . . . *$40.00–$50.00*

McCracken, H. *Charles M. Russell Book*. Garden City. 1957. 1st ed. dj.. . . . .
. . . . *$45.00–$60.00*

McCracken, Harold. *Flaming Bear*. Phila/NY. 1951. 1st ed. presentation copy, sgn. . . . . *$55.00–$75.00*

McCracken, Harold. *Frank Tenny Johnson Book*. NY. 1974. 1st ed. folio, dj. . . . . *$48.00–$65.00*

McCracken, Harold. *George Catlin and the Old Frontier*. NY. 1959. 1st ed. illus. sgn, dj. . . . . *$50.00–$70.00*

McCracken, Harold. *Portrait of the Old West*. NY. McGraw-Hill. (1952). 1st ed. illus. dj. . . . . *$20.00–$75.00*

McCullagh, Rev. Joseph H. *Sunday-School Man of The South....* Phila. 1889. 1st ed. illus. . . . . *$55.00–$75.00*

McCullers, Carson. *Clock Without Hands*. Bos. Houghton Mifflin. 1961. 1st ed. dj. . . . . *$35.00–$80.00*

McCullers, Carson. *Member of the Wedding*. Bos. Houghton Mifflin. 1946. 1st ed. dj. . . . . *$70.00–$150.00*

McCullock, J. R. *Dictionary, Practical, Theoretical, and Historical, of Commerce and Commercial Navigation*. Phila. Thomas Wardle. 1840. 2 vols. 1st Amer ed. . . . . *$200.00–$275.00*

McCullough, Colleen. *Tim*. NY. Harper & Row. 1974. 1st ed. author's first book, dj. . . . . *$25.00–$75.00*

McCurdy, Edward. *Mind of Leonardo Da Vinci*. Lon. Jonathan Cape. 1928. illus. calf with marbled end papers. . . . . *$60.00–$80.00*

McCutcheon, John T. *In Africa: Hunting Adventures in the Big Game Country*. Ind. Bobbs, Merrill. (1910). 1st trade ed. illus. photos, plates. . . . . *$115.00–$150.00*

McDiarmid, Hugh. *Fire of the Spirit*. Glasgow. 1965. wrps. . . . . *$30.00–$45.00*

McDuddie, Franklin. *History of the Town of Rochester, NH*. Manchester. 1892. 2 vols. 1st ed. illus. . . . . *$50.00–$65.00*

McEwan, Ian. *In Between the Sheets*. Lon. 1978. 1st ed. dj. . . . . *$175.00–$250.00*

McGlashan, C. F. *History of the Donner Party: A Tragedy of the Sierra*. SF. A. Carlisle & Co. 1929. 15th ed. inscr by McGlashan. . . . . *$70.00–$100.00*

McGlashan, C. F. *History of the Donner Party: A Tragedy of the Sierra*. SF. A.L. Bancroft & Co. 1881. 4th ed. inscr by McGlashan. . . . . *$125.00–$200.00*

McGowan, Archibald. *Prisoners of War, A Reminiscence of the Rebellion*. NY. 1901. 1st ed. . . . . *$75.00–$100.00*

McGuire, Hunter and George L. Christian. *Confederate Cause and Conduct in the War Between the States*. Richmond. Jenkins. 1907. 1st ed. . . . . . . *$75.00–$125.00*

McGuire, J. *Diary of a Southern Refugee During the War*. NY. 1867. 1st ed. . . . .
. . . . *$150.00–$225.00*

McKay, Claude. *Banjo*. NY. 1929. 1st ed. dj. . . . . *$500.00–$800.00*

McKay, Claude. *Harlem Shadows*. NY. (1922). 1st ed. blue cl dj. . *$800.00–$200.00*

McKay, David O. *Statements on Communism and the Constitution of the United States*. Salt Lake. 1964. 1st ed. wrps. . . . . *$65.00–$85.00*

McKee, Edwin D. *Environment and History of the Toroweap and Kaibgab F orma-tions of Northern Arizona and Southern Utal*. DC. Carnegie Inst. 1938. illus. fold-outs, plates. . . . . *$75.00–$125.00*

McKenney, Thomas L. and James Hall. *History of the Indian Tribes of North America with Biographical Sketches and Anecdotes of the Principal Chiefs....* Phila. Bowen. 1848–1850. 3 vols. 120 hand-clred plates. *$15,000.00–*

McKenney, Thomas L. and Jason Hall. *Indian Tribes of North America..* Ohio. 1978. 2 vols. illus. 120 plates, 1st ed thus, lea, slipcase. . . . . *$400.00–$450.00*

McLean, John, MA, PhD. *Indians of Canada, Their Manner & Customs*. Lon. Kelly. 1892 (1899. illus. 3rd ed. . . . . *$95.00–$125.00*

McMullen, John. *The History of Canada*. Brockville. 1855. . . . . *$75.00–$125.00*

McMullen, Joseph V. *Islamic Carpets*. NY. 1965. . . . . *$150.00–$200.00*

McMurtrie, Douglas C. *Early Printing in Tennessee*. Chi. 1933. . . . .
. . . . *$50.00–$60.00*

McMurtrie, Wm. *Report Upon An Examination of Wool and Other Animal Fibers*. DC. GPO. 1886. illus. . . . . *$70.00–$85.00*

McMurtry, Larry. *Anything for Billy*. Simon & Schuster. (1988). 1st ed. dj. . . . . . .
. . . . *$30.00–$45.00*

McMurtry, Larry. *Desert Rose*. NY. Simon & Schuster. 1983. 1st ltd ed. 250 cc, sgn, slipcase. . . . . *$100.00–$300.00*

McMurtry, Larry. *Last Picture Show*. Dial Press. 1966. 1st ed. dj. . . . .
. . . . *$500.00–$1,000.00*

McMurtry, Larry. *Lonesome Dove*. NY. Simon & Schuster. 1985. 1st ed. paper-cvr bds, dj. . . . . *$125.00–$300.00*

McMurtry, Larry. *Moving On*. NY. Simon & Schuster. 1970. 1st ed. dj. . . . .
. . . . *$100.00–$125.00*

McMurtry, Larry. *Terms of Endearment*. NY. Simon & Schuster. (1975). 1st ed. dj, sgn. . . . . *$50.00–$75.00*

McNemar, Richard. *Concise Answer... Who, or What Are the Shakers.* Stockbridge. 1826. 1st ed. . . . . *$200.00–$250.00*

McPhee, John. *Coming into the Country.* Lon. 1978. 1st ed. dj. . . . *$30.00–$45.00*

McPhee, John. *Deltoid Pumpkin Seed.* Farrar, Straus & Giroux. 1973. 1st ed. dj. . . . . *$24.00–$35.00*

McPhee, John. *Encounters with the Archdruid.* NY. Farrar, Straus & Giroux. (1971). 1st ed. dj. . . . . *$25.00–$75.00*

McPhee, John. *Giving Good Weight.* NY. Farrar, Straus & Giroux. (1979). 1st ed. dj. . . . . *$25.00–$40.00*

McPhee, John. *Headmaster. Frank L Boyden....* NY. Farrar, Strauss & Giroux. 1966. 1st ed. illus. photos, dj. . . . . *$80.00–$100.00*

McPhee, John. *Looking for a Ship.* NY. Farrar Straus Giroux. (1990). 1st ed. sgn, dj. . . . . *$80.00–$125.00*

McPhee, John. *Pine Barrens.* Farrar Straus Giroux. 1968. dj. . . . . . *$75.00–$95.00*

McPhee, William. *Pilgrims of Adversity.* Doubleday Doran. 1928. 1st ed. dj. . . . . *$45.00–$50.00*

McPhee, John. *Roomful of Hovings.* NY. 1968. dj. . . . . *$85.00–$100.00*

McPherson, Edward. *Handbook of Politics for 1878.* DC. 1878. large 8 vo. . . . . *$40.00–$50.00*

McQuarrie. *Star Wars Portfolio–Return of the Jedi.* Ballantine Books. 1983. 1st ed. dj. . . . . *$10.00–$35.00*

McQuire, Hunter. *The Confederate Cause.* Richmond. 1907. . . . *$75.00–$125.00*

Mead, Margaret. *Male And Female.* NY. 1st ed. dj. . . . . *$45.00–$65.00*

Mead, McKim & White. *Monograph of...in Two Volumes.* NY. Architectural Book Pub. 1925. folders with string ties, students ed. . . . . *$200.00–$300.00*

Meany, Edmond S. (ed.). *Mount Rainier: A Record of Exploration.* NY. Macmillan. 1916. 1st ed. presentation copy, dark blue cl. . . . . *$135.00–$200.00*

Medical Society of VA. *Confederate Medicine 1861–1865.* np. 1961. wrps. . . . . *$54.00–$75.00*

Meek, A. S. *A Naturalist in Cannibal Land.* Lon. Unwin. 1913. 1st ed. illus. dark gray cl. . . . . *$45.00–$80.00*

Meigs, Charles D. *Complete Treatise on Midwifery.* Phila. 1852. illus. 4th Amer ed. calf, steel plates. . . . . *$75.00–$200.00*

Meigs, Charles D. *Woman: Her Diseases and Remedies.* Phila. 1851. . . . .
. . . . *$20.00–$100.00*

Meikle, James. *The Traveller.* Albany. E. Torrey & W Seaver. 1812. lea. . . . .
. . . . *$45.00–$85.00*

Mellon, James. *African Hunter.* NY. Harcourt, Brace, Jovanovich. [1975]. 1st ed.
photos, dj. . . . . *$75.00–$150.00*

Melville, Herman. *Journal Up the Straits.* NY. The Colophon. 1935. 1st ed. 182 pp,
paper bds with lea label, 650 cc printed. . . . . *$50.00–$100.00*

Melville, Herman. *Moby Dick; or The Whale.* SF. Arion Press. 1979. ltd 265 cc, blue
mor, slipcase. . . . . *$3,000.00–$5,000.00*

Mencken, H L. *Minority Report—Notebooks:.* NY. 1956. 1st ed. dj. *$30.00–$40.00*

Mencken, H L. *Philosophy of Friedrich Nietzsche.* Bos. 1913. 3rd ed.. . . . .
. . . . *$35.00–$50.00*

Mencken, H L. *Treatise on Right and Wrong.* NY. 1934. 1st ed. dj. . . . .
. . . . *$100.00–$125.00*

Mencken, H. L. *Europe After 8:15.* NY. John Lane. 1914. . . . . . . *$80.00–$125.00*

Mencken, H. L. *Happy Days.* NY. 1940. 1st ed. dj. . . . . *$25.00–$35.00*

Mencken, H. L. *Notes on Democracy.* NY. Knopf. [1926]. 1st ed. *$60.00–$125.00*

Mencken, Henry L. *George Bernard Shaw, His Plays.* Bos. George W. Luce. 1905.
1st ed. black cl. . . . . *$100.00–$200.00*

Menefee, Josephine T. *Virginia Housekeeper's Guide.* Roanoke. Stone Printing.
1935. . . . . *$50.00–$80.00*

Menninger, Karl A. *Man Against Himself.* NY. 1938. sgn. . . . . *$65.00–$95.00*

Menocal, A. G. *Report of the U S Nicaragua Surveying Party 1885.* DC. GPO. 1886.
fldg maps. . . . . *$80.00–$210.00*

Merril, George P. *Contributions to the History of Geology.* DC. GPO. 1906. illus.
780 pp. . . . . *$85.00–$100.00*

Merryman, Richard. *Andrew Wyeth.* Bos. 1968. 1st trade ed. clr plates, oblong, dj.
. . . . *$100.00–$200.00*

Merryweather, James C. *Fire Protection of Mansions.* Lon. 1899. 3rd ed. . . . . . .
. . . . *$60.00–$110.00*

Mertins, Louis & Esther. *Intervals of Robert Frost.* Berkeley. 1947. wrps. . . . . . .
. . . . *$50.00–$65.00*

Merton, H. W. *Descriptive Mentality From the Head, Face and Hand*. Phila. 1899. 1st ed. illus. . . . . *$65.00–$75.00*

Merton, Thomas. *Ascent to Truth*. NY. Harcourt, Brace. (1951). 1st ed. dj. . . . . *$40.00–$60.00*

Merton, Thomas. *Waters of Siloe*. Harcourt. 1949. 1st ed. dj. . . . . . *$50.00–$75.00*

Meyer De Schauensee, R. M. *Birds of China*. Smithsonian.. 1984. illus. 38 clr plates and 30 wash drawings, dj. . . . . *$25.00–$50.00*

Michael Robartes and the Dancer. Dublin. Cuala Press. 1920. ltd 400 cc.. . . . . *$100.00–$145.00*

Michelson, Truman. *Owl Sacred Pack of the Fox Indians*. DC. GPO. 1921. 1st ed. . . . . *$50.00–$120.00*

Michener, James A. *Floating World*. NY. 1954. 1st ed. dj. . . . . *$70.00–$85.00*

Michener, James A. *Hawaii*. NY. Random House. 1959. dj. . . . . . *$45.00–$125.00*

Michener, James A. *Heirs of the Incas*. NY. 1924. 1st ed. dj. . . . . . *$10.00–$20.00*

Michener, James A. *Sayonara*. NY. 1954. 1st ed. dj.. . . . . *$95.00–$125.00*

Michener, James A. *The Drifters*. NY. Random House. (1971). 1st ed. dj. . . . . *$40.00–$70.00*

Micheners, James A. and A. Grove Day. *Rascals in Paradise*. Lon. Secker & Warburg. 1957. 1st UK ed. dj. . . . . *$100.00–$125.00*

Milburn, George. *Hobo's Hornbook*. NY. Ives Washburn. 1930. 1st ed. dj. . . . . *$125.00–$175.00*

Mill, John Stuart. *Autobiography*. NY. 1874. 1st Amer ed.. . . . . . . *$60.00–$85.00*

Mill, John Stuart. *Subjection of Women*. Phila. Lippincott. 1869. 1st Amer ed.. . . . . *$175.00–$500.00*

Millais, J. G. et al. *British Deer & Ground Game, Dogs, Guns & Rifles*. The London & Counties Press Association. 1913. ltd 950 cc, numbered, full lea.. . . . . *$500.00–$650.00*

Millay, Edna St. Vincent. *Buck In The Snow*. Harper. 1928. 1st ed. dj. *$45.00–$60.00*

Millay, Edna St. Vincent. *Fatal Interview*. Harper. 1931. 1st ed. dj. *$25.00–$35.00*

Millay, Edna St. Vincent. *Harp Weaver*. NY. Harper & Bros. 1923. 1st ed. dj. . . . . *$50.00–$90.00*

Millay, Edna St. Vincent. *Mine the Harvest*. NY. 1954. 1st ed. dj. . *$27.00–$35.00*

Miller. *World in the Air: Story of Flying in Pictures.* NY. 1930. 2 vols. . . . .
. . . . *$75.00–$95.00*

Miller, Arthur. *Death of a Salesman.* NY. 1949. 1st ed. dj. . . . . . . *$75.00–$125.00*

Miller, Arthur. *The Price: A Play.* NY. Viking. (1968). 1st ed. dj. . . *$20.00–$65.00*

Miller, Francis Trevelyan (ed.). *Photographic History Of The Civil War.* NY. 1911.
10 vols. illus. dec blue cl. . . . . *$350.00–$500.00*

Miller, Henry. *Black Spring.* NY. Grove Press. 1963. 1st US ed. dj. *$35.00–$50.00*

Miller, Henry. *Tropic of Cancer.* Grove. 1961. dj. . . . . *$20.00–$50.00*

Miller, Henry. *Tropic of Capricorn.* NY. Grove Press. 1961. 1st Us prtg. dj. . . . . .
. . . . *$40.00–$70.00*

Miller, Olive Beaupre. *My Book House: The Treasure Chest.* Chi. 1920. illus. . . .
. . . . *$20.00–$25.00*

Miller, Olive Beaupre. *Nursery Friends From France.* 1927. illus. *$20.00–$35.00*

Miller, Olive Beaupre. *Tales Told in Holland.* 1926. . . . . *$25.00–$35.00*

Miller, Olive Beaupre. *Tales Told in Holland.* The Bookhouse for Children. (1952).
. . . . *$20.00–$30.00*

Miller, Olive Thorne. *Little People of Asia.* NY. Dutton. 1888. 1st ed. illus. wood
engrs. . . . . *$40.00–$50.00*

Miller, William. *Evidence from Scripture and History of the Second Coming of
Christ About the Year 1843.* Troy, NY. Elias Gates. 1838. 2nd ed. cl-backed bds. . .
. . . . *$360.00–$425.00*

Mills, Anson. *My Story.* Wash. 1918. 1st ed. illus. limp cl illus. . . *$110.00–$235.00*

Milne, A. *By Way of Introduction.* NY. 1929. 1st Amer ed. ltd 166 cc, sgn, slipcase.
. . . . *$150.00–$300.00*

Milne, A. A. *Christopher Robin Birthday Book.* Lon. Methuen & Co.. (1930). decorations by Shepard. . . . . *$125.00–$250.00*

Milne, A. A. *Four Days' Wonder.* Lon. 1933. 1st ed. dj. . . . . *$35.00–$45.00*

Milne, A. A. *Fourteen Songs From When We Were Very Young.* Dutton. (1926). bds
and cl spine. . . . . *$20.00–$40.00*

Milne, A. A. *Gallery of Children.* McKay. (1925). 1st Amer ed. . . *$75.00–$125.00*

Milne, A. A. *House at Pooh Corner.* Lon. Methuen & Co. (1928). 1st ed. illus. by
Ernest H. Shepard. pink cl, pict dj. *$1,750.00–$3,000.00*

Milne, A. A. *House at Pooh Corner.* NY. Dutton. (1928). illus. . . *$85.00–$175.00*

Milne, A. A. *King's Breakfast.* Lon. Methuen & Co.. [1925]. illus. pict bds dj.. . . . .
. . . . *$95.00–$175.00*

Milne, A. A. *Now We Are Six.* Lon. 1927. 1st ed. illus. teg. . . . . . *$150.00–$275.00*

Milne, A. A. *Now We Are Six.* Dutton. (1927). 1st Amer ed. illus by Shepard. . . . . .
. . . . *$95.00–$140.00*

Milne, A. A. *Teddy Bear and Other Songs.* Dutton. (1926). bds and cl spine. . . . . .
. . . . *$25.00–$60.00*

Milne, A. A. *Toad of Toad Hall.* Lon. 1929. 1st ed. dj.. . . . . *$65.00–$115.00*

Milne, A. A. *Winnie the Pooh and the Bees.* Dutton. 1952. 4 pop-ups, spiral bound. .
. . . . *$40.00–$55.00*

Milne, A. A. *Winnie-The-Pooh.* Lon. (1926). 1st ed. illus. grn pict cl. . . . .
. . . . *$600.00–$1,000.00*

Miltown, Francis. *Rambles on the Riviera.* 1906. illus. by McManus. . . . .
. . . . *$20.00–$45.00*

Miniatures from Paris, showing the Leading Designs by the Great Parisian Modistes.... Bos. Wm. S. Butler & Co. 1898-99. pict wrps, 32 pp. . . . .
. . . . *$50.00–$75.00*

Minkoff, George R. *Bibliography of the Black Sun Press.* Great Neck. 1970. . . . . .
. . . . *$50.00–$95.00*

Miscellany of Arms & Armor. Presented To Bashford Dean. np. 1927. illus. ltd 150 cc, presentation copy from Hugh Smiley. . . . . *$125.00–$200.00*

Miss Leslie. *Directions for Cookery.* Phila. 1839. 468 pp, 7th ed. . *$75.00–$100.00*

Mitchell's New General Atlas. Phila. 1864. folio, maps. . . . . *$300.00–$400.00*

Mitchell, Margaret. *Gone With the Wind.* NY. 1936. 1st ed. inscr, sgn, gray cl, "Published May 1936" appears on copyright page, pict dj.. . . *$2,500.00–$6,000.00*

Mitchell, Margaret. *Gone With the Wind.* NY. 1936. 2nd ptg, dj.. . . . .
. . . . *$40.00–$60.00*

Mitchener, C. H. (ed.). *Historic Events in the Tuscarawas and Muskingham Valleys.* Dayton. 1876. . . . . *$40.00–$65.00*

Mitford, Mary Russell. *Our Village.* Lon. Macmillan. 1893. illus. by Hugh Thompson, ltd 475 cc, printed Dec 1883.. . . . . *$150.00–$300.00*

Molnar, John Edgar. *Author-Title Index to Joseph Sabin's Dictionary of Books Relating to America.* Metuchen. 1974. . . . . *$100.00–$140.00*

Monroe, James. *Message From the President.* DC. 1821. 1st ed. wrps. sewn. . . . . .
. . . . *$75.00–$95.00*

Monteath, Robert. *Forester's Guide and Profitable Planter.* Edin. Stirling & Kennedy. 1824. 2nd ed. 15 plates. . . . . *$100.00–$200.00*

Montessori, Maria. *Dr. Montessori's Own Handbook.* NY. Stokes. (1914). 1st ed. . . . . *$35.00–$60.00*

Montessori, Maria. *Montessori Method.* NY. Stokes. 1912. illus. 1st US ed. author's first book, 377 pp, scarce. . . . . *$125.00–$150.00*

Montgomery, Frances. *Billy Whiskers Tourist.* Saalfield. 1929. illus. . . . . *$20.00–$35.00*

Montgomery, Frances Trego. *On a Lark to the Planets.* Akron. 1904. 1st ed. illus. by Winifred Elrod. . . . . *$50.00–$60.00*

Montgomery, L. M. *Anne of Avonlea.* NY. Grosset & Dunlap. dj.. . *$10.00–$15.00*

Montgomery, L. M. *Anne of the Island.* NY. Grosset & Dunlap. dj. *$12.00–$15.00*

Montgomery, L. M. *Anne's House of Dreams.* A. L. Burt. dj. . . . . . *$25.00–$37.00*

Montgomery, L. M. *Chronicles of Avonlea.* NY. Grosset & Dunlap. 1940. dj. . . . . *$14.00–$20.00*

Montgomery, L. M. *Jane of Lantern Hill.* NY. Grosset & Dunlap. 1937. dj. . . . . *$10.00–$18.00*

Montgomery, L. M. *Jane of Lantern Hill.* Tor. McClelland & Stewart. 1937. 1st ed. inscr. . . . . *$150.00–$175.00*

Montgomery, L. M. *Rainbow Valley.* NY. 1919. wrps. rprnt.. . . . . . *$30.00–$40.00*

Moore, Albert B. *Conscription & Conflict in the Confederacy.* NY. Macmillan. 1924. dj. . . . . *$40.00–$70.00*

Moore, Brian. *Lonely Passion of Judith Hearne.* Bos. Little, Brown. 1955. 1st Amer ed. dj. . . . . *$125.00–$260.00*

Moore, Clement C. *Night Before Christmas.* Chi. 1908. illus. by J R Neill.. . . . . *$40.00–$50.00*

Moore, Clement C. *Poems.* NY. 1844. 1st ed. presentation copy. . . . . *$3,000.00–$7,000.00*

Moore, Frank. *Rebel Rhymes and Rhapsodies.* NY. 1864. 1st ed. calf spine, bds. . . . . *$55.00–$100.00*

Moore, George Henry. *Notes on The History of Slavery in Massachusetts.* NY. 1866. 1st ed. . . . . *$150.00–$200.00*

Moore, John Hamilton. *Seaman's Complete Daily Assistant & New Mariner's Compass.* Lon. 1796. 5th ed. sailcl over calf. . . . . *$190.00–$235.00*

Moore, Marianne. *Poems.* Lon. Egoist Press. 1921. 1st ed. wrps. author's first book, decorative wrps.. . . . . *$500.00–$900.00*

Moore, Marianne. *Tell Me, Tell Me.* NY. Viking. 1966. 1st ed. dj.. . . . . *$45.00–$90.00*

Moore, William. *Indian Wars of the United States...with Accounts of the Origin, Manners, Superstitions, etc of the Aborigines.* Phila. Leary. 1850. 1st ed. illus. rbnd. . . . . *$80.00–$120.00*

Moorehead, Warren King. *Report of the Susquehanna River Expedition.* Andover, MA. 1938. 1st ed. wrps. illus. photos, maps. . . . . *$110.00–$130.00*

Moravian Tiles. Doylestown, PA. Moravian Pottery and Tile Works. early 20th century. printed wrps, illus, 16 pp. . . . . *$40.00–$50.00*

More, Hannah. *Strictures on the Modern System of Female Education.* Phila. Budd and Bartram. 1800. 2 vols. 1st ed. . . . . *$125.00–$225.00*

More, Jedidiah. *Sermon.* Charlestown. 1799. rprnt by Hudson and Goodwin. . . . . *$150.00–$175.00*

Morgan, Lewis H. *Houses and House-Life of the American Aborigines.* DC. GPO. 1881. illus. litho and photo plates. . . . . *$95.00–$125.00*

Morgan, William. *Personal Reminiscences of the War.* Lynchburg. 1911. . . . . *$100.00–$175.00*

Morley, Christopher. *Haunted Bookshop.* Garden City. Doubleday, Page. 1919. 1st ed. 2nd issue. no # on p. 76, sgn. . . . . *$700.00–$1,000.00*

Morrison, Toni. *Beloved.* NY. Knopf. (1987). 1st ed. sgn, dj. . . . *$300.00–$700.00*

Morrison, Toni. *Beloved.* NY. Knopf. (1987). 1st ed. dj.. . . . . *$50.00–$100.00*

Morrison, Toni. *Bluest Eye.* Lon. 1979. 1st ed. dj. . . . . *$65.00–$75.00*

Morrison, Toni. *Jazz.* NY. Knopf. 1992. 1st ed. dj sgn.. . . . . *$95.00–$125.00*

Morrison, Toni. *Paradise.* NY. Knopf. 1997. 1st ed. dj. . . . . *$18.00–$30.00*

Morrison, Toni. *Song of Solomon.* NY. Knopf. 1977. 1st ed. dj. . . . *$75.00–$125.00*

Morrison, Toni. *Tar Baby.* NY. Knopf. 1981. 1st ed. dj. . . . . *$30.00–$100.00*

Morse Twist Drill & Machine Co., New Bedford, Mass., USA. New Bedford. 1938. wrps. illus. . . . . *$10.00–$20.00*

Morse, A. H. *Radio: Beam and Broadcast.* 1925. 1st ed. illus. . . . . *$70.00–$90.00*

Morse, Edward Lind. *Samuel F. B. Morse: His Letters and Journals.* 1914. 2 vols. 1st ed. illus. . . . . *$65.00–$115.00*

Morse, J. & E. Parish. *Compendious History of New England.* Charlestown. 1820.
.... *$20.00–$30.00*

Morse, Jedidiah. *American Gazeteer.* Bos. 1797. 7 maps. ..... *$250.00–$400.00*

Morse, Jedidiah. *Annals of the American Revolution....* Hartford. 1824. illus. ...
.... *$100.00–$200.00*

Morse, Jedidiah. *Geography Made Easy.* Bos. Thomas & Andrews. 1818. 19th ed.
2 pull-out maps in clr. .... *$150.00–$200.00*

Morse, Jedidiah. *Traveller's Guide.* New Haven. 1823. lea, fldg map..........
.... *$60.00–$75.00*

Moxon, Joseph. *Tutor To Astronomy and Geography.* Lon. S Roycroft. 1686. 4th ed.
enlarged, lea, drawings, diagrams, 271 pp.................. *$500.00–$700.00*

Muir, John. *A Thousand Mile Walk to the Gulf.* Bos. 1916. ltd 550 cc. ....
.... *$60.00–$200.00*

Muir, John. *My First Summer in the Sierra.* Bos. 1911. 1st ed. .. *$95.00–$125.00*

Muir, John. *Our National Parks.* Bos. Houghton Mifflin. 1909. 1st enlarged ed. fldg
map, 31 plates... *$125.00–$300.00*

Muir, John. *The Story of a Dog.* Bos. (1909). .... *$25.00–$30.00*

Muir, John. *Travels in Alaska.* Bos. 1915. 1st ed. illus. .... *$80.00–$150.00*

Muir, John. *Yosemite and the Sierra Nevada.* Bos. Houghton Mifflin. [1948]. 1st ed.
later ptg, photographs by Ansel Adams, dj. .... *$65.00–$130.00*

Muir, John (ed.). *Picturesque California....* NY. 1894. illus. folio.*$140.00–$180.00*

Muir, Leo J. *Century of Mormon Activities in California.* Salt Lake. nd, 1951.
vols 1 & 2. illus. photos, sgn........................... *$100.00–$150.00*

Muir, Percy. *English Children's Books 1600 to 1900.* Lon. Batsford. (1985).
3rd impression, dj... *$30.00–$75.00*

Muir, Percy. *Victorian Illustrated Books.* NY. (1971). 1st ed. dj.... *$40.00–$50.00*

Mulford, Clarence. *Hopalong Cassidy and Lucky at the Double X Ranch.* NY. 1950.
1st ed. illus. by Jack Crowe, 2 pop-ups..................... *$140.00–$160.00*

Mulfurd, Clarence. *Hopalong Cassidy's Coloring Book.* NY. 1951. wrps. ......
.... *$15.00–$20.00*

Mulford, Isaac S. *Civil and Political History of New Jersey.* Phila. 1851. 500 pp. .
.... *$48.00–$60.00*

Mullins, Michael A. *Fremont Rifles: A Hist. of 37th Ill. Vet. Vol. Infantry..* NC. 1990.
illus. sgn, dj. .... *$35.00–$50.00*

Mulvaney, Charles Pelham. *History of the Northwest Rebellion of 1885.* Tor. 1886. 440 pp, maps. . . . . *$40.00–$50.00*

Mumford, John Kimberly. *Oriental Rugs.* NY. 1923. 4th ed.. . . . . *$35.00–$50.00*

Mundy, Talbot. *Ivory Trail.* Ind. Bobbs Merrill. 1919. 1st ed. . . . . *$35.00–$60.00*

Munro, Hector Hugh ("Saki"). *Toys of Peace.* Lon. John Lane. 1919. 1st ed. 303 pp. . . . . *$25.00–$85.00*

Munson, John W. *Reminiscences of a Mosby Guerilla.* NY. 1906. 1st ed. illus. . . . . *$175.00–$300.00*

Munson, Loveland. *Early History of Manchester, VT.* Manchester. 1876. . . . . *$35.00–$55.00*

Murdoch, Iris. *The Unicorn.* Lon. 1963. 1st ed. dj. . . . . *$35.00–$45.00*

Murgatroyd, Madeline. *Tales from the Kraals.* South Africa. Central News Agency. (1944). illus. . . . . *$20.00–$50.00*

Murphy, Robert Cushman. *Oceanic Birds of So. America.* NY. 1936. 2 vols. illus. boxed. . . . . *$80.00–$125.00*

Mussolini, Benito. *Cardinal's Mistress.* NY. 1928. 1st ed. in Eng. . *$45.00–$65.00*

My Cave Life in Vicksburg. NY. Appleton. 1864. 1st ed. . . . . . . *$150.00–$225.00*

Myrick, Herbert. *Cache La Poudre, the Romance of a Tenderfoot in the Days of Custer.* NY. Orange Judd. 1905. 1st ed. . . . . *$50.00–$125.00*

Mytinger, Caroline. *Headhunting in the Solomon Islands.* Macmillan. 1942. 1st ed. illus. dj. . . . . *$18.00–$25.00*

Nabokov, Vladimir. *Invitation to a Beheading.* Putnam. 1959. 1st US ed. dj. . . . . *$30.00–$75.00*

Nabokov, Vladimir. *King, Queen, Knave.* McGraw-Hill. 1968. 1st US ed. dj. . . . . *$25.00–$30.00*

Nabokov, Vladimir. *Lectures on Russian Literature.* 1981. 1st ed. . *$25.00–$30.00*

Nabokov, Vladimir. *Lolita.* Paris. Olympia Press. 1955. 2 vols. 1st ed. wrps. 1st issue. . . . . *$5,000.00–$7,000.00*

Nabokov, Vladimir. *Look At The Harlequins!.* McGraw-Hill. 1974. 1st ed. dj. . . . . *$25.00–$95.00*

Nabokov, Vladimir. *Nabokov's Quartet.* NY. 1966. 1st ed. . . . . . . *$35.00–$55.00*

Nabokov, Vladimir. *Notes on Prosody.* NY. 1964. dj. . . . . *$50.00–$75.00*

Nabokov, Vladimir. *Pale Fire.* NY. Putnam. 1962. 1st US ed. dj. . *$95.00–$125.00*

Nabokov, Vladimir. *Real Life of Sebastian Knight*. Norfolk. New Directions. (1941). 1st Amer ed.. . . . . *$40.00–$75.00*

Nabokov, Vladimir. *The Defense*. NY. Putnam. 1964. 1st ed in Eng, dj. . . . . *$40.00–$125.00*

Naipaul, V. S. *Loss of El Dorado*. Lon. Andre Deutsch. 1960. 1st ed. dj. . . . . *$80.00–$100.00*

Naipaul, V. S. *Loss of El Dorado*. NY. Knopf. 1970. 1st US ed. dj.. *$30.00–$75.00*

Nansen, Dr Fridtjof. *Farthest North.. .1893-96*. NY. Harper & Bros. 1897. 2 vols. 1st Amer ed. 4 fldg maps, 16 clr plates, pict cl, teg. . . . . *$150.00–$300.00*

Nansen, Fridtjof. *Eskimo Life*. Lon. Longmans, Green. 1893. frontis, platew, wood-cuts. . . . . *$130.00–$175.00*

Nansen, Fridtjof. *First Crossing of Greenland*. Lon. 1892. illus. fldg map. . . . . *$45.00–$65.00*

Nansen, Fridtjof. *Through Siberia the Land of the Future*. NY. Stokes. 1914. 1st Amer ed. illus, maps. . . . . *$160.00–$250.00*

Napheys, Geo. H. *Physical Life of a Woman*. Phila. George Maclean. 1870. . . . . *$25.00–$40.00*

Narrative of Five Youths From the Sandwich Islands.... NY. 1816. wrps. . . . . *$50.00–$100.00*

Nash, E. B. *Leaders in Homeopathic Therapeutics*. Phila. 1901. 2nd ed. . . . . *$35.00–$40.00*

Nash, Wallis. *Two Years in Oregon*. Appleton. 1882. 2nd ed.. . . . . . *$60.00–$75.00*

Nasmyth, James & James Carpenter. *The Moon: Considered as a Planet, A World, and A Satellite*. Lon. 1885. illus. 3rd ed. . . . . *$75.00–$150.00*

Nathan, George Jean. *Art of the Night*. NY. 1928. 1st ed. ltd 200 cc, sgn. . . . . *$45.00–$75.00*

Nation, Carry A. *Use and Need of the Life of Carry A. Nation....* Topeka. 1905. wrps. illus. . . . . *$85.00–$125.00*

Nature Library. Doubleday. 1904. 10 vols. . . . . *$200.00–$280.00*

Nature's Romance "Over the Loop". Denver. 1903. wrps. souvenir picture book. . . . . *$65.00–$75.00*

Nautical Almanac and Astronomical Ephemeris for the Year 1837. Lon. John Murray. 1835. 526 pp. . . . . *$35.00–$45.00*

Naylor, E. M. *The Poets and Music*. Lon. 1928. . . . . *$30.00–$50.00*

Near, I. W. *History of Steuben County, NY, and Its People.* Chi. 1911. 2 vols. . . . . .
. . . .*$100.00–$135.00*

Nearing, Scott. *Black America.* NY. Vanguard. 1929. 1st ed. illus. dj. . . . .
. . . .*$125.00–$150.00*

Nearing, Scott. *Black America.* Shocken Books. 1969. illus. rprnt. . *$22.00–$30.00*

Nearing, Scott. *British General Strike.* NY. Vanguard. 1926. 1st ed. *$20.00–$30.00*

Nearing, Scott. *Conscience of a Radical.* MA. 1965. 1st ed. dj. . . . *$22.00–$30.00*

Nearing, Scott. *Europe — West and East.* NY. Vanguard. 1934. 1st ed. wrps. . . . . .
. . . .*$25.00–$40.00*

Nearing, Scott. *From Capitalism to Communism.* DC. World Events. nd. wrps. 24pp.
. . . .*$18.00–$25.00*

Nearing, Scott. *Maple Sugar Book.* John Day. 1950. dj. . . . . *$20.00–$35.00*

Nearing, Scott. *Rise and Decline of Christian Civilization.* Ridgewood. pub by
author. 1940. wrps. 24 pp. . . . . *$20.00–$25.00*

Nearing, Scott. *Victory Without Peace.* DC. World Events. nd. wrps. 16 pp.. . . . . . .
. . . .*$18.00–$25.00*

Nearing, Scott. *Warless World.* NY. Vanguard Press. nd. wrps. 32 pp. . . . .
. . . .*$25.00–$35.00*

Nearing, Scott & Ward Percy. *Would The Practice of Christ's Teachings Make For
Social Progress.* KS. Haldeman Julius Co. nd. pamphle,t wrps. . . . . *$20.00–$25.00*

Neff, Jackob. *Army and Navy of America from the French & Indian Wars....* Phila.
1845. fldg plates. . . . . *$52.00–$60.00*

Neill, Edward. *History of Minnesota....* Phila. 1858. 1st ed. fldg map. . . . .
. . . .*$50.00–$95.00*

Nelson, E. W. *Report Upon the Natural History of Collections....* Alaska. DC. 1887.
illus. . . . . *$85.00–$125.00*

Nelson, Henry Loomis and H. A. Ogden. *Uniforms of the United States Army.* NY.
1959. illus. . . . . *$40.00–$50.00*

Nevins, W. S. *Witchcraft in Salem Village.* Salem/Bos. 1892. illus. . *$60.00–$85.00*

New England Primer. Dodd, Mead. 1899. 2nd rprnt. . . . . *$75.00–$175.00*

Newberger, Richard L. *Royal Canadian Mounted Police.* Random House. 1953. 1st
ed. illus. dj. . . . . *$10.00–$17.00*

Newell, Peter. *Hole Book.* NY. 1908. 1st ed. illus. . . . . *$50.00–$125.00*

Newell, Peter. *Slant Book*. NY. (1910). 1st ed. illus. . . . . *$65.00–$100.00*

Newhall, Walter S. *A Memoir*. Phila. 1864. 1st ed. regimental. . . . . *$60.00–$75.00*

Newton, Edward A. *Amenities of Book Collecting*. Bos. Atlantic Monthly Press. 1918. 1st ed. illus. scarce errata slip present. . . . . *$40.00–$50.00*

Newton, Helmut. *White Women*. 1976. 1st ed. presentation copy, dj. . . . .
. . . . *$75.00–$150.00*

Newton, Isaac. *Opticks or a Treatise of the Reflections Refractions Inflections and Colours of Light*. Lon. G Bell & Sons. 1931. rprnt. . . . . *$65.00–$100.00*

Nichols, Frederick. *Early Architecture of Georgia*. Chapel Hill. Univ N.C. Press. 1957. 1st ed. illus. 292 pp, slipcase. . . . . *$150.00–$200.00*

Nimoy, Leonard. *I Am Not Spock*. Millbrae. 1975. 1st ed. softbound, photos. . . . .
. . . . *$30.00–$40.00*

Nimrod. *The Chase, the Turf and the Road*. Lon. Murray. 1843. 2nd ed. illus. . . . .
. . . . *$70.00–$100.00*

Nin, Anais. *Children Of The Albatross*. Dutton. 1947. 1st US ed. dj. *$50.00–$95.00*

Nin, Anais. *Four Chambered Heart*. 1950. dj. . . . . *$85.00–$250.00*

Nin, Anais. *Ladders to Fire*. Dutton. 1946. 1st ed. dj. . . . . *$50.00–$110.00*

Nin, Anais. *Novel of the Future*. NY. Macmillan. 1968. 1st ed. dj. . . . .
. . . . *$30.00–$55.00*

Nin, Anais. *Spy In The House of Love*. NY. British Book Centre. 1954. 1st Amer ed. dj. . . . . *$35.00–$75.00*

***Ninth Air Force Service Command in the Eropean Theatre of Operations*.** NY. 1945. 1st ed. photos. . . . . *$75.00–$95.00*

Nixon, Richard. *Memoirs of Richard Nixon*. NY. Grosset & Dunlap. 1978. 1st ed. boxed, sgn. . . . . *$145.00–$175.00*

Nobel, Alfred. *Les Explosifs Modernes*. Paris. 1876. 1st ed. . . . . *$200.00–$230.00*

Nordenskjold, N. Otto G. and John Gunnar Anderson. *Antarctica*. Lon. 1905. 1st ed. illus. clr plates, pict green cl, ex lib. . . . . *$185.00–$210.00*

Nordhoff, Charles. *Communistic Societies of the United States*.... NY. Harper & Brothers. 1875. 439 pp. . . . . *$100.00–$200.00*

Norris, Frank. *Octopus, a Story of California*. NY. 1901. 1st ed. claret cl, leaded, decorated in gilt. . . . . *$100.00–$150.00*

Norris, Frank. *The Pit*. NY. 1903. 1st ed. *$50.00–$80.00*

Norris, Thaddeus. *The American Angler's Book...Describing Noted Fishing Places.* Phila. Porter & Coates. (1865). illus. calf & marbled bds. . . . . . . *$100.00–$150.00*

Northrup, Solomon. *Narr. of a Citizen of N.Y. Kidnapped...in 1841, Rescued in 1853.* Derby & Miller. 1853. . . . . *$75.00–$150.00*

Northrup, Solomon. *Twelve Years a Slave.* Baton Rouge. LA State Univ Press. 1968. republication, dj. . . . . *$25.00–$40.00*

Norton, A Tiffany. *History of Sullivan's Campaign Against Iroquois.* Lima, NY. 1879. fldg map. . . . . *$65.00–$70.00*

Norton, Andre. *Cats Eye.* Harcourt. 1961. 1st ed. dj. . . . . *$30.00–$45.00*

Norton, Andre. *Night of Masks.* Harcourt. 1964. 1st ed. dj.. . . . . . . *$65.00–$85.00*

Norton, Andre. *Sword is Drawn.* Bos. Houghton Mifflin. 1944. 1st ed. 180 pp.. . . . . *$30.00–$45.00*

Norton, Andre. *Ware Hawk.* NY. Atheneum. 1983. 1st ed. dj.. . . . . *$25.00–$35.00*

Norton, Andre. *Wraiths of Time.* NY. 1976. 1st ed. dj. . . . . *$50.00–$65.00*

Norton, Andre. *Yankee Privateer.* Cleve. World Pub. (1955). 1st ed. cl, dj. . . . . *$500.00–$800.00*

Norton, Caroline T. *Rocky Mountain Cook Book.* Denver. 1903. . . *$30.00–$40.00*

Norton, John P. *Elements of Scientific Agriculture.* Pease. 1859. 1st ed. 208 pp. . . . . *$60.00–$75.00*

Noyes, A. J. *In the Land of Chinook, or the Story of Blaine County.* Helena. 1917. 1st ed. illus. . . . . *$75.00–$145.00*

Noyes, Katherine M. *Jesse Macy: An Autobiography.* Springfield, Il. 1933. 1st ed. illus. . . . . *$50.00–$75.00*

Nutt, Frederick. *Complete Confectioner....* Lon. 1809. illus. plates, calf. . . . . *$150.00–$225.00*

Nuttall, T. *Manual of Ornithology.* Bos. 1834. . . . . *$45.00–$75.00*

Nutting, Wallace. *American Windsors.* Wallace Nutting. (1917). . . *$65.00–$75.00*

Nutting, Wallace. *Clock Book.* Old America. 1924. 1st ed. . . . . . . *$55.00–$67.00*

Nutting, Wallace. *Furniture of the Pilgrim Century 1620–1720.* Bos. 1921. 1st ed. illus. . . . . *$40.00–$90.00*

Nutting, Wallace. *Massachusetts Beautiful.* NY. 1923. 1st ed. . . . . *$18.00–$40.00*

Nutting, Wallace. *New Hampshire Beautiful.* 1923. 1st ed. . . . . . . *$20.00–$40.00*

Nutting, Wallace. *Photographic Art Secrets.* NY. 1927. 1st ed. illus. . . . .
. . . . *$60.00–$75.00*

Nutting, Wallace. *Vermont Beautiful.* 1st ed. . . . . *$20.00–$35.00*

Nutting, Wallace. *Windsor Handbook.* Saugus, MA. (1917). tan cl. *$40.00–$60.00*

Nutting, Walllace. *Furniture of the Pilgrim Century.* Framingham. Old America Co.
(1924). rprnt. . . . . *$75.00–$125.00*

Nweeya, Samuel. *Persia the Land of the Magi.* Urmia City. (1910). 4th ed. illus.
presentation copy. . . . . *$20.00–$40.00*

O'Brien, Edward J. (ed.). *Best Short Stories of 1922.* NY. 1922. includes Fitzgerald,
Hecht, Lardner. . . . . *$75.00–$100.00*

O'Brien, Edward J. (ed.). *Best Short Stories of 1923.* Bos. (1924). first prntg of
Ernest Hemingway, misspelled "Hemenway". . . . . *$125.00–$400.00*

O'Brien, Geoffrey. *Hardboiled America: The Lurid Years of Paperbacks.* NY.
Van Nostrand, Reinhold. 1981. 1st ed. dj. . . . . *$75.00–$90.00*

O'Brien, Patrick. *H.M.S. Surprise.* Phil. Lippincott. (1973). 1st US ed dj. . . . . . .
. . . . *$125.00–$225.00*

O'Brien, Patrick. *Reverse of the Medal.* Lon. Collins. 1986. 1st ed. dj. . . . .
. . . . *$100.00–$160.00*

O'Brien, Tim. *Things They Carried.* Bos. Houghton Mifflin. 1990. 1st ed. dj. . . . . .
. . . . *$35.00–$90.00*

O'Cathasaigh, P. *Story of the Irish Citizen Army.* Dublin. 1919. 1st ed. wrps. . . .
. . . . *$175.00–$300.00*

O'Connor, Flannery. *Good Man is Hard to Find.* NY. Harcourt, Brace. [1955]. 1st
ed. 251 pp, dj. . . . . *$400.00–$600.00*

O'Connor, Flannery. *Habit of Being.* NY. Farrar, Straus & Giroux. 1979. 1st ed. dj.
. . . . *$25.00–$65.00*

O'Connor, Flannery. *Mysteries and Manners.* NY. 1969. 1st ed. dj. *$45.00–$60.00*

O'Connor, Flannery. *Wise Blood.* NY. 1952. 1st ed. dj. . . . . *$350.00–$725.00*

O'Connor, Frank. *Lords and Commons: Translations from the Irish.* Dublin. Cuala
Press. 1938. 1st ed. ltd 250 cc, dj. . . . . *$150.00–$300.00*

O'Connor, J. *Big Game Animals of North America.* NY. 1961. folio, dj. . . . .
. . . . *$45.00–$60.00*

O'Connor, Jack. *Art of Hunting Big Game in North America.* NY. 1967. 1st ed. illus.
dj. . . . . *$50.00–$100.00*

O'Connor, Jack. *Big Game Rifle.* NY. 1952. 1st ed. dj.. . . . . *$60.00–$100.00*

O'Connor, Jack. *Jack O'Connor's Big Game Hunts.* NY. 1963. illus. . . . .
. . . . *$60.00–$75.00*

O'Connor, Kathryn. *Presidio La Bahia Del Espritu....* 1966. 1st ed. illus. cl. . . . . .
. . . . *$35.00–$50.00*

O'Donnell, Elliott. *Strange Cults and Secret Societies of Modern London.* Dutton.
(1935). 1st ed. dj. . . . . *$25.00–$40.00*

O'Faolain, Sean. *Come Back to Erin.* Viking. 1940. 1st US ed. dj. . *$45.00–$50.00*

O'Faolain, Sean. *Life Story of Eamon De Valera.* Dublin. 1933. 1st ed. . . . .
. . . . *$60.00–$75.00*

O'Hara, Frank. *Lunch Poems.* SF. City Lights Books. (1964). 1st ed. wrps. . . . . . .
. . . . *$25.00–$35.00*

O'Hara, John. *And Other Stories: A Collection of 12 New Stories.* NY. Random
House. (1968). 1st Trade ed. sgn.. . . . . *$35.00–$50.00*

O'Hara, John. *Cape Cod Lighter.* NY. Random House. 1962. 1st ed. dj.. . . . .
. . . . *$20.00–$30.00*

O'Hara, John. *Farmers Hotel.* Random House. 1951. 1st ed. dj. . . *$30.00–$45.00*

O'Hara, John. *From The Terrace.* NY. Random House. 1958. 1st ed. dj.. . . . .
. . . . *$30.00–$60.00*

O'Hara, John. *Instrument.* NY. Random House. (1967). 1st ed. ltd 300 cc, teg, sgn,
slipcase.. . . . . *$90.00–$100.00*

O'Hara, John. *Lovey Childs: A Philadelphian's Story.* NY. Random House. (1969).
1st ed. ltd 200 cc, sgn, slipcase.. . . . . *$40.00–$80.00*

O'Hara, John. *Rage to Live.* NY. Random House. (1949). 1st ed. dj.. . . . .
. . . . *$75.00–$90.00*

O'Hara, John. *Ten North Frederick.* NY. Random House. (1955). 1st ed. dj.. . . . . .
. . . . *$30.00–$45.00*

O'Hara, John. *Waiting for Winter.* NY. Random House. (1966). 1st ed. ltd 300 cc,
teg, sgn, slipcase.. . . . . *$50.00–$80.00*

O'Hara, John. *Waiting for Winter.* NY. 1966. 1st ed. dj.. . . . . *$18.00–$45.00*

O'Keeffe, Georgia. *Georgia O'Keeffe.* NY. 1976. 1st ed. folio, dj. *$75.00–$100.00*

O'Neill, Eugene. *Ah, Wilderness.* Random House. 1933. 1st ed. dj.*$55.00–$175.00*

O'Neill, Eugene. *Anna Christie.* NY. 1930. illus. 775 cc, sgn.. . . . *$95.00–$200.00*

O'Neill, Eugene. *Dynamo.* NY. Horace Liveright. 1929. 1st ed. dj.. *$65.00–$75.00*

O'Neill, Eugene. *Iceman Cometh.* NY. Random House. 1946. dj. . . . *$35.00–$75.00*

O'Neill, Eugene. *Lazarus Laughed.* NY. 1927. 1st ed. dj. . . . . *$75.00–$150.00*

O'Neill, Eugene. *Mourning Becomes Electra.* NY. Horace Liveright. 1931. 1st trade ed. cl, dj. . . . . *$45.00–$185.00*

O'Neill, Eugene. *Strange Interlude.* NY. Boni & Liveright. 1928. 1st ed. dj. . . . . . .
. . . . *$35.00–$95.00*

Oates, Joyce Carol. *Angel of Light.* Dutton. 1981. 1st ed. dj. . . . . . *$20.00–$25.00*

Oates, Joyce Carol. *Goddess and Other Women.* Vanguard. 1974. 1st ed. dj. . . . . .
. . . . *$25.00–$30.00*

Oates, Joyce Carol. *Marriage and Infidelities.* Vanguard. 1972. 1st ed. dj. . . . . . .
. . . . *$25.00–$30.00*

Oates, Joyce Carol. *On Boxing.* NY. 1987. illus. sgn, dj. . . . . *$65.00–$90.00*

Oberholser, Harry. *Bird Life of Texas.* Austin/Lon. Univ of Texas. (1974). 1st ed. illus. by Fuertes 36 col plates, full page maps, slipcase. . . . . *$100.00–$150.00*

Ocker, William. *Blind Flight in Theory and Practice.* The Naylor Co. 1932. 3rd prtg. illus. frontis, cl. . . . . *$18.00–$22.00*

Odets, Clifford. *Clash by Night.* NY. Random House. (c1942). 1st ed. dj. . . . .
. . . . *$50.00–$75.00*

Odets, Clifford. *Golden Boy.* NY. 1937. 1st ed. sgn. . . . . *$500.00–$700.00*

Odets, Clifford. *Paradise Lost: A Play in Three Acts.* NY. Random House. (c1936). 1st ed. dj. . . . . *$125.00–$175.00*

Odum, Howard. *Rainbow Round My Shoulder: The Blue Trail of Black Ulysses.*. Bobbs Merrill. 1928. 1st ed. dj. . . . . *$37.00–$65.00*

Odum, Howard W. *Cold Blue Moon.* Ind. Bobbs-Merril. 1931. 1st ed. . . . .
. . . . *$50.00–$65.00*

Odum, Howard W. and Guy B. Johnson. *Negro and His Songs.* Chapel Hill. Univ of N. C. Press. 1925. 1st ed. . . . . *$125.00–$200.00*

Official Guide of The National Association of Professional Baseball Leagues. NY. Spalding. 1903. wrps. illus. photos. . . . . *$350.00–$450.00*

Official Railway and Steamboat Traveler's Guide . . .Tourists in Japan. Yokahama. 1889. map in pocket. . . . . *$40.00–$55.00*

Ogden, Ruth. *Little Pierre and Big Peter.* Stokes. (1915). illus. by Maria Kirk. green cl with pastedown endpapers, dj. . . . . *$50.00–$60.00*

Ogg, Frederick Austin. *Opening of the Mississippi.* NY. 1904. 1st ed. illus. maps. .
....*$37.00–$50.00*

Old Dame Trot and Her Comical Cat. Lon. nd. illus. ....*$350.00–$450.00*

Oldfield, Otis. *Pictorial Journal of a Voyage About the Three Masted Schooner Louise...as Recorded in 1931 by the Artist Otis Oldfield.* SF. Grabhorn-Hoyem. 1969. illus. half mor & cl, ltd 400 cc. ....*$150.00–$225.00*

Oliver, W. R. B. *New Zealand Birds.* Wellington. 1955. 2nd ed. clr plates.........
....*$67.00–$75.00*

Olney, J. *New and Improved School Atlas to Accompany the Practical System of Modern Geography.* NY. Robinson Pratt. 1837. illus. *$185.00*

Olympia 1936. Germany. 1936. 2 vols. illus. photos 350 tip-in photos...........
....*$200.00–$450.00*

Oration Delivered in Wallingford...Before Republicans of Ct. New Haven. 1801. .
....*$32.00–$45.00*

Orcutt, Samuel. *Indians of the Housatonic & Naugatuck Valleys.* Hartford. 1882. illus. ....*$90.00–$135.00*

Orwell Reader, George Orwell. NY. 1956. 1st ed. wrps. ....*$50.00–$75.00*

Orwell, George. *Animal Farm..* NY. Harcourt. 1946. 1st US ed. dj. .*$75.00–$175.00*

Orwell, George. *England Your England, and other essays.* Lon. Secker & Warburg. 1953. 1st ed. dj...*$50.00–$95.00*

Orwell, George. *Nineteen Eighty-Four.* NY. 1949. 1st Amer ed. red dj..........
....*$150.00–$300.00*

Osler, Sir William. *Student Life.* Bos/NY. 1931. red cl..........*$55.00–$75.00*

Osler, William. *Aeguanimitas.* Phila. 1906. 2nd ed. 475 pp. ......*$60.00–$75.00*

Osler, William. *An Alabama Student and Other Biographical Essays.* Oxford. 1908. ....*$75.00–$150.00*

Osler, William. *Biblioteca Osleriana: a Catalogue of Books Illustrating the History of Medicine & Science.* McGill-Queens Univ Press. 1969. 2nd ed. 792 pp.........
....*$250.00–$375.00*

Osler, William. *Lectures on the Diagnosis of Abdominal Tumors.* NY. 1895. .....
....*$75.00–$125.00*

Osler, William. *Old Humanities and the New Science.* Bos. 1920. dj. ....
....*$75.00–$140.00*

Osler, William. *Principles and Practice of Medicine.* NY. Appleton. 1899. ....
....*$125.00–$250.00*

Osler, William. *Science & Immortality: Ingersoll Lecture.* Bos. 1904. 1st ed. . . . .
. . . . *$60.00–$95.00*

Oswald, John Clyde. *Printing in the Americas.* NY/Lon. 1937. 1st ed. illus. dj. . .
. . . . *$45.00–$85.00*

Otero, Miguel A. *Report of the Governor of New Mexico.* DC. 1903. illus. fldg map.
. . . . *$140.00–$175.00*

Otis, James. *Toby Tyler or Ten Weeks with a Circus.* NY. Harper & Bros. 1881. 1st
ed. illus. . . . . *$135.00–$195.00*

Otis, James. *Toby Tyler or Ten Weeks With a Circus.* NY. Harper. 1881. 1st ed.
scarce. . . . . *$150.00–$300.00*

Otis, Raymond. *Fire in the Night.* NY. 1934. 1st ed. dj. . . . . *$85.00–$100.00*

Otis, Raymond. *Little Valley.* Lon. (1937). 1st ed. dj. . . . . *$135.00–$200.00*

Ottin, J. J. *Manual of Phrenology.* Phila. Carey, Lea & Blanchard. 1835. illus. 2
steel-engr plate. bds. . . . . *$40.00–$60.00*

Our New Friends. Dick & Jane Reader. *1946.* . . . . *$25.00–$30.00*

Overton, Robert. *A Chase Around the World.* Lon. Frederick Warne. 1900. 1st ed.
. . . . *$120.00–$150.00*

Overton, Robert. *A Chase Around the World.* Lon. Frederick Warne. 1900. 1st ed.
. . . . *$100.00–$130.00*

Overton, Robert. *The Mathematics of Guilt.* NY. McBride. 1926. 1st ed. dj. . . . . . .
. . . . *$100.00–$200.00*

Page, Thomas Nelson. *In Ole Virginia.* NY. Scribner's. 1896. 1st ed. thus. plates, teg.
. . . . *$200.00–$300.00*

Paine, Albert Bigelow. *Mark Twain, a Biography.* NY. Harper. 1912. 3 vols. . . . . .
. . . . *$35.00–$60.00*

Paine, Thomas. *Political and Miscellaneous Works.* Lon. Carlile. 1819. vol. 1. bds.
. . . . *$60.00–$75.00*

Paine, Thomas. *Rights of Man.* Lon. 1791. 6th ed. . . . . *$200.00–$225.00*

Paley, Grace. *Enormous Changes at the Last Minute.* NY. Farrar, Straus & Giroux.
1974. 1st ed. author's first book, sgn, dj. *$75.00–$125.00*

Paley, Grace. *Little Disturbances of Man.* Garden City. 1959. 1st ed. dj,. . . . .
. . . . *$25.00–$125.00*

Palmer, Abraham J. *History of theForty-Eighth Regiment of New York State
Volunteers: 1861-1865.* NY. Veterans Assoc. 1885. illus. . . . . *$110.00–$350.00*

Palmer, Brooks. *Book of American Clocks.* NY. 1950. 1st ed. dj. . . *$40.00–$75.00*

Palmer, C. H. *Salmon Rivers of Newfoundland.* Bos. 1928. illus. fldg map. . . . .
. . . . *$75.00–$95.00*

Palmer, Howard & J. Monroe. *Climber's Guide to the Rocky Mountains of Canada.* NY. Knickerbocker Press. 1921. 1st ed. illus. 16mo, 183 pp, maps. *$65.00–$125.00*

Palmer, Julius. *Mushrooms of America.* Bos. Prang. 1885. . . . . . *$130.00–$150.00*

Palmer, R. *Maine Birds.* Museum of Comparative Zoology. 1949. one of the scarcest state bird books.. . . . . *$110.00–$150.00*

Pankhurst, E. Sylvia. *Suffragette Movement.* Lon. Longmans. 1931. 1st ed. 631 pp, dj, scarce. . . . . *$100.00–$125.00*

Parker, Dorothy. *After Such Pleasures.* NY. 1933. ltd 250 cc, slipcase, sgn. . . . . . .
. . . . *$100.00–$125.00*

Parker, Dorothy. *Death and Taxes.* NY. Viking. 1931. 1st ed. dj. *$100.00–$160.00*

Parker, Dorothy. *Laments of the Living.* Viking 1930. . . . . *$35.00–$40.00*

Parker, John (ed.). *The Green Room or Who's Who on the Stage.* Lon. 1908. illus. .
. . . . *$75.00–$100.00*

Parker, Robert B. *Double Deuce.* NY. Putnam. 1992. 1st ed. sgn, dj. *$40.00–$50.00*

Parker, Robert B. *Introduction to Raymond Chandler's Unknown Thriller: the Screenplay of Playback.* NY. Mysterious Press. 1985. 1st ed. wrps. scarce. . . . .
. . . . *$175.00–$225.00*

Parker, Robert B. *Judas Goat.* Bos. Houghton Mifflin. 1978. 1st ed. dj. . . . .
. . . . *$55.00–$125.00*

Parker, Thomas V. *Cherokee Indians...Their Relations With The U.S. Govt.* NY. 1907. 1st ed. illus. . . . . *$65.00–$75.00*

Parkinson, C Northcote. *Devil to Pay.* Bos. Houghton Mifflin. (1973). 1st US ed. dj.
. . . . *$20.00–$40.00*

Parkman, Francis. *Francis Parkman's Works.* Bos. Little, Brown. 1898. 11 vols. illus. frontis, teg. . . . . *$100.00–$130.00*

Parkman, Francis. *History of the Conspiracy of Pontiac.* Bos. Little, Brown. 1855. 4 maps. . . . . *$70.00–$85.00*

Parkman, Francis. *Old Regime in Canada.* Bos. 1874. 1st ed. map. . . . .
. . . . *$20.00–$35.00*

Parkman, Francis. *Oregon Trail.* Bos. Little, Brown. 1892. 1st ed. illus. by Frederick Remington. . . . . *$400.00–$500.00*

Parkman, Francis. *Oregon Trail*. Bos. 1925. illus. by N. C. Wyeth & F. Remington, ltd 975 cc. . . . . *$145.00–$195.00*

Parloa, Maria. *Camp Cookery*. Bos. Graves, Locke & Co. 1878. rbnd. . . . . *$150.00–$200.00*

Parloa, Maria. *Miss Parloa's New Cook Book*. Bos. 1881. 1st ed. . *$50.00–$75.00*

Parlour Magic. Phila. 1938. 1st US ed. . . . . *$50.00–$60.00*

Parrish, Maxfield. *Poems of Childhood*. Scribner's. 1904. 1st ed. *$125.00–$150.00*

Parry, William Edward. *Journal of a Second Voyage for the Discovery of a Northwest Passage from the Atlantic to the Pacific*. Lon. John Murray. 1824. 1st ed. illus. 26 plates, 5 charts, fldg maps. . . . . *$780.00–$925.00*

Parsons, C. G. *Inside View of Slavery*. Bos. 1855. 1st ed. 318 pp. . *$75.00–$135.00*

Partington, Charles F. (ed.). *British Cyclopoedia of Natural History*. Lon. Orr & Smith. 1836. 3 vols. illus. plates, engr, marbled bds. . . . . *$60.00–$100.00*

Partisan Review. John Reed Club of NY. 1934. Vol. I, No. 1. incl "Studs Lonigan" by James T. Farrell. . . . . *$25.00–$30.00*

Parton, James. *General Butler in New Orleans*. Mason Bros. 1864. illus. maps. . . . . *$30.00–$45.00*

Pasternak, Boris. *Doctor Zhivago*. Pantheon. 1959. 1st Amer ed. . . *$45.00–$60.00*

Patch, Edith M. *Holiday Meadow*. NY. Macmillan Co. 1930. 1st ed. illus. yellow cl. . . . . *$15.00–$20.00*

Patchen, Kenneth. *Before the Brave*. NY.Random House. 1936. 1st ed. dj, author's first book. . . . . *$225.00–$400.00*

Patchen, Kenneth. *Hurrah for Anything*. 1957. 1st ed. wrps. . . . . . *$37.00–$45.00*

Paton, Alan. *Cry, The Beloved Country*. NY. 1948. sgn. . . . . *$125.00–$150.00*

Paton, Alan. *Too Late the Phalarope*. Capetown. 1953. 1st ed. dj. . *$65.00–$100.00*

Patten, William (ed.). *The Book of Sport*. NY. Taylor & Co. 1901. ltd 450 cc, folio, gray bds. . . . . *$375.00–$500.00*

Patterson, J. H. *In the Grip of the Nyika*. NY. Macmillan. 1909. 1st Amer ed. illus. photos. . . . . *$70.00–$100.00*

Patterson, J. H. *Man-Eater of Tzavo and Other African Adventures*. NY. Macmillan. 1927. revised. illus. photos. . . . . *$80.00–$110.00*

Patterson, Lawson. *Twelve Years in the Mines of California*. Cambridge. 1862. . . . . *$150.00–$400.00*

Patterson, Robert. *Narrative of the Campaign in the Valley of the Shenandoah.* Phila. 1865. map, sgn. . . . . *$112.00–$120.00*

Paul, Howard and George Gebbie, eds. *Stage and its Stars Past and Present.* Phila. Gebbie & Co. 1889. illus. vol. #1 only, large folio. . . . . *$75.00–$100.00*

Paulding, James K. *Slavery in the United States.* NY. 1836. wrps. 312 pp. . . . . *$100.00–$275.00*

Pauling, Linus and E. Bright Wilson. *Introduction to Quantum Mechanics.* NY/Lon. 1935. dj. . . . . *$30.00–$40.00*

Paulsen, Gary. *Clobbered Dirt, Sweet Grass.* NY. 1992. 1st ed. illus. clr, dj. . . . . *$10.00–$20.00*

Paulsen, Gary. *Eastern Sun, Winter Moon.* NY. 1993. 1st ed. presentation copy, sgn, dj. . . . . *$18.00–$25.00*

Pavlov, Ivan Petrovich. *Lectures on Conditioned Reflexes....* NY. 1928. illus. 1st ed in Eng. . . . . *$125.00–$150.00*

Peabody, F. *Education for Life. The Story of Hampton Institute.* 1918. 1st ed. . . . . *$38.00–$70.00*

Pear, Fern Bissel. *Birds.* Akron. (1943). paintings of 12 birds, stiff linen. . . . . *$18.00–$25.00*

Peary, Robert E. *North Pole.* NY. Stokes. 1910. 1st ed. illus. fldg map. . . . . *$90.00–$150.00*

Peck, J. M. *New Guide for Emigrants to the West.* Bos. 1836. 2nd ed. . . . . *$150.00–$225.00*

Peckham, G. W. and E. G Peckham. *On the Instincts and Habits of the Solitary Wasps.* Madison, Wisc. 1898. . . . . *$30.00–$45.00*

Peer, Frank. *Hunting Field.* NY. Mitchell Kennerly. 1910. 1st ed. cl pict panel. . . . . *$50.00–$75.00*

Pelecanos, George P. *A Firing Offense.* NY. St. Martin's. 1992. 1st ed. uncorrected proof. wrps. . . . . *$150.00–$225.00*

Pelecanos, George P. *Shoedog.* NY. St. Martin's. 1994. 1st ed. dj. . *$100.00–$130.00*

Penn, Irving. *Moments Preserved.* NY. Simon & Schuster. (1960). 1st ed. illus. slipcase. . . . . *$550.00–$600.00*

Pennell, Joseph. *Pen Drawing and Pen Draughtsmen.* NY. Macmillan. 1920. illus. gilt, buckram. . . . . *$35.00–$80.00*

Pennsylvania Tours to the Golden State. Phila. 1890. wrps. illus. fldg map. . . . . *$75.00–$125.00*

Penzer, N. M. *Book of the Wine Label.* Lon. 1947. 1st ed. illus. . . . *$38.00–$45.00*

Percy, Walker. *Last Gentleman.* Farrar, Straus & Giroux. 1966. 1st ed. dj.. . . . . . .
. . . . *$125.00–$185.00*

Percy, Walker. *Love in the Ruins.* 1971. dj.. . . . . *$35.00–$55.00*

Percy, William Alexander. *Lanterns on the Levee.* NY. 1941. 1st ed. sgn, dj. . . . .
. . . . *$50.00–$75.00*

Perelman, S. J. *Chicken Inspector.* Simon & Schuster. 1966. 1st ed. dj.. . . . .
. . . . *$40.00–$50.00*

Perelman, S. J. *Ill-Tempered Clavicord.* Simon & Schuster. 1952. 1st ed. dj.. . . . .
. . . . *$55.00–$70.00*

Perelman, S. J. *Listen to the Mockingbird.* Simon & Schuster. 1949. 1st ed. dj.. . . .
. . . . *$65.00–$75.00*

Perkings, Charles E. *Pinto Horse.* CA. 1927. 1st ed. 76 pp, plates. . *$30.00–$45.00*

Perkins, D. A. W. *History of O'Brien County, Iowa.* Sioux Falls. 1897. illus. . . . .
. . . . *$45.00–$65.00*

Perkins, G. *Report of the State Geologist on the Mineral Industries and Geology of Vermont.* Montpelier. Capital City Press. 1912. . . . . *$30.00–$40.00*

Perkins, James. *Annals of the West.* Cinc. 1846. 1st ed. maps. . . . . *$58.00–$70.00*

Perkins, Lucy Fitch. *Indian Twins.* Houghton. 1930. illus. . . . . . . *$18.00–$35.00*

Perkins, Lucy Fitch. *Italian Twins.* Houghton. 1920. illus. . . . . . . *$22.00–$40.00*

Perkins, Lucy Fitch. *Japanese Twins..* Houghton. 1912. illus. . . . . *$20.00–$40.00*

Perkins, P. D. & Ione Perkins. *Bibliography of Lafcadio Hearne.* NY. 1968. . . . .
. . . . *$45.00–$60.00*

Perry Hand Book of Choice New Fruits, Ornamentals, Roses.... Rochester. Perry Nursery. (1899). illus. . . . . *$80.00–$120.00*

Perry, Anne. *Bethlehem Road.* Ny. St. Martin's. 1990. 1st ed. sgn, dj. . . . .
. . . . *$100.00–$130.00*

Pesci, David. *Amistad.* NY. Marlowe & Co. (1997). 1st ed. dj, sgn. *$55.00–$100.00*

Peterjohn, B. G. *Birds of Ohio.* Ind. University. 1989. dj.. . . . . *$30.00–$45.00*

Peters, Ellis. *Monk's Hood.* Lon. Macmillan. 1980. 1st ed. dj.. . . *$275.00–$500.00*

Peters, Ellis. *One Corpse Too Many.* Lon. Macmillan. 1979. 1st ed. dj. . . . .
. . . . *$800.00–$900.00*

Peters, F. J. *Currier & Ives Railroad, Indian & Pioneer Prints.* NY. 1930. folio, dj.. . . . . *$35.00–$45.00*

Petersen, Wm. J. *Steamboating on the Upper Mississippi.* Iowa City. 1937. 1st ed. 575 pp. . . . . *$65.00–$85.00*

Peterson, R.T. *Field Guide to Western Birds.* Bos. Houghton Mifflin. 1941. 1st ed. . . . . *$55.00–$75.00*

Peto, Florence. *Historic Quilts.* NY. 1939. 1st ed. illus. dj. . . . . . . *$75.00–$150.00*

Phair, Charles. *Atlantic Salmon Fishing.* Camden. John Culler & Sons. 1985. . . . . *$85.00–$125.00*

Pharmacopoeia of the United States. Phila. 1830. . . . . *$150.00–$225.00*

Phillips, John. *China Trade Porcelain.* Harvard Univ Press. 1956. 1st ed. illus. clr & b/w. . . . . *$75.00–$185.00*

Phillips, John C. *Natural History of the Ducks.* Bos. Houghton Mifflin. 1922-26. 4 vols. 1st ed. illus. cl & bds, paper spine. . . . . *$1,700.00–$2,250.00*

Phillips, W. J. *Maori Carvings.* New Plymouth. 1941. photos. . . . . *$45.00–$70.00*

Phister, Harold Francis. *Facing the Light... Daguerreotypes.* DC. Smithsonian. 1978. 1st ed. wrps. . . . . *$40.00–$55.00*

Photographs by Cartier-Bresson. NY. Grossman. 1963. 1st ed. wrps. illus. . . . . *$22.00–$30.00*

Physician's and Dentist's Directory of the State of Pennsylvania. Phila. Galen Gonsier. 1902. 1st prtg, illus, 458 pp. . . . . *$35.00–$48.00*

Piaget, H. E. *The Watch.* 1860. illus. *$100.00–$200.00*

Picard, Mary Ann. *Official Star Trek Cooking Manual.* NY. 1978. 1st ed. paperback, sgn. . . . . *$12.50–$18.00*

Picasso, Pablo. *Desire. A Play.* NY. 1948. 1st ed. dj.. . . . . *$25.00–$35.00*

Pictographic History of the Oglala Sioux. Lincoln. 1967. illus. by Amos Bad Heart Bull, boxed. . . . . *$37.00–$45.00*

Pictorial History of the 69th Infantry Division...15 May, 1943 to 15 May, 1945. np. 1945. 93 pp. . . . . *$70.00–$85.00*

Pictorial History of the Second World War. NY. 1944-65. 5 vols. illus. photos. . . . . *$45.00–$60.00*

Pictures of Old Chinatown. NY. Moffat Jard & Co. 1909. 2nd prtg, 57 pp, photos by Arnold Genthe. . . . . *$135.00–$150.00*

Pierce, Gerald S. *Texas Under Arms... Rep. of Texas, 1836-1846.* Austin. 1969. dj. . . . . *$27.00–$35.00*

Pierce, Justin. *Palestine, or the Holy Land.* Phila. c. 1825. clr, fldg map in lea folder. . . . . *$500.00–$550.00*

Pike, James. *Scout and Ranger.. .in the Indian Wars.* Cinc. 1865. 1st issue, plates. . . . . *$450.00–$500.00*

Pike, Nicholas. *New & Complete System of Arithmetick.* Bos. 1808. 3rd ed. calf.. . . . . *$22.00–$45.00*

Pike, S. & S. Hayward. *Religious Cases of Conscience.* NH. Charles Peirce. 1808. lea. . . . . *$45.00–$70.00*

Pike, Warburton. *Barren Ground of Northern Canada.* Lon. 1892. 1st ed. fldg maps.. . . . . *$85.00–$125.00*

Pike, Zebulon M. *Exploratory Travels Through the Western Territories.* Denver. 1889. . . . . *$125.00–$325.00*

Pilling, James Constantine. *Bibliography of the Eskimo Language.* DC. GPO. 1887. wrps. . . . . *$75.00–$125.00*

Pincus, Gregory. *Eggs of Mammals.* NY. Macmillan Co. 1936. . . . *$35.00–$40.00*

Pinkerton, Alan. *Gypsies and the Detectives.* NY. Carleton. 1880. 1st ed. pict cl. . . . . *$65.00–$100.00*

Pinkerton, Allan. *Strikers, Communists, Tramps and Detectives.* NY. Carlton. 1878. 1st ed. illus. wood engr.. . . . . *$100.00–$200.00*

Pinkham, Lydia E. *Text Book upon Ailments Peculiar to Women.* Lynn, MA. Lydia Pinkham Medicine Co. (c 1875). printed wrps, frontis, 79 pp.. . . . . . *$60.00–$85.00*

Pinkwater, Daniel. *Doodle Flute.* Macmillan. (1991). illus. dj.. . . . *$15.00–$25.00*

Pinkwater, Daniel. *Return of the Moose.* NY. Dodd, Mead. dj.. . . . *$20.00–$35.00*

Pinkwater, Daniel. *The Last Guru.* NY. Bantam Books. (1978). paper back.. . . . . *$8.00–$15.00*

Piper, Watty. *Cock The Mouse and the Little Red Hen.* NY. Platt & Munk Co. 1925. 1st ed. illus. pict bds.. . . . . *$18.00–$30.00*

Pittenger, Peggy. *Morgan Horses.* So Brunswick. Barnes. 1977. 1st ed. . . . . *$50.00–$65.00*

Plath, Sylvia. *Ariel.* NY. Harper & Row. (1966). 1st ed. dj.. . . . . . *$85.00–$100.00*

Plowden, E. *History of Ireland..* Lon. 1812. 2 vols. 2nd ed. 1/4 lea.. . . . . *$50.00–$75.00*

Pneumatic and Electric Tools and Accessories Catalogue No. 560. NY. 1924. illus.
.... *$95.00–$120.00*

Pocock, Roger. *Following the Frontier..* NY. 1903. .... *$85.00–$115.00*

Poe, Edgar Allan. *Fall of the House of Usher.* Cheshire House. 1931. illus. by Abner Epstein. ltd 1200 cc, tan cl. .... *$45.00–$60.00*

Poe, Edgar Allan. *Poetical Works of Edgar Poe.* Lon. 1858. 1st ed. thus, full lea, aeg, 247 pp, illus. .... *$150.00–$225.00*

Poe, Edgar Allan. *Tales of Mystery and Imagination.* NY. Brentano's. (1923). illus. by Harry Clarke. 1st US thus. pict label. .... *$80.00–$120.00*

Poe, Edgar Allan. *Works of Edgar A. Poe.* NY. 1902. 10 vols. lib ed.. ....
.... *$75.00–$100.00*

Poe, Edgar Allan. *Works of....* Chi. Stone & Kimball. 1894. 10 vols. illus. 36 plates, teg, green cl. .... *$275.00–$350.00*

Poe, Edgar Allan. *A Valentine.* Phila. 1849. 1st prtg in Sartains Mag. ....
.... *$50.00–$60.00*

Poe, Edgar Allan. *Tales of Mystery and Imagination.* Tudor. 1935. illus. by Harry Clarke.. .... *$50.00–$100.00*

Pogany, Willy and Elaine. *Golden Cockerel.* NY. Thomas Nelson. 1938. 1st ed. illus. by Willy Pogany, red cl.. .... *$100.00–$175.00*

Poiteau, A. (ed.). *Le Bon Jardinier, Almanach pour l'Annee 1828.* Paris. 1828. rbnd.
.... *$150.00–$250.00*

Polk, James. *Treaty With Mexico....* 30th Congress, 1st Session. 1848. House Executive Document No. 69. 74pp. .... *$145.00–$175.00*

Polk, Willis. *Matter of Taste.* SF. Book Club of California. 1979. ltd 550 cc. illus. dj.
.... *$55.00–$80.00*

Pollard, Edward A. *First Year of the War.* Richmond. 1863. 1st ed. Confederate imprint. .... *$225.00–$300.00*

Pollard, Edward A. *Lost Cause: A New Southern Hist. of War of the Confederates..* NY. 1866. .... *$75.00–$100.00*

Pollard, Edward A. *Southern History of the Great Civil War..* NY. 1865. 2 vols. . .
.... *$100.00–$125.00*

Poole, Ernest. *The Harbor.* NY. Macmillan. 1915. 1st ed. ...... *$75.00–$100.00*

Poortenaar, Jan. *Art of the book and Its Illustration.* Lon. Harrap. (1935). 1st ed. illus. .... *$80.00–$100.00*

Pope, Dudley. *Black Ship.* Phila. Lippincott. (1964). 1st ed. dj..... *$50.00–$75.00*

Pope, Dudley. *Ramage.* Phila. Lippincott. (1965). 1st US ed dj. . . *$55.00–$150.00*

Pope, Dudley. *Ramage and the Rebels.* Lon. Secker & Warburg. (1978). 1st UK ed dj. . . . . *$35.00–$85.00*

Popple, Henry. *Carolinas section Map of the British Empire.* Lon. 1733. includes Georgia and Southern Virginia. . . . . *$2,000.00–$2,200.00*

Porok, Byron Kuhn D. *Digging for Lost African Gods.* NY. Putnam. 1926. 1st ed. photos, fldg map, teg. . . . . *$60.00–$70.00*

Porter, Eliot. *Birds of North America.* E. P. Dutton. 1972. 1st ed. illus. dj. . . . . *$40.00–$60.00*

Porter, Gene. *Music of the Wild.* Garden City. 1910. 1st ed. . . . . . *$95.00–$150.00*

Porter, Gene Stratton. *Birds of the Bible.* Cinc. 1909. 1st ed. . . . . *$200.00–$400.00*

Porter, Gene Stratton. *Laddie. A True Blue Story.* Garden City. Doubleday. 1913. 1st ed. illus. blue cl. . . . . *$40.00–$105.00*

Porter, Gene Stratton. *Magic Garden.* NY. 1927. 1st ed. . . . . *$35.00–$48.00*

Porter, Gene Stratton. *Michael O'Halloran.* Garden City. Doubleday. 1915. illus. 1st Amer ed illus cl. . . . . *$55.00–$65.00*

Porter, Gene Stratton. *Moths of the Limberlost..* NY. Doubleday. 1912. 1st ed. . . . . *$200.00–$300.00*

Porter, Gene Stratton. *Song of the Cardinal.* Ind. Bobbs-Merrill. 1903. illus. buckram. . . . . *$80.00–$90.00*

Porter, Gene Stratton. *What I Have Done With Birds.* Ind. 1907. 1st ed. . . . . *$175.00–$225.00*

Porter, Jane. *The Scottish Chiefs.* NY. Scribner's. 1921. illus. by N. C. Wyeth. blue cl. . . . . *$50.00–$85.00*

Porter, Katherine. *My Chinese Marriage.* NY. 1921. . . . . *$50.00–$65.00*

Porter, Katherine Anne. *Leaning Tower.* NY. Harcourt Brace. (1944). 1st ed. dj. . . . . *$50.00–$100.00*

Porter, Katherine Anne. *Ship of Fools.* Bos. Little, Brown. 1962. 1st ed. dj. . . . . *$40.00–$60.00*

Porter, Kenneth W. *The Jacksons and the Lees...Massachusetts Merchants, 1765–1844.* Camb. 1937. 2 vols. 1st ed. illus. dj. . . . . *$65.00–$100.00*

Potter, Beatrix. *Peter Rabbit Pop-up Book.* Columbia. 1983. . . . . . *$35.00–$45.00*

Potter, Beatrix. *Pie and the Patty Man.* NY. 1905. . . . . *$45.00–$60.00*

Potter, Beatrix. *Story of Peter Rabbit and Other Stories.* Whitman. 1928. . . . .
. . . . *$18.00–$35.00*

Potter, Beatrix. *Tale of Benjamin Bunny.* Lon. 1904. 1st ed. . . . . *$375.00–$495.00*

Potter, Beatrix. *Tale of Mr. Toad.* 1939. illus. dj.. . . . . *$20.00–$35.00*

Potter, Beatrix. *Wag-by-Wall.* Bos. 1944. 1st ed. illus. by J J Lankes. dj.. . . . .
. . . . *$125.00–$200.00*

Pound, Ezra. *70 Cantos.* Lon. 1950. 1st UK ed. ltd 1622cc, dj. . . *$90.00–$120.00*

Pound, Ezra. *Classic Anthology Defined by Confucius.* Harvard Univ Press. 1954.
1st ed. dj.. . . . . *$50.00–$125.00*

Pound, Ezra. *Section: Rock Drill 85-95 de los Cantares.* New Directions. [1956]. 1st
US, 107 pp, dj,. . . . . *$75.00–$125.00*

Powall, Thomas. *Topographical Description of the Dominions of the United States
of America.* Pitts. Univ Pitts Press. 1949. 1st thus, illus.. . . . . *$100.00–$150.00*

Powell, Agnes Baden. *Handbook for Girl Scouts.* 1917. 1st ed. . . . *$30.00–$45.00*

Powell, Anthony. *At Lady Molly's.* Lon. Heinemann. c1957. 1st ed. dj.. . . . .
. . . . *$65.00–$75.00*

Powell, Anthony. *Venusberg & Agents and Patients: Two Novels.* NY. Periscope-
Holliday. (1952). 1st Amer ed. dj. . . . . *$50.00–$65.00*

Powell, J. W. *14th Annual Report of the Bureau of Ethnology.* DC. GPO. 1896. illus.
maps.. . . . . *$65.00–$95.00*

**Powell, J. and Mary C. Rabbitt, Edwin D. McKee, Charles B. Hunt, and Luna
B. Leopold.** *Colorado River Region and John Wesley Powell.* DC. GPO. 1969. 1st ed.
illus. Geological Survery Professional Paper 669. . . . . *$45.00–$60.00*

Powell, John Wesley. *Fourth Annual Report of the Bureau of American Ethnology....*
DC. GPO. 1893. illus. clr lith. . . . . *$100.00–$138.00*

Powell, John Wesley. *Nineteenth Annual Report of the Bureau of Ethnology....* DC.
GPO. 1900. illus. photos.. . . . . *$100.00–$150.00*

Power, John. *Handy-book About Books.* Lon. Wilson. 1870. 1st ed. illus. chro-
molithos. . . . . *$70.00–$100.00*

Poyas, Mrs. Elizabeth A. *Carolina in Olden Time.* Charleston. 1855. 1st ed. . . . . .
. . . . *$50.00–$75.00*

Practical Guide to Homeopathy for Family and Private Use. Bos/Prov/Cinc. Otis
Clapp/A F Worthington. 1892. 180 pp. . . . . *$60.00–$85.00*

Pratt, Joseph. *Year with Osler.* Balt. Johns Hopkins. 1949. fldg chart.. . . . .
. . . . *$65.00–$85.00*

Pratt, Parley P. *Voice of Warning and Instruction to All People*. Liverpool. 1881. full gilt lea. . . . . *$65.00–$75.00*

Prebble, John. *Buffalo Soldiers*. NY. Harcourt, Brace and Co. [1959]. 1st ed. dj.. . . . . *$45.00–$65.00*

Prescott, W H. *Conquest of Mexico*. NY. 1848. 3 vols. 1st ed. . . . . *$110.00–$125.00*

Price, Edith Ballinger. *Four Winds*. NY. Stokes. 1927. 1st ed. illus. sgn. . . . . *$70.00–$100.00*

Price, George. *Modern Factory*. NY. Wiley. 1914. 1st prtg.. . . . . . . *$50.00–$75.00*

Price, Lee & Co. *Map of the City of New London 1890*. np. 1890. fldg map. . . . . *$225.00–$250.00*

Price, Reynolds. *Generous Man*. NY. Atheneum. 1966. 1st ed. dj. . *$35.00–$50.00*

Price, Reynolds. *Permanent Errors*. NY. Atheneum. 1970. 1st ed. sgn, dj. . . . . *$50.00–$75.00*

Price, Vincent and Mary Price. *Treasury of Great Recipes*. NY. Ampersand Press. 1965. 1st ed. dj. . . . . *$50.00–$75.00*

Prideaux, Humphrey. *Old and New Testament....Hist. of Jews and Neighbouring Nations*. Balt. 1833. illus. fldg maps calf. *$50.00–$65.00*

Priest, Josiah. *American Antiquities and Discoveries in the West..* Albany. 1833. illus. fldg map, calf. . . . . *$90.00–$135.00*

Priestley, J. *Discourses Relating to the Evidences of Revealed Religion..* Phila. 1796. 1st ed. lea. . . . . *$95.00–$120.00*

Priestly, J. B. *Dangerous Corner*. Lon. Heinemann. 1932. 1st ed. dj.*$20.00–$30.00*

Prieur, J. C. *Boyer's Royal Dictionary*. Dublin. 1796. full lea, 17th ed. . . . . *$55.00–$85.00*

Prime, Samuel I. *Under the Trees*. NY. Harper. 1874. 1st ed. . . . . . *$50.00–$90.00*

Prime, William C. *Boat Life in Egypt and Nubia*. Harper & Bros. 1857. 1st ed. red cl. . . . . *$85.00–$100.00*

Prime, William C. *Tent Life in the Holy Land*. NY. (1857). sgn. . . *$75.00–$100.00*

Prince, Nancy. *Narrative of the Life and Travels of Mrs. Nancy Prince*. Bos. 1853. original cl 89 pp. . . . . *$250.00–$300.00*

Probable Termination of Mormon Troubles in the Utah Territory. GPO. 1858. . . . . *$55.00–$75.00*

Proceedings of the Exec. of the U.S. Respecting...Insurgents. Phila. 1795. (Whiskey Rebellion).. *$125.00–$175.00*

Proceedings of the Fifth Imperial Konvokation Held in Chicago, Illinois August 18 and 19, 1930. wrps. 16 pp. .... *$40.00–$50.00*

Proctor, R. *Chance & Luck.* Lon. 1887. .... *$50.00–$90.00*

Propert, W. A. *Russian Ballet.* NY. Greenberg. (1932). illus. ... *$150.00–$200.00*

Prosch, Charles. *Reminiscences of Washington Territory....* Seattle. 1904. sgn. ....
.... *$95.00–$125.00*

Proulx, E. Annie. *Complete Dairy Foods Cookbook.* PA. Rodale Press. 1982. 1st ed. illus. bds, sgn. .... *$50.00–$100.00*

Proulx, E. Annie. *Fine Art of Salad Gardening.* PA. Rodale Press. 1985. dj. ......
.... *$75.00–$150.00*

Proulx, E. Annie. *Heart Songs.* NY. Scribner's. 1988. 1st ed. dj.. *$350.00–$400.00*

Proulx, E. Annie. *Postcards.* NY. Scribner's. 1971. 1st ed. dj,. ... *$450.00–$500.00*

Prussian International Literature, Organ of the International Union of Revolutionary Writers. Moscow. 1934. bound vols 1, 2, 3, black cl. . *$50.00–$75.00*

Psalms of David by Isaac Watts. NH. Prentiss. 1803. lea. .... *$65.00–$85.00*

Punkin, Jonathan. *Downfall of Freemasonry.* published for the editor. 1838. 1st ed. illus. 159 pp, cl.................................... *$145.00–$200.00*

Purdy, James. *Day After the Fair.* NY. 1977. 1st ed. dj cl bds. .... *$60.00–$75.00*

Pusey, William Allen. *Wilderness Road to Kentucky..* NY. 1921. dj. . *$58.00–$75.00*

Putnam, Carleton. *Race and Reason.* Wash. Public Affairs Press. 1961. cl........
.... *$60.00–$75.00*

Putnam, George Haven. *Prisoner of War in Virginia.* Putnam. 1912. 1st ed. .....
.... *$60.00–$75.00*

Putnam, George R. *Lighthouses and Lightships of the United States.* 1933. illus.
.... *$30.00–$45.00*

Pyle, Howard. *Howard Pyle's Book of Pirates.* NY/Lon. Harper & Bros. (1921). illus. .... *$50.00–$100.00*

Pyle, Howard. *Men of Iron.* Harper. 1892. 1st ed. illus. .... *$55.00–$75.00*

Pyle, Howard. *Story of the Champions of the Round Table.* NY. Charles Scribner's. 1905. 1st ed. brown cl................................... *$80.00–$120.00*

Pynchon, Thomas. *Crying of Lot 49*. Phila. Lippincott. 1966. 1st ed. dj. . . . . *$250.00–$500.00*

Pynchon, Thomas. *Gravity's Rainbow*. NY. Viking. (1973). 1st ed. spine-faded, dj. . . . . *$650.00–$1,000.00*

Pyne, Henry R. *History of the First New Jersey Cavalry*. Trenton. 1871. 1st ed. . . . . *$150.00–$200.00*

Queen, Ellery. *Devil To Pay*. NY. Stokes. 1938. 1st ed. dj. . . . . *$30.00–$45.00*

Queen, Ellery. *Double, Double*. Bos. Little, Brown. 1950. 1st ed. dj. *$25.00–$30.00*

Queen, Ellery. *Ellery Queen's Double Dozen*. NY. 1964. 1st ed. dj. *$32.00–$40.00*

Queen, Ellery. *Murderer Is a Fox*. Bos. Little, Brown. 1945. 1st ed. dj. . . . . *$20.00–$35.00*

Queen, Ellery. *Origin of Evil*. Bos. Little, Brown. 1951. 1st ed. dj.. *$20.00–$40.00*

Queen, Ellery. *Queen's Bureau of Investigation*. Bos. Little, Brown. 1954. 1st ed. dj. . . . . *$25.00–$35.00*

Queen, Ellery. *Ten Days Wonder*. Bos. Little, Brown. 1948. 1st ed. dj. . . . . *$10.00–$18.00*

Queen, Ellery (ed.). *To The Queen's Taste*. Bos. 1946. 1st ed. dj. . . *$25.00–$75.00*

Queeny, Edgar. *Prairie Wings*. NY. 1946. 1st ed. dj. . . . . *$150.00–$275.00*

Queeny, Edgar M. *Cheechako, The Story of an Alaskan Bear Hunt*. NY. Scribner's. 1941. photos. . . . . *$90.00–$125.00*

Quiller-Couch, A. T. *Sleeping Beauty and Other Fairy Tales*. Lon. nd. illus. by Edmund Dulac. . . . . *$125.00–$175.00*

Quiller-Couch, A. T. *Twelve Dancing Princesses*. NY. nd. illus. tip-in plates, dj.. . . . . *$90.00–$200.00*

Quiller-Couch, Arthur T. *Old Fires & Profitable Ghosts*. NY. Scribner's 1900. 1st Amer ed. 384 pp. . . . . *$100.00–$135.00*

Quincy, John. *Pharmacopoeia Officialis & Extemporanea: or A Complete English Dispensary*....Lon. 1782. 15th ed.. . . . . *$40.00–$60.00*

Quint, Alonzo. *Record of the Second Massachusetts Infantry 1861–65*. Bos. 1867. 528 pp. . . . . *$90.00–$150.00*

Quiz Book upon the U.S.G.A. Rules of Golf. NY. Burr. (1914). 2nd ed. illus. . . . . *$90.00–$316.00*

Raht, C. G. *Romance of Davis Mountains and Big Bend Country*. El Paso. 1919. 1st ed. illus. fldg map, plates. . . . . *$55.00–$100.00*

Railroad Commissioners of New York. *Map of the Rail-Roads of the State of New York*. Albany. 1856. fldg map. . . . . *$425.00–$475.00*

Ralph, Julian. *On Canada's Frontier.* Harper & Bros. 1892. 1st ed. illus. by Remington. . . . . *$75.00–$95.00*

Ramsay, D. *History of the American Revolution.* Trenton. 1811. 2 vols. 2nd ed. lea.. . . . . *$95.00–$125.00*

Ramsdell, Charles W. *Laws and Joint Resolution of Last Session of Confed. Congress.* Durham. 1941. . . . . *$45.00–$70.00*

Ramsey, Charles & Harold Sleeper. *Architectural Graphic Standards.* NY. John Wiley. (1947). illus. 3rd ed. . . . . *$35.00–$65.00*

Rand McNally. *Atlas of the World.* Chi/NY. Rand McNally & Co. 1908. illus. folio clr maps. . . . . *$60.00–$90.00*

Rand McNally & Co's New Dollar Atlas of the US and Canada. Chi. 1884. cl, bds. . . . . *$40.00–$60.00*

Rand, Ayn. *Atlas Shrugged.* NY. Random House. 1957. 1st ed. dj.*$100.00–$250.00*

Rand, Ayn. *The Fountainhead.* Ind. Bobbs Merrill. 1943. 1st ed. dj. . . . . *$1,000.00–$2,000.00*

Rand, Ayn. *We the Living.* NY. Random House. 1936. 1st ed. dj. . . . . *$75.00–$100.00*

Randall, E. O. *History of the Zoar Society from its Commencement to its Conclusion.* Columbus. Press of Fred J Heer. 1899. 100 pp. . . . . *$95.00–$135.00*

Randolph Caldecott Graphic Pictures. Lon. 1883. illus. folio. . . . *$85.00–$115.00*

Randolph, Cornelia J. *Parlor Gardener...* Bos. J. E. Tilton & Co. 1861. illus. 11plates. . . . . *$50.00–$75.00*

Ransom, Arthur. *Swallowdale.* Phila. 1932. 1st ed. . . . . *$30.00–$40.00*

Ransom, John L. *Andersonville Diary.* NY. private printing. 1881. 1st ed. . . . . *$125.00–$250.00*

Ransome, Stafford. *Japan in Transition.* NY. Harper & Bros. 1800. illus. maps, red decorated cl, frontis. . . . . *$50.00–$65.00*

Rarey, John Solomon. *Modern Art of Taming Wild Horses.* Columbus. 1856. 1st ed. wrps. . . . . *$900.00–$1,500.00*

Rasmussen, Wayne D. (ed.). *Agriculture in the United States: a documentary history.* NY. Random House. 4 vols. 1st ed. . . . . *$185.00–$225.00*

Rawling, Charles J. *History of the First Regiment, Virginia Infantry.* Phila. 1887. 1st ed. . . . . *$275.00–$350.00*

Rawlings, Marjorie Kinnan. *Cross Creek Cookery.* NY. Scribner's. 1942. 1st ed. . . . . *$85.00–$125.00*

Rawlings, Marjorie Kinnan. *The Yearling.* Scribner's. 1938. 1st ed. illus. dj. . . . . *$50.00–$60.00*

Rawls, Walton. *Great Book of Currier & Ives America.* NY. Abbeville. (1979). illus. clr plates, folio, dj. . . . . *$85.00–$120.00*

Rawstorne, Lawrence. *Gamonia.* Phila. McKay. 1930. rprnt of 1837 ed. illus. with clr plates. . . . . *$60.00–$100.00*

Ray, J. A. *Compleat Collection of English Proverbs.* Lon. Otridge. 1768. 4th ed. . . . . *$70.00–$100.00*

Reagan, R. *Speaking My Mind.* sgn. . . . . *$98.00–$125.00*

Redding, J. Saunders. *Stranger and Alone.* NY. Harcourt, Brace. 1950. 1st ed. author's only novel, dj. . . . . *$100.00–$150.00*

Redmond, Pat H. *History of Quincy and Its Men of Mark.* Ill. 1869. 1st ed. Howes. . . . . *$50.00–$100.00*

Redpath, James. *Public Life of Captain John Brown. .With and Autobiography of His Childhood and Youth.* Bos. 1860. 1st ed. . . . . *$90.00–$180.00*

Redpath, James. *Roving Editor.* NY. 1859. 1st ed. blue cl, plates. *$200.00–$325.00*

Redpath, John Clark. *James Otis - The Pre Revolutionist.* Milwaukee. Campbell. 1898. . . . . *$30.00–$40.00*

Reed, Earl H. *Sketches in Duneland.* NY/Lon. John Lane Company. 1918. illus. sgn. . . . . *$50.00–$75.00*

Reed, Ishmael. *Mumbo Jumbo.* Garden City. 1972. 1st ed. dj. . . . . . *$55.00–$75.00*

Reed, John. *An Apology For the Rite of Infant Baptism.. Modes of Baptism.* Prov. 1815. calf. . . . . *$25.00–$30.00*

Reed, John. *Daughter of the Revolution and Other Stories.* NY. Vanguard. 1927. 1st ed. uncommon in dj. . . . . *$60.00–$85.00*

Reed, John. *War In Eastern Europe.* NY. Scribner's. 1919. illus. by boardman Robinson. . . . . *$35.00–$95.00*

Reed, John A. *History of the 101st Regiment Pennsylvania Volunteer Infantry.* Chi. 1910. . . . . *$40.00–$50.00*

Reed, William Howell. *Hospital Life in the Army of the Potomac.* Bos. William V Spencer. 1866. 1st ed. . . . . *$95.00–$150.00*

Reeves, J. E. *Hand-Book of Medical Microscopy*. Phila. 1894. 1st ed. illus. . . . . . .
. . . . *$37.00–$45.00*

Reeves, James J. *History of the 24th Regiment New Jersey Volunteers*. Camden, NJ.
1889. 1st ed. wrps. 45 pp. . . . . *$135.00–$250.00*

Regulations for the Care of Camels. Cairo. War Office Prtg Press. 1896. wrps. . . .
. . . . *$55.00–$75.00*

Reichard, Gladys. *Spider Woman: A Story of Navajo Weavers and Chanters*. 1934.
1st ed. . . . . *$25.00–$48.00*

Reichenbach, W. *Six Guns & Bulls Eyes*. Sam Worth. 1936. 1st ed. dj. . . . .
. . . . *$40.00–$50.00*

Reid, W. Max. *Lake George and Lake Champlain*. NY/Lon. Putnam. 1910. 1st ed.
illus. blue cl, small paste-down, gold lettering, teg, frontis, maps. *$100.00–$175.00*

Reid, Carol McMillan. *Our Own Mother Goose*. WI. Whitman Pub. (1934).
1st ed. illus. tall pict wrps. . . . . *$10.00–$20.00*

Reid, Mayne. *White Chief: A Legend of North Mexico*. NY. 1875. . *$22.00–$30.00*

Reid, Mrs . Hugo. *Woman, Her Education and Influence*. NY. 1847. wrps. . . . . . .
. . . . *$30.00–$45.00*

Reifenstahl, Leni. *People of Kau*. NY. Harper & Row. (1976). 1st Amer ed. illus. clr
plates. . . . . *$50.00–$80.00*

Reilly, Catherine W. *English Poetry of the First World War: a Bibliography*. NY. St.
Martin's Press. (1978). 1st ed. . . . . *$50.00–$80.00*

Reinfeld, Fred and Harold M. Phillips. *Book of the Warsaw 1935 International
Chess Team Tournament*. NY. Black Knight Press. 1936. 1st ed. . . . *$40.00–$45.00*

Reinhardt, Col. G. C. and Lt. Col. W. R. Kintner. *Atomic Weapons in Land
Combat*. Harrisburg. 1953. 1st ed. wrps. illus. . . . . *$20.00–$30.00*

Religious Folk Songs of the Negro. Hampton, VA. 1918. new ed.. . *$40.00–$75.00*

Remarks On a Scandalous Libel.... Lon. 1713. wrps. 2nd ed. corrected with additions, 26 pp plus 16 pp List of All The Members of the House of Commons. . . . . . .
. . . . *$75.00–$125.00*

Remarque, Erich Maria. *All Quiet on the Western Front*. Bos. Little, Brown. 1929.
1st ed. dj. . . . . *$65.00–$125.00*

Remarque, Erich Maria. *Road Back*. Bos. Little, Brown. 1931. 1st ed. second book,
dj. . . . . *$60.00–$85.00*

Remey, Charles Mason. *The New Day*. pub by author. 1919. wrps. *$25.00–$50.00*

Remey, Charles Mason. *Universal Conciousness of the Bahai Revelation.* Italy. (1925). tan bds. . . . . *$25.00–$35.00*

Remington, Frederic. *Crooked Trails.* NY. Harper & Bros. 1898. illus. by Remington. . . . . *$200.00–$275.00*

Remington, Frederic. *Done in the Open, Drawings by...* NY. 1904. Folio. . . . . *$120.00–$250.00*

Remington, Frederic. *Way of an Indian.* NY. 1906. 1st ed. illus. by Remington. . . . . *$125.00–$200.00*

Remington, Frederic. *Pony Tracks.* NY. Harper. 1895. 1st ed. illus. by Remington. . . . . *$300.00–$500.00*

Rendell, Ruth. *One Across, Two Down.* Lon. Hutchinson. 1971. 1st ed. dj. . . . . *$400.00–$550.00*

Report of the Cruise of the US Revenue Cutter Bear...November27, 1897 to September 13, 1898. DC. GPO. 1899. blue cl, plates, map. . . . . . . *$85.00–$125.00*

Report of the Secretary of the Navy, Nov. 5, 1864. Richmond. 1864. 1st ed. wrps. 52 pp, Confederate imprint. . . . . *$250.00–$350.00*

Report of the Special Commission Appointed to Investigate the Affairs.... DC. GPO. 1875. illus. cl, sp lettered in gilt. . . . . *$100.00–$175.00*

Report on Indians Taxed and Not Taxed in the United States...Eleventh Census: 1890. DC. GPO. 1894. 683 pp, maps, plates. . . . . *$700.00–$1,200.00*

Report on Japanese Research on Radio Wave Propagation. US Army. 1946. 1st ed. . . . . *$50.00–$65.00*

Report on the Census of Cuba, 1899. DC. GPO. 1900. illus. photos. *$48.00–$60.00*

Report on the Control of the Aborigines of Formosa. 1911. illus. maps. . . . . *$75.00–$100.00*

Report on U. S. Geographical Surveys West of 100th Meridian.... DC. GPO. 1877. illus. . . . . *$80.00–$120.00*

Reports...Joint Palestine Survey Commission, October 1, 1928. Bos. 1928. illus. . . . . *$95.00–$125.00*

Reports of Officers in Relation to Recent Battles at Pittsburg Landing. Wash. 1862. . . . . *$75.00–$100.00*

Revillon, Freres. *Igloo Life: A brief account of a primitive Arctic tribe....* NY. private prtg. 1923. illus. . . . . *$45.00–$100.00*

Revised Regulations for the Army of the United States. Phila. Lippincott. 1862. . .
. . . . *$75.00–$95.00*

Revolutionary Writers, International Literature Organ of the International Union.
Moscow, USSR. 1934. bound, vols 1, 2 & 3, black cl. . . . . *$50.00–$75.00*

Rey, H. A. *Zebrology.* Lon. Chatto & Windus. c 1937. illus. yellow paper. . . . .
. . . . *$75.00–$150.00*

Reynolds, George. *Book of Abraham.* Salt Lake. 1879. 1st ed. printed wrps. . . . . . .
. . . . *$40.00–$50.00*

Reynolds, Quentin. *Fiction Factory.* NY. Random House. 1955. 1st ed. dj. . . . .
. . . . *$35.00–$55.00*

Reznikoff, Nathan and Charles Reznikoff. *Early History of a Sewing Maching
Operator.* NY. Reznikoff. (1936). 1st ed. blue cl, paper label. . . . *$165.00–$200.00*

Rheims, Maurice. *Flowering of Art Nouveau.* NY. nd. dj. . . . . *$85.00–$115.00*

Rhind, William. *History of the Vegetable Kingdom.* Lon. Blackie & Son. 1877.
revised ed. . . . . *$120.00–$140.00*

Rhinegold & The Valkyrie. Lon/NY. 1914. illus. by Arthur Rackham, tip-in plates. .
. . . . *$60.00–$75.00*

Rhoades, J. *Little Flowers of St Francis of Assisi.* Lon. Oxford Univ Press. 1934.
rprnt, 319 pp, full lea, gold tooled, aeg. . . . . *$30.00–$40.00*

Rhode, John. *The Venner Crime.* Lon. Odhams. 1933. 1st ed. dj. . . . *$70.00–$80.00*

Rice, Anne. *Lasher.* Knopf. 1993. 1st ed. dj, sgn. . . . . *$50.00–$60.00*

Rice, Anne. *Memnoch the Devil.* NY. Knopf. 1995. 1st ed. sgn, dj. . *$45.00–$60.00*

Rice, Anne. *Mummy or Ramses the Damned.* NY. Ballantine. [1989]. 1st ed. illus.
Harlan Ellison's copy with his sgn bookplate. . . . . *$35.00–$65.00*

Rice, Anne. *Queen of the Damned.* Knopf. 1988. sgn, dj. . . . . *$45.00–$60.00*

Rice, Anne. *Tale of the Body Thief.* 1992. 1st ed. dj. . . . . *$30.00–$40.00*

Rice, Anne. *The Mummy.* Lon. 1989. 1st Brit ed. dj. . . . . *$175.00–$200.00*

Rice, Anne. *Vampire Lestat.* NY. Knopf. 1985. 1st ed. dj, sgn.. . . *$300.00–$500.00*

Rice, Anne. *Vampire Lestat.* NY. Knopf. 1985. 1st ed. dj. . . . . . . *$150.00–$200.00*

Rich E. E. *Hudson's Bay Company, 1670-1870.* NY. Macmillan Company. [1961]. 3
vols. 1st Amer ed. six plates, two fldg maps. . . . . *$100.00–$150.00*

Rich, Adrienne. *Sources*. Woodside. Heyeck Press. 1983. 1st ed. ltd 300 cc, mor, marbled bds. . . . . *$225.00–$300.00*

Rich, Prof George. *Artistic Horse Shoeing*. NY. 1890. . . . . *$35.00–$45.00*

Richards, Laura. *Captain January*. Bos. 1893. illus. . . . . *$35.00–$45.00*

Richards, Laura E. *Golden Windows*. Little, Brown. 1903. illus. . . . *$30.00–$40.00*

Richards, Laura E. *Silver Crown*. Little, Brown. 1906. illus. . . . . *$20.00–$40.00*

Richards, Laura E. *When I Was Your Age*. Bos. 1849. 1st ed. . . . . *$20.00–$30.00*

Richards, Laura Elizabeth Howe. *Hurdy-Gurdy*. Bos. 1902. illus. *$65.00–$85.00*

Richardson, A. E. *Old Inns of England*. Lon. 1942. . . . . *$25.00–$40.00*

Richardson, Albert D. *Secret Service, the Field, the Dungeon and the Escape*. Hartford. 1865. 1st ed. illus. . . . . *$65.00–$145.00*

Richardson, Frank. *From Sunrise to Sunset: Reminiscence*. Bristol, TN. 1910. 1st ed. illus. . . . . *$90.00–$125.00*

Richardson, Frank. *Secret Kingdom*. Lon. (1911). 3rd prtg. . . . . *$50.00–$75.00*

Richardson, J. *Health & Longevity*. Phila. Home Health Society. 1912. illus. . . . . *$50.00–$75.00*

Richardson, James D. *Messages of the Presidents*. Bureau of National Literature. 22 vols. . . . . *$75.00–$100.00*

Richardson, James (ed.). *Wonders of the Yellowstone*. NY. Scribner, Armstrong. 1875. illus. fldg map. . . . . *$50.00–$80.00*

Richardson, Sir John. *Arctic Searching Expedition for Sir John Franklin*. NY. 1852. . . . . *$60.00–$80.00*

Rickett, H. *Wildflowers of the U.S.: The Southeastern States*. 1966. 2 vols. slipcase. . . . . *$85.00–$120.00*

Riddle, Kenyon. *Records and Maps of the Old Santa Fe Trail*. Fla. priv. pub. 1963. illus. fldg maps in rear pocket, rev. . . . . *$60.00–$75.00*

Riefel, Carlos von. *Folio of Fruit*. Lon. The Ariel Press. 1957. illus. folio dj. . . . . *$50.00–$75.00*

Riggs, Lynn. *Big Lake. A Tragedy in Two Parts*. NY. 1927. 1st ed. dj. . . . . *$45.00–$60.00*

Riggs, Lynn. *Russet Mantle and the Cherokee Night*. NY. 1936. 1st ed. dj. . . . . *$45.00–$125.00*

Riggs, Stephen R. *Dakota Grammar, Texts and Ethnography.* DC. GPO. 1893. . . .
. . . . *$60.00–$95.00*

Rights, Douglas LeTell. *American Indian In North Carolina.* NC. 1947. 1st ed. . . .
. . . . *$50.00–$65.00*

Riis, Jacob A. *How the Other Half Lives. .the Tenements of New York.* NY. 1891. 1st
ed. blue cl, illus. . . . . *$125.00–$175.00*

Riker, James. *Revised History of Harlem.* NY. 1904. fldg map. . . . *$60.00–$95.00*

Riley, James Whitcomb. *Old Swimmin' Hole and 'leven More Poems....* Ind. 1891.
1st ed. 3rd state. . . . . *$50.00–$75.00*

Riley, James Whitcomb. *The Complete Works of James Whitcomb Riley.* Harper.
1916. 10 vols. illus. *$165.00–*

Rinehart, Mary Roberts. *Tenting Tonight.* Bos/NY. 1918. illus. . . *$45.00–$60.00*

Rinehart, Mary Roberts. *The Circular Staircase.* Ind. Bobbs-Merrill. 1908. author's
first mystery. . . . . *$100.00–$175.00*

Rinehart, Mary Roberts. *When a Man Marries.* Tor. 1909. illus. 1st Canadian ed. .
. . . . *$50.00–$65.00*

Rinhart, Floyd and Marion. *American Miniature Case Art.* South Brunswick.
(1969). illus. plates, dj. . . . . *$80.00–$150.00*

Ripley, Eliza McHatton. *From Flag to Flag.* NY. Appleton. 1880. brown pict cl. . .
. . . . *$65.00–$125.00*

Ripley, Henry J. *Sacred Rhetoric.* Bos. Gould, Kendall & Lincoln. 1849. 1st ed. . .
. . . . *$25.00–$35.00*

Ripley, Mary. *Oriental Rug Book.* Stokes. (1904). clr illus.. . . . . . . *$30.00–$45.00*

Ritchie, Leitch. *Ireland Picturesque and Romantic.* Lon. 1837. 1st ed. illus. engr,
aeg. . . . . *$85.00–$125.00*

Rivera, Diego. *Frescoes.* NY. (1929). *$65.00–$135.00*

Rivers, George R. R. *Captain Shays, a Populist of 1786.* Bos. Little, Brown. 1897.
1st ed. . . . . *$65.00–$125.00*

Robbins, R. A. *91st Infantry Division in WW II.* DC. 1947. 1st ed. illus. maps,
photos.. . . . . *$50.00–$60.00*

Roberts, Charles G D. *History of Canada.* Bos. Lamson, Wolfe. 1897. 1st ed. illus.
fldg map.. . . . . *$15.00–$40.00*

Roberts, John. *Modern Medicine and Homeopathy.* Phila. Edwards & Docker. 1895.
1st ed. 69 pp.. . . . . *$90.00–$125.00*

Roberts, John Jr. and others. *Modern Billiards*. Lon. Pearson. 1902. 1st ed. illus. diagrams.. . . . . *$50.00–$85.00*

Roberts, Kenneth. *Arundel*. ME. Kennebunk. 1985. Centennial ed. . *$50.00–$75.00*

Roberts, Kenneth. *Black Magic*. Ind. Bobbs-Merrill. [1924]. 1st ed. author's fifth book, scarce. . . . . *$45.00–$100.00*

Roberts, Kenneth. *Concentrated New England*. Indianapolis. Bobbs-Merrill. [1924]. 1st ed. scarce. . . . . *$260.00–$300.00*

Roberts, Kenneth. *Europe's Morning After*. NY. Harper and Bros. [1921]. 1st ed. author's first book.. . . . . *$100.00–$300.00*

Roberts, Kenneth. *It Must Be Your Tonsils*. NY. 1936. sgn.. . . . . . *$55.00–$100.00*

Roberts, Kenneth. *Lively Lady*. Garden City. Doubleday, Doran. [1931]. 1st ed. . . . . *$30.00–$45.00*

Roberts, Kenneth. *Lydia Bailey*. Garden City. 1947. 1st ed. dj. . . . . *$55.00–$85.00*

Roberts, Kenneth. *Moreau de St. Mary's American Journey*. NY. Doubleday. [1947]. dj, blue cl.. . . . . *$15.00–$22.00*

Roberts, Kenneth. *Northwest Passage*. NY. 1937. 1st ed. wrps. inscr dj.. . . . . *$150.00–$250.00*

Roberts, Kenneth. *Rabble in Arms*. NY. Doubleday, Doran. 1956. dj.. . . . . *$10.00–$20.00*

Roberts, Kenneth. *Trending into Maine*. Bos. 1938. 1st ed. illus. by N. C. Wyeth. dj. . . . . *$150.00–$225.00*

Roberts, Kenneth L. *Why Europe Leaves Home*. Bobbs-Merrill. [1922]. 1st ed. author's second book. no dj. . . . . *$250.00–$325.00*

Roberts, Morley. *Private Life of Henry Maitland: A Record Dictated by J. H.* Lon. Eveleigh Nash. 1912. 1st ed. . . . . *$80.00–$125.00*

Roberts, Thomas S. *Birds of Minnesota*. Minneapolis. 1932. 2 vols. 1st ed. clr plates. . . . . *$100.00–$125.00*

Robeson, Eslanda Goode (Mrs. Paul Robeson). *African Journey*. NY. 1945. 1st ed. dj.. . . . . *$45.00–$65.00*

Robeson, Kenneth. *Quest of the Spider: A Doc Savage Novel*. NY. 1935.. . . . . *$95.00–$130.00*

Robeson, Paul. *Here I Stand*. Lon. Dennis Dobson. 1958. 2nd Brit ed. dj.. . . . . *$35.00–$50.00*

Robie, Virginia. *Historic Styles in Furniture.* Chi. 1905. 1st ed. illus. *$35.00–$40.00*

Robinson, Bert. *Basket Weavers of Arizona.* Albuquerque. 1954. dj. . *$50.00–$75.00*

Robinson, Charles. *Kansas Conflict.* NY. 1892. 1st ed. . . . . *$95.00–$150.00*

Robinson, E. *Map of Bergen County, New Jersey, with a Portion of Passaic County.* NY. 1902. large case map. . . . . *$750.00–$800.00*

Robinson, E. et al. *Palestine.* Bos. Crocker & Brewster. 1856. . . . *$55.00–$100.00*

Robinson, Edward Arlington. *Cavender's House.* 1929. 1st ed. dj. . *$20.00–$30.00*

Robinson, G. *Travels in Palestine and Syria.* Paris. 1837. 2 vols. illus. half calf, maps, plates. . . . . *$150.00–$200.00*

Robinson, Leigh. *South Before and at the Battle of the Wilderness.* Richmond. 1878. wrps. . . . . *$100.00–$250.00*

Robinson, Mabel L. *Runner of the Mountain Tops: the Life of Louis Agassiz.* NY. Random House. (1939). 1st ed. illus. by Lynd Ward. *$35.00*

Robinson, Rowland E. *Sam Lovel's Camps and Other Stories.* Rutland. Tuttle. (1934). Centennial Ed.. . . . . *$30.00–$50.00*

Robinson, Rowland E. *Sam Lovel's Camps.* NY. 1893. . . . . *$20.00–$35.00*

Robinson, Rowland E. *Uncle Lisha's Outing.* Bos/NY. 1897. 1st ed. . . . .
. . . . *$25.00–$35.00*

Robinson, S. *Kansas: Interior & Exterior Life.* Bos. 1856. . . . . . . *$35.00–$45.00*

Robinson, Samuel. *Course of Fifteen Lectures on Medical Botany.* Columbus. Pike, Platt & Co. 1832. . . . . *$125.00–$165.00*

Robinson, Selma. *City Child.* NY. Farrar & Rinehart. 1931. 1st trade ed. illus. by Rockwell Kent, bown cl, dj.. . . . . *$50.00–$100.00*

Robinson, Will. *Story of Arizona.* Phoenix. 1919. . . . . *$30.00–$65.00*

Robison, Capt S. S. *Robison's Manual of Radio Telegraphy And Telephony 1919.* 1919. illus. 5th ed.. . . . . *$30.00–$40.00*

Rockne, Knute. *Coaching.* NY. 1931. *$28.00–$35.00*

Rockwell, A. H. *Improved Practical System of Educating the Horse.* NY. 1971. illus.
. . . . *$25.00–$35.00*

Rockwell, Carey. *Danger in Deep Space.* NY. Grosset & Dunlap. (1954). dj. . . . . .
. . . . *$20.00–$30.00*

Rockwell, Carey. *Robot Racket.* NY. Grosset & Dunlap. (1956). dj. . *$14.00–$10.00*

Rockwell, Carey. *Stand By for Mars.* NY. Grosset & Dunlap. (1953). Tom Corbett, Space Cadet, dj.. *$25.00–$30.00*

Rockwell, Carey. *Treachery in Outer Space.* NY. Grosset & Dunlap. 1952. Tom Corbett #6, dj... *$25.00–$35.00*

Rockwell, George. *History of Ridgefield, Connecticut.* private printing. 1927. illus. blue cl, gold lettering. .... *$40.00–$55.00*

Rockwell, Norman. *My Adventures as an Illustrator.* NY. 1960. 1st ed. slipcase, dj. .... *$40.00–$45.00*

Rockwood, Ray. *The Speedwell Boys on Motorcycles.* Cupples & Lean. 1913. . . . . *$30.00–$45.00*

Rockwood, Roy. *Through the Air to the North Pole..* NY. 1906. 1st ed. illus. . . . . *$32.00–$45.00*

Rocky Mountain Country Club. 1905. .... *$45.00–$60.00*

Rodgers, Otis and Pat Mulkern, eds. *Hobo From Texas.* np. 1950. 1st ed. thus, illus, pict wrps.. *$50.00–$80.00*

Roe, F. G. *North American Buffalo.* Lon. David & Charles. 1972. 2nd ed, dj. . . . . *$35.00–$70.00*

Roeder, Bill. *Jackie Robinson.* A. S. Barnes & Co. (1950). dj...... *$35.00–$80.00*

Roehl, Louis M. *Harness Repairing.* Milw. Bruce. 1921. 1st ed. illus. *$40.00–$65.00*

Roemer, Ferdinand. *Texas With Particular Reference to German Immigration.* San Antonio. 1935. 1st ed. wrps. .... *$100.00–$150.00*

Roeser, C. *State of Wisconsin.* DC. 1878. wall map. .... *$400.00–$450.00*

Rogers, Alice Lang. *Poodles in Particular.* NY. 1951. illus. ...... *$14.00–$18.00*

Rogers, Dale Evans. *Angel Unaware.* Revell. 1953. dj........... *$15.00–$22.00*

Rogers, J. E. *Shell Book.* NY. 1908. illus. .... *$25.00–$50.00*

Rogers, Mrs. Byron. *Cairn and Sealyham Terriers.* NY. McBride. 1922. illus. . . . . *$45.00–$65.00*

Rogers, Samuel. *Recollections of the Table-Talk of Samuel Rogers.* Lon. Moxon. 1856. calf and marbled bds............................... *$100.00–$150.00*

Rohmer, Sax. *Bat Flies Low.* NY. 1935. 1st ed. .... *$35.00–$50.00*

Rohmer, Sax. *Green Eyes of Bast.* NY. 1920. 1st ed. .... *$45.00–$75.00*

Rohmer, Sax. *Grey Face.* NY. Doubleday. 1924. 1st ed. .... *$15.00–$25.00*

Rohmer, Sax. *Hand of Fu Manchu.* McBride. 1917. 1st ed. . . . . . . *$40.00–$75.00*

Rohmer, Sax. *Island of Fu Manchu.* Garden City. 1941. 1st ed. Crime Club, dj. . . .
. . . . *$100.00–$450.00*

Rohmer, Sax. *Moon of Madness.* Garden City. 1927. 1st ed. . . . . *$40.00–$100.00*

Rohmer, Sax. *Return of Dr. Fu Manchu.* NY. Grosset & Dunlap. dj. *$55.00–$75.00*

Rohmer, Sax. *Tales of Chinatown.* NY. Doubleday. 1922. 1st ed. . . *$20.00–$35.00*

Rohmer, Sax. *White Velvet.* Garden City. 1937. dj. . . . . *$25.00–$35.00*

Rollicking Rhymes for Youngsters. Fleming Revell Co. 1902. 1st ed. illus. . . . .
. . . . *$27.00–$55.00*

Rollinson, John K. *Pony Trails in Wyoming..* Caldwell. Caxton Printers. 1941. inscr
by author dj scarce. . . . . *$65.00–$95.00*

Rolvaag, O. E. *Giants in the Earth.* Harper. 1927. dj. . . . . *$65.00–$95.00*

Romance of the Oriental Rug. Tor. Babylon's Ltd. (1925). 1st ed. clr plates. . . . . . .
. . . . *$35.00–$45.00*

Romantic Salt Lake City. Salt Lake. 1927. 1st ed. illus. printed wrps, photos. . . . . .
. . . . *$25.00–$35.00*

Ronalds, Alfred. *Fly-Fisher's Entomology.* Lon. 1883. illus. 9th ed. plates. . . . .
. . . . *$125.00–$180.00*

Roop, Guy. *Villas & Palaces of Andrea Palladio, 1508-1580.* Milano. Arti Grafiche
Francesco Ghezzi. 1968. illus. 1st ed in Eng, slipcase. . . . . *$70.00–$100.00*

Roop, Guy. *Villas and Palaces of Andrea Palladio.* Milano. Arti Grafiche Francesco
Ghezzi. 1968. 1st UK ed. illus. slipcase. *$70.00–$100.00*

Roosevelt, Eleanor. *This Troubled World.* NY. Kinsey. 1938. 1st ed. 47 pp, dj. . . . .
. . . . *$65.00–$75.00*

Roosevelt, Eleanor [Anna]. *It's Up to Women.* NY. Stokes. 1933. . *$20.00–$30.00*

Roosevelt, Franklin D. *Happy Warrior, Alfred E. Smith.* Bos. 1928. 1st ed. . . . . . .
. . . . *$35.00–$50.00*

Roosevelt, Theodore. *African Game Trails.* NY. 1910. 1st ed. illus. . . . .
. . . . *$95.00–$150.00*

Roosevelt, Theodore. *Naval War of 1812.* NY. Haskell House. 1968. reprnt. . . . . . .
. . . . *$30.00–$35.00*

Roosevelt, Theodore. *Outdoor Pastimes of American Hunter.* NY. 1905. 1st ed. illus.
. . . . *$125.00–$400.00*

Roosevelt, Theodore. *Through the Brazilian Wilderness.* NY. 1914. 1st ed. . . . . .
. . . . *$67.00–$75.00*

Roosevelt, Theodore. *Wilderness Hunter.* NY. Putnam. 1893. illus. with b/w plates
by Frost, Beard, Sandham, Eaton and Remington. . . . . *$50.00–$125.00*

Roosevelt, Theodore. *Winning of the West.* NY. 1900. 4 vols. . . . *$70.00–$225.00*

Roosevelt, Theodore & Kermit. *East of the Sun and West of the Moon.* NY.
Scribner's. 1927. 1st ed. photos, maps. . . . . *$60.00–$90.00*

Roosevelt, Theodore & Kermit. *Trailing the Giant Panda.* NY. Scribner's. 1929. 1st
ed. photos, fldg map. . . . . *$50.00–$75.00*

Root, Edward W and Phillip Hooker. *Contribution to the Study of the
Rennaissance in America.* NY. Scribner's. 1929. 1st ed. 242 pp, ltd 750 cc. . . . . . .
. . . . *$175.00–$225.00*

Root, S. *Primary Bible Questions for Young Children.* Atlanta. 1864. 3rd ed. . . . . . .
. . . . *$125.00–$150.00*

Rosch, John. *Historic White Plains.* White Plains. Baletto-Sweetman. 1939. ltd
1000, fldg map. . . . . *$25.00–$40.00*

Roseman, Mill. *Strathmore Century:The 100th Anniversary Issues of the
Strathmorean.* Westfield, MA. Strathmore Paper. 1992. illus. photos, facsimile. . . .
. . . . *$60.00–$90.00*

Rosendahl, Commander C. E. *What About the Airship.* NY. 1938. 1st ed. dj. . . . .
. . . . *$65.00–$80.00*

Rosengarten, A. *Romantic Revolutionary: Biography of John Reed.* NY. Knopf.
1975. 1st ed. illus. photos, dj. . . . . *$35.00–$45.00*

Ross, Alexander. *Adventures of First Settlers on the Oregon or Columbia River.*
Lakeside Press. 1928. . . . . *$40.00–$45.00*

Ross, Alexander. *Birds of Canada.* Tor. 1872. 2nd ed. brown cl. . . . *$30.00–$60.00*

Ross, John. *Narrative of a Second Voyage in Search of a North west Passage.* Lon.
A W Webster. 1835. 2 vols. 1st ed. illus. cl views and charts litho, 9 hand-clred. . .
. . . . *$450.00–$650.00*

Rosser, Mrs. Thomas. *Housekeepers' and Mothers' Manual.* VA. Everett Waddey
Co. 1895. 1st ed. dark green gilt-lettered cvr. . . . . *$40.00–$60.00*

Rossetti, Christina. *A Pageant.* Lon. Macmillan. 1881. 1st ed. 198 pp. . . . .
. . . . *$225.00–$300.00*

Rossi, Mario M. *Pilgrimage in the West.* Dublin. Cuala Press. 1932. 300 cc. . . . . .
. . . . *$85.00–$175.00*

Roth, Cecil (ed.). *Haggadah.* Bos. Little, Brown. 1965. illus. by Ben Shahn.......
.... *$90.00–$100.00*

Roth, Philip. *American Pastoral.* Bos/NY. Houghton Mifflin. 1997. 1st ed. dj. ....
.... *$35.00–$40.00*

Roth, Philip. *Great American Novel.* NY. 1973. 1st ed. dj. .... *$25.00–$55.00*

Roth, Philip. *Operation Shylock.* Simon & Schuster. 1993. 1st ed. dj. ....
.... *$15.00–$25.00*

Roth, Philip. *Our Gang.* NY. Random House. 1971. 1st ed. dj..... *$20.00–$35.00*

Roth, Philip. *Professor of Desire.* NY. 1977. 1st ed. dj........... *$20.00–$35.00*

Roth, Philip. *When She Was Good.* Random House. 1967. 1st ed. dj............
.... *$35.00–$50.00*

Rothstein, T. *From Chartism to Labourism.* International Pub. (1929). black cl. ....
.... *$25.00–$40.00*

Rowe, Samuel. *Perambulation of the Ancient and Royal Forest of Dartmoor.*
Lon/Exeter. 1896. 3rd ed. illus. .... *$50.00–$75.00*

Rowse, A. L. *Homosexuals in History.* Dorset. 1977. 1st Eng ed. dj. . *$40.00–$55.00*

Roy, Arundhati. *God of Small Things.* NY. Random House. (1997). 1st Amer ed...
.... *$35.00–$60.00*

Royce, Sarah. *Frontier Lady: Recollections of the Gold Rush and Early California.*
New Haven. Yale Univ Press. 1932. 1st ed. dj................. *$50.00–$70.00*

Royko, Mike. *I May Be Wrong, But I Doubt It.* Chi. 1968. 1st ed. ....
.... *$24.00–$37.00*

Ruark, Robert. *Honey Badger.* NY. McGraw Hill. 1965. 1st ed. dj. *$12.00–$25.00*

Ruark, Robert. *Old Man's Boy Grows Older.* NY. Holt, Rinehart & Winston. 1961.
1st ed. dj... *$75.00–$195.00*

Ruark, Robert. *Something of Value.* Garden City. 1955. 1st ed. dj.. *$30.00–$45.00*

Ruark, Robert. *Use Enough Gun.* NY. New American Lib. (1966). 1st ed. ....
.... *$45.00–$60.00*

Ruark, Robert. *Women.* NY. 1967. dj. .... *$50.00–$60.00*

Ruark, Robert C. *Horn of the Hunter.* NY. Doubleday. 1953. 1st ed. illus. dj. ....
.... *$70.00–$165.00*

Ruark, Robert C. *The Old Man & the Boy.* NY. 1957. 1st ed. illus. ....
.... *$45.00–$100.00*

Rubaiyat of Omar Khayyam. NY. Doran. nd. illus. by Edmund Dulac. . . . .
. . . . *$45.00–$65.00*

Rubin, Jerry. *We Are Everywhere.* 1971. 1st ed. dj. . . . . *$20.00–$25.00*

Ruess, Everett. *On the Desert Trails with Everett Ruess.* CA. Desert Magazine.
1940. illus. . . . . *$200.00–$250.00*

Rugg, H. W. *History of Freemasonry in Rhode Island.* Prov. 1895. *$30.00–$45.00*

Rukeyser, Muriel. *Green Wave.* NY. Doubleday. 1948. 1st ed. dj.. . *$25.00–$60.00*

Rukeyser, Muriel. *Life of Poetry.* Current Books. 1949. 1st ed. dj. *$75.00–$125.00*

Rukeyser, Muriel. *Selected Poems.* New Directions. 1951. 1st ed. dj. . . . .
. . . . *$25.00–$40.00*

Rules and Regulations for the Field Exercise and Maneuvres of Infantry. NH.
U. S. War Dept. 1817. lea backed bds. . . . . *$75.00–$100.00*

Rundell, Maria. *A New System of Domestic Cookery.* Bos. 1807. . . . .
. . . . *$150.00–$200.00*

Rush, Benjamin. *An Account of the Bilious Remiting Yellow Fever..* Phila. Thomas
Dobson. 1794. 2nd ed. lea, rbckd. . . . . *$150.00–$275.00*

Rush, Benjamin. *Letters of the American Philosophical Society.* Princeton/Phila.
1951. 2 vols. 1st ed. dj. red cl. . . . . *$45.00–$50.00*

Rush, Benjamin. *Medical Inquiries and Observations.* AL. 1979. rprnt. . . . .
. . . . *$50.00–$65.00*

Rushdie, Salman. *Jaguar Smile.* NY. Viking Press. (1987). 1st ed. dj. . . . .
. . . . *$15.00–$35.00*

Rushdie, Salman. *Midnight's Children.* NY. Knopf. 1981. 1st US ed pink dj. . . . .
. . . . *$300.00–$500.00*

Rushdie, Salman. *Moor's Last Sigh.* NY. Pantheon. 1996. 1st US ed. dj, sgn. . . . .
. . . . *$40.00–$65.00*

Rushdie, Salman. *Satanic Verses.* NY. 1989. 1st Amer ed. dj.. . . . . *$30.00–$45.00*

Rushdie, Salman. *Shame.* NY. Knopf. 1983. 1st US ed. dj.. . . . . . . *$25.00–$35.00*

Ruskin, John. *King of the Golden River.* Lon. (1932). 1st ed. wrps. illus. by Arthur
Rackham. dj. . . . . *$150.00–$175.00*

Ruskin, John. *Letters and Advice to Young Girls and Young Ladies.* NY. 1879. . .
. . . . *$35.00–$45.00*

Russell, A. *Grizzly Country.* NY. Knopf. 1967. 2 vols. 1st ed. illus. dj. *$10.00–$20.00*

Russell, Bertrand. *A B C of Atoms*. NY. Dutton. 1923. . . . . *$25.00–$45.00*

Russell, Bertrand. *ABC of Relativity*. NY/Lon. 1925. 1st ed. . . . . *$75.00–$100.00*

Russell, Bertrand. *Analysis of Matter*. NY. Harcourt, Brace. 1927. 1st Amer ed cl. . . . . *$75.00–$125.00*

Russell, Bertrand. *Scientific Outlook*. NY. W. W Norton. 1931. 1st ed. . . . . *$35.00–$45.00*

Russell, Charles M. *Good Medicine*. Garden City. 1930. illus. . . . . *$50.00–$75.00*

Russell, George. *Tour Through Sicily in the Year 1815*. Lon. 1819. plates, clr fldg map. . . . . *$75.00–$100.00*

Russell, Keith. *Duck-Huntingest Gentlemen: Coll. of Waterfowling Stories*. 1977. ltd, slipcase, sgn. . . . . *$85.00–$125.00*

Russell, Prof. William. *Scientific Horse Shoeing*. 1901. illus. 6th ed.. . . . . *$30.00–$45.00*

Russell, William Howard. *My Diary North And South*. NY. 1954. rprnt, dj. . . . . *$18.00–$25.00*

Rutherford, Livingston. *John Peter Zenger: His Press, His Trial...Bibliography of Imprints*. NY. 1904. 1st ed. illus. ltd 325 cc. . . . . *$150.00–$250.00*

Rutledge, Archibald. *An American Hunter*. NY. 1937. illus. by Lynne Bogue Hunt, 2nd prtg. . . . . *$18.00–$45.00*

Rutledge, Archibald. *Brimming Chalice*. NY. 1936. 1st ed. sgn, dj. . . . . *$95.00–$150.00*

Rutledge, Archibald. *Etiquette Among the Beasts*. np. 1981. . . . . . *$18.00–$22.00*

Rutledge, Archibald. *Hunter's Choice*. NY. Barnes. 1946. 1st ed. dj. . . . . *$65.00–$130.00*

Rutledge, Archibald H. *Home by the River*. Ind. 1941. plates, sgn, dj. . . . . *$75.00–$100.00*

Rutter, Owen. *The Monster of Mu*. Lon. 1932. 1st ed. . . . . *$90.00–$110.00*

Ryder, Tom. *On the Box Seat*. Macclesfield. 1972. 2nd ed. dj. . . . . *$45.00–$60.00*

Rye, E. C. *British Beetles*. Lon. Lovell Reeve. 1866. 1st ed. illus. 1st separate ed. 113 pp. . . . . *$40.00–$55.00*

Rynhart, Susie Carson. *With the Tibetans in Tent and Temple*. Revell. 1901. illus. decorative cvrs. . . . . *$45.00–$65.00*

Sabatini, Rafael. *Strolling Saint...Tyrant.* Bos. Houghton Miflin Co. 1925. . . . . . .
. . . . *$10.00–$25.00*

Sabin, Edwin L. *Building the Pacific Railway.* Phila. Lippincott. 1919. . . . .
. . . . *$25.00–$37.00*

Sabin, Joseph. *Dictionary of Books Relating to America.* NY. (1967). 2 vols.
mini-print ed.. . . . . *$270.00–$350.00*

Sabin, Joseph. *Dictionary of Books Relating to America..* Amsterdam. 1961. 15
vols. rprnt. . . . . *$950.00–$1,250.00*

Sachs, B. & L. Hausman. *Nervous & Mental Disorders from Birth Through
Adolescence.* NY. 1926. 1st ed. illus. . . . . *$50.00–$85.00*

Sackville-West, Vita. *Daughter of France.* NY. Doubleday. 1959. 1st US ed. 336 pp,
dj. . . . . *$45.00–$75.00*

Sackville-West, Vita. *Devil at Westease.* NY. 1947. 1st ed. dj.. . . . . *$20.00–$25.00*

Sadler, William S. *Race Decadence.* Chi. 1922. 1st ed. dj. . . . . *$27.00–$35.00*

Sagan, Carl. *Broca's Brain.* NY. (1979). 1st ed. dj.. . . . . *$25.00–$35.00*

Salaman, Malcolm C. *British Book Illustration.* Lon. The Studio. 1923. 1st ed. illus.
. . . . *$80.00–$110.00*

Sale, Edith Tunis (ed.). *Historic Gardens of Virginia.* Richmond. William Byrd
Press. illus. ltd 1000cc. . . . . *$75.00–$95.00*

Salinger, J. D. *Catcher in the Rye.* Bos. 1951. 1st ed. dj, blue cl.. . . . .
. . . . *$5,000.00–$15,000.00*

Salinger, J. D. *Complete Uncollected Short Stories.* vols I and II. wrps, scarce.. . . .
. . . . *$250.00–$475.00*

Salinger, J. D. *Franny and Zooey.* Bos. 1961. 1st ed. dj. . . . . *$65.00–$300.00*

Salinger, J. D. *Kitbook for Soldiers, Sailors & Marines.* 1943. 1st ed. . . . .
. . . . *$60.00–$150.00*

Salinger, J. D. *Nine Stories.* Bos. (1953). 1st ed. dj.. . . . . *$1,250.00–$7,000.00*

Salk & Salk. *World Population and Human Values.* NY. 1981. sgn, dj. . . . .
. . . . *$55.00–$70.00*

Sallis, James. *The Guitar Players.* NY. Morrow. 1982. 1st ed. dj. . *$130.00–$175.00*

Salten, Felix. *Bambi's Children.* Ind. Bobbs-Merill. (1939). 1st ed. scarce dj. . . . .
. . . . *$38.00–$50.00*

Salten, Felix. *Bambi, A Life in the Woods.* Simon & Schuster. 1928. ltd 1000 cc.. . .
. . . . *$50.00–$60.00*

Salten, Felix. *Bambi.* Simon & Schuster. 1928. 1st ed. . . . . *$40.00–$50.00*

Sampson, Ezra. *Youth's Companion.* Hudson. Nathan Elliott. 1816. 3rd ed. lea. . . .
. . . . *$12.00–$25.00*

Samuels, Edward. *Ornithology and Oology of New England...with illustrations of many Species of Birds.* Bos. Nichols & Noyes. 1867. illus. plates, 583 pp. . . . .
. . . . *$75.00–$95.00*

Sanborn, F. B. (ed.). *Life and Letters of John Brown, Liberator of Kansas....* Bos. 1891. 1st ed. . . . . *$45.00–$55.00*

Sanborn, Helen. *Winter in Central America and Mexico.* Bos. 1887. 1st ed. . . . . . .
. . . . *$32.00–$45.00*

Sandberg, Carl. *Breathing Tokens.* NY. Harcourt, Brace & World. 1978. 1st ed. dj. .
. . . . *$12.00–$20.00*

Sandburg, Carl. *Abraham Lincoln: The Prairie Years.* NY. Harcourt, Brace. 1926. 2 vols. 1st trade, sgn. . . . . *$75.00–$100.00*

Sandburg, Carl. *Always the Young Strangers.* NY. 1953. 1st ed. sgn, dj. . . . .
. . . . *$30.00–$50.00*

Sandburg, Carl. *American Songbag.* NY. 1927. . . . . *$25.00–$75.00*

Sandburg, Carl. *Chicago Poems.* Henry Holt. 1916. dj. . . . . *$20.00–$25.00*

Sandburg, Carl. *Early Moon.* NY. Harcourt Brace. (1930). 1st ed. no dj. . . . .
. . . . *$20.00–$50.00*

Sandburg, Carl. *Good Morning America.* NY. Harcourt Brace. 1928. 1st Trade ed. sgn, dj. . . . . *$85.00–$100.00*

Sandburg, Carl. *Good Morning America.* Harcourt. 1928. 1st ed. dj. . . . .
. . . . *$20.00–$45.00*

Sandburg, Carl. *Potato Face.* NY. Harcourt, Brace. 1930. 1st ed. dj. . . . .
. . . . *$50.00–$80.00*

Sandburg, Carl. *Potato Face.* NY. Harcourt, Brace. 1930. 1st ed. dj. *$50.00–$75.00*

Sandburg, Carl. *Remembrance Rock.* NY. 1948. 1st ed. dj. . . . . . . *$20.00–$30.00*

Sandburg, Carl. *Rootabaga Pigeons.* NY. 1923. 1st ed. illus. . . . *$75.00–$110.00*

Sanders, Lawrence. *Anderson Tapes.* NY. Putnam. 1970. 1st ed. author's first book, dj. . . . . *$45.00–$60.00*

Sanderson, G P. *Thirteen Years Amoung the Wild Beasts of India.* Lon. 1893. . . . .
. . . . *$18.00–$25.00*

Sandoz, Mari. *Horse Catcher.* 1957. sgn, dj. . . . . *$25.00–$30.00*

Sandoz, Mari. *Old Jules.* 1935. . . . . *$10.00–$35.00*

Sandoz, Mari. *Son of the Gamblin' Man.* NY. Clarkson and Potter. [1960]. 1st ed. sgn, dj.. . . . . *$100.00–$150.00*

Sandoz, Mari. *The Cattlemen.* NY. 1958. dj.. . . . . *$10.00–$20.00*

Sandoz, Maurice. *Fantastic Memories.* Garden City. Doubleday. 1944. 1st ed. illus. dj. . . . . *$85.00–$125.00*

Sandoz, Maurice. *The Maze.* NY. 1945. 1st ed. illus. by Salvador Dali.. . . . .
. . . . *$40.00–$75.00*

Sanger, Margaret. *An Autobiography.* NY. (1938). 1st ed. 504 pp, dj. . . . .
. . . . *$25.00–$125.00*

Sanger, Margaret. *My Fight For Birth Control.* NY. (1931). 1st ed. 360 pp. . . . . .
. . . . *$65.00–$75.00*

Sanger, Margaret. *Woman and the New Race.* NY. Brentano. 1920. . . . .
. . . . *$50.00–$80.00*

Sanger, William W. *History of Prostitution.* NY. Eugenics Pub. 1939. . . . .
. . . . *$15.00–$30.00*

Sangree, Allen. *Jinx: Stories of the Diamond.* NY. 1911. illus. . . . . *$60.00–$90.00*

Sanial, Lucien. *General Bankruptcy or Socialism?.* NY. Co-operative Press. wrps.
. . . . *$35.00–$50.00*

Sansom, Joseph. *Travels in Lower Canada..* Lon. 1820. 1/4 calf. . *$85.00–$125.00*

Santayana, George. *Sonnets and Other Verses.* Camb. 1894. 1st ed. ltd 450cc. . . .
. . . . *$150.00–$225.00*

Santee, Ross. *Bubbling Spring.* NY. Scribner's (1949). 1st ed. dj. . . *$20.00–$45.00*

Sanz, Carlos. *Bibliografia General de la Carta de Colon.* Madrid. Libreria General. 1958. 1st ed. wrps. 305 pp. . . . . *$125.00–$150.00*

Sarg, Tony. *Tony Sarg's Book of Animals.* Greenberg Pub. 1925. 1st ed. . . . .
. . . . *$30.00–$40.00*

Sarg, Tony. *Tony Sarg's Surprise Book.* np. (1941). pict bds.. . . . . . *$25.00–$50.00*

Sargent, Lyman Towers. *British and American Utopian Literature 1516-1975.* Bos. Hall. (1979). 1st ed. . . . . *$45.00–$80.00*

Saroyan, William. *Daring Young Man on the Flying Trapeze.* NY. Random House. 1934. 1st ed. dj.. . . . . *$300.00–$400.00*

Saroyan, William. *Fiscal Hoboes.* NY. Valenti Angelo. 1949. 1st ed. wrps. ltd 250 cc. sgn. . . . . *$80.00–$100.00*

Saroyan, William. *Human Comedy.* NY. Harcourt, Brace. (1943). 1st ed. illus. author's first novel. dj. . . . . *$35.00–$100.00*

Saroyan, William. *Laughing Matter.* Doubleday. 1953. 1st ed. dj.. . *$30.00–$55.00*

Saroyan, William. *My Heart's in the Highlands.* NY. (1939). dj. . *$75.00–$100.00*

Saroyan, William. *Native American.* SF. George Fields. 1938. 1st ed. illus. ltd 450 cc. sgn. . . . . *$80.00–$115.00*

Saroyan, William. *Rock Wagram.* NY. 1951. 1st ed. dj.. . . . . *$25.00–$100.00*

Saroyan, William. *Saroyan's Fables.* NY. Harcourt, Brace. 1941. 1st ed. illus. ltd 1,000 cc. sgn, slipcase. . . . . *$40.00–$70.00*

Sarton, George. *History of Science.* MA. Harvard Univ Press. 1952. . . . . *$25.00–$45.00*

Sarton, May. *A Reckoning.* NY. W. W. Norton. 1978. 1st ed. dj. . . . *$15.00–$25.00*

Sarton, May. *Anger.* NY. 1982. sgn, dj.. . . . . *$30.00–$50.00*

Sarton, May. *Education of Harriet Hatfield.* NY. W. W. Norton. [1955]. 1st ed. dj. . . . . *$20.00–$30.00*

Sarton, May. *Kinds of Love.* NY. W. W. Norton 1970. 1st ed. dj. . . *$20.00–$30.00*

Sarton, May. *Miss Pickthorn and Mr. Hare.* NY. 1st ed. sgn, dj. . . . *$50.00–$65.00*

Sarton, May. *Plant Dreaming Deep.* NY. W. W. Norton (1968). 1st ed. y. . . . . *$12.00–$25.00*

Sarton, May. *Poet and the Donkey.* NY. 1969. 1st ed. dj. . . . . *$25.00–$30.00*

Sarton, May. *Recovering: A Journal.* NY/Lon. W. W. Norton. (1980). *$20.00–$30.00*

Sarton, May. *Shadow of a Man.* NY. Rinehart. (1950). 1st ed. no dj.*$40.00–$50.00*

Sarton, May. *Shower of Summer Days.* NY. Rinehart. [1952]. 1st ed. 244 pp, dj, scarce. . . . . *$50.00–$75.00*

Sartre, Jean-Paul. *Devil & The Good Lord.* Knopf. 1960. 1st US ed. dj. . . . . *$27.00–$35.00*

Sartre, Jean-Paul. *Existentialism.* Philosophical Library. 1947. 1st US ed. dj. . . . . *$45.00–$55.00*

Sartre, Jean-Paul. *Nausea.* CT. 1949. 1st US ed. dj.. . . . . *$30.00–$55.00*

Sartre, Jean-Paul. *Situations.* 1965. 1st ed. dj.. . . . . *$35.00–$60.00*

Sartre, Jean-Paul. *Theatre: Les Mouches, Huis-clos, Morts san sepulchre, La Putain Respectueuse.* Paris. Gallimard. c1947. 1st ed thus, ltd. . . . . *$75.00–$100.00*

Sartre, Jean-Paul. *Wall and Other Stories.* New Directions. 1948. ltd ed. slipcase. . . . . *$45.00–$75.00*

Sass, Herbert Ravenel. *Hear Me, My Chiefs.* NY. William Morrow. 1940. map frontis 2nd prntg. . . . . *$8.00–$25.00*

Satterlee, L. *American Gun Makers.* NY. 1940. 1st ed. . . . . *$35.00–$40.00*

Saundby, R. *Lectures on Bright's Disease.* Bristol/Lon. 1889. . . . . *$22.00–$25.00*

Saunders, Ann. *Narrative of the Shipwreck & Sufferings of. .* Prov. 1827. 1st ed. wrps. . . . . *$75.00–$85.00*

Saunders, Charles Francis. *Indians of the Terraced Houses.* NY. 1912. . . . . *$30.00–$45.00*

Saunders, Louise. *Knave of Hearts.* Racine, WI. 1925. illus. by Maxfield Parrish, folio, spiral bound. . . . . *$600.00–$750.00*

Saunders, Ruth. *Book of Artists' Own Bookplates.* Claremont. Saunders Studio Press. 1933. 1st ed. ltd 360 cc, sgn and numbered. . . . . *$50.00–$75.00*

Savitt, Sam. *Around the World with Horses.* NY. Dial. 1962. 1st ed. oblong, dj. . . . . *$30.00–$45.00*

Sawtelle, Mrs. M P. *Heroine of '49.* SF. 1891. . . . . *$35.00–$50.00*

Sawyer, Charles Winthrop. *Our Rifles.* The Cornhill Co. 1920. 1st ed. *$45.00–$65.00*

Sawyer, Ruth. *Tale of the Enchanted Bunnies.* NY. (1923). 1st ed. illus. dj, scarce. . . . . *$105.00–$175.00*

Sayer, Robert. *Course of the River Mississippi from the Balise to Fort Charles.. in the Latter End of the Year 1765 by Lieut. Ross of the 34th Regiment.* Lon. 1775. . . . . *$2,000.00–$2,250.00*

Sayers, Dorothy. *Gaudy Night.* NY. Harcourt, Brace. (1936). 1st Amer ed. dj. . . . . *$150.00–$450.00*

Sayers, Dorothy L. *Omnibus of Crime.* NY. Payson & Clarke. 1929. 1st ed. dj. . . . . *$150.00–$200.00*

Sayers, Dorothy L. *Strong Poison.* NY. Brewer & Warren. 1930. 1st Amer ed. . . . . *$40.00–$85.00*

Sayers, R S. *LLoyds Bank in the History of English Banking.* Oxford. Clarendon Press. 1957. cl. . . . . *$40.00–$60.00*

Sayler, Oliver M. *Russian Theatre.* NY. Brentano. 1922. . . . . *$50.00–$80.00*

Schaack, Michael. *Anarchy and Anarchists.* Chi. Schulte. 1889. 1st ed. fine. . . . . *$150.00–$225.00*

Schaeffler, Casper. *Memoirs and Reminiscences together with Sketches of the Early History of Sussex County, NJ.* . Hackensack, NJ. private printing. 1907. illus. ltd 250 cc, 187 pp. . . . . *$35.00–$50.00*

Schaldach, William J. *Coverts and Casts.* NY. 1943. 1st ed. illus. . *$35.00–$45.00*

Schaldach, William J. *Upland Gunning.* VT. 1946. illus. presentation copy, dj.. . . . . *$100.00–$175.00*

Schenck, David. *North Carolina 1780-81.* Raleigh. 1889. 1st ed. . *$75.00–$100.00*

Schley, W S. *Report of Greely Relief Exped. of 1884.* DC. 1887. 1st ed. . . . . *$85.00–$110.00*

Schmookler, Paul. *Salmon Flies of Major John P. Traherne.* 1993. ltd and only ed. 300 cc, photos, lea, French hand-dipped clr paper over bds, slipcase, aeg. . . . . *$350.00–$600.00*

Schoenberger, J. *From Great Lakes to Pacific.* 1934. 1st ed. . . . . . *$50.00–$65.00*

Schoolcraft, Henry R. *American Indians; Their History, Condition and Prospects.* . Rochester. 1851. illus. plates.. . . . . *$150.00–$250.00*

Schoolcraft, Henry R. *New York Historical Society.* NY. 1854. . . . *$30.00–$55.00*

Schoolcraft, Henry R. *View of the Mines of Missouri.* NY. Charles Wiley. 1819. 1st ed. copper engr frontis and pl.. . . . . *$800.00–$1,000.00*

Schooling, William. *Hudson's Bay Company, 1670-1920.* Lon. Hudson Bay Co. 1920. wrps. fldg map, 129 pp.. . . . . *$65.00–$85.00*

Schoonmaker, W. J. *World of the Grizzly Bear.* Phila/NY. 1968. illus. *$30.00–$40.00*

Schoonover, T. *Life of General J. Sutter.* 1895. 1st ed. . . . . *$60.00–$75.00*

Schoonover, T. J. *Life and Times of Gen. John Sutter.* Sacramento. 1907. . . . . *$25.00–$85.00*

Schreiner, Olive. *Story of an African Farm.* Westerham Press. 1961. illus. clr lith, drawings, ltd 1500 cc sgn.. . . . . *$25.00–$35.00*

Schroter, Ludwig and Dr. C. Schroter. *Taschenflora des Alpen-Wanderers.* Zurich. Meyer & Zeller. 1890. illus. . . . . *$50.00–$80.00*

Schulberg, Budd. *Sanctuary V.* Cleve. World. 1969. 1st ed. dj.. . . . *$20.00–$25.00*

Schulthess, Emil. *Antarctica.* NY. 1960. 1st Amer ed. plates. . . . . . *$60.00–$75.00*

Schultz, Charles M. *Good Grief, More Peanuts.* NY. 1956. wrps. . *$30.00–$40.00*

Schulz, Charles M. *Snoopy and the Red Baron.* NY. 1966. 1st ed. dj. *$28.00–$38.00*

Schultz, J. *Blackfeet Tales of Glacier National Park.* Bos. 1916. . . *$45.00–$55.00*

Schuster, Claud. *Peaks and Pleasant Pastures.* Oxford. Clarendon Press. 1911. 1st ed. illus. maps. . . . . *$25.00–$45.00*

Schuyler, George W. *Colonial New York.* NY. 1885. 2 vols. . . . . *$150.00–$175.00*

Schuyler, Keith. *Lures.* Stackpole. (1955. dj. . . . . *$15.00–$22.00*

Schwatka, Frederick. *Summer in Alaska.* St Louis. 1893. illus. . . . *$45.00–$75.00*

Schweinfurth, Charles. *Orchids of Peru.* Chi. 1958. 2 vols. . . . . . *$50.00–$60.00*

Schweizer, Charles H. *Billiard Hints.* LaCrosse, WI. 1906. . . . . . . *$20.00–$28.00*

Scott, Emmett. *Scott's Official History of the American Negro in the World War.* 1919. illus. . . . . *$20.00–$25.00*

Scott, H. *English Song Book.* Lon. 1926. . . . . *$30.00–$50.00*

Scott, Harold (ed.). *English Songbook.* NY. 1926. dj. . . . . *$25.00–$35.00*

Scott, Robert Falcon. *Scott's Last Expedition.* Lon. Smith, Elder. 1913. 2 vols. 3rd ed., teg. . . . . *$200.00–$260.00*

Scott, W. W. *History of Orange County, Virginia.* Richmond. 1907. 1st ed. . . . . . .
. . . . *$90.00–$150.00*

Scott, Winfield. *General Scott and his Staff..* Phila. 1849. illus. . . . *$37.00–$45.00*

Scott, Winfield Townley. *Biography for Traman.* NY. 1937. 1st ed. scarce, dj. . . . .
. . . . *$50.00–$85.00*

Scott, Winfield Townley. *To Marry Strangers.* NY. 1945. 1st ed. dj. *$30.00–$75.00*

Scott, Winfield Townley. *Wind the Clock.* Prairie City, IL. 1941. y. sgn, dj. . . . . . .
. . . . *$95.00–$125.00*

Scouting for Girls. NY. Girl Scouts. 1923. 5th ed.. . . . . *$35.00–$50.00*

Scrivenor, Harry. *History of the Iron Trade.* Lon. 1854. 2nd ed. 321 pp. . . . .
. . . . *$60.00–$75.00*

Scudder, S. H. *Tertiary Insects of North America.* DC. 1890. 4to, 734 pp, map frontis, 28 plates (US Geological Survey, Vol 13). . . . . *$125.00–$250.00*

Seale, Bobby. *Seize the Time.* NY. Random House. 1970. 1st ed. dj. *$25.00–$40.00*

Seale, Bobby. *Seize the Time, the Story of the Black Panther Party.* NY. Random House. (1970). 1st ed. dj. . . . . *$35.00–$50.00*

Seaman, Louis L. *From Tokio Through Manchuria with the Japanese.* NY. 1905. .
. . . . *$22.00–$35.00*

Seawell, Molly. *Ladies' Battle.* NY. 1911. 1st ed. 119 pp. . . . . *$30.00–$45.00*

Second Annual Report...Convict Labor. DC. 1887. . . . . *$30.00–$40.00*

Secret Life of Salvador Dali. NY. Dial Press. 1942. 1st ed. illus. bl cl dj. . . . .
. . . . *$95.00–$130.00*

Sedgwick, James. *Law of Storms.* Lon. Partridge and Oakey. 1852. illus. . . . .
. . . . *$45.00–$85.00*

Seeger, Alan. *Poems.* 1916. 1st ed. . . . . *$30.00–$45.00*

Self, Margaret Cabell. *Morgan Horse in Pictures.* Phila. Macrae Smith. 1967. dj. .
. . . . *$45.00–$65.00*

Sellars, Eleanore Kelly. *Murder a la Mode.* NY. Dodd, Mead. 1941. 1st ed. dj.. . . .
. . . . *$40.00–$50.00*

Selous, Frederick C. *African Nature Notes and Reminiscences.* Lon. Macmillan.
1908. 1st ed. illus. 13 plates. forward by President Roosevelt, cl.. *$225.00–$285.00*

Sendak, Maurice. *In the Night Kitchen.* NY. Harper & Row. 1970. 1st ed. illus.
Caldecott Honor book. . . . . *$75.00–$120.00*

Sendak, Maurice. *Outside Over There.* NY. Harper & Row. [1981]. 1st ed. illus. clr,
dj. . . . . *$35.00–$75.00*

Sendak, Maurice. *Posters by.* Harmony, NY. 1986. 1st ed. dj.. . . . . *$28.00–$35.00*

Sendak, Maurice. *Works of Maurice Sendak 1947-1994.* Portsmouth. Peter Randall.
1995. 1st ed. dj. . . . . *$35.00–$50.00*

Senefelder, Alois. *Invention of Lithography.* NY. Fuchs & Lang. 1911. trans by
Muller.. . . . . *$50.00–$70.00*

Senn, C Herman. *Luncheons and Dinner Sweets. .Ice Making.* Lon. 1st ed. illus. dj.
. . . . *$15.00–$20.00*

Senn, Dr Nicholas. *In the Heart of the Arctics.* Chi. Conkey. 1907. 1st ed. illus. . . .
. . . . *$75.00–$125.00*

Sergeant, F L. *Wright's Usonian House.* 1978. dj. . . . . *$47.00–$60.00*

Serling, Rod. *Season to be Wary.* Bos/Tor. Little, Brown & Co. (1967). 1st ed. dj.. .
. . . . *$25.00–$60.00*

Serling, Rod. *Season to be Wary.* Bos. Little, Brown. (1967). dj. . . *$30.00–$45.00*

Service, Robert. *Ballads of a Cheechako.* NY. 1909. . . . . *$6.00–$12.00*

Service, Robert. *Ballads of a Cheechako.* Tor. William Briggs. 1916. 1st ed. illus.
green cl. . . . . *$40.00–$60.00*

Service, Robert. *Complete Poems of Robert Service.* NY. Dodd, Mead. 1945. 1st ed.
inscr. . . . . *$120.00–$350.00*

Service, Robert. *Rhymes of a Rolling Stone.* Tor. 1912. 1st ed. . . *$60.00–$100.00*

Service, William. *Bar-Room Ballads.* Santa Fe. 1940. 1st UK ed dj. . *$30.00–$40.00*

Seton, E. T. *Woodmyth & Fable.* Century. 1905. 1st ed. . . . . *$115.00–$125.00*

Seton, Ernest Thompson. *Biography of a Grizzly.* NY. Century. 1900. 1st ed. . . .
. . . . *$45.00–$150.00*

Seton, Ernest Thompson. *Book of Woodcraft.* Garden City. 1921. illus. . . . .
. . . . *$30.00–$35.00*

Seton, Ernest Thompson. *Gospel of the Red Man.* NY. Doubleday Doran. 1936. 1st
ed. dj. . . . . *$50.00–$65.00*

Seton, Ernest Thompson. *Lives of the Hunted.* NY. Scribner's. 1901. 1st ed. . . . .
. . . . *$60.00–$80.00*

Seton, Ernest Thompson. *Monarch, The Big Bear of Tallac.* NY. 1904. 1st ed. illus.
1st imp. . . . . *$25.00–$50.00*

Seton, Ernest Thompson. *Rolf in the Woods.* Doubleday. 1911. illus. *$30.00–$45.00*

Seton, Ernest Thompson. *Two Little Savages.* NY. 1903. 1st ed. illus. *$40.00–$55.00*

Seton, Grace Thompson. *Yes, Lady Saheb.* NY/Lon. 1925. 1st ed. illus. photos. . .
. . . . *$25.00–$45.00*

Seton, Grace Thompson. *Yes, Lady Shaheb.* NY. Harper. 1925. 1st ed. 1st prtg. illus.
. . . . *$35.00–$45.00*

Seton, Julia M. *Pulse of the Pueblo.* NM. 1939. presentation copy, sgn. . . . .
. . . . *$25.00–$30.00*

Seuss, Dr. *500 Hats of Bartholomew Cubbins.* NY. Vanguard. (1938). 1st ed. dj. . .
. . . . *$70.00–$200.00*

Seuss, Dr. *Horton Hatches the Egg.* NY. Random House. 1940. dj. . *$25.00–$50.00*

Seuss, Dr. *More Boners.* NY. 1931. . . . . *$40.00–$60.00*

Seuss, Dr. *Seven Lady Godivas.* NY. (1939). 1st ed. dj. . . . . *$150.00–$750.00*

Seuss, Dr. *Thidwick: The Big Hearted Moose.* NY. 1948. 1st ed. . . . *$40.00–$80.00*

Seuss, Dr. *You're Only Old Once.* NY. Random House. 1986. 1st ed. dj. . . . .
. . . . *$15.00–$30.00*

Seutonius, Caius. *History of the Twelve Caesars, Emperors of Rome.* Lon. Starkey.
1672. 12 copper plates. . . . . *$80.00–$115.00*

Sewel, William. *History of the Rise, Increase and Progress of the Christian People
Called Quakers.* Burlington, NJ. Isaac Collins. 1774. 812 pp. . . . *$100.00–$125.00*

Sewell, A. *Black Beauty*. Bos. 1890. illus. 1st Amer ed......... *$200.00–$300.00*

Sewell, Anna. *Black Beauty: His Grooms and Companions.* Bos. 1890. 1st thus, Amer Humane Ed Soc. .... *$150.00–$295.00*

Sextus, Carl. *Hypnotism.* Chi. 1893. 1st ed. illus. .... *$30.00–$45.00*

Seymour, Eaton. *Travelling Bears in New York.* Barse & Hopkins. 1915. illus. frontis... *$90.00–$150.00*

Seymour, George Dudley, et al. *History of the Seymour Family..* New Haven. 1939. .... *$35.00–$50.00*

Seymour, Prof W. P. *Seymour's Key to Electro-Therpeutics.* Newark. 1904. 2nd ed.. .... *$20.00–$30.00*

Sfinde, Julius. *Frau Wilhelmine.* Berlin. 1886. in German. .... *$25.00–$35.00*

Shackleton, E. H. *The heart of the Antarctic Being the Story of the British Antarctic Expedition 1907-1909.* Lon. Heinemann. 1910. revised. bds....... *$35.00–$65.00*

Shackleton, E. H. *The heart of the Antarctic Being the Story of the British Antarctic Expedition 1907-1909.* Heinemann. 1909. 2. 1st ed. printed wrps. .... *$500.00–$5,000.00*

Shackleton, Ernest H. *South.* NY. Macmillan. 1920. 1st Amer ed. illus, map...... .... *$140.00–$165.00*

Shackleton, Ernest H. (ed.). *Aurora Australis.* New Zealand. 1988. illus. rprnt, dj. . ... *$25.00–$30.00*

Shahn, Ben. *Haggadah for Passover.* Bos. Little, Brown. 1965. 1st ed. illus. trans by Roth. white cl, gold lettered. .... *$100.00–$125.00*

Shakespeare's The Merry Wives of Windsor. NY. Stokes. 1910. 1st ed. illus. by Hugh Thomson dec cl. .... *$85.00–$150.00*

Shakespeare, William. *As You Like It.* Lon/NY. Hodder & Stoughton. illus. paste in illus by Hugh Thomson............................... *$100.00–$125.00*

Shakespeare, William. *Comedies, Histories & Tragedies of Wm. Shakespeare.* 1939. 37 vols. illus. Ltd Ed Club, 8 slipcases. .... *$850.00–$950.00*

Shakespeare, William. *Dramatic Works.* Bos. Hilliard Gray. 1839. 8 vols. .... *$75.00–$100.00*

Shakespeare, William. *New Shakespeare.* Camb. Univ Press. 10 vols. 2nd ed. .... *$80.00–$120.00*

Shakespeare, William. *Romeo and Juliet.* NY. 1936. illus. dj. .... *$50.00–$75.00*

Shakespeare, William. *Shakespeare's Comedy As you Like It.* Lon/NY. nd. 1st ed. illus. 39 tip-in clr pls........................... *$250.00–$350.00*

Shakespeare, William. *Shakespeare's Comedy of The Tempest.* Lon. 1915. illus. by Edmund Dulac. . . . . *$250.00–$300.00*

Shakespeare, William. *Tempest.* Lon. Heinneman. (1926). 1st ed thus. illus by Arthur Rackham. decorated black cl. . . . . *$120.00–$195.00*

Shakespeare, William. *Works of Shakespeare.* Lon. 1904. 10 vols. deluxe ed. ltd 500 cc.. . . . . *$120.00–$135.00*

Shakespeare, William. *Works of....* Lon/NY. The Noneshuch Press/Random House. 1929-33. 7 vols. . . . . *$1,200.00–$1,500.00*

Shakespeare, William. *Works.* Lon/NY. 1892. 12 vols. boxed. . . . . *$50.00–$75.00*

Shand, Alex Innes. *Gun Room.* Lon. The Bodley Head. 1905. . . . . *$65.00–$75.00*

Shapiro, Karl. *White-Haired Lover.* NY. 1968. 1st ed. sgn, dj. . . . . *$30.00–$45.00*

Sharp, H. *Modern Sporting Gunnery Manual....* Lon. 1906. folio.. . *$30.00–$40.00*

Sharpe, Philips B. *Rifle in America.* NY. Funk & Wagnalls. 1947. illus. . . . . *$50.00–$60.00*

Shaw, Archer H. *Lincoln Encyclopedia.* NY. 1950. 1st ed. dj.. . . . . *$30.00–$40.00*

Shaw, Edward. *Shaw's Civil Architecture.* Bos. 1852. . . . . *$40.00–$50.00*

Shaw, Edward Richard. *Pot of Gold. A Story of Fire Island Beach.* Chi/NY. 1888. . . . . *$85.00–$125.00*

Shaw, George Bernard. *Adventures of a Black Girl in Her Search of God.* Dodd, Mead. 1933. illus. 1st Amer ed. dj. . . . . *$30.00–$45.00*

Shaw, George Bernard. *Intelligent Woman's Guide to Socialism & Capitalism.* NY. 1928. 1st Amer ed. . . . . *$35.00–$90.00*

Shaw, George Bernard. *Man and Superman.* NY. Heritage. (1962). slipcase. . . . . *$20.00–$40.00*

Shaw, George Bernard. *Quintessence of Ibsenism.* Lon. Walter Scott. 1891. 1st ed. . . . . *$100.00–$150.00*

Shaw, George Bernard. *Two Plays for Puritans.* NY. Limited Editions Club. 1966. illus. drawings by George Him, ltd 1500 cc, sgn slipcase. . . . . *$20.00–$30.00*

Shaw, George Bernard (ed.). *Fabian Essays in Socialism.* Lon. 1899. pict and dec cl. . . . . *$95.00–$120.00*

Shaw, Irwin. *Mixed Company.* Random House. 1950. 1st ed. dj.. . . *$40.00–$50.00*

Shaw, Irwin. *Sailor Off the Bremen and Other Stories.* NY. Random House. (c1939). 1st ed. no dj. . . . . *$35.00–$45.00*

Shaw, Irwin. *Troubled Air.* NY. 1951. 1st ed. dj............... *$35.00–$40.00*

Shaw, Irwin. *Young Lions.* NY. 1st ed. dj.................... *$35.00–$45.00*

Shaw, Robert. *Visits to High Tartary, Yarkand, and Kashgar.* Lon. John Murray. 1871. 1st ed. 2 fldg maps, 7 tinted plates. .... *$300.00–$450.00*

Shaw, Thomas George. *Wine Trade and Its History.* Lon. nd. .... *$37.00–$75.00*

Sheckley, Robert. *Is That What People Do?.* NY. 1984. sgn, dj. ... *$15.00–$20.00*

Sheldon, Charles. *Wilderness of the Upper Yukon.* NY. 1913. illus. maps......... .... *$50.00–$75.00*

Shelley, Mary. *Frankenstein.* Univ CA Press. 1984. 1st ed thus, dj............. .... *$50.00–$65.00*

Shelley, Mary W. *Letters of Mary W Shelley.* Bos. Bibliophile Society. 448 cc..... .... *$50.00–$75.00*

Shelley, Mary Wollstonecraft. *Frankenstein.* Bos. Sever, Francis, &c. 1869. 2nd Amer ed. 177 pp....................................... *$350.00–$450.00*

Shepherd, Sam. *Operation Sidewinder.* NY. 1970. .... *$35.00–$40.00*

Sheridan, P. H. *Personal Memoirs.* NY. 1888. 2 vols. 1st ed. ..... *$40.00–$85.00*

Sherman, Gen. *Memoirs of.* 1891. 2 vols. 4th ed.............. *$40.00–$70.00*

Sherman, John. *Recollections.* 1895. 2 vols. 1st ed. .... *$45.00–$65.00*

Sherman, S. M. *History of the 133rd Regiment, O.V.I.* Columbus. 1896. 1st ed. ... . *$125.00–$200.00*

Sherman, William Tecumseh. *Home Letters of General Sherman.* NY. 1909. 1st ed. .... *$40.00–$50.00*

Sherwen, Grayson. *Romance of St. Sacrement.* Vt. Free Press Printing Co. 1912. 1st ed. illus. blue cl. .... *$12.00–$20.00*

Sherwin, Shapiro. *Davy Crockett's Keelboat Race.* NY. Simon & Schuster. 1955. Mickey Mouse Club book...................................... *$20.00–$30.00*

Sherwood, Mary Martha. *History of Little Henry and His Bearer.* Hartford. George Goodwin & Sons. 1822. 52 pp, 14 x 87 cm. .... *$70.00–$95.00*

Sherwood, Robert Emmet. *Queen's Husband.* NY. 1928. 1st ed. . *$40.00–$45.00*

Shetrone, Henry Clyde. *Mound-Builders: A Reconstruction of the Life of a Prehistoric American Race.* NY. Appleton. 1930. 1st ed. illus. .... *$50.00–$80.00*

Shiel, M. P. *Children of the Wind.* NY. 1923. 1st US ed......... *$30.00–$40.00*

Ship Figureheads and other Wood Carving Art in the Nautical Collection of the
SSTC of Boston. State Street Trust Co. wrps. illus. . . . . *$20.00–$30.00*

Shirley Temple through the day. Ohio/NY. The Saalfield Pub Co. 1936. 1st ed. illus.
pict wrps authorized ed.. . . . . *$125.00–$150.00*

Shirts, Augustus F. *History of...Hamilton County, Indiana (1818 to Civil War).* 1901.
1st ed. illus. . . . . *$65.00–$100.00*

Shoemaker, Henry. *Black Forest Souvenirs.* Reading, PA. Bright-Faust Printing Co.
1914. illus. plates, inscr. . . . . *$60.00–$75.00*

Shriner, C. H. *Birds of New Jersey.* 1896. . . . . *$25.00–$45.00*

Shurtleff, Nathaniel. *Topographical and Historical Description of Boston.* Bos.
1871. . . . . *$45.00–$75.00*

Shuster, George N. *Like a Mighty Army..* NY. Appleton Century. 1935. 1st ed. dj..
. . . . *$30.00–$45.00*

Shute, Miss T. S. *American Housewife Cook Book.* Phila. 1878. . . *$30.00–$40.00*

Shute, Nevil. *On the Beach.* Lon. Heinemann. 1957. 1st ed. dj.. . *$110.00–$150.00*

Shute, Nevil. *Ordeal.* NY. Morrow. 1939. 1st Amer ed. dj. . . . . *$25.00–$50.00*

Shute, Nevil. *Trustee from the Toolroom.* NY. William Morrow. (1960). 1st ed. dj..
. . . . *$30.00–$40.00*

Sidney, M. *Five Little Peppers Grown Up.* Bos. 1892. 1st ed. . . . . . *$20.00–$30.00*

Siebert, Wilbury H. *Vermont's Anti-Slavery and Underground Railroad Record..*
Columbus, OH. 1937. 1st ed. illus. map, plates.. . . . . *$50.00–$75.00*

Siegbahn, M. *Spectroscopy of X-Rays.* Lon. 1925. 1st UK ed. . . . . *$40.00–$50.00*

Sikorsky, Igor I. *Story of the Winged-S with New Material on...Helicopter.* NY.
1942. illus. photos, inscr, dj. . . . . *$40.00–$45.00*

Silko, Leslie marmon. *Ceremony.* NY. Viking. (1977). 1st ed. dj. . *$100.00–$150.00*

Silverberg, Robert. *Lord Valentine's Castle.* Harper & Row. (1980). 1st ed. sgn, dj.
. . . . *$20.00–$25.00*

Silverberg, Robert. *New Springtime.* Warner Books. (1990). 1st US ed. dj.. . . . . .
. . . . *$14.00–$20.00*

Silverberg, Robert. *Shadrach in the Furnace.* Ind. Bobbs-Merrill. (1976). 1st ed. dj.
. . . . *$20.00–$35.00*

Silverberg, Robert. *Starborne.* Norwalk. Easton Press. (1996). 1st ed. ltd 1500 cc,
numbered and sgn, bound-in ribbon bookmark, laid-in Easton Press bookplate (not
issued in dj). . . . . *$75.00–$85.00*

Silverstein, Shel. *Different Dances.* 1978. 1st ed. dj. . . . . *$100.00–$135.00*

Silverstein, Shel. *Giving Tree.* Harper & Row. 1964. . . . . *$20.00–$30.00*

Silverstein, Shel. *Light In the Attic.* Harper & Row. (1981). 1st ed. dj. . . . .
. . . . *$15.00–$25.00*

Silverstein, Shel. *Take Ten.* Tokyo. Pacific Stars and Stripes. 1955. 1st ed. . . . .
. . . . *$75.00–$135.00*

Simenon, George. *The Son.* Lon. Hamish Hamilton. 1958. 1st ed. dj. . . . .
. . . . *$70.00–$80.00*

Simenon, George. *The Venice Train.* Lon. Hamish Hamilton. 1974. 1st UK ed. dj. . .
. . . . *$45.00–$55.00*

Simenon, George. *The Window Over the Way.* Lon. Routledge & Kegan Paul. 1951.
1st UK ed. dj. . . . . *$75.00–$90.00*

Simkins, Francis Butler & James Welch Patton. *Women of the Confederacy.*
Rich/NY. 1936. 1st ed. dj. . . . . *$90.00–$125.00*

Simmon, Albert Dixon. *Wing Shots.* NY. Derrydale. (1936). 1st ed. illus. . . . .
. . . . *$70.00–$100.00*

Simmons, Amelia. *American Cookery.* NY. 1958. ltd 800 cc, boxed. . *$35.00–$50.00*

Simms, Henry H. *Life of Robert M T Hunter.* Wm Byrd Press. . . . *$40.00–$50.00*

Simms, W Gilmore. *Lily & The Totem.* NY. 1850. . . . . *$35.00–$45.00*

Simpson, Charles. *Leicestershire & Its Hunts.* Lon. John Lane. (1926). illus. 28 col.
55 b/w 75 cc sgn.. . . . . *$100.00–$150.00*

Sinclair, John L. *American Outpost.* NY. 1932. 1st ed. dj. . . . . *$70.00–$85.00*

Sinclair, John L. *I, Candidate..* Pasadena. (1935). 1st ed. . . . . *$15.00–$40.00*

Sinclair, Upton. *100%: The Story of a Patriot.* Pasadena. private printing. (1920).
1st ed. . . . . *$100.00–$180.00*

Sinclair, Upton. *Mental Radio.* Lon. Werner Laurie. 1930. 1st ed. dj blue cl. . . . . . .
. . . . *$45.00–$70.00*

Sinclair, Upton. *Millennium.* Viking. 1943. 1st ed. dj. . . . . *$20.00–$30.00*

Sinclair, Upton. *The Jungle.* NY. Doubleday. 1906. 1st ed. olive cl.*$65.00–$150.00*

Singer, Isaac Bashevis. *Gimpel the Fool.* Franklin Center. Franklin Library. 1980. 1st
ed. dj. . . . . *$50.00–$70.00*

Singer, Isaac Bashevis. *Lost in America.* Garden City. Doubleday. 1981. . . . .
. . . . *$10.00–$15.00*

Singer, Isaac Bashevis. *Manor.* NY. Farrar Straus & Giroux. 1967. 1st ed. dj..... . . . . *$20.00–$40.00*

Singer, Isaac Bashevis. *Spinoza of Market Street.* Phila. Jewish Pub. (1961). 1st ed. dj. . . . . *$60.00–$150.00*

Singer, Isaac Bashevis. *Tale of Three Wishes.* NY. (1976). 1st ed. illus. by Irene Lieblich. dj. . . . . *$20.00–$25.00*

Singer, Isaac Bashevis. *The Penitent.* Franklin Center. Franklin Library. 1983. 1st ed. ltd. sgn. . . . . *$70.00–$95.00*

Singer, Isaac Bashevis. *Young Man in Search of Love.* NY. Doubleday. 1978. 1st ed. dj. . . . . *$15.00–$25.00*

Singh, Kesri. *Tiger of Rajasthan.* Lon. Hale. 1959. 1st ed. illus. dj.. *$50.00–$65.00*

Singleton, Esther. *Shakespeare Garden.* NY. 1931. . . . . *$20.00–$25.00*

Singleton, Esther. *Social New York Under the Georges 1714-1776.* NY. 1902. 1st ed. . . . . *$30.00–$40.00*

Sinnett, A. P. *Occult World.* Bos. 1882. 1st ed. . . . . *$45.00–$85.00*

Siringo, Charles A. *History of Billy the Kid.* Austin. 1967. pict cl. . *$30.00–$75.00*

Siringo, Charles A. *Lone Star Cowboy.* Santa Fe. 1919. 1st ed. pict dark red cl. . . . . *$100.00–$400.00*

Siringo, Charles A. *Riata & Spurs.* Bos. 1931. . . . . *$75.00–$135.00*

Siringo, Charles A. *Riata and Spurs.* Bos/NY. Houghton Mifflin. 1927. 1st ed. illus. pict cov. . . . . *$165.00–$275.00*

Siringo, Charles A. *Texas Cowboy.* NY. 1950. illus. by Tom Lea dj. *$40.00–$75.00*

Siringo, Charles A. *Two Evil Isms.* Austin. 1967. illus. bds, facs. . . *$40.00–$50.00*

Sisson, James E. II and Robert W. Martens. *Jack London First Editions.* Oakland. Star Rover House. 1979. 1st ed. illus. ltd 1,000 cc. . . . . *$60.00–$105.00*

Sitwell, Edith. *Shadow of Cain.* Lon. Lehmann. 1947. sgn, presentation copy from Margaret Mead. dj. . . . . *$55.00–$65.00*

Sitwell, Sacheverall. *Dance of the Quick and the Dead.* Lon. Faber & Faber. 1936. 1st ed. illus. dj. . . . . *$35.00–$47.00*

Sitwell, Sacheverell. *Gothick North.* Bos. Houghton Mifflin. 1929. plates.. . . . . *$30.00–$40.00*

Sketch of the 126th Regiment Pennsylvania Volunteers. PA. 1869. 1st ed. . . . . *$125.00–$200.00*

Skinner, Otis. *Footlights and Spotlights.* Bobbs Merrill. 1924. ltd 500 cc, sgn. . . . .
. . . . *$35.00–$45.00*

Skinner, Otis A. *Theory of William Miller, Concerning the End of the World in 1843.*
Bos. Whittemore. 1840. 1st ed. . . . . *$150.00–$200.00*

Slang Dictionary. Lon. 1864. 2nd ed. . . . . *$40.00–$60.00*

Sloane, Eric. *Spirits of '76.* NY. Walker and Co. (1973). illus. white decorated cl over
bds, pict dj. . . . . *$10.00–$24.00*

Sloane, T. O'Connor. *Electric Toy Making for Amateurs.* NY. Munn & Co. 1903.
illus. 25. . . . . *$35.00–$85.00*

Slocum, John and Herbert Cahoon. *Bibliography of James Joyce.* Westport, CT.
(1977). illus. rprnt of 1953 ed. . . . . *$30.00–$60.00*

Slocum, Joshua. *Sailing Alone Around the World.* Lon. Samson, Low, Marston & Co.
c1900. 3rd ed. illus, pict cl, aeg. . . . . *$38.00–$50.00*

Slocum, Joshua. *Sailing Alone Around the World.* NY. Century. 1900. 1st ed. . . . . .
. . . . *$250.00–$400.00*

Slocum, Joshua. *Voyage of the Liberdade.* Bos. 1894. illus. . . . . *$125.00–$255.00*

Slud, Paul. *Birds of Costa Rica.* American Museum of Natural History. 1964. buckram. . . . . *$45.00–$60.00*

Small Homes. Ithaca, NY. Driscoll Bros & Co. c 1940s. pict wrps, for National Plan
Service, 48 pp. . . . . *$35.00–$50.00*

Small, John. *Flora of the Florida Keys.* NY. pub. by author. 1913. *$75.00–$115.00*

Smiley, Jane. *Age of Grief.* NY. Knopf. 1987. 1st ed. dj. . . . . *$60.00–$150.00*

Smith, A. *Dental Microscopy.* Lon/Phila. 1895. plates. . . . . *$35.00–$45.00*

Smith, Adam. *An Inquiry Into the Nature and Causes of the Wealth of Nations.* Lon.
1930. 2 vols. djs. . . . . *$75.00–$130.00*

Smith, Adam. *An Inquiry Into the Nature and Causes of The Wealth of Nations.* Lon.
1811. 2nd Amer ed. . . . . *$300.00–$800.00*

Smith, Amanda. *An Autobiography.* . Chi. 1893. 1st ed. . . . . *$45.00–$175.00*

Smith, Charles W. *Beautiful Virginia.* Beautiful America Pub. illus. *$50.00–$75.00*

Smith, Clark Ashton. *Other Dimensions.* Sauk City. Arkham House. 1970. 1st ed.
dj. . . . . *$30.00–$85.00*

Smith, Clark Ashton. *Tales of Science & Sorcery.* Sauk City. Arkham House. 1964.
1st ed. dj. . . . . *$50.00–$125.00*

Smith, Daniel. *Company K, First Alabama Regiment.*.Prattville, Al. 1885. . . . . *$900.00–$1,000.00*

Smith, George W. *When Lincoln Came to Egypt.* Herrin, IL. Trovillion Private Press. 1940. 498 cc sgn by Smith. . . . . *$50.00–$75.00*

Smith, Gustavus Woodson. *Battle of Seven Pines.* NY. 1891. 1st ed. wrps. . . . .*$175.00–$200.00*

Smith, James Power. *General Lee At Gettysburg.* VA. nd. 1st ed. . *$50.00–$75.00*

Smith, Jerome V. C. *Natural History of the Fishes of Mass...Essay on Angling.* Bos. 1833. . . . .*$150.00–$175.00*

Smith, Joseph. *Pearl of Great Price.* Salt Lake. 1888. brown cl. . *$150.00–$200.00*

Smith, Lawrence B. *American Game Preserve Shooting.* NY. Garden City Pub. 1937. illus. buckram, dj. . . . . *$15.00–$40.00*

Smith, Martin Cruz. *Gorky Park.* NY. Random House. (1981). 1st ed. dj. . . . . *$20.00–$40.00*

Smith, Martin Cruz. *Gypsy in Amber.* NY. (1971). 1st ed. dj. . . . . *$60.00–$75.00*

Smith, Martin Cruz. *Indians Won.* NY. Belmont. (1970). 1st ed. wrps. . . . .*$100.00–$125.00*

Smith, Martin Cruz. *Rose.* NY. Random House. 1996. 1st ed. dj. . *$10.00–$20.00*

Smith, William Jay. *Spectra Hoax.* Ct. Wesleyan Univ Press. (1961). 1st ed. illus. 4 plates. . . . .*$20.00–$55.00*

Smith, Willie. *Match-Winning Billiards.* Lon. Mills & Boon. 1924. 1st ed. illus. diagrams, blue cl. . . . .*$60.00–$95.00*

Smith, Winston O. *Sharps Rifle.* William Morrow. 1943. 1st ed. . . *$60.00–$75.00*

Smucker, Samuel. *Life of Col John Charles Fremont.* NY. Miller, Orton, & Mulligan. 1856. 1st ed. . . . .*$35.00–$65.00*

Smyth, Henry Dewolf. *Atomic Energy for Military Purposes.* 1945. illus. 2nd ed. softcvr. . . . .*$35.00–$55.00*

Smythe, Frank S. *Kamet Conquered.* Lon. Victor Gollancz. 1933. 2nd imp, photos, maps. . . . .*$14.00–$20.00*

Smythe, Sarah M. *Ten Months in the Fiji Islands.* Oxford. John Henry & James Parker. 1864. maps, clr plates. . . . .*$325.00–$385.00*

Smythies, B. E. *Birds of Borneo.* The Sabah Society. 1981. pict bds. . . . . *$75.00–$100.00*

Snow, Alan. *How Dogs Really Work.* Bos. Little, Brown & Co. 1993. 1st ed. illus. dj. .... *$10.00–$25.00*

Snow, Jack. *Magical Mimics of Oz.* Chi. Reilly & Lee. (1946). illus. by Frank Kramer. .... *$75.00–$110.00*

Snow, Jack. *Shaggy Man of Oz.* Chi. Reilly & Lee. (1949). 1st ed. illus. by Frank Kramer. .... *$60.00–$110.00*

Snowden, James H. *Truth About Mormonism.* NY. 1926. 1st ed. illus. photos, scarce in dj. .... *$35.00–$50.00*

Snowden, R. *History of North and South America.* Phila. 1813. 2 vols in one, lea, maps. .... *$75.00–$100.00*

Snyder, Gary. *Earth House Hold.* 1969. 1st ed. sgn, dj. .... *$60.00–$85.00*

Snyder, Gary. *Old Ways.* SF. City Lights. 1977. 1st ed. .... *$20.00–$25.00*

Snyder, Gary. *Regarding Wave.* Lon. 1970. 1st ed. dj. .... *$35.00–$45.00*

Solomon. *Why Smash Atoms?* Camb. 1940. 1st ed. .... *$30.00–$60.00*

Solzhenetsyn, Aleksandr. *Gulag Archipelago.* NY. Harper & Row. 1973. 3 vols. 1st ed. djs. .... *$25.00–$75.00*

Solzhenitsyn, Aleksandr. *Oak and the Calf.* Harper. 1980. 1st US trade ed. dj. . . . . *$15.00–$25.00*

Solzhenitsyn, Alexandr. *Cancer Ward.* Bodley Head. 1968. 1st UK ed. dj. . . . . *$35.00–$40.00*

Solzhenitsyn, Alexandr. *Lenin in Zurich.* Farrar, Straus & Giroux. 1976. 1st US ed. dj. .... *$20.00–$30.00*

Solzhenitsyn, Alexandr. *One Day in the Life of Ivan Denisovich.* NY. Dutton. 1963. 1st ed. dj. .... *$15.00–$50.00*

Solzhenitsyn, Alexandr. *Stories and Prose Poems.* Farrar, Straus & Giroux. 1971. 1st US ed. dj. .... *$15.00–$30.00*

Some Books, Catalogue 56. Austin. Jenkins Company. nd. wrps. bibliography. . . . . *$20.00–$30.00*

Somers, Rev. A. N. *History of Lancaster, New Hampshire.* Rumford Press. 1899. illus. frontis. .... *$50.00–$75.00*

Somerville & Ross. *Sweet Cry of Hounds.* Bos/NY. Houghton Mifflin. 1937. 1st ed. .... *$35.00–$45.00*

Somerville, H. B. *Ashes of Vengeance, a Romance of Old France.* McBride. 1923. illus. rust-clr cl. .... *$25.00–$35.00*

Somerville, Mary. *On the Connexion of the Physical Sciences.* Lon. John Murray. 1836. 3rd ed. . . . . *$30.00–$45.00*

Sommerville, Frankfort. *Spirit of Paris.* Lon. Adam and Charles Black. 1913. decorated cvr, teg, 169 pp, clr plates. . . . . *$60.00–$75.00*

Sonneck, Oscar G. T. *"The Star Spangled Banner.. ".* DC. GPO. 1st ed. illus. . . . . *$25.00–$45.00*

Sontag, Susan. *Trip to Hanoi.* NY. Farrar Straus & Giroux. 1968. 1st ed. paperback. . . . . *$45.00–$85.00*

South, Theophilus (pseud.) *The Fly Fisher's Text Book.* Lon. Ackerman. 1841. 1st ed. illus. steel-engr plates, blindstamped cl. . . . . *$250.00–$350.00*

Southern Songster.... Liverpool. 1864. wrps. . . . . *$175.00–$225.00*

Southern, Terry. *Red Dirt Marijuana.* NAL. 1967. dj. . . . . *$35.00–$60.00*

Southwell, T. *Seals and Whales of the British Seas.* Lon. 1881. illus. . . . . *$175.00–$300.00*

Spalding's Official Base Ball Guide: Golden Jubilee, 1876-1925. NY. American Spotts Publishing. 1925. wrps. illus. . . . . *$80.00–$120.00*

Spargo, John. *Karl Marx. His Life and Work.* NY. Huebsch. 1910. 1st ed. . . . . *$20.00–$65.00*

Spark, Muriel. *Driver's Seat.* NY. Knopf. 1970. 1st US ed. dj. . . . . *$25.00–$30.00*

Spark, Muriel. *Hothouse by the East River.* Lon. Macmillan. (1973). 1st UK ed. . . . . *$35.00–$40.00*

Spark, Muriel. *My Best Mary.* Lon. 1953. 1st ed. dj. . . . . *$25.00–$60.00*

Spark, Muriel. *Prime of Miss Jean Brodie.* NY. Lippincott. 1961. 1st ed. dj. . . . . *$40.00–$75.00*

Spark, Muriel. *Prime of Miss Jean Brodie.* Lon. Macmillan. 1961. 1st UK ed. dj. . . . . *$125.00–$150.00*

Sparks, Jared. *Life of George Washington.* Bos. 1839. 1st ed. illus. *$65.00–$95.00*

Sparks, Jared. *Life of John Ledyard..* Camb. Hilliard & Brown. 1828. 2nd ed. . . . . *$50.00–$100.00*

Sparrow, Walter Shaw. *Book of Sporting Painters.* Lon. The Bodley Head. 1931. illus. col and b/w dj folio. . . . . *$150.00–$200.00*

Spears, John. *Illustrated Sketches of Death Valley.* Chi. 1892. wrps. illus. . . . . *$150.00–$300.00*

Spears, John R. *Illustrated Sketches of Death Valley..* Chi. Rand McNally. 1892. 1st ed. illus. blue cl map. . . . . *$300.00–$500.00*

Specimen Book of Monotype, Linotype & Foundry Type Faces, etc. Bos. 1941. 1st ed. . . . . *$28.00–$35.00*

Speck, Frank G. *Tutelo Spirit Adoption Ceremony.* Harrisburg. 1942. illus. photos.. . . . . *$25.00–$50.00*

Speer, Robert S. *Of One Blood.* Council of Women for Home Missions. (1924). wrps. . . . . *$10.00–$25.00*

Speert, Harold. *Iconographia Gyniatrica.* Phila. F A Davis. (1973). 1st ed. illus. black cl.. . . . . *$60.00–$90.00*

Spence, Lewis. *Encyclopedia of the Occult.* Lon. Bracken Books. 1988. dj.. . . . . *$18.00–$28.00*

Spencer, Ambrose. *Narrative of Andersonville.* NY. 1866. 1st ed. 272 pp.. . . . . *$85.00–$100.00*

Spencer, Robert F. *North Alaskan Eskimo: A Study in Ecology and Society.* DC. GPO. 1959. 1st ed. 490 pp. Bulletin #171. . . . . *$85.00–$115.00*

Spender, Stephen. *Forward from Liberalism.* NY. Random House. c1937. 1st Amer ed. . . . . *$50.00–$65.00*

Spender, Stephen. *New Realism, a Discussion.* Lon. The Hogarth Press. 1939. 1st ed. printed wrps. . . . . *$40.00–$50.00*

Spender, Stephen. *Poems.* Lon. Faber & Faber. (1933). 1st ed. . . . *$70.00–$80.00*

Spender, Stephen. *Poems of Dedication.* Lon. Faber & Faber. (1947). 1st ed. dj.. . . . . *$20.00–$40.00*

Spender, Stephen. *Trial of a Judge: A Tragedy in Five Acts.* Lon. Faber & Faber. (1938). 1st ed. inscr,. . . . . *$55.00–$75.00*

Spenser, Edmund. *Prothalamion: Epithalamion.* Bos/NY. 1902. illus. ltd 400 cc, folio, dj.. . . . . *$67.00–$85.00*

Sperry, Earle E. *Jerry Rescue.* NY. 1921. 16 pp. . . . . *$15.00–$25.00*

Spielmann, M. H & Walter Jerrold. *Hugh Thomson....* Lon. A. & C. Black. 1931. illus. 13 clr plates, dj. . . . . *$85.00–$125.00*

Spielmann, M. H. & G. S. Layard. *Kate Greenaway.* Lon. Adam & Charles Black. 1905. 2nd prtg. blue cl, teg. . . . . *$25.00–$50.00*

Spillane, Mickey. *Kiss Me, Deadly.* NY. 1952. 1st ed. dj. . . . . *$75.00–$200.00*

Spillane, Mickey. *The Deep.* NY. Dutton. 1961. 1st ed. dj. . . . . *$40.00–$65.00*

Spiller, Burton L. *Firelight.* Derrydale. 1937. illus. by Lynn Bogue Hunt, ltd 950 cc.
. . . . *$180.00–$350.00*

Spiller, Burton L. *Grouse Feathers.* NY. 1947. illus. by Lynn Bogue Hunt. . . . . . .
. . . . *$50.00–$60.00*

Spivak, John L. *Georgia Nigger.* Lon. 1933. 1st ed. . . . . *$175.00–$250.00*

Splan, John. *Life With The Trotters.* 1889. presentation copy. . . . *$110.00–$125.00*

Splawn, A. J. *KA-MI-AKIN, the Last Hero of the Yakimas.* Portland. 1917. 1st ed.
illus. photos, lea. . . . . *$90.00–$110.00*

Springs, Elliott White. *Rise and Fall of Carol Banks.* Garden City. Doubleday,
Doran. 1931. ltd 200 cc, gray cl, paper label. . . . . *$75.00–$125.00*

Sprunt, A. *Florida Bird Life.* Coward McCann. 1954. dj. . . . . *$60.00–$75.00*

Sprunt, Alexander Jr. *North American Birds of Prey.* Harper & Bros. 1955. 1st ed.
dj. . . . . *$25.00–$40.00*

Spy, W. J. J. *The Cruise of Her Majesty's Ship "Challenger."* NY. Harper. 1877.
illus. wood-engr plates, fldg map. . . . . *$40.00–$60.00*

Spyri, Johanna. *Heidi.* Phila. 1927. illus. by Jessie Wilcox Smith. 1st ed thus. . . . .
. . . . *$125.00–$175.00*

Squier, Ephraim G. *Lecture of the Condition and True Interests of the Working Man
in America.* Albany. 1843. 16 pp, wrps. . . . . *$45.00–$55.00*

Squier, Ephraim G. *Nicaragua.* NY. Harper. 1860. rev ed. fldg map, 23 plages,
original cl, rbkd. . . . . *$95.00–$120.00*

Squier, Ephraim G. *States of Central America.* NY. 1858. illus. maps. . . . .
. . . . *$30.00–$50.00*

St. John Roosa, D. B. *Practical Treatise on the Diseases of the Ear.* NY. 1876. illus.
. . . . *$42.00–$55.00*

Stafford, Jean. *Catherine Wheel.* NY. 1952. 1st ed. dj. . . . . *$20.00–$45.00*

Stafford, Jean. *Children are Bored on Sunday.* NY. Harcourt & Brace Co. (1953).
1st ed. dj. . . . . *$30.00–$45.00*

Stafford, Jean. *Mountain Lion.* NY. Harcourt Brace & Co. (1947). 1st ed. dj. . . . .
. . . . *$70.00–$85.00*

Stafford, Joseph. *An Astronomical Diary.* New Haven. (1800). . *$100.00–$125.00*

Stafford, Joseph. *An Astronomist's Diary.* New Haven. (1800). . *$100.00–$125.00*

Stalin, Joseph. *Leninism.* NY. International Publishers. 1928. 1st Amer ed. . . . . . .
. . . . *$60.00–$75.00*

Stanley, Dean. *Picturesque Palestine.* Lon. 1880–1884. 5 vols. plates . . . .
. . . . *$275.00–$350.00*

Stanley, Henry M. *Congo and the Founding of its Free State.* NY. Harper & Bros.
1885. 2 vols. 1st Amer ed. illus. maps . . . . *$150.00–$500.00*

Stanley, Henry M. *Congo and the Founding of its Free State.* Lon. 1885. 2 vols.
1st ed. illus. maps, plates, pict cl . . . . *$600.00–$850.00*

Stanley, Henry M. *Livingstone Lost and Found.* Hartford. Mutual Publishing. 1873.
1st ed. illus. 782 pp. . . . . *$70.00–$85.00*

Stanley, Henry M. *Slavery and the Slave Trade in Africa.* NY. Harper & Bros. 1893.
1st Amer ed. illus by Frederick Remington . . . . *$35.00–$50.00*

Stanley, Sir Henry Morton. *Autobiography, edited by His Wife.* Bos. Houghton
Mifflin. 1909. 1st ed. photogravures, fldg map, teg . . . . *$50.00–$70.00*

Stanley, W. H. *My Kalulu Prince, King & Slave.* NY. Scribner's. 1890. illus. . . . . .
. . . . *$100.00–$150.00*

Stansbury, Howard. *Exploration and Survey of the Valley of the Great Salt Lake.*
Phila. 1852. . . . . *$225.00–$500.00*

Star Trek. Random House. 1977. 4 fan-folded pop-ups. . . . . *$40.00–$55.00*

Star Trek Technical Manual. 1975. 1st ed. . . . . *$20.00–$35.00*

Stark, Francis R. *Abolition of Privateering and the Declaration of Paris.* NY. 1897.
. . . . *$30.00–$50.00*

Starkie, Walter. *Scholars and Gypsies.* Berkeley. Univ Calif Press. [1963].
1st Amer ed. sgn, dj. . . . . *$25.00–$30.00*

Stathan, J. C. B. *Through Angola: A Coming Colony.* Edin. William Blackwood.
1922. 1st ed. illus. photos, plates, 2 fldg maps. . . . . *$50.00–$80.00*

Stawell, Mrs. Randolph. *Fabre's Book of Insects.* Lon. Hodder & Stoughton. (1921).
1st ed. illus. clr plates. . . . . *$250.00–$300.00*

Steamboats of Lake George 1817–1832. Albany. 1932. illus. 174 pp, maps, photos . .
. . . . *$500.00–$700.00*

Stearns, Samuel. *American Herbal....* Walpole, MA. 1801. 1st Amer ed. lea. . . . . .
. . . . *$1,000.00–$2,000.00*

Steele, Chester K. *Gold Course Mystery.* NY. George Sully. (1919). 1st ed. illus. . .
. . . . *$35.00–$45.00*

Steele, Matthew Forney. *American Campaigns.* DC. 1909. 2 vols. 1st ed. . . . .
. . . . *$85.00–$125.00*

Stefansson, Vilhjalmu. *Farthest North.* NY/Lon. Harper. 1897. 2 vols. illus. 16 clr plates, 4 fldg maps in pocket. . . . . *$60.00–$90.00*

Stefansson, Vilhjalmur. *Adventure of Wrangle Island.* NY. 1925. 1st ed. illus. fldg clr map, sgn. . . . . *$75.00–$100.00*

Stefansson, Vilhjalmur. *Arctic Manual.* NY. 1944. 1st ed. . . . . . . *$28.00–$100.00*

Stefansson, Vilhjalmur. *Fat of the Land.* NY. 1956. 1st ed. sgn. . . . *$35.00–$45.00*

Stefansson, Vilhjalmur. *Friendly Arctic.* Macmillan. 1944. . . . . . . *$20.00–$25.00*

Stefansson, Vilhjalmur. *My Life With the Eskimo.* NY. 1921. maps, inscr, rprnt. . . . . *$40.00–$60.00*

Stefansson, Vilhjalmur. *Not By Bread Alone.* 1946. 1st ed. . . . . . . *$25.00–$30.00*

Stegner, Wallace. *All the Little Live Things.* NY. 1967. 1st ed. dj. . . *$35.00–$45.00*

Stegner, Wallace. *Beyond the Hundredth Meridian.* Bos. Houghton & Mifflin. 1954. dj. . . . . *$60.00–$85.00*

Stegner, Wallace. *Big Rock Candy Mountain.* NY. Duell, Sloan & Pearce. (1943). 1st ed. deep red cl, dj. . . . . *$675.00–$1,000.00*

Stegner, Wallace. *Crossing to Safety.* Random House. (1987). 1st ed. dj. . . . . *$25.00–$35.00*

Stegner, Wallace. *Discovery! The Search for Arabian Oil.* Middle East Export Press. (1971). 1st ed. wrps. map endpapers, scarce 1st issue. . . . . *$50.00–$60.00*

Steichen, Edward. *Life In Photography.* Garden City. Doubleday. 1963. 1st ed. illus. photos.. . . . . *$50.00–$80.00*

Steig, William. *The Amazing Bone.* Farrar Straus & Giroux. 1976. dj. . . . . *$15.00–$30.00*

Stein, Gertrude. *An Elucidation.* np. Transition. 1927. 1st separate ed. printed wrps. . . . . *$200.00–$300.00*

Stein, Gertrude. *Autobiography of Alice B. Toklas.* NY. Harcourt Brace. 1933. 1st ed. dj. . . . . *$350.00–$400.00*

Stein, Gertrude. *Four in America.* New Haven. 1947. 1st ed. dj. . . *$45.00–$75.00*

Stein, Gertrude. *Lectures in America.* NY. Random House. (1935). 1st ed. dj. . . . . *$75.00–$200.00*

Stein, Gertrude. *Wars I Have Seen.* NY. Random House. (1945). 1st ed. dj. . . . . *$35.00–$45.00*

Stein, Gertrude. *World is Round.* Lon. 1939. dj. . . . . *$20.00–$30.00*

Steinbeck, John. *Burning Bright.* NY. Viking. 1950. 1st ed. dj.... *$80.00–$120.00*

Steinbeck, John. *Cup of Gold.* NY. Robert McBride. 1929. 1st ed. first issue of author's first book, yellow cl, teg, dj, scarce.............. *$600.00–$3,500.00*

Steinbeck, John. *Grapes of Wrath.* Viking Press. (1939). 1st ed. first issue, dj. .... *$750.00–$3,000.00*

Steinbeck, John. *Letters to Elizabeth.* SF. Book Club of California. 1978. ltd 500 cc. dj. .... *$70.00–$100.00*

Steinbeck, John. *Log From the Sea of Cortez.* NY. dj......... *$100.00–$200.00*

Steinbeck, John. *Moon is Down.* NY. Viking. 1942. 1st ed. dj.... *$50.00–$100.00*

Steinbeck, John. *Of Mice and Men.* Covici Friede. 1937. 1st issue, dj. .... *$550.00–$1,000.00*

Steinbeck, John. *Red Pony.* NY. (1945). illus. dj. .... *$50.00–$150.00*

Steinbeck, John. *Sweet Thursday.* NY. Viking. 1954. 1st ed. dj. .. *$85.00–$125.00*

Steinbeck, John. *The Pearl.* NY. Viking. 1947. 1st ed. illus. dj.... *$80.00–$140.00*

Steinbeck, John. *Travels with Charley in Search of America.* NY. Viking. (1962). 1st ed. dj.. *$70.00–$125.00*

Steinbeck, John. *Wayward Bus.* NY. Viking. 1947. 1st ed. dj...... *$40.00–$75.00*

Steinbeck, John. *Winter of Our Discontent.* NY. (1961). 1st ed. dj.. *$45.00–$70.00*

Steinbeck, John & Edward F. Ricketts. *Sea of Cortez.* NY. Viking Press. 1941. 1st ed. dj.. *$100.00–$150.00*

Steiner, Jesse Frederick & Roy M. Brown. *North Carolina Chain Gang....* Chapel Hill. 1927. 1st ed. .... *$100.00–$150.00*

Steiner, Stan. *Last Horse.* NY. Macmillan. 1961. 1st ed. illus. b/w & clr, dj. .... *$25.00–$30.00*

Steinmetz, Andrew. *Sunshine and Showers:Their Influence Throughout Creation: A Compendium of Popular Meteorology.* Lon. 1867. 432 pp........ *$95.00–$150.00*

Stejneger, L. *Poisonous Snakes of North America.* DC. 1895. .... *$40.00–$60.00*

Stemons, James Samuel. *As Victim to Victims....* NY. Fortuny's. 1941. 1st ed. cl. .. .. *$40.00–$50.00*

Stephens, J. *Incidents of Travel in Yucatan.* NY. 1843. 2 vols. 1st ed. foldout plate, xlib.. *$60.00–$85.00*

Stephens, James. *Crock of Gold.* Lon. 1912. 1st ed. dj........ *$125.00–$175.00*

Stephens, James. *Demi-Gods.* Lon. 1914. 1st ed. 1st issue. . . . . . . *$50.00–$75.00*

Stephenson, Neal. *Big U.* NY. Vintage. 1984. 1st ed. paperback scarce. . . . .
. . . . *$225.00–$400.00*

Sterling, Bruce. *Islands in the Net.* NY. Arbor House/William Morrow. (1988). 1st ed. dj. . . . . *$50.00–$100.00*

Sterling, George. *House of Orchids and Other Poems.* SF. Robertson. 1911. 1st ed. sgn, dj. . . . . *$85.00–$150.00*

Sterling, George. *Lilith.* SF. Robertson. 1919. 1st ed. ltd 300 cc. sgn. . . . .
. . . . *$35.00–$60.00*

Sterling, Sara Hawks. *Lady of King Arthur's Court.* Phila. Jacobs. 1907. 1st ed. illus. . . . . *$45.00–$80.00*

Stern, Richard Martin. *Bright Road to Fear.* NY. (1958). 1st ed. dj. . . . .
. . . . *$65.00–$100.00*

Stern, Richard Martin. *High Hazard.* NY. (1962). 1st ed. dj. . . . . . *$20.00–$30.00*

Stern, Richard Martin. *Search for Tabatha Carr.* NY. Scribner's. (1960). 1st ed. dj.
. . . . *$40.00–$75.00*

Sterne, Laurence. *Life and Opinions of Tristram Shandy, Gentleman.* Basil. Legrand. 1803. 2 vols. mor. . . . . *$50.00–$100.00*

Stetson, George R. *Southern Negro As He Is.* Bos. 1877. 1st ed. . . *$75.00–$100.00*

Stevens, Abel. *History of the Methodist Episcopal Church.* NY. 1868. 4 vols. . . . .
. . . . *$30.00–$45.00*

Stevens, Hazard. *Life of Isaac Ingalls Stevens.* Bos. 1900. 2 vols. 1st ed. illus. . .
. . . . *$50.00–$85.00*

Stevens, John L. and W. B. Oleson. *Picturesque Hawaii.* np. Edgewood Pub. blue pict cl. . . . . *$80.00–$100.00*

Stevens, Thomas. *Around the World on a Bicycle, vol.1.* NY. 1889. illus. . . . .
. . . . *$35.00–$50.00*

Stevenson, Robert Louis. *Black Arrow.* Scribner's. 1936. 1st ed. illus. by N. C. Wyeth. . . . . *$500.00–$650.00*

Stevenson, Robert Louis. *Across the Plains.* NY. Scribner's. 1892. 1st Amer ed cl.
. . . . *$75.00–$125.00*

Stevenson, Robert Louis. *Catriona.* Lon. Cassell. 1893. 1st ed. . . *$70.00–$90.00*

Stevenson, Robert Louis. *David Balfour.* Scribner's. 1924. illus. by N. C. Wyeth. .
. . . . *$20.00–$55.00*

Stevenson, Robert Louis. *Kidnapped.* NY. Scribner's Classic. 1913. illus. by N. C. Wyeth. . . . . *$30.00–$200.00*

Stevenson, Robert Louis. *Strange Case of Dr. Jekyll & Mr. Hyde.* NY. 1930. illus. 1st thus. . . . . *$50.00–$65.00*

Stevenson, Robert Louis. *Treasure Island.* Phila. 1930. illus. by Lyle Justis, No 1 of the Anderson Books. . . . . *$45.00–$150.00*

Stevenson, William G. *Thirteen Months in the Rebel Army.. by an Impressed New Yorker.* Lon. 1862. 1st UK ed. rbnd. . . . . *$75.00–$150.00*

Stewart, Elinore Pruitt. *Letters of a Woman Homesteader.* Bos. 1914. 1st ed. illus. by N. C Wyeth. . . . . *$25.00–$37.00*

Stewart, Henry. *Shepherd's Manual.* NY. 1876. illus. . . . . *$27.00–$35.00*

Stewart, John J. *Mormonism and the Negro.* Utah. Community Press. 1963. 3rd ed cl. . . . . *$12.00–$65.00*

Stickley, Gustav. *Craftsman Homes.* NY. 1909. 1st ed. . . . . *$125.00–$250.00*

Stieglitz, Alfred. *Georgia O'Keeffe: a Portrait.* NY. MOMA. 1st ed. illus. dj, slipcase. . . . . *$50.00–$80.00*

Stiles, Henry Reed, M.D. *Bundling, Its Origin, Progress and Decline in America.* Albany. 1869. 1st ed. 139 pp. . . . . *$85.00–$100.00*

Still, A. T. *Autobiography of Andrew T Still.* Kirksville, MO. 1908. illus. 2nd ed. revised, 404 pp. . . . . *$85.00–$145.00*

Stimson, F. J. *My Story.* NY. Scribner's 1917. 1st ed. 3 plates. . . . . *$45.00–$60.00*

Stockham, Alice. *Tokology. A Book for Every Woman.* Chi. Sanitary Pub. 1883. 1st ed. seventh thousand, 277 pp. . . . . *$75.00–$125.00*

Stockham, Alice B. *Tokology.* Chi. 1907. rprnt. . . . . *$30.00–$45.00*

Stocking, Amer Mills. *Saukie Indians and Their Great Chiefs Black Hawk and Keokuk.* Rock Island. Vaile. 1926. illus. red cl, gold lettering. . . . . . *$50.00–$75.00*

Stockley, C. H. *Arican Camera Hunts.* Lon. Country Life, Ltd. (1948). 1st ed. illus. photos. . . . . *$80.00–$100.00*

Stockman, David A. *Triumph of Politics, Why the Reagan Revolution Failed.* 422 pp, photos, dj. . . . . *$10.00–$30.00*

Stockton, Frank. *Pomonas Travels.* Scribner's. 1894. illus. . . . . . . *$50.00–$65.00*

Stockton, Frank R. *Girl at Cobhurst.* NY. 1898. 1st ed. . . . . *$45.00–$50.00*

Stoddard, Herbert. *Bobwhite Quail.* NY. Scribner's. 1932. illus. . . *$50.00–$75.00*

Stoddard, John L. *Stoddard's Lectures.* Balch Bros. 1897. 10 vols. . . . .
. . . . *$150.00–$200.00*

Stoddard, Lothrop. *Rising Tide of Color.* Blue Ribbon Books. (1920). brown cl, dj.
. . . . *$20.00–$50.00*

Stoddard, Solomon. *Guide to Christ..* NY. 1813. small lea. . . . . . . *$30.00–$40.00*

Stoker, Bram. *Dracula.* NY. Grosset & Dunlap. (1931). illus. from the Universal
picture, Photo-play ed. dj. . . . . *$60.00–$125.00*

Stoker, Bram. *Dracula's Guest and Other Weird Stories.* Lon. 1914. rprnt. . . . . . .
. . . . *$35.00–$45.00*

Stoker, Bram. *Jewel of the Seven Stars.* NY. Harper. 1904. 1st Amer ed. . . . .
. . . . *$75.00–$175.00*

Stoker, Bram. *Mystery of the Sea.* NY. Harper. 1904. 1st ed. . . . . *$75.00–$100.00*

Stoker, Bram. *Personal Reminiscences of Henry Irving.* NY. 1906. 2 vols. 1st Amer
ed. illus.. . . . . *$75.00–$125.00*

Stoker, Bram. *Under the Sunset.* Lon. Sampson, Low, Marston. 1882. 1st ed.
author's first book. . . . . *$75.00–$200.00*

Stone, I. F. *Haunted 50s.* NY. 1963. 1st ed. dj. . . . . *$30.00–$40.00*

Stone, I. F. *Hidden History of the Korean War.* NY. Monthly Review Press. (1952).
1st ed. . . . . *$20.00–$35.00*

Stoney, S. G. *Plantations of the Carolina Low Country.* Charleston. 1938. 1st ed. dj,
slipcase.. . . . . *$85.00–$165.00*

Stoppard, Tom. *Arcadia.* Lon/Bos. Faber & Faber. (1993). 1st ed. . *$60.00–$75.00*

Stories by American Authors. NY. Scribner's. 1896. 10 vols. red cl. *$45.00–$55.00*

Stories from the Old Testament. NY. Winston. 1938. illus. in clr by Maud and Miska
Petersham.. . . . . *$25.00–$30.00*

Story of Dark Plot or Tyranny on the Frontier. Warren Press. 1903. . . . .
. . . . *$15.00–$35.00*

Story of King Arthur and His Knights. Scribner's. 1903. 1st ed. illus. by Howard
Pyle. . . . . *$85.00–$115.00*

Story of the Fourth of July. NY. Kiggins & Kellogg. nd. wrps. illus. by Uncle Ned,
16 pp, 9 x 55 cm.. . . . . *$40.00–$25.00*

Story, A T. *Story of Wireless Telegraphy.* 1904. 1st ed. illus. . . . . . . *$45.00–$85.00*

Stout, Rex. *And Four To Go.* NY. Viking. 1958. 1st ed. dj. . . . . . . *$80.00–$125.00*

Stout, Rex. *Before Midnight.* NY. Viking. 1955. 1st ed. dj. . . . . . *$200.00–$275.00*

Stout, Rex. *Black Mountain.* NY. Viking. 1954. 1st ed. dj. . . . . . . *$95.00–$125.00*

Stout, Rex. *Black Orchids.* NY. Collier. 1942. . . . . *$75.00–$125.00*

Stout, Rex. *Death of a Doxy.* Viking. 1966. 1st ed. dj.. . . . . *$50.00–$125.00*

Stout, Rex. *Death of a Dude.* NY. Viking. 1969. 1st ed. dj. . . . . . *$100.00–$130.00*

Stout, Rex. *Double for Death.* NY. Farrar & Rinehart. 1939. 1st ed. no dj.. . . . .
. . . . *$85.00–$175.00*

Stout, Rex. *Family Affair.* Lon. (1975). 1st UK ed dj. . . . . *$35.00–$45.00*

Stout, Rex. *Father Hunt.* NY. Viking. 1968. 1st ed. dj. . . . . *$120.00–$150.00*

Stout, Rex. *Golden Spiders.* NY. Viking. 1953. 1st ed. dj.. . . . . . . *$95.00–$120.00*

Stout, Rex. *Might As Well Be Dead.* Collins. 1957. 1st UK ed. dj.. . *$40.00–$55.00*

Stout, Rex. *Mother Hunt.* NY. Viking. 1963. 1st ed. dj.. . . . . *$32.00–$40.00*

Stout, Rex. *Prisoner's Base.* NY. Viking. 1952. 1st ed. dj.. . . . . . . *$65.00–$125.00*

Stout, Rex. *Red Box.* NY. Farrar & Rinehart. 1937. 1st ed. no dj. *$125.00–$200.00*

Stout, Rex. *The Nero Wolfe Cook Book.* NY. Viking. 1973. 1st ed. dj. . . . .
. . . . *$100.00–$175.00*

Stout, Rex. *Three at Wolfe's Door.* 1960. 1st ed. dj. . . . . *$100.00–$135.00*

Stout, Rex. *Too Many Women.* NY. Viking. 1947. 1st ed. dj. . . . . . *$70.00–$200.00*

Stout, Rex. *Triple Jeopardy.* 1952. 1st ed. dj. . . . . *$20.00–$300.00*

Stowe, Harriet Beecher. *Dred, a Tale of the Great Dismal Swamp.* Bos. 1856. 2 vols.
1st ed.. . . . . *$40.00–$55.00*

Stowe, Harriet Beecher. *Key to Uncle Tom's Cabin.* Bos. 1853. 1st ed. . . . .
. . . . *$300.00–$600.00*

Stowe, Harriet Beecher. *Men of Our Times.* Hartford. Hartford Pub. 1868. 1st ed.
illus.. . . . . *$65.00–$150.00*

Stowe, Harriet Beecher. *Sunny Memories of Foreign Lands.* NY. 1854. 2 vols. illus.
. . . . *$200.00–$300.00*

Strachen, Arthur W. *Mauled by a Tiger.* Edin. 1933. 1st ed. illus. . *$35.00–$55.00*

Strachey, Lionel (trans). *Memoirs of an Arabian Princess.* NY. 1907. . . . .
. . . . *$95.00–$115.00*

Strand, Paul. *Retrospective.1915-1968.* large folio. . . . . *$90.00–$110.00*

Strange, Daniel. *Pioneer History of Eaton County, Michigan, 1833-1866..* 1923. 1st ed. illus. . . . . *$60.00–$85.00*

Stratton, E. M. (ed.). *New York Coach-makers Magazine.* NY. Stratton. 1861. vol. 3. illus. 46 clr plates. . . . . *$150.00–$175.00*

Street, Julian. *Abroad at Home.* NY. Century. 1916. illus. . . . . *$15.00–$30.00*

Striker, Fran. *Lone Ranger and the Silver Bullet.* 1948. 1st ed. dj. . .*$20.00–$35.00*

Striker, Fran. *Lone Ranger and the Gold Robbery.* NY. Grosset & Dunlap. 1939. Lone Ranger #3. . . . . *$18.00–$35.00*

Striker, Fran. *Lone Ranger and the Haunted Gulch.* NY. Grosset & Dunlap. 1941. 1st ed. Lone Ranger #6, dj. . . . . *$35.00–$47.00*

Striker, Fran. *Lone Ranger and the Mystery Ranch.* 1938. 1st ed. dj. . . . . *$25.00–$35.00*

Striker, Fran. *Lone Ranger on Powderhorn Trail.* 1949. 1st ed. dj.. *$20.00–$35.00*

Striker, Fran. *Lone Ranger Traps the Smugglers.* NY. Grosset & Dunlap. 1941. Lone Ranger #7. . . . . *$35.00–$45.00*

Stringer, Arthur. *The Shadow.* NY. Century. 1913. 1st ed. dj. . . . . . *$70.00–$90.00*

Strode, Hudson. *Jefferson Davis, Confederate President.* Harcourt. 1959. wrps. dj. . . . . *$20.00–$30.00*

Strode, Hudson. *Story of Bermuda.* NY. Smith & Haas. 1932. 1st ed. illus. dj. . . . . *$20.00–$30.00*

Strong, Anna Louise. *Children of Revolution..* Seattle. privately printed. 1926. wrps. 2nd print. sgn, scarce pamphlet.. . . . . *$50.00–$60.00*

Strong, Chas. J. & L. S. *Strong's Book of Designs.* Chi. Drake & Co. 1917. illus. oblong. . . . . *$100.00–$250.00*

Stuart, James. *Three Years in America.* NY. 1833. 2 vols. 1st Amer ed. . . . . *$50.00–$90.00*

Stuart, Jesse. *Kentucky Is My Land.* 1952. sgn, dj. . . . . *$50.00–$80.00*

Stuart, Jesse. *Man With a Bull-Tongue Plow.* NY. 1934. 1st ed. sgn, dj.. . . . . *$270.00–$400.00*

Stuart, Jesse. *Ride With Huey the Engineer.* NY. (1966). 1st ed. illus. by Robert Henneberger. dj. . . . . *$50.00–$100.00*

Stuart, Jesse. *Taps for Private Tussie.* NY. Dutton. 1943. 1st ed. dj. *$50.00–$90.00*

Stuart, Moses. *Grammar of the Hebrew Language.* Andover, MA. Gould and Newman. 1838. 6th ed. calf-backed bds. . . . . *$85.00–$125.00*

Studley, Mary. *What Our Girls Ought to Know*. NY. 1878. . . . . . . *$20.00–$25.00*

Sturgeon, Theodore. *More Than Human*. NY. 1953. 1st ed. dj.. . *$100.00–$150.00*

Sturgeon, Theodore. *Sturgeon in Orbit*. Lon. 1970. 1st Brit ed. dj. . . . .
. . . . *$150.00–$200.00*

Sturgeon, Theodore. *Without Sorcery*. np (Phila). Prime Press. 1948. 355 pp, dj. . .
. . . . *$60.00–$200.00*

Styron, William. *Confessions of Nat Turner*. NY. Random House. (1967). 1st ed.
sgn, dj.. . . . . *$75.00–$150.00*

Styron, William. *Confessions of Nat Turner*. NY. Random House. (1967). 1st ed. dj.
. . . . *$40.00–$75.00*

Styron, William. *Lie Down in Darkness*. Ind. Bobbs-Merrill. 1951. 1st ed. author's
first book, dj. . . . . *$120.00–$150.00*

Styron, William. *Set This House on Fire*. NY. Random House. (1960). 1st ed. dj. . .
. . . . *$40.00–$60.00*

Styron, William. *Set This House on Fire*. Lon. Hamish Hamilton. (1961). 1st UK dj.
. . . . *$40.00–$75.00*

Styron, William. *Sophie's Choice*. Random House. 1979. 1st ed. sgn, dj. . . . .
. . . . *$60.00–$75.00*

Suckow, Ruth. *Bonney Family*. NY. 1928. 1st ed. ltd 95 cc, sgn, dj. *$35.00–$40.00*

Sue, Eugene. *Wandering Jew*. Lon. 1844-1845. 1st ed. . . . . *$275.00–$315.00*

Summer, Montague. *Vampire in Europe*. NY. Dutton. 1929. 1st US ed.. . . . .
. . . . *$35.00–$45.00*

Summers, Montague. *History of Witchcraft & Demonology*. Lon. 1973. rprnt of
1926 ed. dj.. . . . . *$8.00–$12.00*

Sumner, Charles. *White Slavery in the Barbary States*. Bos. John P. Jewett. 1853. 1st
ed. illus. wood engr.. . . . . *$80.00–$120.00*

Sun Chief. *Autobiography of a Hopi Indian*. Yale. 1942. 1st ed. illus. 459 pp. . . . . .
. . . . *$28.00–$35.00*

Sunday School Almanac. NY. Carlton & Philips. (1854). wrps. illus. 32 pp, 112 x 73
cm. . . . . *$20.00–$35.00*

Supplement. Wholesale and Retail Catalogue of Military Goods. NY. Francis
Bannerman. 1905. pict wrps, 42 pp, illus. *$40.00–$50.00*

Surtees, R. S. *Hawbuck Grange*. Lon. nd. illus. . . . . *$50.00–$85.00*

Surtees, R. S. *Hunts with Jorrocks*. NY. 1908. illus. . . . . *$50.00–$85.00*

Susann, Jacqueline. *Every Night, Josephine!*. NY. 1963. 1st ed. dj, author's first book. . . . . *$150.00–$190.00*

Sutherland, C. H. V. *Gold: Its Beauty, Power, and Allure*. McGraw-Hill. 1969. 2nd ed. dj. . . . . *$25.00–$35.00*

Suthren, Victor. *In Perilous Seas*. NY. St. Martin's Press. (1983). 1st US ed dj. . . . . *$35.00–$50.00*

Sutton, Margaret. *Mysterious Half Cat*. NY. Grosset & Dunlap. 1936. Judy Bolton #9, dj. . . . . *$20.00–$35.00*

Sutton, Margaret. *Seven Strange Clues*. NY. Grosset & Dunlap. 1932. Judy Bolton #4, dj. . . . . *$20.00–$50.00*

Sutton, Margaret. *Summer on the Farm*. NY. Grosset & Dunlap. 1938. 1st ed. illus. pict dj. . . . . *$40.00–$65.00*

Sutton, Margaret. *The Yellow Phantom*. NY. Grosset & Dunlap. 1933. dj. . . . . *$30.00–$65.00*

Sutton, Margaret. *Trail of the Green Doll*. NY. Grosset & Dunlap. 1956. Judy Bolton #21, dj. . . . . *$25.00–$35.00*

Sutton, Margaret. *Vanishing Shadow*. NY. Grosset & Dunlap. rprnt, Judy Bolton #1, dj. . . . . *$10.00–$15.00*

Sutton, Richard & Emmy Lou Sutton. *An Arctic Safari. With Camera & Rifle.*. St Louis. C V Mosby. 1932. 1st ed. sgn & inscr by author, 100 photos, dj. . . . . *$75.00–$90.00*

Swanton, John. *Indian Tribes of North America*. DC. GPO. 1953. 726 pp, fldg maps. . . . . *$45.00–$65.00*

Swanton, John. *Indian Tribes of the Lower Mississippi Valley.*. DC. 1911. . . . . *$45.00–$60.00*

Sweeney, Robert L. *Frank Lloyd Wright: An Annotated Bibliography*. LA. 1978. dj. . . . . *$35.00–$75.00*

Sweet, Frederick A. *Miss Mary Cassatt*. Norman. (1966). 1st ed. illus. photos col and b/w sgn dj. . . . . *$30.00–$45.00*

Swift, Jonathan. *Gulliver's Travels*. Lon. Ernest Lister. illus. col plates by Jackson. . . . . *$75.00–$125.00*

Swinburne, Algernon. *Bothwell: A Tragedy*. Lon. Chatto & Windus. 1874. 1st ed. . . . . *$50.00–$85.00*

Swinburne, Algernon. *Chastelard: A Tragedy*. Lon. Edward Moxon. 1865. 1st ed. . . . . *$125.00–$165.00*

Swinburne, Algernon Charles. *Century of Roundels and Other Poems.* NY. 1883. 1st Amer ed. dj. . . . . *$40.00–$45.00*

Swinburne, Algernon Charles. *Erechtheus.* Lon. 1876. . . . . *$40.00–$55.00*

Swinburne, Algernon Charles. *Ode on the Proclamation of the French Republic, September 4th, 1879.* Lon. Ellis. 1870. 1st ed. wrps. . . . . *$80.00–$100.00*

Swinburne, Algernon Charles. *Springtide of Life.* Lon. Heinemann. (1918). 1st ed. illus. by Arthur Rackham. ltd 765 cc, sgn by Rackham. . . . . *$800.00–$900.00*

Swinton, George. *Sculpture of the Eskimo.* Tor. McClelland & Stewart. (1972). 1st ed. illus. . . . . *$50.00–$80.00*

Swope, John. *Camera Over Hollywood.* NY. 1939. illus. dj. . . . . . *$95.00–$125.00*

Sylva, Carmen. *Pelefch-Marchen.* Bonn. 1886. author pseudonym for Elizabeth, Queen of Roumania, red cl, gold lettering. . . . . *$25.00–$35.00*

Sylvester, Herbert Milton. *Homestead Highways.* Bos. Ticknor. 1888. 1st ed. teg. . . . . *$25.00–$30.00*

Synge, John M. *Poems and Translations.* Churchtown. Cuala Press. 1909. 1st ed. ltd 250 cc. . . . . *$200.00–$250.00*

Szyk, Arthur. *Haggadah.* Jerusalem. 1956. 1st ed. mor, boxed. . . *$145.00–$225.00*

Szyk, Arthur. *New Order.* NY. 1941. dj. . . . . *$125.00–$200.00*

20 Years, Evergood. NY. ACA Gallery. 1946. illus. ltd 150 cc, sgn, numbered, 108 pp. . . . . *$400.00–$475.00*

Taber, Gladys. *Amber A Very Personal Cat.* Phila. Lippincott. 1970. 1st ed. illus. dj. . . . . *$20.00–$45.00*

Taber, Gladys. *Daisy and Dobbin: Two Little Seahorses.* Phila. 1948. illus. . . . . *$18.00–$25.00*

Taber, Gladys. *Especially Spaniels.* Macrae-Smith. 1945. illus. 4th prntg, photos, dj. . . . . *$10.00–$15.00*

Taber, Gladys. *First Book of Cats.* Franklin Watts. 1950. illus. . . . *$20.00–$35.00*

Taber, Gladys. *First Book of Dogs.* NY. 1949. dj. . . . . *$25.00–$45.00*

Taber, Gladys. *Harvest of Yesterdays.* 1976. 1st ed. dj. . . . . *$10.00–$15.00*

Taber, Gladys. *Mrs. Daffodil.* Phila. Lippincott. 1957. 1st ed. dj. . . *$45.00–$60.00*

Taber, Gladys. *Reveries at Stillmeadow.* 1970. 1st ed. dj. . . . . *$22.00–$30.00*

Taber, Gladys. *Stillmeadow Cook Book.* Lippincott. 1965. 1st ed. dj. . . . . *$25.00–$50.00*

Taber, Gladys. *What Cooks at Stillmeadow.* Phila. 1958. 1st ed. dj. *$45.00–$60.00*

Taber, Grace. *Stillmeadow Kitchen.* MacRae Smith. 1951. illus. enlarged ed. . . . . *$50.00–$85.00*

Tabor, Grace. *One Dozen and One.* Phila. Lippincott. 1966. 1st ed. dj. . . . . *$15.00–$45.00*

Taft, J. A. *Practical Treatise on Operative Dentistry.* Phila. 1868. calf. . . . . *$37.00–$45.00*

Tait, L. *Diseases of Women.* NY. 1879. . . . . *$40.00–$50.00*

Talbot, Eleanor W. *My Lady's Casket of jewels and Flowers..* Bos. Lee & Shepard. 1885. 1st ed. illus. aeg. . . . . *$50.00–$100.00*

Talbot, Ethelbert. *My People of the Plains.* NY. 1906. illus. photos, teg. . . . . *$28.00–$40.00*

Talbot, Ethelbert. *My People of the Plains.* NY. 1906. 1st ed. . . . . *$52.00–$65.00*

Talbot, F. A. *Aeroplanes and Dirigibles of the War.* Phila. 1915. 1st Amer ed. illus. . . . . *$30.00–$40.00*

Tallent, Annie D. *Black Hills: or the Last Hunting Ground of the Dakotas.* Sioux Falls. Brevet Press. 1974. 2nd ed. dj. . . . . *$25.00–$48.00*

Talmage, James E. *Vitality of Mormonism.* Bos. 1919. 1st ed. sgn by President George Albert Smith, rare. . . . . *$180.00–$200.00*

Tan, Amy. *Joy Luck Club.* NY. Putnam's. (1989). 1st ed. author's first book, dj.. . . . . *$100.00–$200.00*

Tan, Amy. *Kitchen God's Wife.* NY. Putnam. 1991. 1st ed. sgn, dj. . .*$50.00–$100.00*

Tanner, Henry S. *Massachusetts and Rhode Island.* Phila. 1833. clr, fldg map in lea folder. *$800.00–*

Tanner, Z. L. *Deep-Sea Exploration.* DC. GPO. 1896. illus. drawings, fldg plates. . . . . *$50.00–$85.00*

Tappan, David. *Lectures on Jewish Antiquities.* Bos. Hilliard and Lincoln. 1807. 1st ed. . . . . *$95.00–$175.00*

Tarbel, Ida. *Business of Being a Woman.* NY. 1919. rprnt. . . . . *$25.00–$35.00*

Tarbell, Ida M. *In the Footsteps of the Lincolns.* NY. 1924. illus. . *$30.00–$40.00*

Tarbell, Ida M. *Life of Abraham Lincoln.* 1924. 4 vols. the Sangamon ed. . . . . *$60.00–$75.00*

Tarbell, Ida M. *Life of Abraham Lincoln.* NY. 1903. 5 vols. . . . . . *$45.00–$80.00*

Targ, W. *Bibliophile in the Nursery.* Cleve. 1957. 1st ed. dj. . . . . . . *$25.00–$35.00*

Tarkington, Booth. *Fascinating Stranger.* NY. Doubleday, Page. 1923. 1st trade ed. dj. . . . . *$60.00–$80.00*

Tarkington, Booth. *Gentle Julia.* Doubleday, Page. 1922. . . . . *$30.00–$40.00*

Tartt, Donna. *Secret History.* NY. Knopf. 1992. 1st ed. dj. . . . . *$50.00–$75.00*

Tasso, Torquato. *Jerusalem Delivered, an Heroic Poem.* Lon. Mawman. 1818. 2 vols. trans. by J. H. Hunt. . . . . *$55.00–$80.00*

Tate, Allen. *The Fathers.* Putnam. (1938). 1st ed. dj. . . . . *$110.00–$140.00*

Tatham, Julie. *Clinic Nurse.* NY. Grosset & Dunlap. 1952. Cherry Ames #13, dj. . . . . *$14.00–$25.00*

Tatham, Julie. *Night Supervisor.* NY. Grosset & Dunlap. 1950. Cherry Ames #11. . . . . *$10.00–$14.00*

Taton, Rene. *General History of the Sciences.* Lon. Thames and Hudson. 1965-66. 3 vols. . . . . *$150.00–$300.00*

Taverner, Eric. *Trout Fishing From All Angles.* Lon. Seeley, Service & Co. 1929. 1st ed. illus. . . . . *$25.00–$60.00*

Taverner, P. A. *Birds of Canada.* 1934. illus. . . . . *$35.00–$40.00*

Taverner, P. A. *Birds of Eastern Canada.* Canada Dept of Mines. 1922. . . . . *$20.00–$25.00*

Tax, Sol (ed.). *Evolution After Darwin.* Chi. Univ of Chi Press. 1960. 1st ed. dj. . . . . *$45.00–$60.00*

Taylor, Edward B. *Primitive Culture: Researches into the Development of Mythology, Philosophy, Religion, Language, Art and Custom.* Lon. John Murray. 1891. 2 vols. 3rd rev ed. dark burgundy cl. . . . . *$100.00–$150.00*

Taylor, Griffith. *With Scott: the Silver Lining.* Lon. 1916. 1st ed. illus. maps. . . . . *$450.00–$0.00*

Taylor, Henry Dixon. *Church Welfare Plan.* np. 1984. illus. inscr. . *$60.00–$75.00*

Taylor, J. *Lives of Virginia Baptist Ministers.* Richmond. 1838. 2nd ed. lea. . . . . *$35.00–$45.00*

Taylor, John L. *Memoir of His Honor Samuel Phillips, LL.D.* Bos. 1856. 1st ed. illus. . . . . *$30.00–$75.00*

Taylor, Peter. *Happy Families are All Alike.* NY. McDowell and Obolensky. (1959). 1st ed. dj. . . . . *$80.00–$125.00*

Taylor, Peter. *Old Forest.* NY. 1985. 1st ed. dj. . . . . *$30.00–$75.00*

Taylor, Peter. *Summons to Memphis.* NY. Knopf. 1986. 1st ed. dj. . *$22.00–$60.00*

Telephone Appeals -1887. 1887. 1st ed. softcvr. . . . . *$125.00–$165.00*

Telephone Catalogue and Students' Manual for the Practical Instruction of Learners of Telegraphy... NY. J H Bunnell & Co. 1900. illus. printed wrps, 112 pp. . . . . *$40.00–$50.00*

Telescopes for Town and Country. Rochester, NY. Bausch & Lomb Optical Co. 1928. pict wrps, illus, 16 pp. . . . . *$40.00–$50.00*

Tell It All: The Story of a Life's Experience in Mormonism. Hartford. 1874. . . . . *$25.00–$35.00*

Teller, Daniel W. *History of Ridgefield, Ct.* Danbury. 1878. illus. 3/4 mor. . . . . *$50.00–$75.00*

Tennien, Mark. *Chungking Listening Post.* NY. Creative Age Press. 1945. 1st ed. illus. red cl, map endpapers dj. . . . . *$12.00–$20.00*

Tennyson, Alfred. *Harold: A Drama.* Lon. Henry S King. 1877. 1st ed. . . . . *$25.00–$50.00*

Tennyson, Alfred. *Ode on the Death of Wellington.* Lon. Edward Moxon. 1853. printed wrps. . . . . *$35.00–$100.00*

Tennyson, Alfred. *Passing of Arthur.* Lon. Macmillan. 1884. 1st ed. printed wrps. . . . . *$200.00–$300.00*

Tennyson, Alfred Lord. *Tiresias and Other Poems.* Lon. 1885. 1st ed. 12mo. . . . . *$60.00–$80.00*

Terhune, Albert Payson. *The Heart of a Dog.* Garden City. 1924. illus. by Kirmse. . . . . *$15.00–$30.00*

Terkel, Studs. *Division Street: America.* Pantheon. 1967. 1st ed. dj. . *$28.00–$35.00*

Terkel, Studs. *Working.* Pantheon. 1974. 1st ed. dj. . . . . *$25.00–$30.00*

Terrell, John Upton. *War for the Colorado River.* CA. Arthur H. Clark Co. 1965. 2 vols. 1st ed. dj. . . . . *$110.00–$125.00*

Terrell, Mary Church. *A Colored Woman in a White World.* DC. National Association of Colored Women's Clubs. 1968. 1st ed. wrps. . . . . . . *$25.00–$35.00*

Terry, Adrian. *Travels in the Equatorial Regions of South America in 1832.* Hartford. 1832. 1st ed. 290 pp. . . . . *$100.00–$150.00*

Terry, Ellen. *Story of My Life.* NY. 1908. . . . . *$20.00–$35.00*

Terry, Ellen. *Story of My Life.* Lon. 1908. illus. ltd 1,000 cc, plates, teg, sgn. . . . . *$125.00–$150.00*

Tesla, Nikola. *Experiments with Alternate Currents of High Potential and High Frequency.* NY. 1896. illus. . . . . *$125.00–$200.00*

Tesla, Nikola. *Lectures, Patents, Articles Published by Nikola Tesla Museum.* CA. 1973. rprnt, illus, wrps. . . . . *$75.00–$100.00*

Tey, Josephine. *The Singing Sands.* Lon. Davies. 1957. 1st ed. dj. . *$200.00–$275.00*

Tey, Josephine. *To Love and Be Wise.* Lon. Davies. 1950. 1st ed. dj. . . . . *$150.00–$180.00*

Thacher, J. *American Revolution.* Hartford. 1861. illus. . . . . *$37.00–$55.00*

Thacher, James. *History of Plymouth Mass.* Bos. 1832. map. . . . . *$75.00–$200.00*

Thatcher, James, M. D. *History of the Town of Plymouth, From Its First Settlement* .. Bos. 1835. illus. in 1620 to the Present Time Map. . . . . *$175.00–$200.00*

Thayer, Tiffany. *Doctor Arnold.* (NY). Julian Messner. 1934. 1st ed. . . . . *$30.00–$45.00*

Thayer, William. *Marvels of the New West.* Norwich. 1889. . . . . . *$50.00–$75.00*

The Allen Press Bibliography: A Facsimile with Original Leaves and Additions to Date Including a Checklist of Ephemera. SF. Book Club of CA. (1985). 2nd ed. illus. ltd 750 cc. tip-in samples, brown cl. . . . . *$175.00–$300.00*

The Century of Queens. NY. Miller. 1872. steel engr pl, mor, embossed and blind tooled, aeg. . . . . *$75.00–$125.00*

The Compact Edition of the Oxford English Dictionary. NY. Oxford University. (1973). 2 vols. cl, slipcase.. . . . . *$50.00–$85.00*

The Coquet-Dale Fishing Songs. Edin. William Blackwood. 1852. 1st ed. marbled endpapers, teg.. . . . . *$75.00–$200.00*

The Encyclopoedia of Sport. Lon. Lawrence & Bullen. 1897-98. 1st ed. illus. aeg. . . . . *$50.00–$250.00*

The Gift: A Christmas, New Year and Birthday Present. Phila. Carey & Hart. 1845. 1st ed. first issue, illus,. . . . . *$200.00–$275.00*

The Gloucester Directory, 1899-1900. Gloucester, MA. Sampson, Murdock & Co. 1899. illus. map, clr litho, bds.. . . . . *$10.00–$35.00*

The Holy Bible. A. J. Holman & Co. 1880. illus. lea. records of Norbert Family, Burlington, VT. . . . . *$130.00–$150.00*

The Roycroft Books. A Catalogue and Some Remarks. 1902. gray wrps. . . . . *$40.00–$50.00*

The Southern Workman. VA. Hampton Institute. 1910. wrps. vol. XXXIX, No. 1-5, Jan-May, 320 pp.. . . . . *$50.00–$100.00*

The Works of Sir William Temple Bar. Lon. 1720. 2 vols. . . . . . *$260.00–$300.00*

Theory of the Universe. NY. 1868. . . . . *$50.00–$65.00*

Theroux, Paul. *Black House.* Houghton Mifflin. 1974. 1st ed. dj. . . *$30.00–$35.00*

Theroux, Paul. *London Embassy.* Bos. Houghton Mifflin. 1983. 1st Amer ed. dj. . . . . *$25.00–$32.00*

Theroux, Paul. *Mosquito Coast.* Houghton Mifflin. 1982. 1st ed. dj.*$20.00–$35.00*

Theroux, Paul. *O Zone.* Lon. Hamish Hamilton. (1986). 1st ed. sgn, dj. . . . . *$40.00–$50.00*

Theroux, Paul. *Saint Jack.* Bos. 1973. 1st ed. dj, sgn. . . . . *$50.00–$100.00*

Thimm, Carl A. *A Complete Biography of Fencing and Duelling.* Lon. Bodley head. 1896. 1st ed. illus. large paper copy. . . . . *$300.00–$475.00*

Third Annual Report of the Geological Survey of Texas. Austin TX. wrps. . . . . *$24.00–$50.00*

Third Marine Division. DC. 1948. 1st ed. . . . . *$42.00–$50.00*

Thirkell, Angela. *High Rising and Wild Strawberries.* NY. 1951. 2 vols. 1st ed. djs. . . . . *$25.00–$40.00*

Thirkell, Angela. *Love at All Ages.* NY. 1959. 1st US ed. . . . . *$18.00–$22.50*

This is Japan. Asahl Shimbun. 1958. illus. slipcase, dj. . . . . *$40.00–$65.00*

Thomas, Dylan. *Adventures in the Skin Trade.* Lon. Putnam. (1955). 1st ed. dj. . . . . *$75.00–$350.00*

Thomas, Dylan. *Beach of Falesa.* NY. Stein and Day. 1963. 1st ed. dj. . . . . *$15.00–$30.00*

Thomas, Dylan. *Child's Christmas in Wales.* CT. New Directions. 1954. 1st ed. dj. . . . . *$50.00–$150.00*

Thomas, Dylan. *New Poems.* CT. New Directions. 1943. 1st ed. purple bds, dj. . . . . *$60.00–$100.00*

Thomas, Dylan. *Portrait of the Artist as a Young Dog.* Norfolk, CT. New Directions. (c1940). 1st Amer ed. dj. . . . . *$250.00–$300.00*

Thomas, Dylan. *Portrait of the Artist as a Young Dog.* CT. New Directions. 1940. 1st Amer ed. sgn. dj. . . . . *$850.00–$1,500.00*

Thomas, Dylan. *Prospect of the Sea.* Lon. Dent. (1955). 1st ed. dj. *$45.00–$60.00*

Thomas, Dylan. *Quite Early One Morning.* CT. New Directions. 1954. 1st Amer ed. dj. . . . . *$100.00–$160.00*

Thomas, Dylan. *Under Milk Wood.* New Directions. 1954. 1st ed. dj. . . . .
. . . . *$70.00–$400.00*

Thomas, Isaiah. *Holy Bible Containing the Old and New Testaments.* Worcester.
1800. . . . . *$120.00–$150.00*

Thomas, John J. *Farm Implements and Farm Machinery.* NY. Judd. 1869. enlarged
ed. illus.. . . . . *$85.00–$125.00*

Thomas, Katherine. *Women in Nazi Germany.* Lon. 1943. 1st ed. . *$25.00–$35.00*

Thomas, Lowell. *Old Gimlet Eye. The Adventures of Smedley D. Butler.* NY. 1933.
1st ed. sgn by author and Butler. . . . . *$125.00–$175.00*

Thomas, Lowell, Jr. *Out of This World.* NY. Greystone Press. (1950). 1st ed. illus. dj,
map endpapers. . . . . *$17.00–$25.00*

Thomas, Ross. *Spies, Thumbsuckers, etc.* Northridge. Lord John Press. 1989. 1st ed.
ltd 300 cc. sgn, dj. . . . . *$100.00–$150.00*

Thomas, Ross. *The Money Harvest.* NY. Morrow. 1975. 1st ed. dj. *$90.00–$120.00*

Thomas, Will. *God is for White Folks.* NY. 1947. 1st ed. dj. . . . . . . *$30.00–$50.00*

Thomas, William Hamilton. *American Negro.* NY. Macmillan. 1901. 1st ed. cl.. . . .
. . . . *$175.00–$250.00*

Thompson Seton, Ernest. *Ernest Thompson Seton's America.* NY. 1954. 1st ed.
1st prtg, dj. . . . . *$20.00–$35.00*

Thompson, D P. *History of the Town of Montpelier.* Montpelier. 1860. . . . .
. . . . *$30.00–$50.00*

Thompson, George. *Narrative of ... Attempting to Aid Some Slaves.* Hartford. 1854.
cl. . . . . *$75.00–$100.00*

Thompson, Hunter S. *Great Shark Hunt.* NY. Summit/Rolling Stone. 1979). 1st ed.
. . . . *$45.00–$75.00*

Thompson, Jim. *Nothing More Than Murder.* NY. Harper & Bros. (1949). 1st ed. .
. . . . *$25.00–$40.00*

Thompson, Laurence. *The Story of Scotland Yard.* Random House. 1952. 1st ed. dj.
. . . . *$15.00–$20.00*

Thompson, Lieut.-Col. R. R. *Fifty-Second (Lowland) Division.* Glasgow. Maclehose
Jackson. 1923. illus. frontis, blue cl, 11maps in back of book.. . . . *$150.00–$230.00*

Thompson, Margaret. *High Trails of Glacier National Park.* Caldwell. Caxton
Printers. 1936. 1st ed. illus. photos, map, cl, dj. . . . . *$80.00–$100.00*

Thompson, Ruth Plumly. *Hungry Tiger of Oz.* Reilly & Lee. 1926. illus. by J R Neill
pict green cvr. . . . . *$75.00–$225.00*

Thompson, Ruth Plumly. *Lost King of Oz.* Chi. (1925). illus. by John R Neill 12 clr plates. . . . .*$140.00–$250.00*

Thompson, Ruth Plumly. *Yellow Knight of Oz.* Chi. Reilly & Lee. 1930. illus. b/w brown cl. . . . .*$200.00–$400.00*

Thompson, W G. *Training-Schools for Nursing.* NY. Putnam. 1883. 1st ed. . . . .*$90.00–$150.00*

Thompson, Zadock. *Geography and Geology of Vermont.. State & County Outline Maps.* VT. 1848. illus. maps. . . . .*$50.00–$85.00*

Thompson, Zadock. *History of Vermont.* Burlington. 1842. illus. engr. . . . .*$75.00–$135.00*

Thomson, J. J. *Corpuscular Theory of Matter.* Lon. 1907. 1st ed. *$55.00–$100.00*

Thoreau, Henry David. *Cape Cod.* Bos. Ticknor & Fields. 1865. 1st ed. . . . .*$500.00–$700.00*

Thoreau, Henry David. *Men of Concord.* Bos. Houghton Mifflin. 1936. illus. by N. C. Wyeth, dj. . . . .*$45.00–$60.00*

Thoreau, Henry David. *Walden, or Life in the Woods.* Peter Pauper Press. illus. slipcase.. . . . .*$15.00–$35.00*

Thoreau, Henry David. *Walden.* Bos. 1854. 1st ed. . . . . *$1,600.00–$3,000.00*

Thorpe, T. E. *Dictionary of Applied Chemistry.* Lon. Longmans Green. 1898. 4th impression. . . . .*$15.00–$22.00*

Thrasher, Halsey. *Hunter & Trapper.* 1863. . . . .*$65.00–$100.00*

Three Bears. Wis. Whitman Pub. (1927). 1st ed. illus. linen-like finish. . . . .*$15.00–$30.00*

Thurber, James. *Fables For Our Time.* NY. 1940. 2nd issue. . . . . . *$25.00–$40.00*

Thurber, James. *Is Sex Necessary.* NY. 1929. author's first book.*$500.00–$700.00*

Thurber, James. *Wonderful O.* NY. Simon & Schuster. (1957). 1st ed. illus. col, dj. . . . .*$25.00–$50.00*

Thurston, Robert. *History of the Growth of the Steam-Engine.* NY. 1878. . . . .*$45.00–$60.00*

Tillotson, John. *Palestine, Egypt and Syria with the History of the Jews.* Phila. clr maps, illus. . . . .*$70.00–$85.00*

Tilman, H. W. *Ascent of Nanda Devi.* NY. Macmillan. 1937. 1st ed. photos, maps, dj. . . . .*$55.00–$75.00*

Tilton, Theodore. *Sexton's Tale.* NY. Sheldon. 1867. 1st ed. author's first book. . . .
. . . . *$35.00–$60.00*

Tjader, Richard. *Big Game of Africa.* NY. Appleton. 1910. 1 vol. 1st ed. map, plates.
. . . . *$225.00–$250.00*

Tocqueville, Alexis de. *Democracy in America.* NY. 1840. 2nd Amer ed. cl. . . . . . .
. . . . *$100.00–$250.00*

Tocqueville, Alexis de. *Democratie en Amerique.* 1849. 2 vols. . . *$50.00–$100.00*

Todd, W. E. C. *Birds of the Labrador Penninsula and Adjacent Areas.* Tor. 1963.
illus. . . . . *$50.00–$75.00*

Todd, W. E. C. *Birds of Western Pennsylvania.* Univ of Pitts. 1940. . . . .
. . . . *$70.00–$85.00*

Toffler, Alvin. *Future Shock.* NY. 1970. dj. . . . . *$15.00–$20.00*

Toklas, Alice B. *Alice B. Toklas Cook Book.* NY. Harper & Bros. 1954. 1st ed. illus.
. . . . *$85.00–$300.00*

Toler, Ernst. *Man and the Masses.* Garden City. 1924. 1st ed. 109 pp, photos. . . . . .
. . . . *$60.00–$75.00*

Tolkien, J. R. R. *Father Christmas Letters.* Bos. Houghton Mifflin. 1976. 1st ed. . . .
. . . . *$55.00–$80.00*

Tolkien, J. R. R. *Pictures.* Bos. Houghton Mifflin. 1979. 1st Amer ed. slipcase. . . . .
. . . . *$65.00–$80.00*

Tolkien, J. R. R. *Smith of Wooton Major.* Bos. Houghton, Mifflin. 1967. illus. by
Pauline Baynes, 1st Amer ed. dj. . . . . *$50.00–$75.00*

Tolkien, J. R. R. *The Hobbit.* Bos. Houghton Mifflin. (1968). green dec cvr. . . . . . .
. . . . *$70.00–$85.00*

Tolkien, J. R. R. *The Hobbitt.* Bos. 1966. illus. no dj. . . . . *$25.00–$50.00*

Tolkien, J. R. R. *The Silmarillion.* 1977. 1st ed. dj. . . . . *$45.00–$100.00*

Tolkien, J. R. R. *Tree and Leaf.* Bos. Houghton Mifflin. 1965. 1st Amer ed. 112 pp,
dj. . . . . *$50.00–$65.00*

Tollemache, Lord. *Croquet.* Lon. Stanley Paul. 1914. 1st ed. illus. plates, diagrams.
. . . . *$250.00–$850.00*

Tolley, Cyril. *Modern Golfer.* NY. 1924. illus. . . . . *$30.00–$50.00*

Tolstoi, Alexis. *Vampires: Stories of the Supernatural.* NY. 1969. 1st Eng language
ed. dj. . . . . *$40.00–$50.00*

Tomes, Robert. *Battles of America by Sea and Land.* NY. 1878. 3 vols. illus. . . . .
. . . . *$145.00–$175.00*

Tooker, William W. *Indian Place-Names on Long Island..* NY. 1911. . . . .
. . . . *$35.00–$40.00*

Tooley, R. V. *Maps and Map-makers.* Lon. B.T. Batsford. [1949]. 1st ed. illus. dj. .
. . . . *$25.00–$35.00*

Towne, H. R. *Treatise on Cranes.* Conn. 1883. . . . . *$40.00–$50.00*

Train, Arthur. *Mortmain.* NY. Appleton. 1907. 1st ed. . . . . *$30.00–$45.00*

Train, Arthur. *Page Mr. Tutt.* NY. Scribner's 1926. 1st ed. dj. . . . . . *$30.00–$35.00*

Train, Arthur. *Yankee Lawyer–The Autobiography of Ephraim Tutt.* NY. 1943.
1st ed. illus. dj. . . . . *$35.00–$50.00*

Travels in South Eastern Asia. NY. Sunday School Union. 1838. illus. . . . .
. . . . *$10.00–$20.00*

Traven, B. *March to Caobaland.* Lon. Robert Hale. 1961. 1st ed in Eng, dj. . . . . .
. . . . *$50.00–$115.00*

Traver, Robert. *Anatomy of a Fisherman.* McGraw Hill. 1964. 1st ed. dj. . . . .
. . . . *$125.00–$250.00*

Travers, P. C. *Maria Poppina..* NY. Harcourt Brace. 1968. 1st ed. illus. by Mary
Shepard dj. . . . . *$30.00–$50.00*

Treece, Henry. *Haunted Garden.* Lon. 1947. 1st ed. dj. . . . . *$30.00–$45.00*

Tremaine, Marie. *Bibliography of Canadian Imprints, 1751-1800.* Tor. 1952. . . .
. . . . *$90.00–$150.00*

Treves, Sir Frederick. *Land That is Desolate.* NY. Dutton. 1912. illus. 1st Amer ed.
. . . . *$30.00–$50.00*

Trevor, William. *Family Sins.* Viking. (1990). 1st Amer ed. dj. . . . . *$25.00–$35.00*

Trevor, William. *Old Boys.* NY. 1964. 1st ed. dj. . . . . *$85.00–$100.00*

Trial of Andrew Johnson, President of the U S. DC. GPO. 1868. 3 vols. . . . .
. . . . *$50.00–$100.00*

Trilling, Lionel. *Liberal Imagination.* NY. Viking. 1950. 1st ed. dj. *$25.00–$35.00*

Trilling, Lionel. *Middle of the Journey.* NY. 1947. 1st ed. sgn. . . . . *$45.00–$65.00*

Trimble, Harvey M. *History of the 93rd Regiment Illinois Volunteer Infantry.* Chi.
1898. illus. fldg map. . . . . *$125.00–$150.00*

Trip Around the World in an Automobile. McLoughlin Bros. 1907. wrps. illus. lithos.
.... *$50.00–$80.00*

Triscott, C. Pette. *Golf in Six Lessons.* Phila. nd. 1st ed. illus. .... *$30.00–$40.00*

Trollope, A. *West Indies and the Spanish Main.* NY. 1860. 1st Amer ed. ....
.... *$70.00–$90.00*

Trollope, Anthony. *Bertrams.* The Folio Society. 1993. .... *$40.00–$55.00*

Trollope, Anthony. *Can You Forgive Her.* Lon. 1864. 2 vols. 1st ed. illus. ....
.... *$135.00–$250.00*

Trollope, Anthony. *Chronicles of Barsetshire.* Bos. Lauriat. 1926. 6 vols. illus. ....
.... *$150.00–$175.00*

Trollope, Anthony. *Last Chronicle of Barset.* Lon. 1867. 2 vols in one. ....
.... *$110.00–$125.00*

Trollope, Anthony. *North America.* Phila. Lippincott. 1862. 2 vols in one. 1st Amer
ed. .... *$100.00–$200.00*

Trollope, Anthony. *Small House At Allington.* NY. Harper & Bros. 1864. 1st Amer
ed cl. .... *$100.00–$150.00*

Trollope, Anthony. *Vicar of Bullhampton.* NY. Harper. 1870. 1st Amer ed. ....
.... *$175.00–$225.00*

Trollope, Frances. *Life and Adventures of Jonathan Jefferson Whitlaw.* Lon. 1836. 3
vols. 15 engrs. .... *$250.00–$350.00*

Trotsky, Leon. *Stalin.* NY. Harper & Bros. 1941. 1st Amer ed. .... *$30.00–$50.00*

Trotter, William. *On the Rearing and Management of Poultry.* Lon. 1852. wrps. illus.
.... *$28.00–$35.00*

Trowbridge, Bertha Chadwick. *Old Houses of Connecticut.* New Haven. Yale Univ
1923. 1000 cc, sgn, teg. .... *$100.00–$150.00*

Trowbridge, J. T. *South: A Tour of Its Battlefields and Ruined Cities..* CT. 1866.
1st ed. illus. .... *$45.00–$55.00*

Trowbridge, J. T. *Vagabonds.* NY. Hurd & Houghton. 1869. 1st ed. illus. ....
.... *$60.00–$90.00*

Truman, Harry. *Memoirs by Harry S. Truman.* Garden City. 1955,1956. 2 vols. 1st
ed. sgn, dj. .... *$350.00–$380.00*

Truman, Margaret. *Harry S. Truman.* NY. 1973. photos. .... *$35.00–$45.00*

Truman, Margaret. *Murder in Georgetown.* NY. Arbor House. 1986. 1st ed. dj. ....
.... *$10.00–$27.00*

Truman, Margaret. *Murder in the CIA*. NY. Random House. 1987. 1st ed. dj. . . .
. . . . *$20.00–$25.00*

Truman, Margaret. *Murder in the Smithsonian*. 1983. 1st ed. dj. . . . .
. . . . *$10.00–$20.00*

Truman, Margaret. *Murder in the White House*. 1980. dj. . . . . . . *$18.00–$25.00*

Truman, Margaret. *Murder on Embassy Row*. 1984. 1st ed. dj. . . . *$12.00–$18.00*

Trumbull, Benjamine. *Compendium of the Indian Wars of New England*. Hartford.
Edwin Valentine Mitchell. 1926. 1st ed. wrps. ltd 400 cc. . . . . *$75.00–$100.00*

Trumbull, James Hammond. *Natick Dictionary*. DC. GPO. 1903. 1st ed. 347pp.
Bulletin 25. . . . . *$50.00–$125.00*

Tschopik, Harry. *Navaho Pottery Making*. Cambridge, MA. 1941. illus. printed
wrps, plates. . . . . *$60.00–$75.00*

Tuckerman, A. *Index to the Literature of Thermodynamics*. DC. 1890. inscr.. . . . .
. . . . *$50.00–$75.00*

Tuckerman, A. *Short History of Architecture*. NY. 1887. illus. calf. *$75.00–$95.00*

Tudor, Tasha. *Corgiville Fair*. Ny. Crowell. 1971. illus. dj. . . . . *$38.00–$50.00*

Tudor, Tasha. *First Delights*. NY. (1966). 1st ed. inscr. . . . . *$130.00–$150.00*

Tudor, Tasha. *Give Us This Day - The Lord's Prayer*. NY. (1987). 1st ed. dj. . . . .
. . . . *$35.00–$65.00*

Tudor, Tasha. *Night Before Christmas*. Chi. Rand McNally. 1975. illus. by Tudor.
tall 4to. . . . . *$65.00–$85.00*

Tudor, Tasha. *Night Before Christmas*. Chi. Rand McNally. 1984. 9th prnt.. . . . . .
. . . . *$35.00–$40.00*

Tullidge, Edward W. *Life of Brigham Young*. NY. 1876. 1st ed. . . . .
. . . . *$60.00–$80.00*

Tunis, Edwin. *Wheels, a Pictorial History*. Cleve. World Pub. 1954. 1st ed. illus. dj.
. . . . *$35.00–$65.00*

Turbott, E. G. (ed.). *Bullers Birds of New Zealand*. East West Center Press. 1967.
dj. . . . . *$60.00–$80.00*

Turner, L. M. *Contributions to the Natural History of Alaska*. DC. GPO. 1886.
1st ed. illus. 26 litho plates. . . . . *$40.00–$80.00*

Turner, William. *Transfer Printing on Enamels, Porcelain & Pottery*. Lon. 1907.
illus. . . . . *$115.00–$150.00*

Tuttle, Charles. *An Illustrated History of the State of Wisconsin.* 1875. . . . .
. . . . *$55.00–$75.00*

Tuttle, Florence Guertin. *Awakening of Woman.* NY. Abingdon Press. (1915). 1st ed.
dj. . . . . *$60.00–$75.00*

Twain, Mark. *Adventures of Huckleberry Finn.* NY. The Heritage Press. (1940).
illus. by Norman Rockwell slipcase. . . . . *$20.00–$40.00*

Twain, Mark. *Adventures of Tom Sawyer.* 1876. 1st Amer ed. 2nd prntg. . . . .
. . . . *$450.00–$500.00*

Twain, Mark. *Curious Republic of Gondour.* NY. Boni & Liveright. 1919. 1st ed.
140 pp, dj. . . . . *$350.00–$800.00*

Twain, Mark. *Dog's Tale.* Lon. Anti-National Vivisection Society. 1903. wrps. First
separate ed, original stiff wrps. . . . . *$200.00–$350.00*

Twain, Mark. *Europe and Elsewhere.* NY. Harper. [1923]. 1st ed. 406 pp, intro by A
B Paine, dj. . . . . *$700.00–$900.00*

Twain, Mark. *Following the Equator.* Hartford. Amer Pub Co. 1897. 1st ed. first
state, 8vo, 712 pp, blue cl. . . . . *$125.00–$250.00*

Twain, Mark. *Innocents Abroad..* NY. Limited Editions Club. 1962. illus. by Fritz
Kredel, ltd 1500 cc, sgn. slipcase. . . . . *$100.00–$200.00*

Twain, Mark. *Letters From the Earth.* NY. Harper & Row. 1962. blue cl, dj.. . . . . .
. . . . *$45.00–$75.00*

Twain, Mark. *Life On the Mississippi.* 1883. 1st Amer ed. 1st issue. . . . .
. . . . *$195.00–$250.00*

Twain, Mark. *Mark Twain's Autobiography.* NY. Harper. 1924. 2 vols. illus. teg. . .
. . . . *$50.00–$75.00*

Twain, Mark. *Mark Twain's Sketches, New and Old.* Hartford. 1875. 1st ed.
2nd state. illus. blue cl. . . . . *$20.00–$40.00*

Twain, Mark. *Prince and the Pauper.* NY. Grosset & Dunlap. 1921. dj. reprnt. . . . .
. . . . *$8.00–$15.00*

Twain, Mark. *Pudd'nhead Wilson..* Hartford. 1894. 1st US ed.. . *$100.00–$185.00*

Twain, Mark. *Roughing It.* NY. Time-Life Books. imitation brown leather. . . . .
. . . . *$15.00–$20.00*

Twain, Mark. *Tom Sawyer Abroad.* NY. Grosset & Dunlap. 1924. illus. dj. . . . .
. . . . *$12.00–$20.00*

Twain, Mark. *Tramp Abroad.* NY. Limited Editions Club. (1966). illus. by David
Knight, ltd 1500 cc, sgn, slipcase. . . . . *$25.00–$35.00*

Twain, Mark [Clemens, Samuel L.]. *Innocents Abroad.* Leipzig. Bernhard Tauchnitz. 1879. 2 vols. in one. Authorized ed. 1st prtg, 16mo, half lea, inscr. . . . . *$800.00–$1,000.00*

Tweedy, Mary Johnson. *Bermuda Holiday.* Crown Pub. (1950). presentation copy, sgn. . . . . *$10.00–$15.00*

Twenty Sixth Annual Catalogue of Fancy Goods and Toys.... Bos. Cutter, Hyde & Co. 1870's. illus. . . . . *$65.00–$75.00*

Twiss, Travers. *Oregon Territory, Its History and Discovery.* . NY. Appleton. 1846. 1st Amer ed. 264 pp. . . . . *$180.00–$225.00*

Tyler, Anne. *Accidental Tourist.* Knopf. 1985. dj. . . . . *$20.00–$35.00*

Tyler, Anne. *Accidental Tourist.* NY. Knopf. 1985. 1st ed. dj. . . . . *$50.00–$175.00*

Tyler, Anne. *Dinner at the Homesick Restaurant.* NY. Knopf. 1982. 1st ed. dj. . . . . *$15.00–$60.00*

Tyler, Anne. *Saint Maybe.* NY. Knopf. 1991. 1st ed. dj. . . . . *$50.00–$85.00*

Tyler, Anne. *Searching for Caleb.* NY. Knopf. 1975. 1st ed. dj.. . *$175.00–$200.00*

Tyler, Benjamin Owen. *Declaration of Independence.* Washington. 1818. mounted on linen. *$1,850.00*

Tytler, Patrick F. *Historical View of the Progress of Discovery on the More Northern Coasts of America.* Edin. 1832. cl fldg map. . . . . *$90.00–$120.00*

U.S. Camera. NY. 1945. . . . . *$30.00–$50.00*

U.S. Camera. NY. 1953. . . . . *$12.00–$20.00*

U.S. Camera. NY. 1936. . . . . *$25.00–$50.00*

U.S. Camera. NY. 1943. . . . . *$15.00–$25.00*

U.S. Cartridge Company's Collection of Firearms. US Cartridge Co. nd. cat. . . . . *$35.00–$50.00*

Ude, Louis Eustache. *French Cook.* Phila. 1828. rebacked w/lea. . *$295.00–$375.00*

Ulrich, Arthur. *Colt: A Century of Achievement.* Hartford. 1936. illus. pict cvr.. . . . . *$40.00–$40.00*

Underhill, Ruth. *Here Come the Navaho.* KA. Bureau of Indian Affairs. 1953. illus. pict wrps.. . . . . *$12.00–$45.00*

Underhill, Ruth. *Workaday Life of the Pueblos.* AZ. Bureau of Indian Affairs. 1954. illus. pict wrps. . . . . *$15.00–$20.00*

Undertakers' Specialties. Catalogue No XVII. Albany or Rochester, NY. National Casket Co. August, 1903. illus. paper-cvr cl wrps,120 pp. . . . . *$50.00–$75.00*

Underwood, L. H. *With Tommy Tompkins in Korea.* Revell. (1905). *$25.00–$35.00*

Underwood, L. H. *With Tommy Tompkins in Korea.* Fleming Revell. (1905). . . . . .
. . . . *$100.00–$300.00*

Underwood, Rev J. L. *Women of the Confederacy.* Neale. 1906. 1st ed. . . . .
. . . . *$145.00–$175.00*

United States Bureau of American Ethnology. *Twenty eighth Annual Report.Smithsonian Institution.* DC. 1912. illus. 102 plates. . . . . . *$125.00–$175.00*

Universal Indian Sign Language. Boy Scouts. 1929. . . . . *$32.00–$45.00*

Untermeyer, Louis (ed.). *The Book of Living Verse.* NY. Harcourt Brace. (1932). mor, aeg, raised bands, bound by Sangorski & Sutcliffe, slipcase. . . . .
. . . . *$75.00–$100.00*

Updike, Daniel Berkeley. *Printing Types.* Camb. 1927. 2 vols. 1st prtg of 2nd ed., dj.
. . . . *$75.00–$100.00*

Updike, Daniel Berkeley. *Some Aspects of Printing, Old and New.* New Haven. Rudge. 1941. 1st ed. . . . . *$30.00–$45.00*

Updike, John. *Bech is Back.* NY. Knopf. 1982. dj. . . . . *$14.00–$35.00*

Updike, John. *Hoping for a Hoopoe.* Lon. Victor Gollancz. 1959. 1st UK ed. author's first book, dj. . . . . *$65.00–$125.00*

Updike, John. *Hugging the Shore.* Knopf. 1983. 1st ed. dj. . . . . *$22.00–$27.00*

Updike, John. *Month of Sundays.* NY. Knopf. 1975. 1st ed. dj. . . . . *$20.00–$35.00*

Updike, John. *Odd Jobs.* NY. Knopf. 1991. 1st ed. dj. . . . . *$40.00–$50.00*

Updike, John. *Of the Farm.* Knopf. 1965. 1st ed. dj. . . . . *$100.00–$125.00*

Updike, John. *Pigeon Feathers.* NY. 1962. 1st ed. dj. . . . . *$40.00–$75.00*

Updike, John. *Poorhouse Fair.* NY. Borzoi. 1959. 1st ed. dj. . . . . *$85.00–$100.00*

Updike, John. *Problems and Other Stories.* NY. Knopf. 1979. 1st ed. dj. . . . .
. . . . *$15.00–$65.00*

Updike, John. *Rabbit at Rest.* NY. Knopf. 1990. 1st ed. dj. . . . . *$20.00–$40.00*

Updike, John. *Rabbit is Rich.* NY. Knopf. 1981. 1st ed. sgn, dj. . *$125.00–$200.00*

Updike, John. *Rabbit Redux.* NY. Knopf. 1971. 1st ed. dj. . . . . *$25.00–$50.00*

Updike, John. *Rabbit Run.* NY. Knopf. 1960. 1st ed. dj. . . . . *$50.00–$100.00*

Updike, John. *Same Door*. NY. Knopf. (1959). 1st ed. cl-backed bds dj. . . . .
. . . . *$85.00–$100.00*

Updike, John. *The Centaur*. NY. Knopf. 1963. 1st ed. dj. . . . . *$35.00–$50.00*

Updike, John. *Trust Me*. NY. 1987. 1st ed. dj. . . . . *$18.00–$25.00*

Updike, John. *Twelve Terrors of Christmas*. NY. Gotham. (1993). 1st ed. wrps. illus. by Edward Gorey. sgn by author and illustrator. . . . . *$100.00–$160.00*

Updike, John. *Witches of Eastwick*. NY. Knopf. 1984. dj. . . . . *$12.00–$30.00*

Updike, Wilkins. *History of the Narragansett Church*. Bos. 1907. 3 vols. . . . .
. . . . *$75.00–$125.00*

Upham, Charles. *Salem Witchcraft....* Bos. Wiggin & Lunt. 1867. 2 vols. wrps. green cl.. . . . . *$175.00–$250.00*

Upham, Elizabeth. *Little Brown Bear*. Platt & Munk. (1942). illus. by Marjorie Hartwell. . . . . *$65.00–$125.00*

Urban, John W. *In Defense of the Union*. DC. 1887. 1st ed. illus. . . . .
. . . . *$35.00–$45.00*

Uris, Leon. *Exodus*. NY. Doubleday. 1st ed. dj.. . . . . *$30.00–$85.00*

Uses of Elleman's Embrocation. Slough. 1902. 3rd ed. illus, 188 pp. . . . .
. . . . *$35.00–$45.00*

Utah. Hastings House. 1941. black cl.. . . . . *$35.00–$45.00*

Utah Beach of Cherbourg. Historical Div., Dept. of the Army. (1947). illus. maps.
. . . . *$10.00–$30.00*

Vaillant, George C. *Aztecs of Mexico*. NY/Garden City. 1950. illus. dj tan dec cvr and endpapers.. . . . . *$25.00–$40.00*

Valk, M. H. A van der. *De Profeet Der Mormonene Joseph Smith Jr*. Kampen. 1921. illus. photos. . . . . *$80.00–$95.00*

Van de Water, Frederic F. *Glory Hunter: a Life of General Custer*. Ind. Bobbs-Merrill. [1934]. 1st ed. illus. plates, maps. . . . . *$85.00–$135.00*

Van Dervoort, Prof. J. W. *The Water World*. Union Pub. House. 1884. . . . .
. . . . *$20.00–$30.00*

Van Dine, S. S. *Green Murder Case*. NY. Scribner's 1928. 1st ed. no dj. . . . .
. . . . *$10.00–$20.00*

Van Dine, S S. *Gracie Allen Murder Case*. NY. Scribner's. 1938. 1st ed. dj. . . . . .
. . . . *$100.00–$250.00*

Van Dine, S. S. *Bishop Murder Case.* NY. Scribners. 1929. 1st ed. dj. . . . .
. . . . *$35.00–$50.00*

Van Dine, S. S. *Dragon Murder Case.* NY. Scribners. 1933. 1st ed. dj. . . . .
. . . . *$200.00–$400.00*

Van Dine, S. S. *Scarab Murder Case.* NY. 1930. 1st ed. dj. . . . . . *$100.00–$225.00*

Van Dine, S. S. *The Canary Murder Case.* NY. Scribner's. 1927. 1st ed. dj. . . . .
. . . . *$90.00–$120.00*

Van Dine, S. S. *The Casino Murder Case.* NY. Scribner's. 1934. 1st ed. dj. . . . .
. . . . *$400.00–$500.00*

Van Dyke, Henry. *Travel Diary of an Angler.* Derrydale Press. 1929. illus. ltd
750 cc. . . . . *$225.00–$250.00*

Van Dyke, Theodore S. *Southern California.* NY. 1886. 1st ed. sgn. . . . .
. . . . *$100.00–$125.00*

Van Gulik, Robert. *Chinese Bell Murders.* Lon. Michael Joseph. 1958. 1st ed. dj. . .
. . . . *$200.00–$300.00*

Van Gulik, Robert. *Chinese Bell Murders.* NY. Harper & Bros. 1959. 1st Amer ed.
dj. . . . . *$55.00–$75.00*

Van Gulik, Robert. *Chinese Lake Murders.* NY. 1960. illus. 1st US ed. . . . .
. . . . *$50.00–$75.00*

Van Gulik, Robert. *Chinese Nail Murders.* NY. Harper. 1961. 1st Amer ed dj. . . . .
. . . . *$65.00–$175.00*

Van Gulik, Robert. *Haunted Monastery.* NY. Scribner's (1969). 1st ed. dj. . . . .
. . . . *$40.00–$65.00*

Van Gulik, Robert. *Judge Dee at Work.* Lon. Heinemann. 1967. 1st UK ed. dj. . . . .
. . . . *$125.00–$140.00*

Van Gulik, Robert. *Judge Dee at Work.* NY. 1973. dj. . . . . *$25.00–$35.00*

Van Gulik, Robert. *Monkey and the Tiger.* NY. Scribner's 1965. 1st US ed. dj. . . . .
. . . . *$40.00–$75.00*

Van Gulik, Robert. *Murder in Canton.* Lon. Heinemann. 1966. 1st UK ed. dj. . . . .
. . . . *$115.00–$140.00*

Van Gulik, Robert. *Murder in Canton.* NY/Lon. 1966. 1st Amer ed. dj. . . . .
. . . . *$30.00–$75.00*

Van Gulik, Robert. *Poets and Murder.* Lon. Heinemann. 1968. 1st UK ed. dj. . . . .
. . . . *$100.00–$125.00*

Van Gulik, Robert. *The Chinese Lake Murders.* Lon. Michael Joseph. 1960. 1st UK ed. dj. . . . . *$175.00–$225.00*

Van Gulik, Robert. *The Emperor's Pearl.* Lon. Heinemann. 1963. 1st ed. dj. . . . . *$150.00–$190.00*

Van Gulik, Robert. *The Given Day.* San Antonio. Dennis McMillan. 1984. 1st Amer ed. ltd 300 cc. sgn, dj. . . . . *$75.00–$90.00*

Van Gulik, Robert. *The Haunted Monestary.* Lon. Heinemann. 1963. 1st UK ed. dj. . . . . *$150.00–$200.00*

Van Gulik, Robert. *The Lacquer Screen.* Lon. Heinemann. 1962. 1st UK ed. dj.. . . . . *$150.00–$200.00*

Van Gulik, Robert. *The Phantom of the Temple.* Lon. Heinemann. 1966. 1st UK ed. dj. . . . . *$70.00–$90.00*

Van Gulik, Robert. *The Red Pavilion.* Kuala Lumpur. Art Printing Works. 1961. 1st ed. cardboard cvrs.. . . . . *$475.00–$550.00*

Van Gulik, Robert. *The Red Pavilion.* Lon. Heinemann. 1964. 1st UK ed. dj. . . . . *$150.00–$200.00*

Van Gulik, Robert. *The Willow Pattern.* Lon. Heinemann. 1965. 1st UK ed. dj. . . . . *$150.00–$175.00*

Van Gulik, Robert. *Willow Pattern.* NY. Scribner's 1965. 1st ed. dj. . *$50.00–$85.00*

Van Loan's Catskill Mountain Guide and Bird's-eye View.... NY. 1879. illus. maps. . . . . *$175.00–$225.00*

Van Urk, J Blan. *Horse, The Valley and the Chagrin Valley Hunt.* NY. Richard Ellis. 1947. 700 cc, teg. . . . . *$75.00–$100.00*

Van Urk, J. Blan. *Story of American Foxhuntin.* NY. Derrydale. 1940 & 1941. 2 vols. ltd 950 cc. sgn, djs. *$450.00–$595.00*

Vanderveer, Helen. *Little Slam Bang.* Volland. 1928. . . . . *$15.00–$30.00*

Vargas, Alberto. *Varga The Esquire Years.* NY. Alfred VAn der Marck editions. 1987. 1st ed. dj.. . . . . *$40.00–$60.00*

Variety Inc. *Radio Directory 1937-1938.* 1937. 1st ed. . . . . *$45.00–$60.00*

Varney, Almon. *Our Homes and Their Adornments; or How to Build, Furnish, and Adorn a Home.* Detroit. J. C. Chilton. 1885. illus. 486 pp.. . . . . *$50.00–$85.00*

Vasari, Giorgio. *Lives of Seventy of the Most Eminent Painters, Sculptors & Architects.* NY. Scribner's. 1896. 4 vols. illus. ltd 500 cc, buckram, teg.. . . . . *$50.00–$75.00*

Vassall, Henry. *Football: The Rugby Game.* NY. 1890. 1st ed. . . . . *$65.00–$95.00*

Vaughan, B. F. *Life and Writings of Rev. Henry R. Rush, D.D.* Dayton, Oh. 1911. 1st ed. . . . . *$55.00–$75.00*

Veblin, Thorstein. *An Inquiry into the Nature of Peace and the Terms of Perpetuation.* NY/Lon. Macmillan. 1917. 1st ed. . . . . *$50.00–$75.00*

Veblin, Thorstein. *Theory of the Leisure Class..* NY/Lon. Macmillan Co. 1917. 1st Amer ed, green cl. . . . . *$100.00–$150.00*

Verdelle, A. J. *Good Negress.* Chapel Hill. Algonquin. 1995. 1st ed. dj. . . . . *$48.00–$60.00*

Verne, Jules. *In Search of the Castaways.* Phila. Lippincott. 1874. illus. 1st Amer ed. . . . . *$200.00–$475.00*

Verne, Jules. *Journey to the Centre of the Earth.* NY. Scribner's 1906. cl. . . . . *$25.00–$40.00*

Verne, Jules. *Michael Strogoff.* 1926. Photoplay ed. dj. . . . . *$75.00–$125.00*

Verne, Jules. *Michael Strogoff.* Paris. 1876. 1st ed. . . . . *$200.00–$350.00*

Verne, Jules. *Mysterious Island.* Scribner's 1875. 1st ed. illus. . . *$100.00–$250.00*

Verne, Jules. *North Against South, a Tale of the American Civil War.* Lon. 1888. illus. by L Benett.. . . . . *$90.00–$125.00*

Verne, Jules. *Their Island Home.* NY. 1924. 1st US ed. . . . . *$40.00–$50.00*

Verne, Jules. *Tour of the World in Eighty Days.* Bos. Osgood. 1873. 1st Amer trade ed. red cl.. . . . . *$150.00–$300.00*

Verne, Jules. *Twenty Thousand Leagues Under the Sea.* NY. Heritage Press. (1956). slipcase.. . . . . *$25.00–$40.00*

Verne, Jules. *Winter In The Ice.* Bos. 1876. . . . . *$25.00–$35.00*

Verne, Jules. *Wreck of the Chancellor.* Bos. 1875. 1st US ed. . . . . . *$20.00–$30.00*

Verplanck, William E. & Collyer, Moses W. *Sloops of the Hudson.* NY/Lon. Putnam. 1908. 1st ed. . . . . *$50.00–$100.00*

Vibert, Henri. *All About Dogs.* Q-W Laboratories. 1921. wrps. illus. . . . . *$18.00–$25.00*

Vickers, Roy. *Seven Chose Murder.* Lon. Faber and Faber. 1959. 1st ed. dj.. . . . . *$90.00–$120.00*

Victor, O. *History of the Southern Rebellion.* NY. Torrey. 1862. 4 vols. 1st ed. illus. . . . . *$165.00–$225.00*

Vidal, Gore. *Dark Green Bright Red.* NY. Dutton. 1950. 1st ed. dj.*$75.00–$130.00*

Vidal, Gore. *Myra Breckinridge.* Little, Brown. 1968. 1st ed. dj.... *$28.00–$35.00*

Vidal, Gore. *Season of Comfort.* NY. 1949. 1st ed. dj. .... *$25.00–$40.00*

Vidal, Gore. *Lincoln.* NY. Random House. (1984). uncorrected proof...........
.... *$40.00–$50.00*

View Book of the Alaska Highway. Tor. nd. wrps. 16 images...... *$35.00–$50.00*

Viollet-Le-Duc, Eugene. *Mont Blanc: A Treatise on its Geodesical and Geological Constitution.* Lon. Sampson Low. 1877. illus. royal blue cl...... *$225.00–$300.00*

Visscher, William Lightfoot. *Thrilling and Truthful History of the Pony Express.* Chi. Rand McNally. 1908. 1st ed. illus. .... *$50.00–$60.00*

Vladislav, Jan. *Italian Fairy Tales.* Lon. Hamlyn Pub Co. 1971. illus. dj. ....
.... *$25.00–$35.00*

Von Chamisso, Adelbert. *Peter Schlemihl.* Lon. Hardwicke. 1861. 3rd ed. illus. by George Cruikshank.. *$50.00–$80.00*

Vonnegut, Kurt. *Player Piano.* NY. Scribner's 1952. 1st ed. of author's first book, dj.. *$600.00–$1,000.00*

Vonnegut, Kurt. *Canary in a Cat House.* NY. 1962. sgn, dj..... *$70.00–$125.00*

Vonnegut, Kurt. *Galapagos.* NY. Delecorte. 1985. 1st ed. dj...... *$25.00–$35.00*

Vonnegut, Kurt. *God Bless You, Mr. Rosewater.* Holt Rinehart Winston. 1965. 1st ed. dj... *$400.00–$650.00*

Vonnegut, Kurt. *Jailbird.* np. 1979. 1st ed. dj. .... *$25.00–$30.00*

Vonnegut, Kurt. *Palm Sunday.* Delacorte. 1981. 1st ed. dj........ *$15.00–$30.00*

Vonnegut, Kurt. *Precautionary Letter to the Next Generation.* np. 1988. ....
.... *$18.00–$30.00*

Vonnegut, Kurt. *Slapstick.* NY. Delacorte. 1973. 1st ed. dj. ...... *$12.00–$35.00*

Vonnegut, Kurt. *Slaughterhouse Five.* NY. 1969. sgn, dj.... *$1,000.00–$1,800.00*

Voth, H. R. *Oraibi Natal Customs and Ceremonies.* Field Columbian Museum. 1905. illus. vol VI, no 2. .... *$35.00–$50.00*

Voth, H. R. *Oraibi Oaqol Ceremony.* Field Columbian Museum. 1903. illus. vol VI, no 1...................................... *$85.00–$130.00*

Voth, H. R. *Oraibi Summer Snake Ceremony.* Field Columbian Museum. 1903. illus. vol III.. *$95.00–$145.00*

Voyage Through the Islands of the Pacific Ocean. NY. Lane & Scott. 1851. rev, cl.
. . . . *$90.00–$120.00*

Vrooman, J. J. *Forts and Firesides of the Mohawk Valley.* Phila. 1943. 1st ed.
ltd 106 cc. . . . . *$65.00–$90.00*

Wa-Sha-Quon-Asin (Grey Owl). *Tales of an Empty Cabin.* Lon. Lovat Dickson.
1936. illus. 2nd prntg, brown cl. . . . . *$35.00–$50.00*

Wack, Henry Wellington. *Story of the Congo Free State.* NY. 1905. 1st ed. illus. .
. . . . *$125.00–$175.00*

Wagner, Charles. *The Simple Life.* McClure, Phillips. 1904. . . . . . . *$5.00–$10.00*

Wagner, Henry R. *The Plains and the Rockies: A Bibliography of Original*
Narratives of Travel and Adventure, 1800–1865. SF. Grabhorn Press. 1937. 2nd ed.
ltd 600 cc. illus. . . . . *$25.00–$50.00*

Wain, Louis. *Fun For Everyone.* Lon. Nister. nd. illus. b/w, clr. . . . *$50.00–$70.00*

Wainwright, John Howard. *Rhymings.* NY. Appleton. 1860. purple cl, sgn. . . . . . .
. . . . *$30.00–$40.00*

Wakefield, H R. *Clock Strikes Twelve.* Sauk City. Arkham House. 1946. 1st US ed,
dj. . . . . *$40.00–$65.00*

Wakefield, H. R. *They Return at Evening.* NY. Appleton. 1928. 1st Amer ed. 266 pp,
no dj. . . . . *$65.00–$75.00*

Wakefield, J. *History of Waupaca County, Wisc.* Waupaca, WI. 1890. 1st ed. . . . . .
. . . . *$60.00–$85.00*

Walcott, Mary Vaus. *Illustrations of North American Pitcherplants.* DC.
Smithsonian Inst. 1935. 1st ed. illus. folio, 34 pp, portfolio with ties, ltd 500 cc. . . .
. . . . *$175.00–$225.00*

Walden, Arthur T. *Dog Puncher on the Yukon.* Bos. Houghton Mifflin. 1928. . . . .
. . . . *$25.00–$35.00*

Waley, Arthur. *More Translations from the Chinese.* NY. Knopf. 1919. 1st Amer ed.
. . . . *$40.00–$50.00*

Walker, Aldace F. *Vermont Brigade in the Shenandoah Valley.* VT. 1869. illus. maps.
. . . . *$35.00–$100.00*

Walker, Alice. *Color Purple.* NY. 1982. sgn, dj. . . . . *$900.00–$3,000.00*

Walker, Alice. *Color Purple.* NY. 1982. 1st ed. dj. . . . . *$600.00–$675.00*

Walker, Alice. *Temple of My Familiar.* Harcourt. 1989. ltd 500 cc, sgn, dj, slipcase. .
. . . . *$85.00–$100.00*

Walkowitz, Abraham. *Faces from the Ghetto.* NY. Machmadim Art. (1946). ltd 500 cc. inscr. illus. . . . . *$35.00–$50.00*

Wallace, Alfred R. *Australia.* Lon. Edward Stanford. 1879. 1st ed. illus., 2 clr maps, pict cl. . . . . *$195.00–$250.00*

Wallace, Alfred Russel. *Darwinism..* Lon. Macmillan. 1889. 1st ed. bds. . . . . *$140.00–$160.00*

Wallace, Alfred Russel. *Malay Archipelago..* NY. Harper & Bros. 1869. 1st Amer ed. . . . . *$75.00–$100.00*

Wallace, Anthony F. C. *King of the Delawares: Teedyuscung 1700–1763.* Phila. 1949. 1st ed. dj. . . . . *$40.00–$60.00*

Wallace, Dillon. *Long Labrador Trail.* Chi. 1923. illus. sgn. . . . . . . *$22.00–$30.00*

Wallace, Dillon. *Lure of the Labrador Wild.* NY. Fleming. [1913]. 11th ed. illus, map. . . . . *$25.00–$35.00*

Wallace, Edgar. *Clever One.* Doubleday Crime Club. 1928. 1st ed. dj. . . . . *$35.00–$50.00*

Wallace, Edgar. *Day of Uniting.* Mystery League. 1930. 1st ed. dj. *$50.00–$60.00*

Wallace, Edgar. *Gunman's Bluff.* Garden City. Doubleday Crime Club. 1929. 1st Amer ed. dj. . . . . *$100.00–$130.00*

Wallace, Edgar. *The Green Ribbon.* Garden City. Doubleday Crime Club. 1930. 1st Amer ed. dj. . . . . *$100.00–$130.00*

Wallace, Edgar. *The Stretelli Case and Other Mystery Stories.* Cleve. World Pub. 1930. 1st Amer ed. dj. . . . . *$30.00–$50.00*

Wallace, Edgar. *White Face.* Garden City. Doubleday Crime Club. 1931. 1st Amer ed. dj. . . . . *$100.00–$130.00*

Wallace, Frederick William. *Wooden Ships & Iron Men.* NY. . . . . *$30.00–$45.00*

Wallace, Isabel. *Life and Letters of General W.H.L. Wallace.* Chi. 1909. 1st ed. illus. . . . . *$95.00–$125.00*

Wallace, Lewis. *Ben-Hur.* NY. Harper. 1880. 1st ed. . . . . *$130.00–$300.00*

Wallace, Lewis. *Ben-Hur.* NY. Harper & Bros. 1908. . . . . *$35.00–$40.00*

Wallace, Susan E. *Land of the Pueblos.* NY. 1888. 1st ed. illus. photos. . . . . *$75.00–$95.00*

Waller, Robert James. *Bridges of Madison County.* NY. Times Warner. 1992. 1st ed. author's first book, dj. . . . . *$70.00–$100.00*

Walsh, J. H. *Every Horse Owner's Cyclopedia.* Phila. Porter & Coates. 1871. 1st ed. illus. . . . . *$30.00–$45.00*

Walt Disney's Pinocchio's Picture Book. Racine, WI. Whitman. 1940. wrps. illus. . . . . *$125.00–$195.00*

Walter Camp's Book of College Sports. NY. 1893. 1st ed. . . . . *$50.00–$75.00*

Walton, Evangeline. *Cross and the Sword.* NY. Bouregy & Curl. (1956). 1st ed. dj. . . . . *$55.00–$65.00*

Walton, Evangeline. *Virgin and the Swine.* Chi. 1936. 1st ed. dj. *$100.00–$175.00*

Walton, Evangeline. *Witch House.* Arkham House. 1945. 1st ed. dj. . . . . *$40.00–$100.00*

Walton, Isaac. *Compleat Angler.* 1931. illus. by Arthur Rackham, ltd 775 cc, sgn by Rackham. . . . . *$200.00–$300.00*

Walton, Isaac & Charles Cotton. *Complete Angler, or Contemplative Man's Recreation.* Lon. 1784. illus. 4th ed. slipcase. . . . . *$350.00–$450.00*

Walton, Isaac & Charles Cotton. *Complete Angler.* NY. 1848. 3/4 lea, bds. . . . . *$50.00–$60.00*

Walton, Izaak. *Compleat Angler.* Lon. J.M. Dent. 1896. illus. . . . . *$45.00–$55.00*

Walton, Izaak. *Universal Angler.* Lon. Marriott & Brome. 1676. *$700.00–$850.00*

Warbey, William. *Vietnam: the Truth.* Lon. 1965. 1st ed. . . . . *$25.00–$30.00*

Ward, Austin. *Male Life Among the Mormons or The Husband in Utah.* Phila. 1863. . . . . *$45.00–$60.00*

Ward, Henshaw. *Charles Darwin..* Ind. Bobbs-Merrill. 1927. . . . . *$20.00–$30.00*

Ward, Maria. *Female Life Among the Mormons: A Narrative of Many Years' Personal Experience, by the Wife of a Mormon Elder.* NY. 1857. . *$75.00–$250.00*

Warhol, Andy. *"A."* NY. 1968. 1st ed. dj. *$35.00–$45.00*

Waring, John Burnley (ed.). *Examples of Weaving and Embroidery.* Lon. Day & Son. illus. 14 chromolith plates, folio. *$100.00–$150.00*

Warren Report. GPO. 1964. 26 vols. *$900.00–$1,500.00*

Warren, John. *The Conchologist.* Bos. 1834. 1st ed. illus. presentation copy, lea, bds. . . . . *$115.00–$130.00*

Warren, Joseph. *Revenge.* NY. Grosset & Dunlap. 1928. 1st ed. dj. . . . . *$140.00–$175.00*

Warren, Lillie E. *Defective Speech and Deafness.* NY. Edgar S Werner. 1895. 116 pp... *$50.00–$75.00*

Warren, Robert Penn. *Meet Me in the Green Glen.* NY. 1971. 1st ed. presentation copy, sgn. .... *$100.00–$225.00*

Warren, Robert Penn. *Wilderness.* Random House. 1961. 1st ed. dj. .... *$50.00–$30.00*

Washington, Booker T. *Up From Slavery.* NY. Doubleday, Page. 1901. 1st ed. photos.. *$40.00–$70.00*

Washington, Booker T. *Working With the Hands.* Doubleday. 1904. 1st ed. .... *$55.00–$75.00*

Washington, Booker T. (ed.). *Negro In Business.* Bos. Hertel, Jenkins. 1907. 1st ed. illus. photos. .... *$145.00–$170.00*

Watanna, Onoto. *Heart of Hyacinth.* Harper. 1903. 1st ed. illus. teg. .... *$25.00–$75.00*

Watanna, Onoto. *Japanese Blossom.* NY. Harper. 1906. 1st ed. clr plates......... .... *$30.00–$50.00*

Waters, Ethel. *His Eye is on the Sparrow.* NY. 1951............. *$25.00–$35.00*

Watson, Francis Sedgwick. *Operative Treatment of the Hypertrophied Prostate.* Cupples & Hurd. 1888. 167 pp, photogravures............... *$100.00–$140.00*

Watson, Wilbur J. *Bridge Architecture.* NY. 1927. illus. .... *$50.00–$75.00*

Watson, William. *Adventures of a Blockade Runner.* Lon. 1892. *$100.00–$155.00*

Watts, Rev. Isaac. *An Arrangement of the Psalms, Hymns and Spiritual Songs of..* Bos. James Loring. 1818. .... *$70.00–$100.00*

Waugh, Evelyn. *Brideshead Revisited.* Bos. Little, Brown. 1946. 1st Amer trade ed. dj. .... *$30.00–$125.00*

Waugh, Evelyn. *Edmund Campion.* NY. Sheed & Ward. (1935). 1st ed. dj....... .... *$30.00–$125.00*

Waugh, Evelyn. *Love Among the Ruins.* Lon. 1953. 1st ed. dj..... *$35.00–$45.00*

Waugh, Evelyn. *Mr. Loveday's Little Outing and Other Sad Stories.* Lon. Chapman & Hall. (1936). 1st ed. .... *$50.00–$125.00*

Waugh, Evelyn. *When the Going Was Good.* Bos. Little, Brown. 1947. dj. .... *$40.00–$55.00*

Waugh, F. A. *Landscape Gardening.* NY. 1899. 1st ed. .... *$32.00–$45.00*

Waugh, Frank A. *Textbook of Landscape Gardening.* NY. Wiley. 1922. 1st ed. illus.
. . . . *$35.00–$45.00*

Weaver, Clarence E. *Sketches of Richmond Virginia..* Central Pub. illus. b/w photos.
. . . . *$50.00–$65.00*

Weaver, Lawrence. *Small Country Houses.* Lon. Country Life. 1914. 1st ed. illus. .
. . . . *$50.00–$100.00*

Weaver, Warren A. *Lithographs of N. Currier and Currier & Ives.* NY. Holport.
(1925). 1st ed. illus. . . . . *$50.00–$80.00*

Webb, Walter Prescott. *Texas Rangers.* Houghton Mifflin. 1935. 1st ed. illus. . . . .
. . . . *$52.00–$60.00*

Weber, Carl J. *Fore-Edge Painting.* Irvington-on-Hudson. 1966. illus. dj. . . . .
. . . . *$165.00–$200.00*

Webster, Daniel. *Private Correspondence of Daniel Webster.* Bos. Little, Brown.
1857. 1st ed. illus. . . . . *$50.00–$100.00*

Webster, Lt. Col. F. A. M. *Olympic Cavalcade.* Lon. Hutchinson. nd. 1st ed. illus.
dark green cl, 80 photo plates. . . . . *$20.00–$35.00*

Webster, Noah. *An American Dictionary of the English Language.* Springfield, MA.
Merriam. 1859. rev. *$75.00–*

Webster, Thomas. *An Encyclopedia of Domestic Economy.* NY. 1845. 1st ed. . . . .
. . . . *$65.00–$125.00*

Wee Gee. *Naked City.* NY. Essential Books. 1945. dj. . . . . *$150.00–$200.00*

Weeden Toy Steam Engines. New Bedford, MA. Weeden Manufacturing Corp. 1939.
pict wrps, illus, 19 pp. . . . . *$65.00–$75.00*

Weeden, Howard. *Songs of the Old South.* NY. 1900. 1st ed. illus. clr plates. . . . . .
. . . . *$85.00–$125.00*

Weeks, John. *History of Salisbury, VT.* Middlebury. 1860. . . . . . . *$90.00–$100.00*

Wehr, Julian. *Popeye and the Pirates.* NY. Duenewald Pub. (1945). illus. by
Sagendorf, with four moveables by Wehr. . . . . *$150.00–$200.00*

Weissl, August. *The Mystery of the Green Car.* Lon. Nelson. 1913. 1st ed. . . . .
. . . . *$80.00–$90.00*

Weld, Isaac. *Travels through the States of North America and the Provinces of Upper
and Lower Canada During the Years 1795, 1796, and 1797.* Lon. 1799. 1st ed. 464
pp, plates, maps laid in, small folio. . . . . *$320.00–$400.00*

Well, Samuel R. *New Physiognomy of Signs of Character.* Fowler & Wells. 1883.
illus. brown decorated cl. . . . . *$40.00–$55.00*

Wellman, Manly Wade. *After Dark*. Garden City. Doubleday. 1980. 1st ed. dj. . . .
. . . . *$35.00–$65.00*

Wellman, Manly Wade. *Lost and the Lurking*. Garden City. Doubleday. 1981). 1st
ed. dj. . . . . *$25.00–$65.00*

Wellman, Manly Wade. *Old Gods Awaken*. Garden City. Doubleday. 1979. 1st ed.
y. . . . . *$30.00–$65.00*

Wells, Carolyn. *Folly for the Wise*. Bobbs Merrill. 1904. 170 pp, illus. . . . .
. . . . *$45.00–$65.00*

Wells, Carolyn. *Marjorie in Command*. NY. Grosset & Dunlap. 1910. . . . .
. . . . *$10.00–$18.00*

Wells, Carolyn. *Merry-Go-Round*. Russell. 1901. 152 pp, illus by Peter Newell. . .
. . . . *$120.00–$150.00*

Wells, Emma M. *History of Roane County, Tennessee, 1801-1870*. Chattanooga.
1927. 1st ed. illus. . . . . *$30.00–$75.00*

Wells, Frederic P. *History of Newbury, Vermont*. St. Johnsbury, VT. 1902. illus. fldg
plans, 3/4 mor. . . . . *$40.00–$55.00*

Wells, H G. *Tono-Bungay*. Lon. Macmillan. 1909. 1st ed. . . . . *$50.00–$75.00*

Wells, H. G. *Ann Veronica*. NY. 1909. 1st ed. dj. . . . . *$75.00–$100.00*

Wells, H. G. *First and Last Things*. NY. 1908. 1st US ed. . . . . *$40.00–$50.00*

Wells, H. G. *Invisible Man*. Lon. 1897. 1st ed. . . . . *$1,000.00–$2,000.00*

Wells, H. G. *Invisible Man*. NY. Edward Arnold. 1897. 1st Amer ed. 279 pp, orange
cl. . . . . *$600.00–$1,150.00*

Wells, H. G. *New Worlds for Old*. Lon. Constable. 1908. 1st ed. red cl. . . . .
. . . . *$85.00–$100.00*

Wells, H. G. *Tales of Space and Time*. NY. Doubleday & McClure. 1899. 1st Amer
ed. . . . . *$45.00–$65.00*

Wells, H. G. *Time Machine*. Lon. 1927. dj. . . . . *$125.00–$165.00*

Wells, H. G. *When the Sleeper Wakes*. Lon/NY. Harper & Bros. 1899. 1st ed. illus.
. . . . *$150.00–$400.00*

Wells, Helen. *Cherry Ames, Visiting Nurse*. NY. Grosset & Dunlap. (1947). dj. . . . .
. . . . *$5.00–$12.00*

Wells, Helen. *Island Nurse*. NY. Grosset & Dunlap. 1960. Cherry Ames #21, dj. . .
. . . . *$14.00–$17.00*

Wells, Helen. *Jungle Nurse.* NY. Grosset & Dunlap. 1965. Cherry Ames #25. . . . . .
. . . . *$30.00–$40.00*

Wells, Helen. *Student Nurse.* NY. Grosset & Dunlap. 1943. Cherry Ames #1, dj. . . .
. . . . *$12.00–$20.00*

Wells, Helen. *Veterans' Nurse.* NY. Grosset & Dunlap. 1946. Cherry Ames, #6, dj. .
. . . . *$8.00–$12.00*

Wells, Henry P. *City Boys in the Woods.* NY. Harper. (1889). 1st ed. illus. . . . .
. . . . *$30.00–$80.00*

Welo, Samuel. *Practical Lettering.* Chi. Drake. (1930). 1st ed. illus. . . . .
. . . . *$30.00–$50.00*

Welty, Eudora. *A Curtain Green: A Book of Stories.* Garden City. Doubleday, Doran.
1941. 1st ed. author's first book, dj. . . . . *$850.00–$1,000.00*

Welty, Eudora. *Delta Wedding.* NY. (1946). 1st ed. dj. . . . . *$125.00–$250.00*

Welty, Eudora. *Golden Apples.* NY. Harcourt, Brace. [1949]. 1st ed. dj. . . . .
. . . . *$125.00–$150.00*

Welty, Eudora. *In Black and White.* Northridge. Lord John Press. 1985. sgn. . . . . .
. . . . *$165.00–$250.00*

Welty, Eudora. *One Writer's Beginnings.* Camb. 1984. dj. . . . . *$30.00–$40.00*

Welty, Eudora. *Robber Bridegroom.* Garden City. Doubleday Doran. 1942. 1st ed.
dj. . . . . *$100.00–$500.00*

Welty, Eudora. *Wide Net and Other Stories.* NY. 1943. 1st ed. dj. . . *$350.00–$500.00*

Wentworth, Patricia. *The Gazebo.* Phila. Lippincott. 1955. 1st ed. dj. . . . .
. . . . *$40.00–$55.00*

Wentz, Robert W., Jr. *Portsmouth A Pictorial History.* Donning. illus. b/wphotos,
sgn, dj. . . . . *$30.00–$45.00*

Weslager, C. A. *Delaware Indians: A History.* New Brunswick. Rutgers Univ Press.
1972. 2nd ed. dj. . . . . *$30.00–$40.00*

West, James E. *Lone Scout of the Sky.* NY. Boy Scouts of America. 1927. 1st ed.
illus. green cl. . . . . *$20.00–$50.00*

West, Jerry. *Happy Hollisters and the Indian Treasure.* Doubleday. 1953. . . . .
. . . . *$10.00–$20.00*

Westermarck, Edward. *Marriage Ceremonies in Morocco.* Lon. Macmillan. 1914.
1st ed. brown cl. . . . . *$80.00–$100.00*

Westerners Brand Book. Chi. 1st ed. vol XV11. . . . . *$40.00–$75.00*

Westminster Shorter Catechism Ratified...Presbyterian Church in Augusta, Georgia. Virginia. [Confederate Imprint]. 1861. wrps. . . . . *$95.00–$125.00*

Westwood, T and T. Satchell. *Biblioteca Piscatoria: A Catalogue of Books on Angling....* Lon. 1883-1901. 1/4 blue mor & blue cl, teg, complete with 1901 supplement, orig supplement wrps preserved. *$150.00–$250.00*

Wetmore, Mrs. Helen C. *Last of the Great Scouts: The Life Story of Buffalo Bill.* Duluth. 1899. 1st ed. illus. plates. . . . . *$50.00–$200.00*

Whalen, Will W. *The Priest Who Vanished or Murderer at Large.* Ozone Park, NY. Catholic Literary Guild. 1942. 1st ed. dj. . . . . *$80.00–$90.00*

Whall, W. B. *Sea Songs & Shanties.* Glasgow. 1920. illus. 4th ed. . *$50.00–$75.00*

Wharton, Edith. *Crucial Instances.* NY. Scribner's. 1901. 1st ed. . . *$85.00–$200.00*

Wharton, Edith. *Custom of the Country.* NY. Scribner's. 1913. 1st ed. . . . .
. . . . *$50.00–$90.00*

Wharton, Edith. *Ethan Frome.* NY. Scribner's. 1911. 1st ed. 2nd issue. . . . .
. . . . *$250.00–$600.00*

Wharton, Edith. *Ethan Frome.* NY. Scribner's. 1911. 1st ed. 1st issue. teg, points.
. . . . *$500.00–$1,150.00*

Wharton, Edith. *Fruit of the Tree.* NY. Scribner's 1907. 1st ed. 633 pp,. . . . .
. . . . *$25.00–$50.00*

Wharton, Edith. *Gods Arrive.* NY. Appleton. 1932. 1st ed. dj. . . . *$125.00–$150.00*

Wharton, Edith. *House of Mirth.* NY. Scribner's. 1905. 1st ed. 1st issue. teg. . . . .
. . . . *$75.00–$150.00*

Wharton, Edith. *Italian Villas and Their Gardens.* NY. 1904. 1st ed. illus. by Maxfield Parrish, dec cl. . . . . *$700.00–$750.00*

Wharton, Edith. *Sanctuary.* NY. Scribner's 1903. 1st ed. illus. by Walter Appleton Clark, 184 pp, scarce. . . . . *$150.00–$250.00*

Wharton, Edith. *Summer.* NY. 1917. 1st ed. dj. . . . . *$65.00–$95.00*

Wharton, Edith. *The Children.* NY. 1928. 1st ed. dj. . . . . *$75.00–$125.00*

Wharton, Edith (ed.). *Book of the Homeless.* Scribner's. 1916. illus. grey bds. . . . .
. . . . *$50.00–$80.00*

Wharton, James George. *What the White Race May Learn from the Indian.* Chi. Forbes. 1908. 1st ed. illus. photos. presentation copy. inscr by James. red cl. . . . . . .
. . . . *$100.00–$150.00*

Wheeler, F. G. *Billy Whiskers at the Fair.* Akron. 1909. 1st ed. illus. plates........
.... *$30.00–$35.00*

Where to Hunt American Game. MA. 1898. 1st ed. illus. .... *$50.00–$75.00*

Whilt, James W. *Mountain Memories.* Chi. W. B. Conkey. 1925. illus. sgn by author.
.... *$20.00–$30.00*

Whipple, Maurine. *Giant Joshua.* Bos. 1941. 1st ed. dj.. .... *$45.00–$60.00*

White, Alma. *Ku Klux Klan In Prophecy.* NJ. Zarephath. 1925. 1st ed. ....
.... *$75.00–$275.00*

White, E. B. *Charlotte's Web.* NY. (1952). 1st ed. illus. by Garth Williams, dj. ....
.... *$200.00–$450.00*

White, E. B. *Stuart Little.* NY. 1945. dj. .... *$50.00–$175.00*

White, James. *Early Life and Later Experiences.. of Elder Joseph Bates.* Battle
Creek. 1877. illus. 320 pp............................... *$115.00–$150.00*

White, Mrs. Alma. *Titantic Tragedy..* Bound Brook. Pentecostal Union. 1913. ....
.... *$25.00–$50.00*

White, Randy Wayne. *North of Havana.* Ny. Putnam's. 1997. 1st ed. sgn, dj......
.... *$30.00–$50.00*

White, Randy Wayne. *The Heat Islands.* NY. St. Martin's. 1992. 1st ed. dj. ......
.... *$190.00–$225.00*

White, Stewart Edward. *The Cabin.* Doubleday Page. 1911. .... *$25.00–$35.00*

White, W. Edward. *Covered Bridges of New Hampshire.* Plymouth, NH. (1942).
illus. pict wrps. .... *$25.00–$40.00*

Whitehead, Alfred North. *Science in the Modern World.* NY. 1925. 1st ed. ......
.... *$40.00–$50.00*

Whitehead, Russell F. *Architecture of the American Colonies and the Early
Republic.* NY. Helburn. (1927). 2 vols. illus. photos. .... *$60.00–$80.00*

Whitehouse, Eula. *Texas Flowers in a Natural Colors.* Austin. 1936. 1st ed. illus. in
clr, illus by author, inscr by author. .... *$35.00–$65.00*

Whitman, Charles F. *A History of Norway, Maine.* ME. 1924. illus. frontis.......
.... *$75.00–$100.00*

Whitman, Roger B. *Motor-Car Principles.* NY. Appleton. 1909. rev. ed. illus. ....
.... *$60.00–$80.00*

Whitman, Walt. *Good-Bye My Fancy: 2nd Annex to Leaves of Grass.* Phila. David
McKay. 1891. 1st ed. teg. .... *$50.00–$100.00*

Whitman, Walt. *Leaves of Grass.* Mount Vernon. Peter Pauper Press. 1943. illus. ltd 1100 cc, folio. . . . . *$95.00–$125.00*

Whitman, Walt. *November Boughs.* Phila. 1888. 1st ed. . . . . *$90.00–$325.00*

Whitney, Ada. *Mother Goose for Grown Folks.* NY. 1859. 1st ed. sgn. . . . . *$125.00–$250.00*

Whitney, Harry. *Hunting with the Eskimos.* NY. Century. 1910. 1st ed. illus. fldg map. . . . . *$50.00–$75.00*

Whitted, J. A. *History of the Negro Baptists of North Carolina.* Raleigh. Edwards & Broughton. 1908. 1st ed. illus. . . . . *$195.00–$225.00*

Whymper, C. *Egyptian Birds for the Most Part Seen in the Nile Valley.* Lon. 1909. illus. . . . . *$70.00–$85.00*

Whymper, Frederick. *Travel and Adventure in the Territory of Alaska.* Harper & Bros. 1871. illus. . . . . *$65.00–$85.00*

Wickersham, Hon James. *Old Yukon.* WA. Washington Law Book Co. 1938. 1st ed. illus. . . . . *$28.00–$75.00*

Wiggin, Kate. *The Story of Patsy.* Bos. 1890. . . . . *$25.00–$40.00*

Wiggin, Kate Douglas. *Birds' Christmas Carol.* 1912. illus. . . . . . *$18.00–$27.00*

Wiggin, Kate Douglas. *Diary of a Goose Girl.* Bos. 1902. 1st ed. . *$20.00–$30.00*

Wiggin, Kate Douglas. *Old Peabody Pew.* Bos/NY. 1907. 1st ed. . *$35.00–$50.00*

Wiggin, Kate Douglas. *Penelope's Irish Experience.* Bos. 1902. illus. aeg. . . . . *$50.00–$60.00*

Wiggin, Kate Douglas. *Rebecca of Sunnybrook Farm.* NY. Houghton Mifflin. 1903. 1st ed. 1st state binding.. . . . . *$150.00–$225.00*

Wight, J. B. *Tobacco: Its Use and Abuse.* Columbia, SC. 1889. . . . *$20.00–$35.00*

Wightman, Orrin. *Diary of an American Physician in the Russian Revolution. 1917.* Brooklyn. Daily Eagle. 1928. 1st ed. photographs,, 230 pp, sgn, presentation copy. . . . . *$95.00–$125.00*

Wilcox, Walter Dwight. *Rockies of Canada.* NY/Lon. 1900. . . . . *$75.00–$100.00*

Wilde, Oscar. *Canterville Ghost.* Bos. J. W. Luce. 1906. 1st separate ed. illus, tri-clr slate cl, teg. . . . . *$100.00–$125.00*

Wilde, Oscar. *Critic in Pall Mall.* Lon. Methuen & Co. (1919). 1st ed. fine. . . . . *$75.00–$150.00*

Wilde, Oscar. *Epigrams and Aphorisms.* Bos. Luce. 1905. 1st ed. *$45.00–$100.00*

Wilde, Oscar. *Fisherman and His Soul.* SF. Ransohoff's. 1939. . *$125.00–$180.00*

Wilde, Oscar. *Intentions: the Decay of Lying, Pen Pencil and Poison, the Critic as Artist, the Truth of Masks.* Lon. Osgood McIlvaine & Co. 1891. 1st ed. green cl, presentation copy. . . . . *$3,000.00–$5,000.00*

Wilder, Thornton. *Angel That Troubled the Waters and Other Plays.* NY. Coward-McCann. 1928. 1st ed. ltd 775 cc. sgn. . . . . *$70.00–$100.00*

Wilder, Thornton. *Bridge of San Luis Rey.* NY. Boni. 1927. 1st ed. . . . . *$200.00–$350.00*

Wilder, Thornton. *Cabala.* NY. Boni. 1926. 1st ed. points.. . . . . . *$50.00–$360.00*

Wilder, Thornton. *Theophilus North.* NY. Harper & Row. (1973). 1st ed. presentation copy, sgn, dj. . . . . *$50.00–$80.00*

Wilke, Charles. *24 Facsimiles of Charts and Maps produced by Wilkes to Accompany his Report on the US Exploring Expedition, 1841.* np. nd. . . . . *$175.00–$250.00*

Willard, Frances E. *Woman in the Pulpit.* Chi. Woman's Temperance Pub Co. 1889. 1st ed. . . . . *$85.00–$125.00*

Willard, Signey. *Hebrew Grammar.* Camb. 1817. 1st ed. calf-backed bds.. . . . . *$225.00–$285.00*

Willett, Mortimer & Peter. *Great Racehorses of the World.* NY. St. Martins. 1970. 1st US ed. . . . . *$35.00–$45.00*

Williams, Garner F. *Diamond Mines of South Africa.* NY. Macmillan. 1902. 1st ed. fldg map, plates. . . . . *$125.00–$200.00*

Williams, J. David (ed.). *America Illustrated.* Ny. Arundel Press. (1880). 1st ed. illus. brown cl, aeg. . . . . *$25.00–$50.00*

Williams, Joseph J. *Hewbrewisms of West Africa. From Nile to Niger with the Jews.* NY. Dial Press. 1930. 1st ed. maps. . . . . *$50.00–$80.00*

Williams, S. Wells. *Middle Kingdom.* NY. 1883. 2 vols. wrps. rev ed. 2 fldg frontis, pocket map. . . . . *$150.00–$225.00*

Williams, Tennessee. *Roman Spring of Mrs. Stone.* NY. 1950. 1st ed. dj.. . . . . *$50.00–$75.00*

Williams, Tennessee. *Cat on a Hot Tin Roof.* NY. 1955. 1st ed. dj. *$75.00–$100.00*

Williams, Tennessee. *Glass Menagerie.* NY. Random House. 1945. 1st ed. dj.. . . . . *$65.00–$80.00*

Williams, Tennessee. *Rose Tattoo.* CT. New Directions. 1951. 1st ed. dj.. . . . . *$60.00–$125.00*

Williams, Tennessee. *Streetcar Named Desire*. [NY]. New Directions. [1947]. 1st ed. 171 pp, bds, dj. . . . . *$900.00–$3,000.00*

Williams, W. *Appleton's Northern and Eastern Traveller's Guide*. NY. 1855. illus. maps. . . . . *$85.00–$130.00*

Williams, Wellington. *The Traveller's and Tourist's Guide through the United States of America, Canada....* Lippincott, Grambo. 1851. brown lea, map. *$1,650.00*

Williams, William Carlos. *Complete Collected Poems, 1906-1938*. Norfolk, CT. New Directions. (c1938). 1st ed. dj. . . . . *$150.00–$225.00*

Williams, William Carlos. *Kora in Hell*. SF. City Lights. (1957). wrps. 2nd ed,. . . . . *$60.00–$75.00*

Williams, William Carlos. *Life Along the Passaic River*. Norfolk, CT. New Directions. 1938. 1st ed. dj. . . . . *$100.00–$400.00*

Williams, William Carlos. *White Mule*. Norfolk, CT. New Directions. 1937. 1st ed. dj. . . . . *$120.00–$200.00*

Williamson, Henry. *Salar the Salmon*. Bos. Little, Brown. 1936. 1st ed. dj. . . . . *$40.00–$50.00*

Williamson, James J. *Mosby's Rangers*. NY. Sturgis & Walton. 1909. rev. and enlarged. . . . . *$125.00–$475.00*

Wilson, Angus. *Hemlock and After*. Viking. 1952. 1st Amer ed, dj. . *$20.00–$25.00*

Wilson, Capt. James. *Missionary Voyage to the South Pacific Ocean, in 1796, 1797 & 1798: In the Ship Duff*. Lon. Chapman. 1799. plates, fold-out charts, 395 pp, very scarce treasure. . . . . *$225.00–$550.00*

Wilson, Colin. *Philosopher's Stone*. NY. Crown. (1971). 1st Amer ed. dj. . . . . *$35.00–$40.00*

Wilson, Dixie. *Pinky Pup*. Chi. Volland. (1922). illus. by Erick Berry. . . . . *$70.00–$125.00*

Wilson, Edmund. *Poets, Farewell*. NY. Scribner's. 1929. 1st ed. dj. . . . . *$475.00–$600.00*

Wilson, Edmund. *Travels in Two Democracies*. NY. Harcourt, Brace. (c1936). 1st ed. dj. . . . . *$125.00–$250.00*

Wilson, Elija N. *Among the Shoshones*. Salt Lake City 1910. 1st ed. . . . . *$200.00–$250.00*

Wilson, F. P. *The Keep*. NY. Morrow. 1981. 1st ed. dj. . . . . *$30.00–$45.00*

Wilson, Joseph Thomas. *Black Phalanx; A History of Negro Soldiers of the U.S.* CT. 1888. 1st ed. illus. . . . . *$175.00–$250.00*

Wilson, Mitchell. *American Science and Invention.* NY. Bonanza Books. 1960. . . .
. . . . *$25.00–$35.00*

Wilson, Rev. Edward F. *Missionary Work Among the Ojebway Indians.* Lon. 1886.
1st ed. illus. . . . . *$75.00–$150.00*

Wilson, T. *Biography of the Principal American Military & Naval Heroes.* NY. 1821.
2 vols. . . . . *$55.00–$65.00*

Wilstock, Frank J. *Wild Bill Hickock.* Garden City. 1926. . . . . *$15.00–$22.00*

***Winchester and Hotchkiss Repeating Fire Arms, Rifled Muskets, Carbines...of All
Kinds.*** New Haven, CT. Winchester Repeating Arms Co. 1884. illus. printed wrps,
68 pp. . . . . *$175.00–$225.00*

Winkfield, Uncle Eliza. *Female American.* Vergennes, VT. Jepthah Shedd. 1814. 2nd
ed. 12mo, 270 pp, calf, scarce. . . . . *$150.00–$250.00*

Winslow, Don. *A Long Walk Up the Water Slide.* NY. St. Martin's. 1994. 1st ed. dj. .
. . . . *$40.00–$50.00*

Winslow, John. *Famous Planes and Famous Flights.* NY. The Platt & Munk Co.
(1940). 1st ed. illus. pict cvr. . . . . *$20.00–$50.00*

Winter, William. *Life of David Belasco.* NY. 1918. 2 vols. 1st ed. illus. . . . .
. . . . *$40.00–$50.00*

Winthrop, Theodore. *Canoe and the Saddle.* Bos. Ticknor & Fields. 1863. . . . . . .
. . . . *$75.00–$100.00*

Wirt, Mildred A. *Ghost Beyond the Gate.* Cupples & Leon. 1943. Penny Parker.
10, dj. . . . . *$13.00–$40.00*

Wodehouse, P. G. *Bachelors Anonymous.* Simon & Schuster. 1974. dj. . . . .
. . . . *$20.00–$30.00*

Wodehouse, P. G. *Bill The Conqueror.* NY. 1924. 1st Amer ed. . . . . *$50.00–$75.00*

Wodehouse, P. G. *Carry On, Jeeves!.* NY. 1927. 1st US ed. . . . . . . *$45.00–$65.00*

Wodehouse, P. G. *Code of the Woosters.* Lon. 1938. 1st ed. . . . . . . *$35.00–$50.00*

Wodehouse, P. G. *Golf Without Tears.* NY. 1924. 1st ed. . . . . *$60.00–$85.00*

Wodehouse, P. G. *Inimitable Jeeves.* Lon. 1923. 1st ed. . . . . *$40.00–$50.00*

Wodehouse, P. G. *Love Among Chickens.* Lon. 1936. . . . . *$35.00–$40.00*

Wodehouse, P. G. *Piccadilly Jim.* Lon. 1924. . . . . *$30.00–$40.00*

Wodehouse, P. G. *Prince and Betty.* 1912. 1st ed. . . . . *$50.00–$65.00*

Wodehouse, P. G. *Thank You, Jeeves.* Lon. 1934. 1st ed. . . . . *$75.00–$85.00*

Wodehouse, P. G. *Uncle Fred in the Springtime.* NY. 1939. 1st ed. dj . . . .
. . . . *$40.00–$55.00*

Wodehouse, P. G. *Uneasy Money.* Lon. 1934. . . . . *$30.00–$35.00*

Wodehouse, P. G. *Very Good, Jeeves.* NY. Doubleday. 1930. 1st US ed. 340 pp . . .
. . . . *$50.00–$65.00*

Wolf, Simon. *American Jew As Patriot, Soldier and Citizen.* Phila. 1895. 1st ed. .
. . . . *$65.00–$75.00*

Wolfe, Humbert. *Troy.* Lon. Faber & Gwyer. 1928. 1st ed. illus. ltd 500 cc. sgn. .
. . . . *$90.00–$150.00*

Wolfe, Thomas. *Of Time and The River.* NY. Scribners. 1935. 1st ed. black cl, green
and gilt-stamped front board and spine, dj . . . . *$100.00–$275.00*

Wolfe, Thomas. *Web and the Rock.* NY. Harper. 1939. 1st ed. 695 pp, dj . . . .
. . . . *$100.00–$250.00*

Wolfe, Thomas. *You Can't Go Home Again.* NY. Scribner's [1940]. 1st ed. 743 pp,
dj . . . . *$110.00–$250.00*

Wolfe, Thomas. *You Can't Go Home Again.* NY. Scribner's (1940. 1st ed. . . . . . .
. . . . *$25.00–$50.00*

Wolfe, Tom. *Bonfire of the Vanities.* 1987. 1st ed. dj . . . . *$40.00–$60.00*

Wolfe, Tom. *In Our Time.* NY. 1980. 1st ed. dj . . . . *$60.00–$75.00*

Wolfe, Tom. *Mauve Gloves & Madmen, Clutter & Vine.* Farrar. 1976. 1st ed. dj . . .
. . . . *$40.00–$50.00*

Wolfe, Tom. *Right Stuff.* NY. Farrar, Straus & Giroux. (1979). 1st ed. inscr, dj. . . .
. . . . *$60.00–$100.00*

Wolff, Tobias. *In the Garden if the North American Martyrs.* Ecco Press. 1981.
1st ed. dj . . . . *$85.00–$600.00*

Wolff, Tobias. *Matters of Life and Death.* Wampeter Press. 1983. 1st ed. dj . . . . .
. . . . *$75.00–$90.00*

Wolff, Tobias. *This Boy's Life.* Lon. 1989. 1st Eng ed, dh. . . . . *$15.00–$35.00*

Wood, Alphonso. *American Botanist and Florist.* NY. A S Barnes. 1875. . . . .
. . . . *$18.00–$25.00*

Wood, Clement. *Double Jeopardy.* Ny. Arcadia House. 1947. 1st ed. dj . . . .
. . . . *$40.00–$50.00*

Wood, Edward J. *Curiosities of Clocks and Watches From the Earliest Times.* Lon.
1866. 1st ed. . . . . *$150.00–$220.00*

Wood, Edward J. *Giants and Dwarfs.* Lon. 1868. 1st ed. . . . . *$58.00–$75.00*

Wood, Nancy. *Hollering Sun.* NY. (1972). 1st ed. illus. photos.. . . . *$55.00–$70.00*

Wood, Wales W. *History of the Ninety-fifth Regiment Illinois Infantry Vols.* Chi. 1865. 1st ed. . . . . *$175.00–$450.00*

Wood, Walter. *Harvesting Machines.* NY. 1882. wrps. . . . . *$30.00–$40.00*

Wood, William. *General Conchology: A Description of Shells.* Lon. 1835. illus. 60 hand-clr plates, 1/2 green mor, marbled bds, xlib. . . . . *$300.00–$400.00*

Woodbridge, Hensley C., John London and George Tweney (comps). *Jack London, A Bibliography.* Georgetown, CA. Talisman Press. 1966. 1st ed. illus. . . . . *$60.00–$120.00*

Woods, Rev James. *Recollections of Pioneer Work in California.* San Francisco. Joseph Winterburn & Co. 1878. 1st ed. . . . . *$85.00–$100.00*

Woods, Stuart. *Deep Lie.* NY. (1986). 1st ed. dj. . . . . *$25.00–$50.00*

Woodworth, Jim. *Kodiak Bear.* Harrisburg. Stackpole. 1958. illus. with b/w photos. dj. . . . . *$75.00–$100.00*

Woolf, Virginia. *Flush.* Lon. 1933. 1st ed. illus. by Vanessa Bell, dj.*$50.00–$75.00*

Woolf, Virginia. *Night and Day.* Lon. 1919. . . . . *$125.00–$275.00*

Woolf, Virginia. *The Waves.* Lon. 1931. 1st ed. dj. . . . . *$75.00–$225.00*

Woolf, Virginia. *The Years.* NY. Harcourt, Brace. 1937. 1st Amer ed. dj. . . . . *$75.00–$100.00*

Woolf, Virginia. *Three Guineas.* Lon. Hogarth. 1938. 1st UK ed. . . *$45.00–$60.00*

Woolf, Virginia. *Writer's Diary: Being Extracts from the Diary of Virginia Woolf.* Lon. Hogarth Press. 1953. 1st ed. dj. . . . . *$70.00–$85.00*

Woolfe, Virginia. *Contemporary Writers.* NY. 1965. 1st US ed. dj. . *$40.00–$50.00*

Woolner, Frank. *Grouse and Grouse Hunting.* NY. Crown Pub. (1970). illus. yellow c,l pict dj. . . . . *$25.00–$45.00*

Worcester, J E. *Geographical Dictionary.* Bos. Cummings & Hilliard. 1823. 2 vols. calf. . . . . *$45.00–$65.00*

Wordsworth, William. *Sonnets of.* NY. Peter Pauper Press. slipcase. . . . . *$15.00–$25.00*

Wordsworth, William. *The Prelude.* NY. Appleton. 1850. 1st US ed. . . . . *$250.00–$300.00*

Work, John W. *American Negro Songs and Spirituals*. NY. Bonanza Books. 1940. illus. dj. . . . . *$55.00–$75.00*

World Encompassed: An Exhibition of the History of Maps. Balt. Walters Art Gallery. 1952. 1st ed. illus. 60 plates, pict wrps. . . . . *$100.00–$150.00*

Wormley, A. E. *Israel Yesterday and Today*. Bos. Beauchamp. 1918. 1st ed. . . . . *$60.00–$80.00*

Worthington, T. *Brief History of the 46th Ohio Volunteers*. DC. 1877-1880. wrps. . . . . *$75.00–$100.00*

Wouk, Herman. *The Caine Mutiny*. Doubleday. 1952. sgn. . . . . . *$200.00–$250.00*

Wouk, Herman. *Caine Mutiny*. Franklin Center. Franklin Library. 1977. ltd, sgn. . . . . *$100.00–$200.00*

WPA. *Alaska*. 1943. . . . . *$25.00–$35.00*

WPA. *Anthology of Writers in Fed. Writer's Project.* . . . . *$50.00–$75.00*

WPA. *Boston Looks Seaward the Story of the Port*. Bos. 1941. illus. *$25.00–$40.00*

WPA. *California*. NY. Hastings House. 1945. 1st ed. 15. . . . . *$30.00–$45.00*

WPA. *Cape Cod*. 2nd prntg. . . . . *$30.00–$35.00*

WPA. *Cavalcade of the American Negro*. Chi. 1940. . . . . *$50.00–$75.00*

WPA. *Iowa*. NY. 1938. 1st ed. pocket map, dj. . . . . *$30.00–$40.00*

WPA. *Key West*. NY. 1949. 2nd ed. dj. . . . . *$14.00–$20.00*

WPA. *Maryland*. NY. 1940. 5th prntg. . . . . *$12.00–$15.00*

WPA. *Michigan*. Ox. 1941. 1st ed. pocket map, dj. . . . . *$30.00–$40.00*

WPA. *Minnesota*. NY. Viking Press. 1938. 1st ed. map, dj. . . . . *$45.00–$50.00*

WPA. *Montana*. 1st ed. map, dj. . . . . *$35.00–$100.00*

WPA. *Negroes of Nebraska*. Lincoln, Nebraska. 1940. 1st ed. . . . . *$45.00–$60.00*

WPA. *New Orleans City Guide*. 1938. map. . . . . *$22.00–$30.00*

WPA. *New York City Guide*. 1939. pocket map. . . . . *$30.00–$40.00*

WPA. *North Dakota*. Fargo. 1938. 1st ed. . . . . *$37.00–$50.00*

WPA. *South Dakota*. NY. 1952. 2nd ed. maps, dj. . . . . *$40.00–$50.00*

WPA. *Texas, A Guide to the Lone Star State*. NY. 1940. 1st ed. illus. dj. . . . . *$24.00–$35.00*

WPA. *Wyoming.* 1st ed. map, dj. . . . . *$60.00–$95.00*

Wren, Percival Christopher. *Mysterious Ways.* NY. Stokes. 1930. 1st Amer ed. dj. .
. . . . *$175.00–$200.00*

Wrensch, Frank A. *Harness Horse Racing in the United States and Canada.* Van
Nostrand. (1951). 2nd ed. illus. . . . . *$20.00–$30.00*

Wright & Ditson's Lawn Tennis Guide for 1895. wrps. . . . . *$25.00–$45.00*

Wright, Frank Lloyd. *Drawings for a Living Architecture.* NY. Horizon Press. 1959.
1st ed. illus. 255pp. . . . . *$600.00–$950.00*

Wright, Frank Lloyd. *Future of Architecture.* NY. Horizon Press. 1953. 1st ed. dj. .
. . . . *$95.00–$115.00*

Wright, Frank Lloyd. *Japanese Print and Interpretation.* NY. 1967. 1st ed. boxed..
. . . . *$90.00–$250.00*

Wright, Frank Lloyd. *Living City.* 1958. 1st ed. dj. . . . . *$55.00–$67.00*

Wright, Frank Lloyd. *Natural House.* NY. Horizon. 1954. 1st ed. illus. . . . .
. . . . *$100.00–$260.00*

Wright, Frank Lloyd. *On Architecture.* NY. 1941. 1st ed. . . . . . . *$95.00–$125.00*

Wright, Frank Lloyd. *Works of.* NY. Bramhall House. 1965. illus. The Wendingen
ed, 163 pp, dj. . . . . *$100.00–$155.00*

Wright, G Frederick. *Ice Age In North America.* Appleton. 1889. 1st ed. . . . .
. . . . *$70.00–$100.00*

Wright, Gordon and the US Equestrian Team. *Horsemanship.* Tryon, NC. Gordon
Wright. 1958. 1st ed. slipcase. . . . . *$45.00–$58.00*

Wright, H. B. *Long Ago Told Legends of the Papago Indians.* 1st ed. illus. facs dj. .
. . . . *$450.00–$675.00*

Wright, H. B. *Shepherd of the Hills.* A. L. Burt. 1907. 1st ed. . . . . *$45.00–$70.00*

Wright, Harold B. *Uncrowned King.* The Book Supply Co. 191o. . . . .
. . . . *$30.00–$40.00*

Wright, Harold Bell. *Devil's Highway.* NY. 1932. dj. . . . . *$150.00–$275.00*

Wright, Harold Bell. *Ma Cinderella.* Harper. 1932. maroon cl. . *$100.00–$450.00*

Wright, Harold Bell. *Mine With The Iron Door.* NY. 1923. 1st ed. dj. . . . .
. . . . *$25.00–$65.00*

Wright, Henry. *History of the Sixth Iowa Infantry.* Iowa City. 1923. . . . .
. . . . *$55.00–$65.00*

Wright, Olgivanna. *Our House*. NY. 1959. 1st ed. dj. . . . . *$50.00–$65.00*

Wright, Richard. *Black Boy*. NY. (1945). 1st ed. dj.. . . . . *$100.00–$200.00*

Wright, Richard. *Black Power*. NY. Harpers. (1954). 1st ed. dj.. . . *$30.00–$60.00*

Wright, Richard. *Native Son*. NY. 1940. 1st ed. 1st binding. dj. . *$200.00–$350.00*

Wright, Richard. *The Outsider*. NY. Harper. 1953. 1st ed. . . . . . . *$20.00–$30.00*

Wright, Thomas. *History of Domestic Manners and Sentiments in England During the Middle Ages*. Lon. Chapman & Hall. 1862. 1st ed. illus. aeg, bound by Zaehnsdorf. . . . . *$100.00–$150.00*

Wright, William. *Grizzly Bear*. NY. Scribner's. 1909. 1st ed. illus. photos by author. . . . . *$75.00–$195.00*

Wroth, Lawrence C. A. *History of Printing*. Balt. 1922. ltd 500 cc, lea, marbled bds. . . . . *$120.00–$150.00*

Wulff, Lee. *Atlantic Salmon*. NY. A.S. Barnes. 1958. illus. b/w, ltd 200 cc, sgn, slipcase. . . . . *$275.00–$325.00*

Wyatt, Thomas. *Manual of Conchology*. NY. 1838. 1st ed. illus. 36 litho plates. . . . . *$65.00–$140.00*

Wyeth, Betsey James. *Wyeth at Kuerners*. Bos. 1976. 1st ed. dj.. . . *$60.00–$90.00*

Wyeth, Betsy James. *Christina's World*. Bos. 1982. 1st ed. illus. oblong folio, dj.. . . . . *$50.00–$75.00*

Wylie, Eleanor. *Orphan Angel*. NY. Knopf. 1926. 1st ed. . . . . *$20.00–$75.00*

Wylie, Elinor. *Collected Poems*. NY. Knopf. 1932. 1st ed. dj. . . . . . *$25.00–$50.00*

Wylie, Elinor. *Mr. Hodge & Mr. Hazard*. NY. Knopf. 1928. 1st ed. *$30.00–$60.00*

Wylie, Elinor. *Nets to Catch the Wind*. NY. Harcourt, Brace. 1921. 1st ed. dj, author's first book. . . . . *$100.00–$175.00*

Wylie, Philip. *Murderer Invisible*. NY. 1931. 1st ed. . . . . *$35.00–$50.00*

Wyss, Johann. *Swiss Family Robinson*. NY. Limited Editions Club. 1963. illus. by David Gentleman, ltd 1500 cc, sgn, slipcase. . . . . *$20.00–$30.00*

X, Malcolm. *Autobiography of Malcolm X*. NY. Grove. 1965. 1st ed. illus. photos, dj. . . . . *$650.00–$800.00*

Yardley, Herbert. *Chinese Black Chamber*. Bos. Houghton & Mifflin. 1893. 1st ed. dj. . . . . *$25.00–$45.00*

Yates, Richard. *Special Providence*. NY. Knopf. 1969. 1st ed. dj.. . *$25.00–$50.00*

Year Book Boston 1913. Boston Architectural Club. blue cl, grey bds, pict pastedown, illus. . . . . *$18.00–$25.00*

Yeats, William Butler. *Hour-Glass*. NY. Macmillan. 1904. 1st Amer ed. . . . . *$75.00–$150.00*

Yeats, William Butler. *Synge and the Ireland of His Time*. Cuala Press. 1911. 1st ed. . . . . *$200.00–$275.00*

Yeats, William Butler. *Words upon the Window Pane: A Play in One Act*. Dublin. Cuala Press. 1934. 1st ed. ltd 350 cc. . . . . *$200.00–$250.00*

Yolen, Jane. *Dragon's Blood*. Delacorte Press. (1980). 1st ed. dj. . . *$20.00–$25.00*

Yolen, Jane. *Neptune Rising, Songs and Tales of the Undersea Folk*. NY. (1982). 1st ed. sgn, dj. . . . . *$25.00–$35.00*

Yolen, Jane. *Sister Light, Sister Dark*. NY. 1988. 1st ed. sgn, dj. . . . *$25.00–$35.00*

York, Alvin C. *Sergeant York*. Garden City. Doubleday Doran & Co. 1928. 1st ed. dec cl, sgn by York. . . . . *$200.00–$300.00*

Youatt, William. *Sheep*. NY. 1865. illus. *$60.00–$85.00*

Youatt, William. *The Horse*. NY. Leavitt & Allen. nd. illus. 448pp. *$55.00–$67.00*

Youmans, Eliza. *Descriptive Botany*. NY. Appleton. 1985. . . . . *$20.00–$25.00*

Young, Alexander A. *Manual of Phrenology*. Phila. Perkins. 1837. 1st ed. wrps. . . . . *$140.00–$175.00*

Young, Ann Elizabeth. *Wife #19*. Hartford. 1876. 1st ed. illus. 605 pp. . . . . *$150.00–$230.00*

Young, Brigham. *The Resurrection*. Salt Lake. 1884. 2nd ed, printed wrps. . . . . *$40.00–$65.00*

Young, Clarence. *Jack Ranger's School Victories*. Cupples & Leon. 1908. Jack Ranger #3, dj. . . . . *$15.00–$35.00*

Young, Clarence. *Motor Boys on the Atlantic*. Cupples & Leon. 1908. Motor Boys #6, dj. . . . . *$40.00–$60.00*

Young, Jesse Bowman. *The Battle of Gettysburg*. NY. 1913. . . . . *$85.00–$125.00*

Younghusband, Ethel. *Glimpses of East Africa and Zanzibar*. Lon. John Long. 1910. 1st ed. illus. photos, fldg map, teg. . . . . *$60.00–$100.00*

Yount, George C. *George C. Yount and His Chronicles of the West*. Rosenstock. 1966. 1st ed. illus. fldg map. . . . . *$40.00–$50.00*

Zabriskie, George. *The Pathfinder*. FL. 1947. dj. . . . . *$65.00–$80.00*

Zaharias, Babe Didrikson. *Championship Golf.* NY. Barnes. 1948. 1st ed. illus. photos.. . . . . *$25.00–$40.00*

Zaharias, Babe Didrikson. *This Life I've Led.* NY. Barnes. 1955. 1st ed. illus. photos dj. . . . . *$25.00–$95.00*

Zahm, J A. *Quest of El Dorado.* NY. Appleton. 1917. 1st ed. cl.. . . *$40.00–$75.00*

Zahm, The Reverend J. A. *Through South America's Southland.* Appleton. 1916. illus. frontis, teg, blindstamped. . . . . *$20.00–$35.00*

Zangwill, Israel. *Children of the Ghetto.* Lon. 1892. 3 vols. 1st ed. . . . . *$125.00–$150.00*

Zeisberger's Indian Dictionary. Cambridge. John Wilson & Son. 1887. . . . . *$140.00–$160.00*

Zelazny, Roger. *Doorways in the Sand.* Harper & Row. (1976). 1st ed. dj.. . . . . *$25.00–$35.00*

Zelazny, Roger. *Eye of Cat.* NY. Timescope Books. (1982). 1st ed. dj, sgn. . . . . *$15.00–$25.00*

Zelazny, Roger. *Sign of Chaos.* NY. Arbor House. (1987). 1st ed. dj.*$12.00–$25.00*

Zelazny, Roger. *Sign of the Unicorn.* Garden City. 1975. 1st ed. dj. . *$30.00–$45.00*

Zelazny, Roger. *Trumps of Doom.* NY. (1985). 1st ed. dj. . . . . *$25.00–$35.00*

Zeller, Mrs. H. *Wild Flowers of Holy Land.* Lon. 1876. illus. 2nd ed. 54 plates. . . . . *$95.00–$120.00*

Ziegler, Rev Winfred. *Wyoming Indians.* Laramie. 1947. wrps. illus. . . . . *$20.00–$30.00*

Zilahy, Lajos. *Century in Scarlet.* NY. McGraw-Hill. 1965. 1st ed. dj.. . . . . *$15.00–$25.00*

Zimmer, Dave. *Crosby Stills and Nash.* NY. 1984. 1st ed. wrps. . . *$16.00–$40.00*

Zinkersen, Doris. *Designing for the Stage.* Lon. illus. . . . . *$55.00–$95.00*

Zobelin, Jennifer. *Dinosaurs.* Kansas City. (1971). illus. dj. . . . . . *$75.00–$125.00*

Zogbaum, Rufus Fairchild. *Horse, Foot, and Dragoons.* . NY. Harper & Bros. 1888. 1st ed. illus. by the author, 176 pp, pict cl, teg.. . . . . *$175.00–$225.00*

Zolotow, Charlotte. *I Have a Horse of My Own.* Crowell. 1964. 1st ed. dj, sgn. . . . . *$18.00–$45.00*

Zolotow, Charlotte. *Mr. Rabbit and the Lovely Present.* NY. Harper & Row. (1962). illus. in clr by Maurice Sendak. sgn by Sendak. pict bds. . . . . *$100.00–$150.00*

Zolotow, Charlotte. *New Friend.* NY. Abelard & Schuman. 1968. 1st ed. dj. . . . . . .
. . . . *$14.00–$22.00*

Zolotow, Charlotte. *River Winding.* NY. Crowell. (1970). dj, inscr.. *$25.00–$35.00*

Zolotow, Charlotte. *Sky Was Blue.* Harper & Row. 1963. 1st ed. illus. dj, sgn. . . . .
. . . . *$35.00–$40.00*

Zolotow, Charlotte. *White Marble.* NY. Abelard-Schuman. 1963. 1st ed. dj. . . . . . .
. . . . *$20.00–$25.00*

Zouch, Thomas. *Life of Isaac Walton.* Lon. 1823. . . . . *$200.00–$300.00*

Zuckerman, Solly. *Monkeys Men and Missiles.* NY. W W Norton. 1989. . . . .
. . . . *$20.00–$25.00*

Zweig, Stefan. *Amok.* NY. Viking. 1931. dj. . . . . *$30.00–$50.00*

Zweig, Stephen. *Marie Antoinette.* NY. 1933. dj. . . . . *$20.00–$35.00*

Zwemmer, Samuel. *Arabia: The Cradle of Islam.* NY/Chi/Tor. Fleming Revell.
(1900). 1st ed. illus. red pict cl, maps, photos. . . . .`. . . . . . . *$35.00–$75.00*

BIBLES

That Book in many eyes doth share the glory
That in gold clasps locks in the golden story
—SHAKESPEARE

Although the Bible has been on the bestseller list since Gutenberg made it readily available, Bibles in general are not collectible. Even so, collector interest in notable Bibles remains high. To separate the wheat from the chaff in this area of interest, a few caveats for the novice are in order.

American Bibles dated 1800 or later are far less likely to have any collectible value than those printed earlier. That is, unless they are associated with a notable event or family. For instance, a Bible that chronicles family births, marriages and deaths written in Mary Todd Lincoln's hand would certainly qualify.

On the other hand, European Bibles should be published before 1700 to qualify for collectibility. Yet, again, after 1800, ask for counsel from a credible bookseller on whether or not you have a prize. Some later editions have association or special publication value, so don't discard a fine Bible indiscriminately based on its date.

What else makes a Bible valuable beside it's age? Well, you might one day run across the first Bible printed in a particular place, country, state, or city. Or the first Bible printed in any language, such as the Eliot or Natick Bible printed for the Natick colony of "praying Indians," west of Boston, completed in 1663. The first Bible printed, translated or edited by a woman would be a prime example of a significant exception. Also, Bibles owned by

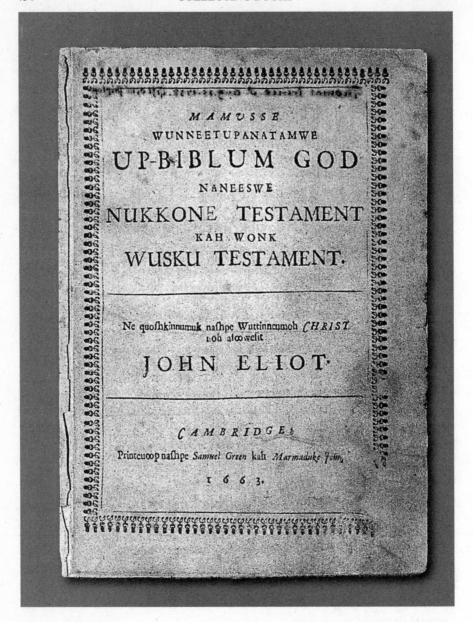

The earliest example in history of an entire Bible translated into a new language. By John Eliot, known as the "Eliot Bible" or "Natick Bible," it was printed for the Natick Colony of "praying Indians" west of Boston, Massachusetts, and completed in 1663.

Courtesy of the Trustees of the Boston Public Library. Photo by Marilyn Green.
Digital enhancement by Jonathan Draudt, Tamarac Arts

famous people, miniature Bibles called "thumb-Bibles," hieroglyphic Bibles, or other unusual volumes in fine bindings, or those printed for children.

Most people think of the family Bible, old, leather-worn and bearing the ancient script of a long-deceased ancestor, as surely a valuable treasure. Indeed, it is a treasure, not in dollars—but in the pleasure and fortune of having a precious family heirloom tucked away safely or prominently spotlighted in your home.

Listed below are some collectible Bibles and Bible-related volumes:

American Bible. The "Eliot" or "Natick Bible." Cambridge, MA. 1663. Indian language translation. Scarce. As we go to press, at least one excellent copy of this Bible is currently offered for sale and the price it realizes could change these estimates. *$175,000.00–$250,000.00*

American Bible. Phila. 1790. 2 vols. 1st Amer ed of the Douai or Roman Catholic Bible. . . . . *$6,500.00–$10,000.00*

American Bible. Trenton. 1791. . . . . *$1,000.00–$2,000.00*

American Bible. Phila. 1794. pocket size. . . . . *$100.00–$175.00*

American Bible. Windsor, Vt. 1812.. . . . . *$800.00–$1,000.00*

Bible. NY. American Bible Society. 1831. lea. . . . . *$24.00–$35.00*

Bible in English. Oxford. Baskett. 1717. 2 vols. large folio. many errors. called the "Vinegar Bible" for a proofreading error in Luke XX, word "vinegar" substituted for "vineyard." . . . . *$800.00–$1,000.00.*

Holy Bible. Phila. Bible Society of Phila. 1812. lea. stereotype ed. . . . . *$125.00–$225.00.*

Holy Bible. Phila. Woodward. 1819. red morocco. . . . . . *$150.00–$175.00*

The New Testament of Our Lord and Saviour Jesus Christ...in Pitman's Shorthand. "The Shorthand Bible." Lon. Pitman and Sons. c. 1888. lea. . . . . *$50.00–$75.00*

"Nonesuch Bible." Lon. Nonesuch Press. 1924-27. 5 vols. *$400.00–$500.00*

Psalms of David. Golden Cockerel Press. 1927. ltd 500 cc. blue buckram. . . . . *$100.00-$130.00*

A collectible reference that includes information on the topic is:

Dibden, Rev. Thomas Frognall. *An Introduction to the Knowledge of Rare and Valuable Editions of the Greek and Latin Classics* .... Lon. 1827. 2 vols. 4th ed.. . . . . **$300.00–$400.00**

GLOSSARY

All the world knows me in my book
And my book in me.

—MICHEL DE MONTAIGNE

ADDENDA (or ADDENDUM). Supplemental material inserted at the end of a book.

ADVANCE COPY. Copies of a book issued ahead of schedule to gain final approval from the author or to send to reviewers before the edition is released. Sometimes the advance copies will be identical to the regular edition, but often they are not, at least to the extent that they are labeled advance copies. If the only difference is in style or color of binding, it may be difficult to determine later if the copies are an advance issue or simply a binding variant, which could be part of a normal trade run.

Collectors often value advance copies since they represent an early state of the text and, however rare the case, they may contain notations by the author.

ALL EDGES GILT. Indicates that all three edges of the leaves (top, bottom, and fore-edge) have been gilded. The term is abbreviated a.e.g. or, if only the top edge is gilded, t.e.g.

AMERICANA. In the strict sense, refers to material dealing with the American hemisphere. But today, the term more often refers narrowly and loosely to books, documents, pamphlets and other printed material that shows why, how, when and by whom the United States was developed.

ANA (or IANA). Suffix denoting items related to a particular subject, be it a person, a time or place in history, or some such. For instance, Joyceiana is material relating in some way to James Joyce, even if the connection is remote. The heading covers such things as pamphlets, books, newspaper accounts, artifacts, and letters by, about, or to the subject.

Collecting ana (or iana) is widespread among those interested in a particular author or historical time or personality. Even those who have written only one book (or none) can be the subject of an extensive collection of written and artifact items. Institutions and libraries are notable collectors of ana.

ANTHOLOGY. A collection of short works, by one or more writers, in one book or set of volumes. Anthologies are most often collections of work that has appeared elsewhere.

ANTIQUARIAN BOOKSELLING. Sale of used, old, and rare books, printed fare and related items; usually refers to trade in books out of print.

Until about the 12th century, most books were handcrafted in monasteries and churches and remained their property. Except to those who owned them and valued the information they contained, books had no intrinsic value unless they contained gold gilt or were inlaid with precious stones. Not until sometime around the 13th century, when craftspeople in the secular world began to make and sell books, adding topics like philosophy and literature, did books take on a broader commercial value.

Michael Olmert, author of the *Smithsonian Book of Books* (1992) remarks, "An intriquing question is when did books become valuable enough to steal?" Olmert says that thieves profited from stealing books once a commercial market for them was established. As proof that books were taking on value, he reports book owners of the 12th century began writing curses on their flyleaves to discourage theft, warning that whoever steals the books would be damned to hellfire.

Even as the first commercial markets were growing, bookmaking was done slowly by hand, comparatively few books were produced, and those were often custom made for specific buyers. Bookselling was primarily a second-hand business but was not yet antiquarian bookselling. Since bound books were still in their infancy, you wouldn't term their trade antiquarian.

By the 17th century, enough time had elapsed, printing had become mechanized, and enough books were in circulation for true antiquarian bookselling to arise in England, France, and elsewhere.

Few catalogues were issued at first. Most early shops gathered in clusters, such as those that sprang up in St. Paul's Churchyard, London. Most shopkeepers were located in large cities, primarily in stalls with much of their material displayed on the sidewalk and very little within. The **PENNY BOXES** that became such a favorite of the bargain hunters in later years were probably not present early on. Prints, engravings, maps and such were sold by at least some dealers.

The emergence of the scholar-dealer—the collector at heart who studied his merchandise with interest—did not occur until the early part of the 19th century. By this time, bookselling was big business. The Bohn brothers of

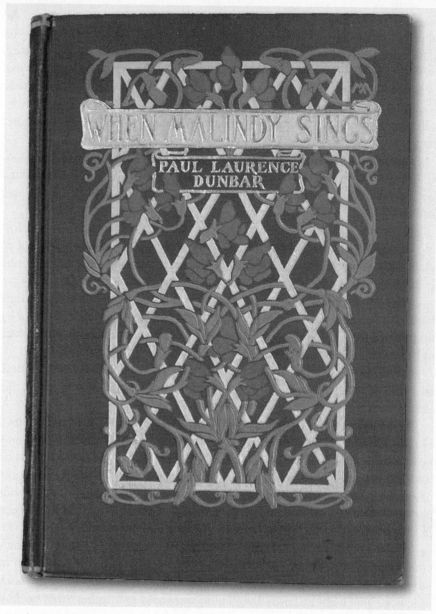

When Malindy Sings, *with cloth binding decorations by Margaret Armstrong, is by Paul Lawrence Dunbar, Dodd Mead & Co., Chicago, 1903.*
Photography and digital enhancement by Jonathan Draudt, Tamarac Arts

London are generally credited with giving birth to modern rare-book dealing. By 1900, at least a half dozen English dealers boasted inventories in excess of half-a-million volumes. Several German booksellers by this time had stocks even larger.

APPRAISAL. Estimation of the value of a book or a collection. An appraisal should be made by a qualified professional in the antiquarian book trade with the tools and the experience to do the job right. Some appraisers will offer an opinion based on a mere list and description of volumes, but that is not recommended. The value of a book depends on many factors, not the least of which is its condition. The best appraisals are done by experts who can hold the books in their hands and examine them in fine detail. This can't be done with a list.

AQUATINT. A method of etching that stresses soft tones and shades, resembling wash paintings. The French artist LePrince is generally credited with perfecting the process during the late 18th century. The technique became popular in Britain during the 18th and 19th centuries.

Sometimes aquatint printing was done in color and sometimes the coloring was added by hand later. When printing in colored aquatint, a separate plate for each color is necessary. A few famous artists such as Goya and Picasso experimented with the process.

ART PAPER. Shiny, coated stock on which most art books (or at least the illustrations) are printed. The paper ages badly and is easily damaged by moisture. Also, dirt stains cannot be removed without damaging the surface of the paper.

AS NEW. Showing no signs of wear; the book doesn't look used. Basically a British expression. Americans prefer **MINT**, which carries the same meaning.

ASSOCIATION COPY. A book that was part of the author's own library or was associated in one way or another with a famous person. It may be that the author inscribed the book to a friend, or the book may contain an inscription by another famous owner, perhaps a dedication or a presentation, or the book was merely included—without any inscriptions—in a famous person's library. But the point is, there must be proof that the book has been in the possession of someone famous.

The value of association copies to the collector derives from the book's connection to history, or in modern times, to people who are perceived as larger than life. If we were to learn that Abraham Lincoln had a favorite book of sonnets that he daily carried with him, we would love to have that book. It would be an association copy.

Association copies should be distinguished from signed copies, which proliferate these days with the popularity of book tours and autograph signings. And beware the forgeries! Experts in the trade can help you weed them out.

AUTHORIZED EDITION. Usually refers to biographies written with the approval or even help of the subject. The term is intended to draw attention and interest, but a drawback to authorized editions is the public perception that if the subject of a biography authorized the work, it wouldn't tell tales of the subject's secret life.

B.A.L. The Bibliography of American Literature, authored by Jacob Nathaniel Blanck and published in 1955 by the Yale Univerisity Press for the Bibliographical Society of America. Virginia Smyers and Michael Winship edited the work and later added a final volume. The seven volume work is a detailed bibliography of important American literature through much of the 20th century and an indispensable research tool for the serious book person.

BASTARD TITLE. Another name for the **HALF-TITLE PAGE**, the leaf preceding the title page that carries the title in small print but no other information. Use of this page is a holdover from the incunabula days when the title page consisted of only this. It has no other real purpose and is retained in many volumes merely because old habits die hard. With a nod to decorum, many bibliographers refered to this as the "bas. title."

BAY PSALM BOOK. The first full-length American-printed book. Issued at Cambridge, Massachusetts, in 1640 by Stephen Daye, the name derives from the Massachusetts Bay Colony. Only 11 volumes are known to remain, all but one in public or institutional collections. The total number of copies printed isn't known, but is guessed to be from 100 to 300. Though the usual press run at the time was considerably more, experts theorize that Daye would not have had a large market for books printed locally and would have printed less than the usual number. The book was collected as a rarity as early as the mid-1700s. The actual title of Daye's volume is *The Whole Booke of Psalmes Faithfully Translated into English Metre*, but printers in Europe had produced works with similar titles, and therefore *Bay Psalm Book* more clearly distinguishes Daye's work from the others.

BEVELED EDGES. Angle-cut edges on wooden boards once used in bookbindings. They're of little consequence when judging the value of an antiquarian book.

BIBLIOGRAPHY. Commonly, a list of books organized by subject or author. For instance, libraries consider an author bibliography to be a list, as complete as possible, of all specimens of an author's work that have appeared in print.

The term has taken on an alternate meaning coming into its own now as the study of books themselves, including their origins, history, development, physical appearance, construction, and value.

BIBLIOMANIA. A preoccupation with books, a compulsion to be around them, learn about them and own them. Booksellers and collectors are prone to this disease. The malady can be observed at library sales, auctions and house sales.

BIBLIOTHECA AMERICANA. A comprehensive directory of books on Americana, 29 volumes in all, dating from the coming of the Europeans to the 20th century. Begun by Joseph Sabin, who completed the first thirteen volumes, the work was continued by Wilberforce Eames and completed by R. W. G. Vail.

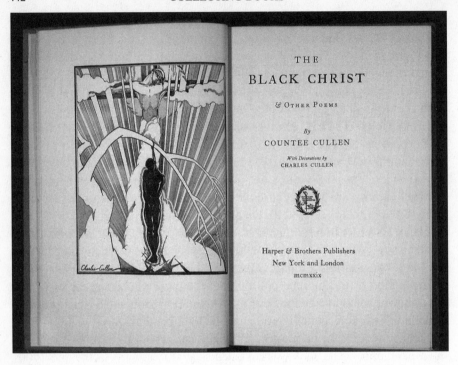

The Black Christ, *Harper Brothers, NY/London, 1929, is a first edition of this book of poetry by African-American poet Countee Cullen.*

BIBLIOPHILE. An ardent and avid book collector. One who loves books. A person having a mild, benign form of bibliomania.

BINDING COPY. A book in need of a new binding. A British term.

BINDINGS. The permanent cover of a book, not to be confused with a dust jacket. As soon as books were made of folded leaves instead of scrolls, they needed a proper covering. The earliest bindings were probably uncovered wooden boards with a hide spine—what we call today a **HALF-LEATHER** binding. This evolved into a full leather binding. Early ornamentation on books consisted of painting and encrusting with jewels and bone carvings. In time, these gave way to **BLINDSTAMPING** and finally goldstamping.

Materials used over the centuries for binding books are numerous and even macabre. Most common were vellum, pigskin, calf, morocco and various types of cloth or muslin. A practice arose during the Middle Ages of occasionally stripping the skin of slain enemy soldiers. One use of the leather made out of these skins: book bindings. (In some cathedrals in Europe one can still see doors covered in these human hides. Tour guides often hesitate to mention this fact.)

Collecting fine bindings is a major area of book collecting.

BLINDSTAMPING. Recessed or raised impressions on the bindings of books which are not inked or colored. Blindstamping did not originate with bookbinding but was long a popular means of hand-decorating leather. As a decoration for bindings, the process did not begin until the 12th century.

BOARDS. Uncovered hard cardboard, wooden boards, or boards covered with thin paper, linen, buckrum, etc., used as front and back covers in bindings. The term is a holdover from the early days of printing when books were bound with actual wooden boards held together by leather or buckram at the spine. In the bookselling trade today, "boards" refers to stiff bindings covered in paper instead of the more common cloth or even leather.

BOOK OF HOURS. Iluminated medieval prayer books. During the Middle Ages, wealthy patrons commissioned these stunning books for their personal use. They were prized for their calendars, which frequently featured pictures of month-by-month activities–planting in spring, harvesting in fall, etc.–providing historians with valuable insights into medieval society and habits. Small in size, handy to carry to church services, the books included psalms, litanies, and various offices of the church. The organization of these books was based on the church's prescribed daily schedule for devotions, hence the name *Book of Hours*.

BOOK OF KELLS. An Irish manuscript of Christian scripture from the 8th century. The opening page of each Gospel is lavishly illustrated with brightly colored designs and images of saints and religious persons and events. Depictions of nature, such as animals, fish and trees, abound throughout. The art of the monks and their use of color and whimsey shows the attainment of the Irish artists of the early Middle Ages. By the way figures are depicted in the hand illuminations, it is obvious artists of the day had not perfected the study of anatomy but that deficiency was made up for in their exquisite concepts of color and design. The folio manuscript is housed in the Library of Trinity College, Dublin, Ireland.

BOOKPLATES. A label identifying ownership usually pasted on the inside of a book cover. Older, intricately designed and executed bookplates are collector's items in their own right. Some are delightful examples of art. Their use dates from the 15th century. If a modern bookplate is inserted by a person of no particular renown, the plate does not detract from the book; when properly applied, they do no harm, but they should not be affixed over existing plates or in such a way that they obscure important inscriptions or writings.

Plates of antiquity, either engraved by some famous craftsman or showing possession by some notable person, are highly sought after by collectors of bookplates but they really should not be removed from the books. Contrary to common belief, this practice damages the books and destroys evidence of a book's **PROVENANCE,** or history, an important phase of bibliography.

BOOK SCOUT. A person who beats the bushes looking for saleable books who then markets these finds to booksellers. Since a bookseller is often tied down with a shop, scheduling time for a buying trip can be a problem. Enter the bookscout. With no overhead and unfettered by the minutiae of a bookseller's store, scouts have time to ferret out books sitting on somebody's shelf, in an attic, or at the eternal Friends of the Library book sale.

A bookseller might have several scouts scattered in different parts of the country haunting the flea markets, Salvation Army stores, and estate sales. But for the most part, scouts work independently, seeking out the bookseller with the strongest interest in their finds.

Often a person starting out as a scout develops into a fulltime bookseller. Scouts of the seedy, unsavory character described by John Dunning in his mystery novel, *Booked to Die* (1992), may exist somewhere, but our experience of scouts in New England (Marie started out as a scout 20 years ago) reveals a type of person who loves books to begin with and is delighted to chase them for booksellers.

BOOK SIZES. Industry terms loosely describing the size of volumes. The terms describe books according to their **FORMAT** (the way they are printed and bound) rather than actual measurements, giving the practiced professional only an indication of how big the books really are.

The common book size formats are folio, quarto, octavo and duodecimo, indicating the manner in which the printer folds the paper sheets, on which a book is printed, to create leaves (pages). Regardless of the planned format, all sheets are fed through a press in full size and folded later into "quires." These are collected and bound together, the closed edges of the folded sheets are slit, and—presto—you have a book.

If each printed sheet is folded once to create two leaves, the book becomes a folio, the largest format. If folded twice, we get four leaves, or a quarto, written "4to." Fold again and there are eight leaves, an octavo, or "8vo;" twelve leaves are duodecimo, "12mo." Keep going and you have progressively smaller sizes and larger numbers: 16mo, 24mo, 32mo, and 64mo. A 128mo format exists, but it's only seen in the very tiniest of miniature volumes.

You can't divine the actual measure of a book from the format, but it isn't a useless convention. What you can reliably ascertain from a statement of format is something about the shape of a volume. Octavos tend to be sleek, at least 1 1/2 times as tall as they are wide. Quartos tend to be squarish and dumpy. Folios are tall and well-proportioned. The Gutenberg Bible is a folio. Most modern novels are 8vo's. Coffee table art books are folios and large quartos.

BOOKWORMS. The larval stage of a beetle that likes to eat books, a pesty little worm that feeds upon the bindings and leaves. They've been preying on libraries since the very earliest times. These maggots were the scourge of monastic libraries in the Middle Ages. No area of Europe was free of the bookworm, and contrary to some beliefs, they did not seek out only filthy habitations but ate books in fine homes and libraries as well. Modern chemicals have virtually exterminated them.

BREAKER. Someone who takes books apart and then sells the parts separately, especially the illustrations. Breaking a book may bring a higher price for the parts than the book would fetch as a whole. When a book is so badly damaged that it cannot be repaired or recovered as a book, breaking is a way of preserving the plates and putting them into circulation.

Breaking books that are not otherwise damaged is looked down on by serious antiquarian booksellers and collectors as a horrendous practice.

BROADSIDE. A poster, announcement, or proclamation, usually printed on one side of a sheet and meant to be posted on a wall. Many a political statement was brought to the people's attention in this manner even after the advent of newspapers. Old auction posters, especially horse auctions, might be adorned with an illustrated display of wares adding to the value and desirability of the artifact.

Broadsides are popular with collectors today.

BUCKRAM. A modern binding material very much like cloth but tougher and somewhat more attractive. Libraries most always have their books rebound in buckram. Inexpensive, buckram can be dyed all the colors of the rainbow, as well as goldstamped. The natural shade, which is rather like a cross between straw and wheat, is preferred by many.

Buckram bindings are often described in catalogues as cloth and vice-versa, a fact of life that collectors must endure.

CALF. Leather used for bookbindings.

CALLED FOR. Points mentioned in bibliographies that determine the edition of a book. For instance, if a handbook written by Smith says that a blank leaf follows the title in a certain edition of a certain book, then the blank leaf is "called for" for that edition and must be there for the book to be complete.

CAXTON, WILLIAM. First English printer. Born at Kent, he started his business life as a mercer, or dealer in yarn goods, a trade he followed for most of his life, showing no particular mechanical skills or flair for literature. Around 1441, Caxton went to Burgundy. He spent most of his adult life on the continent. In 1471, he entered the service of the Duchess of Burgundy and, under her influence, he performed his first effort with books, translating the *Recuyell of the Historyes of Troye*.

On a visit to Cologne that year, he was apparently introduced to the art of printing, which he brought back to Bruges, setting about to give the city a printing press. Together with a Flemish calligrapher, Colard Mansion, Caxton issued the first English language book, the same *Recuyell*. After printing two more books with Mansion, Caxton returned alone to England and founded a printing office in the parish of Westminster.

Compared to the best French and Italian printing of the time, Caxton's books come off a sorry second. His fame has led many to assume that his talent as a craftsman and type designer must have been extraordinary, but this was not the case. He did however exert much influence upon his contemporaries and followers. He began with types modeled on German gothic and stuck with them to the end. This set the trend for English printers and it was not until a century after his death that the types were replaced by the more graceful Roman.

A craze for Caxtons among collectors began in the early part of the 19th century and has gathered steam ever since. The finest collections are at the British Museum and John Rylands Library. In the U.S., the Morgan and Huntington libraries are notable for their Caxtons.

CHAPBOOK. A small pamphlet or booklet usually associated with children's stories or rhymes. Most are diminutive in size and illustrated with woodcuts. In the 18th century, itinerant peddlers, or "chapmen," hawked the booklets door to door. Because they were cheaply made, many of the books have not survived in very good condition, but those that have are highly prized and collectible.

CHEAP COPY. A defective copy which is being offered at a discount. The dealer wants the prospective buyer to be aware of the poor condition.

CLOTH BINDING. The ideal binding substance, cheap, durable, easy to apply, comes in a variety of colors. For modern books, cloth has replaced leather as the binding of choice. True, the disappearance of leather is lamentable, but the cost of leather binding would prohibit ownership of books to all but a limited class of collectors.

In the first years of cloth binding, publishers let their imaginations run wild. Every effort was made to ornament the bindings lavishly. The books were gilded and blindstamped using patterns copied from notable bindings of earlier ages. But unlike the books of old, gilding was done with large panel stamps impressed by machine rather than with tools worked by hand. The purpose was to make the public forget leather. It succeeded; out of sight, out of mind. In time, only connoisseurs who kept fine libraries retained any affection for leather. That is not to say, however, that we have become so undiscriminating that we cannot still appreciate a book bound in fine, soft leather.

CODEX. Applies to leaves bound in book form—this book, you are holding, for example—as opposed to scrolls or tablets. The invention is generally credited to Roman legal clerics who grew weary of cumbersome scrolls and cut them down to convenient size. The practice made sense at a time when the whole process of managing information was time-consuming and laborious.

COLLATED. Inspected from cover to cover to be sure all pages, plates, maps and the like are present, intact, and in their proper place. In the case of earlier books, a perfect copy—or comprehensive knowledge of one—is necessary to make a comparison when collating.

A good practice when purchasing a book is to check out the list of illustrations numbered in the contents and confirm that they are all there. If maps should be present, check them out. Nothing is more frustrating when you get home than to discover pages missing from a book you were all excited about purchasing.

And never, never send out a book to a dealer or customer before collating it. Selling a book with missing pages could be cause for manslaughter, or, more seriously, labeling yourself unprofessional.

COLOPHON. The "finishing touch." The tradition of medieval scribes when completing their manuscripts was to record, on the last page, their name and place of residence and, sometimes, the day on which the book was finished.

At times, the addition of a colophon was done out of vanity but, more often than not, such information was necessary. Without it, a printer or publisher could not identify an edition as his own, which might result in legal difficulties if the book were pirated or stolen by another printer.

The average colophon was a model of simplicity, one sentence or so, giving the essential facts. Colophons were replaced after the 16th century by information included on the title page. However, some modern books, usually limited editions, still add a colophon, perhaps out of respect for tradition. You might find one that starts out: "This book was set on the monotype in Fournier . . ."

CONDITION. The general state of a book. This singularly most important point cannot be overemphasized when considering whether to buy or sell a collectible book.

Like people, books are either in fine shape, very good shape, bad shape, or various states in between. As no hard and fast definitions exist, the terms used to designate a book's condition are subject to personal opinion. Having said that, we hasten to add that there is some agreement in the booktrade as to what the terms mean.

•Mint. As new. Right off the press.

•Fine. Nearly new. Sometimes a dealer might overlap this with mint.

•Very Good. Definitely showing wear, but not damaged. Usually a clean, tight copy. Most collectible books fit this category.

•Good. Obviously read. Perhaps the covers show moderate wear, a hinge is cracked in front or back, some minor spine fading might be present, the binding scuffed. Perhaps the book is even a little shaken, not quite as tight as it used to be. All in all, the condition shows the book has been around for a while and used. No really major defects.

•Fair. Worn and used. Cover soiled, scuffed, evidence of repairs, shaken, perhaps a page torn here or there. The book has definitely been around the block.

•Reading copy. About all it is good for. Or, it may interest collectors of modern first editions who keep their pristine copies on a shelf safe from prying hands but who may still want to read Hemingway or Faulkner. Reading copies come in handy for research.

Now when all is said and done, should a disheveled rare book come up at auction, you can bet your bottom dollar—and you might have to—that book will not lack for spirited bidding. So extenuating circumstances call for common sense. If a book is being purchased for investment, then by all means, abide by the most rigid rules of condition.

COPPER PLATE ENGRAVING. A process for producing prints and book illustrations. Plates were prepared by a battery-hammer method, then smoothed by rubbing with pumice and oilstone. Though costly and time-consuming, this method gave the best possible surface for engraving. The majority of English illustrated books of the 18th century used copper plates.

COPYRIGHT. The equivalent of a patent on a work of literature. A copyright prohibits anyone from reproducing the work, either in whole or in part, without consent of the copyright holder.

CURIOSA. In today's market, books that deal with off-beat subjects like a monograph on foot fetishes or the psychology of wearing hats. During the Victorian age, anything of a sexual nature was hidden under the heading of curiosa. Today's bookseller has no problem with that subject and classifies erotic material where it belongs, under erotica.

C.W.O. Cash with order. Most booksellers append this to their ads, safeguarding their interests, choosing not to send a book out to a customer before they have payment in hand. Payment under C.W.O may be in the form of cash, checks, money orders or credit cards.

But through the years, we have never encountered a deadbeat customer or bookseller. We have sent out books before the check arrives, in particular, a $5,000 sporting book to a dealer with a fine reputation.

At times, we need to have a little faith in our fellow human beings. Of course, in this case, it was easy as we knew the man's character.

DAMP STAINS. Damage caused by excessive humidity, but not water as is sometimes thought. Books damaged by damp are ragged and musty rather than crisp.

Improper ventilation can cause as much damage as water. Humidity constantly above 70% can damage a book as it stands untouched in a bookcase. In a book with lovely plates, dampness can cause the pages to stick together. Pulling them apart damages the plates, thus greatly altering the value and esthetics of the book.

DAYE, STEPHEN. An important individual, the first man to print mechanically in America. Daye, a British locksmith, came to the Massachusetts Bay Colony in 1633. He and his son, Matthew, a printer's apprentice, set up a printing shop in Cambridge at Harvard College. The earliest surviving book of the Dayes' press is commonly known as the *Bay Psalm Book,* after the colony where it was printed.

DELUXE EDITION. Meant to imply extraordinary production qualities; those books which, by superior design, type, paper, binding, or other factors, are set above the pale.

DISBOUND. Refers to a pamphlet or other brief work that once was part of a larger work and has been separated. Purists look down on this practice of removing the piece from the larger collection much as they look down on breaking a book.

DISCARD STAMP. A mark used by libraries when they are culling their collections to show the books have been released for sale or distribution. This is a matter of procedure to guard against theft and to show the book is legitimately no longer a part of the library collection. How nice when a librarian thinks like a book collector and carefully selects an inobtrusive place for the stamp.

DOG-EARED. Originally referred to the corners of pages that have become ragged or creased. Now, it applies to any pages that have the appearance of heavy use. One of the causes of dog-earing is the regrettable habit many readers have of turning down the corner of a page to mark their place. Thank goodness not all readers are guilty of this barbaric practice, choosing instead to use bookmarks.

DÜRER, ALBRECHT. A German artist, painter, and book illustrator at the turn of the 16th century, he was famous and in great demand for quality woodcuts used in book illustrations. Among his early works are the woodcuts for Sebastian Brant's famous *Ship of Fools.*

Most of Dürer's fame came after 1500 when he was prolific in his output not only in book illustration but working in oils, watercolor, silverpoint, and other artistic media.

DUST JACKET (or DUSTWRAPPER). The decorative paper cover that protects the binding from soil and wear. Jackets were sometimes used during the 19th century and if you found a volume with a jacket of such antiquity, hooray for you. Jackets for books dating back to the early part of the 20th century, too, are like icing on the cake. They're desirable, but hard to come by. For newer books, however—the **MODERN FIRST EDITIONS**—jackets are a must.

If a book such as William Faulkner's *Light in August* has no dust jacket, it can lose half or more of its value. Even reprints of Zane Grey or Edgar Rice Burroughs command higher prices when accompanied by dust jackets. A modern book with a jacket missing can be likened to an antique table without its legs.

EDGES. Refers to the three outer edges of the leaves. Style of edges is a very important part of a book's makeup, especially in fine or rare editions. New books are delivered to the binder in folded but uncut sheets, or gatherings, and the binder must separate the leaves by cutting the folds. The edges are usually trimmed to make them perfectly even. Books bound without trimming the edges, showing the original state of the paper with all its irregularities, are valued by some collectors. But then there is a collector for just about anything.

ELSE FINE. A term used after a recitation of a book's faults indicating that, otherwise, something is right with the book. The phrase "o/w very good," is more common.

ENGRAVING. Ilustrations printed from a metal plate or wood-block. Engravings on steel were developed in the 15th century, an improvement over wood that permitted more fine detail and delicate shading.

Collectors of engravings seek the early impressions in a print run, those among the first taken from a plate, as the fine lines of the engraved image sometimes wear down with repeated use.

EPHEMERA. Items that were meant to last a short time. Some booksellers abhor the myriad post cards, sheet music, and advertising paper that appear at book shows under this heading. But many of these items are extensions of book collecting that we accept as not only legitimate but desirable. Say you are putting together a collection of P. G. Wodehouse. Why would you reject the sheet music he wrote? Or the Christmas cards by Robert Frost to round out a collection of his books of poetry? Or the screen scripts written by now famous authors when they were down on their luck and needed to eat?

Ephemera is fun and exciting and some very famous artists like Maxfield Parrish produced beautiful ads as well as book illustrations for some of the most sought after children's books. Tucked into old volumes, many ephemera treasures have come to light. A stevensgraph, or a hollow-cut silhouette, even a letter with historical information, are some of the bonuses possible when turning the pages of an old book.

A Burlington, Vermont, bookseller was a little chagrined when she learned she'd sold a book on Calvin Coolidge with a holograph letter tucked unnoticed among the leaves. The next day the customer returned and asked, did she have any more of those books with letters of the presidents inside?

ERASURES. Removal of underlining or notations with an eraser, discussed further under "Notations and Underlining" in the section on Care and Repair of Books.

A bookseller may resort to erasing pencil or pen markings made by former owners of a book, generally by use of a wad of art gum or pencil eraser. Collectors have mixed feelings about notations and whether or not they should be removed. The value and rarity of a book will influence whether a book is rejected due to the presence of notations or purchased and lived with as is. For the bibliophile, a notation might suggest some continuity with the former owners and be cherished.

The erasures themselves should be clean and not leave unsightly blotches or destroy the print.

ERRATA. Mistakes in printing. The "errata leaf" is still used in cases where a blooper was spotted too late to correct the print run but early enough to bind a note into the book stating the error and correction. More frequently seen is the "errata slip," a small strip of paper containing the correction which may be pasted in the book, or laid-in loosely, after the book has been bound.

EX-LIBRIS (EX-LIBRARY, EX-LIB). Indicates the book belonged to a library or bears evidence of having been in a library collection, e.g., the library stamp, card pockets, or identifying marks on the spine. These books, unless they are exceedingly rare, are not often sought by collectors as they usually show considerable wear and damage due to use and library mutilation.

Ex-lib books are almost as difficult to sell as Book of the Month Club or Reader's Digest editions, although many catalogues feature ex-lib books.

FINE PRINTING. Any book in which the quality of type and layout are a main consideration. Books printed by individuals or presses which design their own type may rate as fine printing if the type is well designed. Such books do not necessarily have to be limited editions or kept from public sale. All the products of early typographers were sold on the general market, yet some represent excellent presswork. Had these men bought their types from foundries rather than having a hand in their design, their books might not be so respected.

FIRST EDITION. The first appearance of a book in print. Collectors refer to the first impression (print run) of the book as a true first edition. Identification of true first editions can be an art and even the most experienced booksellers and collectors run the risk of making an error.

The way printers specify the edition somewhere inside the book—or fail to give any indication at all of which edition it is—varies widely from printer to printer, era to era, and country to country. Best to go prepared with a pocket guide on the subject when browsing for books, for you could not possibly keep in mind the vast number of codes that publishers have used or the legions of points that identify specific titles. Unfortunately, if a book does not readily admit in print to being a second or a third or a 15-thousandth edition, the uninformed public automatically assumes the book is a first. The collector or bookseller cannot afford this casual assumption as most collectors acquire first editions for many reasons, not least among them, investment.

FIRST IMPRESSION. The first time a set of plates has been used to print a book. Also called a **PRINTING**.

All impressions using the same set of plates constitute one edition, thus each edition can include more than one impression. Most sellers and collectors are speaking of the first impression of the first edition when discussing collectible **FIRST EDITIONS**.

FIRST THUS. Not the first edition, but you may see this used to describe an altered edition of an old book. Since the revised book is an edition unlike the original, perhaps issued by a different publishing house or illustrated by some other artist, the book can be presented as first thus. Like a distant cousin to the first edition.

FLYLEAF. Blank leaf after the front free endpaper, not always present. The term is often misapplied to the front endpaper.

FOLDING PLATES. Plates which fold out to a larger size than the book leaves. Volumes published by the Government Printing Office during the 19th century have many folding maps and color illustrations bound into the books. Guide books are designed with folding illustrations and maps, too. Through the years, unfortunately, folding plates begin to show wear and tear from handling.

FOLIO. A standard book size, measuring from about 12" tall on up. An atlas folio is 24", and an elephant folio is 20" or more. Audubon's *Birds of America* is a most valued natural history book measuring 37" tall.

FORE-EDGE. The outer edge of a book, opposite the spine.

FORE-EDGE PAINTING. Painting the edges of a book's leaves with a scene or other picture. The book must be held in a special press and while the leaves are slightly fanned out the artist paints or decorates the exposed fore-edges of the leaves. When the book is fully closed, the edge is gilded to conceal traces of the painting. But lightly fan out the edges, and the fore-edge painting can be a lovely surprise. Because the painting is hidden, a book with a fore-edge painting can go undetected, even by a knowledgable bookseller, until the book is opened.

FORMAT. The size of a book determined by the specific number of times the original printed sheet of paper has been folded to form the leaves. For standard format sizes used in the booktrade, see **BOOK SIZE.**

FOXED. Discoloration with brown spots and blotches caused by microorganisms that find the paper in certain books appetizing. Dampness can encourage the problem. The spots are often dark and, when the foxing is heavy, can seriously detract from the value of an otherwise good book.

FRAKTUR. A German style of gothic or black-letter type. Fraktur was most prevalent at Augsburg and Nuremburg in the post-incunabula period when gothic had been almost totally dropped by French and Italian printers. Popular with the Pennsylvania Dutch, early birth certificates decorated and embellished with fraktur are becoming harder to find and more expensive to buy.

FRONTISPIECE. An illustration appearing opposite the title page. More often than not, the frontis (as abbreviated) is a portrait of the author, but in many books, the frontis is a lovely color plate or a steel engraving.

GILT EDGES. Gold applied to all three edges of a book's leaves. In book parlance, teg means top edge gilt, and aeg means all edges gilt.

HALF-BOUND. A book with leather extending over the spine and about an inch or so along the front and back covers. The rest of the binding is either cloth or paper. If the spine is leather and the four corners of the book are covered in leather triangles, you have a book which is called three-quarter leather. Thought to be an English custom, the practice goes back to the 17th century, but did not become popular until the 18th century.

HALF-TITLE. Usually the first appearance of print in a volume, the title printed on an otherwise blank sheet before the title page. This is a holdover from the days of early printing when the title was the only information given on the title page.

The half-title is also known as **BASTARD TITLE.** Grant Uden in his book *Understanding Book Collecting*, puts this appelation down to the insensitivity of Americans who he says often adopt their own bibliographical terminology. But whosoever puts these terms together, all you have to remember is that the half-title is most often the first appearance of print in a volume.

In the past, when restoring a book, binders often discarded the half-title page. They may have considered it superfluous, and well it might be, unless you are a collector, and then that half-title page had better be there.

HEADBAND. A (usually) colorful band inside of the spine, sewn across the top of the leaves. In modern bindery, it has no function and is primarily decorative, if it is present at all. Headbands are more often seen in older books. The term is used to include the tailband (sewn across the bottom inside of the spine) as well.

HINGE. The ridge where the front or back cover meets the spine. When a book has a hinge crack, the cover is intact but loose. It definitely needs attention before worse can happen, which is separation of the covers from the book.

HOLOGRAPH. A document written wholly in the hand of the author. Although autograph collectors use the term more frequently, booksellers find it helpful to indicate more than mere inscription or presentation material on the flyleaf of a book; specifically, a laid-in letter or a **MANUSCRIPT.**

HORNBOOK. A sheet of paper, printed on one side with the alphabet or some other rudiments of school work, pasted onto a handled piece of wood then covered with transparent horn. In colonial America, these were a child's first school books. Used from the 16th to the 18th century, genuine hornbooks are rare, but imitation copies turn up now and then, no doubt prompted by the high price an original would command.

ILLUMINATED MANUSCRIPT. A work containing dazzling letters, initials, and sentence openings, hand decorated in bold colors and finished off with gold and silver. Spectacular and colorful, the art work did, in essense, brilliantly shed light upon the text. Manuscript illumination is known to have been practiced as early as the 5th century. Monks in the 7th and 8th centuries produced specimens of great artistry in Ireland, including the awe-inspiring *Book of Kells*.

Illuminating manuscripts remained the province of monastic scribes until the end of the 14th century when the commercial manuscript industry came into its own and the secular world took a serious interest in book ownership. Unfortunately, the invention of printing, which literally set the book business on it's head, also contributed to the demise of the manuscript trade. By 1470, the German manuscript industry had virtually ceased to function; those of Italy and Spain gave way soon after. France was the last stronghold of illuminated manuscripts, turning out specimens of quality even after the age of **INCUNABULA.** But in the end, the writing was on the wall and manuscripts were only hand-illuminated by special request.

IMPRESSION. In the strictest sense, a run of copies, large or small, ordered by a publisher from the printer at one time. Traditionally, after the first impression of a book has come off the press, other runs may be printed from the same setting of type, and are usually so noted. Collectors of first editions are looking for the first impression of the first edition of a volume, as all impressions taken from one setting of type constitute an edition.

In days past, when type was set in metal and was ungainly and difficult to store for long periods, a book that remained in demand after its first edition sold out was likely to need resetting before it could be reissued.

IMPRINT. The information at the foot of the title page that refers to the publisher or the place of publication. The book industry includes collectors who specialize in imprints. Those of the Revolutionary period and the Confederacy are especially prized.

INCUNABULA (INCUNABLE). Books printed on presses in the 15th century. The word is derived from the Latin root meaning "in the cradle," and indicates printing in its infancy. Incunabula is automatically valuable and collectible.

INDIAN BIBLE. The name commonly given to an edition of the *Bible* in a Native American language, an Algonquin dialect, translated and compiled by the Rev. John Eliot and published at Cambridge, Massachusetts in 1663. The bible is also known as the "Natick Bible" and the "Eliot Bible."

INSCRIBED COPY. A book carrying a signed inscription, usually saying something like "with regards to" or "for a special friend." Should the author of the inscription be famous, the book's value is enhanced. However, simply an inscription by the former owner, who may be a nice person, does not constitute an inscribed copy.

ISSUE. A term applied to a second printing (impression) of an edition that includes a change or correction—but not a complete resetting of type—made after the first impression is printed. Adding to the confusion are "states," or printings in which changes have been made during the print run. The terms are technical but important to the identification of older first editions. Many booksellers use "issue" and "state" interchangeably.

LAID IN. Refers to a piece of paper, such as a letter or a photo, placed in the book but not attached.

LEAF. A single sheet of paper, with a **RECTO** (front) page and a **VERSO** (back) page. Many people confuse pages and leaves. Pages are just one side of a leaf.

LIBRARY OF CONGRESS. America's largest library, located in Washington, D.C. Once founded as a working library for members of Congress, the library now holds not only government documents, but one of the largest collections of incunabula in the U.S.

LIMITED EDITION. Special printing of a limited number of books. Printing and binding is often of a higher quality than the usual trade books or may be the product of a **PRIVATE PRESS.** The books are often numbered and signed by the author and illustrator, if there is one.

LIMP. Refers to bookbindings made of material that is not supported by boards. The cover is literally hanging limp. Limp vellum was first used as a trade binding for printed books almost since the beginning of typography and remained popular in Italian, Spanish, and Portuguese bindery during the 15th to 17th centuries. Limp bindings were often fitted with leather thong ties in place of clasps.

In the 19th century, limp leather was often used as a binding for Bibles, giving way to imitation leather in later years.

LITHOGRAPHY. A principal method of printing developed in the 19th and 20th centuries, especially suited to reproducing drawings and illustrations. The process consists of printing from an impression drawn on smooth lithographic limestone using chemical inks. Many artists came to use the process to replace engraving, including the reknowned Currier and Ives. Lithography is now a prominent art form.

LOOSE. A book that is in danger of separating from its binding. No longer held tight by the spine, the joints cannot support the weight of the book.

MANUSCRIPT. In the book world, refers to a handwritten document. Technically, a work written by hand, but in the modern world, a manscript can be typewritten and still be considered a manuscript. The distinction is that it was not typeset or printed. If the writing is in the author's hand, it's termed a **HOLOGRAPH** manuscript. In the Middle Ages, monks copying sacred texts created **ILLUMINATED** (illustrated) manuscripts of great beauty, but with the invention and proliferation of mechanical printing, the practice died out.

MARBLED. A technique of decorating paper to create the effect of marble, mostly used for endpapers. Some examples have intriguing patterns that craftspeople today are duplicating to frame or to function as bookcovers.

MEZZOTINT. The process of engraving on copper plates.

MINIATURE. Actually not what you'd think, derived from "miniate" which means to paint with vermilion. The ancient artists who used this red paint were called miniators. Originally, miniatures referred to the colored drawings in early manuscripts.

MINT CONDITION. Like new. Right off the press.

MISPRINT. An error in printing, very important when identifying first editions. For instance, in the first American edition of Mark Twain's *Adventures of Huckleberry Finn* the word "saw" was printed incorrectly as "was" on line 23, page 57. Misprints are often among the important **POINTS** which must be present if a book is a true first edition.

MODERN FIRST EDITIONS. Includes books published since the turn of the 20th century. Here again in book parlance, phrases are evolving with time and most people use the term in reference to books from the 1920's on.

MOROCCO. Leather made from goatskin.

ND. No date of publication is given.

NP. No place of publication is given.

OCTAVO. The most common size/format of books. Usually seen expressed as "8vo," the most common octavos measure approximately 8" high.

OUT OF PRINT. No longer obtainable from the publisher.

PAMPHLET. A small work, issued unbound or in wraps, and usually sewn or stapled together.

PAPERBACK. Softcovered books, primarily books bound in heavy paper, published from the 1930's on. Today, early paperbacks are collectible and sought after, especially the horror and science fiction genres.

The term is not to be confused with WRAPS, a thin paper cover.

PARTS. Books released in serial form or in installments. Many books started out this way and were only later published in book form. The works of Dickens followed this pattern—his *Dombey and Son* was printed in parts, 19 of the 20 parts in green pictorial wrappers, as were several of his other works. Amassing all the parts can be a daunting task since unprotected paper is fragile and many did not survive.

PENNY BOXES. Trays or boxes outside antiquarian bookshops where the bookseller puts cheap, miscellaneous stock to attract browsers.

PLATE. A full page devoted to an illustration, separate from the text pages of the book. The verso is blank.

POINTS. Characteristics which determine whether or not a book is a first edition. For instance, the first edition of a book may contain a specific spelling or other publishing mistake on a certain page that was corrected in later editions. The presence of the mistake is a point.

PRESENTATION COPY. Inscribed by the author as a gift. Not to be confused with a signature acquired by a total stranger who asked for the author's autograph in the book.

PRESS BOOK. A finely produced book, published by a private press, an individual or established publisher for the sake of excellence in printing and binding and not necessarily for the book's literary value. Prices run high on these specialties—from the outset, not just as collectibles—again for the high manufacturing standard, not because the book is wonderful literature, though it might be.

PRINT RUN. The number of volumes of a book run off the press at one time.

PRIVATELY PRINTED. Not produced by a publisher. The author pays for the publication out of his own pocket. Quite often in the past, privately printed books were produced for the author's friends and family. This remains true today, but in response to changes in the publishing industry, private printings are becoming more common for trade sales, as well.

Some very collectible books have been privately published, not the least of which was Edgar Allan Poe's *Tamerlane*, a copy of which sold at auction for a quarter of a million dollars in the late 20th century.

PRIVATE PRESS. Publishers of limited editions or, simply, a single person producing (publishing) books.

PROVENANCE. The history of a book's ownership. Provenance may add to value if it shows prized associations. Many bibliophiles like information on the provenance of a book for its own sake. A love of old books and their history seem to go hand in hand.

QUARTER BOUND. Only the spine of a book is leather. The rest is boards or cloth.

QUOTES. The backbone of the bookseller's trade, a written description of a book with the asking price of the book stated. This can be communicated to the prospective buyer in paper form or over the Internet.

When quoting, include all pertinent information about the book: the title, author, publisher, date, edition, number of pages, whether or not illustrations or maps are present, and the type of binding. Then carefully describe the condition. It is here a book professional appreciates full disclosure of the defects. Even if you are as accurate as you know how to be, sometimes a buyer will envision something different and find the quote wanting. Include your name, address, and sale requirements and state whether the transaction is **C.W.O.** (Cash With Order) or future billing.

READING COPY. A book that has seen better days, worn from use and in less than good condition. They're appreciated by scholars for research, but not by collectors unless the volume is exceedingly rare.

REBACKED. Fitted with a new spine and hinges. When considering such repairs, be prepared to pay well for a competent job. Unless you have a personal affinity for the book, before ordering any restoration by a professional book binder, have your volume appraised to see if it is worth the preservation cost.

REBOUND. Fitted with a new binding. Here again, as in the rebacked book, we are talking restoration and expensive repairs. Whenever this route is undertaken, opt for re-attaching the original covers, if that is possible. Again, if you are selling the book, value should be there to justify the expense.

RECTO. In a book, the right-hand page, the front of the leaf.

REMAINDER. Selling book stock to a distributor at a considerable discount when the publisher believes the title has sold as many copies as it is likely to sell at full price in bookstores.

REPRINT. A re-issue of a book previously published. A. L. Burt and Grosset & Dunlap reissued and made available many famous works to those who otherwise could not afford the first editions. In an elderly farm woman's house we visited in Vermont, the shelves in an upstairs bedroom were lined with books, reprints by Zane Grey, E. R. Burroughs, Dixon, Henty, Horatio Alger, and more. And proud she was that she had read them all.

REVIEW COPY. Complimentary copies of books sent to editors, journalists, and institutions, hoping for a review or at least a mention in their publications or programs.

RUBBED. Scratches or wear spots on leather bindings.

SABIN, JOSEPH. An English bookseller who emigrated to the United States and became one of the foremost authorities on Americana, setting about to publish a comprehensive bibliography of the genre. Unfortunately, Sabin lived to see only the first thirteen volumes realized. Wilberforce Eames and R. W. G. Vail completed the monumental work, finishing with a total of twenty-nine volumes.

SCUFFED. Worn, scratched, nicked.

SEARCH SERVICE. Precisely what the term implies, initiating a search for a title through dealership and trade channels. In the recent past, if you wanted a particular book and you could not find it in a used bookstore, a bookseller would print an inquiry in the trade journals welcoming quotes from other dealers. Since the advent of the Internet, many of these trade journals are no longer available. For instance, AB Bookman, which was the Bible of the collectible book industry, has stopped publishing.

Now, dealers and collectors go directly to book-finding web sites on the Internet where they can almost instantaneously collect information on books available worldwide.

Booksellers continue to offer professional search services for a fee whether or not a book is found. Back in the good old days, Wright Howes noted in his Fall, 1933 catalogue "out of print and scarce books sought for and reported free of charge." The times, they are a changing.

SPINE. The backstrip of a book.

STATE. Changes or corrections made during a print run. Sometimes used interchangeably with "issue," which indicates changes or corrections, but not a full resetting of the type, made between impressions.

SUNNED. Faded. The original color of the book loses brightness and freshness when exposed to direct bright light, especially sunlight.

THREE-QUARTER LEATHER. Leather on the spine and about an inch beyond, along with triangles of leather at the corners of the book. The rest of the binding could be cloth or boards.

TIPPED-IN. Glued in, as when illustrations are not bound into a book but glued in after binding. The technique is most often used to add glossy pictures or maps, with glue applied to the back of the illustration at the top only. Tipping-in was used to incorporate illustrations that would have been too expensive to print and bind into the book.

TISSUE GUARDS. Tissue paper bound into the book that protects the plates.

TITLE PAGES. The page at the front of each book which gives the title, author, publisher and, sometimes, the printing date. In most books, this information in on a recto page. Always consult the title page for pertinent information about a book, never depend upon what is printed on the spine or cover.

TOOLING. Impressing a design by hand in leather.

UNCUT. Untrimmed leaves. When sheets are printed, folded, and bound, the trimming process to open the leaves can miss some folds, leaving the pages uncut and unopened.

UNOPENED. Uncut leaves. Tearing can open them, but they remain uncut, though opened.

VELLUM. Calfskin binding. Also sometimes called parchment. Vellum and other leather bindings should be carefully cared for to keep them from drying and cracking (see Care and Repair of Books).

VERSO. Left-hand page of a book, the back side of a leaf.

WANT LIST. A listing of books needed either to fill a dealer's bookshelves or to accommodate customers looking for particular works. Booksellers periodically send out want lists to other dealers. Often the bookseller will include a "permanent want list" in which case there is no cut-off date for acquiring those books, and duplicates may even be welcome.

In today's computer environment, both collectors and dealers look to the Internet to fill their want lists. However, a collector who is not knowledgeable would do better to consult a bookdealer to search his wants. Established dealers have additional resources for finding collectible books.

WESTERN AMERICANA. The genre covering the settling of the American west and American western culture, including indigenous peoples. Everyone seems to want this category, and the prices are high for the really good stuff. The collector, of course, is looking for pioneer imprints, broadsides, handbills, documents, hand-written journey narratives or ledgers. Books on Indians, explorations, out-laws, mining, and whatever else attested to the westward push are collectible.

WRAPPERS. Paper binding. This does not refer to modern paperbacks, which are bound in stiff paper with illustrations. The term refers to simple paper covering, sometimes plain paper serving also as a title page. Before modern bindings, books were often published with plain paper covers. Customers brought the works to their own binderies to have custom leather or cloth covers put on. Older pamphlets were often published with thin paper covers, or wrappers.

WRAPS. Same as wrappers.

RECOMMENDED
PERIODICALS AND
RESEARCH RESOURCES

PRINT RESOURCES:

The Antiquarian Booksellers Association of America (ABAA) Membership Directory. 50 Rockefeller Plaza. New York, NY 10020.

A comprehensive listing of dealers in the association.

American Book Prices Current. Box 1236. Washington, CT 06793.

The annual compilation of realized prices of books sold at auction. It lists sales of $50 or more. While an excellent investment, the volumes are expensive and your best bet is to find a good library that carries the books in the reference department.

The Used Book Price Guide. Compiled by Mildred Mandeville.
P.O. Box 82525. Kenmore, WA 98028.

"Mandeville" has been a standard for dealers for decades, offering extensive lists of books and current prices, but subject to the usual cautions as to errors or fluctuations in the markets that pertain to any regularly produced price guides. When we went to press, the 1998 (3-year) edition was available.

Identification of First Editions–A Pocket Guide. By Bill McBride. Hartford, CT. 06105.

Pointers for identifying first editions from various publishers over the years. This book has been available through new book dealers.

Book Prices Used and Rare. E. Zempel and L. A. Verkler (eds.)
Includes 800 pages and over 30,000 entries. When we went to press, the 1999 edition was available from Spoon River Press. 2319-C West Rohmann. Peoria, IL. 61604-5072.

Book Collecting as a Hobby. By P. H. Muir.
Out of print, but worth finding.

Bookman's Price Index. Gale Research Inc. Detroit, Mich. 48226-4094.
A pricing resource.

US-Iana. Wright Howes. R. R. Bowker, Co. New York.
A bibliography of books on the United States.

Synsine Press. Box 6422. Rheem Valley, CA 94570.
Children's series book.

A Collector's Guide to Hard Cover Boy's Series Books 1872-1993. E. Christian Mattson and Thomas B. Davis. Mad Book Co. 273 Pollydrummond Rd. Newark, DE 19711. (302) 738-0532.

The Insider's Guide to Old Books, Magazines, Newspapers and Trade Catalogs. by Ron Barlow and Ray Reynolds. Windmill Publishing Company. El Cajon, CA 92020.

Civil War Books, Confederate and Union. Ronald R. Seagrave. Sgt. Kirkland's Museum and Historical Society, Inc. 912 Lafayette Blvd. Fredericksburg, VA 22401-5617.

Civil War Books. Tom Broadfoot. 1907 Buena Vista Circle. Wilmington, NC 28405.

Price Guide for Children's & Illustrated Books for the Years 1850-1960. E. Lee Baumgarten.

Collected Books. The Guide to Value. Allen and Patricia Ahearn.
This guide offeres information identifying first editions of books in hand.

Book Collecting. Allen Ahearn.
This is a guide to values for the first book by an author.

A Primer of Book Collecting. John T. Winterich, New York, Greenberg, 1926.

INTERNET WEBSITE RESOURCES:
Advanced Book Exchange
Book listings, dealerships, information
www.abebooks.com

BiblioFinder
Search engine
www.bibliofinder.com

Aleph Bet Books
Book listings and genre information
www.alephbet.com

Swann Galleries
Fine Book Auction House
www.swanngalleries.com

Pacific Book Auction Galleries
Book Auction House and website
www.pacificbook.com

John Zubal Books, Inc
Book Auction House and website
www.zubal.com

Bookseller Monthly
Listings and Book Information
www.booksellermonthly.com
and
www.bookgraveyard.com

DEALERS AND AUCTION HOUSES

We wish to thank the dealers listed below who responded to our request for information. Most of them, except where a specialty is noted, are general booksellers covering a broad field of subjects.

American Booksellers
102 West 11th St.
Aberdeen, WA 98520

Antiquarian and Collector Books
Rodger & Joan Bassett
P. O. Box 536
Fullerton, NE 68638
308-536-2377

Abracadabra Booksearch
International
Alan & Mary Culpin, Booksellers
32 S. Broadway
Denver, CO 80209
1-800-545-2665

Abracadabra Booksearch
International
3606 Chalkstone Cove
Austin, TX 78730
512-502-9042

An Uncommon Vision
1425 Greywall Ln.
Wynnewood, PA 19096-3811
610-658-0953

Artis Books
201 N. Second Ave.
Alpena, MI 49707
517-354-3401

Barbara B. Harris Books
8 Morgan Way
Gilford, NH 03246
603-524-5405

Barry and Hillary Anthony
Milford Book Cellar and
Church Street Books
201 West Hartford St.
Milford, PA 18337

Barry R. Levin
Science Fiction & Fantasy
720 Santa Monica Blvd.
Santa Monica, CA 90401
310-458-6111

Benchmark Books
3269 S. Main St., Suite 250
Salt Lake City, UT 84115
801-486-3111

Bev Chaney Jr. Books
73 Croton Ave.
Ossining, NY 10562

Bibliomania
129 Jay St.
Schenectaday, NY 12305
518-393-8069

Bolerium Books
2141 Mission, Suite 300
San Francisco, CA 94110
1-800-326-6353

Bookcell Books
Box 506
Haverford, PA 19041
610-649-4933

Bookseller Monthly and
Bookseller Marketplace
Joe Spoor, editor
P. O. Box 266
Rockwood, MI 48173
734-586-1318
info@booksellermonthly.com

Brick House Bookshop
RFD 3 Box 3020
Morrisville, VT 05661
802-888-4300

Callahan & Co. Booksellers
P. O. Box 505
Peterborough, NY 03458
603-924-3726

Cattermole
20th Century Children's Books
9880 Fairmont Rd.
Newberry, OH 44065
216-338-3253

Center for Western Studies
Box 727, Augustana College
Sioux Falls, SD 57197
605-336-4999 or 1-800-727-2844

Dan Wyman, Books
47 Dartmouth St.
Springfield, MA 01109
413-733-9065

David M. Lesser
One Bradley Rd., #302
Woodbridge, CT 06525
203-389-8111

DeWolfe & Wood
P. O. Box 425
Alfred, ME 04002
207-490-5572

Edwin Glaser
P. O. Box 1765
Sausalito, CA 94966
415-332-1194

Emmett Harrington
P. O. Box 27236
San Francisco, CA 94127
415-587-4604

Ethnographic Arts Publication
1040 Erica Rd.
Mill Valley, CA94941
415-383-2998, 332-1646

Foundations Antiques
Stephen Smith
148 North Main St.
Fair Haven, VT 05743
802-265-4544

Frances L. Robinson
US Rt 2, 81 South St.
South Hero, VT 05486
802-372-6622

Freeman Fine Arts of
Philadelphia, Inc.
1808 Chestnut St.
Philadelphia, PA 19103
215-563-8236

George Kolbe
Fine Numismatic Books
P. O. Drawer 3100
Crestline, CA 92325-3100
909-338-6527

Heinoldt Books
1325 W. Central Ave.
South Egg Harbor, NJ 08215
609-965-2284

High Meadows Natural History
Books
1198 Clear Creek
Boise, ID 82709
208-323-0328

Hurley Books
1752 Rt. 12
Westmoreland, NH 033467
603-399-4342

J & J House
731 Unionville Rd.
Rt. 82, Box 919
Unionville, PA 19375
215-444-0490

James Cummins, Bookseller
699 Madison Ave.
New York, NY 10021
212-688-6441

James W. Beattie Rare Books
105 N. Wayne Ave.
Wayne, PA 19087
215-687-3347

Julian J. Nadolny
121 Hickory Hill Rd.
Kensington, CT 06037
203-225-5353

Just Good Books
P. O. Box 232
Belgrade MT 59714-0232

Ken Andersen
Ken Andersen Books
P. O. Box 621
Auburn, MA 01501
802-388-8412

Ken Lopez
51 Huntington Rd.
Hadley, MA 01035

Knollwood Books
P. O. Box 197
Oregon, WI 53575-0197
608-835-8861

L & T Resspess Books
P. O. Box 1604
Charlottesville, VA 22902
804-293-3553

L. W. Currey, Inc.
Water St., Box 187
Elizabethtown, NY 12932
518-873-6477

Lyders Fine Books
P.O. Box 250
Peacham, VT 05862
802-592-3086

Michael Canick Booksellers
80 East 11th St., Room 430
New York, NY 10003
e-mail: canick@panix.com

Monroe Street Books
Dick & Flanzy Chodkowski
7 Monroe St.
Middlebury, VT 05753
802-388-1622

Mordita Books
P. O. Box 79322
Houston, TX 77279
713-467-4280

Nouveau Rare Books
P. O. Box 12471
5005 Meadows Oak Park Dr.
Jackson, MS 39211

October Farm
2609 Branch Rd.
Raleigh, NC 27610
919-772-0482

Orpheus Books
11522 NE 20th St.
Bellevue, WA 98004-3005
360-776-4912

Pacific Book Auction Galleries
415-989-2665
133 Kearny St., 4th Floor
San Francisco, CA 94108
pba@pacificbook.com

Peninsula Books
451 North Madison
Traverse City, MI 49684-2112
1-800-530-6737

Philadelphia Rare Books and
Manuscripts Company
P. O. Box 9536
Philadelphia, PA 19125
215-744-6734
rarebks@prbm.com

Poor Richard's Books, Ltd.
968 Balmoral Rd.
Victoria B.C. Canada V8T 1AB
604-384-4411

Richard Adelson Antiquarian
Booksellers
Jane & Richard Adelson
HC 69 Box 23
North Pomfret, VT 05053
802-457-2608

Roy C. Kulp
Handwritten Americana
Box 264
Hatfield, PA 19440
215-362-0732

Rudolph Wm. Sabbat
6821 Babcock Ave.
N. Hollywood, CA 91605
818-982-4911

Ruth Woods, Oriental Books & Art
266 Arch Rd.
Englewood, NJ 07631
201-567-0149

Second Life Books, Inc.
P. O. Box 242, 55 Quarry Rd.
Lanesborough, MA 01237
413-447-8010

Stan Clark Military Books
915 Fairview Ave.
Gettysburg, PA 17325
717-337-1728

Steve Finer
Box 758
Greenfield, MA 01302
413-773-5811

Swann Galleries
104 East 25th Street
New York, NY 10010
212-254-4710
swann@swanngalleries.com

The Eloquent Page
Donna & Marilyn Howard
21 Catherine St.
St. Albans, VT 05478
802-527-7243

The Inquisitive Sportsman Books
Box 1811
Granite Falls, WA 98252
360-691-7540

The Printer's Shop
4546 El Camino Real B10 #207
Los Altos, CA 94022
415-941-0433

The Unique Antique
Jonathan Flaccus
P. O. Box 485 Main St.
Putney, VT 05346
802-387-4488

T. N. Luther, Books
P. O. Box 429
Taos, NM 87571
505-776-8117

Tom Munnerlyn Books
P. O. Drawer 15247
Austin, TX 78761-5247
e-mail: thomas@texas.net

Waverly Auctions
4931 Cordell Ave
Bethesda, MD 20814
www.waverlyauctions.com

Thomas Cullen
Rockland Bookman
Box 134
Cattaraugus, NY 14719
716-257-9116

Trotting Hill Park Books
P. O. Box 1324
Springfield, MA 01101
413-567-6466

William L. Parkinson, Books
P. O. Box 40
Hinesburg, VT 05461
802-482-3113

John T. Zubal, Inc.
2969 West 25th St.
Cleveland, Ohio 44113
Fax: 216-241-6966
infor@zubal.com

INDEX OF AUTHORS AND TITLES BY POPULAR GENRE

Illustrators

Literature

Medicine/Scientific

Military/Civil War

Modern First Editions

0-609-80820-6

THE COMIC BOOK COLLECTOR'S BIBLE!

The Official® Overstreet Comic Book Price Guide is the most comprehensive sourcebook in the field!

- Detailed information on comic books and graphic novels from the 1800s to the present

- Up-to-the-minute market reports

- Special exclusives on The Fantastic Four's fortieth anniversary, Wonder Woman's sixtieth anniversary, and more

- Directory of comic book fan websites

- Important tips on grading and caring for your comics

- More than 1,500 photographs *plus* 33 pages in full color

Buy It • Use It • Become an Expert™

HOUSE OF COLLECTIBLES

Available at bookstores everywhere!